Dina Goldin · Scott A. Smolka · Peter Wegner (Eds.)

T0140349

Dina Goldin
Scott A. Smolka
Peter Wegner (Eds.)

Interactive Computation

The New Paradigm

With 84 Figures

 Springer

Editors

Dina Goldin
Brown University
Computer Science Department
Providence, RI 02912
USA
dqg@cs.brown.edu

Scott A. Smolka
State University of New York at Stony Brook
Department of Computer Science
Stony Brook, NY 11794-4400
USA
sas@cs.sunysb.edu

Peter Wegner
Brown University
Computer Science Department
Providence, RI 02912
USA
pw@cs.brown.edu

ACM Computing Classification (1998): F, D.1, H.1, H.5.2

ISBN 978-3-642-07102-7   e-ISBN 978-3-540-34874-0

Springer is a part of Springer Science+Business Media

springer.com

© Springer-Verlag Berlin Heidelberg 2010

Cover design: KünkelLopka Werbeagentur, Heidelberg

This book is dedicated to our families, and to the memory of our former colleague and advisor Paris Kanellakis.

Preface

Interaction is an emerging paradigm of models of computation that reflects the shift in technology from mainframes to networks of intelligent agents, from number-crunching to embedded systems to graphical user interfaces, and from procedure-oriented to object-based distributed systems. Interaction-based models differ from the Turing-machine-based algorithmic models of the 1960s in interesting and useful ways:

Problem Solving: Models of interaction capture the notion of performing a task or providing a service, rather than algorithmically producing outputs from inputs.

Observable Behavior: In models of interaction, a computing component is modeled not as a functional transformation from input to output, but rather in terms of observable behavior consisting of interaction steps. For example, interactions may consist of interleaved inputs and outputs modeled by dynamic streams; future input values can depend on past output values.

Environments: In models of interaction, the world or environment of the computation is part of the model and plays an active part in the computation by dynamically supplying the computational system, or agent, with inputs, and consuming the output values the system produces. The environment cannot be assumed to be static or even effectively computable; for example, it may include humans or other real-world elements.

Concurrency: In models of interaction, computation may be concurrent; a computing agent can compute in parallel with its environment and with other agents.

The interaction paradigm provides a new conceptualization of computational phenomena that emphasizes interaction rather than algorithms. Concurrent, distributed, reactive, embedded, component-oriented, agent oriented and service-oriented systems all exploit interaction as a fundamental paradigm.

This book thus challenges traditional answers to fundamental questions relating to problem solving or the scope of computation. It aims to increase the awareness of interaction paradigms among the wider computer-science community and to stimulate practice and theoretical research in interactive computation.

This book consists of 18 chapters that are divided into four sections: (I) introduction, (II) theory, (III) applications, and (III) new directions. The three chapters in Sect. I introduce interactive computation and explore its fundamental principles. The six chapters in Sect. II discuss the formalization of different aspects of interaction. The five chapters in Sect. III present some applications of interactive computation within various subdisciplines of computer science. Finally, the four chapters in Sect. IV move beyond computer science to consider the multidisciplinary implications of this new paradigm.

Each chapter makes a different contribution to the study of interactive computing, collectively providing a broad overview of the field that will help in the evolution of this increasingly important discipline. A brief overview of each chapter follows.

I. Introduction

1. Robin Milner, *Turing, Computing, and Communication*

In this chapter, Milner discusses how computer science has changed substantially since Turing's founding ideas, advancing from prescription to description, from hierarchical to heterarchical design, from determinism to nondeterminism, and from end results to interaction. The evolution of computer science to include interaction would have excited and been approved by Turing.

2. Farhad Arbab, *Computing and Interaction*

This chapter offers a rough sketch of the landscape of computing with the specific aim of interrelating well established topics such as computability and concurrency to newer areas such as interaction and composition of behavior.

3. Peter Wegner and Dina Goldin, *Principles of Interactive Computation*

This chapter explores Wegner and Goldin's contributions to interactive computing, with special emphasis on the philosophical question of how truth has been used (and misused) in computing and other disciplines. They suggest that interaction provides an empiricist model of computation that differs from rationalist mathematical algorithms models proposed in the 1960s by theoretical computer scientists, and point out that the Strong Church–Turing thesis, which reinterprets the Church–Turing thesis by applying it to all computation, contradicts the original thesis and is technically incorrect.

II. Theory

4. Manfred Broy, *A Theory of System Interaction: Components, Interfaces, and Services*

This chapter studies models, specification, and refinement techniques for distributed interactive software systems composed of interfaces and components. A theory for the interaction between such systems is given which refers to the interaction among systems and their environments, as well as the interaction among the components of systems. Interfaces and interactions are modeled by logical formulas in the style of design by contract, by state machines, and by streams of messages and signals. This leads to a theory of interface abstraction of systems that is essential for an interaction view. In particular, this theory treats interaction refinement and introduces a service concept based purely on interaction.

5. Orna Kupferman and Moshe Vardi, *Verification of Open Systems*
This chapter considers the verification of interactive systems. In formal verification, one verifies that a system meets a desired property by checking that a mathematical system model satisfies a formal specification of the property. Since assumptions about the environment and its interaction a system are a natural part of the specification in robust model checking, the model studied in this chapter subsumes extensions that can be expressed in terms of properties of the environment and its interaction with the system.

6. Jan van Leeuwen and Jiří Wiedermann, *A Theory of Interactive Computation*
This chapter asks what a computational theory of interactive, evolving programs should look like. The authors point out that a theory of interactive computation must necessarily lead beyond the classical, finitary models of computation. A simple model of interactive computing is presented consisting of one component C and an environment E, interacting using single streams of input and output signals. This model elegantly characterizes interactive computation in a stream setting and enables the authors to study the computational implications of interaction, building on the theory of ω-automata. Viewing components as interactive transducers, they obtain several interesting theoretical results.

7. Susanne Albers, *Online Algorithms*
Online algorithms are a theoretical framework for studying problems in interactive computing. They model the situation in which the input to an interactive system arrives not as a batch but as a sequence of input portions, and in which at any point in time the future input is unknown. This chapter explores online algorithms for diverse applications, including resource management in operating systems, data structuring, scheduling, networks, and computational finance.

8. Yuri Gurevich, *Interactive Algorithms 2005*
In this chapter, Gurevich asserts that computer science is largely about algorithms, and broadens the notion of algorithms to include interaction by allowing intrastep interaction of an algorithm with its environment. This chapter discusses various forms of intrastep interaction and shows that numerous disparate phenomena are best understood as special cases of it. A survey of recent work on interactive algorithms follows.

9. Giorgi Japaridze, *Computability Logic: A Formal Theory of Interaction*
This chapter presents an introduction to computability logic, which is a formal theory of interactive computability in the same sense as classical logic is a formal theory of truth. It views computational problems as games played by a

machine against the environment: if there exists a machine that always wins the game, then the problem is computable.

III. Applications

10. Michel Beaudouin-Lafon, *Human–Computer Interaction*

Human–computer systems are systems with a human user in the loop; to give the user a sense of control, they must be prepared to receive virtually any input at any moment and react to it in a way the user can understand. In this chapter, Beaudouin-Lafon evaluates some unique aspects of human–computer systems with respect to these characteristics. The chapter covers a wide range of user-interface styles and techniques, from traditional graphical user interfaces to advanced research, and considers the full life-cycle of human–computer systems from design to evaluation.

11. Shriram Krishnamurthi, Robert Findler, Paul Graunke and Matthias Felleisen, *Modeling Web Interactions and Errors*

Interactive web programs permit consumers to navigate at whim among the various stages of a dialogue, leading to unexpected outcomes. In this chapter, the authors develop a model of web interactions that reduces the panoply of browser-supported user interactions to three fundamental ones. The model is used to formally describe two classes of errors in Web programs and to suggest techniques for detecting and eliminating these errors.

12. Farhad Arbab, *Coordination of Interacting Computations*

Coordination models and languages are a recent approach to design and development of concurrent systems. In this chapter, Arbab presents a brief overview of coordination models and languages and a framework for their classification. He then focuses on a specific coordination language, called Reo, that serves as a good example of a constructive model of computation in which interaction is treated as a first-class concept, and demonstrates that it provides a powerful and expressive model for flexible composition of behavior through interaction.

13. Rahul Singh and Ramesh Jain, *From Information-Centric to Experiential Environments*

User expectations of information-management systems are changing: rather than providing answers in response to queries, users want the system to let them interact with the data so that they can gain insights about it. In this chapter, the authors explore the paradigm of experiential computing for designing information-management systems.

14. Chris Barrett, Stephen Eubank, and Madhav Marathe, *Modeling and Simulation of Large Biological, Information and Socio-Technical Systems: An Interaction-Based Approach*

In this chapter, the authors describe an interaction-based approach to computer modeling and simulation systems composed of a large number of interacting components—be they biological, physical, or informational. Examples of such systems are transportation systems, electric power grids, gene regulatory networks, and the Internet. Their approach allows the authors to specify, design, and analyze simulations of extremely large systems, and implement them on massively parallel architectures.

IV. New Directions

15. Andrea Omicini, Alessandro Ricci, and Mirko Miroli, *The Multidisciplinary Patterns of Interaction from Sciences to Computer Science*
In this chapter, Omicini et al. take a multidisciplinary view of interaction by drawing parallels between research outside and within computer science. They point out some of the basic patterns of interaction emerging from a number of heterogeneous research fields, and show how they can be brought to computer science to provide new insights on interaction in complex computational systems.

16. Peter Denning and Thomas Malone, *Coordination*
This chapter discusses coordination, an area of computing concerned with managing the interactions among multiple activities so that they achieve a single, collective result. Principles of coordination have been employed for many years by those who design, build, and evaluate interactive systems. Coordination plays a similarly fundamental role in management science. The chapter presents two complementary views of coordination in human–machine systems, in the belief that coordination principles will play a central role in the new theoretical paradigms of interactive computation.

17. Eric Pacuit and Rohit Parikh, *Social Interaction, Knowledge, and Social Software*
Social procedures are interactions in which humans must engage to reach some goal, whether to build a house or take a train. The authors ask whether it is possible to create a theory of how social procedures work, with a view to creating better ones and ensuring the correctness of the ones we have. This chapter surveys some of the logical and mathematical tools that address this question.

18. Lynn Stein, *Interaction, Computation, and Education*
This volume as a whole documents a fundamental shift in the culture of computation from a focus on algorithmic problem solving to a perspective in which interaction plays a central role. In this chapter, Stein points out that such a shift must be accompanied by a corresponding shift in computer science education, in the fundamental "story" we tell our students in their introductory courses.

We are proud that such distinguished authors have written about this area, and we hope this book will encourage the evolution of interaction as a fundamental principle of computing.

Newton, MA; Port Jefferson, NY; Providence, RI   *Dina Goldin*
March 2006   *Scott Smolka*
                                                         Peter Wegner

Supported by NSF award 0545489.

Contents

Part I

Introduction

Turing, Computing and Communication

Robin Milner

Cambridge University, Cambridge, United Kingdom

Summary. This essay is a slightly edited transcription of a lecture given in 1997 in King's College, Cambridge, where Alan Turing had been a Fellow. The lecture was part of a meeting to celebrate the 60th anniversary of the publication of Turing's paper *On computable numbers, with an application to the Entscheidungsproblem*, published in the *Proceedings of the London Mathematical Society* in 1937.

1 Introduction

How has computer science developed since Turing's founding ideas? His thinking bore strongly both upon the possibility of mechanical intelligence and upon logical foundations. One cannot do justice to both in a short lecture, and I shall continue the discussion of logical foundations begun in the previous lecture.

Physical stored-program computers came to exist some ten years after Turing's paper on the *entscheidungsproblem*, notably with the EDSAC in the Cambridge Mathematical Laboratory in 1949, under the leadership of Maurice Wilkes; a great engineering achievement. Thus logic and engineering are the two foundation stones of computer science; our constructions rest firmly on both foundations, and thereby strengthen both. I shall discuss how the logical foundation has developed through practical experience.

My thesis is that this logical foundation has changed a lot since Turing, but harks back to him. To be more precise:

THESIS:
1 Computing has grown into *informatics*,
   the science of interactive systems.

2 Turing's logical computing machines are matched
   by a *logic of interaction*.

My message is that we must develop this logical theory, partly because otherwise the interactive systems which we build, or which just happen, will escape our understanding and the consequences may be serious, and partly because it is a new scientific challenge. Besides, it has all the charm of inventing the science of navigation while already onboard ship.

2 Concepts in Computer Science

In natural science, concepts arise from the urge to understand observed phenomena. But in computer science, concepts arise as distillations of our design of systems. This is immediately evident in Turing's work, most strikingly with the concept of a *universal logical computing machine*.

By 1937 there was already a rich repertoire of computational procedures. Typically they involved a hand calculating machine and a schematic use of paper in solving, say, a type of differential equation following a specific algorithm. Turing's class of logical computing machines—which he also called "paper machines"—was surely distilled from this repertoire of procedures. But he distilled more, namely the idea of a *universal* paper machine which can analyse and manipulate descriptions of members of the class, even of itself. This demonstrated the logical possibility of the general-purpose stored-program computer.

Turing also, among others, distilled the idea of the *subroutine* in computing. The distillation of this idea was a continuing affair, and didn't happen all at once. Turing's term for subroutine was "subsidiary operation"; anyone familiar with numerical methods must have known exactly what that meant when referring to humanly performed operations.

A concept rarely stands clear unless it has been reached from different angles. The gene is a prime example; it was seen first logically, then physically. So each computer design, whether logical or—like the EDSAC—physical, was a step in the distillation of the notion of subroutine. The distillation continued with the notion of *parametric procedure* in high-level programming languages such as ALGOL, where the humble subroutine was endowed with a rich taxonomy which might have surprised Turing himself. Each high-level language is, at least, a universal paper machine; but each one also expresses higher-level concepts distilled from practice.

In modern computing we build and analyse huge systems, equal in complexity to many systems found in nature—e.g., an ecology. So in computing, as in natural science, there must be many levels of description. Computer science has its organisms, its molecules and its elementary particles—its biology, chemistry and physics:

Levels of Description

Natural Science		Computer Science
Biology	ORGANISMS	Databases, networks, ...
Chemistry	MOLECULES	Metaphors of programming
Physics	PARTICLES	Primitives of programming
	(ELEMENTS)	

At the level of organism we find, for example, species of database and net-work, each with a conceptual armoury. At the level of molecule we find the metaphors, like parametric procedure, provided by programming languages. At the particle level we find—as it were—the most basic parts of speech. (I make no apology for talking so much in terms of language. Computers like screwdrivers are prosthetic devices, but the means to control them is linguistic, not muscular.) The best of these parts of speech and the best of the metaphors become accepted modes of thought; that is, they become concepts.

3 From Metaphor to Concept

I shall now discuss a couple of molecular concepts or metaphors, distilled over the last thirty years, in which the notion of interaction is prominent.

There is a Babel of programming languages. This is not surprising; much of the world we live in can be modelled, analysed or controlled by program, and each application domain has its own structure. But sometimes a central idea finds its first clear expression in a language designed for a particular problem domain. Such was the case with the problem domain of *simulation*.

In the 1960s there was a great vogue in simulation languages. New ones kept emerging. They all gave you ways of making queues of things (in the process which you wished to simulate), giving objects attributes which would determine how long it took to process them, giving agents attributes to determine what things they could process, tossing coins to make it random, and recording what happened in a histogram. These languages usually did not last; one can simulate so many real-world processes that no single genre of language can cover them all. So simulation languages merged into the general stream.

But not without effect. One of them highlighted a new metaphor: the notion of a community of agents all *doing* things to each other, each persisting in time but changing state. This is the notion known to programmers as an *object*, possessing its own state and its repertoire of activities, or so-called *methods*; it is now so famous that even non-programmers have heard of it. It originated in the simulation language known as Simula, invented by Ole-Johann Dahl and Kristen Nygaard. *Object-oriented programming* is now a widely accepted metaphor used in applications which have nothing to do with simulation. So the abstract notion of agent or active object, from being a convenient metaphor, is graduating to the status of a concept in computer science.

Even more fundamental to computing, at the molecular level, is the time-honoured concept of *algorithm*. Until quite recently it could be defined no better than "the kind of process enacted by a computer program", which is no help at all if we are trying to understand what computational processes are! But recently algorithms have come to be characterized precisely as *game-theoretic interactions*. We could hardly wish for better evidence that the notion of interaction is basic to computer science.

4 Concurrent Processes

The notion of *agent* or *active object* brings programming ontology—if you like, the metaphors programmers use in design—much closer to the real world. So why, you may ask, did we not *always* write programs in terms of interactive agents? The answer lies partly in von Neumann's so-called bottleneck, and I want to describe this before I talk about new parts of speech, or elements.

The early computers all followed the model of John von Neumann, in which—as far as the programmer was concerned—only one thing could happen at once; at any given time only one agent could be active. So the possibility of *concurrent activity* or even *co-existence* of such agents could not be expressed in a program—even though underneath, as it were in the machine's subconscious, many wheels would whirr and circuits cycle simultaneously. One can speculate why this sequential discipline was adopted. The familiar calculational procedures, which computers were designed to relieve us of, were all inherently sequential; not at all like cooking recipes which ask you to conduct several processes at once—for example, to slice the beans *while* the water is coming to the boil. This in turn may be because our conscious thought process is sequential; we have so little short term memory that we can't easily think of more than one thing at once.

The bursting of von Neumann's bottleneck is due in part to the premature birth and later triumph of the metaphor of object-oriented programming. But a river never breaks its banks in one place. In the 1960s and 1970s the designers of computer operating systems, people like Edsgar Dijkstra and Tony Hoare, were ill-content with sequential programming metaphors. Programming in the von Neumann model was too much like a child's construction kit; you can build the lorry but you can't build the engine. Consider several programs running simultaneously inside a computer. They may only *appear* to run simultaneously, by virtue of time-slicing, but in any case you need to write the master program—the so-called operating system—which controls them all by interacting with them. This is not *sequential* but *concurrent* activity; you need new language to express concurrent activity, and new theory for it. You cannot decently express it as a metaphor in a sequential language.

Indeed, in the same period, Carl-Adam Petri developed a new model of concurrent processes not only to describe computational behaviour, but also to model office information systems. He was among the first to point out that concurrency is the norm, not the exception.

What this amounts to is that computer scientists began to invent new parts of speech, new elements, to express the metaphors suitable for interactive concurrent systems.

5 The Old and the New Computer Science

The first part of my thesis was that the river of computer science has indeed burst its von Neumann banks, and has become a structural theory of interaction. I call it *informatics* here; I don't know a better word which is as free of misleading connotation. It goes far beyond describing what programs do; it claims that the kind of interactions which go on under the bonnet of a sequential program are no different from those which occur —even involving human components— in the world outside. For example, we have no need to describe these two systems in different terms, if we are thinking of information-flow:

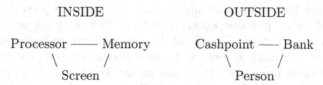

Thus software, from being a *prescription* for how to do something —in Turing's terms a "list of instructions"— becomes much more akin to a *description* of behaviour, not only programmed *on* a computer, but occurring by hap or design *inside* or *outside* it. Here is a set of contrasts, distinguishing the old computer science as a limiting case of the new:

Old Computing		New Computing
Prescription	···	Description
Hierarchical design	···	Heterarchical phenomena
Determinism	···	Nondeterminism
End-result	···	Continuing interaction
(Extension)		(Intension)

Take the first line: Software no longer just *prescribes* behaviour to take place inside a computer; instead, it *describes* information flow in wider systems.

Take the second line: We can no longer confine ourselves to systems which are neatly organised, like an army with colonels and platoons. Consider the Internet; it is a linkage of autonomous agents, more of an informatic rabble than an army. Of course we built many of its parts; but the whole is a heterarchical assembly—something of a *natural* phenomenon.

Take the third line: We can never know enough about an assembly of autonomous agents to predict each twist in its behaviour. We have to take non-determinism as elementary, not just temporary laziness which we can amend later by supplying values for all the hidden variables.

Take the fourth line: The meaning of a conventional computer program, as far as a user is concerned, is just the mathematical function it evaluates. But we users are *inside* our interactive systems; we care about what continually goes on. The meaning surely lies in the whole conversation, not just its end-result. (Indeed there may be no end-result, since there may have been no goal.)

Now, here are some sharper contrasts which hint at what might be the elements of a mathematical theory of interactive systems:

	Computation	Interaction
ACTIVE ENTITY P:	program	active object, agent
ITS MEANING:	function	process
STATICS (COMBINATION):	sequential composition	parallel composition
	$P_1; P_2$	$P_1 \parallel P_2$
DYNAMICS (ACTION):	operate on datum	send/receive message

In the first line, note especially that all *programs* are prescriptive—they are designed with a purpose; *agents* need be neither designed nor purposeful. As for *meanings*, there is a big knowledge gap; we have an impressive mathematical theory of functions, but we still have no consensus on a corresponding theory of discrete processes. (Of course we are working on it.) The *composition* of programs emphasizes the sequentiality imposed by the designer; but in interactive systems everything can happen as soon as the interactions which trigger it have occurred. Finally, concerning *action*, note the asymmetry in computation between an active operator and a passive operand; in an interactive system, messages pass between active peers.

6 Elements of Interaction

Now, what are the new particles —parts of speech, or elements— which allow one to express interaction? They lie at the same elementary level as the operation of a Turing machine on its tape, but they differ. For much longer than the reign of modern computers, the basic idiom of algorithm has been the asymmetric, hierarchical notion of operator acting on operand. But this does not suffice to express interaction between agents as peers; worse, it locks the mind away from the proper mode of thought.

So we must find an elementary model which does for *interaction* what Turing's logical machines do for *computation*. The second part of my thesis was that there is a logic of informatic action, and in my view it is based upon two fundamental elements:

Logical Elements of Interaction
Synchronized action
Channel, or vocative name

These two fit together perfectly; indeed, like quarks, they hardly exist apart. Synchronization is between an action—the vocative use of a name—by one agent, and a reaction by another. At this level, *names* and *channels* are the same thing; in fact, they are the essence of several superficially different things which computer scientists have called *links*, *pointers*, *references*, *identifiers*, *addresses*, ..., and so on. These elements seem slight in themselves, but they serve to unify our theory; they can form the basis of a logical calculus not only for traditional computation but for the wider range of interactive systems.

There are many systems of increasing importance in our lives which show the pervasive role played by naming and synchronized action. We don't have to look far for an example; consider simply a document—not a paper copy, but the virtual kind that exists on the Internet:

- A piece of hypertext representing a document exists nowhere in linear form. It's a mass of pointers, or names, which link its parts in a tree-like way.
- But it does not stop at tree-like structures. Parts of the document will be links into other structures; many links to one structure, for economy.
- When you "click" on such a link, you synchronize your action with an action by the document.
- It does not stop at static structures; some links may command a translation or even a summarization of the text-agent which they call.
- Not all parts reside at one site; some parts may lie across the Atlantic.
- It does not stop at textual structures. Some links will call up animated pictures, others will provide exercises for the reader, games to play, and so on.

All this, just starting from the notion of a document! The web will be much more tangled for other applications. But the point is that you don't just *read* a document like this—you *interact* with it.

I ask you to think of the term "information" actively, as the *activity of informing*. An atomic message, then, is not a passive datum but an action which synchronizes two agents. Our example of active documents has shown that the active/passive polarization between operator and operand, between process and data, is no longer realistic—and we have removed this limitation.

7 Reflection: Back to Turing

We have briefly explored what computer science has become, having been launched logically by Turing, and physically by the earliest computers. The technological story is of course a marvel, and has been a prerequisite for the informatic story, which is what concerns us here. To summarize: Turing's *paper machines* have evolved into the kind of informatic web in which we now live. They are truly virtual, not physical; they are webs of naming, calling, migrating in a sense which has little to do with where they reside, or with how they are physically represented.

Can we ask about these webs the kind of question Turing asked about his paper machines? Both Turing machines and informatic webs are what Herbert Simon and Allen Newell have called *symbol systems*. In each class of symbol systems, one can ask whether a member of the class can represent and manipulate some property of the class itself. Such a phenomenon is called *reflection*. In particular, consider the following:

- A computing entity can *compute a means of computing* (consider the universal Turing machine).
- Can a cognitive entity *know about knowing*?
- Can a learning entity *learn how to learn*?

... and so on. If the answer is "yes", we are inclined to think that the class of entities is properly adult, has come of age. Consider then:

- Can a communicating entity *communicate a means of communicating*?

This question differs intriguingly from the one about computing entities, because it concerns systems of agents in a heterarchy. In a heterarchy you cannot manipulate another agent, in the sense that a universal Turing machine interprets another. The concept of a universal Turing machine relies on a sharp distinction between passive data (e.g., the description of a machine) and active agent (e.g., the machine itself), and I have made a case for eroding this distinction. But in an interactive system you can, by communicating with your neighbour, acquire new links and relinquish old ones. So distributed computing is also adult, in the above sense. In our informatic webs, agents can acquire new contacts by link-manipulation, and so realize new forms of behaviour. That is, a web can spin itself.

To conclude: I believe that computing has evolved in a direction which would excite Alan Turing. His search for primitives continues to inspire our search. He would surely agree that these primitives must relate to computing practice, since he himself spent much effort on plans to build a physical computer, the ACE, not just logical ones. In the same way, but in a wider sense, our primitives relate to informatic practice. So I shall be sorry if computer science ever flies apart into two disciplines, one theoretical and one technological. We are back to our two foundation stones, logic and engineering; among all his other legacies, Turing embodies the wisdom of arching between them.

Computing and Interaction

Farhad Arbab[1,2]

[1] Center for Mathematics and Computer Science (CWI), Amsterdam, The Netherlands
[2] Leiden University, Leiden, The Netherlands

Summary. This chapter offers a rough sketch of the landscape of computing with the specific aim of identifying and interrelating well-established topics such as computability and concurrency to newer areas such as interaction and composition of behavior.

1 Introduction

The size, speed, capacity, and price of computers have all dramatically changed in the last half-century. Still more dramatic are the subtle changes in society's perception of what computers can, should, and are expected to do. Clearly, this change of perception would not have been possible without the technological advances that reduced the size and price of computers, while increasing their speed and capacity. Nevertheless, the social impact of this change of perception and its feedback influence on the advancement of computer science and technology, are too significant to be regarded as mere by-products of those technological advances.

The term *computer* today has a very different meaning than it did in the early part of the twentieth century. Even after such novelties as mechanical and electromechanical calculators had become commonplace in the 1960s, the arithmetic involved in engineering calculations and book-keeping was a time consuming and labor intensive endeavor for businesses and government agencies alike. Analogous to *typist pools* that lingered on until much later, enterprises from engineering and accountant firms to banks and insurance companies employed armies of people to process, record, and extract the large volumes of essentially numerical data that were relevant for their business. Since in the early part of the twentieth century, *computer* was the term that designated these professionals, the machine that could clearly magnify their effectiveness and held the promise of replacing them altogether became known as the *electronic computer*[1].

The social perception of what computers are (to be used for) has evolved through three phases:

1. computers as fast number crunchers;
2. computers as symbol manipulators;
3. computers as mediators and facilitators of interaction.

Two specific transformations marked the above phase transitions. The advent of fast, large main memory and mass-storage devices suitable to store and access the significantly more voluminous amounts of data required for non-numerical symbol manipulation made symbolic computation possible. The watershed that set forth the second transition was the availability of affordable personal computers and digital telecommunication that together fueled the explosion of the Internet.

In spite of the fact that from the beginning, symbol manipulation was as much an inherent ability of electronic computers the juggling of numbers, the perception that computers are really tools for performing fast numerical computations was prevalent. Problems such as information retrieval that did not involve a respectable amount of number crunching were either rejected outright as non-problems, or were considered as problems not worthy of attempts to apply computers and computing to. Subscribers to such views were not all naive outsiders, many an insider considered such areas as business and management, databases, and graphics, to be not only on the fringes of computer applications, but also on the fringes of legitimacy. As late as 1970, James E. Thornton, vice president of Advanced Design Laboratory of Control Data Corporation, who was personally responsible for most of the detailed design of the landmark CDC 6600 computer system, wrote [1]:

> There is, of course, a class of problems which is essentially *noncompu-tational* but which requires a massive and sophisticated storage system. Such uses as inventory control, production control, and the general category of information retrieval would qualify. *Frankly, these do not need a computer.* There are, however, legitimate justifications for a large computer system as a "partner" with the computational usage. [*Emphasis added.*]

---

[1] As of the date of this writing, on the etymology of the word "computer" the free encyclopedia Wikipedia (http://en.wikipedia.org/) says: "The word was originally used to describe a person who performed arithmetic calculations and this usage is still valid. The OED2 lists the year 1897 as the first year the word was used to refer to a mechanical calculating device. By 1946 several qualifiers were introduced by the OED2 to differentiate between the different types of machine. These qualifiers included *analogue, digital* and *electronic*." According to the free English dictionary Wiktionary (http://en.wiktionary.org), however, the usage of the word "computer" as "a person employed to perform computations" is obsolete.

Of course, by that time many people were not only convinced that legitimate computational applications need not involve heavy number crunching, but were already actively working to bring about the changes that turned fringe activities such as databases and graphics into the core of computing, and reshaped it both as *science* as well as by expanding its domain of applications. Nevertheless, Thornton's statement at the time represented the views of a non-negligible minority that has only gradually diminished since. While the numerical applications of computing have steadily grown in number, size, and significance, its non-numerical applications have simply grown even faster and vaster.

We are still at the tail-end of the second transition (from symbolic computation to interaction) and trying come to terms with its full implications on computer science and technology. This involves revisiting some established areas, such as concurrency and software composition, from a new perspective, and leads to a specific field of study concerned with theories and models for *coordination* of interactive concurrent computations. Pragmatic concerns in software engineering have often driven the advancement of computer science. The transition from symbolic computation to interaction involves, among others, coarse-grain reuse in component based software and (third-party) composition of the behavior of services while their actual software cannot be composed.

Already, a growing number of vendors offer an increasing number of useful computations and services packaged in various forms as specialized hardware and/or software. Together with advanced communication networks, this sets the stage to realize all sorts of new complex applications, from embedded systems with demanding timing requirements to geographically distributed, always-on, dynamically evolving cooperation networks of mobile autonomous agents. Tackling the architectures of complex systems whose organization and composition must dynamically change, e.g., to accommodate mobility, or evolve and be reconfigured to adapt to short- as well as long-term changes in their environment, presents new challenges in software engineering.

Two key concepts emerge as core concerns: (1) interaction, and (2) compositionality. While researchers have worked on both individually in the past, we propose that their combination deserves still more serious systematic study because it offers insight into new approaches to coordination of cooperating interacting components that comprise such complex systems.

2 Computing

The formal notions of *computing* and *computability* were introduced by Alonzo Church (1903–1995), in terms of λ-calculus, and Alan Turing (1912–1954), in terms of Turing machines. Both Church and Turing were inspired by David Hilbert's (1862–1943) challenge proposed in his 1900 lecture delivered before the International Congress of Mathematics at Paris, to define a solid foundation for (mechanical) effective methods of finding mathematical truth.

Hilbert's program consisted of finding a set of axioms as the unassailable foundation of mathematics, such that only mathematical truths could be derived from them by the application of any (truth preserving) mechanical operation, and that all mathematical truths could be derived that way.

But, what exactly is a mechanical operation? This was what Church, Turing, and others were to define. Turing himself also intended for his abstract machine to formalize the workings of the human mind. Ironically, his own reasoning on the famous halting problem can be used to show that Turing machines cannot find all mathematical truths, let alone model the workings of the human mind[2]. Kurt Godel's (1906–1978) incompleteness theorem of 1931, which brought the premature end of Hilbert's program for mathematics, clearly shows the limits of formal systems and mechanical truth derivation methods. By his halting problem, Turing intended to provide a constructive proof of Godel's incompleteness theorem: they both show that there are (even mathematical) truths that cannot be derived mechanically, and interestingly in both cases, the crucial step in the proof is a variation of the diagonalization technique first used by Georg Cantor (1845–1918) to show that the infinity of real numbers between any two numbers is greater than the infinity of natural numbers.

It is far from obvious why Turing's simple abstract machine, or Church's λ-calculus, is a reasonable formalization of what we intuitively mean by any mechanical operation. However, all extensions of the Turing machine that have been considered, are shown to be mathematically equivalent to, and no more powerful than, the basic Turing machine. Turing and Church showed the equivalence of Turing machines and λ-calculus. This, plus the fact that other formalizations, e.g., Emil Post's (1897–1954), have all turned out to be equivalent, has increased the credibility of the conjecture that a Turing machine can actually be made to perform any mechanical operation whatsoever. Indeed, it has become reasonable to mathematically define a mechanical operation as any operation that can be performed by a Turing machine, and to accept the view known as the Church–Turing thesis: that the notion of Turing machines (or λ-calculus, or other equivalents) mathematically defines the concept of an algorithm (or an effective, or recursive, or mechanical procedure).

---

[2] Intuitively, human beings believe that the human mind can perceive truths beyond mathematics. If so, the working of the human mind is likely beyond the scope of our formal systems. This may be because as Penrose argues [2], what goes on in the human mind is substantially different than what our formal systems express. He proposes that to comprehend the human mind, we require a hitherto lacking, fundamentally important insight into physics, which is also a prerequisite for a unified theory of everything.

3 Interaction

The Church–Turing thesis can simply be considered as a mathematical definition of what computing is in a strictly technical sense; it reflects the notion of computing of functions. Real computers, on the other hand, do much more than mere computing in this restrictive sense. Among other things, they are sources of heat and noise, and have always been revered (and despised) as (dis)tasteful architectural artifacts, or pieces of furniture. More interestingly, computers also interact: they can act as facilitators, mediators, and coordinators that enable the collaboration of other agents. These other agents may in turn be other computers (or computer programs), sensors and actuators that involve their real world environment, or human beings. The role of a computer as an agent that performs computing, in the strict technical sense of the word, should not be confused with its role as a mediator agent that, e.g., empowers its human users to collaborate with one another (including, for instance, word-processing, where a single user engages in self-collaboration over a span of time). The fact that the computer, in this case, may perform some computation in order to enable the collaboration of other agents, is ancillary to the fact that it needs to interact with these agents to enable their collaboration. To emphasize this distinction, Wegner proposes the concept of an interaction machine [3, 4, 5]. Some of the formal aspects of interaction machines are discussed in [6, 7, 8, 9]. Here we focus on the essential difference between interaction machines and Turing machines.

A Turing machine operates as a closed system: it receives its input tape, starts computing, and (hopefully) halts, at which point its output tape contains the result of its computation. In every step of a computation, the symbol written by a Turing machine on its tape depends only on its internal state and the current symbol it reads from the tape. An interaction machine is an extension of a Turing machine that can interact with its environment with new input and output primitive actions. Unlike other extensions of the Turing machine (such as more tapes, more controls, etc.) this one actually changes the essence of the behavior of the machine. This extension makes interaction machines *open systems.*

Consider an interaction machine I operating in an environment described as a dynamical system E. The symbol that I writes on its tape at a given step, not only depends on its internal state and the current symbol it reads from the tape, but can also depend on the input it obtains directly from E. Because the behavior of E cannot be described by a computable function, I cannot be replaced by a Turing machine. The best approximation of I by a Turing machine, T, would require an encoding of the actual input that I obtains from E, which can be known only *after* the start of the computation. The computation that T performs, in this case, is the same as that of I, but I does more than T because it interacts with its environment E. What T does, in a sense, is analogous to predicting yesterday's weather: it is interesting that it can be done (assuming that it can be done), but it doesn't quite pass muster! To emphasize the distinction, we can imagine that the interaction of *I* with *E* is not limited to just one input: suppose *I* also does a direct output to *E*, followed by another direct input from *E*. Now, because as a dynamical system, *E* is non-computable, and the value of the second input from *E* to *I* depends on the earlier interaction of *E* and *I*, no input tape can encode this "computation" for any Turing machine.

It is the ability of computers (as interaction machines) to interact with the real world, rather than their ability (as mere Turing machines) to carry on ever-more-sophisticated computations, that is having the most dramatic impact on our society. In the traditional models of human–computer interaction, users prepare and consume the information needed and produced by their applications, or select from the alternatives allowed by a rigid structure of computation. In contrast to these models, the emerging models of human–computer interaction remove the barriers between users and their applications. The role of a user is no longer limited to that of an observer or an operator: increasingly, users become active components of their running applications, where they examine, alter, and steer on-going computations. This form of cooperation between humans and computers, and among humans via computers, is a vital necessity in many contemporary applications, where realistic results can be achieved only if human intuition and common-sense is combined with formal reasoning and computation.

For example, *computational steering* allows human experts to intervene and guide an on-going computation with which they interact through visualizations of various scalar, vector, and tensor fields. Construction and manipulation of complex simulation models that use numerical approximation and solutions of partial differential equations, e.g., in computational fluid dynamics and biology, already benefit from such techniques. The applications of computer facilitated collaborative work are among the increasingly important areas of activity in the foreseeable future. They can be regarded as natural extensions of systems where several users simultaneously examine, alter, interact, and steer on-going computations. The promise of *ubiquitous computing* requires the full harnessing of the potential of these combinations. Interaction machines are suitable conceptual models for describing such applications.

Interaction machines suggest a new perspective on composition. Traditionally, software composition has focused on *composition of algorithms*, where (the designer of) one algorithm, as part of its own internal logic, decides to engage another algorithm, e.g., through a function call or a method invocation. Composed behavior ensues as a consequence of composing algorithms and its implied flow of control. Interaction machines are self-contained entities that directly neither offer nor engage algorithms. They can be arranged by third parties to engage one another only through their mutual interactions, which involve no flow of control. This leads to *composition of behavior* where the algorithms (embedded in the individual interaction machines) involved in a composed system do not directly engage each other and (their designers) remain oblivious to their composition.

Van Leeuwen and Wiedermann offer a formal treatment of some of the implications of interactive computing and its relationship with the more traditional views of computability in [10]. Goldin et al. [11] propose persistent Turing machines (PTMs) as a stream-based extension to the Turing machine model with persistence and the same notion of interaction as in interaction machines. They investigate the "minimal" changes to the Turing machine model necessary for capturing the extra expressive power conjectured by Wegner for interaction machines over Turing machines, using a general kind of transition system called interactive transition systems (ITSs) as reference. They show an isomorphism that implies every equivalence result over PTMs carries over to ITSs, and vice versa.

Interaction machines have unpredictable input from their external environment, and can directly affect their environment, unpredictably, due to such input. Because of this property, interaction machines may seem too open for formal studies: the unpredictable way that the environment can affect their behavior can make their behavior underspecified, or even ill-defined. But, this view is misleading. Interaction machines are both useful and interesting for formal studies.

On the one hand, the openness of interaction machines and their consequent underspecified behavior is a valuable true-to-life property. Real systems are composed of components that interact with one another, where each is an open system. Typically, the behavior of each of these components is ill-defined, except within the confines of a set of constraints on its interactions with its environment. When a number of such open systems come together as components to comprise a larger system, the topology of their interactions forms a context that constrains their mutual interactions and yields well-defined behavior.

On the other hand, the concept of interaction machines suggests a clear separation of concerns for the formal study of their behavior, both as components in a larger system, as well as in isolation. Just like a Turing machine, the behavior of an interaction machine can be studied as a computation (in the sense of the Church–Turing thesis) between each pair of its successive interactions. More interestingly, one can abstract away from all such computations, regarding them as internal details of individual components, and embark on a formal study of the constraints, contexts, and conditions on the interactions among the components in a system (as well as between the system and its environment) that ensure and preserve well-behavedness.

Consider, for example, constructing a simple system using three black-box components: a clock, a thermometer, and a display. The clock has an output port through which it periodically produces a string of characters that represents the current time. Similarly, the thermometer has an output port through which it periodically produces a string of characters that represents the current temperature. The display has an input port through which it periodically consumes a string of characters and displays it. Our goal is to build a system—similar to what one finds on top of some tall bank buildings—

that alternately displays the current time and current temperature. It is the constraints on the periods and the relative order of exchanges between these three components that together shape the desired alternating behavior in our composed system. It is at least as essential to study and express these intercomponent constraints that define the behavior of a composed system, as it is to study and specify the computation carried out by each of its individual components. It is even more sensible to focus on such protocols and constraints in isolation from intracomponent computation concerns. And this material is the thread that weaves the fabric of *coordination*.

4 Concurrency

The concept of interaction is closely related to concurrency. Concurrency means that different computations in a system overlap in time. The computations in a concurrent system may be interleaved with one another on a single processor or actually run in parallel (i.e., use more than one physical processor at a time). Parallelism introduces extra concerns (over monoprocessor computing) such as interprocessor communication, the links that carry this communication, synchronization, exclusion, consensus, and graceful recovery or termination in case of partial failures. The parallel computations in a system may or may not be geographically distributed. Geographic distribution escalates the significance of the extra concerns in parallel computing by increasing communication link delays, potential for partial failures, and the difficulty of maintaining consistency, which together make schemes based on central control and global views less tenable in practice.

Nevertheless, concurrency in itself does not change the essence of computing. Clearly, interleaving is but one specific regiment for programming a Turing machine. Parallelism, on the other hand, involves multiple Turing machines. Although not obvious at the outset, it turns out that involving multiple Turing machines does not increase their expressiveness: parallel systems are mathematically equivalent to a single Turing machine. This is not so for interactive systems. What distinguishes an interactive system from other concurrent systems is the fact that an interactive system has unpredictable input from an external environment that it does not control.

The theoretical equivalence of (closed) concurrent systems and a Turing machine is of little practical use. It is far more difficult to consider, design, and reason with a set of concurrent activities than it is to do so with individual sequential activities; the whole, in this case, is considerably more (complex) than the sum of its parts.

The study and the application of concurrency in computer science have a long history. The study of deadlocks, the dining philosophers problem, and the definition of semaphores and monitors were all well established by the early 1970s. Theoretical work on concurrency, e.g., CSP [12, 13], CCS [14], process algebra [15], and π-calculus [16], has helped to show the difficulty of dealing with concurrency, especially when the number of concurrent activities becomes large. Most of these models are more effective for describing closed systems. A number of programming languages have been based upon some of these theoretical models, e.g., Occam [17] uses CSP and LOTOS [18] uses CCS. However, it is illuminating to note that the original context for the interest in concurrency was somewhat different than the demands of the applications of today in two respects:

- In the early days of computing, hardware resources were prohibitively expensive and had to be shared among several programs that had nothing to do with each other, except for the fact that they were unlucky enough to have to compete with each other for a share of the same resources. This was *concurrency of competition*. Today, it is quite feasible to allocate tens, hundreds, and thousands of processors to the same task (if only we could do it right). This is *concurrency of cooperation*. The distinction is that whereas it is sufficient to keep independent competing entities from trampling on each other over shared resources, cooperating entities also depend on the (partial) results they produce for each other. Proper passing and sharing of these results require more complex protocols, which become even more complex as the number of cooperating entities and the degree of their cooperation increase.

- It was only in the 1990s that the falling costs of processor and communication hardware dropped below the threshold where having very large numbers of "active entities" in an application makes pragmatic sense. Massively parallel systems with thousands of processors are a reality today. Current trends in processor hardware and operating system kernel support for threads make it possible to efficiently have in the order of hundreds of active entities running in a process on each processor. Thus, it is not unrealistic to think that a single application can be composed of hundreds of thousands of active entities. Compared to classical uses of concurrency, this is a jump of several orders of magnitude in numbers. When a phenomenon is scaled up by several orders of magnitude, originally insignificant details and concerns often add up to the extent that they can no longer be ignored; we have not just a quantitative change (i.e., more of the same thing), but rather a qualitative change (i.e., involving new properties, or even a whole new phenomenon). In our view, grappling with massive concurrency requires a qualitative change in (classical) models of concurrency.

The primary concern in the design of a concurrent application must be its model of cooperation: how the various active entities comprising the application are to cooperate with each other. Eventually, a set of communication primitives must be used to implement whatever model of cooperation application-designers opt for; the concerns for performance may indirectly affect their design.

It is important to realize that the conceptual gap between the system supported communication primitives and a concurrent application must often be filled with a nontrivial model of cooperation. Ideally, one should be able to design and understand a concurrent system by separately understanding its individual active entities, and how they cooperate. Precise description of how this cooperation is to materialize has a shorter history than models, methods, and languages for precise descriptions of individual active entities. Various ad hoc libraries of functions (e.g., PVM [19], MPI [20], and CORBA [21]) have emerged as the so-called *middle-ware* layer of software to fill this conceptual gap by providing higher-level support for developing concurrent (and especially distributed) applications on top of the lower-level communication models offered by operating system platforms.

The two classical approaches to construction of concurrent systems are shared memory and message passing. In the shared memory model, a piece of real, virtual, or conceptual memory is simultaneously made available to more than one entity, which share accessing and modifying its contents through atomic read/write or store/load operations. In the message-passing model, entities communicate and synchronize by explicit exchange of messages.

In the shared memory model, communication is only a side effect of the timing of the memory access operations that its subscribing entities perform, and of the delay patterns induced by the inherent synchronization imposed by their atomicity. Participation of an entity in any specific exchange, and the whole communication protocol, are strongly influenced by ephemeral timing dependencies. These dependencies are equally likely to arise out of errors, (lucky or unfortunate) coincidences, or subtle implicit ordering and data dependencies that emerge from the global semantics of an application. The shared memory model inherently supports indirect, anonymous communication among participating entities whose activities are decoupled from one another in the temporal domain. But communication is not always explicitly obvious in shared memory models.

Communication is the primary concern in message passing models, and the synchronization involved, if any, is only a side effect of what it takes to realize communication. There are indeed many substantially different variants of message passing. Messages can be targeted or untargeted and the exchange of a message may or may not involve a synchronizing rendezvous between its sender and receiver. Object oriented programming ties the semantics of message passing together with method invocation. This further complicates the semantics of message passing by implicating the semantics of the invoked method and the states of the entities involved in its execution. For instance, when an object invokes a method m of another object, o, it expects o to perform something "meaningful" as suggested by the name of the method m. The (future) state of the calling object may depend on the fulfillment of this expectation, which itself involves assumptions about the actual semantics of the method m, as well as the state of the object o.

While each of the variants of shared memory and message passing communication models is useful for construction of concurrent systems, composition of systems involving many active entities raises a number of issues that go beyond concerns for communication of their constituent entities. We address this in the next section.

5 Composition

From houses and bridges to cars, aircraft, and electronic devices, complex systems are routinely constructed by putting simpler pieces together. This holds for software construction as well. We call a software construction compositional (with respect to a set of properties) only if the properties of the resulting system can be defined as a composition of the properties of its constituent parts. For instance, given the memory requirements M_p and M_q of two programs p and q, the memory requirement of a system constructed by composing p and q can be computed as a composition of M_p and M_q (e.g., $M_p + M_q$, $\max(M_p, M_q)$, etc., depending on how they are composed). On the other hand, the deadlock-freedom property of a system composed out of p and q cannot always be derived as a composition of the deadlock-freedom properties of p and q.

According to one trivial interpretation of this definition, all software construction is compositional: every complex piece of software eventually consists of some composition of a set of primitive instructions, and in principle, its properties can always be derived by applying its relevant rules of composition to the properties of those primitives. This is precisely how one formally derives the semantic properties of relatively simple programs from those of their primitive instructions. However, this trivial interpretation of compositionality quickly becomes uninteresting and useless for complex concurrent systems, for the same reason that deriving interesting properties of a complex piece of mechanical machinery from those of its constituent atoms is intractable. With only a smidgen of exaggeration, one can say that attempting to derive the dynamic run-time behavior of such software in this way is as hopelessly misguided as trying to derive the properties of a running internal combustion engine from an atomic particle model of the engine, its fuel, air, and electricity.

To be useful, our definition of compositionality must be augmented with appropriate definitions of "its constituent parts" and "the properties" that we are interested in. Both of these notions are manifestations of abstraction. Instead of considering individual primitive instructions as the constituents of a complex system, we must identify parts of the system such that each part consists of a (large) collection of such primitives whose precise number and composition we wish to abstract away as internal details of that part. The properties of a collection of primitive instructions that are abstracted away as internal details of a part, versus those that are exposed as the properties of the part, play a crucial role in defining the effectiveness of an abstraction and the flexibility of a composition. The more properties we hide, the more effective an abstraction we have, allowing more freedom of choice in selecting the precise collection or sequence of instructions that comprise an implementation of a part. On the other hand, the less properties we expose, the less of an opportunity we leave for individual parts to affect and be affected by the exposed properties of other parts. This, in turn, restricts the possibility of influencing the role that a given part can play in different compositions.

To identify the exposed properties of a part that can and cannot be influenced through its composition with other parts, we distinguish between its behavior versus its semantics. To show the usefulness of this distinction, consider a simple adder as a (software) part (for instance, consider this adder as a process, an agent, an object, a component, etc.). This adder takes two input values, x and y, and produces a result, z, which is the sum of x and y. For this adder to be useful, it must expose its property of how it relates the values x, y, and z, that is $z = x + y$. We call this the *semantics* of the adder because it reflects the meaning of what it does. In addition to this semantics, successful composition of this adder as a part in any larger system requires the knowledge of certain other properties of the adder that must also be exposed. For instance, we need clear answers to the following questions:

- Does the adder consume x and y in a specific order, or does it consume whichever arrives first?
- Does it consume x and y only when both are available?
- Does it consume x and y atomically, or in separate steps that can potentially be interleaved with other events?
- Does it produce z in a separate step, with possible interleaving of other events, or does it compute and produce z atomically together with:
  - the atomic consumption of both x and y, or
  - the consumption of x or y, whichever is consumed last?

The answers to such questions define the (externally observable) *behavior* of the adder, above and beyond its mere semantics. It is clear that even in the simple case of our trivial adder, different alternative answers to the above questions are possible, which means we can have different adders, each with its own different (externally observable) behavior, all sharing (or implementing) the same semantics, i.e., $z = x + y$.

The distinction between behavior and semantics is important in composition of all concurrent systems. However, it becomes essential in concurrent systems where autonomy, anonymity, and reuse of parts comprise a primary concern. Such is the case for a system composed of interacting machines, which we contend serves as the best model for component-based concurrent software. Components are expected to be independent commodities, viable in their binary forms in the (not necessarily commercial) marketplace, developed, offered, deployed, integrated, and maintained, by separate autonomous organizations in mutually unknown and unknowable contexts, over long spans of time. It is impossible to determine the properties of a system composed out of a set of components without explicit knowledge of both (1) the relevant behavioral properties of the components, and (2) the composition scheme's rules that affect those properties.

Traditional schemes for composition of software parts into more complex systems rely on variants of procedure call (including method invocation of object oriented models). Typically, each such scheme specifies much of the extra-semantic properties of the behavior of the composed system by pre-defining aspects of composition such as the (non)atomicity of the call and its return result, synchronization points, permissible concurrency, etc. This limits composition alternatives and restricts the possible behavior that can be obtained by composing a given set of software part to the choices prescribed in that scheme. Moreover, composition through procedure calls requires an intimate familiarity of the caller with the semantics of the called procedure (or method), which creates an asymmetric semantic dependency between the two. This semantic dependency, together with the unavailability of (or stringent restrictions on) the means to control the extra-semantic behavioral properties of a software composition at its composition time, severely limit the range of possible variations that can be composed out of the same set of software parts, which in turn limits the reusability of those software parts.

Component composition is expected to be more flexible than other forms of software composition, such as module interconnections, method invocations, or procedure calls. It is expected to allow the same components to play different roles in different compositions. This flexibility requires the ability to influence the behavior of components at the time of their composition and places the emphasis in composition on interaction. Coordination models and languages [22] address precisely the issues involved in managing the interactions among the constituents of a concurrent system into a coherently coordinated cooperation. However, the different mechanisms that various coordination models offer to manage interaction do not all equally support the increased level of flexibility required in component composition.

In the chapter "Composition of Interacting Computations" in this book, we present a brief overview of coordination models and languages and offer a framework for their classification. We then describe a specific model, called Reo [23], that uniquely uses interaction as its only primitive concept for compositional construction of component coordination protocols.

6 Discussion

The classical notion of computing was forged to formalize and study the algorithmic aspects of computing mathematical functions. Real computers do more than compute mathematical functions; they also interact. Interaction is an increasingly important aspect of the behavior of our modern (hardware and software) computing devices, which often act as agents that engage and communicate with other agents in the real world. Interaction is also the key concern in the composition of complex computing systems out of independent building block components that often run concurrently with one another. The model of interaction machines extends the notion of computing, as what real computing devices do, beyond the classical notion of computing, as algorithmic evaluation of mathematical functions.

Our society increasingly relies on computing devices not only as number crunchers and symbol manipulators, but more importantly, as mediators and facilitators of interaction. Models of computation that incorporate interaction as a primitive concept on a par with that of algorithmic computing form the foundation for study, understanding, and reliable construction of modern computing.

References

1. Thornton, J.: Design of a Computer: The Control Data 6600. Scott, Foresman and Company, 1970.
2. Penrose, R.: The Emperor's New Mind. Oxford University Press, 1990.
3. Wegner, P.: Interaction as a basis for empirical computer science. ACM Computing Surveys **27**, 1995, pp. 45–48.
4. Wegner, P.: Interactive foundations of computing. Theoretical Computer Science **192**, 1998, pp. 315–351.
5. Wegner, P., Goldin, D.: Computation beyond Turing machines. Communications of the ACM **46**, 2003.
6. Wegner, P., Goldin, D.: Coinductive models of finite computing agents. In: Proc. Coalgebraic Methods in Computer Science (CMCS). Volume 19 of Electronic Notes in Theoretical Computer Science (ENTCS), Elsevier, 1999.
7. van Leeuwen, J., Wiedermann, J.: On the power of interactive computing. In van Leeuwen, J., Watanabe, O., Hagiya, M., Mosses, P.D., Ito, T., eds.: Proceedings of the 1st International Conference on Theoretical Computer Science — Exploring New Frontiers of Theoretical Informatics, IFIP TCS'2000 (Sendai, Japan, August 17-19, 2000. Volume 1872 of LNCS. Springer-Verlag, Berlin-Heidelberg-New York-Barcelona-Hong Kong-London-Milan-Paris-Singapore-Tokyo, 2000, pp. 619–623.
8. van Leeuwen, J., Wiedermann, J.: Beyond the turing limit: Evolving interactive systems. In Pacholski, L., Ruicka, P., eds.: SOFSEM 2001: Theory and Practice of Informatics: 28th Conference on Current Trends in Theory and Practice of Informatics. Volume 2234 of Lecture Notes in Computer Science. Springer-Verlag, 2001, pp. 90–109.
9. Wegner, P., Goldin, D.: Interaction, computability, and church's thesis. British Computer Journal, 2005 (to appear).
10. van Leeuwen, J., Wiedermann, J.: A Theory of Interactive Computation. In: [24], 2006.
11. Goldin, D., Smolka, S., Attie, P., Sonderegger, E.: Turing machines, transition systems, and interaction. Information and Computation Journal **194**, 2004, pp. 101–128.
12. Hoare, C.: Communicating Sequential Processes. Communications of the ACM **21**, 1978.
13. Hoare, C.: Communicating Sequential Processes. Prentice Hall International Series in Computer Science. Prentice-Hall, 1985.

14. Milner, R.: Communication and Concurrency. Prentice Hall International Series in Computer Science. Prentice Hall, 1989.
15. Bergstra, J., Klop, J.: Process algebra for synchronous communication. Information and Control **60**, 1984, pp. 109–137.
16. Milner, R.: Elements of interaction. Communications of the ACM **36**, 1993, pp. 78–89.
17. INMOS Ltd.: OCCAM 2, Reference Manual. Series in Computer Science. Prentice-Hall, 1988.
18. Bolognesi, T., Brinksma, E.: Introduction to the ISO specification language LOTOS. Computer Networks and ISDN Systems **14**, 1986, pp. 25–59.
19. (PVM) http://www.csm.ornl.gov/pvm.
20. (MPI) http://www-unix.mcs.anl.gov/mpi/.
21. (CORBA) http://www.omg.org.
22. Papadopoulos, G., Arbab, F.: Coordination models and languages. In Zelkowitz, M., ed.: Advances in Computers – The Engineering of Large Systems. Volume 46. Academic Press, 1998, pp. 329–400.
23. Arbab, F.: Reo: A channel-based coordination model for component composition. Mathematical Structures in Computer Science **14**, 2004, pp. 329–366.
24. Goldin, D., Smolka, S., Wegner, P., eds.: Interactive Computation: The New Paradigm. Springer-Verlag, 2006 (this volume).

Principles of Interactive Computation

Dina Goldin and Peter Wegner

Brown University, Providence, RI, USA

Summary. This chapter explores the authors' 10-year contributions to interactive computing, with special emphasis on the philosophical question of how truth has been used and misused in computing and other disciplines. We explore the role of *rationalism* and *empiricism* in formulating true principles of computer science, politics, and religion. We show that interaction is an empiricist rather than rationalist principle, and that rationalist proponents of computing have been the strongest opponents of our belief that interaction provides an empirical foundation for both computer problem solving and human behavior. The rationalist position was adopted by Pythagoras, Descartes, Kant, and many modern philosophers; our interactive approach to computing suggests that empiricism provides a better framework for understanding principles of computing.

We provide an empirical analysis of questions like "can machines think", and "why interaction is more powerful than algorithms". We discuss *persistent Turing machines* as a model of sequential interaction that formally proves the greater power of interaction over algorithms and Turing machines. We explain that the *Strong Church–Turing Thesis*, formulated by theorists in the 1960s, violates Turing's original thesis about unsolvability of the decision problem and is a myth, in the sense that it departs from the principles of Turing's unsolvability result in his 1936 paper. Our analysis contributes to the book's goals towards the acceptance of interactive computing as a principle that goes beyond Turing machine models of computer problem solving.

1 Scientific, Political, and Religious Truth

Alan Turing's 1936 paper "On computable numbers with an application to the *Entscheidungsproblem* (decision problem)" [12] played a central role in the 1960s in establishing a mathematical paradigm of computation. Turing's goal was to show that Hilbert's decision problem was unsolvable in the sense that computers could not prove the truth or falsity of mathematical theorems. His paper strengthened Godel's earlier proof that mathematical theorems were not provable by logic, and weakened the belief in strong mental mathematical ability, showing that human mathematical theorem proving through logic or computing was mentally incomplete.

However, such weakness in modeling mathematics was unwelcome to mathematical thinkers who believed that human reasoning could completely express mathematical ideas about the world. They believed that mathematics was a widespread scientific method for reasoning about physics and computation and that human thought provided a basis for scientific, philosophical, political, and religious understanding. They reinterpreted Turing's paper proving that computers could not solve all mathematical theorems, wrongly asserting that computers could in fact solve all computable problems (including mathematical problems), and that all computation could be done by Turing machines through algorithmic solution methods. Though Turing clearly showed this to be untrue, the desire to believe that computers and rationalist humans could solve a complete range of problems was so strong that Turing's counterarguments could easily be brushed aside and ignored.

There are many applications where humans consider it more important to adopt and justify principles rather than to prove them true. This is so in politics, where politicians have tenaciously preserved dubious principles in order to consolidate their power, regardless of whether the principles are true or ethical. This occurred in Germany under Hitler's Nazi principles, which he retained as a justification for dominating Germany and Europe until he was defeated in a costly war. It occurred under Stalin, who used Communist principles to eliminate his adversaries until he was himself eliminated, and more recently under Saddam Hussein and other democratically elected dictators. It has led to a decline of European scientific principles about the world in favor of extraneous political ideas.

Religions also seek to retain strongly established a priori beliefs independently of their truth. Christianity, Judaism, and Islam preserve their belief in God and in the validity of biblical texts that distinguish their religion from other religions, and can eliminate and kill nonbelievers simply because their beliefs differ, independently of their truth. Truth is adjusted so that religious belief is inherently true and is used to destroy alternative ideas about society independently of the truth or falsity of religious or secular ideas. For example it is appropriate to discredit Darwin's evolution theory because it negates the biblical account of creation in spite of its experimental validity, just as Copernican and Galilean models were discredited three hundred years earlier.

The questionable manipulation of truth in politics and religion is widely acknowledged, but is nevertheless accepted and practiced by particular political and religious organizations. Scientists have assumed that truth is more often falsified by philosophical experts than by scientific researchers, but careful analysis shows that this is not always the case and that truth claims among scientists like Newton and Einstein, or mathematicians like Hilbert, can be as false as the truth claims of political and religious experts. Newtonian physics was assumed indubitably true for 200 years until modified by Einstein's theory of relativity, while Descartes philosophical assumption that "Cogito Ergo

Sum" is indubitably true is seen in retrospect as a questionable assumption that has been used to support many untrue beliefs on the basis of rationalist principles that can be easily disproved by empiricism.

2 Rationalism Versus Empiricism

Rationalism holds that truth is determined by the human mind in terms of "a priori" (predetermined) insight about knowledge, while empiricism holds that knowledge is confirmed only by experience of actual perceptions that determine knowledge. Rationalism implies that people can strongly advocate scientific, political, or religious knowledge through "a priori" mental properties of the brain that are inherently true and cannot be changed by experiments, while empiricism implies that experiments are more effective than predetermined a priori properties of the brain in determining scientific, political, or religious knowledge. Since rationalists believe humans have smarter forms of understanding than do empiricists, and can ignore empirical forms of knowledge, rationalism is often adopted as a broader and more complete form of knowledge, even though it can support wrong and sometimes disastrous principles.

The adoption of rationalism by Pythagoras as an a priori basis for mathematical truth led to its adoption by Plato, who focused on geometry as a central rationalist discipline whose a priori truth implied that a priori principles were a central justification of human knowledge. Aristotle accepted Plato's rationalist view of truth, though his idea of the syllogism was in part empiricist (Socrates mortality was due to the empirical fact that all men are mortal). Though some scientists and philosophers accepted empiricism, the much greater practical power of rationalism helped to establish its role as a primary basis for knowledge about the world and society. This was strengthened by the choice of rationalism as a primary basis for religious beliefs like the existence of God, and the truth of biblical narrative (which could not be proved by empiricism though easily acceptable through rationalism).

St. Augustine (fifth century) and St. Thomas Aquinas (thirteenth century) developed rationalist philosophical models of religion that redefined Christian beliefs in ways that are still accepted today. Descartes is considered the world's greatest modern philosopher primarily because his Jesuit upbringing allowed him to define philosophy in terms of rationalist religious principles at a time when it was being questioned both by scientists like Galileo and by religious dissenters like Martin Luther. Newton solidified scientific principles of Galileo, but spent the last 30 years of his life studying religion. Detailed analysis of philosophers like Descartes and Kant makes it clear that the basis for acceptance of philosophical ideas had more to do with their contributions to religious thought than with their inherent truth or the strength of their arguments.

Locke, Berkeley, and Hume are among the few widely studied empiricist philosophers who contributed substantially to human and political thought. All three were strongly challenged by rationalist opponents, but contributed to the strength of British and US politics though not to European politics. Locke had to flee to Holland during the short Catholic reign of James II (1685–88) to avoid imprisonment and potential death in the Tower of London as a Protestant dissenter. His ideas contributed to the power of the British Parliament, to the Bank of England, and to the US Constitution. His essay on religious toleration, written while in exile in Holland to support toleration between Protestants and Catholics, was used in the US Constitution to support separation of church and state. Locke's contributions to both the growth and power of the British empire and the rise of US democracy suggests that empiricism properly applied can contribute to both the quality and the persistence of political democracies.

Though empiricism has enhanced both scientific research and political democracy, it could not displace rationalism in European politics or in widespread religious beliefs. Kant's early work was influenced by Hume's empiricism, but his later written *Critique of Pure Reason* was strongly rationalist, advocating a priori knowledge over experiment as a basis for acceptance of reason and truth. Kant's model led to the rationalist philosophy of Hegel, which in turn influenced the communist rationalism of Marx and the Nazi rationalism of Hitler. Contemporary politicians like US president Bush are strongly rationalist, using a priori political and religious certainty to support principles like the war in Iraq or the sanctity of marriage in contradicting empiricist assertions about human nature raised by their opponents.

Mathematicians have traditionally believed that mathematics is justified by rationalist rather than empiricist principles because properties of numbers, geometry, and equations are a priori and therefore rational. Hilbert's assumption that all mathematical assertions could be logically proved was considered an a priori idea, and its empirical disproof by Godel and Turing was considered suspect because empiricism should not intrude on a priori inherently rationalist principles. Turing's proof that computers could not automatically decide all mathematical theorems was likewise an empiricist disproof of an a priori rationalist idea, and the fast and loose idea that Turing machines can solve all computable problems was a return from empiricist to previously accepted rationalist a priori results.

The choice of interaction as a computational extension of Turing machines can be viewed as an empiricist model of computing associated with Turing's original empiricist assertion. The strong resistance to this view is in part due to the idea that empiricist models should not intrude on a priori rationalist assumptions about the nature of computation. It is for this reason that we have begun this chapter with a philosophical discussion of the role of empiricism and rationalism in processes of computation and human thought.

3 Turing's 90th Birthday

Turing was born in 1912 and died tragically in 1954 around his 42nd birthday, committing suicide because he was being prosecuted by the police as a homosexual. His 90th birthday conference in Lausanne in 2002 yielded a book about his life and legacy [11] with articles by Andrew Hodges, Martin Davis, Daniel Dennett, Jack Kopeland, Ray Kurzweil, and many other writers including the editor Christof Teuscher and the authors of this chapter.

Andrew Hodges, author of a comprehensive book on Turing, reviews his life and examines what Turing might have contributed had he lived longer. Copeland explores Turing's contributions to artificial intelligence, artificial life, and the Turing Test of whether machines can think. Teuscher explores his contributions to neural networks and unorganized machines. The authors show that Turing's contributions are much broader than Turing machines, and include interaction as a super-Turing model that Turing had already examined through choice machines, oracles, and unorganized machines.

Several writers used this opportunity to explore the pros and cons of hypercomputation as an extension of Turing machines. Martin Davis claimed that hypercomputation simply shows that noncomputable inputs may yield noncomputable outputs and that all computable problems can in fact be solved by Turing machines. We show that algorithms can express only a subset of computable problems and that interaction provides a framework for expressing non-algorithmic problems and extending Turing machine models.

Turing machines and algorithms must completely specify all inputs before they start computing, while *interaction machines* [17] can add actions occurring during the course of the computation. Driving home from work is an example of a computation where actions observed during the course of driving must be included in deciding how to drive and is therefore an example of an interactive non-algorithmic computation. Drivers must observe the road conditions, the cars in front of them, the traffic lights, and pedestrians crossing the street in order to decide how to drive and whether to change the speed or the direction of driving. This eliminates a predefined algorithmic specification of exactly how and where to drive and shows that interaction is more expressive than algorithms in the context of driving home.

Other similar extensions of interactive over algorithmic specification include operating systems, managing a company, fighting opponents in a war, or even aiding one's partner in a marriage. Interactive computations are more powerful than algorithmic computations of Turing machines in many practical situations that occur frequently in computing. Their power does not depend on the quality of prior inputs as suggested by Martin Davis, but it does depend on the degree to which the environment can be observed and acted upon during the course of the computation.

4 Can Machines Think?

Turing in his 1950 paper "Machinery and intelligence" [14] suggests that intelligence should be defined by the ability of machines to respond to questions exactly like humans, so that their ability to think and understand cannot be distinguished from that of humans. Turing not unexpectedly equated "machines" with "Turing machines". He permitted machines to delay their answer to mimic the slower response time of humans in games or mathematical computing, but did not consider that machines can sometimes be inherently slower than humans, or require hidden interfaces from agents or oracles when they answer questions.

Skeptics who believe that machines cannot think can be divided into two classes:

- *intentional skeptics* who believe that that machines that simulate thinking cannot think, because their behavior does not completely capture inner (intentional) awareness or understanding;
- *extensional skeptics* who believe that machines have inherently weaker extensional behavior than humans, because they cannot completely model physics or consciousness.

Searle is an intentional skeptic who argues that passing the test intentionally did not constitute thinking because competence did not constitute inner understanding, while Penrose [7] asserts that machines are not extensionally as expressive as physical or human mental models.

We agree with Penrose that Turing machines cannot model the real world, but disagree that this implies extensional skepticism because interaction machines can model physical behavior of the real world and mental behavior of the brain. Our assertion that interaction is more powerful than algorithms implies not only greater computing power but also greater thinking power of interactive machines.

Penrose builds an elaborate house of cards on the noncomputability of physics by Turing machines. However, this house of cards collapses if we accept that Turing machines do not model all of computation. Penrose's argument that physical systems are subject to elusive noncomputable laws yet to be discovered is wrong, since interaction is sufficiently expressive to describe physical phenomena like action at a distance, nondeterminism, and chaos, which Penrose cites as examples of physical behavior not expressible by computers. Penrose's error in equating Turing machines with the intuitive notion of computing is similar to Plato's identification of reflections on the walls of a cave with the intuitive richness of the real world. Penrose is s self-described Platonic rationalist whose arguments based on the acceptance of Church's thesis are disguised forms of rationalism, denying first-class status to empirical models of interactive computation.

Penrose's dichotomy between computing on the one hand and physics and cognition on the other is based on a misconception concerning the nature of computing that was shared by the theorists of the 1960s and has its roots in the rationalism of Plato and Descartes. The insight that the rationalist/empiricist dichotomy corresponds to algorithms and interaction and that "machines" can model physics and cognition through interaction, allows computing to be classified as empirical along with physics and cognition. By identifying interaction as an ingredient that distinguishes empiricism from rationalism and showing that interaction machines express empirical computer science, we can show that the arguments of Plato, Penrose, and rationalist computer scientists of the 1960s are rooted in a common fallacy concerning the role of noninteractive algorithmic abstractions in modeling computation in the real world.

5 Why Interaction is More Powerful than Algorithms

The paper by this title [16] was a primary early attempt to explore the distinction between algorithms and interaction. It was widely praised by practical programmers but criticized by mathematical rationalists who believed that Turing machines express all forms of problem solving and computation. However, algorithms yield outputs completely expressible by memoriless, history-independent inputs, while interactive systems like personal computers, airline reservation systems, and robots provide history-dependent services over time that can learn from and adapt to experience.

Algorithms are "sales contracts" that deliver outputs in exchange for an input, while interactive system specifications are "marriage contracts" that specify their behavior for all contingencies (in sickness and in health) over the lifetime of the object (till death do us part). The folk wisdom that marriage contracts cannot be reduced to sales contracts is made precise by showing that interaction cannot be reduced to algorithms.

Interaction provides a better model than Turing machines for object-oriented programming. Objects are interactive agents that can remember their past and provide time-varying services to their clients not expressible by algorithms. It is fashionable to say that everyone talks about object-oriented programming but no one knows what it is. But knowing what it is has proved elusive because of the implicit assumption that explanations must specify what it is by algorithms, that excludes specifyng what it is through interaction. The better explanation of computational behaviors through interaction is similar to that used in better expressing the notion "can machines think", and occurs also in many other descriptions of computing.

Interactive extensions of Turing machines through dynamic external environments can be called interaction machines. Interaction machines may have single or multiple input streams, synchronous or asynchronous actions, and can differ along many other dimensions. Interaction machines transform closed to open systems and express behavior beyond that computable by algorithms in the following ways:

Claim: Interaction machine behavior is not expressible by Turing machine
  behavior.
Informal evidence of richer behavior: Turing machines cannot handle the passage of time or interactive events that occur during computation.
Formal evidence of irreducibility: Input streams of interaction machines are
  not expressible by finite inputs, since any finite representation can be
  dynamically extended by uncontrollable adversaries.

The radical view that Turing machines are not the most powerful computing mechanism has a distinguished pedigree. It was accepted by Turing who
assumed in 1936 that choice machines were not expressible by Turing machines
and showed in 1939 that oracles for predicting noncomputable functions were
not Turing machines. Milner noticed as early as 1975 that concurrent processes cannot be expressed as algorithms, while Manna and Pnueli showed in
1980 that nonterminating reactive processes like operating systems cannot be
modeled by algorithms.

Input and output actions of processes and objects are performed with
logical sensors and effectors that change external data. Objects and robots
have very similar interactive models of computation: robots differ from objects
only in that their sensors and effectors have physical rather than logical effects.
Interaction machines can model objects, software engineering applications,
robots, intelligent agents, distributed systems, and networks like the Internet
and the World-Wide Web.

6 Theory of Sequential Interaction

The hypothesis that interactive computing agents are more expressive than
algorithms requires fundamental assumptions about models of computation
to be reexamined. What are the minimal extensions necessary to Turing machines to capture the salient aspects of interactive computing? This question
serves as a motivation for a new model of computation called *persistent Turing
machines* (PTMs), introduced by Goldin et al. [3]; van Leeuwen and Wiedermann's chapter in this book provides a related model, with similar motiva-
tions [15]. PTMs allow us to formally prove Wegner's hypothesis regarding
the greater expressiveness of interaction.

PTMs are interaction machines that extend Turing machine semantics in
two different ways, with dynamic streams and persistence, capturing sequential interactive computations. A PTM is a nondeterministic three-tape Turing
machine (N3TM) with a read-only input tape, a read/write work tape, and
a write-only output tape. Its input is a *stream of tokens* (strings) that are
generated *dynamically* by the PTM's environment during the computation.

A PTM computation is an infinite sequence of *macrosteps*; the i'th
macrostep consumes the i'th input token a_i from the input stream, and produces the i'th output token for the output stream. Each macrostep is an

N3TM computation consisting of multiple N3TM transitions (microsteps), just as each input and output token is a string consisting of multiple characters. The input and output tokens are temporally interleaved, resulting in the interaction stream $\{(a_1, o_1), (a_2, o_2), ...\}$. This stream represents the *observed behavior* of the PTM during the computation.

PTM computations are *persistent* in the sense that a notion of "memory" (work-tape contents) is maintained from one macrostep to the next. Thus the output of each macrostep o_i depends both on the input a_i and on the work tape contents at the beginning of the macrostep. However, the contents of the worktape is hidden internally, and is not considered observable. Thus this contents is not part of interaction streams, which only reflect input and output (observable) values.

Persistence extends the effect of inputs. An input token affects the computation of its corresponding macrostep, including the work tape. The work tape in turn affects subsequent computation steps. If the work tape were erased, then the input token could not affect subsequent macrosteps, but only "its own" macrostep. With persistence, a macrostep can be affected by all preceeding input tokens; this property is known as *history dependence*.

Three results concerning the expressiveness of PTMs are discussed below. The first result is that the class of PTMs is isomorphic to *interactive transition systems* (ITSs), which are effective transition systems whose actions consist of input/output pairs, thereby allowing one to view PTMs as ITSs "in disguise". This result addresses an open question concerning the relative expressive power of Turing machines and transition systems. It has been known that transition systems are capable of simulating Turing machines. The other direction, namely "What extensions are required of Turing machines so they can simulate transitions systems?", is solved by PTMs.

The second result is the greater expressiveness of PTMs over *amnesic Turing machines* (ATMs), which are a subclass of PTMs that do not have persistence, in effect by erasing their work tape. ATMs extend Turing machines with dynamic streams but without memory. An example is a squaring machine, whose input and output are streams of numbers; at i'th macrostep, if the input number is a_i, the output is its square a_i^2. While some have found it tempting to think that only dynamic streams are needed to model interaction, such as [9], our results show that persistence (memory) is also necessary. Furthermore, since ATMS are an extension of Turing machines, the strictly greater expressiveness of PTMs over ATMs also implies that PTMs are more expressive than Turing machines.

The third result proves the existence of a *universal* PTM; similarly to a universal Turing machine, a universal PTM can simulate the behavior of any arbitrary PTM.

PTMs perform sequential interactive computations, defined as follows:

Sequential Interactive Computation: A sequential interactive computation continuously interacts with its environment by alternately accepting an input string and computing a corresponding output string. Each output-string computation may be both nondeterministic and history-dependent, with the resultant output string depending not only on the current input string, but also on all previous input strings.

PTMs do not capture all forms of interactive computation. Interaction encompasses nonsequential computation as well, specifically multistream, or multiagent, computation [17]. However, examples of sequential interactive computation abound, including Java objects, static C routines, single-user databases, and network protocols. A "simulator PTM" can be constructed for each of these examples, similarly to the construction of the universal PTM. The result is a sequential interactive analogue to the Church–Turing thesis, stating that PTMs capture all sequential interaction:

Sequential Interaction Thesis: Any sequential interactive computation can be performed by a persistent Turing machine.

This hypothesis establishes the foundation of the theory of sequential interaction, with PTMs and ITSs as its alternative canonical models of computation. Since PTMs are more expressive than amnesic TMs and Turing machines, this theory represents a more powerful problem-solving paradigm than the traditional theory of computation (TOC), confirming the conjecture that "interaction is more powerful than algorithms". We also expect that this theory will prove as robust as TOC, with appropriate analogues to fundamental TOC concepts such as logic and complexity.

7 The Church–Turing Thesis Myth

The greater expressiveness of interaction over Turing machines is often viewed as violating the *Church–Turing thesis* (CTT). This is a misconception, due to the fact that the Church–Turing thesis has been commonly reinterpreted; we call this reinterpretation the *Strong Church–Turing thesis* (SCT). In this section, we show that the equivalence of the two theses is a myth; a longer discussion can be found in [4]. Our work disproves SCT, without challenging the original Church–Turing thesis.

The Church–Turing thesis, developed when Turing visited Church in Princeton in 1937–38 and included in the opening section of [13], asserted that Turing machines and the lambda calculus could compute all algorithms for effectively computable, recursive, mathematical functions.

Church–Turing thesis (CTT): Whenever there is an effective algorithm for computing a mathematical function it can be computed by a Turing machine or by the lambda calculus.

While *effectiveness* was a common notion among mathematicians and logicians of early twentieth century, it lacked a formal definition. By identifying the notion of effective function computability with the computation of Turing machines (as well as the lambda calculus and recursive functions), the Church–Turing thesis serves to provide a formal definition in the case of effective computation of functions, based on transformations of inputs to outputs. However this thesis was extended in the 1960s to a broader notion of computability, which we call the Strong Church–Turing thesis.

Strong Church–Turing thesis (SCT): A Turing machine can compute anything that any computer can compute. It can solve all problems that are expressible as computations (well beyond computable functions).

While the Church–Turing thesis is correct, this later version is not equivalent to it; in fact, PTMs prove it wrong. Since they are inequivalent, a proof that SCT is wrong does not challenge the original thesis. However, the Strong Church–Turing thesis is still widely accepted as an axiom that underlies theoretical computer science, and establishes a mathematical principle for computing analogous to those underlying physics and other sciences.

The equivalence of the Strong Church–Turing thesis to the original is a myth, clearly refuted by interactive models of computation. The widespread acceptance of this myth rests on the following beliefs:

1. All computable problems are mathematical problems expressible by functions from integers to integers, and therefore captured by Turing machines.
2. All computable problems can be described by algorithms (the primary form of all computation).
3. Algorithms are what computers do.

The first of these beliefs views computer science as a mathematical discipline. According to this world-view, mathematics strengthens the form of computing just as it has strengthened scientific models of physics and other disciplines. Though Turing was educated as a mathematician, he did not share the mathematical world-view [1]. However, mathematicians like Martin Davis, Von Neumann, Karp, Rabin, Scott, and Knuth accepted the mathematical ideas of Pythagoras, Descartes, Hilbert, and others that mathematics was an a priori rationalist principle that lay at the root of philosophy and science. They ignored Godel and Turing's proofs that mathematics was too week to be a universal problem solving principle in favor of the old a priori belief that mathematics was at the foundation of science in general and computer science in particular.

The second of these beliefs positions algorithms at the center of computer science; it ties the first and the third beliefs together, resulting in the Strong Church–Turing thesis. This central position of algorithms was a deliberate historical development of the 1960s, when the discipline of computer science was still in its formative stages. While there was an agreement on the strong role of algorithms, there was no agreement on their definition; two distinct and incompatible interpretations can be identified. The first interpretation, found in Knuth [5], defines algorithms as function-based transformations of inputs to outputs; the second, found in less theoretical textbooks such as [8], defines them as abstract descriptions of the behavior of a program. Yuri Gurevich's chapter in this book [2] also reflects this second view of algorithms.

While the former interpretation of the notion of algorithm is consistent with the rationalist approach of the first belief, the latter interpretation is consistent with the empiricist approach of the third belief. The incompatibility of these interpretations pulls apart the three beliefs, bringing down the Strong Church–Turing thesis.

Hoare, Milner, and other Turing award winners realized in the 1970s that Turing machines do not model all problem solving, but believed it was not yet appropriate to challenge TMs as a complete model of computation. They separated interaction from computation, thereby avoiding the view that interaction was an expanded form of computation, raised by Wegner in 1997 [16].

The interactive view of computation is now widely accepted by many programmers, but is strongly disputed by adherents of the Turing machine model who regard the interaction model as an unnecessary and unproven paradigm shift. We believe it is now appropriate to accept the legitimacy of interactive models of computation, since new applications of agents, embedded systems, and the Internet expand the role of interaction as a fundamental part of computation.

8 Conclusion

Interaction provides an expanded model of computing that extends the class of computable problems from algorithms computable by Turing machines to interactive adaptive behavior of airline reservation systems or automatic cars. The paradigm shift from algorithms to interaction requires a change in modes of thought from a priori rationalism to empiricist testing that impacts scientific models of physics, mathematics, or computing, political models of human behavior, and religious models of belief. The substantive shift in modes of thought has led in the past to strong criticism by rationalist critics of empiricist models of Darwinian evolution or Galilean astronomy. Our chapter goes beyond the establishment of interaction as an extension of algorithms computable by Turing machines to the question of empiricist over rationalist modes of thought.

This chapter contributes to goals of this book by establishing interaction as an expanded form of computational problem solving, and to the exploration of principles that should underlie our acceptance of new modes of thought and behavior. Our section on persistent Turing machines (PTMs) examines the proof that sequential interaction is more expressive than Turing machine computation, while our section on the Church–Turing thesis shows that the Strong version of this thesis, with its assumption that Turing machines completely express computation, is both inaccurate and a denial of Turing's 1936 paper.

Our chapter has been influenced by Russell's *History of Western Philosophy* [10], whose articles on Descartes, Kant, and other philosophers support our philosophical arguments, and by Kuhn, whose book on scientific revolutions [6] supports the view that paradigm changes in scientific disciplines may require changes in modes of thought about the nature of truth.

References

1. E. Eberbach, D. Goldin, P. Wegner. Turing's Ideas and Models of Computation. In *Alan Turing: Life and Legacy of a Great Thinker*, ed. Christof Teuscher. Springer 2004.
2. Y. Gurevich. Interactive Algorithms 2005. In current book.
3. D. Goldin, S. Smolka, P. Attie, E. Sonderegger. Turing Machines, Transition Systems, and Interaction. *Information & Computation J.*, Nov. 2004.
4. D. Goldin, P. Wegner. The Church-Turing Thesis: Breaking the Myth. *LNCS 3526*, Springer, June 2005, pp. 152-168.
5. D. Knuth. *The Art of Computer Programming, Vol. 1: Fundamental Algorithms*. Addison-Wesley, 1968.
6. T. S. Kuhn. *The Structure of Scientific Revolutions*. University of Chicago Press, 1962.
7. R. Penrose. *The Emperor's New Mind*, Oxford, 1989.
8. J. K. Rice, J. N. Rice. *Computer Science: Problems, Algorithms, Languages, Information and Computers*. Holt, Rinehart and Winston, 1969.
9. M. Prasse, P. Rittgen. Why Church's Thesis Still Holds - Some Notes on Peter Wegner's Tracts on Interaction and Computability, *Computer Journal* 41:6, 1998, pp. 357–362.
10. B. Russell. *History of Western Philosophy*. Simon and Schuster, 1945.
11. C. Teuscher, editor. *Alan Turing: Life and Legacy of a Great Thinker*. Springer 2004
12. A. Turing. On Computable Numbers, with an Application to the Entscheidungsproblem, *Proc. London Math. Soc.*, 42:2, 1936, pp. 230-265; A correction, ibid, 43, 1937, 544–546.
13. A. Turing. Systems of logic based on ordinals, *Proc. London Math. Soc.*, 45:2, 1939, 161–228.
14. A. Turing. Computing Machinery and Intelligence, *Mind*, 1950.
15. J. van Leeuwen, J. Wiedermann. A Theory of Interactive Computation. In current book.
16. P. Wegner. Why Interaction is More Powerful Than Algorithms. *Comm. ACM*, May 1997.
17. P. Wegner. Interactive Foundations of Computing. *Theoretical Computer Science* 192, Feb. 1998.

Part II

Theory

A Theory of System Interaction: Components, Interfaces, and Services

Manfred Broy

Institut für Informatik, München, Germany

Summary. We study models, specification, and refinement techniques of distributed interactive software systems composed of interfaces and components. A theory for the interaction between such systems is given. We concentrate on the interaction between systems and their environments as well as the interaction between the components of systems. We show how to model interfaces and interactions by logical formulas in the style of design by contract, by state machines, and streams of messages and signals. This leads to a theory interface abstraction of systems, which is essential for an interaction view. In particular, we treat interaction refinement. We introduce a service concept that is purely based on interaction.

1 Introduction: Basics of a Theory of Interaction

Today's systems are distributed and connected by networks. Typically systems are decomposed into a family of components that are distributed and interact by exchanging messages. Such systems show a number of interfaces to the outside world such as user interfaces or interfaces to other system. Also the interaction between a system and its environment is carried out by message exchange.

A scientifically based modular development of this type of systems requires a mathematical theory. Such a theory aims at a clear notion of interaction, of an interactive component and of ways to manipulate and to compose interactions and components.

In this chapter, we outline a theory and a mathematical model of interactions and components with the following characteristics:

- A system interacts with its environment by message exchange via input and output channels.
- An interaction is a pattern of messages on channels.
- Interaction takes place in a time frame.
- A system can be decomposed into a distributed family of subsystems called components or represented by a state machine with input and output.

- A component is again a system and *interactive*.
- A component interacts with its environment exclusively by its *interface* formed by named and typed *channels*. Channels are communication links for asynchronous, buffered message exchange.
- A component *encapsulates* a state that cannot be accessed from the outside directly.
- A component receives *input messages* from its environment on its *input* channels and generates *output messages* to its environment on its *output* channels.
- A component can be *underspecified* and thus *nondeterministic*. This means that for a given input history there may exist several output histories representing possible reactions of the component.
- The interaction between the component and its environment takes place *concurrently* in a *global time frame*. In the model, there is a global notion of time that applies both to the component and its environment.
- Each system can be used as a component again in a large system; systems can be formed hierarchically.
- An interaction can be refined.
- A component offers a set of services.
- A service is a set of patterns of interactions.

Throughout this chapter we work exclusively with a simple model of discrete (also called sparse) time. Discrete time is a satisfactory model for most of the typical applications of digital information processing systems.

Our approach is based on a model that incorporates a number of simple assumptions about systems. In addition to the ones mentioned above we are working with the following assumptions that are significant for our semantic model:

- We strictly distinguish input from output.
- We assume a notion of causality between input and output.
- We assume that causality is reflected by the timing model.

Based on the ideas of an interactive component we define forms of composition. We basically introduce only one powerful composition operator, namely *parallel composition with interaction*.

For establishing a relation between interactions and services *interaction refinement*. These notions of refinement typically occur in a systematic top down system development.

2 Central Model of Interaction: Streams

A *stream* is a finite or infinite sequence of elements of a given set. In interactive systems streams are built over sets of messages or actions. Streams are used that way to represent interaction patterns by communication histories for channels or histories of activities.

2.1 Types of Models for Interactive Systems

There are many different theories and fundamental models of interactive systems. Most significant for them are their paradigms of interaction and composition. We identify three basic concepts of communication in distributed systems that interact by message exchange:

- *Asynchronous communication* (message asynchrony): a message is sent as soon as the sender is ready, independent of the fact whether a receiver is ready to receive it or not. Sent messages are buffered (by the communication mechanism) and can be accepted by the receiver at any later time; if a receiver wants to receive a message but no message was sent it has to wait. However, senders never have to wait (see [18], [21]) until receivers are ready since messages may be buffered.
- *Synchronous communication* (message synchrony, rendezvous, handshake communication): a message can be sent only if both the sender and the receiver are simultaneously ready to communicate; if only one of them (receiver or sender) is ready for communication, it has to wait until a communication partner gets ready (see [15], [16]).
- *Time synchronous communication* (perfect synchrony): several interaction steps (signals or atomic events) are conceptually gathered into one time slot; this way systems are modeled with the help of sequences of sets of events (see [6] as a well-known example).

In the following, we work with asynchronous message passing since this model has fine properties for our purpose. We follow the system model given in [11] basing our approach on a concept of a component that communicates messages asynchronously with its environment via named channels within a synchronous time frame.

2.2 Types, Streams, Channels and Histories

A type is a name for a set of data elements. Let TYPE be the set of all types. With each type $T \in$ TYPE we associate a set CAR(T) of data elements. CAR(T) is called the carrier set for T.

By ID we denote a set of identifiers. A typed identifier is a pair (x, T) consisting of an identifier $x \in$ ID and a type $T \in$ TYPE. We write also x : T to express that the identifier x has type T.

We use the following notation:

M^* denotes the set of finite sequences over M including the *empty* sequence $\langle \rangle$,

M^∞ denotes the set of infinite sequences over M (that are represented by the total mappings $\mathbb{N} \to M$).

By

$$M^\omega \times M^* \cup M^\infty$$

we denote the set of streams of elements taken from the set M. Streams of elements from M are finite or infinite sequences of elements of the set M.

By $\langle \rangle$ we denote the empty stream m. The set of streams has a rich algebraic and topological structure. We introduce concatenation ˆ as an operator:

$$M^\omega \times M^\omega \to M^\omega$$

On finite streams concatenation is defined as usual on finite sequences x, y $\in$ M*:

$$\langle x_1 \ldots x_n \rangle \,\hat{}\, \langle y_1 \ldots y_m \rangle = \langle x_1 \ldots x_n y_1 \ldots y_m \rangle$$

where $\langle x_1 \ldots x_n \rangle$ denotes a finite sequence of length n with $x_1, \ldots, x_n$ as its elements. For infinite streams

r, s: $\mathbb{N} \to M$

we define sˆx, xˆs, sˆr to be infinite streams as follows:

$$s\hat{}x = s,$$
$$s\hat{}r = s,$$
$$[\langle x_1 \ldots x_n \rangle \hat{}s](t) = \begin{cases} x_t & \text{if } t \leq n \\ s(t+n) & \text{otherwise} \end{cases}$$

We may see finite streams as partial functions $\mathbb{N} \to M$ and infinite streams as total functions.

Based on concatenation we introduce the prefix order $\sqsubseteq$ prefix as a relation on streams s, r $\in M^\omega$

$$s \sqsubseteq r \Leftrightarrow_{def} \exists z \in M^\omega \colon s\hat{}z = r$$

$(M^\omega, \sqsubseteq)$ is a partially ordered set with $\langle \rangle$ as its least element, complete in the sense that every chain $x_t \in M^\omega \colon t \in \mathbb{N}$ has a least upper bound.

A stream represents the sequence of messages sent over a channel during the lifetime of a system. Of course, in concrete systems this communication takes place in a time frame. Hence, it is often convenient to be able to refer to this time. Moreover, as we will see the theory of feedback gets much simpler. Therefore we work with *timed streams*.

Streams are used to represent histories of communications of data messages transmitted within a time frame. Given a message set M of type T we define a *timed stream* by a function

s: $\mathbb{N} \to M^*$

For each time t the sequence s(t) denotes the sequence of messages communicated at time t in the stream s. The set of all timed streams forms the carrier set of type Stream T.

The t-th sequence s.t in a timed stream s $\in (M^*)^\infty$ represents the sequence of messages appearing on a channel in the t-th time interval or, if the stream represents a sequence of actions, the sequence of actions executed in the t-th time interval.

Throughout this chapter we work with a couple of simple basic operators and notations for streams and timed streams respectively that are summarized below:

$\langle \rangle$	empty sequence or empty stream,
$\langle m \rangle$	one-element sequence containing m as its only element
x.t	t-th element of the stream x,
$\#x$	length of the stream x,
$x\,\hat{}\,z$	concatenation of the sequence x to the sequence or stream z,
$x{\downarrow}t$	prefix of length t of the stream x,
S©x	stream obtained from x by deleting all its messages that are not elements of the set S,
S#x	number of messages in x that are elements of the set S,
$\bar{x}$	finite or infinite stream that is the result of concatenating all sequences in the timed stream x. Note that $\bar{x}$ is finite if x carries only a finite number of nonempty sequences.

In a timed stream $x \in (M^*)^\infty$ we express at which times which messages are transmitted. As long as the timing is not relevant for a system it does not matter if a message is transmitted a bit later (scheduling messages earlier may make a difference with respect to causality—see later). To take care of this we introduce a *delay closure*. For a timed stream $s \in (M^*)^\infty$ we define the set $x{\uparrow}$ of timed streams that carry the same stream of messages but perhaps with some additional time delay as follows:

$$x{\uparrow} = \{x' \in (M^*)^\infty : \forall\, t \in \mathbb{N}:\ \overline{x' \downarrow t} \sqsubseteq \overline{x \downarrow t} \wedge \bar{x} = \bar{x}'\}$$

Obviously we have

$$x \in x{\uparrow}$$

and for each $x' \in x{\uparrow}$ we have $x'{\uparrow} \subseteq x{\uparrow}$ and $\bar{x} = \bar{x}'$. The set $x{\uparrow}$ is called the *delay closure* for the stream x. The delay closure is easily extended to sets of streams as follows (let $S \subseteq (M^*)^\infty$)

$$S{\uparrow} = \bigcup_{s \in S} s{\uparrow}$$

We may also consider timed streams of states to model the traces of state-based system models (see [12]). In the following, we restrict ourselves to message passing systems and therefore to streams of messages, however.

Throughout this chapter, we use streams exclusively to model the communication histories of sequential communication media called *channels*. In general, in a system several communication streams occur. Therefore we work with channels to refer to individual communication streams. Accordingly, in Focus, a channel is simply an identifier in a system that evaluates to a stream in every execution of the system.

A channel is an identifier for streams. A channel is a name of a stream. Formally it is an identifier of type Stream T with some type T. The concept of a stream is used to define the concept of a channel history. A channel history is given by the messages communicated over a channel.

Definition. Channel history

Let C be a set of channels; a channel history is a mapping (let $\mathbb{U}$ be the universe of all data elements)

$$x : C \to (\mathbb{N} \to \mathbb{U}^*)$$

such that x.c is a stream of type Type(c) for each $c \in C$. Both by $\mathbb{H}(C)$ as well as by $\overrightarrow{C}$ the set of channel histories for the channel set C is denoted.   □

All operations and notation introduced for streams generalize in a straight-forward way to histories applying them element wise. Given two disjoint sets C and C' of channels with $C \cap C' = \varnothing$ and histories $z \in \mathbb{H}(C)$ and $z' \in \mathbb{H}(C')$ we define the *direct sum* of the histories z and z' by $(z \oplus z') \in \mathbb{H}(C \cup C')$. It is specified as follows:

$$(z \oplus z').c = z.c \Leftarrow c \in C, \qquad\qquad (z \oplus z').c = z'.c \Leftarrow c \in C'$$

The notion of a stream is essential for defining the behavior of components as shown the following chapter.

3 Components and Services

In this section we introduce the syntactic and semantic notion of a *component interface* and that of a *service*. Since services are partial functions, a suggestive way to describe them are assumption/commitment specifications. We show how the notion of a service is related to state machines. State machines are one way to describe services.

We closely follow the FOCUS approach explained in all its details in [14]. It provides a flexible modular notion of a component and of a service, too.

3.1 Specification of Components

An I/O-behavior represents the behavior of a component. Using logical means, an I/O-behavior F can be described by a logical formula Φ relating the streams on the input channels to the streams on the output channels. In such a formula channel identifiers occur syntactically as identifiers (variables) for streams of the respective type. The specifying formulas are interpreted in the standard way of typed higher order predicate logic (see [4]).

An abstract interface specification of a component provides the following information:

- its syntactic interface, describing how the component interacts with its environment via its input and output channels;

- its behavior by a specifying formula Φ relating input and output channel valuations.

This leads to a specification technique for components (see [14] for lots of examples). In FOCUS we specify a component by a scheme of the following form:

⟨name⟩

in ⟨input channels⟩   **out** ⟨output channels⟩
⟨specifying formula⟩

The shape of the scheme is inspired by well-known specification approaches like Z (see [22]).

Example. Transmission, merge and fork

As simple but quite fundamental examples of components we specify a merge component MRG, a transmission component TMC, and a fork component FRK. In the examples let T1, T2, and T3 be types (recall that in our case types are simply sets) where T1 and T2 are assumed to be disjoint and T3 is the union of the sets of elements of type T1 and T2. The specification of the merge component MRG (actually the specification relies on the fact that T1 and T2 are disjoint which should be made explicit in the specification in a more sophisticated specification approach) reads as follows:

MRG

in x: T1, y: T2   **out** z: T3
$\overline{x} = T1 \; \copyright \; \overline{z} \wedge \overline{y} = T2 \; \copyright \; \overline{z}$

In this specification we do not consider the time flow and therefore refer only to the time abstractions of the involved streams. As a result we get a time independent specification The causality of the time flow is considered in detail in the following subsection.

We specify the proposition $x \sim y$ for timed streams x and y of arbitrary type T; $x \sim y$ is true if the messages in x are a permutation of the messages in y. Formally we define by the following logical equivalence:

$$x \sim y \equiv (\forall \, m \in T: \{m\} \copyright \overline{x} = \{m\} \copyright \overline{y})$$

Based on this definition we specify the component TMC.

Often it is helpful to use certain channel identifiers both for input channels and for output channels. These are then two different channels, which may have different types. To distinguish these channels in the specifying formulas, we use a well-known notational trick. In a specification it is sometime convenient to use the same channel name for an input as well as for an output channel. Since these are different channels with identical names we have to distinguish them in the body of a specification. Hence, in the body of a specification, we write for a channel c that occurs both as input and as output channel simply c to denote the stream on the input channel c and c' to denote the stream on the output channel c. Thus in the following specification z is the outside name of the output channel z and z' is its local name.

TMC	
in z: T3	
out z: T3	
$z \sim z'$	

This simple specification expresses that every input message is forwarded eventually also as output message, and vice versa. Nothing is specified about the timing of the messages. In particular, messages may be arbitrarily delayed and overtake each other. If no restriction is added output messages may even be produced earlier than they are received. This paradox is excluded by causality in the following section.

The following component FRK is just the "inversion" of the component merge. Its specification reads as follows.

FRK	
in z: T3	
out x: T1, y: T2	
$\bar{x} = T1 © \bar{z}$	
$\bar{y} = T2 © \bar{z}$	

Note that the merge component MRG as well as the TMC component and the fork component FRK as they are specified here are "fair". Every input is eventually processed and reproduced as output.   □

Based on the specifying formula given in a specification of an I/O-behavior F we may prove properties about the function F.

3.2 Interfaces, I/O-Behaviors, Time, and Causality

In this section we introduce a theory of component behaviors and interface abstraction. Then we discuss issues of time and causality.

3.2.1 Interfaces

We start with a syntactic, "static" view on components in terms of syntactic interfaces and continue with a more semantic view.

Definition. Syntactic interface

Let $I = \{x_1 : IT_1, \ldots , x_m : IT_m\}$ be a set of typed input channels and $O = \{y_1 : OT_1, \ldots , y_n : OT_n\}$ be the set of typed output channels. The pair (I, O) characterizes the syntactic interface of a component. By $(I \blacktriangleright O)$ this *syntactic interface* is denoted.   □

The syntactic interface does not say much about the behavior of a component. It basically only fixes the basic steps of information exchange possible for the component and its environment.

Definition. Semantic interface

A component interface (behavior) with the syntactic interface $(I \blacktriangleright O)$ is given by a function

$$F : \overrightarrow{I} \to \wp(\overrightarrow{O})$$

For each input $x \in \overrightarrow{I}$ we denote by F.x the output histories that may be returned for the input history x. The set F.x can be empty.   □

By this definition we basically define a relation between input and output histories. We do not distinguish semantically so far between input and output. In the next section we introduce the notion of causality as an essential semantic differentiation between input and output.

3.2.2 Causality

For input/output information processing devices there is a crucial dependency of output from input. Certain output messages depend on certain input messages. A crucial notion for interactive systems is therefore *causality*. Causality indicates dependencies between the messages exchanged within a system.

So far I/O-behaviors are nothing but relations represented by set valued functions. In the following we introduce and discuss the notion of causality for I/O-behaviors.

I/O-behaviors generate their output and consume their input in a time frame. This time frame is useful to characterize causality between input and output. Output that depends causally on certain input cannot be generated before this input has been received.

Definition. Causality

An I/O-behavior $F : \overrightarrow{I} \to \wp(\overrightarrow{O})$ is called *causal* (or *properly timed*), if for all times $t \in \mathbb{N}$ we have

$$x{\downarrow}t = z{\downarrow}t \Rightarrow (F.x){\downarrow}t = (F.z){\downarrow}t$$ □

F is causal if the output in the t-th time interval does not depend on input that is received after time t. This ensures that there is a proper time flow for the component modeled by F.

If F is not causal, there exists a time t and input histories x and x' such that $x{\downarrow}t = x'{\downarrow}t$ holds but $(F.x){\downarrow}t \neq (F.x'){\downarrow}t$. A difference between x and x' occurs only after time t but at time t the reactions of F in terms of output messages are already different.

Nevertheless, causality permits instantaneous reaction [6]: the output at time t may depend on the input at time t. This may lead into problems with causality between input and output, if we consider in addition delay free feedback loops known as causal loops. To avoid these problems we either have to introduce a sophisticated theory to deal with such causal loops for instance by domain theory and least fixpoints or we strengthen the concept of proper time flow to the notion of strong causality.

Definition. Strong causality

An I/O-behavior F is called *strongly causal* (or *time guarded*), if for all times $t \in \mathbb{N}$ we have

$$x{\downarrow}t = z{\downarrow}t \Rightarrow (F.x){\downarrow}t{+}1 = (F.z){\downarrow}t{+}1 \qquad \square$$

If F is strongly causal then the output in the t-th time interval does not depend on input that is received after the $(t{-}1)$-th time interval. Then F is strongly causal and in addition reacts to input received in the $(t{-}1)$-th time interval not before the t-th time interval. This way causality between input and output is guaranteed.

A function f: $\overrightarrow{\mathsf{I}} \to \overrightarrow{\mathsf{O}}$ is called *strongly causal* (and properly timed respectively) if the deterministic I/O-behavior F: $\overrightarrow{\mathsf{I}} \to \wp(\overrightarrow{\mathsf{O}})$ with F.x = f.x for all $x \in \overrightarrow{\mathsf{I}}$ has the respective properties.

By $[\![F]\!]$ we denote the set of strongly causal total functions f: $\overrightarrow{\mathsf{I}} \to \overrightarrow{\mathsf{O}}$, with f.x $\in$ F.x for all input histories $x \in \overrightarrow{\mathsf{I}}$.

3.2.3 Realizability

A nondeterministic specification F defines a set $[\![F]\!]$ of total deterministic behaviors. A specification is only meaningful if the set $[\![F]\!]$ is not empty. This idea leads to the following definition.

Definition. Realizability

An I/O-behavior F is called *realizable*, if there exists a strongly causal total function f: $\overrightarrow{\mathsf{I}} \to \overrightarrow{\mathsf{O}}$ such that

$$\forall\, x \in \overrightarrow{\mathsf{I}}: f.x \in F.x. \qquad \square$$

A strongly causal function f: $\overrightarrow{\mathsf{I}} \to \overrightarrow{\mathsf{O}}$ provides a deterministic *strategy* to calculate for every input history a particular output history which is correct with respect to F. Every input $x{\downarrow}t$ till time point t fixes the output till time point t+1 and in particular the output at time t+1. Actually f essentially defines a deterministic automata with input and output.

Obviously, partial I/O-behaviors are not realizable. But there are more sophisticated examples of behaviors that are not realizable. Consider for instance the following example of a behavior F: $\overrightarrow{I} \to \wp(\overrightarrow{I})$ that is not realizable (the proof of this fact is left to the reader, a proof is given in [14]):

$$F.x = \{x' \in \overrightarrow{I} : x \neq x'\}$$

Note that F.x is strongly causal.

Definition. Full realizability

An I/O-behavior F is called *fully realizable*, if it is realizable and if for all input histories $x \in \overrightarrow{I}$:

$$F.x = f.x: f \in \llbracket F \rrbracket$$

holds.   □

Full realizability guarantees that for every output histories there is a strategy (a deterministic implementation) that computes this output history. In fact, nondeterministic state machines are not more powerful than sets of deterministic state machines.

3.2.4 Time Independence

All the properties of I/O-behavior defined so far are closely related to time. To characterize whether the timing of the messages is essential for a component we introduce notions of time dependencies of components. *Time independence* expresses that the timing of the input histories does not restrict the choice of the messages but at most their timing in the output histories. We give a precise definition of this notion as follows.

Definition. Time independence

An I/O-function F is called *time independent,* if for all its input histories x, x' $\in \overrightarrow{I}$

$$\bar{x} = \bar{x}' \Rightarrow \overline{F.x} = \overline{F.x'}$$

holds.   □

Time independence means that the timing of the input histories does not influence the messages produced as output. We use this notion also for functions

$$f: \overrightarrow{I} \to \overrightarrow{O}$$

By analogy, f is time independent, if for all its input histories x, x' $\in \overrightarrow{I}$

$$\bar{x} = \bar{x}' \Rightarrow \overline{f.x} = \overline{f.x}'$$

holds.

Definition. Time independent realizability

An I/O-behavior F is called *time independently realizable*, if there exists a time independent, time guarded total function f: $\vec{I} \rightarrow \vec{O}$ such that

$$\forall\, x \in \vec{I}: f.x \in F.x \qquad\qquad \square$$

By $[\![F]\!]_{ti}$ we denote the set of time guarded, time independent total functions f: $\vec{I} \rightarrow \vec{O}$, where f.x $\in$ F.x for all input histories x $\in \vec{I}$.

Definition. Full time independent realizability

An I/O-behavior F is called *fully time independently realizable*, if it is time independent and time independently realizable and if for all input histories x $\in \vec{I}$:

$$F.x = \{f.x: f \in [\![F]\!]_{ti}\} \qquad\qquad \square$$

Full time independent realizability guarantees that for all output histories there is a strategy that computes this output history and does not use the timing of the input.

Our component model has a built-in notion of time. This has the advantage that we can explicitly specify timing properties. However, what if we want to deal with systems where the timing is not relevant? In that case we use a special subclass of specifications and components called time permissive.

Definition. Time permissivity

An I/O-behavior F is called *time permissive*, if for all input histories x $\in \vec{I}$:

$$F.x = (F.x)\!\uparrow \qquad\qquad \square$$

This means that for every output history y $\in$ F.x any delay is tolerated but not acceleration since this may lead to conflicts with causality.

If we want to specify a component for an application that is not time critical, the I/O-behavior should be fully time independently realizable and time permissive. This means that

- the timing of the input does not influence the timing of the output,
- the timing of the output is only restricted by causality, but apart from that any timing is feasible.

This way we specify components for which time is only relevant with respect to causality. This corresponds to functions that are fully time independently realizable and time permissive. Such components are easily specified by predicates that refer only to the time abstractions of the streams on the channels.

3.3 Inducing Properties on Specifications

A specifying formula for a component with the set of input channels I and the set of output channels O defines a predicate

$$p: \vec{I} \times \vec{O} \to \mathbb{B}$$

This predicate defines an I/O-behavior (not taking into account causality)

$$F: \vec{I} \to \wp(\vec{O})$$

by the equation (for $x \in \vec{I}$)

$$F.x = \{y \in \vec{O}: p(x, y)\}$$

For a component specification, we also may carefully formulate the specifying formula such that the specified I/O-behavior fulfills certain of the properties such as causality or time independence as introduced above. Another option is to add these properties, if wanted, as schematic requirements to specifications. This is done with the help of closures for specified I/O-behaviors F. By closures with a given I/O-behavior either the inclusion greatest or the inclusion least I/O-behavior is associated that has the required property and is included in the I/O-behavior F or includes the I/O-behavior F, respectively. We demonstrate this idea for strong causality.

3.3.1 Imposing Causality

Adding strong causality as a requirement on top of a given predicate p specifying the I/O-behavior F leads to a function F' that is strongly causal. F' is to guarantee all the restrictions expressed by the specifying predicate p and by strong causality but not more. Following this idea F' is defined as the inclusion greatest function F' where $F'.x \subseteq F.x$ for all input histories x such that F' is strongly causal and $y \in F'.x$ implies $p(x, y)$. This characterization leads to the following recursive definition for the function F' written in the classical way that is commonly used to define a closure.

Definition. Causality restriction

Given an I/O-behavior F the *causality restriction* F' is the inclusion greatest function such that the following equation holds:

$$F'.x = \{y \in \vec{O}: p(x, y) \land \forall x' \in \vec{I}, t \in \mathbb{N}:$$
$$x{\downarrow}t = x'{\downarrow}t \Rightarrow \exists y' \in F'.x': y{\downarrow}t+1 = y'{\downarrow}t+1\}$$

Since the right-hand side of this equation is inclusion monotonic in F' this definition is proper.   □

Obviously, the behavior F' is included in F, since $y \in F'.x$ implies $p(x, y)$ and thus $y \in F.x$. In other words, $F'.x = F'.x$ for all histories x. Since the formula to the right of this equation is inclusion monotonic in F' such a function exists and is uniquely determined.

Theorem. Causality restriction is strongly causal

For every I/O-behavior F its causality restriction F' is strongly causal.

Proof. Given

$$y \in F'.x \wedge x{\downarrow}t = x'{\downarrow}t$$

we conclude by the definition of F':

$$\exists\, y' \in \overrightarrow{O}\colon y'{\downarrow}t{+}1 = y{\downarrow}t{+}1 \wedge y' \in F'.x'$$

Thus we obtain

$$(F'.x){\downarrow}t{+}1 \subseteq (F'.x'){\downarrow}t{+}1$$

Vice versa if

$$y'' \in F'.x'$$

then by $x{\downarrow}t = x'{\downarrow}t$ we get

$$\exists\, y' \in \overrightarrow{O}\colon y''{\downarrow}t{+}1 = y'{\downarrow}t{+}1 \wedge y' \in F'.x$$

Thus we obtain

$$(F'.x'){\downarrow}t{+}1 \subseteq (F'.x){\downarrow}t{+}1$$

Hence

$$(F'.x){\downarrow}t{+}1 = (F'.x'){\downarrow}t{+}1$$

which shows that F' is strongly causal. $\square$

Note that the causality restriction F' may be the trivial function $F'.x = \varnothing$ for all $x \in \overrightarrow{I}$, if there is a contradiction between strong causality and the specifying predicate p. An example is given the following. We abbreviate for a given function F the causality restriction by TG[F].

Example. Conflict with strong causality

Consider the specification

CTG

in x: T1
out y: T1

$\forall\, t \in \mathbb{N}\colon x.t{+}1 = y.t$

The component CTG is required to show at time t always as output what it receives as input at time t+1. This specification is obviously in conflict with strong causality.

Adding strong causality as a requirement to CTG we derive for every input history x and every output history y:

$$[\forall\ t \in \mathbb{N}: x.t{+}1 = y.t]$$
$$\wedge \quad \forall\ t \in \mathbb{N},\ x' \in (T1^*)^\infty:\ x{\downarrow}t = x'{\downarrow}t \Rightarrow \exists\ y':\ y{\downarrow}t{+}1 = y'{\downarrow}t{+}1$$
$$\wedge \quad \forall\ t \in \mathbb{N}:\ x'.t{+}1 = y'.t$$

If we choose $x.t{+}1 \neq x'.t{+}1$ (assuming $T1 \neq \varnothing$) we get by the formula

$$x.t{+}1 = y.t = y'.t = x'.t{+}1$$

which is a contradiction to the assumption $x.t{+}1 \neq x'.t{+}1$. Thus there does not exist any output history for TG[CTG] if we assume causality.   □

If an I/O-behavior F is strongly causal, then obviously $F = TG[F]$. But also in some other cases TG[F] can be easily identified. If a function F'' defined as follows:

$$F''.x = y:\ p(x, y) \wedge \forall\ x' \in \overrightarrow{\mathsf{I}},\ t \in \mathbb{N}:$$
$$x{\downarrow}t = x'{\downarrow}t \Rightarrow \exists\ y' \in \overrightarrow{\mathsf{O}}:\ y{\downarrow}t{+}1 = y'{\downarrow}t{+}1 \wedge p(x', y')$$

fulfills the defining equation for TG[F], then F'' is the required function, that is $F'' = TG[F]$; otherwise, $TG[F].x \subseteq F''.x$ for all x.

Example. Transmission component

Consider the transmission component TMC given in the example above. In this case we have $p(x, y) = (x.z \sim y.z)$, where z is the only channel for the histories x and y and x.z and y.z are the streams for channel z. Adding strong causality to the specification TMC we get the function (with $I = \{z\}$)

$$TG[TMC].x = y:\ p(x, y) \wedge \forall\ t \in \mathbb{N},\ x' \in \overrightarrow{\mathsf{I}}:$$
$$x{\downarrow}t = x'{\downarrow}t \Rightarrow \exists\ y':\ y{\downarrow}t{+}1 = y'{\downarrow}t{+}1 \wedge p(x', y')$$

From this we easily prove the formula

$$y \in TG[TMC].x \Rightarrow \forall\ m \in T3,\ t \in \mathbb{N}:$$
$$\#\{m\}\copyright\overline{x.z \downarrow t} \geq \#\{m\}\copyright\overline{y.z \downarrow t + 1}$$

which expresses that at every point in time t the number of messages in y at time $t{+}1$ is less or equal to the number of messages m in x at time t. This formula is a simple consequence of the fact that for each input history x and each time t we can find an input history x' such that

$$\overline{x.z \downarrow t} = \overline{x'z \downarrow t}$$

and

$$\overline{x'.z \downarrow t} = \overline{x'z}$$

$\overline{x'z}$ is the finite sequence of messages in $\overline{x.z \downarrow t}$. For all $y' \in TG[TMC].x'$ we have $y' \sim x'$. Moreover, for $y \in TG[TMC].x$ there exists $y' \in TG[TMC].x'$ with $y{\downarrow}t{+}1 = y'{\downarrow}t{+}1$. We get for all $m \in T3$:

$$\#\{m\}\copyright\overline{y.z \downarrow t + 1}$$
$$= \#\{m\}\copyright y\tilde{\mathsf{O}}.z \downarrow t + 1$$
$$\leq \#\{m\}\copyright\overline{y'z}$$

$$= \#\{m\}\copyright\overline{x'z}$$
$$= \#\{m\}\copyright x.z \downarrow t \qquad\qquad \square$$

Strong causality is an essential property both for the conceptual modeling aspects and for the verification of properties of specifications. Strong causality models the causal dependencies between input and output and in this way the asymmetry between input and output

For time permissive, strongly causal systems there is a strong relationship to *prefix monotonicity* for nontimed streams. By causality we also rule out the merge anomaly (see [7]).

3.3.2 A Short Discussion of Time and Causality

As pointed out above, notions like time independence and time permissiveness, and strong causality are logical properties that can either be added as properties to specifications explicitly or proved for certain specifications. It is easy to show for instance that MRG, TMC, and FRK are time permissive. If we add strong causality as a requirement then all three specified I/O-behaviors are fully realizable.

We may add also other properties of I/O-behaviors in a schematic way to specifications. For instance, adding time permissiveness can be interpreted as a weakening of the specification by ignoring any restrictions with respect to timing. We define for an I/O-behavior F a time permissive function F' by the equation

$$F'.x = (F.x)\uparrow$$

As pointed out, we do not require that an I/O-behavior described by a specification has always all the properties introduced above. We are more liberal and allow for more flexibility. We may add specific properties to specifications freely (using key words, see [14]) whenever appropriate and therefore deal in a schematic way with all kinds of specifications of I/O-behaviors and timing properties.

A special case of I/O-behaviors is partial functions, which are functions that for certain input histories have an empty set of output histories. Note that partial functions are never realizable. An extreme case of partiality is a function that maps every input history onto the empty set. Partial I/O-behaviors are not interesting when used for modeling the requirements for an implementation of a component, since an implementation shows at least one output history for each input history.

Let us investigate the case where $F.x = \varnothing$ holds for a component with behavior F for some input history x, If we assume strong causality. In this case, since $x\downarrow 0 = \langle\rangle$ for all streams x, we get $x\downarrow 0 = z\downarrow 0$ for all streams z and since we assume $F.x = \varnothing$ we get

$$\{y\downarrow 1 : y \in F(x)\} = \varnothing$$

by causality since $\{y{\downarrow}1: y \in F(x)\} = \{y{\downarrow}1: y \in F(z)\}$

$$\{y{\downarrow}1: y \in F(z)\} = \varnothing$$

holds we get $F.z = \varnothing$ for all histories z. Therefore, the result of the application of a strongly causal function is either empty for all its input histories or F is "total", in other words $F.x \neq \varnothing$ for all x. In the first case we call the interface function *inconsistent*. In the latter case we call the interface function *total*.

Thus also intuitively partial I/O-behaviors are never realizable. However, partial functions may be of interest as intermediate steps in the specification process, since based on these functions we construct other functions that are not partial and more adequate for composition and implementation. We come back to that under the keyword services.

3.4 Services

A service has a syntactic interface like a component. Its behavior, however, is "partial" in contrast to the totality of a component interface. Partiality here means that a service is defined only for a subset of its input histories according to its syntactic interface. This subset is called the service domain (see [13], [17]).

Definition. Service interface

A service interface with the syntactic interface $(I \blacktriangleright O)$ is given by a function

$$F : \overrightarrow{I} \to \wp(\overrightarrow{O})$$

that fulfills the *timing property* only for the input histories with nonempty output set (let x, z $\in \overrightarrow{I}$, y $\in \overrightarrow{O}$, t $\in \mathbb{N}$):

$$F.x \neq \varnothing \neq F.z \wedge x{\downarrow}t = z{\downarrow}t \Rightarrow$$
$$\{y{\downarrow}t+1: y \in F(x)\} = \{y{\downarrow}t+1: y \in F(z)\}$$

The set

$$\mathrm{Dom}(F) = \{x: F.x \neq \varnothing\}$$

is called the *service domain*. The set

$$\mathrm{Ran}(F) = \{y \in F.x: x \in \mathrm{Dom}(F)\}$$

is called the *service range*. By

$$\mathbb{F}[I \blacktriangleright O]$$

we denote the set of all service interfaces with input channels I and output channels O. By $\mathbb{F}$ we denote the set of all interfaces for arbitrary channel sets I and O.   □

In contrast to a component, where the causality requirement implies that for a component F either all output sets F.x are empty for all input histories x or none, a service may be a partial function. To get access to a service, in general, certain access conventions have to be observed. We speak of a *service protocol*. Input histories x that are not in the service domain do not fulfill the service access assumptions. This gives a clear view: a nonparadoxical component is total, while a service may be partial. In other words a nonparadoxical component represents a total service.

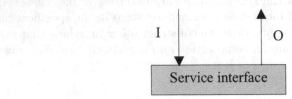

Fig. 1. Service interface

A service is close to the idea of a use case in object oriented analysis. It can be seen as the formalization of this idea. A service provides a partial view onto a component.

Example. Queue service

A Queue service allows one to store elements of type Data and to request them in a Queue fashion. We first define the involved data types:

type QIn = req ∪ Data
type QOut = Data

Based on these data types we write the specification template:

Queue

in x: QIn
out y: QOut
{req}#x = Data#y ∧ y ⊑ Data©x

This is the specification of a partial behavior. If the input stream x has the form

$$x = \langle d1 \rangle \,\hat{}\, \langle req \rangle \,\hat{}\, \langle req \rangle \,\hat{}\, \langle d2 \rangle \,\hat{}\, \langle req \rangle \,\hat{}\, \ldots$$

then the condition for x cannot be made valid. There is no output history that fulfils the specification. We may characterize the set of input histories in the service domain as follows:

Queue_Aspt(x) = ∃ y : Stream Qout: {req}#x = Data#y ∧ y ⊑ Data©x

The assumption here is:

$$\forall \, x': x' \sqsubseteq x \Rightarrow \text{req} \# x \le \text{Data} \# y$$

This predicate is called the service assumption.   □

The characterization of the service domain can be used in service specifications by formulating assumptions about the input histories; we will elaborate on this in the next section.

Definition. Splicing

Let $F \in \mathbb{F}[I \blacktriangleright O]$ and a subset of the input channels $I' \subseteq I$ and a subset of the output channels $O' \subseteq O$ be given, we define a service function

$$F' \in \mathbb{F}[I' \blacktriangleright O']$$

called the *splicing* of F to the syntactic interface $(I'' \blacktriangleright O')$ by the specification

$$F'.x' = \{y|O': \exists \, x: x' = x|I \wedge y \in F.x\}$$

Splicing derives a subinterface from a given service. It is an abstraction of F. We denote F' as defined above in this case also by $F\dagger(I' \blacktriangleright O')$.   □

An easy proof shows that the behavior obtained by F', the splicing of a service F, is strongly causal again due to the causality of F and thus F' is a service provided F is a service.

3.5 Assumption/Commitment Specification of Services

There are many ways to specify components or services. All techniques for component specifications (see [14]) can be used for services, in principle, too. Services can be specified by logical formulas defining the relation between input and output streams, by state machines, or by a set of message sequence diagrams specifying the dialogue between the service user and the service provider. In a service dialogue we observe the input and output history between the service provider and its environment. We assume that only special input is allowed in such a dialogue.

In the following we discuss in detail an assertion technique for describing services. Actually, it addresses explicitly the partiality of I/O-functions representing the behavior of services. Since a service is represented by a partial function we put specific emphasis on characterizing its domain.

We discuss two kinds of assertions, *input assumptions* and *output commitments*. Input assumptions speak about the question whether some input is in conformance to the service dialog. Since the conformance of input histories to service dialogues may depend also on the previous output history the input assumptions are predicates with two parameters, which may be surprising for some readers.

Let $F \in \mathbb{F}[I \blacktriangleright O]$ be a service and $x \in \mathbb{H}[I]$ be an input history, if there exists an input history $x' \in \mathbb{H}[I]$ such that for a time $t \in \mathbb{N}$

$$x{\downarrow}t = x'{\downarrow}t$$

and y ∈ F.x but there does not exist an output history y' ∈ F.x' such that
y↓t = y'↓t then we may conclude, that x↓t is a proper input for output y↓t,
but something in x' is not. We define for each time t ∈ ℕ a predicate

$$A_t: \overrightarrow{I} \times \overrightarrow{O} \to \mathbb{B}$$

by the formula

$$A_t(x, y) = \exists\, x' \in \mathbb{H}[I],\ y' \in F.x': x{\downarrow}t = x'{\downarrow}t \wedge y{\downarrow}t = y'{\downarrow}t$$

The formula $A_{t+1}(x, y)$ expresses that after input of x↓t that has caused
output y↓t there exists an output y.t for input x.t. A_t is called the *input
assumption at time t*. We easily prove for all times t ∈ ℕ:

$$A_{t+1}(x, y) \Rightarrow A_t(x, y)$$

In addition to A_t we define a predicate

$$A: \overrightarrow{I} \to \mathbb{B}$$

by the formula

$$A(x) = \exists\, y \in \mathbb{H}[O]: y \in F.x$$

A is called the *input assumption*. We easily prove for all t ∈ ℕ:

$$A(x) \Rightarrow \exists\, y \in \mathbb{H}[O]: A_t(x, y)$$

This shows that in the logical sense of implication the predicate A is stronger
than all the predicates A_t.

Furthermore for each time t ∈ ℕ we define a predicate

$$G_t: \overrightarrow{I} \times \overrightarrow{O} \to \mathbb{B}$$

by the formula

$$G_t(x, y) = \exists\, x' \in \mathbb{H}[I],\ y' \in F.x': x{\downarrow}t = x'{\downarrow}t \wedge y{\downarrow}t{+}1 = y'{\downarrow}t{+}1$$

G_t is called the *output commitment at time t*. We easily prove for all times t
∈ ℕ:

$$G_{t+1}(x, y) \Rightarrow G_t(x, y)$$

and also

$$G_t(x, y) \Rightarrow A_t(x, y)$$

Finally we define a predicate

$$G: \overrightarrow{I} \times \overrightarrow{O} \to \mathbb{B}$$

by the formula

$$G(x, y) = y \in F.x$$

G is called the *output commitment*. We easily prove for all $t \in \mathbb{N}$:

$$G(x, y) \Rightarrow G_t(x, y)$$

and

$$G(x, y) \Rightarrow A(x)$$

Often we are interested to derive the predicates G and A not from the specification of F but to specify F in terms of the predicates A and G. Then we speak of an *assumption/commitment specification*.

Definition. Assumption/commitment specifications

Given the predicates as defined above, we specify the service function F as follows:

$$F.x = \{y: A(x) \wedge G(x, y)\}$$

and a component F' by

$$F'.x = \{y: (A(x) \Rightarrow G(x, y)) \wedge \forall\, t \in \mathbb{N}: A_t(x, y) \Rightarrow G_t(x, y)\}$$

In both cases we speak an assumption/commitment specification of the service F and the component F' respectively.   □

In an assumption/commitment specification the assumption A characterizes for which input histories x the set F.x is empty. More precisely $F.x = \varnothing$ if $\forall\, y: \neg G(x, y)$. Since $G(x, y) \Rightarrow A(x)$ we can actually drop $A(x)$ in the service specification.

Example. Indexed access

Assume we define a component for indexed access to data. We use the following two types

Type In = put(i:Index, d:Data) | get(i:Index) | del(i:Index)
Type Out = out(d:Data) | fail(i:In) | ack(i:In)

It is specified as follows (using the scheme of [14]):

IndAcc C
in x: In **out** z: y: Out
sel(σ_0, x, y)

Let σ be a mapping

$$\sigma: \text{Index} \rightarrow \text{Data} \cup \{\text{fail}\}$$

where for all $i \in \text{Index}$:

$$\sigma_0(i) = \text{fail}$$

We define:

$$sel(\sigma, \langle a \rangle \hat{\ } x, \langle b \rangle \hat{\ } y) = [sel(\sigma', x, y) \land \exists \, i : Index, d : Data:$$
$$(a = put(i, d) \land (b = fail(i) \lor (b = ack(i) \land \sigma' = \sigma[i := d]))$$
$$\lor (a = get(i) \land \sigma[i] \neq fail \land (b = fail(i) \lor (b = out(d) \land d = \sigma[i]))$$
$$\lor (a = del(i) \land \sigma[i := fail]) \land b = ack(i)]$$

where we specify

$$(\sigma[i := d])[j] = \begin{cases} d & \text{if } i = j \\ \sigma[j] & \text{otherwise} \end{cases}$$

This specification expresses that the message get(i) must not be sent if $\sigma[i]$ = fail. In all other cases, the answer may be fail.   □

In the definition of assumption/commitment specifications as given above F$'$ is a component. The definition of F$'$ has carefully be done in a way that makes sure that F$'$ is total and strongly causal.

Theorem. Consistency of assumption/commitment specification

Let all the definitions be as above. Then F$'$ is total and strongly causal.

Proof. For every input history x we can construct an output history y $\in$ F$'$.x. We define y inductively by defining y.k in terms of y.1, ..., y.k as follows:

$$y \downarrow 0 = \langle \rangle;$$

given y$\downarrow$k we construct y$\downarrow$k+1 as follows:

If $A_k(x, y)$ holds then there exists a sequence s = y.k+1 such that $G_k(x, y)$ holds; if $\neg A_k(x, y)$ holds then we can choose y.k+1 arbitrarily.

This construction yields an output history y. We show that F$'$.x $\neq \varnothing$. We consider three cases.
(1) A(x) holds; then by definition there exists y $\in$ F.x $\subseteq$ F$'$.x.
(2) $\neg$A(x) holds; we consider two subcases
 (2a) $A_k(x, y)$ and $G_k(x, y)$ hold for all k; then y $\in$ F$'$.x.
 (2b) $\neg A_k(x, y)$ and $A_{k'}(x, y)$ and $G_{k'}(x, y)$ for all k$'$ < k; again by definition y $\in$ F$'$.x.

It remains to show the strong causality of F$'$: If x$\downarrow$k = z$\downarrow$k then we can use the same construction as above to construct a history y for x and y$'$ for z. If we do the same choices for y.1, ..., y.k+1 and y$'$.1, ..., y$'$.k+1 yields some y and y$'$ where y$\downarrow$k+1 = y$'\downarrow$k+1 and y $\in$ F$'$.x and y$'$ $\in$ F$'$.z.   □

Which input is feasible at a certain time point may depend on the previous output, the service reaction till that time point. Given an input history x and an output history y the function

$$A_t(x, y)$$

yields true, if the input till time point t is in conformance with the service dialogue provided the service output history was y$\downarrow$t. For nonpardoxical services we trivially obtain $A_0(x, y)$ = false. This expresses that every input is incorrect. The service domain is empty.

The expression

$$G_t(x, y)$$

yields true, if the output y till time point t is correct according to the given service behavior.

Finally the proposition

$$A(x)$$

expresses, that the input history x is a correct input history for the service.

Given a correct input history x the expression

$$G(x, y)$$

yields true, if the output y is correct for input x according to the service.

As we will show in the following the notion of partiality and that of input assumptions is essential for services. We define the chaos closure of a service F as follows

$$F_{chaos}.x = \{y: (A(x) \Rightarrow G(x, y)) \wedge \forall t \in \mathbb{N}: A_t(x, y) \Rightarrow G_t(x, y)\}$$

It turns a service into a component. F_{chaos} is a refinement of F. In fact it is the least refinement of the service F that is a component. According to its definition a service F is always strongly causal. Note that a naive chaos completion by the formula

$$F_{chaosnaive}.x = \{y: A(x) \Rightarrow G(x, y)\}$$

would lead to a contradiction to the requirement of strong causality.

From the chaos closure F_{chaos} we can reconstruct the service F only under the simple assumption that the formula

$$A_t(x, y) \Rightarrow (\forall y': y{\downarrow}t = y'{\downarrow}t \Rightarrow G_t(x, y))$$

is never a tautology for any input history x. In other words, in the service function F there is no chaotic behavior which means that every input history x in the service domain actually restricts the output.

For a consistent service, we require a number of healthiness conditions for the specification of services listed in the following:

- there exists at least one feasible input history and a correct output history $(\text{dom}(F) \neq \varnothing)$

$$\exists\, x, y: A(x) \wedge G(x, y)$$

- every finite feasible input history can be extended to an infinite feasible input history

$$A_t(x, y) \Rightarrow \exists\, x', y': x{\downarrow}t{+}1 = x'{\downarrow}t\, {+}1 \wedge y{\downarrow}t{+}1 = y'{\downarrow}t{+}1 \wedge G(x', y')$$

- for every feasible input history there exists a correct output history

$$A(x) \Rightarrow \exists\, y: G(x, y)$$

- if there exists an output history y for some input history x the assumption is fulfilled

$$G(x, y) \Rightarrow A(x)$$

If we construct the assertions A and G as described above from a consistent service function with a nonempty domain, all these conditions are valid.

Note that the predicates A, G, A_t and G_t are only of interest for the component specification but not for the service specification. They can be extracted from a given service specification.

3.6 State Transition Specifications

Often a component can be described in a well-understandable way by a state transition machine with input and output.

3.6.1 State Machines

We describe the data state of a transition machine by a set of typed attributes V that can be seen as *program variables*. A data state is given by the mapping

$$\eta: V \to \bigcup_{v \in V} \text{type}(v)$$

It is a valuation of the attributes in the set V by values of the corresponding type. $\overrightarrow{V}$ denotes the set of valuations of the attributes in V. In addition, we use a finite set K of control states. Then each state of the component is a pair (k, η) consisting of a *control state* k and a *data state* η. Σ denotes the set of all states.

A state machine with input and output (see [20]) is given by a set $\Lambda \subseteq \Sigma \times (O \to M^*)$ of pairs (σ_0, y_0) of initial states $\sigma_0 \in \Sigma$ and initial output sequences $y_0 \in (O \to M^*)$ as well as a state transition function

$$\Delta: (\Sigma \times (I \to M^*)) \to \wp(\Sigma \times (O \to M^*))$$

Given a state $\sigma \in \Sigma$ and a valuation u: $I \to M^*$ of the input channels by sequences every pair $(\sigma', r) \in \Delta(\sigma, u)$ represents a successor state σ' and a valuation r: $O \to M^*$ of the output channels representing the sequences produced by the state transition.

3.6.2 Interface Abstractions for State Machines

The state transition function Δ induces a function

$$B_\Delta: \Sigma \to ((O \to M^*) \to (\overrightarrow{I} \to \wp(\overrightarrow{O})))$$

B_Δ provides the black-box view onto the state transition function Δ. For each state $\sigma \in \Sigma$, each initial output $y_0 \in (O \to M^*)$, each input pattern $z \in (I \to M^*)$, and each input channel valuation $x \in \overrightarrow{I}$, the black-box function B_Δ is the inclusion maximal solution of the equation

$B_\Delta(\sigma, y_0).(\langle z \rangle \hat{} x) =$
$\{\langle y_0 \rangle \hat{} y : \exists \, \sigma' \in \Sigma, r \in (O \to M^*):(\sigma', r) \in \Delta(\sigma, z) \land y \in B_\Delta(\sigma', r).x\}$

Note that the right hand side of the equation above is inclusion monotonic in B_Δ. If we add elements to $B_\Delta(\sigma, y_0).x$ the set is also increased. B_Δ is recursively defined by an inclusion monotonic function, which even is guarded. Hence there exists a unique inclusion maximal solution. $B_\Delta(\sigma, y_0)$ defines an I/O-behavior for the state σ and the initial output y_0, which represents the behavior of the component described by the state machine Δ if initialized by the state σ. Note that $B_\Delta(\sigma, y_0)$ is always fully realizable. Introducing oracles into the states can prove this leading to a deterministic behavior for each state.

The guardedness of the recursion guarantees time guardedness of the I/O-behavior $B_\Delta(\sigma, y_0)$. B_Δ generalizes to sets Λ of pairs of states and initial output sequences:

$$B_\Delta(\Lambda).x = y \in B_\Delta(\sigma_0, y_0): (\sigma_0, y_0) \in \Lambda$$

Based on these definitions we relate state machines and I/O-behavior (see also [20]).

Given a state transition function Δ and a set Λ of pairs (σ_0, y_0) of initial states $\sigma_0 \in \Sigma$ and initial output sequences $y_0 \in (O \to M^*)$, $B_\Delta(\Lambda)$ provides the black-box view on the behavior of the state transition machine Δ for the set Λ of pairs of states and initial output sequences.

3.6.3 State Transition Diagrams

We describe state machines often by state transition diagrams. A state transition diagram consists of a number of nodes representing control states and a number of transition rules represented by labeled arcs between the control states.

Example. State transition specification

The simple component SWT (switching transmission) receives two input streams one of that has priority until in one time interval its input is empty, then the priority changes to the other channel. It has only one attribute val of sort T3*. The specification of SWT is given in a graphical style by Fig 2. A short explanation of the notation is found in [9].

Here the arrow starting from the dot indicates the initial state and initial output. The component SWT always forwards the input of one of its input channels until it gets empty. Then it switches to the transmission of the input on the other channel. □

In fact, the component SWT can also be specified by predicates on the input and output streams. This leads, however, to a quite involved specification.

A state transition diagram is defined as follows. Given a finite set K of control states (which are nodes in the state transition diagram) and a set V of typed attributes our state space Σ is defined by

(a)

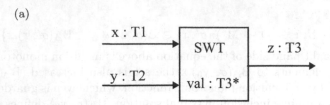

(b)

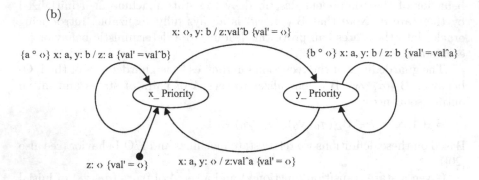

Fig. 2 (a). SWT as data flow node; **(b).** state transition diagram for SWT

$$\Sigma = K \times \vec{V}$$

For each control state $k \in K$ we define a set of transition rules. Each transition rule leads to a control state $k' \in K$ and is labeled by a transition expression

$$\{P\} \, x_1 : a_1, ..., x_n : a_n \, / \, y_1 : b_1, ..., y_m : b_m \{Q\}$$

where P is a logical expression called the *guard* that contains only the attributes from V as logical variables and some auxiliary variables that are bound variables to the transition rule. The $x_1, ..., x_n$ are the input channels (pairwise distinct) and the $y_1, ..., y_m$ are the output channels (pairwise distinct). The $a_1, ..., a_n$ and $b_1, ..., b_m$ are terms denoting sequences of messages of the types of the respective channels. Q is a logical expression called the post condition that contains besides the local variables of the transition rule the attributes in V as logical variables, also in a primed form.

The transition rule can only fire, if the machine is in control state k, if the guard evaluates to true and if all the input $a_1, ..., a_n$ is available on the channels $x_1, ..., x_n$ and if there exist $b_1, ..., b_m$ such that Q holds. For all technical details see [9].

3.6.4 Proofs about State Machines

State transition systems own certain invariants. An invariant is a logical formula that refers to the state of a component. These states are composed of the control state, the state attributes, and the streams associated with the input and output channels. Invariants provide an effective method for proving safety properties for components described by state machines.

3.6.5 Interfaces are State Machines

In this section we show that an interface abstraction defines itself an abstract state machine. Given an interface function

$$F: \overrightarrow{I} \to \wp (\overrightarrow{O})$$

we define the state space by the function space

$$\Sigma = \overrightarrow{I} \to \wp (\overrightarrow{O})$$

We get a state machine

$$\Delta: (\Sigma \times (I \to M^*)) \to \wp(\Sigma \times (O \to M^*))$$

by the following definition (let $G \in \overrightarrow{I} \to \wp (\overrightarrow{O})$, $z \in (I \to M^*)$)

$$\Delta(G, z) =$$
$$\{(H,s) \in (\overrightarrow{I} \to \wp (\overrightarrow{O})) \times (O \to M^*) : \forall x \in \overrightarrow{I} : \{\langle s \rangle \hat{\ } y : y \in H(x)\} = G(\langle z \rangle \hat{\ } x)\}$$

The function H in the formula above is called a *resumption* and s is called the output. H represents the new state of the machine after the transition represented by an I/O-function. If G is strongly causal, then the set of pairs (H, s) related with G do not depend on z and define the initial states and the initial outputs of the state machine related with G.

However, this construction does not necessarily yield a state machine, the interface abstraction of which is G again. The reason lies in specific liveness properties. We illustrate the problem by a simple example.

Example. Liveness properties and interface abstraction
We consider a simple behavior given by the specification template:

LS
in x: {a}   **out** y: {b}
{a}#x ≤ {b}#y

The component LS may produce an arbitrary number of messages b. It produces at least as many messages b as it receives messages a. Of course it may produce in the first time interval no output or an arbitrary number of messages b. Obviously LS is for the empty output a possible resumption for LS. This shows that the constructed state machine may produce no output at all for one of its runs.   □

However, if we consider only deterministic resumptions, the problem disappears. We define the state machine associated with following definition (let $G \in \vec{I} \to \wp(\vec{O})$, $z \in (I \to M^*)$)

$$\Delta_{det}(G, z) = \{(h,s) \in (\vec{I} \to \vec{O}) \times (O \to M^*): \forall x \in \vec{I}: \langle s \rangle \hat{\ } h(x) \in G(\langle z \rangle \hat{\ } x)\}$$

Each function h in the formula above is called a *deterministic resumption*.

Example. Deterministic resumptions

Consider the component LS in the example above. Let ls be a deterministic resumption for the empty input. It produces at least as many messages b as it receives messages a. Of course it may produce in the first time interval no output or an arbitrary number of messages b. According to the definition of ls the output ls.x fulfills the property

$$\{a\}\#x \leq \{b\}\#ls.x.$$ □

This construction shows the significance of realizability. A fully realizable behavior defines with the help of its deterministic resumptions a state machine the interface abstraction of which is the behavior again. In each deterministic resumption all decisions due to nondeterminism have been fixed in a fair way.

4 Composition Operators

In this section we introduce an operator for the *composition* of components. We prefer to introduce only one very general powerful composition operator.

Given I/O-behaviors with disjoint sets of output channels

$$F_1: \vec{I}_1 \to \wp(\vec{O}_1), \qquad\qquad F_2: \vec{I}_2 \to \wp(\vec{O}_2)$$

where the sets of output channels are disjoint $O_1 \cap O_2 = \varnothing$ we define the parallel composition with feedback as it is illustrated by Fig. 3 by the I/O-behavior

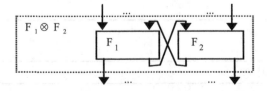

Fig. 3. Parallel composition with feedback

$$F_1 \otimes F_2: \overrightarrow{I} \to \wp\,(\overrightarrow{O})$$

where the syntactic interface is specified by the equations:

$$I = (I_1 \cup I_2)\backslash(O_1 \cup O_2), \; O = (O_1 \cup O_2)\backslash(I_1 \cup I_2)$$

The resulting function is specified by the following equation (here $y \in \overrightarrow{C}$ where the set of channels C is given by $C = I_1 \cup I_2 \cup O_1 \cup O_2$):

$$(F_1 \otimes F_2).x = \{y|O: y|I = x|I \wedge y|O_1 \in F_1(y|I_1) \wedge y|O_2 \in F_2(y|I_2)\}$$

Here y denotes a valuation of all the channels in C of F_1 and F_2. $y|C'$ denotes the restriction of the valuation y to the channels in $C' \subseteq C$. The formula essentially says that all the streams on output channels of the components F_1 and F_2 are feasible output streams of these components.

Let Φ_1 and Φ_2 be the specifying formulas for the functions F_1 and F_2 respectively; the specifying formula of $F_1 \otimes F_2$ reads as follows:

$$\exists\, z_1, ..., z_k: \Phi_1 \wedge \Phi_2$$

where $z_1, ..., z_k = (I_1 \cup I_2) \cap (O_1 \cup O_2)$ are the internal channels of the system.

This shows a beautiful property of our approach: parallel composition corresponds to the conjunction of the specifying formulas where channel hiding is expressed by existential quantification.

4.1 Composed Systems: Architectures

An interactive distributed system consists of a family of interacting components (in some approaches also called *agents*, *modules*, or *objects*). These components interact by exchanging messages over the channels that connect them. A *structural system view*, also called a *system architecture*, consists of a network of communicating components. Its nodes represent components and its arcs represent communication lines (channels) on which streams of messages are sent.

Let Com[I, O] denote the set of components with syntactic interface I ▶ O and Com denote the set of all components. We model distributed systems by data flow nets. Let K be a set of identifiers for components and I and O be sets of input and output channels, respectively. A distributed system (ν, O), an architecture, with syntactic interface (I, O) is represented by the mapping

$$\nu: K \to \text{Com}$$

that associates with every node a component behavior in the form of a black-box view, formally, an interface behavior given by an I/O-function.

The formation of a system from a given set of components is simple. Fig. 4 shows such a set of components.

We can form a network from a set of components by connecting all output channels with input channels with identical names provided the channel types

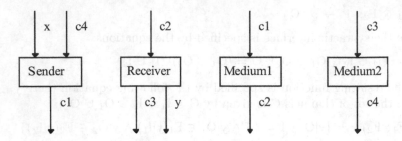

Fig. 4. Graphical illustration of a set of components with their channels

are consistent and that there are no name clashes for the output channels. For the set of components shown in Fig. 4 we obtain a net as shown in Fig. 5. A rearrangement of the components yields the more readable data flow diagram describing a system architecture shown in Fig. 6.

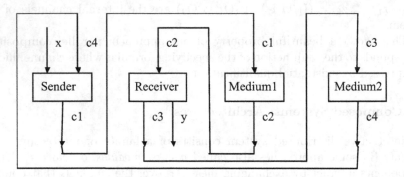

Fig. 5. Forming a data flow net from the components in Fig. 2

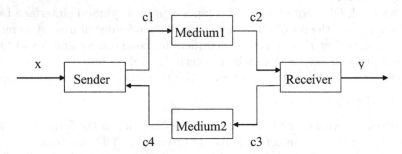

Fig. 6. Data flow net of Fig. 5 in a better readable form

As a well-formedness condition for a net formed by a set of components K, we require that for all component identifiers i, j $\in$ K (with i $\neq$ j) the sets of output channels of the components ν(i) and ν(j) are disjoint. This is formally guaranteed by the condition

$$i \neq j \Rightarrow \text{Out}(\nu(i)) \cap \text{Out}(\nu(j)) = \emptyset$$

In other words, each channel has a uniquely specified component as its source[1]. We denote the set of all (internal and external) channels of the net by the equation

$$\text{Chan}((\nu,O)) = O \cup \{c \in \text{In}(\nu(i)): i \in K\} \cup \{c \in \text{Out}(\nu(i)): i \in K\}$$

The set

$$I = \text{Chan}((\nu,O)) \setminus \{c \in \text{Out}(\nu(i)): i \in K\}$$

denotes the set of input channels of the net. The channels in the set $\{c \in \text{Out}(\nu(i)): i \in K\} \setminus (I \cup O)$ are called *internal*.

Each data flow net describes an I/O-function. This I/O-function is called the *interface abstraction* or the *black-box* view of the distributed system described by the data flow net. We get an abstraction of a distributed system to its black-box view by mapping it to a component behavior in Com[I, O] where I denotes the set of input channels and O denotes the set of output channels of the data flow net. This black-box view is represented by the component behavior f $\in$ Com[I, O] specified by the following formula (note that y $\in \overrightarrow{C}$ where C $\equiv$ Chan((ν, O)) as defined above):

$$f(x) = \{y|_O: y|_I = x \wedge \forall\, i \in K: y|_{\text{Out}(\nu(i))} \in \nu(i)(y|_{\text{In}(\nu(i))})\}$$

Here, we use the notation of function restriction. For a function g: D $\rightarrow$ R and a set T $\subseteq$ D we denote by g$|_T$: T $\rightarrow$ R the restriction of the function g to the domain T. The formula essentially expresses that the output history of a data flow net is the restriction of a fixpoint for all the net-equations for components and their output channels.

5 Layers and Layered Architectures

In this section we introduce the notion of a *service layer* and that of a *layered architecture* based on the idea of a component interface and that of a service. Roughly speaking a layered software architecture is a family of components forming layers in a component hierarchy. Each layer defines an upper interface called the *export interface* and makes use of a lower interface called the *import interface*.

---

[1] Channels that occur as input channels but not as output channels have the environment as their source.

5.1 Service Layers

In this section we introduce the notion of a service layer. A service layer is a service with a syntactic interface decomposed into two complementary subinterfaces. Of course, one might consider not only two but many separate interfaces for a system building block—however, considering two interfaces is enough to discuss most of the interesting issues of layers.

5.1.1 Service Users and Service Providers

In practically applications, services are often structured into service providers and service users. What is the difference between a service provider $F \in \mathbb{F}[I \blacktriangleright O]$ and a service user $G \in \mathbb{F}[O \blacktriangleright I]$? A service user G is, in general, highly nondeterministic. G can use the service in many different ways, in general. It has only to follow the service access protocol making sure that the service input history that it issues is in the service domain. By using F according to G we get two histories x and by the formula:

$$y \in F.x$$

Thus the most general user G of the service F is obviously

$$G.y = \{x: y \in F.x\}$$

A more specific user therefore is given by a refinement G' of G. It may use F only in a restricted form, but it has to be able to accept all output services generated by F on its input histories.

Thus we require

$$Ran(G') \subseteq Dom(F)$$
$$\{y: \exists x: y \in F.x \land x \in Ran(G)\} \subseteq Dom(G)$$

The second formula means that the service user is prepared to handle every output of the service provider produced as reaction on input of G.

5.1.2 Service Layers

A layer is a service with (at least) two syntactic interfaces. Therefore all the notions introduced for services apply also for service layers.

Definition. Service layer

Given two syntactic service interfaces $(I \blacktriangleright O)$ and $(O' \blacktriangleright I')$ where we assume $I \cap O' = \varnothing$ and $O \cap I' = \varnothing$; the behavior of a service layer L is represented by a service interface

$$L \in \mathsf{F}[I \cup O' \blacktriangleright O \cup I']$$

For the service layer the first syntactic service interface is called the syntactic *upward interface* and the second one is called the syntactic *downward interface.* The syntactic service layer interface is denoted by $(I \blacktriangleright O/O' \blacktriangleright I')$. We denote the set of layers by $\mathbb{L}[I \blacktriangleright O/O' \blacktriangleright I']$.   □

The idea of a service layer interface is well illustrated by Fig. 7. It shows the service layer with its two interfaces. The upward interface is also called export interface. The downward interface is also called the import interface.

From a behavioral point of view a service layer itself is nothing but a service, with its syntactic interface divided into an upper and a lower part.

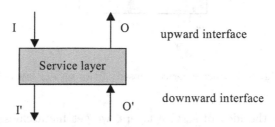

Fig. 7. Service layer

5.1.3 Composition of Service Layers

A service layer can be composed with a given service to provide an upper service. Given a service interface $F' \in \mathbb{F}[I' \blacktriangleright O']$ called the *import service* and a service layer $L \in \mathbb{L}[I \blacktriangleright O/O' \blacktriangleright I']$ we define its composition by the term (for simplicity we assume that the channel sets I, O, I', O' are pairwise disjoint):

$L \otimes F'$

This term corresponds to the small system architecture shown in Fig. 9. We call the layered architecture correct with respect to the *export service* $F \in \mathbb{F}[I \blacktriangleright O]$ for a provided import service F' if the following equation holds:

$F = L \otimes F'$

The idea of the composition of layers with services is illustrated in Fig. 9. This is the parallel composition as introduced before. But now we work with a structured view on the two interfaces.

We may also compose two given service layers $L \in \mathbb{L}[I \blacktriangleright O/O' \blacktriangleright I']$ and $L' \in \mathbb{L}[O' \blacktriangleright I'/O'' \blacktriangleright I'']$ into the term (for simplicity we assume that I, O, I', O', I'' O'' are pairwise disjoint)

$L \otimes L'$

This term denotes a layer in $\mathbb{L}[I \blacktriangleright O/O'' \blacktriangleright I'']$. The composition of layers is illustrated in Fig. 8.

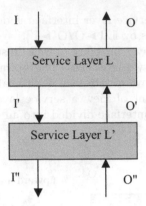

Fig. 8. Service layer composed of two service layers

If we iterate the idea of service layers, we get hierarchies of layers also called *layered architectures* as shown in Fig. 11.

With Fig. 9 we associate three services involved in a layer pattern for the service layer L:

- The *import* service $F' \in \mathbb{F}[I' \blacktriangleright O']$.
- The *export* service $F \in \mathbb{F}[I \blacktriangleright O]$ with $F = L \otimes F'$.
- The *downward* service $G \in \mathbb{F}[O' \blacktriangleright I']$ with $G = L\dagger(O' \blacktriangleright I')$.

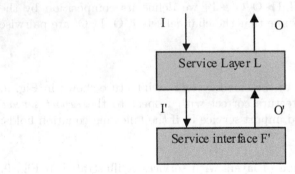

Fig. 9. Layered architecture formed of a service and service layer

The downward service G is the service "offered" (or more precisely the counterpart of the required service) by L to the downward layer; it uses the import service F'. We assume that all inputs to the downward service are within its service domain. Thus the proposition

$$\mathrm{Ran}(G) \subseteq \mathrm{Dom}(F') \qquad\qquad (*)$$

is required. Vice versa all the output produced by F' on input from G is required to be in the domain of G:

$$\{y \in F'.x : x \in Ran(F')\} \subseteq Dom(G)$$

Actually the requirement (*) is stronger than needed, in general! If G does not use its whole range due to the fact, that F' does not use the whole domain of G then we can weaken the requirement $Ran(G) \subseteq Dom(F')$. In fact, we may use a kind of invariant that describes the interactions between services F' and G. However in top down system design it is more convenient to work with (*). This introduces a methodologically remarkable asymmetry between the services downward service G and the import service F'. We come back to this issue!

Another issue is the engineering of layered architectures. Each layer adds to the functionality of the system. Therefore an interesting question is how the export services should be an extension of the import services.

The idea of a layered architecture is illustrated in Fig. 10. It is characterized best by the family of export services $F_j \in \mathbb{F}[I_j \blacktriangleright O_j]$ for $0 \le j \le n$. We get for each layer $L_{j+1} \in \mathbb{L}[I_{j+1} \blacktriangleright O_{j+1}/O_j \blacktriangleright I_j]$:

- The *export* service $F_{j+1} \in \mathbb{F}[I_{j+1} \blacktriangleright O_{j+1}]$ is given by $F_{j+1} = L_{j+1} \otimes F_j$.
- Its the *import* service is $F_j \in \mathbb{F}[I_j \blacktriangleright O_j]$.
- The *downward* service $G_j \in \mathbb{F}[O_j \blacktriangleright I_j]$ is given by $G_j = L_{j+1}\dagger(O_j \blacktriangleright I_j)$.

In the following we deal with the interaction between layers of layered architectures. We, in particular, study the specification of service layers.

5.2 Specifying Service Layers

In this section we discuss how to characterize and to specify service layers. As we have shown, one way to specify layers is the assumption/commitment style. We concentrate here on the specification of layers in terms of services.

5.2.1 Characterizing Layers by their Import and Export Services

The idea of a layer is characterized best as follows: a service layer $L \in \mathbb{L}[I \blacktriangleright O/O' \blacktriangleright I']$ offers an export service $F = L \otimes F'$ provided an adequate import service $F' \in \mathbb{F}[I' \blacktriangleright O']$ is available. In general, a layer shows only a sensible behavior for a small set of import services F'. Therefore the idea of a layer is best communicated by the characterization and the specification of its required import and its provided export services.

Note, however, that a layer $L \in \mathbb{L}[I \blacktriangleright O/O' \blacktriangleright I']$ is not uniquely characterized by a specification of its import and export service. In fact, given two services, an import service $F' \in \mathbb{F}[I' \blacktriangleright O']$ and an export service $F \in \mathbb{F}[I \blacktriangleright O]$ there exist, in general, many layers $L \in \mathbb{L}[I \blacktriangleright O/O' \blacktriangleright I']$ such that the following equation holds

$$F = L \otimes F'$$

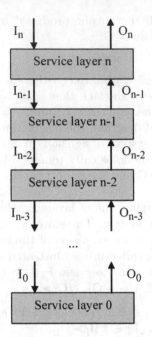

Fig. 10. Layered architecture

In the extreme, the layer L is never forced to actually make use of its import service. It may never send any messages to F' but realize this service by itself internally. This freedom to use an import service or not changes for two or multi-SAP layers (SAP = service access point) that support communication.

5.2.2 Interaction Interfaces between Layers

In a layered architecture two families of streams pointing in different directions connect each pair of consecutive layers. Next we concentrate on this idea of an interface between two layers (see Fig. 11).

Definition. Service interaction interface

Let I, I', I'', O, O', and O'' be sets of channels; a service interaction interface between two layers in $L \in \mathbb{L}(I \blacktriangleright O/O' \blacktriangleright I')$ and $L' \in \mathbb{L}(I' \blacktriangleright O'/O'' \blacktriangleright I'')$ with the syntactic interface $(I \blacktriangleright O)$ is given by a set

$$S \subseteq \mathbb{H}(I' \cup O')$$

of channel histories which fulfills the following strong causality property

$\forall z, z' \in S, \forall t \in \mathbb{N}:$
$(z|I')\!\downarrow\!t = (z'|I')\!\downarrow\!t \Rightarrow \{(y|O')\!\downarrow\!t{+}1 : y \in S$
$\wedge (y|I') = z \mid I'\} = \{(y|O')\!\downarrow\!t{+}1 : y \in S \wedge (y|I') = z'|I'\}$
$\wedge (z|O')\!\downarrow\!t = (y'|O')\!\downarrow\!t \Rightarrow \{(z|I') \downarrow t{+}1 : z \in S$
$\wedge (z|O') = y|O'\} = \{(z|I') \downarrow t{+}1 : z \in S \wedge (z|O') = y'|O'\}$ □

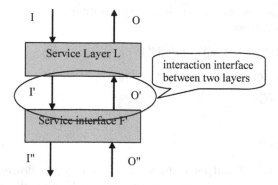

Fig. 11. Service layer composed of two service layers

Figure 11 shows the interaction interface between two layers.

If we concentrate on the interaction going on between the layers L and L' we isolate their downward and upward services $F = L\dagger(I' \blacktriangleright O')$ and $G = L'\dagger(I' \blacktriangleright O')$ respectively.

From an interaction interface S we can derive two corresponding services $F \in \mathbb{F}[I' \blacktriangleright O']$ and $G \in \mathbb{F}[O' \blacktriangleright I']$ as follows:

$$F.x = \{z|O': z \in S \wedge x = z|I'\}$$
$$G.y = \{z|I': z \in S \wedge y = z|O'\}$$

The definition of an interaction interface guarantees that both functions G and F are actual strongly causal on their domains and thus define services. This way we can see an interaction interface as the specification of two services.

Sets of message sequence charts nicely describe interaction interfaces. An interaction interface deals with the communication protocols between two subinterfaces of two components (in our case the interfaces between two layers). This idea is also called a *connector* in software architecture.

5.2.3 Matching Services

Figure 9 shows that there are three services involved in a layer specification pattern for the layer $L \in \mathbb{L}[I \blacktriangleright O/O' \blacktriangleright I']$:

- The *import* service $F' \in \mathbb{F}[I' \blacktriangleright O']$.
- The *export* service $F \in \mathbb{F}[I \blacktriangleright O]$ with $F = L \otimes F'$.
- The *downward* service $G \in \mathbb{F}[O' \blacktriangleright I']$ with $G = L\dagger(O' \blacktriangleright I')$.

If we compose two service interfaces for instance when composing two layers as shown in Fig. 9 we have two syntactically corresponding services $F' \in \mathbb{F}[I' \blacktriangleright O']$ and $G \in \mathbb{F}[O' \blacktriangleright I']$.

If we compose the two services, we get an interaction history $S \subseteq I\!H(I' \cup O')$ specified as follows:

$$S = \{z \in I\!H(I' \cup O'): z|I' \in G(z|O') \wedge z|O' \in F' (z|I')\}$$

We call the two services F' and G matching if

$$S|O' \subseteq Dom(G)$$

and

$$S|I' \subseteq Dom(F')$$

In other words, all output histories produced by the downward service G are required to be in the domain of the service F' and all output histories produced by F' are required to be in the domain of G. In fact, in general, not all input histories in the domain of F and of G do actually occur in S. However, that either F' or G produce output histories in S that are not in the domain of the corresponding service is seen as a design error.

Note the symmetry between the services F' and G here. We cannot actually say that the service F uses the service G or that the service G uses F. This symmetry is broken in the case of import and export services as follows.

We look again at the question whether there is a difference between offering a service for usage (which is the role of an export service) and the idea of using a service (which is the role of the downward service). In fact, if we introduce an asymmetry by stating that the service F uses G, we require the following conditions.

The downward service G uses the import service F'. Thus

$$Ran(G) \subseteq Dom(F') \; (*)$$

is required. Vice versa all the output produced by F' on input from G is required to be in the domain of G:

$$\{y \in F'.x: x \in Ran(F')\} \subseteq Dom(G)$$

By this requirement we break the symmetry between the imported service and the downward service. We do not describe the downward service G but rather the import service.

As noted before actually the requirement (*) is stronger than needed, in general! If G does not use its whole range in the domain of F' due to the fact, that F' does not use the whole domain of G then we can weaken the requirement $Ran(G) \subseteq Dom(F')$.

5.2.4 Specification of Interactions

Looking at the interaction that takes place between two layers of a layered architecture, we speak of an interaction interface. We consider the composition

$$F = L \otimes F'$$

We have to deal with three interfaces F, L and F'. F is a "subinterface" of L. In the classical top down design process we assume that F is given by a requirements specification, and if we are interested in a design, given by L and F'. In a design, we either assume that the service F' is given (as in a bottom up proceeding) and we want to specify layer L or that we do a free decomposition of F into L and F'.

Given the composition above for every input history x for F we get interaction interfaces for L and F' defined by the set of histories

$$\{z \in H[O' \cup I']: \exists\, x \in H[I],\ y \in H[O]:$$
$$y \oplus (z|I') \in L(x \oplus (z|O')) \land z|O' \in F'(z|I')\}$$

This expression defines a set of histories for the channels between the layer L and the service interface F'. This set of histories is called interaction interface. From the interaction interface we can derive the specification of the interface F'.

5.3 Export/Import Specifications of Layers

Typically not all input histories are good for an access to a service. Only those that are within the service domain and thus fulfill certain service assumptions lead to a well controlled behavior. This suggests the usage of assumption/commitment specifications for services as introduced above. The specification of layers is based on the specification of services.

A layer is a bridge between two services. In a layered architecture a layer exhibits several interfaces:

- the upward interface, also called the *export* service interface;
- the downward interface, the converse of which is also called the *import* service interface.

More precisely, the upward interface is a function of the downward interface and vice versa. From a methodological point of view we work according to the following idea:

- the upward service interface corresponds to the service interface specification, provided the downward service interface requirements are fulfilled;
- for the export and the import service interface we assume another form of an assumption/commitment specification.

In particular, in such a specification we do not force a layer to actually make usage of the import interface. It can make use of the interface but it does not need to. This is different for double layered architectures (see later).

If we specify the interaction at the interface between two layers by an interaction interface, we give another form of a specification of a layered architecture. The interaction interface between two layers has to fulfill certain rules and show certain properties. These rules induce specifications for the upper and the lower level.

Since a layer is strictly speaking a service with a more structured syntactic interface the techniques of assumption/commitment specifications can immediately be transferred to this situation.

Each layer interaction is completely separated from the layer interactions above or below. This allows an independent specification and implementation. In other words, to understand the downward interface of a layer L we have only to study the service $L{\dagger}(O' \blacktriangleright I')$. We do not have to take into account the rather complex service $L{\dagger}(I \blacktriangleright O)$. The relationship between the export service $(O \blacktriangleright I)$ and the downward service $L{\dagger}(O' \blacktriangleright I')$ is the responsibility of the layer.

In a requirement specification of a layer we do not want to describe all behaviors of a layer and thus see the layer as a component, but only those that fit into the specific scheme of interactions. We are, in particular, interested in the specification of the behavioral relationship between the layer and its downward layer. There are three principle techniques to specify these aspects of a layer:

- We specify the interaction interface $S \subseteq \mathbb{H}(I' \cup O')$ between the layer and its downward service.
- We specify the layer $L \in \mathbb{L}[I \blacktriangleright O / O' \blacktriangleright I']$ indirectly by specifying the export service $F \in \mathbb{F}[I \blacktriangleright O]$ and the import service $F' \in \mathbb{F}[I' \blacktriangleright O']$ such that $F \approx> L \otimes F'$.
- We specify the layer $L \in \mathbb{L}[I \blacktriangleright O / O' \blacktriangleright I']$ as a service $F_L \in \mathbb{F}[I \cup O' \blacktriangleright O \cup I']$.

All three techniques work in principle and are related. However, the second one seems from a methodological point of view most promising. In particular, to specify a layered architecture, we only have to specify for each layer the export service.

An interesting and critical question is the methodological difference we make between the two services associated with a layer, the export service and downward service.

5.4 Designing Layered Architectures

In the design of a layered architecture we have to carry out the following steps:

- specification of the overall service interface ("top service");
- decomposition of the system into layers of a layered architecture;
- specification of the export service of each layer.

These steps can be done fully systematically within our approach. Its essence is a sequence of (export) service specifications.

6 System Development by Refinement

In requirements engineering and in the design phase of system development many issues have to be addressed such as requirements elicitation, conflict identification and resolution, information management as well as the selection of a favorable software architecture (see [19]). These activities are connected with development steps. Refinement relations (see [8]) are the medium to formalize development steps and in this way the development process.

In FOCUS we formalize the following basic ideas of refinement:

- *property refinement*—enhancing requirements—allows us to add properties to a specification;
- *glass box refinement*—designing implementations—allows us to decompose a component into a distributed system or to give a state transition description for a component specification;
- *interaction refinement*—relating levels of abstraction—allows us to change the representation of the communication histories, in particular, the granularity of the interaction as well as the number and types of the channels of a component (see [8]).

In fact, these notions of refinement describe the steps needed in an idealistic view of a strict hierarchical top down system development. The three refinement concepts mentioned above are formally defined and explained in detail in the following.

6.1 Property Refinement

Property refinement is a well-known concept in structured programming. It allows us to replace an I/O-behavior with one having additional ("refined") properties. This way a behavior is replaced by a more restricted one. In FOCUS an I/O-behavior

$$F: \vec{I} \to \wp(\vec{O})$$

is refined by a behavior

$$\hat{F}: \vec{I} \to \wp(\vec{O})$$

if

$$\hat{F} \subseteq F$$

This relation stands for the proposition

$$\forall x \in \vec{I}: \hat{F}.x \subseteq F.x$$

Obviously, property refinement is a partial order and therefore reflexive, asymmetric, and transitive. Moreover, the inconsistent specification logically described by false refines everything.

A property refinement is a basic refinement step adding requirements as it is done step by step in requirements engineering. In the process of requirements engineering, typically the overall services of a system are specified. Requiring more and more sophisticated properties for components until a desired behavior is specified, in general, does this.

Example. A specification of a component that transmits its input from its two input channels to its two output channels (but does not necessarily observe the order) is specified as follows.

TM2
in x: T1, y: T2
out x: T1, y: T2

$x' \sim x \wedge y' \sim y$

We refine this specification to the simple specification of the time permissive identity TII that reads as follows:

TII
in x: T1, y: T2
out x: T1, y: T2

$\bar{y}' = \bar{y} \wedge \bar{x}' = \bar{x}$

TII is a property refinement of TM2, formally expressed

$$TII \subseteq TM2$$

A proof of this relation is straightforward (see below).   □

The verification conditions for property refinement are easily generated as follows. For given specifications S_1 and S_2 with specifying formulas Φ_1 and Φ_2, the specification S_2 is a property refinement of S_1 if the syntactic interfaces of S_1 and S_2 coincide and if for the specifying formulas Φ_1 and Φ_2 the proposition

$$\Phi_1 \Leftarrow \Phi_2$$

holds. In our example the verification condition is easily generated. It reads as follows:

$$x' \sim x \wedge y' \sim y \Leftarrow \bar{y}' = \bar{y} \wedge \bar{x} = \bar{x}$$

The proof of this condition is obvious. It follows immediately from the definitions of the time abstraction $\bar{x}$ and $x' \sim x$.

The property refinement relation is verified by proving the logical implication between the specifying formulas.

Property refinement is useful to relate composed components to components specified by logical formulas (see also glass box refinement in Sect. 6.3). For instance, the following refinement relation

$$(MRG \circ FRK) \subseteq TII$$

holds. Again the proof is straightforward.

As demonstrated the additional assumptions of schematic properties such as strong causality or realizability is an strengthening of the specifying predicate. Therefore it is also a step in the property refinement relation.

Property refinement is characteristic for the development steps in requirements engineering. It is also used as the baseline of the design process where decisions being made introduce further properties of the components.

6.2 Compositionality of Property Refinement

For FOCUS, the proof of the compositionality of property refinement is straightforward. This is a consequence of the simple definition of composition. The rule of compositional property refinement reads as follows:

$$\frac{\hat{F}_1 \subseteq F_1 \qquad \hat{F}_2 \subseteq F_2}{\hat{F} \otimes \hat{F}_2 \subseteq F_1 \otimes F_2}$$

The proof of the soundness of this rule is straightforward due to the monotonicity of the operator $\otimes$ with respect to set inclusion. Compositionality is often called *modularity* in system development. Modularity guarantees that separate refinements of the components of a system lead to a refinement of the composed system. Thus modularity allows for a separate development of components.

Example. For our example the application of the rule of compositionality reads as follows. Suppose we use a specific component MRG1 for merging two streams. It is defined as follows (recall that T1 and T2 form a partition of T3)

MRG1
in x: T1, y: T2
out z: T3
$z = \langle\langle\rangle\rangle\hat{}f(x, y)$
where $\forall\, s \in T1^*, t \in T2^*, x \in (T1^*)^\infty, y \in (T2^*)^\infty:$
$\qquad f(\langle s\rangle\hat{}x, \langle t\rangle\hat{}y) = \langle s\hat{}t\rangle\hat{}f(x, y)$

Note that this merge component MRG1 is deterministic and not time independent. According to the FOCUS rule of compositionality and transitivity of refinement, it is sufficient to prove

$$MRG1 \subseteq MRG$$

to conclude

$$MRG1 \circ FRK \subseteq MRG \circ FRK$$

and by the transitivity of the refinement relation

MRG1 ∘ FRK ⊆ TII

This shows how local refinement steps that are refinements of subcomponents of a composed system and their proofs are schematically extended to global proofs.   □

The composition operator and the relation of property refinement leads to a design calculus for requirements engineering and system design. It includes steps of decomposition and implementation that are treated more systematically in the following section.

6.3 Glass Box Refinement

Glass box refinement is a classical concept of refinement used in the design phase. In this phase we typically decompose a system with a specified interface behavior into a distributed system architecture or we represent (implement) it by a state transition machine. In other words, a glass box refinement is a special case of a property refinement that is of the form

$$F_1 \otimes F_2 \otimes ... \otimes F_n \subseteq F \quad design \ of \ an \ architecture \ for \ a \ system \ F$$

or of the form

$$B_\Delta(\Lambda) \subseteq F \qquad\qquad implementation \ of \ system \ F \ by \ a \ state \ machine$$

where the I/O-behavior $B_\Delta(\Lambda)$ is defined by a state machine Δ (see also [23]) with Λ as its initial states and outputs.

Glass box refinement means the replacement of a component F by a property refinement that is given by a design. A design is represented by a network of components $F_1 \otimes F_2 \otimes ... \otimes F_n$ or by a state machine Δ with I/O-function B_Δ. The design is a property refinement of F provided the interface behavior of the net or of the state machine respectively is a property refinement of the component F.

Accordingly, a glass box refinement is a special case of property refinement where the refining component has a specific syntactic form. In the case of a glass box refinement that transforms a component into a network, this form is a term shaped by the composition of a set of components. The term describes an architecture that fixes the basic implementation structure of a system. These components have to be specified and we have to prove that their composition leads to a system with the required functionality.

Again, a glass box refinement can be applied afterwards to each of the components F_i in a network of components. The components $F_1, ..., F_n$ can be hierarchically decomposed again into a distributed architecture in the same way, until a granularity of components is obtained which is not to be further decomposed into a distributed system but realized by a state machine. This form of iterated glass box refinement leads to a hierarchical, top down refinement method.

Example. A simple instance of such a glass box refinement is already shown by the proposition

MRG ∘ FRK ⊆ TII

It allows us to replace the component TII by a network of two components.   □
Note, a glass box refinement is a special case of a property refinement.

It is not in the center of this chapter to describe in detail the design steps leading from a interface specification to distributed systems or to state machines. Instead, we take a purist's point of view. Since we have introduced a notion of composition we consider a system architecture as being described by a term defining a distributed system by composing a number of components.

A state machine is specified by a number of state transition rules that define the transitions of the machine (see Sect. 2.6).

Example. Glass box refinement by state machines

The state machine specification SWT is a glass box refinement for the component UFM. We have

SWT ⊆ UFM

The proof of this formula is a simple consequence of the invariant proved for SWT.   □

In fact we may also introduce a refinement concept for state machines explicitly in terms of relations between states leading to variations of simulations and bisimulations (see [1], [2], [5], and also [3]). This is useful if components are refined by state machines. We call a relation between state machines with initial states σ and σ', initial output y and y' and transition function Δ and Δ' a refinement if

$$B_{\Delta'}(\sigma', y') \subseteq B_{\Delta}(\sigma, y)$$

Glass box refinement is a special case of property refinement. Thus it is compositional as a straightforward consequence of the compositionality of property refinement.

6.4 Interaction Refinement

In FOCUS interaction refinement is the refinement notion for modeling development steps between levels of abstraction. Interaction refinement allows us to change for a component

* the number and names of its input and output channels,
* the types of the messages on its channels determining the granularity of the messages.

A pair of two functions describes an interaction refinement

$$A: \overrightarrow{C'} \to \wp(\overrightarrow{C}) \qquad R: \overrightarrow{C} \to \wp(\overrightarrow{C'})$$

that relate the interaction on an abstract level with corresponding interaction on the more concrete level. This pair specifies a development step that is leading from one level of abstraction to the other as illustrated by Fig. 12.

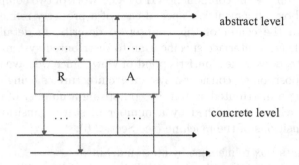

Fig. 12. Communication history refinement

Given an abstract history $x \in \overrightarrow{C}$ each $y \in R.x$ denotes a concrete history representing x. Calculating a representation for a given abstract history and then its abstraction yields the old abstract history again. Using sequential composition, this is expressed by the requirement:

$$R \circ A = Id$$

Let Id denote the identity relation. A is called the *abstraction* and R is called the *representation*. R and A are called a *refinement pair*. For nontimed components we weaken this requirement by requiring $R \circ A$ to be a property refinement of the time permissive identity TII (as a generalization of the specification TII given in Sect. 6.1 to arbitrary sets of channels), formally expressed by

$$\overline{(R \circ A).x} = \{\overline{x}\}$$

Choosing the component MRG for R and FRK for A immediately gives a refinement pair for nontimed components.

Interaction refinement allows us to refine components, given appropriate refinement pairs for their input and output channels. The idea of an interaction refinement is visualized in Fig. 13 for the so-called U^{-1}-simulation. Note that here the components (boxes) A_I and A_0 are no longer definitional in the sense of specifications, but rather methodological, since they relate two levels of abstraction. Nevertheless, we specify them as well as by the specification techniques introduced so far.

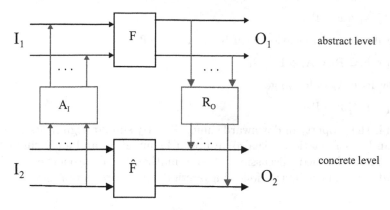

Fig. 13. Interaction refinement (U^{-1}-simulation)

Given refinement pairs

$$A_I: \vec{I}_2 \to \wp(\vec{I}_1) \qquad\qquad R_I: \vec{I}_1 \to \wp(\vec{I}_2)$$
$$A_O: \vec{O}_2 \to \wp(\vec{O}_1) \qquad\qquad R_O: \vec{O}_1 \to \wp(\vec{O}_2)$$

for the input and output channels we are able to relate abstract to concrete channels for the input and for the output. We call the I/O-behavior

$$\hat{F}: \vec{I}_2 \to \wp(\vec{O}_2)$$

an *interaction refinement* of the I/O-behavior

$$F: \vec{I}_1 \to \wp(\vec{O}_1)$$

if the following proposition holds:

$$\hat{F} \subseteq A_I \circ F \circ R_O \qquad\qquad U^{-1}\text{-simulation}$$

This formula essentially expresses that $\hat{F}$ is a property refinement of the component $A_I \circ F \circ R_O$. Thus for every "concrete" input history $\hat{x} \in \vec{I}_2$ every concrete output $\hat{y} \in \vec{O}_2$ can be also obtained by translating $\hat{x}$ onto an abstract input history $x \in A_I.\hat{x}$ such that we can choose an abstract output history $y \in F.x$ such that $\hat{y} \in R_O.y$.

There are three further versions of interaction refinement obtained by replacing in Fig. 13 the upward function A_I by the downward function R_I or the upward function A_O by the downward function R_O or both:

$$R_I \circ \hat{F} \subseteq F \circ R_O \qquad\qquad \textit{Downward simulation}$$

$$\hat{F} \circ A_O \subseteq A_I \circ F \qquad\qquad \textit{Upward simulation}$$

$$R_I \circ \hat{F} \circ A_O \subseteq F \qquad\qquad \textit{U-simulation}$$

These are different relations to connect levels of abstractions. We prefer U^{-1}-simulation as the most restrictive, "strongest" notion which implies the other three. This fact is easily demonstrated as follows. From

$$\hat{F} \subseteq A_I \circ F \circ R_O$$

we derive by multiplication with R_I from the left

$$R_I \circ \hat{F} \subseteq R_I \circ A_I \circ F \circ R_O$$

and by $R_I \circ A_I = \mathrm{Id}$ we get

$$R_I \circ \hat{F} \subseteq F \circ R_O$$

which is the property of downward simulation. By similar arguments we prove that an U^{-1}-simulation $\hat{F}$ is also an upward simulation and an U-simulation.

A more detailed discussion of the mathematical properties of U^{-1}-simulation is given in the following section and more details are found in [8].

Example. For the time permissive identity for messages of type T3 a component specification reads as follows:

TII3
in z: T3
out z: T3
$\bar{z} = \bar{z}'$

We obtain

$$\mathrm{MRG} \circ \mathrm{TII3} \circ \mathrm{FRK} \subseteq \mathrm{TII}$$

as a simple example of interaction refinement by U-simulation. The proof is again straightforward.

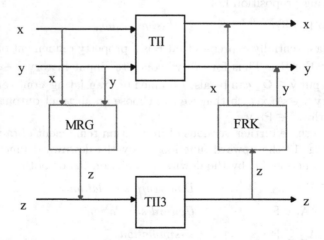

Fig. 14. Graphical representation of an interaction refinement

Figure 7 shows a graphical description of this refinement relation.   □

The idea of interaction refinement is found in other approaches like TLA, as well. It is used heavily in practical system development, although it is hardly ever introduced formally there. Examples are the communication protocols in the ISO/OSI hierarchies. Interaction refinement formalizes of the relationship between layers of abstractions in system development.

This way it can be used to relate the layers of protocol hierarchies, the change of data representations for the messages or the states as well as the introduction of time in system developments.

We show in the sequel that in FOCUS an interaction refinement in fact is a Galois connection. This indicates that interaction refinement maintains reasonable structural properties. It shows in particular that under the conditions given below U-simulation and U^{-1}-simulation are in fact equivalent.

Theorem. Interaction refinement is a Galois connection

Let the two function spaces

$$S_1 = (\overrightarrow{I}_1 \to \wp(\overrightarrow{O}_1))$$
$$S_2 = (\overrightarrow{I}_2 \to \wp(\overrightarrow{O}_2))$$

be given and the functions A_I, R_I, A_O, R_O be defined as above. The condition of a Galois connection then reads as follows

$$\forall\, F \in S_1, \hat{F} \in S_2: (A_I \circ F \circ R_O \supseteq \hat{F}) \equiv (F \supseteq R_I \circ \hat{F} \circ A_O)$$

This condition is fulfilled if

$$R_I \circ A_I \subseteq Id \qquad\qquad A_I \circ R_I \supseteq Id$$

$$R_O \circ A_O \subseteq Id \qquad\qquad A_O \circ R_O \supseteq Id$$

$$(*)$$

Proof. The proof for the direction from left to right reads as follows:

$$A_I \circ F \circ R_O \supseteq \hat{F}$$

$\Rightarrow$ {monotonicity of "$\circ$" with respect to "$\supseteq$"}

$$R_I \circ A_I \circ F \circ R_O \circ A_O \supseteq R_I \circ \hat{F} \circ A_O$$

$\Rightarrow$ {$R_I \circ A_I \subseteq Id$ and $R_O \circ A_O \subseteq Id$}

$$F \supseteq R_I \circ \hat{F} \circ A_O$$

The proof for the direction from right to left reads as follows:

$$F \supseteq R_I \circ \hat{F} \circ A_O$$

$\Rightarrow$ {monotonicity of "$\circ$" with respect to "$\supseteq$"}

$$A_I \circ F \circ R_O \supseteq A_I \circ R_I \circ \hat{F} \circ A_O \circ R_O$$

$\Rightarrow$ {$A_I \circ R_I \supseteq Id$ and $A_O \circ R_O \supseteq Id$,

transitivity of "$\supseteq$", monotonicity of "$\circ$" with respect to "$\supseteq$"}

$$A_I \circ F \circ R_O \supseteq \hat{F}$$

This completes the proof that an interaction refinement forms a Galois connection.   □

Since it is easy to show that under the conditions (*) downward simulation implies U-simulation and also that upward simulation implies U-simulation we get that under these conditions in fact all four notions of simulations are equivalent. So we speak generally of interaction refinement and refer to any of the cases.

Compositionality of U^{-1}-Simulation

Interaction refinement is formulated with the help of property refinement. In fact, it can be seen as a special instance of property refinement. This guarantees that we can freely combine property refinement with interaction refinement in a compositional way.

Example. In a property refinement, if we replace the component TII3 by a new component TII3′ (for instance along the lines of the property refinement of TII into MRG ∘ FRK), we get by the compositionality of property refinement

$$\text{MRG} \circ \text{TII3}' \circ \text{FRK} \subseteq \text{TII}$$

from the fact that TII3 is an interaction refinement of TII.   □

We concentrate on U^{-1}-simulation in the following and give the proof of compositionality only for that special case. To keep the proof simple we do not give the proof for parallel composition with feedback but give the proof in two steps for two special cases, first defining the compositionality for parallel composition without any interaction which is a simple straightforward exercise and then give a simplified proof for feedback.

For parallel composition without feedback the rule of compositional refinement reads as follows:

$$\hat{F}_1 \subseteq A_I^1 \circ F_1 \circ R_O^1$$
$$\hat{F}_2 \subseteq A_I^2 \circ F_2 \circ R_O^2$$

$$\hat{F}_1 \parallel \hat{F}_2 \subseteq (A_I^1 \parallel A_I^2) \circ$$
$$(F_1 \parallel F_2) \circ (R_O^1 \parallel R_O^2)$$

where we require the following syntactic conditions (let (I_k, O_k) be the syntactic interface of F_k for $k = 1, 2$):

$$O_1 \cap O_2 = \varnothing \quad \text{and} \quad I_1 \cap I_2 = \varnothing \quad \text{and} \quad (I_1 \cup I_2) \cap (O_1 \cup O_2) = \varnothing$$

and analogous conditions for the channels of $\hat{F}_1$ and $\hat{F}_2$. These conditions make sure that there are no name clashes.

It remains to show the compositionality of feedback. Let $F \in \mathbb{F}[I \blacktriangleright O]$; we write $\mu\,F \in \mathbb{F}[I \backslash Z \blacktriangleright O]$ for the component where all the output channels of F that are also input channels are fed back. Let $Z = I \cap O$; then $\mu\,F$ is defined by

$$(\mu\ F).x = \{y|_O\colon y|_{I\backslash z} = x \wedge y|_O \in F.(y|_I)\}$$

The general case reads as follows:

$$\frac{\hat{F} \subseteq (A_I \parallel A) \circ F \circ (R_O \parallel R)}{\mu\ \hat{F} \subseteq A_I \circ (\mu\ F) \circ (R_O \parallel R)} \quad \text{where we require the syntactic conditions}$$

$$\mathrm{Out}(R) = \mathrm{In}(A) = \mathrm{In}(\hat{F}) \cap \mathrm{Out}(\hat{F}),$$
$$\mathrm{Out}(A) = \mathrm{In}(R) = \mathrm{In}(F) \cap \mathrm{Out}(F).$$

For independent parallel composition the soundness proof of the compositional refinement rule is straightforward. For simplicity, we consider the special case where

$$\mathrm{In}(F) = \mathrm{Out}(F)$$

In other words, we give the proof for only the feedback operator and only for the special case where the channels coming from the environment are empty. This proof generalizes without difficulties to the general case. In our special case the set I is empty and thus A_I can be dropped. We write for simplicity only R instead of R_0. The compositional refinement rule reads as follows:

$$\frac{\hat{F} \subseteq A \circ F \circ R}{\mu\ \hat{F} \subseteq (\mu\ F) \circ R}$$

where $R \circ A = \mathrm{Id}$. The proof of the soundness of this rule is shown as follows. Here we use the classical relational notation:

$$xFy$$

that stands for $y \in F.x$.

Proof. Soundness for the rule of U^{-1}-simulation:

If we have:	$\hat{z} \in \mu\ \hat{F}$
then by the definition of μ	$\hat{z}\ \hat{F}\ \hat{z}$
and by the hypothesis:	$\exists\ x, y\colon \hat{z}Ax \wedge xFy \wedge yR\hat{z}$
then by $R \circ A = \mathrm{Id}$:	$y\ R\ \hat{z} \wedge \hat{z}\ A\ x \Rightarrow x = y$
we obtain:	$\exists\ x, y\colon \hat{z}Ax \wedge xFy \wedge yR\hat{z} \wedge x = y$
and thus:	$\exists\ x\colon \hat{z}Ax \wedge xFx \wedge xR\hat{z}$
therefore:	$x \in \mu\ F$
and finally:	$\hat{z} \in \mu\ F \circ R$

$\square$

The simplicity of the proof of our result comes from the fact that we have chosen such a straightforward denotational model of a component and of composition. In the FOCUS model, in particular, input and output histories are represented explicitly. This allows us to apply classical ideas of data refinement to communication histories. Roughly speaking: communication histories are nothing else than data structures that can be manipulated and refined like other data structures, too.

Remark. Compositionality is valid for the other forms of refinement only under additional conditions (see [8]).

Example. To demonstrate interaction refinement let us consider the specification of two trivial delay components. They forward their input messages to their output channels with some delay.

D3
in c, z: T3
out c, z: T3
$\bar{c}' = \bar{z}$
$\bar{z}' = \bar{c}$

D
in x, c: T1, y, d: T2
out x, c: T1, y, d: T2
$\bar{c}' = \bar{x}, \ \bar{x}' = \bar{c}$
$\bar{d}' = \bar{y}, \ \bar{y}' = \bar{d}$

We have (see Fig. 16)

$$(\text{MRG} \parallel \text{MRG}[c/x, d/y, c/z]) \circ \text{D3} \circ (\text{FRK} \parallel \text{FRK}[c/x, d/y, c/z]) \subseteq \text{D}$$

and in addition (here we write μ^c for a feedback only on channel c, see Fig. 15)

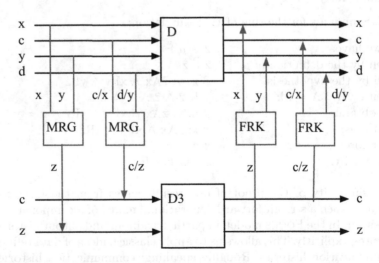

Fig. 15. Interaction refinement

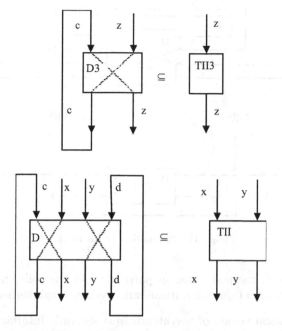

Fig. 16. Refinement relations

$$(\mu^c D3)\backslash\{c\} \subseteq TII3, \qquad\qquad (\mu^{c,d}D)\backslash\{c, d\} \subseteq TII$$

and so finally we obtain (see Fig. 16) by applying the rule of the compositionality of refinement for feedback to

$$MRG \circ (\mu^c D3)\backslash\{c\} \circ FRK \subseteq (\mu^{c,d}D)\backslash\{c, d\} \subseteq TII$$

This shows the power of the compositionality rule for interaction refinement. □

We obtain a refinement calculus, which can also be supported by a CASE tool. All the refinement rules are transformation rules. Their verification can be supported by a interactive theorem prover, their application by a transformation system.

7 Discussion and Conclusions

The previous sections introduce a comprehensive mathematical and logical theory of interaction as a foundation for a component-oriented system modeling. It addresses all the steps of a hierarchical stepwise refinement development method. It is compositional and therefore supports all the modularity requirements that are generally needed. The FOCUS refinement calculus leads to a logical calculus for "programming in the large" to argue about software architectures and their refinement.

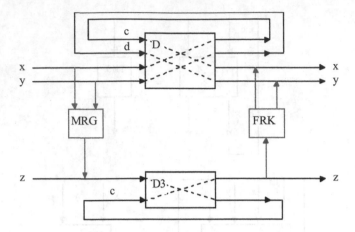

Fig. 17. Interaction refinement

The presented method aims, in particular, at the following logical and mathematical foundations for software and systems engineering:

- a mathematical notion of a syntactic and semantic interface of a component;
- a formal specification notation and method;
- a precise notion of composition;
- a mathematical notion of refinement and development;
- a compositional development method;
- a flexible concept of software architecture;
- concepts of time and the refinement of time.

What we did not mention throughout the paper are concepts that are also available and helpful from a more practical point of view including

- systematic combination with tables and diagrams,
- tool support in the form of AutoFocus.

In fact, there are other system models that can perhaps provide a similar fundamental framework. But this is not obvious as indicated in the discussion above.

The simplicity of our results is a direct consequence of the specific choice of the semantic model for FOCUS. The introduction of time makes it possible to talk about causality, which makes the reasoning about feedback loops in the model robust and expressive. The fact that communication histories are explicitly included into the model allows us to avoid all kinds of complications like prophecies or stuttering and leads to an abstract relational view of systems.

What we have presented is just the scientific kernel and justification of method. More pragmatic ways to describe specifications are needed.

An attempt to specialize the presented work also to component concepts used in practice such as object-oriented analysis, design, and programming is found in [10]. It leads there, in particular, to an abstract method for interface specifications for classes and objects. Whether this method is of practical value is another question that can only be answered after more experimentation.

Acknowledgements

It is a pleasure to thank Andreas Rausch and Bernhard Rumpe for stimulating discussions and helpful remarks on draft versions of the manuscript.

8 References

1. M. Abadi, L. Lamport: The Existence of Refinement Mappings. Digital Systems Research Center, SRC Report 29, August 1988.
2. M. Abadi, L. Lamport: Composing Specifications. Digital Systems Research Center, SRC Report 66, October 1990.
3. L. Aceto, M. Hennessy: Adding Action Refinement to a Finite Process Algebra. *Proc. ICALP 91*, LNCS 510, Springer 1991, 506-519.
4. P. Andrews: *An Introduction to Mathematical Logic and Type Theory: To Truth Through Proof. Computer Science and Applied Mathematics.* Academic Press 1986.
5. R.J.R. Back: Refinement Calculus, Part I: Sequential Nondeterministic Programs. REX Workshop. In: J. W. deBakker, W.-P. deRoever, G. Rozenberg (eds): *Stepwise Refinement of Distributed Systems.* LNCS 430, Springer 1989, 42-66 // R.J.R. Back: Refinement Calculus, Part II: Parallel and Reactive Programs. REX Workshop. In: J. W. de Bakker, W.-P. de Roever, G. Rozenberg (eds): Stepwise Refinement of Distributed Systems. LNCS 430, Springer 1989, 67-93.
6. G. Berry, G. Gonthier: The ESTEREL Synchronous Programming Language: Design, Semantics, Implementation. *INRIA Research Report* 842, 1988.
7. J. D. Brock, W. B. Ackermann: Scenarios: A Model of Nondeterminate Computation. In: J. Diaz, I. Ramos (eds): *Formalization of Programming Concepts.* LNCS 107, Springer 1981, 225-259.
8. M. Broy: Compositional Refinement of Interactive Systems. Digital Systems Research Center, *SRC Report 89*, July 1992, Also in: *J. ACM*, Vol. 44, No. 6 (Nov. 1997), 850-891.
9. M. Broy: The Specification of System Components by State Transition Diagrams. Technische Universität München, Institut für Informatik, *TUM-I9729*, May 1997.
10. M. Broy: Towards a Mathematical Concept of a Component and its Use. First Components' User Conference, Munich 1996. Revised version in: *Software - Concepts and Tools* 18, 1997, 137-148.
11. M. Broy: Compositional Refinement of Interactive Systems Modelled by Relations. In: W.-P. de Roever, H. Langmaack, A. Pnueli (eds.): *Compositionality: The Significant Difference.* LNCS 1536, Springer 1998, 130-149.

12. M. Broy: From States to Histories. In: D. Bert, Ch. Choppy, P. Mosses (eds.): *Recent trends in Algebraic Development Techniques. WADT'99*, LNCS 1827, Springer 2000, 22-36.
13. M. Broy: Multi-view Modeling of Software Systems. Keynote. FM2003 Satellite Workshop on Formal Aspects of Component Software, 8-9 September 2003, Pisa, Italy.
14. M. Broy, K. Stølen: *Specification and Development of Interactive Systems:* Focus *on Streams, Interfaces, and Refinement.* Springer 2001.
15. C.A.R. Hoare: *Communicating Sequential Processes.* Prentice Hall, 1985
16. R. Milner: *A Calculus of Communicating Systems.* LNCS 92, Springer 1980.
17. D. Herzberg, M. Broy: Modelling Layered Distributed Communication Systems. To appear in *Formal Aspects of Computer Programming.*
18. G. Kahn: The Semantics of a Simple Language for Parallel Processing. In: J.L. Rosenfeld(ed.): *Inf. Processing 74.* Proc. of the IFIP Congress 74, Amsterdam: North Holland 1974, 471-475.
19. D. C. Luckham, J. J. Kenney, L. M. Augustin, J. Vera, D. Bryan, W. Mann: Specification and Analysis of System Architecture Using Rapide. *IEEE Trans. Software Engr., Special Issue on Software Architecture*, 21(4): 336-355, April 1995
20. N. A. Lynch, E. W. Stark: A Proof of the Kahn Principle for Input/Output Automata. *Inf. \& Computation* 82(1): 81-92, 1989.
21. Specification and Description Language (SDL), Recommendation Z.100. *CCITT Technical report*, 1988.
22. M. Spivey: Understanding Z - A Specification Language and Its Formal Semantics. *Cambridge Tracts in Theoretical Comp. Science* 3, Cambridge Univ. Press 1988.

Verification of Open Systems[*]

Orna Kupferman[1] and Moshe Y. Vardi[2]

[1] Hebrew University, Jerusalem, Israel
[2] Rice University, Houston, TX, USA

Summary. In order to check whether an open system satisfies a desired property, we need to check the behavior of the system with respect to an arbitrary environment. In the most general setting, the environment is another open system. Given an open system M and a property ψ, we say that M *robustly satisfies* ψ iff for every open system M', which serves as an environment to M, the composition $M \| M'$ satisfies ψ. The problem of *robust model checking* is then to decide, given M and ψ, whether M robustly satisfies ψ. In essence, robust model checking focuses on reasoning algorithmically about interaction. In this work we study the robust-model-checking problem. We consider systems modeled by nondeterministic Moore machines, and properties specified by branching temporal logic (for linear temporal logic, robust satisfaction coincides with usual satisfaction). We show that the complexity of the problem is EXPTIME-complete for CTL and the μ-calculus, and is 2EXPTIME-complete for CTL*. Thus, from a complexity-theoretic perspective, robust satisfaction behaves like satisfiability, rather than like model checking.

1 Introduction

Today's rapid development of complex and safety-critical systems requires reliable verification methods. In formal verification, we verify that a system meets a desired property by checking that a mathematical model of the system satisfies a formal specification that describes the property. We distinguish between two types of systems: *closed* and *open* [22]. (Open systems are called *reactive* systems in [22].) A closed system is a system whose behavior is completely determined by the state of the system. An open system is a system that interacts with its environment and whose behavior depends on this interaction. Thus, while in a closed system all the nondeterministic choices are internal, and resolved by the system, in an open system there are also external nondeterministic choices, which are resolved by the environment [24].

---

[*] The chapter is based on our paper *Robust Satisfaction*, Proceedings of the 10th Conference on Concurrency Theory, volume 1664 of Lecture Notes in Computer Science, pages 383–398, Springer-Verlag, Berlin, 1999.

Since an open system has control only about its internal nondeterminism, and should be able to function correctly with respect to all possible ways in which its external nondeterminism is resolved, the term *angelic* nondeterminism is used for nondeterminism that is resolved by the system, while *demonic* nondeterminism is nondeterminism that is resolved by the environment [37].

In order to check whether a closed system satisfies a desired property, we translate the system into a formal model, typically a state-transition graph, specify the property as a temporal-logic formula, and check formally that the model satisfies the formula. Hence the name *model checking* for the verification methods derived from this viewpoint [4, 43]. In order to check whether an open system satisfies a desired property, we need to check the behavior of the system with respect to an arbitrary environment [15]. In the most general setting, the environment is another open system. Thus, given an open system M and a specification ψ, we need to check whether for every (possibly infinite) open system M', which serves as an environment to M, the composition $M\|M'$ satisfies ψ. If the answer is yes, we say that M *robustly satisfies* ψ. The problem of *robust model checking*, initially posed in [18], is to determine, given M and ψ, whether M robustly satisfies ψ. In essence, robust model checking focuses on reasoning algorithmically about interaction.

Two possible views regarding the nature of time induce two types of temporal logics [35]. In *linear* temporal logics, time is treated as if each moment in time has a unique possible future. Thus, linear temporal logic formulas are interpreted over linear sequences and we regard them as describing a behavior of a single computation of a system. In *branching* temporal logics, each moment in time may split into various possible futures. Accordingly, the structures over which branching temporal logic formulas are interpreted can be viewed as infinite computation trees, each describing the behavior of the possible computations of a nondeterministic system. We distinguish here between *universal* and *nonuniversal* temporal logics. Formulas of universal temporal logics, such as LTL, ∀CTL, and ∀CTL⋆, describe requirements that should hold in all the branches of the tree [19]. These requirements may be either linear (e.g., in all computations, only finitely many requests are sent) as in LTL, or branching (e.g., in all computations we eventually reach a state from which, no matter how we continue, no requests are sent) as in ∀CTL. In both cases, the more behaviors the system has, the harder it is for the system to satisfy the requirements. Indeed, universal temporal logics induce the *simulation* order between systems [38, 6]. That is, a system M simulates a system M' if and only if all universal temporal logic formulas that are satisfied in M' are satisfied in M as well. On the other hand, formulas of nonuniversal temporal logics, such as CTL and CTL⋆, may also impose possibility requirements on the system (e.g., there exists a computation in which only finitely many requests are sent) [9]. Here, it is no longer true that simulation between systems corresponds to agreement on satisfaction of requirements. Indeed, it might be that adding behaviors to the system helps it to satisfy a possibility requirement or, equivalently, that disabling some of its behaviors causes the requirement not to be satisfied.

It turned out that model-checking methods are applicable also for verification of open systems with respect to universal temporal-logic formulas [36, 29]. To see this, consider an execution of an open system in a maximal environment; i.e., an environment that enables all the external nondeterministic choices. The result is a closed system, and it simulates any other execution of the system in some environment. Therefore, one can check satisfaction of universal requirements in an open system by model checking the system viewed as a closed system (i.e., all nondeterministic choices are internal). This approach, however, cannot be adapted when verifying an open system with respect to nonuniversal requirements. Here, satisfaction of the requirements with respect to the maximal environment does not imply their satisfaction with respect to all environments. Hence, we should explicitly make sure that all possibility requirements are satisfied, no matter how the environment restricts the system.

To see the difference between robust satisfaction and usual satisfaction, consider the open system M described in Fig. 1. The system M models a

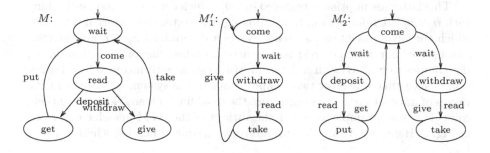

Fig. 1. An ATM and two environments for it

cash machine (ATM). Each state of the machine is labeled by the signal that the machine outputs when it visits the states. Each transition is labeled by the signal that the machine reads when the transition is taken. At the state labeled *wait*, M waits for customers. When a customer comes, M moves to the state labeled *read*, where it reads whether the customer wants to *deposit* or *withdraw* money. According to the external choice of the customer, M moves to either a *get* or *give* state, from which it returns to the *wait* state. An environment for the ATM is an infinite line of customers, each with his depositing or withdrawing plans. Suppose that we want to check whether the ATM can always get money eventually; thus, whether it satisfies the temporal logic formula $\psi = AGEF\,get$. Verification algorithms that refer to M as a closed system perform model checking in order to verify the correctness of the ATM.

Since $M \models \psi$, they get a positive answer to this question. Nonetheless, it is easy to see that the ATM does not satisfy the property ψ with respect to all environments. For example, the composition of M with the environment M_1', in which all the customers only withdraw money, does not satisfy ψ. Formally, M_1' never supplies to M the input *deposit*, thus M_1' disables the transition of M from the *read* state to the *get* state. Consequently, the composition $M \| M_1'$ contains a single computation, in which *get* is not reachable.

A first attempt to solve the robust-model-checking problem was presented in [29, 34], which suggested the method of *module checking*. In this algorithmic method we check, given M and ψ, whether, no matter how an environment disables some of M's transitions, it still satisfies the property. In particular, in the ATM example, the module-checking paradigm takes into consideration the fact that the environment can consistently disable the transition from the *read* state to the *get* state, and detects the fact that the ATM cannot always get money eventually. Technically, allowing the environment to disable some of M's transitions corresponds to restricting the robust-satisfaction problem to environments M' that are both *deterministic* and *have complete information*, in the sense that all the output variables of the system are read by the environment, thus the system has no internal variables.

This latter assumption is removed in [30], which considers module checking with *incomplete information*. In this setting, the system has internal variables, which the environment cannot read. While a deterministic environment with a complete information corresponds to arbitrary disabling of transitions in M, the composition of M with a deterministic system with incomplete information is such that whenever two computations of the system differ only in the values of internal variables along them, the disabling of transitions along them coincide. As an example, consider the variant of the ATM machine described in Fig. 2. Here, the ATM I has an internal variable indicating whether it has

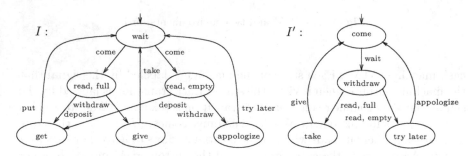

Fig. 2. An ATM with internal variables and an environment for it

money to give. The fact the variable is internal introduces nondeterminism in the description of I. Thus, I waits for customers, and when a customer comes, I consults the internal variable and moves accordingly to either the state labeled *read, full* or to the state labeled *read, empty*. The customer does not know whether the system is empty or full, and his choice is independent of this information. Only after the choice is made, the system shares this information with the customer (in fact, in the fortunate cases of the system being full or the customer depositing money, the information is kept internal). The environment I' corresponds to the case where all customers withdraw money. Note that only after the choice is made, the customers may discover that the ATM has no money. Thus, technically, when we consider the composition of I with an environment I', we cannot consider, for example, environments in which the transition from the state labeled *read, full* to the state labeled *give* is enabled while the transition from the state labeled *read, empty* to the state labeled *apologize* is disabled, or vice versa.

While the setting in [30] is more general, it still does not solve the general robust-model-checking problem. To see this, let us go back to the ATM M from Fig. 1. Suppose that we want to check whether the ATM can either move from all the successors of the initial state to a state where it gets money, or it can move from all the successors of the initial state to a state where it gives money. When we regard M as a closed system, this property is satisfied. Indeed, M satisfies the temporal-logic formula $\varphi = AXEX\,get \vee AXEX\,give$. Moreover, no matter how we remove transitions from the computation tree of M, the trees we get satisfy either $AXEX\,get$ or $AXEX\,give$[1]. In particular, $M\|M_1'$ satisfies $AXEX\,give$. Thus, if we follow the module-checking paradigm, the answer to the question is positive. Consider now the environment M_2' described in Fig. 1. The initial state of $M\|M_2'$ has two successors. One of these successors has a single successor in which the ATM gives money and the second has a single successor in which the ATM gets money. Hence, $M\|M_2'$ does not satisfy φ. Intuitively, while the module-checking paradigm considers only disabling of transitions, and thus corresponds to the composition of M with all deterministic environments, robust model checking considers all, possibly nondeterministic, environments. There, the composition of the system with an environment may not just disable some of the system's transitions, but may also, as in the example above, increase the nondeterminism of the system.

In this chapter we study the robust-satisfaction problem and describe a unified approach and solution for it. Thus, given an open system M and a specification ψ, we solve the problem of determining whether M robustly satisfies ψ. Both M and its environment are nondeterministic Moore machines. They communicate via input and output variables and they both may have private variables and be nondeterministic. Our setting allows the environment to be infinite, and to have unbounded branching degree. Nevertheless, we show that if there is some environment M' for which $M\|M'$ does not satisfy ψ, then there is also a finite environment M'' with a bounded branching degree (which depends on the number of universal requirements in ψ) such that $M\|M'$ does not satisfy ψ.

---

[1] We assume that the composition of the system and the environment is *deadlock free*, thus every state has at least one successor.

We solve the robust-model-checking problem for branching temporal specifications. As with module checking with incomplete information, *alternation* is a suitable and helpful automata-theoretic mechanism for coping with the internal variables of M and M'. In spite of the similarity to the incomplete information setting, the solution the robust model-checking problem is more challenging, as one needs to take into consideration the fact that a module may have different reactions to the same input sequence, yet this is possible only when different nondeterministic choices have been taken along the sequence. Using *alternating tree automata*, we show that the problem of robust satisfaction is EXPTIME-complete for CTL and the μ-calculus, and is 2EXPTIME-complete for CTL*. The internal variables of M make the time complexity of the robust-model-checking problem exponential already in the size of M. The same complexity bounds hold for the problem of module checking with incomplete information [30]. Thus, on the one hand, the problem of robust model checking, which generalizes the problem of module checking with incomplete information, is not harder than the latter problem. On the other hand, keeping in mind that the system to be checked is typically a parallel composition of several components, which by itself hides an exponential blow-up [21], our results imply that checking verification of open systems with respect to nonuniversal branching temporal specifications is rather intractable. From a complexity-theoretic perspective, robust satisfaction behaves like satisfiability [14, 9, 46, 10], rather than like model checking [5, 12].

In the discussion, we compare robust model checking with previous work about verification of open systems as well as with the closely-related area of supervisory control [45, 3]. We also refine the classification of specifications into universal and nonuniversal ones and show that the existential fragment of nonuniversal specifications is insensitive to the environment being nondeterministic. Finally, we argue for the generality of the model studied in this paper and show that it captures settings in which assumptions about the environment are known, as well as settings with global actions and possible deadlocks.

2 Preliminaries

2.1 Trees and Automata

Given a finite set Υ, an Υ-*tree* is a set $T \subseteq \Upsilon^*$ such that if $x \cdot \upsilon \in T$, where $x \in \Upsilon^*$ and $\upsilon \in \Upsilon$, then also $x \in T$. When Υ is not important or clear from the context, we call T a tree. The elements of T are called *nodes*, and the empty word ϵ is the *root* of T. For every $x \in T$, the nodes $x \cdot \upsilon \in T$ where $\upsilon \in \Upsilon$ are the *children* of x. Each node $x \neq \epsilon$ of T has a *direction* in Υ. The direction of a node $x \cdot \upsilon$ is υ. We denote by $dir(x)$ the direction of node x. An Υ-tree T is a *full infinite tree* if $T = \Upsilon^*$. Unless otherwise mentioned, we consider here full infinite trees. A *path* η of a tree T is a set $\eta \subseteq T$ such that

$\epsilon \in \eta$ and for every $x \in \eta$ there exists a unique $\upsilon \in \Upsilon$ such that $x \cdot \upsilon \in \eta$. The i'th *level* of T is the set of nodes of length i in T. Given two finite sets Υ and Σ, a Σ-*labeled* Υ-*tree* is a pair $\langle T, V \rangle$ where T is an Υ-tree and $V : T \to \Sigma$ maps each node of T to a letter in Σ. When Υ and Σ are not important or clear from the context, we call $\langle T, V \rangle$ a labeled tree.

Alternating tree automata generalize nondeterministic tree automata and were first introduced in [39]. An alternating tree automaton $\mathcal{A} = \langle \Sigma, Q, q_0, \delta, \alpha \rangle$ runs on full Σ-labeled Υ-trees (for an agreed set Υ of directions). It consists of a finite set Q of states, an initial state $q_0 \in Q$, a transition function δ, and an acceptance condition α (a condition that defines a subset of Q^ω).

For a set Υ of directions, let $\mathcal{B}^+(\Upsilon \times Q)$ be the set of positive Boolean formulas over $\Upsilon \times Q$; i.e., Boolean formulas built from elements in $\Upsilon \times Q$ using $\wedge$ and $\vee$, where we also allow the formulas **true** and **false** and, as usual, $\wedge$ has precedence over $\vee$. The transition function $\delta : Q \times \Sigma \to \mathcal{B}^+(\Upsilon \times Q)$ maps a state and an input letter to a formula that suggests a new configuration for the automaton. For example, when $\Upsilon = \{0, 1\}$, having

$$\delta(q, \sigma) = (0, q_1) \wedge (0, q_2) \vee (0, q_2) \wedge (1, q_2) \wedge (1, q_3)$$

means that when the automaton is in state q and reads the letter σ, it can either send two copies, in states q_1 and q_2, to direction 0 of the tree, or send a copy in state q_2 to direction 0 and two copies, in states q_2 and q_3, to direction 1. Thus, unlike nondeterministic tree automata, here the transition function may require the automaton to send several copies to the same direction or allow it not to send copies to all directions.

A *run of an alternating automaton* $\mathcal{A}$ on an input Σ-labeled Υ-tree $\langle T, V \rangle$ is a tree $\langle T_r, r \rangle$ in which the root is labeled by q_0 and every other node is labeled by an element of $\Upsilon^* \times Q$. Unlike T, in which each node has exactly $|\Upsilon|$ children, the tree T_r may have nodes with many children and may also have *leaves* (nodes with no children). Thus, $T_r \subset \mathbb{N}^*$ and a path in T_r may be either finite, in which case it contains a leaf, or infinite. Each node of T_r corresponds to a node of T. A node in T_r, labeled by (x, q), describes a copy of the automaton that reads the node x of T and visits the state q. Note that many nodes of T_r can correspond to the same node of T; in contrast, in a run of a nondeterministic automaton on $\langle T, V \rangle$ there is a one-to-one correspondence between the nodes of the run and the nodes of the tree. The labels of a node and its children have to satisfy the transition function. Formally, $\langle T_r, r \rangle$ is a Σ_r-labeled tree where $\Sigma_r = \Upsilon^* \times Q$ and $\langle T_r, r \rangle$ satisfies the following:

1. $\epsilon \in T_r$ and $r(\epsilon) = (\epsilon, q_0)$, for some $q_0 \in Q_0$.
2. Let $y \in T_r$ with $r(y) = (x, q)$ and $\delta(q, V(x)) = \theta$. Then there is a (possibly empty) set $S = \{(c_0, q_0), (c_1, q_1), \ldots, (c_{n-1}, q_{n-1})\} \subseteq \Upsilon \times Q$, such that the following hold:

- S satisfies θ, and
- for all $0 \leq i < n$, we have $y \cdot i \in T_r$ and $r(y \cdot i) = (x \cdot c_i, q_i)$.

For example, if $\langle T, V \rangle$ is a $\{0, 1\}$-tree with $V(\epsilon) = a$ and $\delta(q_0, a) = ((0, q_1) \vee (0, q_2)) \wedge ((0, q_3) \vee (1, q_2))$, then the nodes of $\langle T_r, r \rangle$ at level 1 include the label $(0, q_1)$ or $(0, q_2)$, and include the label $(0, q_3)$ or $(1, q_2)$. Note that if $\theta = \mathbf{true}$, then y need not have children. This is the reason why T_r may have leaves. Also, since there exists no set S as required for $\theta = \mathbf{false}$, we cannot have a run that takes a transition with $\theta = \mathbf{false}$.

Each infinite path ρ in $\langle T_r, r \rangle$ is labeled by a word $r(\rho)$ in Q^ω. Let $inf(\rho)$ denote the set of states in Q that appear in $r(\rho)$ infinitely often. A run $\langle T_r, r \rangle$ is accepting iff all its infinite paths satisfy the acceptance condition. In *Büchi* alternating tree automata, $\alpha \subseteq Q$, and an infinite path ρ satisfies α iff $inf(\rho) \cap \alpha \neq \emptyset$. In *parity* alternating tree automata, $\alpha = \langle F_1, F_2, \ldots, F_{2k} \rangle$, with $F_1 \subset F_2 \subset \cdots \subset F_{2k} = Q$, and and infinite path ρ satisfies α iff the minimal index i for which $inf(\rho) \cap F_i \neq \emptyset$ is even. As with nondeterministic automata, an automaton accepts a tree iff there exists an accepting run on it. We denote by $\mathcal{L}(\mathcal{A})$ the language of the automaton $\mathcal{A}$; i.e., the set of all labeled trees that $\mathcal{A}$ accepts. We say that an automaton is *nonempty* iff $\mathcal{L}(\mathcal{A}) \neq \emptyset$.

Formulas of branching temporal logic can be translated to alternating tree automata [11, 33]. Since the modalities of conventional temporal logics, such as CTL* and the μ-calculus, do not distinguish between the various successors of a node (that is, they impose requirements either on all the successors of the node or on some successor), the alternating automata that one gets by translating formulas to automata are of a special structure, in which whenever a state q is sent to direction v, the state q is sent to all the directions $v \in \Upsilon$, in either a disjunctive or conjunctive manner. Formally, following the notations in [17], the formulas in $\mathcal{B}^+(\Upsilon \times Q)$ that appear in the transitions of such alternating tree automata are members of $\mathcal{B}^+(\{\Box, \Diamond\} \times Q)$, where $\Box q$ stands for $\bigwedge_{v \in \Upsilon}(v, q)$ and $\Diamond q$ stands for $\bigvee_{v \in \Upsilon}(v, q)$. As we shall see in Sect. 3, this structure of the automata is crucial for solving the robust model-checking problem. We say that an alternating tree automaton is *symmetric* if it has the special structure described above. Theorem 1 below reviews the known constructions.

Theorem 1. [11, 33]

(1) A CTL or an alternation-free μ-calculus formula ψ can be translated to a symmetric alternating Büchi automaton with $O(|\psi|)$ states.

(2) A μ-calculus formula ψ can be translated to a symmetric alternating parity automaton with $O(|\psi|)$ states and index $O(|\psi|)$.

(3) A CTL* formula ψ can be translated to a symmetric alternating parity automaton with $2^{O(|\psi|)}$ states and index 3.

2.2 Modules

A *module* is a tuple $M = \langle I, O, W, w_{\text{in}}, \rho, \pi \rangle$, where I is a finite set of Boolean input variables, O is a finite set of Boolean output variables (we assume that $I \cap O = \emptyset$), W is a (possibly infinite) set of states, $w_{\text{in}} \in W$ is an initial state, $\rho : W \times 2^I \to 2^W \setminus \{\emptyset\}$ is a nondeterministic transition function, and $\pi : W \to 2^O$ is a labeling function that assigns to each state its output. Note that we require that for all $w \in W$ and $\sigma \in 2^I$, the set $\rho(w, \sigma)$ is not empty. Thus, the module can always respond to external inputs, though the response might be to enter a "bad" state. The module M starts its execution in w_{in}. Whenever M is in state w and the input is $\sigma \subseteq I$, it moves nondeterministically to one of the states in $\rho(w, \sigma)$. A module is *open* if $I \neq \emptyset$. Otherwise, it is *closed*. The *degree* of M is the minimal integer k such that for all w and σ, the set $\rho(w, \sigma)$ contains at most k states. If for all w and σ the set $\rho(w, \sigma)$ contains exactly k states, we say that M is of *exact degree k*.

Consider two modules $M = \langle I, O, W, w_{\text{in}}, \rho, \pi \rangle$ and $M' = \langle I', O', W', w'_{\text{in}}, \rho', \pi' \rangle$, such that $I \subseteq O'$ and $I' \subseteq O$. Note that the all the inputs of M are the outputs of M' and vice versa. The *composition* of M and M' is the closed module $M \| M' = \langle \emptyset, O \cup O', W'', w''_{\text{in}}, \rho'', \pi'' \rangle$, where

- $W'' = W \times W'$.
- $w''_{\text{in}} = \langle w_{\text{in}}, w'_{\text{in}} \rangle$.
- For every state $\langle w, w' \rangle \in W''$, we have $\rho''(\langle w, w' \rangle, \emptyset) = \rho(w, \pi'(w') \cap I) \times \rho'(w', \pi(w) \cap I')$.
- For every state $\langle w, w' \rangle \in W''$, we have $\pi''(\langle w, w' \rangle) = \pi(w) \cup \pi'(w')$.

Note that since we assume that for all $w \in W$ and $\sigma \in 2^I$, the set $\rho(w, \sigma)$ is not empty, the composition of M with M' is *deadlock free*, thus every reachable state has at least one successor. Note also that the restriction to M' that closes M does not effect the answer to the robust-model-checking problem. Indeed, if there is some M' such that $M \| M'$ is open and does not satisfy ψ, we can easily extend M' so that its composition with M would be closed and would still not satisfy ψ.

We now define when a closed module M satisfies a formula. A closed module $M = \langle \emptyset, O, W, w_{\text{in}}, \rho, \pi \rangle$ can be induces an *enabling tree* $\langle T, V \rangle$. The enabling tree of M is a full infinite $\{\top, \bot\}$-labeled W-tree, thus $T = W^*$. Intuitively, $\langle T, V \rangle$ indicates which behaviors of M are enabled by labeling with $\top$ nodes that correspond to computations that M can traverse, and labeling other

Every closed module $M = \langle \emptyset, O, W, w_{\text{in}}, \rho, \pi \rangle$ induces an *enabling tree* $\langle T, V \rangle$. The enabling tree of M is a full infinite $\{\top, \bot\}$-labeled W-tree, thus $T = W^*$. Intuitively, $\langle T, V \rangle$ indicates which behaviors of M are enabled by labeling with $\top$ nodes that correspond to computations that M can traverse, and labeling other computations with $\bot$. Formally, we define $dir(\epsilon)$ to be w_{in}, and we label ϵ by $\top$. Consider a node $x \in T$ such that $dir(x) = w$ and $V(x) = \top$. For every state $w' \in W$, we define

$$V(x.w') = \begin{bmatrix} \top & \text{if } w' \in \rho(w, \emptyset). \\ \bot & \text{otherwise.} \end{bmatrix}$$

Consider a node $x = w_1, w_2, \ldots, w_m \in T$. By the definition of V, the module M can traverse the computation $w_{in}, w_1, w_2, \ldots, w_m$ iff all the prefixes y of x have $V(y) = \top$. Indeed, then and only then we have $w_1 \in \rho(w_{in}, \emptyset)$, and $w_{i+1} \in \rho(w_i, \emptyset)$ for all $1 \leq j \leq m - 1$.

Following the definition of a product between two modules, the enabling tree of $M_1 \| M_2$ is a $\{\top, \bot\}$-labeled $(W_1 \times W_2)$-tree. Intuitively, M_2 supplies to M_1 its input (and vice versa). Note that while every state in M_1 may read $2^{|I_1|}$ different inputs and move to $|W_1|$ successors, every state in $M_1 \| M_2$ may have $|W_1| \cdot |W_2|$ successors. Note also that M_2 may be nondeterministic. Accordingly, M_2 cannot only prune transitions of M_1 (by not providing the input with which this transition is taken, causing the transition not to contribute to a transition in the product); it can also split transitions of M_1 (by reacting nondeterministically to some output, causing a transition of M_1 to contribute several transitions in the product).

We now define when a closed module M satisfies a formula. Recall that the enabling tree of M is a full infinite $\{\top, \bot\}$-labeled W-tree. As we shall see in Sect. 3, the fact that the tree is full circumvents some technical difficulties. In order to define when M satisfies a formula, we prune from the full tree nodes that correspond to unreachable states of M. Since each state of M has at least one successor, every node in the pruned tree also has at least one successor. Consequently, we are able, in Sect. 3, to duplicate subtrees and go back to convenient full trees. For an enabling tree $\langle T, V \rangle$, the $\top$-*restriction* of $\langle T, V \rangle$ is the $\{\top\}$-labeled tree with directions in W that is obtained from $\langle T, V \rangle$ by pruning subtrees with a root labeled $\bot$. For a closed module M with output signals in O, the *computation tree* of M is a 2^O-labeled W-tree obtained from the $\top$-restriction of M's enabling tree by replacing the $\top$ label of a node with direction w by the label $\pi(w)$. We say that M satisfies a branching temporal logic formula ψ over O iff M's computation tree satisfies ψ. The problem of *robust model checking* is to determine, given M and ψ, whether for every M', the composition $M \| M'$ satisfies ψ (we assume that the reader is familiar with branching temporal logic. We refer here to the logics CTL, CTL*, and the μ-calculus [8, 26]).

3 Robust Model Checking

In this section we solve the robust-model-checking problem and study its complexity. Thus, given a module M and a branching temporal logic formula ψ, we check whether for every M', the composition $M \| M'$ satisfies ψ. We assume that M has finitely many states, but we allow M' to have infinitely many states. Nevertheless, we show that if some environment that violates ψ exists, then there exists also a violating environment with finitely many states and a bounded branching degree. For a branching temporal logic formula ψ, we denote by $\mathcal{E}(\psi)$ the number of existential subformulas (subformulas of the form $E\xi$) in ψ. The "sufficient branching-degree" property for branching temporal logics states that if a CTL* or a μ-calculus formula ψ is satisfiable, then ψ is also satisfiable in a computation tree of branching degree $\mathcal{E}(\psi) + 1$ [14, 9, 46]. We now extend this result and show that in robust model checking of a module M with state space W it suffices to consider environments of degree $|W|(\mathcal{E}(\psi) + 1)$. We note that while this bound is good enough for obtaining tight complexity bounds for the robust satisfaction problem (other factors of the problem dominate the complexity), we do not know whether the bound is tight.

Note that, unlike the classical sufficient branching-degree property for branching temporal logic, here we want to bound the branching degree of the environment, rather than that of the composition $M\|M'$. Consider, for example, a module M with an initial state s_0 that has two successors: a state s_1 with $p \in \pi(s_1)$ and a state s_2 with $p \notin \pi(s_2)$ In order for M to satisfy the formula $\psi = EX(p \wedge q) \wedge EX(p \wedge \neg q)$, for an input variable q, we have to split the state s_1. Though $\mathcal{E}(\psi) = 2$, such a split may result in a composition of branching degree 4. It can, however, be achieved by composing M with an environment M' of branching degree 2, say $\rho'(s_0', p) = \{s_1', s_2'\}$, with $q \in \pi'(s_1)$ and $q \notin \pi(s_2)$. Theorem 2 below shows that it is sufficient to compose M with an environment of branching degree $|W|(\mathcal{E}(\psi) + 1)$. Intuitively, it follows from the fact that we never have to split a state into more than $|W|(\mathcal{E}(\psi) + 1)$ states.

Theorem 2. *Consider a module M and a branching temporal logic formula ψ over $I \cup O$. If there exists M' such that $M\|M' \models \psi$, then there also exists M'' of exact degree $|W|(\mathcal{E}(\psi) + 1)$ such that $M\|M'' \models \psi$.*

Proof (sketch):   A temporal logic formula ψ is satisfiable iff there is a module M of branching degree $\mathcal{E}(\psi) + 1$ satisfying it. The proof is based on the definition of a choice function, which maps each state and subformula that is satisfied in the state and involves a disjunction (either an explicit disjunction like $\varphi_1 \vee \varphi_2$ or an explicit disjunction like existential formulas or least fixed-point) to the way it is satisfied (for example, to φ_1 or φ_2 in case of an explicit disjunction, and to a particular successor in the case of an existential formula). For CTL and the μ-calculus, it is shown in [9] and [46], respectively, that the choice function may require a state s to have at most $\mathcal{E}(\psi)$ successors in order to satisfy all the formulas that are satisfied in s. For CTL*, the need is for $\mathcal{E}(\psi) + 1$ successors [14], where the additional branch guarantees we do not block the path along which path formulas are satisfied.

Our case is more complicated, as we need to bound the branching degree of the model with which we compose M. By increasing the bound by a $|W|$ factor, we can use the techniques of [9, 46, 14]: the $|W|$ factor guarantees that if ψ is satisfied in $M\|M'$ for some M', and the choice function with respect to $M\|M'$ maps different existential formulas that are associated with state $\langle s, s' \rangle$

to successors $\langle t_1, t_1' \rangle, \ldots, \langle t_k, t_k' \rangle$ of $\langle s, s' \rangle$ with the same W-component (that is, there is $t \in W$ such that $t_i = t$ for several i's), then the choice function for $M \| M''$ can use the same W-component as well. $\qquad \square$

We now use Theorem 2 to show that the robust-satisfaction problem for branching temporal logics can be reduced to the emptiness problem for alternating tree automata. For an integer $k \geq 1$, let $[k] = \{1, \ldots, k\}$.

Theorem 3. *Consider a module M with state space W and branching temporal logic formula ψ over $I \cup O$. Let $\mathcal{A}_\psi$ be the symmetric alternating tree automaton that corresponds to ψ and let $k = |W|(\mathcal{E}(\psi) + 1)$. There is an alternating tree automaton $\mathcal{A}_{M,\psi}$ over 2^I-labeled $(2^O \times [k])$-trees such that*

1. *$\mathcal{L}(\mathcal{A}_{M,\psi})$ is empty iff M robustly satisfies $\neg\psi$.*
2. *$\mathcal{A}_{M,\psi}$ and $\mathcal{A}_\psi$ have the same acceptance condition.*
3. *The size of $\mathcal{A}_{M,\psi}$ is $O(|M| \cdot |\mathcal{A}_\psi| \cdot k)$.*

Proof: Before we describe $\mathcal{A}_{M,\psi}$, let us explain the difficulties in the construction and why alternation is so helpful solving them. The automaton $\mathcal{A}_{M,\psi}$ searches for a module M' of exact degree k for which $M \| M' \in \mathcal{L}(\mathcal{A}_\psi)$. The modules M and M' interacts via the sets I and O of variables. Thus, M' does not know the state in which M is, and it only knows M's output. Accordingly, not all $\{\top, \bot\}$-labeled $(W \times W')$-trees are possible enabling trees of a product $M \| M'$. Indeed, $\mathcal{A}_{M,\psi}$ needs to consider only trees in which the behavior of M' is consistent with its incomplete information: if two nodes have the same output history (history according to M''s incomplete information), then either they agree on their label (which can be either $\bot$ or a set of input variables), or that the two nodes are outcomes of two different nondeterministic choices that M' has taken along this input history. This consistency condition is nonregular and cannot be checked by an automaton [47]. It is this need, to restrict the set of candidate enabling trees to trees that meet some non-regular condition, that makes robust model checking in the branching paradigm so challenging. The solution is to consider $(2^O \times [k])$-trees, instead of $(W \times W')$-trees. Each node in such a tree may correspond to several nodes in a $(W \times W')$-tree, all with the same output history. Then, alternation is used in order to make sure that while all these nodes agree on their labeling, each of them satisfy requirements that together guarantee the membership in $\mathcal{A}_\psi$.

Let $M = \langle I, O, W, w_{in}, \rho, \pi \rangle$. For $w \in W$, $\sigma \in 2^I$, and $\upsilon \in 2^O$, we define

$$s(w, \sigma, \upsilon) = \{w' \mid w' \in \rho(w, \sigma) \text{ and } \pi(w') = \upsilon\}.$$

That is, $s(w, \sigma, \upsilon)$ contains all the states with output υ that w moves to when it reads σ. The definition of the automaton $\mathcal{A}_{M,\psi}$ can be viewed as an extension of the product alternating tree automaton obtained in the alternating-automata theoretic framework for branching time model checking [33]. There, as we are concerned with model checking, there is a single computation tree with respect to which the formula is checked, and the automaton obtained is a 1-letter automaton. The difficulty here, as we are concerned with robust model checking, is that each environment induces a different computation tree, so there are many computation trees to check, and a 1-letter automaton does not suffice. Let $\mathcal{A}_\psi = \langle 2^{I \cup O}, Q, q_0, \delta, \alpha \rangle$. We define $\mathcal{A}_{M,\psi} = \langle 2^I, Q', q_0', \delta', \alpha' \rangle$, where

- $Q' = W \times Q$. Intuitively, when the automaton is in state $\langle w, q \rangle$, it accepts all trees that are induced by an environment M' for which the composition with M with initial state w is accepted by $\mathcal{A}$ with initial state q.
- $q_0' = \langle w_{\text{in}}, q_0 \rangle$.
- The transition function $\delta' : Q' \times 2^I \to \mathcal{B}^+((2^O \times [k]) \times Q')$ is defined as follows.
  For all w, q, and σ, the transition $\delta'(\langle w, q \rangle, \sigma)$ is obtained from $\delta(q, \sigma \cup \pi(w))$ by replacing:
  - a conjunction $\Box q'$ by the conjunction $\bigwedge_{v \in 2^O} \bigwedge_{j \in [k]} \bigwedge_{w' \in s(w, \sigma, v)} (\langle v, j \rangle, \langle w', q' \rangle)$, and
  - a disjunction $\Diamond q'$ by the disjunction $\bigvee_{v \in 2^O} \bigvee_{j \in [k]} \bigvee_{w' \in s(w, \sigma, v)} (\langle v, j \rangle, \langle w', q' \rangle)$.

  Consider, for example, a transition from the state $\langle w, q \rangle$. Let $\sigma \in 2^I$ be such that $\delta(q, \sigma \cup \pi(w)) = \Box s \wedge \Diamond t$. The successors of w that are enabled with input σ should satisfy $\Box s \wedge \Diamond t$. Thus, all these successors should satisfy s and at least one successor should satisfy t. The state w may have several successors in $\rho(w, \sigma)$ with the same output $v \in 2^O$. These successors are indistinguishable by M'. Therefore, if M' behaves differently in such two successors, it is only because M' is in a different state when it interacts with these successors. The number k bounds the size of $\rho(w, \sigma)$. Accordingly, M' can exhibit k different behaviors when it interacts with indistinguishable successors of w. For each $j \in [k]$, the automaton sends all the successors of w in $s(w, \sigma, v)$ to the same direction $\langle v, j \rangle$, where they are going to face the same future. Since $\delta(q, \sigma \cup \pi(w)) = \Box s \wedge \Diamond t$, a copy in state s is sent to all the successors, and a copy in state t is sent to some successor. Note that as M is deadlock free, thus for all $w \in W$ and $\sigma \in 2^I$, the set $s(w, \sigma, v)$ is not empty for at least one $v \in 2^O$, the conjunctions and disjunctions in δ cannot be empty.
- α' is obtained from α by replacing every set participating in α by the set $W \times \alpha$.

We now prove that $\mathcal{L}(\mathcal{A}_{M,\psi})$ is empty iff M robustly satisfies $\neg\psi$. Assume first that $\mathcal{L}(\mathcal{A}_{M,\psi})$ is not empty. We prove that there is an environment M' such that $M \| M' \models \psi$, thus M does not robustly satisfy $\neg\psi$. Let $\langle T, V \rangle$ be a 2^I-labeled $(2^O \times [k])$-tree accepted by $\mathcal{A}_{M,\psi}$. We define $M' = \langle O, I, (2^O \times [k])^*, \epsilon, \rho, \pi' \rangle$, where for all states $y \in (2^O \times [k])^*$, we have $\pi'(y) = V(y)$, and for all $v \in 2^O$, we have $\rho(y, v) = \{y \cdot \langle v', j \rangle : v' \in 2^O \text{ and } j \in [k]\}$. Thus, the output of the environment M' is induced by $\langle T, V \rangle$, and regardless of its input, M' branches to $2^{|O|}k$ successor, each extending the current state by a different pair in $2^O \times [k]$.

In order to prove that $M \| M'$ satisfies ψ, we show how the accepting run of $\mathcal{A}_{M,\psi}$ on $\langle T, V \rangle$ induces an accepting run of $\mathcal{A}_\psi$ on the computation tree of $M \| M'$. Let $\langle T_r, r \rangle$ be the accepting run of $\mathcal{A}_{M,\psi}$ on $\langle T, V \rangle$. Consider the $((W \times (2^O \times [k])^*)^* \times Q)$-labeled tree $\langle T_r, r' \rangle$ in which for all $x \in T_r$, if $r(x) = \langle y, \langle w, q \rangle \rangle$, then $r'(x) = \langle \langle w, y \rangle, q \rangle$. We claim that $\langle T_r, r' \rangle$ is an accepting run of $\mathcal{A}_\psi$ on the computation tree of $M \| M'$. In order to see that, note that the state space of $M \| M'$ is $W \times (2^O \times [k])^*$ and its transition function ρ'' is such that $\rho''(\langle w, y \rangle, \emptyset) = \rho(w, \pi'(y)) \times \rho'(y, \pi(w)) = \bigcup_{v \in 2^O}(s(w, \pi'(y), v) \times \{y \cdot \langle v', j \rangle : v' \in 2^O$ and $j \in [k]\})$. Consider a node $x \in T_r$ with $r(x) = \langle y, \langle w, q \rangle \rangle$. Let $v \in 2^O$ be such that $dir(y) = \langle v, j \rangle$ for some $j \in [k]$. Each conjunction $\Box q'$ in $\delta(q, v \cup \pi(w))$ induces $|\rho(w, v) \times 2^O \times [k]|$ successors to x, labeled by exactly all the elements in $\{\langle y \cdot \langle v', j \rangle, \langle w', q' \rangle \rangle : v' \in 2^O, j \in [k]$, and $w' \in \rho(w, v)\}$. Similarly, each disjunction $\Diamond q'$ in $\delta(q, v \cup \pi(w))$ induces a single successor to x, labeled by $\langle y \cdot \langle v', j \rangle, \langle w', q' \rangle \rangle$, for some $v' \in 2^O, j \in [k]$, and $w' \in \rho(w, v)$. Now, in r', we have $r'(x) = \langle \langle w, y \rangle, q \rangle$, and each conjunction $\Box q'$ in $\delta(q, v \cup \pi(w))$ induces $|\rho(w, v) \times 2^O \times [k]|$ successors to x, labeled by exactly all the elements in $\{\langle \langle w', y \cdot \langle v', j \rangle \rangle, q' \rangle : v' \in 2^O, j \in [k]$, and $w' \in \rho(w, v)\}$. Similarly, each disjunction $\Diamond q'$ in $\delta(q, v \cup \pi(w))$ induces a single successor to x, labeled by $\langle \langle w', y \cdot \langle v', j \rangle \rangle, q' \rangle$, for some $v' \in 2^O, j \in [k]$, and $w' \in \rho(w, v)$. Thus, r' is a legal run of $\mathcal{A}_\psi$ on the computation tree of $M \| M'$. Finally, by the definition of α', the fact that $\langle T_r, r \rangle$ is accepting implies that so is $\langle T_r, r' \rangle$.

For the other direction, assume that M does not robustly satisfy $\neg \psi$. Then, by Theorem 2, there is an environment M' of branching degree k such that $M \| M' \models \psi$. Let $M' = \langle O, I, W', w'_{in}, \rho', \pi' \rangle$. We define a 2^I-labeled $(2^O \times [k])$-tree $\langle T, V \rangle$ accepted by $\mathcal{A}_{M,\psi}$. Intuitively, $\langle T, V \rangle$ is an unwinding of M', and we first define it as a W'-labeled tree $\langle T, f \rangle$ as follows. For the root, we have $f(\epsilon) = w'_{in}$. For a node $y \cdot \langle v, j \rangle$, with $f(y) = w'$, let $\langle w'_1, \ldots, w'_k \rangle$ be an ordering on the k successors of w' in $\rho'(w', v)$. We define $f(y \cdot \langle v, j \rangle) = w'_j$. In order to get from $\langle T, f \rangle$ the 2^I-labeled tree $\langle T, V \rangle$, we define $V(y) = \pi'(f(y))$ for all $y \in T$. In the product of M with M', a node y in $\langle T, V \rangle$ may be paired with several states of M. In order to prove that $\langle T, V \rangle$ is accepted by $\mathcal{A}_{M,\psi}$, we show how an accepting run $\langle T_r, r \rangle$ of $\mathcal{A}_\psi$ on the computation tree of $M \| M'$ induces an accepting run $\langle T_r, r' \rangle$ of $\mathcal{A}_{M,\psi}$ on $\langle T, V \rangle$. Intuitively, a copy of $\mathcal{A}_\psi$ in state q that reads a node $x \in (W \times W')^*$ with direction $\langle w, w' \rangle$ induces a copy of $\mathcal{A}_{M,\psi}$ in state $\langle w, q \rangle$ that reads a node $y \in T$ for which $f(y) = w'$ and y is paired with w (and possibly with other states of M, which induce additional copies that read y) in the product of M with M'. Let $\langle T, g \rangle$ be a 2^W-labeling of T in which each node y is labeled by the set of states that y is paired with in the product of M with M'. Thus, $g(\epsilon) = \{w'_{in}\}$ and $g(y \cdot \langle v, j \rangle) = \bigcup_{w \in g(y)} s(w, \pi'(f(y)), v)$. For a node $y = \langle v_1, j_1 \rangle \cdot \langle v_2, j_2 \rangle \cdots \langle v_l, j_l \rangle$ and $0 \leq i \leq l$, let $y[i]$ denote the prefix of length i of y; thus $y[i] = \langle v_1, j_1 \rangle \cdot \langle v_2, j_2 \rangle \cdots \langle v_i, j_i \rangle$. We say that a node $y \in T$ corresponds to a node $z = \langle w_0, w_0' \rangle, \langle w_1, w_1' \rangle, \ldots, \langle w_l, w_l' \rangle$ in the computation tree of $M \| M'$ if $|y| = l$ and for all $0 \leq i \geq l$, we have that $f(y[i]) = w_i'$ and $w_i \in g(y[i])$. In addition, for all $0 \leq i \leq l - 1$, we have that $w_{i+1} \in \rho(w_i, \pi'(w_i))$. Note that y corresponds to $|g(y)|$ nodes. On the other hand, only a single node $y \in T$ corresponds to z; indeed, $w_0', w_1', \ldots, w_l'$ fix a single sequence of output signals (the 2^O elements) and nondeterministic choices (the $[k]$ elements). We can now define the accepting run $\langle T_r, r' \rangle$ of $\mathcal{A}_{M,\psi}$ on $\langle T, V \rangle$. Consider a node $x \in T_r$ with $r(x) = \langle z, q \rangle$. Let $dir(z) = \langle w, w' \rangle$ and let y be the single node in T that corresponds to z. Then, $r'(x) = \langle y, \langle w, q \rangle \rangle$. The fact that $\langle T_r, r' \rangle$ is a legal run follows from the way we define the transition function of $\mathcal{A}_{M,\psi}$ and the labeling f and g. Finally, by the definition of α', the fact that $\langle T_r, r \rangle$ is accepting implies that so is $\langle T_r, r' \rangle$.   □

We now consider the complexity bounds for various branching temporal logics that follow from our algorithm.

Theorem 4. *Robust model checking is*

(1) EXPTIME-complete for CTL, μ-calculus, and the alternation-free μ-calculus.

(2) 2EXPTIME-complete for CTL.*

Proof: Consider a branching temporal logic formula ψ of length n. Let $\mathcal{A}_\psi$ be the symmetric alternating tree automaton that corresponds to ψ. By Theorem 1, $\mathcal{A}_\psi$ is a Büchi automaton with $O(n)$ states for ψ in CTL or in the alternation-free μ-calculus, $\mathcal{A}_\psi$ is a parity automaton with $O(n)$ states and index $O(n)$ for ψ in μ-calculus, and $\mathcal{A}_\psi$ is a parity automaton with $2^{O(n)}$ states and index 3 for ψ in CTL*. In Theorem 3, we reduced the robust-model-checking problem of M with respect to $\neg\psi$ to the problem of checking the nonemptiness of the automaton $\mathcal{A}_{M,\psi}$, which is of size $|M| \cdot |\mathcal{A}_\psi| \cdot |W| \cdot (\mathcal{E}(\psi)+1)$, and which has the same type as $\mathcal{A}_\psi$. The upper bounds then follow from the fact the nonemptiness problem for alternating Büchi tree automata can be solved in exponential time, whereas the one for an alternating parity automaton with m states and index h can be solved in time $m^{O(h)}$ [40, 48, 31].

For the lower bounds, one can reduce the satisfiability problem for a branching temporal logic to the robust-model-checking problem for that logic. The details are similar to the reduction from satisfiability described for the related problem of module checking in [34]. Essentially, by the "bounded-degree property" of branching temporal logic, a search for a satisfying model for ψ can be reduced to a search for a satisfying $2^{I \cup O}$-labeling of a tree with branching degree $(\mathcal{E}(\psi) + 1)$. Then, one can relate the choice of the labels to choices made by the environment.   □

The *implementation complexity* of robust model checking is the complexity of the problem in terms of the module, assuming that the specification is fixed. As we discuss in Sect. 4, there are formulas for which robust model checking coincide with module checking with incomplete information. Since module checking with incomplete information is EXPTIME-hard already for CTL formulas of that type, it follows that the implementation complexity of robust model checking for CTL (and the other, more expressive, logics) is EXPTIME-complete.

In our definition of robust satisfaction, we allow the environment to have infinitely many states. We now claim that finite environments are strong enough. The proof is based on a "finite-model property" of tree automata, proven in [44] for nondeterministic tree automata and extended in [40, 30] to alternating tree automata. As we discuss in Sect. 4, this result is of great importance in the dual paradigm of supervisory control, where instead of hostile environments we consider collaborative controllers.

Theorem 5. *Given a module M and a branching temporal logic formula ψ, if there is an infinite module M' of degree k such that $M\|M'$ satisfies ψ, then there also exists a finite module M'' of degree k such that $M\|M''$ satisfies ψ.*

The alternating-automata-theoretic approach to CTL and CTL* model checking is extended in [28] to handle Fair-CTL and Fair-CTL* [13]. Using the same extension, we can solve the problem of robust model checking also for handle modules augmented with fairness conditions.

4 Discussion

Different researchers have considered the problem of reasoning about open systems. The distinction, in [22], between closed and open systems first led to the realization that *synthesis* of open systems corresponds to a search for a winning strategy in a *game* between the system and the environment [42], in which the winning condition is expressed in terms of a linear temporal logic formula. Transformation of the game-theoretic approach to model checking and adjustment of verification methods to the open-system setting started, for linear temporal logic, with the problem of *receptiveness* [7, 1, 16]. Essentially, the receptiveness problem is to determine whether every finite prefix of a computation of a given open system can be extended to an infinite computation that satisfies a linear temporal property irrespective of the behavior of the environment. In *module checking* [29, 34], the setting is again game-theoretic: an open system is required to satisfy a branching temporal property no matter how the environment disables its transitions. Verification of open systems was formulated in terms of a game between agents in a multiagent system in [2]. *Alternating-time temporal logic*, introduced there, enables path quantifiers to range over computations that a team of agents can force the system into, and thus enables the specification of multiagent systems.

Unlike [2], in which all the agents of the system are specified, our setting here assumes that only one agent, namely the system, is given. We ask whether there exists another agent, namely the environment, which is not yet known, such that the composition of the system and the environment violates a required property. Thus, while the outcome of the games that correspond to alternating temporal logic are computations, here the outcomes are trees[2]. The unknown environment may be nondeterministic, thus the branching structure of the trees is not necessarily a restriction of the branching structure of the system. Since the properties we check are branching, the latter point is crucial.

Robust satisfaction is closely related to *supervisory control* [45, 3]. Given a finite-state machine whose transitions are partitioned into controllable and uncontrollable, and a specification for the machine, the control problem requires the construction of a controller that chooses the controllable transitions so that the machine always satisfies the specification. Clearly, checking whether all the compositions $M \| M'$ of a system M with an environment M' satisfies a property ψ is dual to checking whether there is a controller M' such that $M \| M'$ satisfy the property $\neg \psi$. Thus, from a control-theory point of view, the results of this paper generalize known supervisory-control methods to the case where both the system and the controller are nondeterministic Moore machines. In particular, our results imply that nondeterministic controllers are more powerful than deterministic ones, and describe how to synthesize finite-state controllers. An extension to our setting here, described from the control-theory point of view, is the case where the controlled system may work in a nonmaximal environment. Thus, we would like to know whether M has a controller M' such that for all environments M'', the composition $M \| M' \| M''$ satisfies the specification. This setting is studied, for specifications in CTL and CTL*, in [27], where it is shown that the additional requirement makes the problem exponentially harder. Intuitively, the exponential increase in the complexity follows from the extra nesting of alternating "exists" and "for alls" in the description of the problem.

Recall that only nonuniversal specification formalisms are sensitive to the distinction between open and closed systems. In particular, specifications in linear temporal logic are not sensitive. One of the main advantages of branching temporal logics with respect to linear temporal logic is, however, the ability to mix universal and *existential* properties; e.g., in possibility properties like $AGEFp$. Existential properties describe requirements that should hold in *some* computations of the system. In [32], we show that nonuniversal properties can be partitioned into two classes, each with a different sensitivity to the distinction between open and closed systems. We say that a temporal-logic formula φ is *existential* if it imposes only existential requirements on the system, thus $\neg\varphi$ is universal. The formula φ is *mixed* if it imposes both existential and universal requirements, thus φ is neither universal nor existential. While universal formulas are insensitive to the system being open, we show that existential formulas are insensitive to the environment being nondeterministic.

---

[2] Game logic [2] considers games in which the output are trees, yet both players are known.

Thus, for such formulas, one can use the module-checking method. We study the problems of determining whether a given formula is universal or mixed, and show that they are both EXPTIME-complete. These result are relevant also in the contexts of modular verification [19] and backwards reasoning [23].

Often, the requirement that M satisfies ψ in all environments is too restrictive, and we are really concerned in the satisfaction of ψ in compositions of M with environments about which some *assumptions* are known. In the *assume-guarantee* paradigm to verification, each specification is a pair $\langle \varphi, \psi \rangle$, and M satisfies $\langle \varphi, \psi \rangle$ iff for every M', if $M \| M'$ satisfies φ, then $M \| M'$ also satisfies ψ. When φ and ψ are given in linear temporal logic, M satisfies $\langle \varphi, \psi \rangle$ iff M satisfies the implication $\varphi \to \psi$ [41] (see also [25]). The situation is different in the branching paradigm. For universal temporal logic, M satisfies $\langle \varphi, \psi \rangle$ iff ψ is satisfied in the composition $M \| M_\varphi$, of M with a module M_φ that embodies all the behaviors that satisfy φ [19, 28]. For general branching temporal logic, the above is no longer valid. Robust model checking can be viewed as a special case of the assume-guarantee setting, where φ is **true**. Robust model checking, however, can be used to solve the general assume-guarantee setting. Indeed, M satisfies $\langle \varphi, \psi \rangle$ iff M robustly satisfies the implication $\varphi \to \psi$. Thus, while in the linear framework the assume-guarantee paradigm corresponds to usual model checking, robustness is required in the branching framework.

Since assumptions about the environment and its interaction with the systems are natural part of the specification in robust model checking, the model studied in this chapter subsumes extensions that can be expressed in terms properties of the environment and its interaction with the system. For example, recall that our compositions here are deadlock free, thus deadlock is modeled by entering some "bad" state. In order to check that M satisfies a property ψ in all the compositions $M \| M'$ in which this bad state is not reachable, we have to perform robust model checking of M with respect to the property $(AG\theta) \to \psi$, with $\theta = \neg bad$, assuming that the bad state is labeled by bad. In a similar way, we can specify in θ other global assumptions about the composition, and thus model settings that support handshaking or other forms of coordinations between processes, as well as more general global actions, as in [20].

References

1. M. Abadi and L. Lamport. Composing specifications. *ACM Transactions on Programming Languages and Systems*, 15(1):73–132, 1993.
2. R. Alur, T.A. Henzinger, and O. Kupferman. Alternating-time temporal logic. *Journal of the ACM*, 49(5):672–713, September 2002.
3. M. Antoniotti. *Synthesis and verification of discrete controllers for robotics and manufacturing devices with temporal logic and the Control-D system*. PhD thesis, New York University, New York, 1995.

4. E.M. Clarke and E.A. Emerson. Design and synthesis of synchronization skeletons using branching time temporal logic. In *Proc. Workshop on Logic of Programs*, volume 131 of *Lecture Notes in Computer Science*, pages 52–71. Springer-Verlag, 1981.

5. E.M. Clarke, E.A. Emerson, and A.P. Sistla. Automatic verification of finite-state concurrent systems using temporal logic specifications. *ACM Transactions on Programming Languages and Systems*, 8(2):244–263, January 1986.

6. E.M. Clarke, O. Grumberg, and M.C. Browne. Reasoning about networks with many identical finite-state processes. In *Proc. 5th ACM Symp. on Principles of Distributed Computing*, pages 240–248, Calgary, Alberta, August 1986.

7. D.L. Dill. *Trace theory for automatic hierarchical verification of speed independent circuits*. MIT Press, 1989.

8. E.A. Emerson. Temporal and modal logic. In J. Van Leeuwen, editor, *Handbook of Theoretical Computer Science*, volume B, chapter 16, pages 997–1072. Elsevier, MIT Press, 1990.

9. E.A. Emerson and J.Y. Halpern. Sometimes and not never revisited: On branching versus linear time. *Journal of the ACM*, 33(1):151–178, 1986.

10. E.A. Emerson and C. Jutla. On simultaneously determinizing and complementing ω-automata. In *Proc. 4th IEEE Symp. on Logic in Computer Science*, pages 333–342, 1989.

11. E.A. Emerson and C. Jutla. Tree automata, μ-calculus and determinacy. In *Proc. 32nd IEEE Symp. on Foundations of Computer Science*, pages 368–377, San Juan, October 1991.

12. E.A. Emerson and C.-L. Lei. Modalities for model checking: Branching time logic strikes back. In *Proc. 20th ACM Symp. on Principles of Programming Languages*, pages 84–96, New Orleans, January 1985.

13. E.A. Emerson and C.-L. Lei. Temporal model checking under generalized fairness constraints. In *Proc. 18th Hawaii International Conference on System Sciences*, North Holywood, 1985. Western Periodicals Company.

14. E.A. Emerson and A. P. Sistla. Deciding branching time logic. In *Proc. 16th ACM Symp. on Theory of Computing*, Washington, April 1984.

15. M.J. Fischer and L.D. Zuck. Reasoning about uncertainty in fault-tolerant distributed systems. In M. Joseph, editor, *Proc. Symp. on Formal Techniques in Real-Time and Fault-Tolerant Systems*, volume 331 of *Lecture Notes in Computer Science*, pages 142–158. Springer-Verlag, 1988.

16. R. Gawlick, R. Segala, J. Sogaard-Andersen, and N. Lynch. Liveness in timed and untimed systems. In *Automata, Languages, and Programming, Proc. 21st ICALP*, volume 820 of *Lecture Notes in Computer Science*, pages 166–177. Springer-Verlag, 1994.

17. E. Graedel and I. Walukiewicz. Guarded fixed point logic. In *Proc. 14th Symp. on Logic in Computer Science*, July 1999.

18. O. Grumberg and D.E. Long. Model checking and modular verification. In *Proc. 2nd Conference on Concurrency Theory*, volume 527 of *Lecture Notes in Computer Science*, pages 250–265. Springer-Verlag, 1991.

19. O. Grumberg and D.E. Long. Model checking and modular verification. *ACM Trans. on Programming Languages and Systems*, 16(3):843–871, 1994.

20. J.Y. Halpern and R. Fagin. Modelling knowladge and action in distributed systems. *Distributed Computing*, 3(4):159–179, 1989.

21. D. Harel, O. Kupferman, and M.Y. Vardi. On the complexity of verifying concurrent transition systems. In *Proc. 8th Conference on Concurrency Theory*, volume 1243 of *Lecture Notes in Computer Science*, pages 258–272, Warsaw, July 1997. Springer-Verlag.

22. D. Harel and A. Pnueli. On the development of reactive systems. In K. Apt, editor, *Logics and Models of Concurrent Systems*, volume F-13 of *NATO Advanced Summer Institutes*, pages 477–498. Springer-Verlag, 1985.

23. T.A. Henzinger, O. Kupferman, and S. Qadeer. From pre-historic to postmodern symbolic model checking. In *Computer Aided Verification, Proc. 10th International Conference*, volume 1427 of *Lecture Notes in Computer Science*. Springer-Verlag, 1998.

24. C.A.R. Hoare. *Communicating Sequential Processes*. Prentice-Hall, 1985.

25. B. Jonsson and Y.-K. Tsay. Assumption/guarantee specifications in linear-time temporal logic. In P.D. Mosses, M. Nielsen, and M.I. Schwartzbach, editors, *TAPSOFT '95: Theory and Practice of Software Development*, volume 915 of *Lecture Notes in Computer Science*, pages 262–276, Aarhus, Denmark, May 1995. Springer-Verlag.

26. D. Kozen. Results on the propositional μ-calculus. *Theoretical Computer Science*, 27:333–354, 1983.

27. O. Kupferman, P. Madhusudan, P.S. Thiagarajan, and M.Y. Vardi. Open systems in reactive environments: Control and synthesis. In *Proc. 11th International Conference on Concurrency Theory*, volume 1877 of *Lecture Notes in Computer Science*, pages 92–107. Springer-Verlag, 2000.

28. O. Kupferman and M.Y. Vardi. On the complexity of branching modular model checking. In *Proc. 6th Conference on Concurrency Theory*, volume 962 of *Lecture Notes in Computer Science*, pages 408–422, Philadelphia, August 1995. Springer-Verlag.

29. O. Kupferman and M.Y. Vardi. Module checking. In *Computer Aided Verification, Proc. 8th International Conference*, volume 1102 of *Lecture Notes in Computer Science*, pages 75–86. Springer-Verlag, 1996.

30. O. Kupferman and M.Y. Vardi. Module checking revisited. In *Computer Aided Verification, Proc. 9th International Conference*, volume 1254 of *Lecture Notes in Computer Science*, pages 36–47. Springer-Verlag, 1997.

31. O. Kupferman and M.Y. Vardi. Weak alternating automata and tree automata emptiness. In *Proc. 30th ACM Symp. on Theory of Computing*, pages 224–233, Dallas, 1998.

32. O. Kupferman and M.Y. Vardi. Robust satisfaction. In *Proc. 10th Conference on Concurrency Theory*, volume 1664 of *Lecture Notes in Computer Science*, pages 383–398. Springer-Verlag, August 1999.

33. O. Kupferman, M.Y. Vardi, and P. Wolper. An automata-theoretic approach to branching-time model checking. *Journal of the ACM*, 47(2):312–360, March 2000.

34. O. Kupferman, M.Y. Vardi, and P. Wolper. Module checking. *Information and Computation*, 164:322–344, 2001.

35. L. Lamport. Sometimes is sometimes "not never" - on the temporal logic of programs. In *Proc. 7th ACM Symp. on Principles of Programming Languages*, pages 174–185, January 1980.

36. Z. Manna and A. Pnueli. Temporal specification and verification of reactive modules. Technical report, Weizmann Institute, 1992.

37. A.K. McIver and C. Morgan. Demonic, angelic and unbounded probabilistic choices in sequential programs. *Acta Informatica*, 37(4-5):329–354, 2001.

38. R. Milner. An algebraic definition of simulation between programs. In *Proc. 2nd International Joint Conference on Artificial Intelligence*, pages 481–489. British Computer Society, September 1971.

39. D.E. Muller and P.E. Schupp. Alternating automata on infinite trees. *Theoretical Computer Science*, 54:267–276, 1987.

40. D.E. Muller and P.E. Schupp. Simulating alternating tree automata by nondeterministic automata: New results and new proofs of theorems of Rabin, McNaughton and Safra. *Theoretical Computer Science*, 141:69–107, 1995.

41. A. Pnueli. In transition from global to modular temporal reasoning about programs. In K. Apt, editor, *Logics and Models of Concurrent Systems*, volume F-13 of *NATO Advanced Summer Institutes*, pages 123–144. Springer-Verlag, 1985.

42. A. Pnueli and R. Rosner. On the synthesis of a reactive module. In *Proc. 16th ACM Symp. on Principles of Programming Languages*, pages 179–190, Austin, January 1989.

43. J.P. Queille and J. Sifakis. Specification and verification of concurrent systems in Cesar. In *Proc. 5th International Symp. on Programming*, volume 137 of *Lecture Notes in Computer Science*, pages 337–351. Springer-Verlag, 1981.

44. M.O. Rabin. Weakly definable relations and special automata. In *Proc. Symp. Math. Logic and Foundations of Set Theory*, pages 1–23. North Holland, 1970.

45. P.J.G. Ramadge and W.M. Wonham. The control of discrete event systems. *IEEE Transactions on Control Theory*, 77:81–98, 1989.

46. R.S. Streett and E.A. Emerson. An automata theoretic decision procedure for the propositional μ-calculus. *Information and Computation*, 81(3):249–264, 1989.

47. J.W. Thatcher. Tree automata: an informal survey. In A.V. Aho, editor, *Currents in the theory of computing*, pages 143–172. Prentice-Hall, Englewood Cliffs, 1973.

48. M.Y. Vardi and P. Wolper. Automata-theoretic techniques for modal logics of programs. *Journal of Computer and System Science*, 32(2):182–221, April 1986.

A Theory of Interactive Computation*

Jan van Leeuwen[1] and Jiří Wiedermann[2]

[1] Utrecht University, Utrecht, The Netherlands
[2] Academy of Sciences, Prague, Czech Republic

Summary. Many embedded systems behave very differently from classical machine models: they interact with an unpredictable environment, they are "always on", and they change over time. This leads to the interesting question of what a computational theory of interactive, evolving programs should look like. While the behavior of such programs has been well-studied in concurrency theory, there has been much less emphasis on their computational aspects. A theory of interactive computation must necessarily lead beyond the classical, finitary models of computation.

We describe a simple model of interactive computing consisting of one component C and an environment E, interacting using single streams of input and output signals and with a number of realistic conditions in effect. The model enables us to study the computational implications of interaction, building on the theory of ω-automata. Viewing components as interactive transducers, we show that the interactive capabilities of components for recognition and generation are equivalent. We also show that all interactively computable functions are limit-continuous and that interactively computable bijections have interactively computable inverses. The model elegantly characterizes interactive computation in a stream setting.

1 Introduction

Modern computer systems are built from components that communicate and compute, while interacting with their environment. Consequently, many interactive systems behave very differently from traditional models of computation: their input is unpredictable and is not specified in advance, they never terminate (unless a fault occurs), and they may even change over time. In this chapter we derive some general results for the kind of interactive computing behavior which (components of) interactive systems can exhibit.

* This research was partially supported by project BRICKS (Basic Research for Creating the Knowledge Society), by Institutional Research Plan AV0Z10300504 and by grant No. 1ET100300517 within the National Research Program "Information Society".

The purpose of an interactive system is usually not to compute some final result, but to react to or interact with the environment in which the system is placed and to maintain a well-defined action–reaction behavior. This is an essential feature of e.g., embedded systems (cf. [18, 19]). In the late 1970s and early 1980s, this reactive behavior of systems received much attention in the theory of concurrent processes (see Manna and Pnueli [11] and Milner [12, 13]). Pnueli [15] (p. 511) writes:

> *Reactivity characterizes the nature of interaction between the system and its environment. It states that this interaction is not restricted to accepting inputs on initiation and producing outputs on termination. In particular, it allows some of the inputs to depend on intermediate outputs.*

Wegner [32, 33] called for a more computational view of reactive systems, claiming that "the intuition that computing corresponds to formal computability by Turing machines ... breaks down when the notion of what is computable is broadened to include interaction" ([33], p. 318). Formal aspects of Wegner's theory of interaction were studied in, e.g., Wegner and Goldin [34, 35] and in Goldin *et al.* [5].

Irrespective of the claim, it is of great interest to study the computational features of reactive, or interactive, systems. In [28] we argued that Turing machines indeed do not seem to fully adequately model the features of modern computing systems anymore and that, under suitable but realistic assumptions, modern systems may have super-Turing capabilities, at least theoretically (see also [36]). Stepney et al. [21] went even further and identified six classical paradigms in computing that we should no longer take for granted, including the Turing machine paradigm, posing it as a *grand challenge* for computer science to develop a general theory of "nonclassical" computation.

In this chapter we give a simple model of interactive computing, consisting of a component C and an environment E interacting using single streams of input and output signals and with a number of realistic conditions in effect. The notion of "component" that we use is very similar to Broy's [1] but we restrict ourselves to *deterministic* components. We identify a special condition, called the *interactiveness condition*, which will be imposed throughout. The condition states that C is guaranteed to always give a meaningful output within a finite amount of time after receiving a meaningful input from E and vice versa. The model is described in detail in Sect. 2. Our aim is only to analyze the capabilities of the model from the perspective of computability theory.

In the model we prove a number of general results for the interactive computing behavior which a component C can exhibit, assuming that E can behave arbitrarily and unpredictably. In most results we assume that C is a program with unbounded memory, with a memory contents that is building up over time and that is never erased unless the component explicitly does so. This compares to the use of persistent Turing machines by Goldin [4] (see also [6]) and Kosub[9]. No special assumptions are made about the 'speed' at which C and E operate and generate responses, except that they are using some common underlying clock. In Sects. 3 and 4 we show how interactive computing can lead to super-Turing behavior.

Viewing components as interactive transducers of the signals that they receive we show in Sect. 5 that, using suitable definitions, recognition and generation coincide just like they do for Turing machines. The proof is more intricate than in the latter case and depends on the special operational assumptions in the model. Finally, in Sect. 6 we define a general notion of interactively computable functions. We prove that interactively computable functions are limit-continuous, using a suitable extension of the notion of continuity known from the semantics of computable functions. We also prove an interesting inversion theorem which states that interactively computable 1-1 functions have interactively computable inverses.

The study of machines working on infinite input streams or ω-words is by no means new and has a sizable literature, with the first studies dating back to the nineteen sixties and seventies (cf. Thomas [22], Staiger [20], or Perrin and Pin [14]). The model studied in the present chapter exploits ideas from the theory of ω-automata, but a number of features are added to better capture the intuitive notions of interactiveness. We prove that, using analogs from the classical theory of ω-languages, the recognition and generation capabilities are equivalent for interactive components and e.g., that the interactively recognizable languages are topologically closed, considering $\{0,1\}^\omega$ as a topological space with the normal product topology. These connections provide the theory of interactive computing with a firm basis in the known framework of ω-computations. A preliminary version of the material in this chapter appeared in [25, 26].

2 A Model of Interactive Computation

Let C be a component (a software agent or a computational device) that interacts with an environment E. We assume that C and E interact by exchanging signals (symbols). Although general interactive systems do not need to have a limit on the nature and the size of the signals that they exchange, we assume here that the signals are taken from a fixed and finite alphabet. More precisely:

(*Alphabet*) C and E interact by exchanging symbols from the alphabet $\Sigma = \{0, 1, \tau, \sharp\}$.

Here 0 and 1 are the classical bits, τ is the "silent" or empty symbol, and $\sharp$ is the fault or error symbol. Instead of the bits 0 and 1, one could use any larger, finite choice of symbols but this is easily coded back into bits.

In order to describe the interactions between C and E we assume a uniform time-scale of discrete moments. C and E are assumed to interact in the following sense. At any time t, E can send a symbol of Σ to C and C can send a symbol of Σ to E. It is possible that E or C remains silent for a certain amount a time, i.e., that either of them does not send any active signal during some consecutive time moments. During these moments E or C is assumed to send the symbol τ, just to record this. For the symbol $\sharp$ a special convention is used:

(*Fault rule*) If C receives a symbol $\sharp$ from E, then C will output a $\sharp$ within a finite amount of time after this as well (and vice versa).

If no $\sharp$'s are exchanged, the interaction between E and C is called fault-free (error-free).

Some further assumptions are necessary. First of all, we assume that when E (C) sends a signal to C (E) during time t, then C (E) "knows" this signal from the next time-moment onward. This does not necessarily mean that E or C has processed the symbol in any meaningful way by time $t+1$, but we assume that the signal has entered their circuitry somehow. Second, to disambiguate the interaction, we assume that the interaction is always initiated by E, i.e., at any moment E sends its signal to C first and C sends its signal to E next. It means that the communication between E and C can be described by two sequences $e = e_0 e_1 \ldots e_t \ldots$ and $c = c_0 c_1 \ldots c_t \ldots$, with e_t denoting the signal that E sends to C at time t and c_t denoting the signal that C sends to E at time t. Here e may also be regarded as the "interactive input stream" and c as the corresponding "interactive output stream". When E or C is silent at time t, then the corresponding symbol is τ ("empty"). If two infinite sequences e and c correspond to the actual interactions that take place over time, we say that the sequences represent an *interactive computation* of C in response to the (unpredictable) environment E. C is called an *interactive component*. We let $\bar{e}$ and $\bar{c}$ denote the sequences e and c *without* the τ's.

In an interactive computation, we assume that C acts according to some program that may evolve deterministically over time, in a way depending on the history of its interaction with E. We assume likewise that the signal E sends to C during time t depends on what E remembers from the interaction with C and on c_{t-1}, but also on its "mood" or the situation (which may vary over time) which can lead it to send any symbol it wants. Thus, E can be totally indeterministic and unpredictable in generating its next signal. For later reference we write this as $E_{t-1}(c_{t-1}) \ni e_t$, where E_{t-1} represents all "knowledge" that E possesses at the moment that it generates the response for output to C at time t and all situations that can lead it to generate e_t (which will be an unpredictable choice from the symbols of Σ). The signal C subsequently sends to E during time t depends deterministically on the internal state of C at time $t-1$ and on the signal C received at that time.

Note that at time t, E and C can in principle be assumed to know all signals that were sent at previous times. Thus, C's output at time t can depend on C's program, on $e_0 e_1 \ldots e_{t-1}$ and, implicitly, on $c_0 c_1 \ldots c_{t-1}$. The same holds for E, except that one would also have to know the "situations" of E that underly its unpredictable response at the earlier time moments. We assume that E and C somehow generate their e_0 and c_0 signals spontaneously, with C always generating c_0 deterministically, e.g., always as τ.

We assume the following property as being characteristic for interactive computations: E sends signals to C infinitely often, and C is guaranteed to always send a nonempty (non-τ) output signal within a finite mount of time after receiving a nonempty (non-τ) input signal from E.

> (*Interactiveness*) For all times t, when E sends a non-τ signal to C at time t, then C sends a non-τ signal to E at some time t' with $t' > t$ (and vice versa).

The condition of interactiveness is assumed throughout this chapter. Note that, in the given definition, we do not assume any special causal relationship between the signal sent (by E or C) at time t and the signal sent (by C or E respectively) at time t'. Assuming interactiveness, the behavior of a component C with respect to E is a relation on infinite sequences over Σ. It consists of the (deterministic) responses that C may have to all possible behaviors that E may exhibit. We assume that E sends a non-τ signal at least once, thus always triggering an interaction sequence with infinitely many nonempty signals. The question whether a given component fulfills the interactiveness condition is in general undecidable (cf. Theorem 3).

Definition 1. *An* interaction pair *of C and E is any pair (e, c) such that $e = e_0 e_1 \ldots e_t \ldots$ and $c = c_0 c_1 \ldots c_t \ldots$ represent an interactive computation of C in response to E.*

Sequences of τ's can be meaningful to C and E, e.g., for internal computation or timing purposes. A given infinite sequence of nonempty input signals may lead to a multitude of different sequences c, depending on the way E cares to intersperse the sequence with silent steps. Note again that E is fully unpredictable in this respect. However, the assumed interactiveness forces E to keep sequences of intermittent silent steps finite. For the purposes of this chapter we assume that E sends a nonempty signal at every moment in time, i.e., $e = \bar{e}$ for all sequences of environment input that we consider in the model.

> (*Full environmental activity*) At all times t, E sends a non-τ signal to C.

We retain the possibility for C to emit τ's and do internal computations for some time without giving nonempty output, even though interactiveness forces C to give some nonempty output after some finite amount of time.

We assume that C's behavior can be effectively simulated, in the context of a simulation of any behavior of E. We make the following further assumptions about C: it has only one channel of interaction with E, it admits multithreading (allowing it to run several internal processes simultaneously), and it has a fixed but otherwise arbitrary speed of operation (i.e., any nonzero speed is allowed which comes with the component). As a consequence it will be possible for C to have a foreground process doing e.g., the I/O-operations very quickly and have one or more background processes running, at a slower pace. The following crucial assumption is made, as in classical computability theory:

> (Unbounded component memory) C works without any a priori bounds on the amount of available memory, i.e., its memory space is always finite but potentially unbounded.

Thus C's memory is never reset during an interactive computation, unless its program explicitly does so. We allow C to build up an "infinite" database of knowledge that it can consult in the course of its interactions with E.

Despite the assumed generality, it is conceivable that E is constrained in some way and can generate at some or any given moment only a *selection* of the possible signals from Σ. (We assume that the interactiveness is never in danger, i.e., there should always be at least one allowable nonempty symbol that E can send.) In this case a component may be acting on a very irregular subset of the possible input sequences. If this is the case, one may wish to assume that the constrained behavior of E can be checked algorithmically afterwards (i.e., every time after E has generated a response).

> (*Algorithmicity of environmental input*) When an arbitrary infinite sequence over Σ is supplied as input to C, symbol after symbol, it can be algorithmically verified alongside of it whether this sequence could have been output by E, taking into account the stepwise interaction of C and E and any constraint which may have restricted E's choice of signals at any given moment.

Algorithmicity means that there is some program $\mathcal{E}$ which evolves over time and which answers, possibly after some finite delay, whether $E_{t-1}(c_{t-1}) \ni e_t$ or not, given t and e_t as input and knowing the whole interaction history up until $t - 1$ and assuming the given sequence was correct up until then.

The assumption of algorithmicity does not interfere with or change the unpredictability of E as it generates its signals in any interactive computation. The assumption only implies that, regardless of E's actual behavior, there is an algorithmic way to verify *afterwards* that a sequence *could* have been generated by E, e.g., in a simulation. As soon as the sequence deviates and becomes inconsistent with E's possible actions, the verifier is assumed to output an error message from that point onward. Without constraints there is no need for a special verifier, but when constraints are in effect there is.

It will be helpful to describe an interactive computation of C and E also as a mapping (transduction) of streams e (of environment inputs) to streams c (of component responses). In this way C acts as an ω-transducer on infinite sequences, with the additional interactive behavior as described. In the following definition, recall that we assumed that $e = \bar{e}$.

Definition 2. *The* behavior *of C with respect to E is the set* $T_C = \{(e, \bar{c}) | (e, c)$ is an interaction pair of C and $E\}$. *If* (e, c) *is an interaction pair of C and E,* *then we also write* $T_C(e) = \bar{c}$ *and say that* $\bar{c}$ *is the* interactive transduction *of* e *by C.*

Definition 3. *A relation T on infinite sequences is called* interactively computable *if and only if there is an interactive component C such that* $T = T_C$.

Seemingly simple transductions may be impossible in interactive computation, due to the strict requirement of interactiveness and the unpredictability of the environment. Let $0^\star$ denote the set of finite sequences of 0's (including the empty sequence), $\{0, 1\}^\star$ the set of all finite sequences over $\{0, 1\}$, and $\{0, 1\}^\omega$ the set of infinite sequences or streams over the alphabet $\{0, 1\}$.

Example. We claim that no (interactive) component C can exist that transduces input streams of the form $1\alpha 1\beta 1\gamma$ to output streams of the form $1\beta 1\alpha 1\gamma$, with $\alpha, \beta \in 0^\star$ and $\gamma \in \{0, 1\}^\omega$. Note that the mapping would amount to swapping the first and the second block of zeroes in a sequence starting with a 1, empty blocks allowed. Suppose by way of contradiction that there was a component C that could do this. Consider how C would respond to an input $100\ldots$ from E, assuming that E keeps sending 0's until further notice. By interactiveness, C must send a nonempty signal to E at some time, and we may assume without loss of generality that the first nonempty signal it sends is a 1. By interactiveness C must generate further nonempty signals. Denote the second nonempty symbol it sends by σ. Now let E act as follows. If $\sigma = 0$ (meaning that C's output starts with 10), then let E switch to sending 11 (implying that β is empty) and anything it wants after that. If $\sigma = 1$ (meaning that C's output starts with 11), then let E switch to sending 101 (implying that $\beta = 0$) and anything it wants after that. If $\sigma = \sharp$, the computation clearly is not fault-free. It follows that in all cases C has been fooled into sending the wrong output.

3 Interactively Computable Relations

Given a stream $y \in \{0, 1\}^\omega$ and $t \geq 0$, let $pref_t(y)$ be the length-t prefix of y. For finite and infinite sequences y we write $x \prec y$ if x is a finite and strict prefix of y. We write $x \preceq y$ if $x \prec y$ or $x = y$. We rephrase the common definition of monotonic functions (cf. [37]) for the case of partial functions as follows.

Definition 4. *A partial function* $g : \{0, 1\}^\star \to \{0, 1\}^\star$ *is called* monotonic *if for all* $x, y \in \{0, 1\}^\star$, *if* $x \prec y$ *and* $g(y)$ *is defined then* $g(x)$ *is defined as well and* $g(x) \preceq g(y)$.

The following observation captures that interactive computations can be viewed as classical, monotonic computations taken to infinity.

Theorem 1. *If a relation $T \subseteq \{0,1\}^\omega \times \{0,1\}^\omega$ is interactively computable, then there exists a classically computable, monotonic partial function g : $\{0,1\}^\star \to \{0,1\}^\star$ such that $(u,v) \in T$ if and only if for all $t \geq 0$: $g(pref_t(u))$ is defined, $\lim_{t \to \infty} |g(pref_t(u))| = \infty$ and for all $t \geq 0$, $g(pref_t(u)) \prec v$.*

Proof. Let $T = T_C$. We define g by designing a Turing machine M_g for it. Given an arbitrary finite sequence $x = x_0 x_1 \ldots x_{t-1} \in \{0,1\}^\star$ on its input tape, M_g operates as follows. M_g simulates C using the program of C, feeding it the consecutive symbols of x as input and checking every time it does so whether the next symbol is an input signal that E *could* have given on the basis of the interaction with C up until this moment. To check this, M_g employs the verifier $\mathcal{E}$ which exists by the assumed algorithmicity of E (and which adapts along with the simulation). As long as no inconsistency is detected, M_g continues with the simulation of the interaction of E and C. Whenever the simulation leads C to output a signal 0 or 1, M_g writes the corresponding symbol to its output tape. When the simulation leads C to output a τ, M_g writes nothing. When the simulation leads C to output a $\sharp$ or when the verifier detects that the input is not consistent with E's possible behavior, then M_g is sent into an indefinite loop. If M_g has successfully completed the simulation up to and including the processing of the final input symbol x_{t-1}, then M_g halts. It follows that M_g terminates if and only if x is a valid beginning of an interaction of E with C, with C's response appearing on the output tape when it halts. The result now follows by observing what properties of g are implied when $(u,v) \in T$. The constraints capture the interactiveness of C and E and the fact that the interaction must be indefinite. It is clear from the construction that g is monotonic. $\qquad\square$

For at least one type of interactively computable relation can the given observation be turned into a complete characterization. Let a relation $T \subseteq \{0,1\}^\omega \times \{0,1\}^\omega$ be called *total* if for every $u \in \{0,1\}^\omega$ there exists a $v \in \{0,1\}^\omega$ such that $(u,v) \in T$. Behaviours of interactive components in environments without constraints are always total relations. In the following result the monotonicity of g is *not* assumed beforehand.

Theorem 2. *Let $T \subseteq \{0,1\}^\omega \times \{0,1\}^\omega$ be a total relation. T is interactively computable if and only if there exists a classically computable total function $g : \{0,1\}^\star \to \{0,1\}^\star$ such that $(u,v) \in T$ if and only if $\lim_{t \to \infty} |g(pref_t(u))| = \infty$ and for all $t \geq 0$, $g(pref_t(u)) \prec v$.*

Proof. The "only if" part follows from the proof of Theorem 1. If T is total, then the constructed function g is seen to be total and the stated conditions are satisfied.

For the "if" part, assume that $T \subseteq \{0,1\}^\omega \times \{0,1\}^\omega$ is a total relation, that g is a computable total function and that for all $(u,v) \in \{0,1\}^\omega \times \{0,1\}^\omega$, $(u,v) \in T$ if and only if $\lim_{t \to \infty} |g(pref_t(u))| = \infty$ and for all integers $t \geq 0$, $g(pref_t(u)) \prec v$. To prove that T is interactively computable, design a component C that operates as follows.

While E feeds input, a foreground process of C keeps buffering the input symbols in a queue $q = q_0 q_1 \ldots q_t$ for $t \to \infty$. Let $r \in \{0,1\}^\star$ be the finite output generated by C at any given moment. We will maintain the following invariant: q is a prefix of u and r a prefix of v, for some pair $(u,v) \in T$. Letting q grow into "u" by the input from E, we let r grow into "v" by letting C carry out the background process P explained below every once in a while. C keeps a counter c_q that is initialized to 1 before any call to P has occurred. C outputs "empty" signals as long as a call to P is running.

When called, P copies the length-c_q prefix of q into the variable x, it increments c_q by 1, and computes $g(x)$ using the subroutine for g. (Note that the sequence now in x extends the sequence on which the previous call of P operated by precisely one symbol.) By totality of g the subroutine ends in finitely many steps. Let $y = g(x)$ be the output sequence. By totality of T and the second condition on g only two cases can occur: $r \prec y$ or $y \preceq r$. If $r \prec y$, then C outputs the symbols by which y extends r one after the other, updates r to account for the new output, and calls P again after it has done so. If $y \preceq r$, C does not generate any special output and simply moves on to another call of P, provided at least one further input symbol has entered the queue in the meantime (which will be so by the assumed environmental activity). Note that every call to P maintains the invariant.

Because $\lim_{t \to \infty} |g(pref_t(u))| = \infty$, there will be infinitely many calls to P in which the case $r \prec y$ occurs. Thus r will grow to infinity, with the output generated by C being precisely $\lim_{t \to \infty} r = v$.   □

For total relations $T \subseteq \{0,1\}^\omega \times \{0,1\}^\omega$, we say that T is *implied in the limit* by g if T and g are related as in Theorem 2. Combining Theorems 1 and 2 we can express the relationship between interactive computability and monotonicity very succinctly: *the interactively computable total relations are precisely the relations implied in the limit by classically computable, monotonic total functions on* $\{0,1\}^\star$. We return to this characterization in Sect. 6.

It is realistic to assume that the initial specification of C is a program written in some acceptable programming system. For example, the internal operation of C might be modeled by a persistent Turing machine of some sort (as in [4, 34]). In our model, the underlying program itself may evolve as well but we assume that it does so only in a way that can be simulated. It is easily argued that interactiveness, as a property of arbitrary component programs, is recursively undecidable. The following stronger but still elementary statement can be observed.

Theorem 3. *The set of interactive programs is not recursively enumerable.*

Proof. Let $S = \{\pi | \pi$ is the program of a component C that is interactive$\}$. Suppose that S is recursively enumerable. We use a simple diagonal argument to obtain a contradiction. Let $\pi_1, \pi_2, \ldots$ be a recursive enumeration of S. Consider the programs π_i and observe how they operate when the environment just feeds 1's to them (without empty signals). We now construct the following program π, designed to be different from all π_i's. We let π react the same regardless of the input that it receives from E, but it is useful to imagine it working under the same environment input of all 1's. Let r and r_i denote the finite sequences of output generated by π and π_i in the course of the computation.

As soon as π receives signals from E, it starts. Now π proceeds in *stages*, starting with stage 1. During stage i, π simulates the interactive computation of π_i until its output sequence $\overline{r_i}$ has become longer than $\overline{r}$ (the output of π so far). During the simulation π only outputs τ's. If, during the simulation of π_i, E would decide to stop inputting 1's based on π_i's response and switch to giving an input signal different from a 1, then the simulation is also stopped, at this point.

Consider the cases that can occur in stage i. Assume that E could input 1's all the way (in the simulation of π_i). Then the situation that $\overline{r_i}$ becomes longer than $\overline{r}$ will occur. We can assume w.l.o.g. that, when this happens, $\overline{r_i} = \alpha\delta$ with $|\alpha| = |\overline{r}|$ and $\delta \in \{0,1\}$. At this point, let π output a signal $\delta^c \in \{0,1\}$ different from δ (turning $\overline{r}$ into $\overline{r}\delta^c$). If E could not/did not input 1's the whole way in the simulation, let π output any nonempty symbol, say a 1. After this, π goes to stage $i + 1$.

By interactiveness, every stage of π is finite and thus π itself is interactive. The construction guarantees that π is different from every π_i and thus $\pi \notin S$. This contradicts the definition of S.   □

4 Interactive Recognition

Interactive systems typically perform tasks in *monitoring*, i.e., in the online perception or recognition of patterns in infinite streams of signals from the environment. The notion of recognition is well-studied in the theory of ω-automata (cf. [10, 20, 22, 23]). It is usually based on the automaton passing an infinite number of times through one or more accepting states during the processing of the infinite input sequence. In interactive systems this is not detectable and thus this kind of criterion is not applicable. Instead, a component is normally placed in an environment that has to follow a certain specification and the component has to observe that this specification is adhered to. This motivates the following definition.

Definition 5. *An infinite sequence $\alpha \in \{0,1\}^\omega$ is said to be recognized by C if $(\alpha, 1^\omega) \in T_C$.*

The definition states that, in interactive computation, an infinite sequence α is recognized if C outputs a 1 every once in a while and *no* other symbols except τ's in between, where E generates the infinite sequence α as input during the computation. The criterion is closely related to the notion of $1'$-*acceptance* for ω-sequences [10, 20] which requires an ω-automaton to accept by always staying in a designated subset of states while processing the infinite input sequence.

In interactive computation, a recognized sequence can never contain a $\sharp$ because in finite time it would lead C to output a $\sharp$ as well, causing C to reject the input from E. We can also assume that C does not output any $\sharp$ itself either for, if it did, we might as well have it output a 0 instead without affecting the definition of recognition.

Definition 6. *The set interactively recognized by C with respect to E is the set $J_C = \{\alpha \in \{0,1\}^\omega | \alpha$ is recognized by $C\}$.*

Definition 7. *A set $J \subseteq \{0,1\}^\omega$ is called* interactively recognizable *if there exists an interactive component C such that $J = J_C$.*

Considering Wegner's claim that interactive computing is more powerful than classical computation (cf. Sect. 1), the question arises whether this is somehow reflected in the recognition power of interactive components. To a large extent the super-Turing power of interactive computation comes from the infinite behavior, but at the same time there are new limitations. We prove a number of results that all have their analogies for ω-automata but which we show here for the case of interactive components.

Lemma 1. *The following sets are interactively recognizable:*
(i) $J = \{\alpha \in \{0,1\}^\omega | \alpha$ contains at most k ones\}, for any fixed integer k,
(ii) $J = \{\alpha \in \{0,1\}^\omega | \alpha$ has a 1 only in the prime number positions\}.
The following sets are not *interactively recognizable:*
(iii) $J = \{\alpha \in \{0,1\}^\omega | \alpha$ contains finitely many 1's\},
(iv) $J = \{\alpha \in \{0,1\}^\omega | \alpha$ contains infinitely many 1's\},
(v) $J = \{\alpha \in \{0,1\}^\omega | \alpha$ contains precisely k ones\}, for any fixed integer $k \geq 1$,
(vi) $J = \{\alpha \in \{0,1\}^\omega | \alpha$ contains at least k ones\}, for any fixed integer $k \geq 1$.

Proof. *(i)* Let C output a 1 with every 0 that it receives from E, and let it continue doing so until after the k'th 1 that it sees. Let C switch to outputting 0's after it receives the $(k+1)$-st 1. C is interactive and precisely recognizes the set J.
(ii) Left to the reader.
(iii) Suppose there was an interactive component C that recognized J. Let E input 1's. By interactiveness C must generate a nonempty signal σ sometime. E can then fool C as follows. If $\sigma = 0$, then let E switch to inputting 0's from this moment onward: the resulting input belongs to J but C does not respond with all 1's. If $\sigma = 1$, then let E continue to input 1's. Possibly C outputs a few more 1's but there must come a moment that it outputs a 0. If it didn't then C would recognize the sequence $1^\omega \notin J$. As soon as C outputs a 0, let E switch to inputting 0's from this moment onward: the resulting input still belongs to J but C does not recognize it properly. Contradiction.
(iv) Suppose there was an interactive component C that recognized J. Let E input 0's. Now argue as in the preceding case.

(v) Suppose there was an interactive component C that recognized J, the set of infinite sequences with precisely k 1's. Let E input $k - 1$ 1's followed by all 0's for a while from then onward. By interactiveness C must generate a nonempty signal σ at some moment in time. E can now fool C as follows. If $\sigma = 0$, then let E send a 1 followed by all 0's from then onward: the input sequence clearly belongs to J but isn't recognized properly by C. If $\sigma = 1$, then let E continue to send 0's. Possibly C outputs a few more 1's but there must come a moment that it outputs a 0. If it didn't then C would recognize the sequence $1^{k-1}0^\omega \notin J$. As soon as C outputs a 0, let E switch to inputting a 1 followed by all 0's from then onward: the input sequence again clearly belongs to J but isn't recognized properly by C.

(vi) Analogous to *(v)*. With $k = 1$ this example was shown not to be 1'-definable in [2], Lemma 7.17 (b).   □

The proof of Lemma 1 is based the following underlying fact: if $J \subseteq \{0,1\}^\omega$ contains $\alpha 0^*1M$ as a sublanguage for some nonempty set $M \subseteq \{0,1\}^\omega$ but does *not* contain $\alpha 0^\omega$ for some finite $\alpha \in \{0,1\}^*$, then J is not interactively recognizable.

The power of interactive recognition is expressed in the following observations. We assume again that the internal operation of the components we consider is specified by some program in an acceptable programming system.

Theorem 4. $J = \{0^n1\{0,1\}^\omega | n \in A\} \cup 0^\omega$ *is interactively recognizable if and only if A is the complement of a recursively enumerable set.*

Proof. Let J be of the given form and let C interactively recognize the sequences of J. Observe that C must have the following behavior: if E has sent input 0^n1 at some point in time, then $n \in A$ if and only C recognizes the sequence no matter what further input signals follow. Likewise $n \notin A$ if and only if C does *not* recognize the sequence, no matter what further signals follow. Let π be the program of C.

Now recursively enumerate the complement of A as follows. Enumerate the integers n and for every n simulate π on the input 0^n1 from the environment, using any extension of the sequence when these inputs are called for by π (noting here that E must be able to generate any such extension). After the simulation of C has received the complete 0^n1 as input, output n if, or otherwise as soon as, the simulation of C has led to an output symbol 0. The latter happens only for the elements of the complement of A.

Conversely, let A be the complement of a recursively enumerable set. Let π be the program enumerating A's complement $\overline{A}$. Design a component C that operates as follows. If the first symbol that it receives is a 1, then C outputs 0's forever. (The case $n = 0$ cannot occur as we are only considering subsets of N.) If the first symbol that it receives is a 0, then C outputs 1's until it receives a first 1. If no 1 is ever received, it effectively means that C recognizes 0^ω. If C does receive a 1, let $n \geq 0$ be the number of 0's that it has received until this first 1. Now C switches to the program π that enumerates

$\overline{A}$. C continues to output 1's while it is running π, until it encounters n in the enumeration. If n is encountered, C stops running π and starts outputting 0's instead. Clearly C recognizes $0^n 1 \ldots$ precisely if $n \notin \overline{A}$, i.e., if $n \in A$. This shows that C recognizes J. $\square$

For sets $J \subseteq \{0,1\}^\omega$, let $Init(J)$ be the set of all finite prefixes of sequences from J. Theorem 4 leads to the observation that in interactive computation the initial parts of an environment input do not necessarily hold any clue about the recognizability of the input "in the limit", just as one would expect. The result parallels the one for $1'$-definable ω-Turing machine languages by Cohen and Gold [2], Theorem 7.22.

Corollary 1. *There are interactively recognizable sets J such that Init(J) is not recursively enumerable.*

Proof. Consider the set $J = \{0^n 1 \{0,1\}^\omega | n \in A\} \cup 0^\omega$ for an arbitrary non-recursively enumerable set A whose complement is recursively enumerable (cf. Rogers [17]). By Theorem 4, J is interactively recognizable. Note that $Init(J) \cap 0^* 1 = \{0^n 1 | n \in A\}$. Hence, if $Init(J)$ were recursively enumerable, then so would A be. Contradiction. $\square$

A further characterization of interactive recognizability is implied by the following result. For $1'$-definable ω-Turing machine languages the corresponding fact was shown Cohen and Gold [2], Theorem 7.16 (b).

Theorem 5. *$J \subseteq \{0,1\}^\omega$ is interactively recognizable if and only if there exists a recursively enumerable language $A \subseteq \{0,1\}^*$ such that $J = \{u \in \{0,1\}^\omega | u$ has no prefix in A$\}$.*

Proof. Let $J \subseteq \{0,1\}^\omega$ be interactively recognizable, and C a component that interactively recognizes J. Let A consist of all sequences $\alpha \in \{0,1\}^*$ that lead C to output a 0, after E has interactively fed it α and C has output only τ's and 1's so far. (Thus, α leads C to output its first 0.) By simulating and dovetailing the interactive computations between E and C on all possible finite input segments, A is seen to be recursively enumerable (using our assumptions). J precisely consist of all sequences $\in \{0,1\}^\omega$ that do not begin with a sequence in A.

Conversely, let $A \subseteq \{0,1\}^*$ be recursively enumerable and J as defined. Design a component C that operates as follows. As soon as C receives input, it starts buffering the input in a queue q. At the same time it starts the recursive enumeration of A and it starts outputting 1's. Every time the enumeration of A outputs a sequence α, C adds it to a list L_A. Every once in a while, C checks whether any prefix of the current q happens to occur in L_A. If this is the case, C stops the enumeration and switches to outputting 0's from here onwards. Otherwise C continues with the procedure, and keeps on outputting 1's. Clearly C is interactive, and C recognizes precisely the set J. $\square$

The given characterization together with Cohen and Gold's result show that, with unconstrained environments and recursively evolving C's, *interactive recognizability and $1'$-definability essentially coincide*. Theorem 5 has another consequence when we view $\{0,1\}^\omega$ as a topological space with the usual product or Cantor topology (cf. [10]). The following result was observed by Landweber [10] (cor. 3.2) for $1'$-definable ω-regular languages and Staiger (cf. [20]) for $1'$-definable (deterministic) ω-Turing machine languages. Recall that an open set $\subseteq \{0,1\}^\omega$ is said to have a (minimal) basis $B \subseteq \{0,1\}^*$ if $L = B\{0,1\}^\omega$ (and B is prefix-free).

Corollary 2. $J \subseteq \{0,1\}^\omega$ *is interactively recognizable if and only if J is closed and $\bar{J}$ has a recursively enumerable basis.*

Finally we note some rules for constructing new interactively recognizable sets from old ones. Again a similar result exists for $1'$-definable ω-Turing machine languages, see [2], Theorem 7.20 (a). The proofs here are tedious because the outputs of a component may feed back to E.

Lemma 2. *The family of interactively recognizable sets is*
(i) closed under $\cup$ and $\cap$, but
(ii) not closed under ω-complement.

Proof. (i) We only prove closure under $\cup$, leaving the similar argument for closure under $\cap$ to the reader. Let J_1 and J_2 be interactively recognized by components C_1 and C_2, respectively. A component C recognizing $J_1 \cup J_2$ is obtained as follows. C buffers the input that it receives from E in a queue q, symbol after symbol. In conjunction with this, C simulates the programs of both C_1 and C_2 simultaneously, simulating the input from E by the consecutive symbols from q. C keeps C_1 in the foreground and outputs what C_1 outputs *until* the environment input (which can be influenced by C_1's output) is about to be inconsistent with q or C_1 is about to output a 0 for the first time. (C outputs finitely many τ's to account for the simulation overhead). If the simulation never reaches a point where this occurs, then C works completely like C_1 all the way and recognizes the input as an element of J_1. Every element of J_1 can be recognized this way.

If either one of the two special situations does occur during the simulation, then C tries to switch to C_2. In case the environment input was about to become inconsistent with q (due to C_1's output and E's response to it), C checks whether the environment input in the simulation of C_2 is still consistent with q. If it is, it subsequently checks whether C_2 (running in the background) has output a 0 in the simulation so far. If not, C switches to the simulation of C_2, otherwise it switches to outputting 0's from this moment onward, effectively rejecting the whole input sequence. In case the simulation was interrupted because C_1 was about to output a 0 for the first time, then C does *not* output the 0 but makes a similar check as described before, to see if it can bring the simulation of C_2 to the foreground and switch. If the simulation switches successfully to C_2, then the same constraints continue to be observed. Clearly, if no further exception is reached, C works completely like C_2 all the way and recognizes the input as an element of J_2. Note that every element of $J_2 \setminus J_1$ can be recognized this way.

It is easily seen that C is interactive. Note also that, when C switches from C_1 to C_2 as described, both C_1 and C_2 must have been outputting τ's and 1's until this point and thus, when the simulation of C_2 takes over, it is like C_2 has been running from the beginning as far as the recognition process is concerned. C thus recognizes precisely $J_1 \cup J_2$.

(ii) Consider the set $J = 0^\omega \cup 0^\star 10^\omega$. By Lemma 1 (i) the set is interactively recognizable, but Lemma 1 (vi) shows that its ω-complement is not.   □

5 Interactive Generation

Interactive components typically also perform tasks in *controlling* other components. This involves the online processing of infinite streams into other, more specific streams of signals. In this section we consider what infinite streams of signals an interactive component can *generate*. The notion of generation is well-known in automata theory and related to matters of definability and expressibility, but it seems not to have been studied extensively in the theory of ω-automata (cf. Staiger [20]). Our aim is to prove that generation and recognition are *duals* in our model.

Definition 8. *An infinite sequence $\beta \in \{0,1\}^\omega$ is said to be generated by C if there exists an environment input $\alpha \in \{0,1\}^\omega$ such that $(\alpha, \beta) \in T_C$.*

Unlike the case for recognition (cf. Sect. 4) one cannot simplify the output capabilities for components C now. In particular one has to allow C to outputs $\sharp$-symbols, for example to signify that the generation process has gotten off on some wrong track. If C outputs a $\sharp$-symbol, E will produce a $\sharp$ some finite amount of time later and thus invalidate the current run.

Definition 9. *The set interactively generated by component C is the set $L_C = \{\beta \in \{0,1\}^\omega | \beta$ is generated by $C\}$.*

Formally, the definition should constrain the sequences β to those sequences that can be generated using *allowable* inputs α from E only. Observe that, as in recognition, C may need to make silent steps while generating. It means that interactive generation is not necessarily a "real-time" process. Nevertheless, the interactiveness condition implies that the generation process will output nonempty signals, with finite delay only.

Definition 10. *A set $L \subseteq \{0,1\}^\omega$ is called interactively generable if there exists an interactive component C such that $L = L_C$.*

In the context of generating ω-sequences, it is of interest to know what finite *prefixes* an interactive component C can generate. To this end we consider the following problem:

(*Reachability*) Given an interactive component C and a finite sequence $\gamma \in \{0,1\}^\star$, is there an interactive computation of C such that the sequence of nonempty symbols generated and output by C at some finite moment equals γ.

Lemma 3. *The reachability problem for interactive components C is effectively decidable.*

Proof. Let C and γ be given. Consider the (infinite) binary tree T with left branches labeled 0 and right branches labeled 1. Every node q of T represents a finite input of E, namely the sequence α_q of 0's and 1's leading from the root of T to q, and every finite input that E can provide is so represented. Label/prune T as follows. Label the root by "n". Work through the unlabeled nodes q level by level down the tree and simulate C while E supplies α_q as input to C, halting the simulation when E reaches the end of α_q or when E wants to deviate from giving the next symbol of α_q as input based on C's response. Then do the following:

- label q by "Y" and prune the tree below it if the simulation at q leads C to output a sequence r such that γ is a prefix of $\bar{r}$;
- label q by "N" and prune the tree below it if the simulation at q leads C to output a sequence r of which γ is not a prefix (which certainly can be decided as soon as $|\bar{r}| \geq |\gamma|$);
- label q by "N" and prune the tree below it if the simulation halts before E could input all of α_q; and
- just label q by "n" otherwise (and thus the subtree at q is *Not* pruned yet in this case).

Denote the pruned tree by $\overline{T}$. Clearly the reachability problem is equivalent to the problem of deciding whether there exists a Y-labeled node in $\overline{T}$.

We claim that $\overline{T}$ is finite and, hence, that the algorithm terminates in finitely many steps. Suppose $\overline{T}$ was infinite. By *König's Unendlichkeitslemma* ([7, 8]) it follows that in this case $\overline{T}$ must contain an infinite path from the root down. But by interactiveness the simulations of C along this path must eventually either halt or lead to output sequences r with $|\bar{r}|$ exceeding any fixed bound. This means that some node on the path must lead the algorithm to prune the tree below it, contradicting the fact that the remainder of the path is still in $\overline{T}$.

Because $\overline{T}$ is finite, it can be decided in finite time whether there exists a Y-labeled node in it and thus whether γ can be obtained as output of C. □

We now show that the fundamental law that "what can be generated can be recognized and vice versa" holds in our model of interactive computing. We prove it in two steps.

Lemma 4. *For all sets $J \subseteq \{0,1\}^\omega$, if J is interactively generable then J is interactively recognizable.*

Proof. Let J be interactively generated by means of some component C, i.e., $J = L_C$. To show that J can be interactively recognized, design the following component C'. Let the input from E be β. C' buffers the input that it receives from E symbol after symbol, and goes through the following cycle of activity: it takes the sequence γ that is currently in the buffer, decides whether γ is reachable for C by applying the procedure of Lemma 3, and outputs a 1 if it is and a 0 if it is not. This cycle is repeated forever, each time taking the new (and longer) sequence γ that is in the buffer whenever a new cycle is executed.

Because the reachability problem is decidable in finite time, C' is an interactive component. Clearly, if an ω-sequence β belongs to J then all its prefixes are reachable for C, and C' recognizes it. Conversely, if an ω-sequence β is recognized by C' then it must be interactively generated by C and hence belong to J. We argue this point somewhat more precisely.

Suppose that β is recognized by C'. Take a new instance S of the infinite binary tree and label its nodes as follows. Every time C' carries out its cycle on a next sequence γ (a longer prefix of β) it runs the labeling/pruning algorithm of Lemma 3 on a copy of T to completion and identifies one or more nodes that are to be labeled Y. (This follows because, by assumption, C' identifies every prefix that it checks as reachable.) Copy the labels 'Y' to the corresponding nodes of S. Do not label a node again if it was already labeled at an earlier stage. This process will lead to infinitely many Y-labeled nodes in S, because the prefixes of β that C' checks and finds reachable have a length going to infinity (and this leads to Y-labeled nodes lower and lower in the tree even though some overlaps may occur). By *König's Unendlichkeitslemma*, S must contain an infinite path from the root down with the property that every node on the path has a Y-labeled node as descendent. Let $\alpha \in \{0,1\}^\omega$ be the infinite sequence corresponding to this path. It follows from the definition of the Y-label that C transduces α to β and hence that $\beta \in J$. $\square$

Lemma 5. *For all sets $J \subseteq \{0,1\}^\omega$, if J is interactively recognizable then J is interactively generable.*

Proof. Let J be interactively recognizable. Let C be an interactive component such that $J = J_C$. To show that J can be interactively generated, design the following component C'. C' buffers the input that receives from E symbol after symbol, and copies it to output as well (at a slower pace perhaps). At the same time C' runs a simulation of C in the background, inputting the symbols from the buffer to C one after the other as if they were directly input from E. By algorithmicity it can be checked alongside of this whether the input is indeed a sequence that E could input when taking the responses of C into account.

Let C' continue to copy input to output as long as (a) no inconsistency between the buffered input and the verification of E arises and (b) the simulation of C outputs only τ's and 1's. If anything else occurs, C' switches to outputting ♯'s. C' is clearly interactive, and the generated sequence are precisely those that C recognizes.   □

The lemmas lead to the following basic result, showing that the concepts of interactive recognition and generation as defined are well-chosen.

Theorem 6. *For all sets $J \subseteq \{0,1\}^\omega$, J is interactively generable if and only if J is interactively recognizable.*

6 Interactive Translations

As an additional task, interactive components typically perform the online translation of infinite streams into other infinite streams of signals. We consider this in more detail, viewing components as interactive transducers and viewing the translations (or: transductions) they realize as interactive mappings defined on infinite sequences of 0's and 1's. The related notion of ω-transduction in the theory of ω-automata has received quite some attention before (cf. Staiger [20]). In this section we present some basic observations on interactive mappings. Let C be an interactive component, and let T_C be the behavior of C.

Definition 11. *The* interactive mapping *computed by C is the partial function $f_C : \{0,1\}^\omega \to \{0,1\}^\omega$ such that $f_C(\alpha) = \beta$ if and only if $(\alpha, \beta) \in T_C$.*

If $f_C(\alpha) = \beta$ is defined, then in response to input α, C outputs a sequence $r \in \{0,1,\tau\}^\omega$ such that $\bar{r} = \beta$.

Definition 12. *A partial function $f : \{0,1\}^\omega \to \{0,1\}^\omega$ is called* interactively computable *if there exists an interactive component C such that $f = f_C$.*

Computable functions on infinite sequences should be continuous in the sense that, any time after some finite sequence has been input, any further extension of the input should only lead to an extension of the output generated so far and vice versa, without retraction of any earlier output signals. Interactively computable functions clearly all have this property on defined values, which can be more precisely formulated as follows. We rephrase the classical definition of continuous functions (cf. [37]) for the case of functions on infinite sequences.

Definition 13. *A partial function $f : \{0,1\}^\omega \to \{0,1\}^\omega$ is called* limit-continuous *if there exists a classically computable partial function $g : \{0,1\}^\star \to \{0,1\}^\star$ such that the following conditions are satisfied: (1) g is monotonic, and (2) for all strictly increasing chains $u_1 \prec u_2 \prec \ldots \prec u_t \prec \ldots$ with $u_t \in \{0,1\}^\star$ for $t \geq 1$, one has $f(\lim_{t \to \infty} u_t) = \lim_{t \to \infty} g(u_t)$.*

In condition (2) the identity is assumed to hold as soon as the left- or right-hand side is defined.

Clearly, monotonic functions map chains into chains, if they are defined on all elements of a chain. However, monotonic functions do not necessarily map strictly increasing chains into strictly increasing chains again. Definition 13 implies however that if a total function f is limit-continuous, then the underlying g must be total as well and map strictly increasing chains into ultimately increasing chains. In the terminology of [20], Sect. 2.2, g is 'totally unbounded'. Using Theorem 1 and 2, one easily concludes the following facts.

Theorem 7. If $f : \{0,1\}^\omega \to \{0,1\}^\omega$ is interactively computable, then f is limit-continuous.

Theorem 8. Let $f : \{0,1\}^\omega \to \{0,1\}^\omega$ be a total function. Then f is interactively computable if and only if f is limit-continuous.

Several other properties of interactively computable functions are of interest. The following observation is elementary but is spelled out in some detail so as to show how the assumptions in our model of interactive computing play a role and how only generic properties of the internal functioning of components are needed. In the following results we do not assume any of the interactively computable functions to be total. Let $\circ$ denote composition of functions.

Theorem 9. If f and g are interactively computable, then so is $f \circ g$.

Proof. Let $f = f_{C'}$ and $g = f_C$. To show that $f \circ g$ is interactively computable, design a component C'' that works as follows. C'' runs a foreground process that works exactly like C. On top of that it runs a verifier that observes the incoming symbols and the output of C and verifies that the input is consistent with the behavior E would or could have (which can be done by algorithmicity). Note that this is necessary, because the output of the foreground process is not visible to E directly, and we have to make sure that the interaction between E and C is simulated correctly. If the verifier ever observes an inconsistency, C'' immediately stops the foreground process and outputs ♯'s from this moment onward.

The foreground process feeds its output into an internal buffer $\mathcal{B}$, which only records the non-τ symbols. C'' runs a background process that takes its inputs from $\mathcal{B}$ and simulates the operation of C' just like the foreground process did with C. In particular it (also) runs the verifier to see that the input taken from $\mathcal{B}$ is consistent with the behavior of E, including its response to the output of C' (which can be done by algorithmicity of E again). The background process cannot make steps with every time-tick like C' would. Instead it has to follow/operate on the time-ticks defined by the appearance of symbols in $\mathcal{B}$, to adequately simulate the environmental activity and keep the same timing relationships between E's input and the action of C'. The output of the background process, i.e., of the simulation of C', is the output of C''.

It is easily verified that C'' must be interactive. Whenever an inconsistency in the simulated actions of C and C' is discovered, a $\natural$ is generated and fed into the further simulation and thus eventually to output. Note that the whole process is triggered by the input from E to C'', i.e., to the simulation of C and only this input has a variable aspect. Internally everything runs deterministically (aside from any unpredictable time-delays). It is easily seen that C'' correctly computes the value of $f \circ g$ on the input stream from E. $\square$

The following result is more tedious and relies on the machinery which we developed in the previous section.

Theorem 10. *Let f be interactively computable and $1 - 1$. Then f^{-1} is interactively computable as well.*

Proof. Let $f = f_C$ and assume f is $1 - 1$. If $f(\alpha) = \beta$ (defined) then $f^{-1}(\beta) = \alpha$. Design a component C' to realize the mapping of β's into α's as follows.

Let the input supplied so far be γ, a finite prefix of "β". Assume the environment supplies further input symbols in its own way, reveiling to C' the longer and longer prefixes γ of the β to which an original under f is sought. Let C' buffer γ internally. We want the output σ of C' at any point to be a finite (and growing) prefix of "α" (ignoring any τ's in σ). Let this be the case at some point. Let C' do the following, as more and more symbols are coming in and reveal more and more of β and outputting τ's until it knows better.

The dilemma C' faces is whether to output a 0 or a 1 (or, of course, a $\natural$). In other words, C' must somehow decide whether $\sigma 0$ or $\sigma 1$ is the next longer prefix of the original α under f as β is unfolding. We argue that this is indeed decidable in finite time. The idea is to look "into the future" and see which of the two possibilities survives. To achieve it, create a process P_b that explores the future for σb, for every $b \in \{0, 1\}$. Remember that symbols continue to come into γ.

P_b works on the infinite binary tree $\mathcal{T}$ defined in Lemma 3. Remember that every node q of $\mathcal{T}$ corresponds to a finite sequence α_q, consisting of the 0's and 1's on the path from the root down to q. P_b labels the root by "Y". Then it works through the unlabeled nodes q level by level down the tree, testing for every node q whether the sequence $\sigma b \alpha_q$ is output (i.e., is reached) by C *as it operates on (a prefix of) the sequence* γ, i.e., on a prefix of β. (P_b does this in the usual way, by running the simulation of the interactive computation of C and E and using the algorithmicity of E to properly test for the corresponding behavior of E on C's output.) If $\sigma b \alpha_q$ is reached, then label q by "Y". If the output of C does not reach the end of $\sigma b \alpha_q$ but is consistent with it as far as it gets, then P_b waits (at q) and only continues the simulation when more symbols have come into γ. (By interactivity, γ will eventually be long enough for C to give an output at least as long as $\sigma b \alpha_q$.) If the output of C begins to differ from $\sigma b \alpha_q$ before the end of $\sigma b \alpha_q$ is reached, then label q by "N" and prune the tree below it. If the simulation runs into an inconsistency between

E's behavior and the γ that is input, then label q by "N" and prune the tree below it as well. If P_b reaches a tree level where all nodes have been pruned away, it stops. Denote the tree as it gets labeled by P_b by T_b.

Let C' run P_0 and P_1 "in parallel". We claim that one of the two processes must stop in finite time. Suppose that neither of the two stopped in finite time. Then T_0 and T_1 would both turn into infinite trees as γ extends to "infinity" (i.e., turns into the infinite sequence β). By the *Unendlichkeitslemma*, T_0 will contain an infinite path δ_0 and likewise T_1 will contain an infinite path δ_1. This clearly implies that both $\sigma 0 \delta_0$ and $\sigma 1 \delta_1$ would be mapped by C to β, which contradicts that f is $1-1$. It follows that at least one of the processes P_0 and P_1 must stop in finite time. (Stated in another way, the process that explores the wrong prefix of α will die out in finite time.) Note that both processes could stop, which happens at some point in case the limit sequence β has *no* original under f.

Thus letting C' run P_0 and P_1 in parallel, do the following as soon as one of the processes stops. If both processes stop, C' outputs $\sharp$. If P_0 stopped but P_1 did not, then output 1. If P_1 stopped but P_0 did not, then output 0. If C' output a b (0 or 1), then it repeats the whole procedure with σ replaced by σb. If it output a $\sharp$ it continues to output $\sharp$'s from this moment onwards and does not repeat the above procedure anymore. It is easily seen that C' is interactive and that it computes precisely the inverse of f.   □

7 Conclusions

Interactive computing and its formal study have received much attention since the late 1960s, usually within the framework of reactive and concurrent systems. In this chapter we considered a simple model of interactive compution, consisting of one component and an environment acting together on infinite streams of input and output symbols that are exchanged in an on-line manner and with a number of realistic assumptions into effect. The motivation stems from the interest in capturing the computation-theoretic capabilities of interactive computing.

In the model we have identified a number of properties which one would intuitively ascribe to a component of any system that interacts with the environment in which it is placed. In [28] we have carried this further, to model some interactive features of the Internet and of 'global computing'. In the latter case, the model includes the possibility of letting external information enter into the interaction process and of many components influencing each other. In the present study we have concentrated purely on the property of *interactiveness* for a single component, implying that both the component and its environment always react within some (unspecified) finite amount of time. As components operate on infinite streams, there are various intimate connections to the classical theory of ω-automata.

We have given definitions of interactive recognition, generation and translation that are inspired by realistic considerations of how the various tasks would proceed in an interactive setting. The definition of interactive recognition leads to a useful, machine-independent analogue of the notion of $1'$-definability as known for ω-automata. The definitions allow a proof that interactive recognition and interactive generation are equally powerful in the given model of interactive computation. We also proved that (total) functions are interactively computable if and only they are limit-continuous, using a simple extension of the common definitions of continuity. Among the further results we showed that interactively computable (partial) functions that are 1-1 have interactively computable inverses. Many interesting computational problems seem to remain in the further analysis of the model.

In this chapter we have attempted to capture the power of reactive computation in a simple model. Regarding the claims concerning the greater computational power of interactive computations and insofar as our model captures real interactive systems, the results can be interpreted as follows. When considering only finite computations, there is no difference between the power of classical and interactive computations. Keeping the classical computation time-bounded on the one hand and considering infinite interactive computations on the other, is to draw a comparison between two incomparable things: while the former computes with finite objects (finite streams), the latter operates on infinite objects. Thus, the two modes are incomparable; each of them computes with different entities. Therefore it is not possible to say which of the two has a greater computational power. However, our results show that in the limit the computational power in both modes tends to coincide. The further analysis of the model quickly leads to the consideration of nonuniformly evolving, interactive machines and programs. The prospects of a theory that takes this into account are sketched in [28] and in a different, general framework also in [29].

References

1. M. Broy. A logical basis for modular software and systems engineering, in: B. Rovan (Ed.), *SOFSEM'98: Theory and Practice of Informatics*, Proc. 25th Conference on Current Trends, Lecture Notes in Computer Science, Vol. 1521, Springer-Verlag, Berlin, 1998, pp. 19-35.
2. R.S. Cohen, A.Y. Gold. ω-Computations on Turing machines, *Theor. Comput. Sci.* 6, 1978, pp. 1-23.
3. J. Engelfriet, H.J. Hoogeboom. X-automata on ω-words, *Theor. Comput. Sci.* 110, 1993, pp. 1-51.
4. D.Q. Goldin. Persistent Turing machines as a model of interactive computation, in: K-D. Schewe and B. Thalheim (Eds.), *Foundations of Information and Knowledge Systems*, Proc. First Int. Symposium (FoIKS 2000), Lecture Notes in Computer Science, vol. 1762, Springer-Verlag, Berlin, 2000, pp. 116-135.

5. D.Q. Goldin, S.A. Smolka, P.C. Attie, E.L. Sonderegger. Turing machines, transition systems, and interaction, *Information and Computation* 192, 2004, pp. 101-128.

6. D. Goldin, P. Wegner. Persistence as a form of interaction, Techn. Report CS-98-07, Dept. of Computer Science, Brown University, Providence, RI, 1998.

7. D. König. Sur les correspondances multivoques des ensembles, *Fundam. Math.* 8, 1926, pp. 114-134.

8. D. König. Über eine Schlussweise aus dem endlichen ins Unendliche (Punktmengen. – Kartenfärben. — Verwantschaftsbeziehungen. – Schachspiel), *Acta Litt. Sci.* (Sectio Sci. Math.) 3, 1927, pp. 121-130.

9. S. Kosub. Persistent computations, Techn. Report No. 217, Institut für Informatik, Julius-Maximilians-Universität Würzburg, 1998.

10. L.H. Landweber. Decision problems for ω-automata, *Math. Systems Theory* 3, 1969, pp. 376-384.

11. Z. Manna, A. Pnueli. Models for reactivity, *Acta Informatica* 30, 1993, pp. 609-678.

12. R. Milner. *A calculus of communicating systems*, Lecture Notes in Computer Science, Vol. 92, Springer-Verlag, Berlin, 1980.

13. R. Milner. Elements of interaction, *Comm. ACM* 36:1, 1993, pp. 78-89.

14. D. Perrin, J-E. Pin. *Infinite words: automata, semigroups, logic and games*, Academic Press, New York, 2003.

15. A. Pnueli. Applications of temporal logic to the specification and verification of reactive systems: a survey of current trends, in: J.W. de Bakker, W.-P. de Roever and G. Rozenberg, *Current Trends in Concurrency*, Lecture Notes in Computer Science, Vol. 224, Springer-Verlag, Berlin, 1986, pp. 510-585.

16. A. Pnueli. Specification and development of reactive systems, in: H.-J. Kugler (Ed.), *Information Processing 86*, Proceedings IFIP 10th World Computer Congress, Elsevier Science Publishers (North-Holland), Amsterdam, 1986, pp. 845-858.

17. H. Rogers. *Theory of recursive functions and effective computability*, McGraw-Hill, New York, 1967.

18. G. Rozenberg, F.W. Vaandrager (Eds.). *Lectures on embedded systems*, Lecture Notes in Computer Science, Vol. 1494, Springer-Verlag, Berlin, 1998.

19. L. Sekanina, V. Drábek. Theory and applications of evolvable embedded systems, in: *Proc. 11th IEEE Int. Conference and Workshop on the Engineering of Computer-Based Systems*, IEEE press, Los Alamitos, 2004, pp. 186-193.

20. L. Staiger. ω-Languages, in: G. Rozenberg and A. Salomaa (Eds.), *Handbook of Formal Languages*, Vol. 3: *Beyond Words*, Chapter 6, Springer-Verlag, Berlin, 1997, pp. 339-387.

21. S. Stepney *et al.*. Journeys in non-classical computation I: A grand challenge for computing research, *Int. J. Parallel, Emergent and Distributed Systems* 20, 2005, pp. 5-19.

22. W. Thomas. Automata on infinite objects, in: J. van Leeuwen (Ed.), *Handbook of Theoretical Computer Science*, Vol. B: *Models and Semantics*, Elsevier Science Publishers, Amsterdam, 1990, pp. 135-191.

23. W. Thomas. Languages, automata, and logic, in: G. Rozenberg and A. Salomaa (Eds.), *Handbook of Formal Languages*, Vol. 3: *Beyond Words*, Chapter 7, Springer-Verlag, Berlin, 1997, pp. 389-455.

24. B.A. Trakhtenbrot. Automata and their interaction: definitional suggestions, in: G. Ciobanu and G. Păun (Eds.), *Fundamentals of Computation Theory*, Proc. 12th International Symposium (FCT'99), Lecture Notes in Computer Science, Vol. 1684, Springer-Verlag, Berlin, 1999, pp. 54-89.

25. J. van Leeuwen, J. Wiedermann. On the power of interactive computing, in: J. van Leeuwen et al (Eds), *Theoretical Computer Science - Exploring New Frontiers of Theoretical Computer Science*, Proc. IFIP TCS 2000 Conference, Lecture Notes in Computer Science Vol. 1872, Springer-Verlag, Berlin, 2000, pp. 619-623.

26. J. van Leeuwen, J. Wiedermann. A computational model of interaction in embedded systems, Techn. Report UU-CS-2001-02, Dept of Computer Science, Utrecht University, 2001.

27. J. van Leeuwen, J. Wiedermann. On algorithms and interaction, in: M. Nielsen and B. Rovan (Eds), *Mathematical Foundations of Computer Science 2000*, 25th Int. Symposium (MFCS 2000), Lecture Notes in Computer Science Vol. 1893, Springer-Verlag, Berlin, 2000, pp. 99-112.

28. J. van Leeuwen, J. Wiedermann. The Turing machine paradigm in contemporary computing, in: B. Enquist and W. Schmidt (Eds), *Mathematics Unlimited - 2001 and Beyond*, Springer-Verlag, Berlin, 2001, pp. 1139-1155.

29. P. Verbaan, J. van Leeuwen, J. Wiedermann. Complexity of evolving interactive systems, in: J. Karhumaki *et al.* (Eds.), *Theory is forever*, Festschrift, Lecture Notes in Computer Science Vol. 3113, Springer-Verlag, Berlin, 2004, pp. 268-281.

30. K. Wagner, L. Staiger. Recursive ω-languages, in: M. Karpinsky (Ed.), *Fundamentals of Computation Theory*, Proc. 1977 Int. FCT-Conference, Lecture Notes in Computer Science, Vol. 56, Springer-Verlag, Berlin, 1977, pp. 532-537.

31. P. Wegner. Interaction as a basis for empirical computer science, *Comput. Surv.* 27, 1995, pp. 45-48.

32. P. Wegner. Why interaction is more powerful than algorithms, *Comm. ACM* 40, 1997, pp. 80-91.

33. P. Wegner. Interactive foundations of computing, *Theor. Comp. Sci.* 192, 1998, pp. 315-351.

34. P. Wegner, D. Goldin. Co-inductive models of finite computing agents, in: B. Jacobs and J. Rutten (Eds.), *CMCS'99-Coalgebraic Methods in Computer Science*, TCS: Electronic Notes in Theoretical Computer Science, Vol. 19, Elsevier, 1999.

35. P. Wegner, D. Goldin. Interaction as a framework for modeling, in: P. Chen *et al.* (Eds.), *Conceptual Modeling - Current Issues and Future Directions*, Lecture Notes in Computer Science, Vol. 1565, Springer-Verlag, Berlin, 1999, pp. 243-257.

36. P. Wegner, D. Goldin. Computation beyond Turing machines, *Comm. ACM* 46, 2003, pp. 100-102.

37. G. Winskel. *The formal semantics of programming languages: an introduction*, The MIT Press, Cambridge (Mass.), 1993.

Online Algorithms

Susanne Albers

University of Freiburg, Freiburg, Germany

1 Introduction

This chapter reviews fundamental concepts and results in the area of online algorithms. We first address classical online problems and then study various applications of current interest.

Online algorithms represent a theoretical framework for studying problems in interactive computing. They model, in particular, that the input in an interactive system does not arrive as a batch but as a sequence of input portions and that the system must react in response to each incoming portion. Moreover, they take into account that at any point in time future input is unknown. As the name suggests, online algorithms consider the algorithmic aspects of interactive systems: We wish to design strategies that always compute good output and keep a given system in good state. No assumptions are made about the input stream. The input can even be generated by an adversary that creates new input portions based on the system's reactions to previous ones. We seek algorithms that have a provably good performance.

Formally, an online algorithm receives a *sequence of requests* $\sigma = \sigma(1), \ldots, \sigma(m)$. These requests must be served in the order of occurrence. When serving request $\sigma(t)$, an online algorithm does not know requests $\sigma(t')$ with $t' > t$. Serving requests incurs cost and the goal is to minimize the total cost paid on the entire request sequence. This process can be viewed as a *request answer game*. An adversary generates requests and an online algorithm has to serve them one at a time. The performance of online algorithms is usually evaluated using *competitive analysis* [65]. Here an online algorithm ALG is compared to an optimal offline algorithm OPT that knows the entire request sequence σ in advance and can serve it with minimum cost. Given a sequence σ, let $ALG(\sigma)$ and $OPT(\sigma)$ denote the costs incurred by ALG and OPT, respectively. Algorithm ALG is called c-competitive if there exists a constant b such that $ALG(\sigma) \leq c \cdot OPT(\sigma) + b$, for all sequences σ. The constant b must be independent of the input σ. We note that competitive analysis is a strong worst-case performance measure.

Over the past 15 years online algorithms have received tremendous research interest. Online problems have been studied in many application areas including resource management in operating systems, data structuring, scheduling, networks, and computational finance. In the following sections we first survey fundamental results. We address the paging problem, self-organizing lists, the k-server problem as well as metrical task systems. Then we review a number of new results in application areas of current interest. We focus on algorithmic problems in large networks and competitive auctions. Finally we present refinements of competitive analysis and conclude with some remarks.

2 Basic Results

Paging is an extensively studied problem and perhaps one of the oldest examples of an interactive computing problem. It arises when a CPU communicates with the underlying memory hierarchy. Paging is also an excellent problem to illustrate basic concepts in the theory of online algorithms and we therefore study it in the rest of this section.

In paging we have to maintain a two-level memory system consisting of a small fast memory and a large slow memory. The memory is partitioned into pages of equal size. The system receives a sequence of requests, where each request specifies a page in the memory system. A request can be served immediately if the referenced page is available in fast memory. If the requested page is not in fast memory, a *page fault* occurs. The missing page is then loaded from slow memory into fast memory so that the request can be served. At the same time a page is evicted from fast memory to make room for the missing one. A paging algorithm decides which page to evict on a fault. This decision must usually be made online, i.e., without knowledge of any future requests. The cost to be minimized is the number of page faults.

The two most popular online paging algorithms are LRU and FIFO.

LRU (Least Recently Used): On a fault, evict the page in fast memory that was requested least recently.

FIFO (First-In First-Out): Evict the page that has been in fast memory longest.

Sleator and Tarjan [65] analyzed the performance of the two algorithms. Let k be the number of pages that can simultaneously reside in fast memory.

Theorem 1. [65] *LRU and FIFO are k-competitive.*

There exists a more general class of algorithms that achieve a competitiveness of k.

Marking: A *Marking* strategy processes a request sequence in phases. At the beginning of each phase all pages in the memory system are unmarked. Whenever a page is requested, it is *marked*. On a fault, an arbitrary unmarked page in fast memory is evicted. A phase ends when all pages in fast memory are marked and a page fault occurs. Then all marks are erased and a new phase is started.

It is not hard to see that LRU is in fact a *Marking* algorithm. *Marking* strategies were considered in [24, 37]. Torng [67] explicitly observed that any *Marking* strategy is k-competitive. This factor is best possible for deterministic paging algorithms.

Theorem 2. [65] *No deterministic online algorithm for the paging problem can achieve a competitive ratio smaller than k.*

An optimal offline algorithm for the paging problem was presented by Belady [17]. The algorithm is called MIN and works as follows.

MIN: On a fault, evict the page whose next request occurs furthest in the future.

Belady showed that on any sequence of requests, MIN incurs the minimum number of page faults.

In many problems, such as paging, online algorithms can achieve a better performance if they are allowed to make random choices. The competitive ratio of a randomized online algorithm ALG is defined with respect to an adversary. The adversary generates a request sequence σ and also has to serve σ. When constructing σ, the adversary always knows the description of ALG. The crucial question is: When generating requests, is the adversary allowed to see the outcome of the random choices made by A on previous requests? Oblivious adversaries do not have this ability while adaptive adversaries do. In the literature there exist three kinds of adversaries, which were introduced by Ben-David et al. [19].

Oblivious adversary: The oblivious adversary has to generate the entire request sequence in advance before any requests are served by the online algorithm. The adversary is charged the cost of the optimum offline algorithm for that sequence.

Adaptive online adversary: This adversary may observe the online algorithm and generate the next request based on the algorithm's (randomized) answers to all previous requests. The adversary must serve each request online, i.e., without knowing the random choices made by the online algorithm on the present or any future request.

Adaptive offline adversary: This adversary also generates a request sequence adaptively. However, it may serve the sequence offline and hence is charged the optimum offline cost for that sequence.

A randomized online algorithm ALG is called c-competitive against oblivious adversaries if there is a constant b such that, for all request sequences σ generated by an oblivious adversary, $E[ALG(\sigma)] < c \cdot OPT(\sigma) + b$. The expectation is taken over the random choices made by ALG.

Given a randomized online algorithm ALG and an adaptive online (adaptive offline) adversary ADV, let $E[ALG(\sigma)]$ and $E[ADV(\sigma)]$ denote the expected costs incurred by ALG and ADV in serving a request sequence generated by ADV. Algorithm ALG is called c-competitive against adaptive online (adaptive offline) adversaries if there is a constant b such that, for all adaptive online (adaptive offline) adversaries ADV, $E[ALG(\sigma)] \leq c \cdot E[ADV(\sigma)] + b$ where the expectation is taken over the random choices made by ALG.

Ben-David et al. [19] investigated the relative strength of the adversaries and proved the following results.

Theorem 3. [19] *If there is a randomized online algorithm that is c-competitive against adaptive offline adversaries, then there also exists a c-competitive deterministic online algorithm.*

Theorem 4. [19] *If ALG is a c-competitive randomized algorithm against adaptive online adversaries and if there is a d-competitive algorithm against oblivious adversaries, then ALG is $(c \cdot d)$-competitive against adaptive offline adversaries.*

Theorem 3 implies that randomization does not help against adaptive offline adversaries, and we can ignore them when in search for improved competitive ratios. An immediate consequence of the two theorems above is:

Corollary 1. *If there exists a c-competitive randomized algorithm against adaptive online adversaries, then there is a c^2-competitive deterministic algorithm.*

A result by Raghavan and Snir [61] implies that against adaptive online adversaries, no randomized online paging strategy can be better than k-competitive. Hence we concentrate on oblivious adversaries and show that we can achieve an exponential improvement over the deterministic bound of k. The most popular randomized online paging algorithm is the *Randomized-Marking* strategy presented by Fiat et al. [37]. It is optimal up to a constant factor.

Randomized-marking: The algorithm is a *Marking* strategy. On a fault, a page is chosen uniformly at random from among the unmarked pages in fast memory, and that page is evicted.

Let $H_k = \sum_{i=1}^{k} 1/i$ be the k-th harmonic number, which is closely approximated by $\ln k$, i.e., $\ln(k+1) \leq H_k \leq \ln k + 1$.

Theorem 5. [37] *Randomized-Marking is $2H_k$-competitive against oblivious adversaries.*

Theorem 6. [37] *The competitive ratio of randomized online paging algorithms against oblivious adversaries is not smaller than H_k.*

More complicated algorithms achieving an optimal competitiveness of H_k were presented in [1, 58].

3 Self-Organizing Data Structures

Data structuring is a classical field where many online problems arise. We have to maintain a given structure not knowing which items in the structure will be accessed next. There has been a lot of research on self-organizing lists and trees.

The problem of self-organizing lists, also called the *list update problem*, consists in maintaining a set of items as an unsorted linear list. We are given an unsorted linear linked list of items. As input we receive a sequence of requests, where each request specifies an item in the list. To serve a request, we have to access the requested item. We start at the front of the list and search linearly through the items until the desired item is found. Serving a request to an item that is currently stored at position i in the list incurs a cost of i. Immediately after a request, the referenced item may be moved at no extra cost to any position closer to the front of the list. This can lower the cost of subsequent requests. However, the decision where to move an item must be made online, without knowledge of any future requests. At any time, two adjacent items in the list may be exchanged at a cost of 1. The goal is to serve the request sequence so that the total cost is as small as possible.

Self-organizing lists are useful when maintaining a small dictionary consisting of only a few dozens of items and, moreover, have interesting applications in data compression [5, 20, 27].

With respect to the list update problem we require that a c-competitive online algorithm has a performance ratio of c, for *all size lists*. There exist three very well-known deterministic algorithms.

Move-to-front: Move the requested item to the front of the list.
Transpose: Exchange the requested item with the immediately preceding item in the list.
Frequency-count: Maintain a frequency count for each item in the list. Whenever an item is requested, increase its count by 1. Maintain the list so that the items always occur in nonincreasing order of frequency count.

Sleator and Tarjan analyzed these three algorithms. It shows that Move-To-Front achieves an optimal competitiveness of 2 while the other strategies are not competitive at all.

Theorem 7. [65] *The Move-To-Front algorithm is 2-competitive.*

Theorem 8. [50] *The competitive ratio of any deterministic online algorithm is not smaller than 2.*

Proposition 1. *The algorithms Transpose and Frequency-Count are not c-competitive, for any constant c.*

Ambühl [8] showed that the offline variant of the list update problem is NP-hard. Thus, there is no efficient algorithm for computing an optimal service schedule.

We next consider the influence of randomization. Against adaptive online adversaries no randomized strategy can be better than 2-competitive [62]. However, against oblivious adversaries we can improve the factor of 2. A number of randomized strategies have been proposed in the literature. We mention here only the two most important ones. Reingold et al. [62] presented counter-based algorithms, which move an item to the front of the list if its counter takes a certain value. Using mod 2 counters, we obtain the elegant *Bit* algorithm.

Bit: Each item in the list maintains a bit that is complemented whenever the item is accessed. If an access causes a bit to change to 1, then the requested item is moved to the front of the list. Otherwise the list remains unchanged. The bits of the items are initialized independently and uniformly at random.

Theorem 9. [62] *The bit algorithm is 1.75-competitive against oblivious adversaries.*

The best randomized algorithm known to date combines *Bit* with a deterministic 2-competitive online algorithm called *Timestamp* proposed in [2].

Timestamp (TS): Insert the requested item, say x, in front of the first item in the list that precedes x and that has been requested at most once since the last request to x. If there is no such item or if x has not been requested so far, then leave the position of x unchanged.

Combination: With probability 4/5 serve a request sequence using *Bit*, and with probability 1/5 serve it using *TS*.

Theorem 10. [6] *The algorithm Combination is 1.6-competitive against oblivious adversaries.*

This factor of 1.6 is close to the best lower bound known.

Theorem 11. [9] *Let A be a randomized online algorithm for the list update problem. If A is c-competitive against oblivious adversaries, then $c \geq 1.50084$.*

The latest results on the list update problem are by Blum et al. [21]. Using techniques from learning theory, they gave a randomized online algorithm that, for any $\epsilon > 0$, is $(1.6 + \epsilon)$-competitive and at the same time $(1 + \epsilon)$-competitive against an offline algorithm that is restricted to serving a request sequence with a static list. The main open problem with respect to the list update problem is to develop tight upper and lower bounds on the performance of randomized algorithms.

Many of the concepts shown for self-organizing linear lists can be extended to binary search trees. The most popular version of self-organizing binary search trees are the *splay trees* presented by Sleator and Tarjan [66]. In a splay tree, after each access to an element x in the tree, the node storing x is moved to the root of the tree using a special sequence of rotations that depends on the structure of the access path. Sleator and Tarjan [66] showed that on any sequence of accesses a splay tree is as efficient as the optimum static search tree. The famous splay tree conjecture is still open: It is conjectured that on any sequence of accesses splay trees are as efficient as any dynamic binary search tree.

4 The k-Server Problem

The k-server problem is one of the most famous online problems. It has received a lot of research interest, partly because proving upper bounds on the performance of k-server algorithms is a very challenging task. The k-server problem generalizes paging as well as other caching problems. It can also be viewed as an online vehicle routing problem.

In the k-server problem we are given a metric space S and k mobile servers that reside on points in S. As usual we receive a sequence of requests, where each request specifies a point $x \in S$. In response, a server must be moved to the requested point, unless a server is already present. Moving a server from point x to point y incurs a cost equal to the distance between the two points. The goal is to minimize the total distance traveled by all servers.

It is easy to see that the k-server problem models paging: Consider a metric space in which the distance between any two points in 1. Each point in the metric space represents a page in the memory system and the pages covered by servers are those that reside in fast memory. The k-server problem was introduced in 1988 by Manasse et al. [57] who showed a lower bound for deterministic k-server algorithms.

Theorem 12. [57] *Let A be a deterministic online k-server algorithm in an arbitrary metric space. If A is c-competitive, then $c \geq k$.*

Manasse et al. also conjectured that there exist k-competitive deterministic online algorithms. This conjecture essentially is still open. In 1995, however, Koutsoupias and Papadimitriou [53] achieved a breakthrough. They showed that the *Work Function* algorithm is $(2k - 1)$-competitive. Before, k-competitive algorithms were known only for special metric spaces (e.g., trees [29] and resistive spaces [31]) and special values of k ($k = 2$ and $k = n - 1$, where n is the number of points in the metric space [57]).

The *Work Function* algorithm tries to mimic the optimal offline algorithm and at the same time incorporates aspects of the *Greedy* strategy. Let X be a configuration of the servers. Given a request sequence $\sigma = \sigma(1), \ldots, \sigma(t)$, the *work function* $w(X)$ is the minimal cost of serving σ and ending in configuration X. For any two points x and y in the metric space, let $dist(x, y)$ be the distance between x and y.

Work Function: Suppose that the algorithm has served $\sigma = \sigma(1), \ldots, \sigma(t-1)$ and that a new request $r = \sigma(t)$ arrives. Let X be the current configuration of the servers and let x_i be the point where server s_i, $1 \leq i \leq k$, is located.

Serve the request by moving the server s_i that minimizes $w(X_i) + dist(x_i, r)$, where $X_i = X - \{x_i\} + \{r\}$.

Theorem 13. [53] *The Work Function algorithm is* $(2k - 1)$*-competitive in an arbitrary metric space.*

An interesting open problem is to show that the *Work Function* algorithm is indeed k-competitive or to develop an other deterministic online k-server algorithm that achieves a competitive ratio of k.

Next we turn to randomized k-server algorithms. Against adaptive online adversaries, no randomized strategy can be better than k-competitive. Against oblivious adversaries the best lower bound currently known is due to Bartal et al. [15].

Theorem 14. [15] *The competitive ratio of a randomized online algorithm in an arbitrary metric space is* $\Omega(\log k / \log^2 \log k)$ *against oblivious adversaries.*

The bound can be improved to $\Omega(\log k)$ if the metric space consists of at least $k^{\log^\epsilon k}$ points, for any $\epsilon > 0$ [15]. It is conjectured that $\Theta(\log k)$ is the true competitiveness of randomized algorithms against oblivious adversaries. Bartal et al. [14] presented an algorithm that has a competitive ratio of $O(c^6 \log^6 k)$ in metric spaces consisting of $k + c$ points. Seiden [64] gave an algorithm that achieves a competitive ratio polylogarithmic in k for metric spaces that can be decomposed into a small number of widely separated subspaces. A very challenging open problem is to develop randomized online algorithms that have a competitive ratio of $c < k$ in an arbitrary metric space.

5 Metrical Task Systems

So far we have presented a number of online problems and related results. A natural question is if there exists a more general framework for studying online algorithms. Borodin et al. [25] developed *metrical task systems* that can model a very large class of online problems.

A metrical task system is defined by a metric space (S, d) and an associated set $\mathcal{T}$ of tasks. The space (S, d) consists of a finite set S of, say, n states and a distance function $d : S \times S \longrightarrow \mathbb{R}_0^+$, where $d(i, j) \geq 0$ denotes the cost of changing from state i to state j. Since the space is metric, d is symmetric, satisfies the triangle inequality and $d(i, i) = 0$, for all states i. The set $\mathcal{T}$ is the set of allowable tasks. A task $T \in \mathcal{T}$ is a vector $T = (T(1), T(2), \ldots, T(n))$, where $T(i) \in \mathbb{R}_0^+ \cup \{\infty\}$ denotes the cost of processing the task while in state i. A request sequence is a sequence of tasks $\sigma = T^1, T^2, T^3, \ldots, T^m$ that must be served starting from some initial state $s(0)$. When receiving a new task, an algorithm may serve the task in the current state or may change states at a cost. Thus the algorithm must determine a schedule of states $s(1), s(2), \ldots, s(m)$, such that task T^i is processed in state $s(i)$. The cost of serving a task sequence is the sum of all state transition costs and all task processing costs: $\sum_{i=1}^{m} d(s(i-1), s(i)) + \sum_{i=1}^{m} T^i(s(i))$. The goal is to process a given task sequence so that the cost is as small as possible.

Borodin et al. [25] settled the competitiveness of deterministic online algorithms. Interestingly, the best competitiveness is achieved by a *Work Function* algorithm. Given a request sequence $\sigma = \sigma(1), \dots, \sigma(t)$, let the *work function* $w_t(s)$ be the minimum cost to process σ starting from $s(0)$ and ending in state s.

Work Function: Suppose that the algorithm has served the first t requests $\sigma(1), \dots, \sigma(t)$ of a request sequence and that it is currently in state s_t. To process the next task T^{t+1}, move to state the $s_{t+1} = s$ that minimizes $w_{t+1}(s) + d(s_t, s)$.

Theorem 15. [23, 25] *The Work Function algorithm is $(2n - 1)$-competitive for any metrical task system with n states.*

Theorem 16. [25] *Any deterministic online algorithm for the metrical task systems problem has a competitive ratio of at least $2n - 1$, where n is the number of task system states.*

Unfortunately, the competitive factor of $2n - 1$ often does not provide meaningful bounds when special online problems are investigated. Consider the list update problem. Here the given list can be in $n!$ states. Hence, we obtain a bound of $(2n! - 1)$ on the competitive factor of a deterministic online algorithm for the list update problem. However, *Move-To-Front* achieves a competitive factor of 2.

For randomized algorithms against oblivious adversaries, the known bounds are tight up to a logarithmic factor.

Theorem 17. [39] *There exists a randomized online algorithm that is $O(\log^2 n / \log^2 \log n)$-competitive against oblivious adversaries, for any metrical task system with n states.*

Theorem 18. [15] *Any randomized online algorithm for the metrical task systems problem has a competitive ratio of at least $\Omega(\log n / \log^2 \log n)$ against oblivious adversaries, where n is the number of task system states.*

Better bounds hold for uniform metrical task systems, where the cost $d(i, j)$ of changing states is equal to 1, for all $i \neq j$. Borodin et al. [25] gave a lower bound of H_n, where H_n is the n-th harmonic number. The best upper bound currently known was presented by Irani and Seiden [46] and is equal to $H_n + O(\sqrt{\log n})$.

6 Application Areas

In the previous sections we presented a selection of important results for classical online problems. In this section we study two application areas that have received a lot of research interest recently, namely large networks and competitive auctions.

6.1 Large Networks

With the advent of the Internet, researchers started investigating algorithmic problems that arise in large networks. There exists a host of interesting online problems addressing, e.g., the construction of networks, the maintenance of TCP connections or the management of local caches and buffers. Due to space limitations we only address a few recent problems here.

Network Switches

The performance of high-speed networks critically depends on switches that route data packets arriving at the input ports to the appropriate output ports so that the packets can reach their correct destinations in the network. To reduce packet loss when the traffic is bursty, ports are equipped with buffers where packets can be stored temporarily. However the buffers are of limited capacity so that effective buffer management strategies are important to maximize the throughput at a switch. As a result there has recently been considerable research interest in various single and multibuffer management problems.

We first study single buffer problems, which arise, e.g., when maintaining an output port queue. Consider a buffer that can simultaneously store up to B data packets. Packets arrive online and can be buffered if space permits. More specifically, at any time step t let $Q(t)$ be the set of packets currently stored in the buffer and let $A(t)$ be the set of newly arriving packets. Each packet p has a value $v(p)$ that represents a QoS parameter. If $|Q(t)| + |A(t)| \leq B$, then all new packets can be admitted to the buffer; otherwise $|Q(t)| + |A(t)| - B$ packets from $Q(t) \cup A(t)$ must be dropped. In the time step we can select one packet from the buffer and transmit it through the output port. We assume that the packet arrival step precedes the transmission step. The goal is to maximize the total value of the transmitted packets.

Several problem variants are of interest. In a FIFO model packets must be transmitted in the order they arrive. If packet p is transmitted before p', then p must not have arrived later than p'. In a non-FIFO model there is no such restriction. In a preemptive model we may drop packets from the buffer, while in a nonpreemptive model this is not allowed.

Kesselman et al. [51] analyzed a natural *Greedy* algorithm in the preemptive FIFO model and proved that it is 2-competitive.

Greedy: In the event of buffer overflow, drop the packets with the smallest values.

In the following let α be the ratio of the largest to smallest packet value.

Theorem 19. [51] *Greedy achieves a competitive ratio of* $\min\{2 - \frac{1}{B+1}, 2 - \frac{2}{\alpha+1}\}$.

Recently Bansal et al. [13] gave an algorithm that achieves an improved competitiveness of 1.75. Kesselman et al. [52] showed a lower bound of 1.419.

Aiello et al. [7] investigated nonpreemptive single buffer problems. In this case the buffer can simply be maintained as a FIFO queue. Andelman et al. [10] gave asymptotically tight bounds for this scenario. They analyzed the following algorithm. Suppose that the packet values are in the range $[1, \alpha]$.

Exponential-Interval-Round-Robin: Divide the buffer into k partitions of size B/k, where $k = \lceil \ln \alpha \rceil$. Split the interval $[1, \alpha]$ into k subintervals $[\alpha_0, \alpha_1), [\alpha_1, \alpha_2), \ldots, [\alpha_{k-1}, \alpha_k)$, where $\alpha_j = \alpha^{j/k}$. Each partition of the buffer is associated with one of the subintervals, accepting in a greedy manner packets from that subinterval. The partitions take turn in sending packets. If a partition is empty, its turn is passed to the next partition.

Theorem 20. [10] *Exponential-Interval-Round-Robin achieves a competitive ratio of* $e \lceil \ln \alpha \rceil$.

Theorem 21. [10] *No online algorithm can achieve a competitive ratio smaller than* $1 + \ln \alpha$ *in the nonpreemptive model.*

Kesselman et al. [51] also introduced a *bounded delay model* where packets have deadlines. A packet that has not been transmitted by its deadline is lost. There is no bound on the buffer size and packets may be reordered. Kesselman et al. analyzed a *Greedy* strategy which at any time transmits the packet of highest value among those with unexpired deadlines. This strategy is 2-competitive.

Azar and Richter [12] extended many of the results mentioned so far to multibuffer problems. Consider a switch with m input ports, each of which is equipped with a buffer that can simultaneously store up to B packets. These buffers serve a common output port. At any time t, let $Q_i(t)$ be the set of packets stored in buffer i and let $A_i(t)$ be the set of packets arriving at that buffer. If $|Q_i(t)| + |A_i(t)| \leq B$, then all arriving packets can be admitted to buffer i; otherwise $|Q_i(t)| + |A_i(t)| - B$ packets must be dropped. At any time, the switch can select one nonempty buffer and transmit the packet at the head through the output port. The goal is to maximize the total value of the transmitted packets.

Azar and Richter presented a general technique that transforms a buffer management strategy for a single queue (for both the preemptive and nonpreemptive models) into an algorithm for m queues. The technique is based on the algorithm *Transmit-Largest* that works in the preemptive non-FIFO model.

Transmit-Largest (TL):

1. Admission control: Use *Greedy* for admission control in any of the m buffers. More precisely, enqueue a packet arriving at buffer i if buffer i

is not full or if the packet with the smallest value in the buffer has a lower value than the new packet. In the latter case the packet with the smallest value is dropped.

2. Transmission: In each time step transmit the packet with the largest value among all packets in the m queues.

Using this algorithm, Azar and Richter designed a technique *Generic-Switch* that takes a single buffer management algorithm A as input parameter. We are interested in the preemptive FIFO and the nonpreemptive models. Here packets are always transmitted in the order they arrive (w.l.o.g., in the nonpreemptive model) and only A's admission control strategy is relevant to us.

Generic-Switch:

1. Admission control: Apply admission control strategy A to any of the m buffers.
2. Transmission: Run a simulation of TL (in the preemptive non-FIFO model) with online paket arrival sequence σ. In each time step transmit the packet from the head of the queue served by TL.

The main result by Azar and Richter is as follows.

Theorem 22. [12] *If A is a c-competitive algorithm, then Generic-Switch is 2c-competitive.*

Using this statement, one can derive a number of results for multiqueue problems. In the preemptive FIFO model *Greedy* achieves a competitiveness of $\min\{4 - \frac{2}{B+1}, 4 - \frac{4}{\alpha+1}\}$. The improved algorithm by Bansal et al. [13] gives a 3.5-competitive strategy. In the nonpreemptive setting we obtain a $2e\lceil \ln \alpha \rceil$-competitive strategy.

TCP Acknowledgement

In large networks data transmission is performed using the Transmission Control Protocol (TCP). If two network nodes wish to exchange data, then there has to exist an open TCP connection between these two nodes. The data is partitioned into packets which are then sent across the connection. A node receiving data must acknowledge the receipt of each incoming packet so that the sending node is aware that the transmission was successful. In most TCP implementations today data packets do not have to be acknowledged individually. Instead, there is some delay mechanism which allows the TCP to acknowledge multiple packets with a single acknowledgement and, possibly, to piggyback the acknowledgement on an outgoing data packet. This reduces the number of acknowledgements sent and hence the network congestion as well as the overhead at the network nodes for sending and receiving acknowledgements. On the other hand, by reducing the number of acknowledgements, we add latency to the TCP connection, which is not desirable. Thus, the goal is to balance the reduction in the number of acknowledgements with the increase in latency.

Dooly et al. [34] formulated the following TCP acknowledgement problem. A network node receives a sequence of m data packets. Let a_i denote the arrival time of packet i, $1 \leq i \leq m$. At time a_i, the arrival times a_j, $j > i$, are not known. We have to partition the sequence $\sigma = (a_1, \ldots, a_m)$ of packet arrival times into n subsequences $\sigma_1, \ldots, \sigma_n$, for some $n \geq 1$, such that each subsequence ends with an acknowledgement. We use σ_i to denote the set of arrivals in the partition. Let t_i be the time when the acknowledgement for σ_i is sent. We require $t_i \geq a_j$, for all $a_j \in \sigma_i$. If data packets are not acknowledged immediately, there are acknowledgement delays. Dooley et al. [34] considered the objective function that minimizes the number of acknowledgements and the sum of the delays incurred for all of the packets, i.e., we wish to minimize $f = n + \sum_{i=1}^{n} \sum_{a_j \in \sigma_i} (t_i - a_j)$. It turns out that a simple *Greedy* strategy is optimal for this problem.

Greedy: Send an acknowledgement whenever the total delay of the unacknowledged packets is equal to 1, i.e., equal to the cost of an acknowledgement.

Theorem 23. [34] *The Greedy algorithm is 2-competitive and no deterministic online algorithm can achieve a smaller competitive ratio.*

Noga [59] and independently Seiden [63] showed that no randomized algorithm can achieve a competitive ratio smaller than $e/(e-1) \approx 1.58$ against oblivious adversaries. Karlin et al. [48] presented a randomized strategy that achieves this factor. Let $P(t, t')$ be the set of packets that arrive after time t but up to (and including) time t. The following algorithm works for positive real numbers between 0 and 1. It sends an acknowledgement when, in hindsight, z time units of latency could have been saved by sending an earlier acknowledgement.

Save(z): Let t be the time when the last acknowledgement was sent. Send the next acknowledgement at the first time $t' > t$ such that there is a time τ with $t \leq \tau \leq t'$ and $P(t, t')(t' - \tau) = z$.

Theorem 24. [48] *If z is chosen according to the probability density function $p(z) = e^z/(e-1)$, Save(z) achieves a competitive ratio of $e/(e-1)$.*

Albers and Bals [3] investigate another family of objective functions that penalize long acknowledgement delays of individual data packets more heavily. When TCP is used for interactive data transfer, long delays are not desirable as they are noticeable to a user. Hence we wish to minimize the function $g = n + \max_{1 \leq i \leq n} d_i$, where $d_i = \max_{a_j \in \sigma_i} (t_i - a_j)$ is the maximum delay of any packet in σ_i. The following family of algorithms is defined for any positive real z.

Linear-Delay(z): Initially, set $d = z$ and send the first acknowledgement at time $a_1 + d$. In general, suppose that the i-th acknowledgement has just been sent and that j packets have been processed so far. Set $d = (i+1)z$ and send the $(i+1)$-st acknowledgement at time $a_{j+1} + d$.

Theorem 25. [3] *Setting $z = \pi^2/6 - 1$, Linear-Delay(z) achieves a competitive ratio of $\pi^2/6 \approx 1.644$ and no deterministic strategy can achieve a smaller competitiveness.*

It is well known that $\pi^2/6 = \sum_{i=1}^{\infty} 1/i^2$. Additionally, Albers and Bals [3] investigate a generalization of the objective function g where delays are taken to the p-th power and hence are penalized even more heavily. They proved that the best competitive ratio is an alternating sum of Riemann's zeta function. The ratio is decreasing in p and tends to 1.5 as $p \to \infty$. Frederiksen and Larsen [41] studied a variant of the TCP acknowledgement problem, where it is required that there is some minimum delay between sending two acknowledgements to reflect the physical properties of the network.

6.2 Competitive Auctions

In electronic markets goods are often sold using protocols that resemble classical auctions. The goods available for distribution are not physical but digital and may include, e.g., electronic books, software and digital copies of music or movies. The players who are interested in buying such goods send bids to an auctioneer, who then decides which bidders receive goods at which price. The mechanisms by which resources are transferred should be *truthful* and *competitive*, i.e., players should place bids which reflect their true valuations of the goods and the revenue of the auction should be close to the optimal one. There has recently been considerable research interest in designing truthful competitive auctions [22, 35, 42, 43, 44, 55, 56] and we consider two basic settings here.

Lavi and Nisan [56] were among the first who studied truthful auction mechanisms. In their model k identical invisible goods are to be sold. The players arrive online. When player i arrives he has valuations for buying various quantities of the good. More precisely, let $v_i(q)$ be the additional benefit gained from a q-th item of the good. The total valuation from receiving q goods is $\sum_{j=1}^{q} v_i(j)$. We assume $v_i(q+1) \le v_i(q)$, which is a common assumption in economics. The valuations are only known to the player himself. To buy goods the player sends bids $b_i(q), q = 1, \ldots, k$, where $b_i(q)$ is the bid made for receiving a q-th item. The auctioneer then determines a quantity q_i to be sold to the player as well as a price p_i. The utility of player i is $U_i(q_i, p_i) = \sum_{j=1}^{q_i} v_i(j) - p_i$. As mentioned already before, we are interested in mechanisms where bidders declare their true valuations. More formally a bidding strategy $b_i(q)$ of player i is *dominant* if $U_i(q_i, p_i) \ge U_i(q_i', p_i')$, for any other strategy $b_i'(q)$ that results in quantity q_i' and price p_i'. Using this definition, an auction is called *truthful* if, for each player, declaring true valuations $b_i(q) = v_i(q)$ is a dominant strategy.

Lavi and Nisan give an exact characterization of truthful auctions in the setting under consideration. An auction is based on *supply curves* if before receiving the i-th bids $b_i(q)$, the auctioneer fixes prices $P_i(q)$. The quantity q_i sold to player i is the value q that maximizes $\sum_{j=1}^{q}(b_i(j) - P_i(j))$ and the prize to be paid is $\sum_{i=1}^{q_i} P_i(j)$.

Theorem 26. [56] *An auction is truthful if and only if it is based on supply curves.*

Lavi and Nisan consider two performance measures of an auction, namely *revenue* and *social efficiency*. Suppose that the valuations are in the range $[p_{\min}, p_{\max}]$. For any auction A and valuation sequence σ, the revenue $R_A(\sigma)$ to the auctioneer is defined as $R_A(\sigma) = \sum_i p_i + p_{\min}(k - \sum_i q_i)$, i.e., we sum up the prices paid by the players and the minimum value of the unsold items. The social efficiency is $E_A(\sigma) = \sum_i \sum_{j=1}^{q_i} v_i(j) + p_{\min}(k - \sum_i q_i)$, i.e., we sum up the valuations of all players and the auctioneer. Lavi and Nisan compare an auction to the k-item Vickrey auction. This offline truthful auction sells the k items to the k highest bids at the price of the $(k+1)$-st highest bid. An online auction A is c-competitive with respect to revenue if, for every valuation sequence σ, $R_A(\sigma) \geq R_{VIC}(\sigma)/c$. Similarly, A is c-competitive with respect to social efficiency if, for every σ, $E_A(\sigma) \geq E_{VIC}(\sigma)/c$.

Based on these definitions Lavi and Nisan present a truthful competitive auction for selling k identical invisible goods. We only have to specify the supply curve.

Discrete-Online-Auction: Let $\Phi = p_{\max}/p_{\min}$. Use the supply curve $P(j) = p_{\min}\Phi^{\frac{j}{k+1}}$.

Theorem 27. [56] *The Discrete-Online-Auction achieves a competitive ratio of $k\Phi^{\frac{1}{k+1}}$ with respect to revenue and social efficiency.*

Theorem 28. [56] *The competitive ratio of any truthful online auction with respect to revenue and social efficiency is at least $\max\{\Phi^{\frac{1}{k+1}}, c\}$, where c is the solution of the equation $c = \ln(\frac{\Phi-1}{c-1})$.*

The second scenario we study here are single-round, sealed-bid competitive auctions as introduces by Goldberg et al. [43]. We first consider the offline problem, which is interesting and instructive in itself. Then we discuss the online variant. There are n players, each of whom is interested in buying one item of a given good. An auctioneer has available n items so that each player can potentially receive one copy. Player $i, 1 \leq i \leq n$, submits a bid b_i representing the maximum amount that he is willing to pay for an item. Given the vector B of bids, the auctioneer computes an allocation $X = (x_1, \ldots, x_n) \in \{0,1\}^n$ and prices $P = (p_1, \ldots, p_n)$. If $x_i = 1$, then player i receives an item, i.e., he *wins*, and pays a cost of p_i. We assume $0 \leq p_i \leq b_i$. If $x_i = 0$, then the player does not receive an item, i.e., he loses, and $p_i = 0$. The utility of player i is $v_i x_i - p_i$. The profit of the auction is $\sum_i p_i$. An auction is *truthful* if, for each player i and any choice of bid values of the other players, the utility of the i-th player is maximized by setting $b_i = v_i$.

Given a bid vector B and an auction A, let $A(B)$ be the profit of A on input B. If A is randomized, then $A(B)$ is a random variable. Goldberg et al. [43] define competitiveness with respect to the *optimal single price omniscient auction* F, which is defined as follows. In a bid vector B, let l_i be i-th largest bid. Auction F determines the largest k such that $k\ell_k$ is maximized. All players with $b_i \geq l_k$ win; the remaining players lose. The profit of F on B is $F(B) = \max_{1 \leq i \leq n} i\ell_i$. A truthful auction is called c-competitive against F if, for all bid vectors B, the expected profit of A on B satisfies $E[A(B)] \geq F(B)/c$.

Goldberg et al. give an exact characterization of truthful auctions based on the notion of *bid-independence*. Let $f_i, 1 \leq i \leq n$, be a family of functions from bid vectors to prices. The deterministic bid-independent auction defined by functions f_i has the following property for each player i.

Let $p_i = f_i(B_{-i})$, where $B_{-i} = (b_1, \ldots, b_{i-1}, b_{i+1}, \ldots, b_n)$. If $b_i \geq p_i$, player i wins at a price of p_i; otherwise player i loses.

Theorem 29. [43] *An auction is truthful if and only if it is bid-independent.*

Goldberg et al. presented an elegant randomized 4-competitive truthful auction which is based on the following cost-sharing mechanism.

Cost-Share(C): Given bid vector B, find the largest k such that the highest k bidders can equally share the cost of C. Charge each C/k.

The actual auction then works as follows.

Sampling-Cost-Sharing:
1. Partition B uniformly at random into two sets, resulting in bid vectors B' and B''.
2. Compute $F' = F(B')$ and $F'' = F(B'')$.
3. Compute the auction results by running *Cost-Share(F')* on B'' and *Cost-Share(F'')* on B'.

Theorem 30. [43] *Sampling-Cost-Sharing is a truthful 4-competitive auction.*

Recently Goldberg and Hartline [42] presented a randomized auction that achieves a competitiveness of 3.39 and uses only two random bits.

Bar-Yossef et al. [16] investigated the online variant of the above problem setting where players arrive one by one. A player has access to all prior bids in determining his own bid. When player i has submitted his bid, the auctioneer must fix a price p_i before any other player arrives. If $p_i \leq b_i$, player i wins; otherwise he loses. In the online scenario an auction A is called bid-independent if the price for player i depends only on the previous bids and not on b_i. That is, for any sequence of bids $b_1, \ldots, b_{i-1}$ and for any two choices of the i-th bid b_i and b'_i, $f_i(b_1, \ldots, b_{i-1}, b_i) = f_i(b_1, \ldots, b_{i-1}, b'_i)$. Bar-Yossef et al. show that an online auction is truthful if and only if it is bid-independent.

Assume that all bids are in the range $[1, h]$. Furthermore, let $B_{<i} = (b_1, \ldots, b_{i-1})$ be the bids up to player i. Bar-Yossef et al. presented the following randomized auction. The parameter d will be determined later.

Weighted-Interval-Auction(d): Partition the range $[1, h]$ into $l = \lfloor \log h \rfloor + 1$ subintervals $I_0, \ldots, I_{l-1}$ with $I_k = [2^k, 2^{k+1})$. When player i arrives, determine the set of previous players with bids in I_k, for any k. More precisely, let $S_k = \{j \mid j \leq i - 1, \ b_j \in I_k\}$ and compute the weight $w_k(B_{<i}) = \sum_{j \in S_k} b_j$. Choose the price $p_i = 2^k$ with probability

$$\text{Prob}[p_i = 2^k] = \frac{w_k(B_{<i})^d}{\sum_{r=0}^{l-1} w_r(B_{<i})^d}.$$

Theorem 31. [16] *Weighted-Interval-Auction(d) is a truthful auction. Restricting to bidding sequences with $F(B) \geq 9h$ and setting $d = \sqrt{\log \log h}$, the competitive ratio is $O(\exp(\sqrt{\log \log h}))$.*

Using methods from learning theory, Blum et al [22] developed a constant competitive truthful auction.

7 Refinements of Competitive Analysis

Competitive analysis is a worst-case performance measure. Unfortunately, for some online problems, the competitive ratios of online algorithms are much higher than the performance ratios observed in practice. The reason is, typically, that a competitive algorithm considers arbitrary request sequences whereas in practice only restricted classes of input occur.

We consider the paging problem in more detail. In Sect. 2 we saw that the best competitiveness of deterministic online algorithms is equal to k, where k is the number of pages that can be stored in fast memory. Both LRU and FIFO achieve this bound. From a practical point of view the bound of k is not very meaningful as a fast memory can usually store several hundreds or thousands of pages. On the other hand, the performance ratios of LRU and FIFO in practice are much lower. An experimental study by Young [68] reports ratios in the range between 1.5 and 4. Moreover, in practice, LRU performs better than FIFO. This is not evident in competitive analysis, either. In the paging problem standard competitive analysis ignores the fact that request sequences generated by real programs exhibit locality of reference: Whenever a page is requested, the next request is to an associated page.

Borodin et al. [24] introduced *access graphs* for modeling locality of reference. In an access graph the nodes represent the memory pages. Whenever a page p is requested, the next request must be to a page that is is adjacent to p in the access graph. A number of results have been developed in this model [24, 30, 36, 38, 45]. It has been shown that, for any access graph, LRU is never worse than FIFO. For access graphs that are trees, LRU is in fact an optimal algorithm. Moreover, a number of improved paging algorithms have been proposed that take into account the structure of the access graph.

Karlin et al. [49] modeled locality of reference by assuming that request sequences are generated by a Markov chain. They evaluate paging algorithms in terms of their *fault rate* which is the performance measure preferred by practitioners. In particular, they developed an algorithm that achieves an optimal fault rate, for any Markov chain. Torng [67] analyzed the *total access time* of paging algorithms. He assumes that the service of a request to a page in fast memory costs 1, whereas a fault incurs a penalty of p, $p > 1$. In his model a request sequence exhibits locality of reference if the average length of a subsequence containing requests to m distinct pages is much larger than m.

Recently, Albers et al. [4] proposed another framework for modeling locality of reference that goes back to the working set concept by Denning [32, 33]. In practice, during any phase of execution, a process references only a relatively small fraction of its pages. The set of pages that a process is currently using is called the *working set*. Determining the working set size in a window of size n at any point in a request sequence, one obtains, for variable n, a function that is increasing and concave. Albers et al. restrict the input to request sequences in which the maximum or the average number of distinct pages referenced in windows of size n is bounded by $f(n)$, f being a concave function. They give tight upper and lower bounds on the page fault rates achieved by popular paging algorithms. It shows that LRU is an optimal online algorithm whereas other algorithms, such as FIFO, are not optimal in general.

With respect to arbitrary online problems, other refinements of competitive analysis include extra resource analyses, see e.g., [47, 65], statistical adversaries [28, 60], accomodating functions [26] and the max/max ratio [18]. Koutsoupias and Papadimitriou [54] introduced the *diffuse adversary model*. An adversary must generate an input according to a probability distribution D that belongs to a class Δ of possible distributions known to the online algorithm. We wish to determine, for the given class Δ of distributions, the performance ratio

$$R(\Delta) = \min_{A} \max_{D \in \Delta} \frac{\mathrm{E}_D[A(\sigma)]}{\mathrm{E}_D[OPT(\sigma)]}.$$

Secondly, Koutsoupias and Papadimitriou [54] introduced *comparative analysis*, which compares the performance of online algorithms from given classes of algorithms.

8 Concluding Remarks

In this chapter we have presented a number of fundamental results in the area of online algorithms and studied some applications that have received a lot of research attention lately. There are several important application areas that we have not addressed here. Online bin packing is a fundamental problem where we have to pack a sequence of items into bins so that the number of bins is minimized. Problems in online scheduling are still actively investigated. Here a sequence of jobs has to be scheduled on a number of machines so that a given objective function is optimized. Online coloring and online matching are two classical online problems related to graph theory. In these problems, the vertices of a graph arrive online and must be colored respectively matched immediately. The book by Fiat and Woeginger [40] contains a collection of survey articles on these and many other topics. More generally, an excellent text book on online algorithms was written by Borodin and El-Yaniv [23].

References

1. D. Achlioptas, M. Chrobak, J. Noga. Competitive analysis of randomized paging algorithms. *Theoretical Computer Science*, 234:203–218, 2000.
2. S. Albers. Improved randomized on-line algorithms for the list update problem. *SIAM J. Computing* 27:670–681, 1998.
3. S. Albers, H. Bals. Dynamic TCP acknowledgement: Penalizing long delays. *Proc. 14th ACM-SIAM Symp. on Theory of Computing*, 47–55, 2003.
4. S. Albers, L. M. Favrholdt, O. Giel On paging with locality of reference. *Proc. 34th ACM Symp. on Theory of Computing*, 258–268, 2002.
5. S. Albers, M. Mitzenmacher. Average case analyses of list update algorithms, with applications to data compression. *Algorithmica* 21:312–329, 1998.
6. S. Albers, B. von Stengel, R. Werchner. A combined BIT and TIMESTAMP algorithm for the list update problem. *Information Processing Letters* 56:135–139, 1995.
7. W. Aiello, Y. Mansour, S. Rajagopolan, A. Rosén. Competitive queue policies for differentiated services. *Proc. INFOCOM*, 431–440, 2000.
8. C. Ambühl. Offline list update is NP-hard. *Proc. 8th Annual European Symp. on Algorithms*, Springer LNCS 1879, 42–51, 2001.
9. C. Ambühl, B. Gärtner, B. von Stengel. Towards new lower bounds for the list update problem. *Theoretical Computer Science* 268:3–16, 2001.
10. N. Andelman, Y. Mansour, A. Zhu. Competitive queueing policies in QoS switches. *Proc. 14th ACM-SIAM Symp. on Discrete Algorithms*, 761–770, 2003.
11. A. Archer, C. Papadimitriou, K. Talwar, E. Tardos. An approximate truthful mechanism for combinatorial auctions with single parameter agents. *Proc. 14th ACM-SIAM Symp. on Discrete Algorithms*, 205–214, 2003.
12. Y. Azar, Y. Richter. Management of multi-queue switches in QoS networks. *Proc. 35th Annual ACM Symp. on Theory of Computing*, 82–89, 2003.
13. N. Bansal, L. Fleischer, T. Kimbrel, M. Mahdian, B. Schieber, M. Sviridenko. Further improvements in competitive guarantees for QoS buffering. *Proc. 31st Int'l Colloquium on Automata, Languages and Programming*, Springer LNCS 3142, 196-207, 2004.
14. Y. Bartal, A. Blum, C. Burch, A. Tomkins. A polylog(n)-competitive algorithm for metrical task systems. *Proc. 29th Annual ACM Symp. on Theory of Computing*, 711–719, 1997.

15. Y. Bartal, B. Bollobás, M. Mendel. A Ramsey-type theorem for metric spaces and its applications for metrical task systems and related problems. *Proc. 42nd IEEE Annual Symp. on Foundations of Computer Science*, 396–405, 2001.

16. Z. Bar-Yossef, K. Hildrum, F. Wu. Incentive-compatible online auctions for digital goods. *Proc. 13th Annual ACM-SIAM Symp. on Discrete Algorithms*, 964–970, 2002.

17. L. A. Belady. A study of replacement algorithms for virtual storage computers. *IBM Systems J.* 5:78–101, 1966.

18. S. Ben-David, A. Borodin. A new measure for the study of on-line algorithms. *Algorithmica* 11:73–91, 1994.

19. S. Ben-David, A. Borodin, R. M. Karp, G. Tardos, A. Wigderson. On the power of randomization in on-line algorithms. *Algorithmica* 11:2–14, 1994.

20. J. L. Bentley, D. S. Sleator, R. E. Tarjan, V. K. Wei. A locally adaptive data compression scheme. *Comm. ACM* 29:320–330, 1986.

21. A. Blum, S. Chawla, A. Kalai. Static optimality and dynamic search-optimality in lists and trees. *Algorithmica* 36:249–260, 2003.

22. A. Blum, V. Kumar, A. Rudra, F. Wu. Online learning in online auctions. *Proc. 14th Annual ACM-SIAM Symp. on Discrete Algorithms*, 202–204, 2003.

23. A. Borodin, R. El-Yaniv. *Online computation and competitive analysis*. Cambridge University Press, Cambridge, 1998.

24. A. Borodin, S. Irani, P. Raghavan, B. Schieber. Competitive paging with locality of reference. *J. Computer and System Sciences* 50:244–258, 1995.

25. A. Borodin, N. Linial, M. Saks. An optimal online algorithm for metrical task systems. *J. ACM* 39:745–763, 1992.

26. J. Boyar, K. S. Larsen, M. N. Nielsen. The accommodating function: A generalization of the competitive ratio. *SIAM J. on Computing* 31:233–258, 2001.

27. M. Burrows, D. J. Wheeler. A block-sorting lossless data compression algorithm. *DEC SRC Research Report* 124, 1994.

28. A. Chou, J. Cooperstock, R. El Yaniv, M. Klugerman, T. Leighton. The statistical adversary allows optimal money-making trading strategies. *Proc. 6th Annual ACM-SIAM Symp. on Discrete Algorithms*, 467–476, 1995.

29. M. Chrobak, L. L. Larmore. An optimal online algorithm for k servers on trees. *SIAM J. on Computing* 20:144–148, 1991.

30. M. Chrobak, J. Noga. LRU is better than FIFO. *Algorithmica* 23:180–185, 1999.

31. D. Coppersmith, P. Doyle, P. Raghavan, M. Snir. Random walks on weighted graphs, and applications to on-line algorithms. *J. ACM* 40:421–453, 1993.

32. P. J. Denning. The working set model of program behavior. *Comm. ACM* 11:323–333, 1968.

33. P. J. Denning. Working sets past and present. *IEEE Trans. Software Engineering* 6:64–84, 1980.

34. D. R. Dooly, S. A. Goldman, D. S. Scott. On-line analysis of the TCP acknowledgment delay problem. *J. ACM* 48:243–273, 2001.

35. A. Fiat, A. Goldberg, J. Hartline, A. Karlin. Competitive generalized auctions. *Proc. 34th Annual ACM Symp. on Theory of Computing*, 72–81, 2002.

36. A. Fiat, A. Karlin. Randomized and multipointer paging with locality of reference. *Proc. 27th Annual ACM Symp. on Theory of Computing*, 626–634, 1995.

37. A. Fiat, R. M. Karp, L. A. McGeoch, D. D. Sleator, N. E. Young. Competitive paging algorithms. *J. Algorithms* 12:685–699, 1991.

38. A. Fiat, M. Mendel. Truly online paging with locality of reference. *Proc. 38th Annual Symp. on Foundations of Computer Science*, 326–335, 1997.

39. A. Fiat, M. Mendel. Better algorithms for unfair metrical task systems and applications. *Proc. 32nd Annual ACM Symp. on Theory of Computing*, 725–734, 2000.

40. A. Fiat, G. Woeginger. *Online Algorithms: The State of the Art,* Springer LNCS 1442, 1998.

41. J. S. Frederiksen, K. S. Larsen. Packet bundling. *Proc. 8th Scandinavian Workshop on Algorithm Theory*, Springer LNCS 2368, 328–337, 2002.

42. A. Goldberg, J. Hartline. Competitiveness via consensus. *Proc. 14th Annual ACM-SIAM Symp. on Discrete Algorithms*, 215–222, 2003.

43. A. V. Goldberg, D. S. Hartline, A. Karlin, A. Wright. Competitive auctions. Extended version of [44], 2001.

44. A. V. Goldberg, D. S. Hartline, A. Wright. Competitive auctions of digital goods. *Proc. 12th Annual ACM-SIAM Symp. on Discrete Algorithms*, 735–744, 2001.

45. S. Irani, A. R. Karlin, S. Phillips. Strongly competitive algorithms for paging with locality of reference. *SIAM J. on Computing* 25:477–497, 1996.

46. S. Irani, D. S. Seiden. Randomized algorithms for metrical task systems. *Theoretical Computer Science* 194:163–182, 1998.

47. B. Kalyanasundaram, K. Pruhs. Speed is as powerful as clairvoyance. *J. ACM* 47:617–643, 2000.

48. A. R. Karlin, C. Kenyon, D. Randall. Dynamic TCP acknowledgement and other stories about $e/(e-1)$. *Algorithmica* 36:209–224, 2003.

49. A. Karlin, S. Phillips, P. Raghavan. Markov paging. *SIAM J. on Computing* 30:906–922, 2000.

50. Karp R, Raghavan P From a personal communication cited in [62], 1990.

51. A. Kesselman, Z. Lotker, Y. Mansour, B. Patt-Shamir, B. Schieber, M. Sviridenko. Buffer overflow management in QoS switches. In: *Proc. 33rd Annual ACM Symp. on Theory of Computing*, 520–529, 2001.

52. A. Kesselman, Y. Mansour, R. van Stee. Improved competitive guarantees for QoS buffering. *Proc. 11th European Symp. on Algorithms*, Springer LNCS 2832, 361–372, 2003.

53. E. Koutsoupias, C. H. Papadimitriou. On the k-server conjecture. *J. ACM* 42:971–983, 1995.

54. E. Koutsoupias, C. H. Papadimitriou. Beyond competitive analysis. *SIAM J. on Computing* 30:300–317, 2000.

55. R. Lavi, A. Mu'alem, N. Nisan. Towards a characterization of truthful combinatorial auctions. *Proc. 44th Annual IEEE Symp. on Foundations of Computer Science*, 574-583, 2003.

56. R. Lavi, N. Nisan. Competitive analysis of incentive compatible on-line auctions. *Proc. 2nd ACM Conf. on Electronic Commerce*, 2000.

57. M. S. Manasse, L. A. McGeoch, D. D. Sleator. Competitive algorithms for on-line problems. *Proc. 20th Annual ACM Symp. on Theory of Computing*, 322–333, 1988.

58. L. A. McGeoch, D. D. Sleator. A strongly competitive randomized paging algorithm. *Algorithmica* 6:816–825, 1991.

59. J. Noga. Private communication, 2001.

60. P. Raghavan. A statistical adversary for on-line algorithms. *On-Line Algorithms*, DIMACS Series in Discrete Mathematics and Theoretical Computer Science, 79–83, 1991.

61. P. Raghavan, M. Snir. Memory versus randomization in on-line algorithms. *IBM J. of Research and Development* 38:683–708, 1994.
62. N. Reingold, J. Westbrook, D. D. Sleator. Randomized competitive algorithms for the list update problem. *Algorithmica* 11:15–32, 1994.
63. S. S. Seiden. A guessing game and randomized online algorithms. *Proc. 32nd Annual ACM Symp. on Theory of Computing*, 592–601, 2000.
64. S. S. Seiden. A general decomposition theorem for the *k*-server problem. *Proc. 9th Annual Symp. on Algorithms*, Springer LNCS 2161, 86–97, 2001.
65. D. D. Sleator, R. E. Tarjan. Amortized efficiency of list update and paging rules. *Comm. ACM* 28:202–208, 1985.
66. D. D. Sleator, R. E. Tarjan. Self-adjusting binary search trees. *J. ACM* 32:652–686
67. E. Torng. A unified analysis of paging and caching. *Algorithmica* 20:175–200, 1998.
68. N. Young. The *k*-server dual and loose competitiveness for paging. *Algorithmica* 11:525–541, 1994.

Interactive Algorithms 2005
with Added Appendix

Yuri Gurevich

Microsoft Research, Redmond, WA, USA

Summary. A sequential algorithm just follows its instructions and thus cannot make a nondeterministic choice all by itself, but it can be instructed to solicit outside help to make a choice. Similarly, an object-oriented program cannot create a new object all by itself; a create-a-new-object command solicits outside help. These are but two examples of intrastep interaction of an algorithm with its environment. Here we motivate and survey recent work on interactive algorithms within the Behavioral Computation Theory project.

1 Introduction

This is essentially article [14] except that we have added an appendix called "What is interaction anyway?" that can be read independently.

In 1982, the University of Michigan hired this logician on his promise to become a computer scientist. The logician eagerly wanted to become a computer scientist. But what is computer science? Is it really a science? What is it about?

After thinking a while, we concluded that computer science is largely about algorithms. Operating systems, compilers, programming languages, etc. are all algorithms, in a wide sense of the word. For example, a programming language can be seen as a universal algorithm that applies the given program to the given data. In practice, you may need a compiler and a machine to run the compiled program on, but this is invisible on the abstraction level of the programming language.

A problem arises: What is an algorithm? To us, this is a fundamental problem of computer science, and we have been working on it ever since.

But didn't Turing solve the problem? The answer to this question depends on how you think of algorithms. If all you care about is the input-to-output function of the algorithm, then yes, Turing solved the problem. But the behavior of an algorithm may be much richer than its input-to-output function. An algorithm has its natural abstraction level, and the data structures employed by an algorithm are intrinsic to its behavior. The parallelism of a parallel algorithm is an inherent part of its behavior. Similarly, the interactivity of an interactive algorithm is an inherent part of its behavior as well.

Is there a solution à la Turing to the problem of what an algorithm is? In other words, is there a state-machine model that captures the notion of algorithm up to behavioral equivalence? Our impression was, and still is, that the answer is yes. In [11], we defined sequential abstract state machines (ASMs) and put forward a sequential ASM thesis: for every sequential algorithm, there is a sequential ASM with the same behavior. In particular, the ASM is supposed to simulate the given algorithm step-for-step. In [12], we defined parallel and distributed abstract state machines and generalized the ASM thesis for parallel and distributed algorithms. Parallel ASMs gave rise to a specification (and high-level programming) language AsmL [2] developed by the group of Foundations of Software Engineering of Microsoft Research.

At this point, the story forks. One branch leads to experimental evidence for the ASM thesis and to applications of ASMs [1, 2, 7]. Another branch leads to behavioral computation theory. We take the second branch here and restrict attention to *sequential time algorithms* that compute in a sequence of discrete steps.

In Sect. 2 we discuss a newer approach to the explication of the notion of algorithm. The new approach is axiomatic, but it also involves a machine characterization of algorithms. This newer approach is used in the rest of the article.

In Sect. 3 we sketch our explication of sequential (or small-step) algorithms [13]. We mention also the explication of parallel (or wide-step) algorithms in [3] but briefly. In either case, the algorithms in questions are *isolated-step algorithms* that abstain from intrastep interaction with the environment. They can interact with the environment in the interstep manner, however.

Section 4 is a quick introduction to the study of intrastep interaction of an algorithm with its environment; much of the section reflects [5, Part I]. We motivate the study of intrastep interaction and attempt to demonstrate how ubiquitous intrastep interaction is. Numerous disparate phenomena are best understood as special cases of intrastep interaction. We discuss various forms of intrastep interaction, introduce the query mechanism of [5, Part I] and attempt to demonstrate the universality of the query mechanism: the atomic interactions of any mechanism are queries. In the rest of the article, we concentrate on intrastep interaction; by default interaction means intrastep interaction. To simplify the exposition, we consider primarily the small-step (rather than wide-step) algorithms; by default algorithms are small-step algorithms.

Section 5 is devoted to the explication of *ordinary interactive algorithms* [5]. Ordinary algorithms never complete a step until all queries from that step have been answered. Furthermore, the only information from the environment that an ordinary algorithm uses during a step is answers to its queries.

Section 6 is devoted to the explication of general interactive algorithms [6, Article 1-3]. Contrary to ordinary interactive algorithms, a general interactive algorithm can be *impatient* and complete a step without waiting for all queries from that step to have been answered. It also can be *time sensitive*, so that its actions during a step depend not only on the answers to its queries but also on the order in which the answers have arrived. We mention also the explication of general wide-step algorithms [6, Article 4] but briefly.

Section 7 is a concluding remark to the main part of this article, that is the whole article minus the appendix.

Finally the appendix compares our approach to interactive computing with that of the Wegner school presented in this volume by article [10].

Much of this article reflects joint work with Andreas Blass, Benjamin Rossman and Dean Rosenzweig.

2 Explication of Algorithms

The theses mentioned in the introduction equate an informal, intuitive notion with a formal, mathematical notion. You cannot prove such a thesis mathematically but you can argue for it. Both Church and Turing argued for their theses. While their theses are equivalent, their arguments were quite different [4]. The ASM theses, mentioned in the introduction, have the following form.

ASM Thesis Form

1. Describe informally a class **A** of algorithms.
2. Describe the behavioral equivalence of **A** algorithms. Intuitively two algorithms are behaviorally equivalent if they do the same thing in all circumstances. Since **A** is defined informally, the behavioral equivalence may be informal as well.
3. Define a class **M** of abstract state machines.
4. Claim that $M \subseteq A$ and that every $A \in A$ is behaviorally equivalent to some $M \in M$.

The thesis for a class **A** of algorithms explicates algorithms in **A** as abstract state machines in **M**. For example, sequential algorithms are explicated as sequential ASMs. The thesis is open to criticism. One can try to construct an ASM in **M** that falls off **A** or an algorithm in **A** that is not behaviorally equivalent to any ASM in **M**.

Since the ASM thesis for **A** cannot be proven mathematically, experimental confirmation of the thesis is indispensable; this partially explains the interest in applications of ASMs in the ASM community. But one can argue for the thesis, and we looked for the best way to do that. Eventually we arrived at a newer and better explication procedure.

Algorithm Explication Procedure

1. Axiomatize the class **A** of the algorithms of interest. This is the hardest part. You try to find the most convincing axioms (or postulates) possible.
2. Define precisely the notion of behavioral equivalence. If there is already an ASM thesis T for **A**, you may want to use the behavioral equivalence of T or a precise version of the behavioral equivalence of T.
3. Define a class **M** of abstract state machines. If there is already an ASM thesis T for **A**, you may want to use the abstract state machines of T.
4. Prove the following characterization theorem for **A**: **M** $\subseteq$ **A** and every $A \in$ **M** is behaviorally equivalent to some $M \in$ **M**.

The characterization provides a theoretical programming language for **A** and opens a way for more practical languages for **A**. Any instance of the explication procedure is open to criticism of course. In particular, one may criticize the axiomatization and the behavioral equivalence relation.

If an explication procedure for **A** uses (a precise version of) the behavioral equivalence and the machines of the ASM thesis for **A**, then the explication procedure can be viewed as a proof of the thesis given the axiomatization.

A priori it is not obvious at all that a convincing axiomatization is possible. But our experience seems to be encouraging. The explication procedure was used for the first time in [13] where sequential algorithms were axiomatized and the sequential ASM thesis proved; see more about that in the next section. In [3], parallel algorithms were axiomatized and the parallel ASM thesis was proved, except that we slightly modified the notion of parallel ASM. Additional uses of the explication procedure will be addressed in Sects. 4–6.

In both, [13] and [3], two algorithms are behaviorally equivalent if they have the same states, initial states and transition function. It follows that behaviorally equivalent algorithms simulate each other step-for-step. We have been criticized that this behavioral equivalence is too fine, that step-for-step simulation is too much to require, that appropriate bisimulation may be a better behavioral equivalence. We agree that in some applications bisimulation is the right equivalence notion. But notice this: the finer the behavioral equivalence, the stronger the characterization theorem.

3 Isolated-Step Algorithms

As we mentioned above, sequential algorithms were explicated in [13]. Here we recall and motivate parts of that explication needed to make our story self-contained.

Imagine that you have some entity E. What does it mean that E is a sequential algorithm? A part of the answer is easy: every algorithm is a (not necessarily finite-state) automaton.

Postulate 1 (Sequential time) *The entity E determines*

- *a nonempty collection of states,*
- *a nonempty collection of initial states, and*
- *a state-transition function.*

The postulate does not say anything about final states; we refer the interested reader to [13, Sect. 3.3.2] in this connection. This single postulate allows us to define behavioral equivalence of sequential algorithms.

Definition 1. Two sequential algorithms are *behaviorally equivalent* if they have the same states, initial states and transition function.

It is harder to see what else can be said about sequential algorithms in full generality. Of course, every algorithm has a program of one kind or another, but we don't know how to turn this into a postulate or postulates. There are so many different programming notations in use already, and it is bewildering to imagine all possible programming notations.

Some logicians, notably Andrey A. Markov [18], insisted that the input to an algorithm should be *constructive*, like a string or matrix, so that you can actually write it down. This excludes abstract finite graphs for example. How would you put an abstract graph on the Turing machine tape? It turned out, however, that the constructive input requirement is too restrictive. Relational databases for example represent abstract structures, in particular graphs, and serve as inputs to important algorithms.

Remark 1 You can represent an abstract graph by an adjacency matrix. But this representation is not unique. Note also that it is not known whether there is a polynomial-time algorithm that, given two adjacency matrices, determines whether they represent the same graph.

A characteristic property of sequential algorithms is that they change their state only locally in any one step. Andrey N. Kolmogorov, who looked into this problem, spoke about "steps whose complexity is bounded in advance" [15]. We prefer to speak about bounded work instead; the amount of work done by a sequential algorithm in any one step is bounded, and the bound depends only on the algorithm and not on the state or the input. But we don't know how to measure the complexity of a step or the work done during a step. Fortunately we found a way around this difficulty. To this end, we need two additional postulates.

According to the abstract state postulate, all states of the entity E are structures (that is first-order structures) of a fixed vocabulary. If X is an (initial) state of A and a structure Y is isomorphic to X then Y is an (initial) state of A. The abstract state postulate allows us to introduce an abstract notion of location and to mark locations explored by an algorithm during a given step. The bounded exploration postulate bounds the number of locations explored by an algorithm during any step; the bound depends only on the algorithm and not on the state or the input. See details in [13].

Definition 2. A sequential algorithm is any entity that satisfies the sequential-time, abstract-state and bounded-exploration postulates.

A *sequential abstract state machine* is given is by a program, a nonempty isomorphism-closed collection of states and a nonempty isomorphism-closed subcollection of initial states. The program determines the state transition function.

Like a Turing machine program, a sequential ASM program describes only one step of the ASM. It is presumed that this step is executed over and over again. The machine halts when the execution of a step does not change the state of the machine. The simplest sequential ASM programs are assignments:

$$f(t_1, \ldots, t_j) := t_0$$

Here f is a j-ary *dynamic function* and every t_i is a ground first-order term. To execute such a program, evaluate every t_i at the given state; let the result be a_i. Then set the value of $f(a_1, \ldots, a_j)$ to a_0. Any other sequential ASM program is constructed from assignments by means of two constructs: if-then-else and do-in-parallel. Here is a sequential ASM program for the Euclidean algorithm: given two natural numbers a and b, it computes their greatest common divisor d.

Example 1 (Euclidean algorithm 1).

```
if a = 0 then d := b
else do in-parallel
    a := b mod a
    b := a
```

The do-in-parallel constructs allows us to compose and execute in parallel two or more programs. In the case when every component is an assignment, the parallel composition can be written as a simultaneous assignment. Example 1 can be rewritten as

```
if a = 0 then d := b
else a, b := b mod a, a
```

A question arises what happens if the components perform contradictory actions in parallel, for example,

```
do in-parallel
    x := 7
    x := 11
```

The ASM breaks down in such a case. One can argue that there are better solutions for such situations that guarantee that sequential ASMs do not break down. In the case of the program above, for example, one of the two values, 7 or 11, can be chosen in one way or another and assigned to x. Note, however, that some sequential algorithms do break down. That is a part of their behavior.

If sequential ASMs do not ever break down, then no sequential ASM can be behaviorally equivalent to a sequential algorithm that does break down.

In the Euclidean algorithm, all dynamic functions are nullary. Here is a version of the algorithm where some of dynamic functions are unary. Initially $mode = s = 0$.

Example 2 (Euclidean algorithm 2).

```
if mode = 0 then a(s), b(s), mode := Input1(s), Input2(s), 1
elseif mode = 1 then
    if a(s) = 0 then d(s), s, mode := b(s), s+1, 0
    else a(s), b(s) := b(s) mod a(s), a(s)
```

Theorem 1 (Sequential characterization theorem). *Every sequential ASM is a sequential algorithm, and every sequential algorithm is behaviorally equivalent to a sequential ASM.*

We turn our attention to parallel algorithms and quote from [4]: "The term 'parallel algorithm' is used for a number of different notions in the literature. We have in mind sequential-time algorithms that can exhibit unbounded parallelism but only bounded sequentiality within a single step. Bounded sequentiality means that there is an *a priori* bound on the lengths of sequences of events within any one step of the algorithm that must occur in a specified order. To distinguish this notion of parallel algorithms, we call such parallel algorithms *wide-step*. Intuitively the width is the amount of parallelism. The 'step' in 'wide-step' alludes to sequential time." Taking into account the bounded sequentiality of wide-step algorithms, they could be called "wide and shallow step algorithms".

4 Interaction

4.1 Interstep Interaction

One may have the impression that the algorithms of the previous section do not interact at all with the environment during the computation. This is not necessarily so. They do not interact with the environment during a step; we call such algorithm *isolated step algorithms*. But the environment can intervene between the steps of an algorithm. The environment preserves the vocabulary of the state but otherwise it can change the state in any way. It makes no difference in the proofs of the two characterization theorems whether interstep interaction with the environment is or is not permitted.

In particular, Euclidean algorithm 2 could be naturally interstep interactive; the functions Input1 and Input2 do not have to be given ahead of time. Think of a machine that repeatedly applies the Euclidean algorithm and keeps track of the number s of the current session. At the beginning of session s, the user provides numbers Input1(s) and Input2(s), so that the functions Input1(s) and Input2(s) are *external*. The interstep interactive character of the algorithm becomes obvious if we make the functions Input1, Input2 nullary.

Example 3 (Euclidean algorithm 3).

```
if mode = 0 then a(s), b(s), mode := Input1, Input2, 1
elseif mode = 1 then
   if a(s) = 0 then d(s), s, mode := b(s), s+1, 0
   else a(s), b(s) := b(s) mod a(s), a(s)
```

4.2 Intrastep Interaction

In applications, however, much of the interaction of an algorithm with its environment is intrastep. Consider for example an assignment

```
x := g(f(7))
```

where $f(7)$ is a remote procedure call whose result is used to form another remote procedure call. It is natural to view the assignment being done within one step. Of course, we can break the assignment into several steps so that interaction is interstep but this forces us to a lower abstraction level. Another justification of intrastep interaction is related to parallelism.

Example 4. This example reflects a real-world AsmL experience. To paint a picture, an AsmL application calls an outside paint applications. A paint agent is created, examines the picture and repeatedly calls the algorithm back: what color for such and such detail? The AsmL application can make two or more such paint calls in parallel. It is natural to view parallel conversations with paint agents happening intrastep.

Proviso 1 In the rest of this article, we concentrate on intrastep interaction and ignore interstep interaction. By default, interaction is intrastep interaction.

4.3 The Ubiquity of Interaction

Intrastep interaction is ubiquitous. Here are some examples.

- Remote procedure calls.
- Doing the following as a part of expression evaluation: getting input, receiving a message, printing output, sending a message, using an oracle.
- Making nondeterministic choices among two or more alternatives.
- Creating new objects in the object-oriented and other paradigms.

The last two items require explanation. First we address nondeterministic choices. Recall that we do not consider distributed algorithms here. A sequential-step algorithm just follows instructions and cannot nondeterministically choose all by itself. But it can solicit help from the environment, and the environment may be able to make a choice for the algorithm. For example, to evaluate an expression

```
any x | x in {0, 1, 2, 3, 4, 5} where x > 1
```

an AsmL program computes the set $\{2, 3, 4, 5\}$ and then uses an outside pseudorandom number generator to choose an element of that set. Of course an implementation of a nondeterministic algorithm may incorporate a choosing mechanism, so that there is no choice on the level of the implementation.

Re new object creation. An object-oriented program does not have the means necessary to create a new object all by itself: to allocate a portion of the memory and format it appropriately. A create-a-new-object command solicits outside help. This phenomenon is not restricted to the object-oriented paradigm. We give a non-object-oriented example. Consider an ASM rule

```
import v
  NewLeaf := v
```

that creates a new leaf say of a tree. The import command is really a query to the environment. In the ASM paradigm, a state comes with an infinite set of so-called reserve elements. The environment chooses such a reserve elements and returns it as a reply to the query.

4.4 Interaction Mechanisms

One popular interaction form is exemplified by the Remote Procedure Call (RPC) mechanism. One can think of a remote procedure call as a query to the environment where the caller waits for a reply to its query in order to complete a step and continue the computation. This interaction form is often called synchronous or blocking. Another popular interaction form is message passing. After sending a message, the sender proceeds with its computation; this interaction form is often called asynchronous or nonblocking. The synchronous/asynchronous and blocking/nonblocking terminologies may create an impression that every atomic intrastep interaction is in one of the two form. This is not the case. There is a spectrum of possible interaction forms. For example, a query may require two replies: first an acknowledgment and then an informative reply. One can think of queries with three, four or arbitrarily many replies.

Nevertheless, according to [5, Part I], there a universal form of atomic intrastep interaction: not-necessarily-blocking single-reply queries. In the previous paragraph, we have already represented a remote procedure call as a query. Sending a message can be thought of as a query that gets an immediate automatic reply, an acknowledgment that the query has been issued. Producing an output is similar. In fact, from the point of view of an algorithm issuing queries, there is no principal difference between sending a message and producing an output; in a particular application of course messages and outputs may have distinct formats.

What about two-reply queries mentioned above? It takes two single-reply queries to get two answers. Consider an algorithm A issuing a two-reply query q and think of q as a single-reply query. When the acknowledgment comes back, A goes to a mode where it expects an informative answer to q. This expectation can be seen as implicitly issuing a new query q'. The informative reply ostensibly to q is a usual reply to q'. In a similar way, one can explain receiving a message. It may seem that the incoming message is not provoked by any query. What query is it a reply to? An implicit query. That implicit query manifests itself in A's readiness to accept the incoming message. Here is an analogy. You sleep and then wake up because of the alarm clock buzz. Have you been expecting the buzz? In a way you were, in an implicit sort of way. Imagine that, instead of producing a buzz, the alarm clock quietly produces a sign "Wake up!" This will not have the desired effect, would it?

In general we do not assume that the query issuer has to wait for a reply to a query in order to resume its computation. More about that in Sect. 6.

What are potential queries precisely? This question is discussed at length in [5, Part I]. It is presumed that potential answers to a query are elements of the state of the algorithm that issued the query, so that an answer makes sense to the algorithm.

5 Ordinary Interactive Small-Step Algorithms

Proviso 2 To simplify the exposition, in the rest of the article we speak primarily about small-step algorithms. By default, algorithms are small-step algorithms.

Informally speaking, an interactive algorithm is *ordinary* if it has the following two properties.

- The algorithm cannot successfully complete a step while there is an unanswered query from that step.
- The only information that the algorithm receives from the environment during a step consists of the replies to the queries issued during the step.

Ordinary interactive algorithms are axiomatized in [5, Part I]. Some postulates of [5, Part I] refactor those of [13]. One of the new postulates is this:

Postulate 2 (Interaction Postulate) *An interactive algorithm determines, for each state X, a causality relation $\vdash_X$ between finite answer functions and potential queries.*

Here an answer function is a function from potential queries to potential replies. An answer function α is *closed* under a causality relation $\vdash_X$ if every query caused by α or by a subfunction of α is already in the domain of α. Minimal answer functions closed under $\vdash_X$ are *contexts* at X.

As before, behaviorally equivalent algorithms do the same thing in all circumstances. To make this precise, we need a couple of additional definitions. Given a causality relation $\vdash_X$ and an answer function α, define an α-*trace* to be a sequence $\langle q_1, \ldots, q_n \rangle$ of potential queries such that each q_i is caused by the restriction α_i of α to $\{q_j : \ j < k\}$ or by some subfunction of α_i. A potential query q is *reachable* from α under $\vdash_X$ if it occurs in some α-trace. Two causality relations are *equivalent* if, for every answer function α, they make the same potential queries reachable from α.

Definition 3. Two ordinary interactive algorithms are *behaviorally equivalent* if

- they have the same states and initial states,
- for every state, they have equivalent causality relations, and
- for every state and context, they both fail or they both succeed and produce the same next state. □

We turn our attention to ordinary abstract state machines. Again, a machine is given by a program, a collection of states and a subcollection of initial states. We need only to describe programs.

The syntax of ordinary ASM programs is nearly the same as that of isolated state algorithms, the algorithms of [13]. The crucial difference is in the semantics of external functions. In the case of isolated step algorithms, an invocation of an external function is treated as a usual state-location lookup; see Euclidean algorithm 2 or 3 in this connection. In the case of interactive algorithms, an invocation of an external function is a query.

The new interpretation of external functions gives rise to a problem. Suppose that you have two distinct invocations $f(3)$ of an external function $f( )$ in your program. Should the replies be necessarily the same? In the case of an isolated-step program, the answer is yes. Indeed, the whole program describes one step of an algorithm, and the state does not change during the step. Two distinct lookups of $f(3)$ will give you the same result. In the case of an interactive program, the replies don't have to be the same. Consider

Example 5 (Euclidean algorithm 4).

```
if mode = 0 then a, b, mode := Input, Input, 1
elseif mode = 1 then
   if a = 0 then d, mode := b, 0
   else a, b := b mod a, a
```

The two invocations of input are different queries that may have different results. Furthermore, in the object-oriented paradigm, two distinct invocations of the same create-a-new-object command with the same parameters necessarily result in two distinct objects. We use a mechanism of template assignment to solve the problem in question [5, Parts II and III].

The study of ordinary interactive algorithms in [5] culminates in

Theorem 2 (Ordinary interactive characterization theorem). *Every ordinary interactive ASM is an ordinary interactive algorithm, and every ordinary interactive algorithm is behaviorally equivalent to an ordinary interactive ASM.*

6 General Interactive Algorithms

Call an interactive algorithm *patient* if it cannot finish a step without having the replies to all queries issued during the step. While ordinary interactive algorithms are patient, this does not apply to all interactive algorithms. The algorithm

Example 6 (Impatience).

```
do in parallel
    if α or β then x:=1
    if ¬α and ¬β then x:=2
```

issues two Boolean queries α and β. If one of the queries returns "true" while the other query is unanswered, then the other query can be aborted.

Call an interactive algorithm *time insensitive* if the only information that it receives from the environment during a step consists of the replies to the queries issued during the step. Ordinary algorithms are time insensitive. Since our algorithms interact with the environment only by means of queries, it is not immediately obvious what information the algorithm can get from the environment in addition to the replies. For example, time stamps, reflecting the times when the replies were issued, can be considered to be parts of the replies.

The additional information is the order in which the replies come in. Consider for example an automated financial broker with a block of shares to sell and two clients bidding for the block of shares. If the bid of client 1 reaches the broker first, then the broker sells the shares to client 1, even if client 2 happened to issue a bid a tad earlier.

An algorithm can be impatient and time sensitive at the same time. Consider for example a one-step algorithm that issues two queries, q_1 and q_2, and then does the following. If q_i is answered while q_{3-i} is not, then it sets x to i and aborts q_{3-i}. And if the queries are answered at the same time, then it sets x to 0.

The following key observation allowed us to axiomatize general interactive algorithms. Behind any sequential-step algorithm there is a single executor of the algorithm. In particular, it is the executor who gets query replies from the environment, in batches, one after another. It follows that the replies are linearly preordered according to the time or arrival. In [6, Article 1], we successfully execute the algorithm explication procedure of Sect. 2 in the case of general interactive algorithms.

Theorem 3 (Interactive characterization theorem). *Every interactive ASM is an interactive algorithm, and every interactive algorithm is behaviorally equivalent to an interactive ASM.*

A variant of this theorem is proved in [6, Article 2]. The twist is that, instead of interactive algorithms, we speak about their components there.

Patient (but possibly time sensitive) interactive algorithms as well as time insensitive (but possibly impatient) interactive algorithms are characterized in [6, Article 3].

These variants of the interactive characterization theorem as well as the theorem itself are about small-step algorithms. The interactive characterization theorem is generalized to wide-step algorithms in [6, Article 4].

7 Perspective

The behavioral theory of small-isolated-step algorithms [13] was an after-the-fact explanation of what those algorithms were. Small-isolated-step algorithms had been studied for a long time.

The behavioral theory of wide-isolated-step algorithms was developed in [3]. Wide-isolated-step algorithms had been studied primarily in computational complexity where a number of wide-isolated-step computation models had been known. But the class of wide-isolated-step algorithms of [3] is wider. The theory was used to develop a number of tools [1], most notably the specification language AsmL [2]. Because of the practical considerations of industrial environment, intrastep interaction plays a considerable role in AsmL. That helped us to realize the importance and indeed inevitability of intrastep interaction.

The behavioral theory of intrastep interactive algorithms is developed in [5, 6]. While intrastep interaction is ubiquitous, it has been studied very little if at all. We hope that the research described above will put intrastep interaction on the map and will give rise to further advances in specification and high-level programming of interactive algorithms.

Appendix: What Is Interaction Anyway?

The main part of this article presented our approach to interactive computing. There is another approach to interactive computing pioneered by Peter

Wegner [21, 20], developed in particular in article [9], and presented in this volume by Dina Goldin and Peter Wegner [10]. The editors of this volume suggested that a comparison of the two approaches would be useful; hence this appendix. The appendix refers to the main part of this article but can be read independently. The version of article [10] available to us when this appendix is being written (the first part of December 2005) does not have references to the ASM approach.

What is an Algorithm?

The two schools use the term algorithm differently. The Wegner school uses the term algorithm in the classical sense of Turing's article [19]. This is perfectly legitimate. But Turing explicated the notion of string-to-string computable function rather than the notion of algorithm. Even in Turing's time, the term algorihm had a wider meaning; recall the Gauss elimination procedure or geometric compass-and-ruler constructions. And the meaning of the term algorithm in computer science has been expanding. People speak of parallel and distributed algorithms; see [16, 17] for example. Our usage of the term algorithm is the convergence point for that expansion. For us, an algorithm is a (real or imaginable, physical or abstract) computer system at an abstraction level where its behavior—possibly interactive, possibly parallel, etc.—is given or can be given by a program. We devoted much attention to explicating the notion of algorithm [4].

Can an Algorithm be Interactive?

Our answer to the title question is positive of course. The title "Why Interaction is More Powerful than Algorithms" of [21] may suggest the opposite. Wegner's school speaks about interactive computing but not about interactive algorithms. Taking into account the philosophical character of article [10], we note that the discrepancy is terminological, not philosophical. The term interactive algorithm is used in the rest of this appendix.

Note 1 Even classical Turing machines are somewhat interactive because it is the environment that provides the input and presumably consumes the ouput. Nondeterministic Turing machines, which seem to be accepted as algorithms by the Wegner school [9], need additional interaction to resolve nondeterministic choices; see Sect. 4.3 above in this connection.   □

We distinguish between two kinds of interaction of an algorithm with the environment. One kind is *interstep* interaction, when the environment modifies the state of the algorithm (to a legitimate state) before, after, or between the steps of the algorithm. The other kind is *intrastep* interaction that takes place during a step. An algorithm that is not intrastep interactive is an *isolated-step* algorithm. Abstract state machines have been intrastep interactive (by means of external functions) from the beginning [11].

Two Distinct Theses

Can one capture the behavior of interactive algorithms in the same way that Church and Turing captured the computability of string-to-string functions? Both, the ASM school and the Wegner school, attempt to meet the challenge. Article [9] defines persistent Turing machines (PTMs). A PTM is a non-deterministic Turing machine with three one-way-infinite tapes: a read-only input tape, a read/write work tape, and a write-only output tape. PTMs are interstep interactive in the following sense. The computation of a PTM splits into macrosteps, and the environment intervenes between the macrosteps. The environment

- puts a new input on the input tape and resets the input-tape head to the initial position,
- removes the output from the output tape and resets the output-tape head to the initial position,
- but leaves the work tape intact (that is the persistent aspect of PTMs).

Article [10] asserts that "any sequential interactive computation can be performed by a persistent Turing machine."

We put forward a similar thesis where the role of persistent Turing machines is played by interactive abstract state machines (interactive ASMs); see the main part of this article. Either thesis is meaningful but they are not equivalent. Interactive ASMs are more powerful and more interactive than PTMs.

Interactive ASMs Faithfully Simulate PTMs

A simulation of an interactive algorithm A by an interactive algorithm B is *faithful* if B can replace A in every legal enviroment of A. In other words, every legal enviroment **E** of A is a legal enviroment of B, and the interactive behavior of B in **E** coincides with that of A. In the case of PTMs, interactive behaviors are defined as interactive streams [9]. An interactive stream is essentially the first input followed by the first output, followed by the second input, and so on.

Claim 1 *For every PTM P, there is an interactive ASM A that faithfully simulates P.*

Proof. Employ bounded-choice ASMs of [13, Sect. 9.2]. Bounded choice gives the necessary nondeterminism, and interactive runs [13, Sect. 8.2] provide the necessary intermacrostep interaction. The simulation is step-for-step (that is microstep for microstep) and preserves the interaction stream.   □

Alternatively we can employ the *ordinary* ASMs of [5] that don't have the bounded-choice construct and do not need interstep interaction. Instead two external functions are used, one to resolve nondeterminism, and another to access input. Again the simulation is step for step and preserves the interaction stream.

PTMs Cannot Faithfully Simulate Interactive ASMs

Claim 2 *There is a sequential ASM A_1 such that (i) A_1 is noninteractive (except that the environment provides input and consumes output) and (ii) there is no PTM with the same input/output behavior.*

Proof Sketch. We exploit the higher abstraction level of ASMs. For example, the desired A_1 may express the Euclidean algorithm that works with any Euclidean domain. A_1 has a variety of initial states. One initial state of A_1 could include the ring of integers and two distinguished integers (whose greatest common divisor A_1 is supposed to find), and another initial state of A_1 could include the ring of polynomials over some field K and two distinguished polynomials. □

But let's concentrate on interaction. In most cases, a legal environment **E** of an interactive ASM A is not a legal environment of any PTM B. The messages that **E** sends to A are illegible to B. Even if there is a canonic translation of messages to input string, somebody should do that translation work. In other words, B requires a more hardworking environment. We will return to this issue in Note 2 below.

Besides, the interactive behaviors of ASMs [6, Article 1] are more complicated than PTM interaction streams. Here is a simple example. Consider an interactive ASM

```
do in parallel
    if α ≺ β then x := 1
    if β ⪯ α then x := 2
```

Call it A_2. It makes only one step. It issues two queries α and β but cares only about the reply times; otherwise it does not care about the returned values (so that there is no problem of transforming those values to PTM input). The symbols $\prec$ and $\preceq$ compare the times when the answers are returned. If α is answered before β then β is ignored and x gets 1; it will make no difference whether β is eventually answered or not. If β is answered before or simultaneously with α then x gets 2 (and α is ignored in case β is answered earlier). In our terms, this ASM is time (that is message arrival time) sensitive. Time sensitivity is important in applications. See the automated broker example in Sect. 6 above in this connection.

An appropriate PTM can simulate A_2 in two macrosteps. It writes the two queries on the output tape and then examines the input provided by the environment. But this simulation is not faithful. No PTM B can faithfully simulate A_2. Consider an environment that provides A_2 with one or two answers. A_2 realizes immediately how many replies are there, and, in the case of single reply, what query is this reply to. In order for a PTM to understand this information, it should be transformed into a PTM input, and somebody should do the transformation job.

Note 2 Classical Turing machines suffer from a similar limitation. Consider a noninteractive algorithm A that takes graphs as inputs. No Turing machine can simulate A directly. Somebody has to transform the input graph into a string. Interaction exacerbates the problem for PTMs. Consider an interactive algorithm A and a PTM that is supposed to simulate A. Not only inputs should be coded and outputs decoded, but also every message sent to A should in general be coded and every information sent by A should in general be decoded. In addition, as we have seen in the example above, there may be need to code some information related to the arrival times of various messages.   □

Thesis Justification

In [4], we mentioned how differently Church and Turing arrived at their respective theses. Church made a good guess, but Turing convincingly argued his thesis. In particular, Gödel was not convinced by Church's guess but was convinced by Turing's analysis. Inspired by Turing's analysis, we have been trying hard to justify the interactive ASM thesis from first principles; see the main part of this article. It would be interesting to see a justification of the PTM thesis from first principles.

Of course nothing can replace experimental evidence for a thesis, but we will not address that issue here.

Acknowledgment This appendix benefited from discussions with Andreas Blass and Satya Lokam.

References

1. ASM Michigan webpage, http://www.eecs.umich.edu/gasm/, maintained by J. K. Huggins.
2. The AsmL webpage, http://research.microsoft.com/foundations/AsmL/.
3. A. Blass and Y. Gurevich. "Abstract State Machines Capture Parallel Algorithms," *ACM Trans. on Computational Logic*, 4:4, 2003, pp. 578–651.
4. A. Blass and Y. Gurevich. "Algorithms: A Quest for Absolute Definitions," Bull. Euro. Assoc. for Theor. Computer Science Number 81, October 2003, pp. 195–225. Reprinted in *Current Trends in Theoretical Computer Science: The Challenge of the New Century*, Vol. 2, eds. G. Paun et al., World Scientific, 2004, pp. 283–312.
5. A. Blass and Y. Gurevich. "Ordinary Interactive Small-Step Algorithms", parts I, II, III, *ACM Trans. on Computational Logic*, to appear. Microsoft Research Technical Reports MSR-TR-2004-16 and MSR-TR-2004-88.
6. A. Blass, Y. Gurevich, D. Rosenzweig and B. Rossman. Four articles on interactive algorithms, in preparation. Article 1: "General Interactive Small-Step Algorithms". Article 2: "Composite Interactive Algorithms". Article 3: "Interactive Algorithms: Impatience and Time Sensitivity". Article 4: "Interactive Wide-Step Algorithms". The last three titles are tentative.

7. E. Börger and R. Stärk. "Abstract State Machines: A Method for High-Level System Design and Analysis", Springer-Verlag, 2003.

8. T. H. Cormen, C. E. Leiserson and R. L. Rivest. "Introduction to Algorithms" MIT Press, 1990.

9. D. Q. Goldin, S. A. Smolka, P. C. Attie, E. L. Sonderegger. "Turing Machines, Transition Systems, and Interaction", *Information and Computation* 194:2, 2004, pp. 101–128.

10. D. Q. Goldin and P. Wegner. "Principles of Interactive Computation", this volume.

11. Y. Gurevich. "Evolving Algebras: An Introductory Tutorial", Bull. Euro. Assoc. for Theor. Computer Science 43, February 1991, pp. 264–284. A slightly revised version is published in *Current Trends in Theoretical Computer Science*, eds. G. Rozenberg and A. Salomaa, World Scientific, 1993, pp. 266–292.

12. Y. Gurevich. "Evolving Algebra 1993: Lipari Guide," in *Specification and Validation Methods*, ed. E. Börger, Oxford University Press, 1995, pp. 9–36.

13. Y. Gurevich. "Sequential Abstract State Machines Capture Sequential Algorithms," *ACM Trans. on Computational Logic* 1:1, 2000, pp. 77–111.

14. Y. Gurevich. "Interactive Algorithms 2005", Proceedings of the 2005 conference on Mathematical Foundations of Computer Science, Springer Lecture Notes in Computer Science 3618, 2005, pp. 26–38, eds. J. Jedrzejowicz and A. Szepietowski.

15. A. N. Kolmogorov. "On the Concept of Algorithm", *Uspekhi Mat. Nauk* 8:4, 1953, pp. 175–176, Russian.

16. F. T. Leighton. "Introduction to Parallel Algorithms and Architectures; Arrays, Trees, Hypercubes", MIT Press, 1992.

17. N. A. Lynch. "Distributed Algorithms", Morgan Kaufmann Publishers, 1996.

18. A. A. Markov. "Theory of Algorithms", Transactions of the Steklov Institute of Mathematics, vol. 42, 1954, Russian. Translated to English by the Israel Program for Scientific Translations, Jerusalem, 1962.

19. A. M. Turing. "On Computable Numbers, with an Application to the Entscheidungsproblem", *Proceedings of London Mathematical Society*, series 2, vol. 42, 1936, pp. 230–265; correction, *ibidem*, vol. 43, pp. 544–546.

20. P. Wegner. "Interactive Foundation of Computing", *Theoretical Computer Science* 192, 1998, pp. 315–351.

21. P. Wegner. "Why Interaction is More Powerful than Algorithms", *Communications of ACM*, May 1997, pp. 81–91.

Computability Logic: A Formal Theory of Interaction*

Giorgi Japaridze

Villanova University, Villanova, PA, USA

Summary. Generalizing the traditional concepts of predicates and their truth to interactive computational problems and their effective solvability, computability logic conservatively extends classical logic to a formal theory that provides a systematic answer to the question of what and how can be computed, just as traditional logic is a systematic tool for telling what is true. The present chapter contains a comprehensive yet relatively compact overview of this very recently introduced framework and research program. It is written in a semitutorial style with general computer science, logic and mathematics audiences in mind.

1 Introduction

In the same sense as classical logic is a formal theory of truth, the recently initiated approach called *computability logic* (CL) is a formal theory of computability—in particular, a theory of interactive computability. It understands computational problems as games played by a machine against the environment, their computability as existence of a machine that always wins the game, logical operators as operations on computational problems, and validity of a logical formula as being a scheme of "always computable" problems. The paradigm shift in computer science towards interaction provides a solid motivational background for CL. In turn, the whole experience of developing CL presents additional strong evidence in favor of the new paradigm. It reveals that the degree of abstraction required at the level of logical analysis makes it imperative to understand computability in its most general—interactive—sense: the traditional, noninteractive concept of computability appears to be too narrow, and its scope delimitation not natural enough, to induce any meaningful logic.

Currently computability logic is at its very first stages of development, with open problems and unverified conjectures prevailing over answered questions.

* This material is based upon work supported by the National Science Foundation under Grant No. 0208816

A fundamental, 99-page-long introduction to the subject has been given in [6]. The present chapter reintroduces CL in a more compact and less technical way, being written in a semitutorial style with a wider computer science audience in mind.

The traditional Church–Turing approach to computational problems assumes a simple interface between a computing agent and its environment, consisting in asking a question (input) and generating an answer (output). Such an understanding, however, only captures a modest fraction of our broader intuition of computational problems. This has been not only repeatedly pointed out by the editors and authors of the present collection [4, 5, 6, 8, 12, 16] but, in fact, acknowledged by Turing [15] himself. The reality is that most tasks that computers perform are interactive, where not only the computing system but also its environment remain active throughout a computation, with the two parties communicating with each other through what is often referred to as *observable actions* [12, 16]. Calling sequences of observable actions *interaction histories*, a computational problem in a broader sense can then be understood as a pair comprising a set of all "possible" interaction histories and a subset of it of all "successful" interaction histories; and the computing agent considered to be solving such a problem if it ensures that the actual interaction history is always among the successful ones.

As was mentioned, technically CL understands interactive problems as *games*, or *dialogues*, between two agents/players: *machine* and *environment*, symbolically named as $\top$ and $\bot$, respectively. Machine, as its name suggests, is specified as a mechanical device with fully determined, effective behavior, while the behavior of the environment, which represents a capricious user or the blind forces of nature, is allowed to be arbitrary. Observable actions by these two agents translate into game-theoretic terms as their *moves*, interaction histories as *runs*, i.e., sequences of moves, "possible" interaction histories as *legal runs*, and "successful" interaction histories as *won* (by $\top$) *runs*.

Computational problems in the Church–Turing sense are nothing but dialogues/games of depth 2, with the first legal move ("input") by the environment and the second legal move ("output") by the machine. The problem of finding the value of a function f is a typical task modeled by this sort of games. In the formalism of CL this problem is expressed by the formula

$$\sqcap x \sqcup y \big(y = f(x)\big).$$

It stands for a two-move-deep game where the first move—selecting a particular value m for x—must be made by $\bot$, and the second move—selecting a value n for y—by $\top$. The game is then considered won by the machine, i.e., the problem solved, if n really equals $f(m)$. So, computability of f means nothing but existence of a machine that wins the game $\sqcap x \sqcup y \big(y = f(x)\big)$ against any possible (behavior of the) environment.

Generally, $\sqcap x A(x)$ is a game where the environment has to make the first move by selecting a particular value m for x, after which the play continues—and the winner is determined—according to the rules of $A(m)$; if $\bot$ fails to make an initial move, the game is considered won by the machine as there was no particular (sub)problem specified by its adversary that it failed to solve. $\sqcup x A(x)$ is defined in the same way, only here it is the machine who makes an initial move/choice and it is the environment who is considered the winner if such a choice is never made. This interpretation makes $\sqcup$ a constructive version of existential quantifier, while $\sqcap$ is a constructive version of universal quantifier.

As for standard atomic formulas, such as $n = f(m)$, they are understood as games without any moves. This sort of games are called *elementary*. An elementary game is automatically won or lost by the machine depending on whether the formula representing it is true or false (true = won, false = lost). This interpretation makes the classical concept of predicates a special case of games.

The meanings of the propositional counterparts $\sqcup$ and $\sqcap$ of $\sqcup$ and $\sqcap$ are not hard to guess. They, too, signify a choice by the corresponding player. The only difference is that while in the case of $\sqcup$ and $\sqcap$ the choice is made among the objects of the universe of discourse, $\sqcup$ and $\sqcap$ mean a choice between *left* and *right*. For example, the problem of deciding predicate $P(x)$ could be expressed by $\sqcap x\big(P(x) \sqcup \neg P(x)\big)$, denoting the game where the environment has to select a value m for x, to which the machine should reply by one of the moves *left* or *right*; the game will be considered won by the machine if $P(m)$ is true and the move *left* was made or $P(m)$ is false and the choice was *right*, so that decidability of $P(x)$ means nothing but existence of a machine that always wins the game $\sqcap x\big(P(x) \sqcup \neg P(x)\big)$.

The above example involved classical negation $\neg$. The other classical operators will also be allowed in our language, and they all acquire a new, natural game interpretation. The reason why we can still call them "classical" is that, when applied to elementary games—i.e., predicates—they preserve the elementary property of their arguments and act exactly in the classical way. Here is an informal explanation of how the "classical" operators are understood as game operations:

The game $\neg A$ is nothing but A with the roles of the two players switched: $\top$'s moves or wins become $\bot$'s moves or wins, and vice versa. For example, where *Chess* is the game of chess (with the possibility of draw outcomes ruled out for simplicity) from the point of view of the white player, $\neg Chess$ is the same game from the point of view of the black player.

The operations $\wedge$ and $\vee$ combine games in a way that corresponds to the intuition of parallel computations. Playing $A \wedge B$ or $A \vee B$ means playing the two games A and B simultaneously. In $A \wedge B$ the machine is considered the winner if it wins in both of the components, while in $A \vee B$ it is sufficient to win in one of the components. Thus we have two sorts of conjunction: $\sqcap$, $\wedge$ and two sorts of disjunction: $\sqcup$, $\vee$. Comparing the games *Chess* $\vee \neg$*Chess* and *Chess* $\sqcup \neg$*Chess* will help us appreciate the difference. The former is, in fact, a parallel play on two boards, where $\top$ plays white on the left board and black on the right board. There is a strategy for $\top$ that guarantees an easy success in this game even if the adversary is a world champion. All that $\top$ needs to do is to mimic, in *Chess*, the moves made by $\bot$ in $\neg Chess$, and vice versa. On the other hand, winning the game *Chess* $\sqcup \neg Chess$ is not easy at all: here, at the very beginning, $\top$ has to choose between *Chess* and $\neg Chess$ and then win the chosen one-board game. Generally, the principle $A \vee \neg A$ is valid in the sense that the corresponding problem is always solvable by a machine, whereas this is not so for $A \sqcup \neg A$.

While all the classical tautologies automatically hold when classical operators are applied to elementary games, in the general case the class of valid principles shrinks. For example, $\neg A \vee (A \wedge A)$ is not valid. The above "mimicking strategy" would obviously be inapplicable in the three-board game $\neg Chess \vee (Chess \wedge Chess)$: the best that $\top$ can do here is to pair $\neg Chess$ with one of the two conjuncts of $Chess \wedge Chess$. It is possible that then $\neg Chess$ and the unmatched *Chess* are both lost, in which case the whole game will be lost.

The class of valid principles of computability forms a logic that resembles linear logic [3] with $\neg$ understood as linear negation, $\wedge, \vee$ as multiplicatives and $\sqcap, \sqcup, \bigsqcap, \bigsqcup$ as additives. It however should be pointed out that, despite similarity, these computability-logic operations are by no means "the same" as those of linear logic (see Sect. 7). To stress the difference and avoid possible confusion, we refrain from using any linear-logic terminology, calling $\sqcap, \sqcup, \bigsqcap, \bigsqcup$ *choice operations* and $\wedge, \vee$ *parallel operations*.

Assuming that the universe of discourse is $\{1, 2, 3, \ldots\}$, obviously the meanings of $\bigsqcap x A(x)$ and $\bigsqcup x A(x)$ can be explained as $A(1) \sqcap A(2) \sqcap A(3) \sqcap \ldots$ and $A(1) \sqcup A(2) \sqcup A(3) \sqcup \ldots$, respectively. Similarly, our parallel operations $\wedge$ and $\vee$ have their natural quantifier-level counterparts $\bigwedge$ and $\bigvee$, with $\bigwedge x A(x)$ understood as $A(1) \wedge A(2) \wedge A(3) \wedge \ldots$ and $\bigvee x A(x)$ as $A(1) \vee A(2) \vee A(3) \vee \ldots$. Hence, just like $\wedge$ and $\vee$, the operations $\bigwedge$ and $\bigvee$ are "classical" in the sense that, when applied to elementary games, they behave exactly as the classical universal and existential quantifiers, respectively.

The *parallel implication* $\rightarrow$, yet another "classical" operation, is perhaps most interesting from the computability-theoretic point of view. Formally $A \rightarrow B$ is defined as $\neg A \vee B$. The intuitive meaning of $A \rightarrow B$ is the problem of *reducing* problem B to problem A. Putting it in other words, solving $A \rightarrow B$ means solving B having A as an (external) *resource*. "Resource" is symmetric to "problem": what is a problem (task) for the machine, is a resource for the environment, and vice versa. To get a feel of $\rightarrow$ as a problem reduction operator, consider the reduction of the acceptance problem to the halting problem. The halting problem can be expressed by

$$\bigsqcap x \bigsqcap y \big(Halts(x, y) \sqcup \neg Halts(x, y) \big),$$

where $Halts(x, y)$ is the predicate "Turing machine x halts on input y". And the acceptance problem can be expressed by

$$\bigsqcap x \bigsqcap y \big(Accepts(x, y) \sqcup \neg Accepts(x, y) \big),$$

with $Accepts(x, y)$ meaning "Turing machine x accepts input y". While the acceptance problem is not decidable, it is effectively reducible to the halting problem. In particular, there is a machine that always wins the game

$$\sqcap x \sqcap y \big(Halts(x,y) \sqcup \neg Halts(x,y)\big) \rightarrow \sqcap x \sqcap y \big(Accepts(x,y) \sqcup \neg Accepts(x,y)\big).$$

A strategy for solving this problem is to wait till $\perp$ specifies values m and n for x and y in the consequent, then select the same values m and n for x and y in the antecedent (where the roles of $\top$ and $\perp$ are switched), and see whether $\perp$ responds by *left* or *right* there. If the response is *left*, simulate machine m on input n until it halts and then select, in the consequent, *left* or *right* depending on whether the simulation accepted or rejected. And if $\perp$'s response in the antecedent was *right*, then select *right* in the consequent.

What the machine did in the above strategy was indeed a reduction of the acceptance problem to the halting problem: it solved the former by employing an external, environment-provided solution to the latter. A strong case can be made in favor of the thesis that $\rightarrow$ captures our ultimate intuition of reducing one interactive problem to another. It should be noted, however, that the reduction captured by $\rightarrow$ is stronger than Turing reduction, which is often perceived as an adequate formalization of our most general intuition of reduction. Indeed, if we talk in terms of oracles that the definition of Turing reduction employs, specifying the values of x and y as m and n in the antecedent can be thought of as asking the oracle whether machine m halts on input n. Notice, however, that the usage of the oracle here is limited as it can only be employed once: after querying regarding m and n, the machine would not be able to repeat the same query with different parameters m' and n', for that would require having two "copies" of the resource $\sqcap x \sqcap y \big(Halts(x,y) \sqcup \neg Halts(x,y)\big)$ (which could be expressed by their $\wedge$-conjunction) rather than one. On the other hand, Turing reduction allows recurring usage of the oracle, which the resource-conscious CL understands as reduction not to the halting problem $\sqcap x \sqcap y \big(Halts(x,y) \sqcup \neg Halts(x,y)\big)$ but to the stronger problem expressed by $\lambda \sqcap x \sqcap y \big(Halts(x,y) \sqcup \neg Halts(x,y)\big)$. Here λA, called the *parallel recurrence* of A, means the infinite conjunction $A \wedge A \wedge \ldots$. The λ-prefixed halting problem now explicitly allows an unbounded number of queries of the type "does m halt on n?". So, Turing reducibility of B to A, which, of course, is only defined when A and B are computational problems in the traditional sense, i.e., problems of the type $\sqcap x \big(Predicate(x) \sqcup \neg Predicate(x)\big)$ or $\sqcap x \sqcup y Predicate(x,y)$, means computability of $\lambda A \rightarrow B$ rather than of $A \rightarrow B$, i.e., reducibility of B to λA rather than to A. To put this intuition together, consider the Kolmogorov complexity problem. It can be expressed by $\sqcap t \sqcup z\, K(z,t)$, where $K(z,t)$ is the predicate "z is the smallest (code of a) Turing machine that returns t on input 1". Having no algorithmic solution, the Kolmogorov complexity problem, however, is known to be Turing reducible to the halting problem. In our terms, this means nothing but that there is a machine that always wins the game

$$\lambda \sqcap x \sqcap y \big(Halts(x,y) \sqcup \neg Halts(x,y)\big) \quad \rightarrow \quad \sqcap t \sqcup z\, K(z,t). \tag{1}$$

Here is a strategy for such a machine: Wait till $\perp$ selects a value m for t in the consequent. Then, starting from $i = 1$, do the following: in the ith $\wedge$-conjunct of the antecedent, make two consecutive moves by specifying x and y as i and 1, respectively. If $\perp$ responds there by *right*, increment i by one and repeat the step; if $\perp$ responds by *left*, simulate machine i on input 1 until it halts; if you see that machine i returned m, make a move in the consequent by specifying z as i; otherwise, increment i by one and repeat the step.

One can show that Turing reduction of the Kolmogorov complexity problem to the halting problem essentially requires unlimited usage of the oracle, which means that, unlike the acceptance problem, the Kolmogorov complexity problem is not reducible to the halting problem in our sense, and is only reducible to the parallel recurrence of it. That is, (1) is computable but not with λ removed from the antecedent. One might expect that $\lambda A \rightarrow B$ captures the intuition of reducing an interactive problem B to an interactive problem A in the *weakest* sense, as Turing reduction certainly does for noninteractive problems. But this is not so. While having λA in the antecedent, i.e., having it as a resource, indeed allows an agent to reuse A as many times as it wishes, there is a stronger—in fact the strongest—form of reusage, captured by another operation $\flat$ called *branching recurrence*. Both λA and $\flat A$ can be thought of as games where $\perp$ can restart A as many times as it likes. The difference is that in $\flat A$, unlike λA, A can be restarted not only from the very beginning, but from any already reached state/position. This gives $\perp$ greater flexibility, such as, say, the capability to try different answers to the same (counter)question by $\top$, while this could be impossible in λA because $\top$ may have asked different questions in different conjuncts of λA. Section 2 will explain the differences between λ and $\flat$ in more detail. Our claim that $\flat$ captures the strongest sort of resource-reusage automatically translates into another claim, according to which $\flat A \rightarrow B$ captures the weakest possible sort of reduction of one interactive problem to another. The difference between $\flat$ and λ is irrelevant when they are applied to two-step "traditional" problems such as the halting problem or the Kolmogorov complexity problem: for such a "traditional" problem A, λA and $\flat A$ turn out to be logically equivalent, and hence both $\lambda A \rightarrow B$ and $\flat A \rightarrow B$ are equally accurate translations for Turing reduction of B to A. The equivalence between $\flat$ and λ, however, certainly does not extend to the general case. For example, the principle $\flat(A \sqcup B) \rightarrow \flat A \sqcup \flat B$ is valid while $\lambda(A \sqcup B) \rightarrow \lambda A \sqcup \lambda B$ is not. Among the so far unverified conjectures of CL is that the logical behavior of $\flat A \rightarrow B$ is exactly that of the implication $A \circ\!\!-\, B$ of (Heyting's) intuitionistic logic.

Another group of operations that play an important role in CL comprises $\forall$ and its dual $\exists$ (with $\exists x A(x) = \neg \forall x \neg A(x)$), called *blind quantifiers*. $\forall x A(x)$ can be thought of as a "version" of $\sqcap x A(x)$ where the particular value of x that the environment selects is invisible to the machine, so that it has to play blindly in a way that guarantees success no matter what that value is. This way, $\forall$ and $\exists$ produce games with *imperfect information*.

Compare the problems $\sqcap x (Even(x) \sqcup Odd(x))$ and $\forall x (Even(x) \sqcup Odd(x))$. Both of them are about telling whether a given number is even or odd; the difference is only in whether that "given number" is known to the machine or not. The first problem is an easy-to-win, two-move-deep game of a structure that we have already seen. The second game, on the other hand, is one-move deep with only by the machine to make a move—select the "true" disjunct, which is hardly possible to do as the value of x remains unspecified.

Of course, not all nonelementary $\forall$-problems will be unsolvable. Here is an example:

$$\forall x \Big(Even(x) \sqcup Odd(x) \; \rightarrow \; \sqcap y \big(Even(x \times y) \sqcup Odd(x \times y) \big) \Big).$$

Solving this problem, which means reducing the consequent to the antecedent without knowing the value of x, is easy: $\top$ waits till $\bot$ selects a value n for y. If n is even, then $\top$ makes the move *left* in the consequent. Otherwise, if n is odd, $\top$ continues waiting until $\bot$ selects one of the $\sqcup$-disjuncts in the antecedent (if $\bot$ has not already done so), and then $\top$ makes the same move *left* or *right* in the consequent as $\bot$ made in the antecedent. Note that our semantics for $\sqcap, \sqcup, \rightarrow$ guarantees an automatic win for $\top$ if $\bot$ fails to make either selection.

Both $\forall x A(x)$ and $\wedge x A(x)$ can be shown to be properly stronger than $\sqcap x A(x)$, in the sense that $\forall x A(x) \rightarrow \sqcap x A(x)$ and $\wedge x A(x) \rightarrow \sqcap x A(x)$ are valid while $\sqcap x A(x) \rightarrow \forall x A(x)$ and $\sqcap x A(x) \rightarrow \wedge x A(x)$ are not. On the other hand, the strengths of $\forall x A(x)$ and $\wedge x A(x)$ are mutually incomparable: neither $\forall x A(x) \rightarrow \wedge x A(x)$ nor $\wedge x A(x) \rightarrow \forall x A(x)$ is valid. The big difference between $\forall$ and $\wedge$ is that, while playing $\forall x A(x)$ means playing one "common" play for all possible $A(c)$ and thus $\forall x A(x)$ is a one-board game, $\wedge x A(x)$ is an infinitely-many-board game: playing it means playing, in parallel, game $A(1)$ on board #1, game $A(2)$ on board #2, etc. When restricted to elementary games, however, the distinction between the blind and the parallel groups of quantifiers disappears and, just like $\neg, \wedge, \vee, \rightarrow, \wedge, \vee$, the blind quantifiers behave exactly in the classical way. Having this collection of operators makes CL a conservative extension of classical first-order logic: the latter is nothing but CL restricted to elementary problems and the logical vocabulary $\neg, \wedge, \vee, \rightarrow, \forall$ (and/or $\wedge$), $\exists$ (and/or $\vee$).

As the above examples illustrate, what can be considered an adequate formal equivalent of our broad intuition of computational problems goes far beyond the traditional, two-step, input/output problems. Computational problems of higher degrees of interactivity emerge naturally and have to be addressed in any more or less advanced study in computability theory. So far this has been mostly done in an ad hoc manner as there has been no standard way for specifying interactive problems. The formalism of CL offers a convenient language for expressing interactive computational problems and studying them in a systematic way. Finding effective axiomatizations of the corresponding logic or, at least, some reasonably rich fragments of it, is expected to have not only theoretical, but also high practical significance. Among the applications would be the possibility to build CL into a machine and then use such a machine as a universal problem-solving tool.

Outlining the rest of this chapter: Sections 2–4 provide formal definitions—accompanied with explanations and illustrations—of the basic concepts on interactive computational problems understood as games, including the main operations on such problems/games. Section 5 introduces a model of interactive computation that generalizes Turing machines and, allowing us to extend the Church–Turing thesis to interaction, serves as a basis for our definition of interactive computability. Sections 6 and 7 present sound and complete axiomatizations of various fragments of CL. Section 8 discusses, using ample examples and illustrations, potential applications of CL in the areas of (interactive) knowledgebase systems, planning systems and constructive applied theories.

2 Constant Games

Our ultimate concept of games will be defined in the next section in terms of the simpler and more basic class of games called constant games. To define this class, we need some technical terms and conventions. Let us agree that by a **move** we mean any finite string over the standard keyboard alphabet. A **labeled move** is a move prefixed with $\top$ or $\bot$, with its prefix (**label**) indicating which player has made the move. A **run** is a (finite or infinite) sequence of labeled moves, and a **position** is a finite run.

We will be exclusively using letters Γ, Υ as metavariables for runs, Φ, Ψ for positions, $\wp$ for players, and α for moves. Runs will be often delimited with "$\langle$" and "$\rangle$", with $\langle\rangle$ thus denoting the **empty run**. The meaning of an expression such as $\langle\Phi, \wp\alpha, \Gamma\rangle$ must be clear: this is the result of appending to $\langle\Phi\rangle$ $\langle\wp\alpha\rangle$ and then $\langle\Gamma\rangle$.

Definition 1. A **constant game** *is a pair* $A = (\mathbf{Lr}^A, \mathbf{Wn}^A)$, *where:*

1. $\mathbf{Lr}^A$ *is a set of runs satisfying the condition[1] that a (finite or infinite) run* Γ *is in* $\mathbf{Lr}^A$ *iff all of its nonempty finite initial segments are in* $\mathbf{Lr}^A$.

2. $\mathbf{Wn}^A$ *is a function of the type* $\mathbf{Lr}^A \to \{\top, \bot\}$. *We use* $\mathbf{Wn}^A\langle\Gamma\rangle$ *to denote the value of* $\mathbf{Wn}^A$ *at* Γ.

The intuitive meaning of the $\mathbf{Lr}^A$ component of a constant game A, called the **structure of** A, is that it tells us what runs are legal. Correspondingly, we call the elements of $\mathbf{Lr}^A$ the **legal runs** of A, and call all other runs **illegal**. For a player $\wp$, a run Γ is said to be a $\wp$-**legal** run of A iff either Γ is a legal

---

[1] [6] imposes an additional condition according to which there is a special move that no element of $\mathbf{Lr}^A$ contains. The only result of [6] that appeals to that condition is Lemma 4.7. In the present exposition we directly incorporate the statement of that lemma into the definition of static games (page 201), and thus all results of [6]—in particular, those that rely on Lemma 4.7—remain valid. This and a couple of other minor technical differences between our present formulations from those given in [6] only signify presentational and by no means conceptual variations.

run of A or otherwise the label of the last move of the shortest illegal initial segment of Γ is not $\wp$. Understanding an *illegal move* by player $\wp$ in position Φ as a move α such that adding $\wp\alpha$ to Φ makes this position illegal, the condition of clause 1 of Definition 1 corresponds to the intuition that a run is legal iff no illegal moves have been made in it, which automatically implies that the empty position $\langle\rangle$ is a legal run of every game. And a $\wp$-legal run of A is a run where $\wp$ has not made any illegal moves in any of the legal positions—in other words, a run where, if there are illegal moves at all, $\wp$ is not the first to have made such a move. When modeling real-life interactive tasks, such as server-client or robot-environment interaction, illegal moves will usually mean actions that can, will or should never be performed. For generality, flexibility and convenience, our approach however does not formally exclude illegal runs from considerations.

As for the $\mathbf{Wn}^A$ component of a constant game A, called the **content** of the game, it tells us who has won a given legal run. A run $\Gamma \in \mathbf{Lr}^A$ with $\mathbf{Wn}^A\langle\Gamma\rangle = \wp$ will be said to be a $\wp$-**won** run of A.

We say that a constant game A is **elementary** iff $\mathbf{Lr}^A = \{\langle\rangle\}$. Thus, elementary games have no legal moves: the empty run $\langle\rangle$ is the only legal run of such games. There are exactly two elementary constant games, for which we use the same symbols $\top$ and $\bot$ as for the two players. They are defined by stipulating that $(\mathbf{Lr}^\top = \mathbf{Lr}^\bot = \{\langle\rangle\}$ and) $\mathbf{Wn}^\top\langle\rangle = \top$, $\mathbf{Wn}^\bot\langle\rangle = \bot$. Below comes an official definition of some of the basic game operations informally explained in Section 1.

Definition 2. *In each of the following clauses, Φ ranges over nonempty positions—in view of Definition 1, it would be sufficient to define $\mathbf{Lr}$ only for this sort of Φ, for then $\mathbf{Lr}$ uniquely extends to all runs. Γ ranges over the legal runs of the game that is being defined. A, A_1, A_2 are any constant games. The notation $\bar{\Phi}$ in clause 1 means the result of interchanging $\top$ with $\bot$ in all labeled moves of Φ. And the notation $\Phi^{i\cdot}$ in clauses 2 and 3 means the result of removing from Φ all labeled moves except those of the form $\wp i.\alpha$ ($\wp \in \{\top, \bot\}$), and then deleting the prefix "$i.$" in the remaining moves, i.e., replacing each such $\wp i.\alpha$ by $\wp\alpha$. Similarly for $\bar{\Gamma}$, $\Gamma^{i\cdot}$.*

1. **Negation** $\neg A$:
   - $\Phi \in \mathbf{Lr}^{\neg A}$ *iff* $\bar{\Phi} \in \mathbf{Lr}^A$;
   - $\mathbf{Wn}^{\neg A}\langle\Gamma\rangle = \top$ *iff* $\mathbf{Wn}^A\langle\bar{\Gamma}\rangle = \bot$.
2. **Parallel conjunction** $A_1 \wedge A_2$:
   - $\Phi \in \mathbf{Lr}^{A_1 \wedge A_2}$ *iff every move of Φ starts with "1." or "2." and, for each* $i \in \{1,2\}$, $\Phi^{i\cdot} \in \mathbf{Lr}^{A_i}$;
   - $\mathbf{Wn}^{A_1 \wedge A_2}\langle\Gamma\rangle = \top$ *iff, for each $i \in \{1,2\}$,* $\mathbf{Wn}^{A_i}\langle\Gamma^{i\cdot}\rangle = \top$.
3. **Parallel disjunction** $A_1 \vee A_2$:
   - $\Phi \in \mathbf{Lr}_e^{A_1 \vee A_2}$ *iff every move of Φ starts with "1." or "2." and, for each* $i \subset \{1,2\}$, $\Phi^i \in \mathbf{Lr}^{A_i}$;
   - $\mathbf{Wn}^{A_1 \vee A_2}\langle\Gamma\rangle = \bot$ *iff, for each $i \in \{1,2\}$,* $\mathbf{Wn}^{A_i}\langle\Gamma^{i\cdot}\rangle = \bot$.

4. **Choice conjunction** $A_1 \sqcap A_2$:

- $\Phi \in \mathbf{Lr}^{A_1 \sqcap A_2}$ *iff* $\Phi = \langle \perp i, \Psi \rangle$, *where* $i \in \{1, 2\}$ *and* $\Psi \in \mathbf{Lr}^{A_i}$;
- $\mathbf{Wn}^{A_1 \sqcap A_2} \langle \Gamma \rangle = \perp$ *iff* $\Gamma = \langle \perp i, \Upsilon \rangle$, *where* $i \in \{1, 2\}$ *and* $\mathbf{Wn}^{A_i} \langle \Upsilon \rangle = \perp$.

5. **Choice disjunction** $A_1 \sqcup A_2$:

- $\Phi \in \mathbf{Lr}^{A_1 \sqcup A_2}$ *iff* $\Phi = \langle \top i, \Psi \rangle$, *where* $i \in \{1, 2\}$ *and* $\Psi \in \mathbf{Lr}^{A_i}$;
- $\mathbf{Wn}^{A_1 \sqcup A_2} \langle \Gamma \rangle = \top$ *iff* $\Gamma = \langle \top i, \Upsilon \rangle$, *where* $i \in \{1, 2\}$ *and* $\mathbf{Wn}^{A_i} \langle \Upsilon \rangle = \top$.

6. **Parallel implication,** *or* **reduction** $A_1 \rightarrow A_2$ *is defined as* $(\neg A_1) \vee A_2$.

The operations $\wedge, \vee, \sqcap, \sqcup$ naturally generalize from binary to n-ary (any natural number n) or even infinite-ary, where the 0-ary $\wedge$ and $\sqcap$ should be understood as $\top$ and the 0-ary $\vee$ and $\sqcup$ as $\perp$. Alternatively, $A_1 \wedge \ldots \wedge A_n$ with $n > 2$ can be understood as an abbreviation for $A_1 \wedge (A_2 \wedge \ldots (A_{n-1} \wedge A_n) \ldots)$. Similarly for $\vee, \sqcap, \sqcup$. For simplicity, officially we will stick to the binary version.

Notice the perfect symmetry/duality between $\wedge$ and $\vee$, or $\sqcap$ and $\sqcup$: the definition of each of these operations can be obtained from the definition of its dual by interchanging $\top$ with $\perp$. We earlier characterized legal plays of $A_1 \wedge A_2$ and $A_1 \vee A_2$ as plays "on two boards". According to the above definition, making a move α on "board" #i is technically done by prefixing α with "i.".

Exercise 1. Verify the following equalities (any constant games A,B):

1. $\perp = \neg \top$; $\top = \neg \perp$;
2. $A = \neg\neg A$;
3. $A \wedge B = \neg(\neg A \vee \neg B)$; $A \vee B = \neg(\neg A \wedge \neg B)$;
4. $A \sqcap B = \neg(\neg A \sqcup \neg B)$; $A \sqcup B = \neg(\neg A \sqcap \neg B)$.

Exercise 2. Verify that both $\langle \perp 1.1, \top 2.1.2 \rangle$ and $\langle \top 2.1.2, \perp 1.1 \rangle$ are (legal and) $\top$-won runs of the game $(\top \sqcup \perp) \rightarrow ((\perp \sqcup \top) \wedge \top)$, i.e., by Exercise 1, of the game $(\perp \sqcap \top) \vee ((\perp \sqcup \top) \wedge \top)$. How about the runs $\langle \rangle$, $\langle \perp 1.1 \rangle$, $\langle \top 2.1.2 \rangle$?

An important game operation not mentioned in Section 1 is that of prefixation, which is somewhat reminiscent of the modal operator(s) of dynamic logic. This operation takes two arguments: a constant game A and a position Φ that must be a legal position of A (otherwise the operation is undefined).

Definition 3. *Let* A *be a constant game and* Φ *a legal position of* A. *The* Φ-*prefixation of* A, *denoted* $\langle \Phi \rangle A$, *is defined as follows:*

- $\mathbf{Lr}^{\langle \Phi \rangle A} = \{ \Gamma \mid \langle \Phi, \Gamma \rangle \in \mathbf{Lr}^A \}$;
- $\mathbf{Wn}^{\langle \Phi \rangle A} \langle \Gamma \rangle = \mathbf{Wn}^A \langle \Phi, \Gamma \rangle$ (*any* $\Gamma \in \mathbf{Lr}^{\langle \Phi \rangle A}$).

Intuitively, $\langle \Phi \rangle A$ is the game playing which means playing A starting (continuing) from position Φ. That is, $\langle \Phi \rangle A$ is the game to which A evolves (will be "*brought down*") after the moves of Φ have been made. We have already used this intuition when explaining the meaning of choice operations: we said that after $\perp$ makes an initial move $i \in \{1, 2\}$, the game $A_1 \sqcap A_2$ continues as A_i. What this meant was nothing but that $\langle \perp i \rangle (A_1 \sqcap A_2) = A_i$. Similarly, $\langle \top i \rangle (A_1 \sqcup A_2) = A_i$.

Exercise 3. Verify that, for arbitrary constant games A, B, we have:
1. Where $\langle \wp_1 \alpha_1, \ldots, \wp_n \alpha_n \rangle \in \mathbf{Lr}^A$, $\langle \wp_1 \alpha_1, \ldots, \wp_n \alpha_n \rangle A = \langle \wp_n \alpha_n \rangle \ldots \langle \wp_1 \alpha_1 \rangle A$.
2. Where $\langle \top \alpha \rangle \in \mathbf{Lr}^{\neg A}$, $\langle \top \alpha \rangle \neg A = \neg \langle \perp \alpha \rangle A$. Same with $\top, \perp$ interchanged.
3. Where $\langle \wp 1.\alpha \rangle \in \mathbf{Lr}^{A \wedge B}$, $\langle \wp 1.\alpha \rangle (A \wedge B) = (\langle \wp \alpha \rangle A) \wedge B$. Similarly for $\langle \wp 2.\alpha \rangle$. Similarly for $A \vee B$.

Prefixation is very handy in visualizing legal runs of a given game A. In particular, every (sub)position Φ of such a run can be represented by, or thought of as, the game $\langle \Phi \rangle A$.

Example 1. Let $G_0 = (A \sqcap (B \sqcup C)) \wedge (D \vee (E \sqcup F))$. $\langle \top 2.2.1, \perp 1.2, \top 1.2 \rangle$ is a legal run of G_0, and to it corresponds the following sequence of games:

$G_0 : (A \sqcap (B \sqcup C)) \wedge (D \vee (E \sqcup F))$, i.e., G_0,   i.e., $\langle \rangle G_0$;
$G_1 : (A \sqcap (B \sqcup C)) \wedge (D \vee E)$,   i.e., $\langle \top 2.2.1 \rangle G_0$, i.e., $\langle \top 2.2.1 \rangle G_0$;
$G_2 : (B \sqcup C) \wedge (D \vee E)$,   i.e., $\langle \perp 1.2 \rangle G_1$,   i.e., $\langle \top 2.2.1, \perp 1.2 \rangle G_0$;
$G_3 : C \wedge (D \vee E)$,   i.e., $\langle \top 1.2 \rangle G_2$,   i.e.,

$$\langle \top 2.2.1, \perp 1.2, \top 1.2 \rangle G_0.$$

The run stops at $C \wedge (D \vee E)$, and hence the winner is the player $\wp$ with $\mathbf{Wn}^{C \wedge (D \vee E)} \langle \rangle = \wp$. Note how the $\wedge, \vee$-structure of the game was retained throughout the play.

Another constant-game operation of high interest is **branching recurrence** $\overset{\downarrow}{\circ}$. A strict formal definition of this operation, together with detailed discussions and illustrations of the associated intuitions, can be found in Sect. 13 of [6].[2] Here we only give a brief informal explanation. A legal run of $\overset{\downarrow}{\circ} A$ can be thought of as a tree rather than sequence of labeled moves (with those labeled moves associated with the edges—rather than nodes—of the tree), where each branch of the tree spells a legal run of A. $\top$ is considered the winner in such a game iff it wins A in *all* of the branches. The play starts with the root as the only node of the tree, representing the empty run; at any time, $\top$ can make any legal move of A in any of the existing branches. So can $\perp$, with the difference that $\perp$—and only $\perp$—also has the capability, by making a special "splitting" move (that we do not count as a move of A), to fork any given branch into two, thus creating two runs of A out of one that share the same beginning but from now on can evolve in different ways. So, $\overset{\downarrow}{\circ}$ allows $\perp$ to replicate/restart A as many times as it wishes; furthermore, as noted in Sect. 1, $\perp$ does not really have to restart A from the very beginning every time it "restarts" it; instead, $\perp$ may choose to continue a new

---

[2] [6] used the terms and notation *"branching conjunction"*, *"branching disjunction"*, "!" and "?" for our present "branching recurrence", "branching coreccurrence", "$\overset{\downarrow}{\circ}$" and "$\overset{\downarrow}{?}$", respectively.

run of A from any already reached position Φ of A, i.e., replicate $\langle\Phi\rangle A$ rather than A, thus depriving $\top$ of the possibility to reconsider its previously made moves while giving itself the opportunity to try different strategies in different continuations of Φ and become the winner as long as one of those strategies succeeds. This makes $\circ\!\!\!\!,\, A$ easier for $\bot$ to win than the infinite conjunction $A \wedge A \wedge A \wedge \ldots$ that we call **parallel recurrence** $\wedge A$. The latter can be considered a restricted version of $\circ\!\!\!\!,\, A$ where all the branching happens only at the root. The dual operator $\circ\!\!\!\!,$ of $\circ\!\!\!\!,$, called **branching corecurrence**, is defined in a symmetric way with the roles of the two players interchanged: here it is $\top$ who can initiate new branches and for whom winning in one of the branches is sufficient. Alternatively, $\circ\!\!\!\!,\, A$ can be defined as $\neg\circ\!\!\!\!,\neg A$. Again, winning $\circ\!\!\!\!,\, A$ is easier for $\top$ than winning the infinite disjunction $A \vee A \vee A \vee \ldots$ that we call **parallel corecurrence** $\mathsf{Y} A$ $(= \neg\wedge\neg A)$. To feel this, let us consider the bounded versions $\circ\!\!\!\!,^2$ and Y^2 of $\circ\!\!\!\!,$ and Y, in which the total number of allowed branches is limited to 2. We want to compare $\circ\!\!\!\!,^2 B$ with $\mathsf{Y}^2 B$, i.e., with $B \vee B$, where

$$B = (Chess \sqcup \neg Chess) \sqcap (Checkers \sqcup \neg Checkers).$$

Here is $\top$'s strategy for $\circ\!\!\!\!,^2 B$: Wait till $\bot$ chooses one of the $\sqcap$-conjuncts of B. Suppose the first conjunct is chosen (the other choice will be handled in a similar way). This brings the game down to $Chess \sqcup \neg Chess$. Now make a splitting move, thus creating two branches/copies of $Chess \sqcup \neg Chess$. In one copy choose $Chess$, and in the other copy choose $\neg Chess$. From now on the game continues as a parallel play of $Chess$ and $\neg Chess$, where it is sufficient for $\top$ to win in one of the plays. Hence, applying the "mimicking strategy" described in Section 1 for $Chess \vee \neg Chess$ guarantees success. On the other hand, winning $B \vee B$ is not easy. A possible scenario here is that $\bot$, by making different choices in the two disjuncts, brings the game down to $(Chess \sqcup \neg Chess) \vee (Checkers \sqcup \neg Checkers)$. Unless $\top$ is a champion in either chess or checkers, (s)he may find it hard to win this game no matter what choices (s)he makes in its two disjuncts.

3 Not-Necessarily-Constant Games

Classical logic identifies propositions with their truth values, so that there are exactly two propositions: $\top$ (true) and $\bot$ (false), with the expressions "snow is white" or "$2 + 2 = 4$" simply being two different names of the same proposition $\top$, and "elephants can fly" being one of the possible names of $\bot$. Thinking of the classical propositions $\top$ and $\bot$ as the games $\top$ and $\bot$ defined in Sect. 2, classical propositions become a special—elementary—case of our constant games. It is not hard to see that our game operations $\neg, \wedge, \vee, \rightarrow$, when applied to $\top$ and $\bot$, again produce $\top$ or $\bot$, and exactly in the way their same-name classical counterparts do. Hence, the $(\neg, \wedge, \vee, \rightarrow)$-fragment of CL, restricted to elementary constant games, is nothing but classical propositional logic. The expressive power of propositional logic, however, is very limited.

The more expressive version of classical logic—first-order logic—generalizes propositions to predicates. Let us fix two infinite sets of expressions: the set $\{v_1, v_2, \ldots\}$ of **variables** and the set $\{1, 2,, \ldots\}$ of **constants**. Without loss of generality here we assume that the above collection of constants is exactly the universe of discourse, i.e., the set over which the variables range, in all cases that we consider. By a **valuation** we mean a function that sends each variable x to a constant $e(x)$. In these terms, a classical **predicate** P can be understood as a function that sends each valuation e to either $\top$ (meaning that P is true at e) or $\bot$ (meaning that P is false at e). Say, the predicate $x < y$ is the function that, for a valuation e, returns $\top$ if $e(x) < e(y)$, and returns $\bot$ otherwise. Propositions can then be thought of as special, *constant* cases of predicates—predicates that return the same proposition for every valuation.

The concept of games that we define below generalizes constant games in exactly the same sense as the above classical concept of predicates generalizes propositions:

Definition 4. *A* **game** *is a function from valuations to constant games. We write $e[A]$ (rather than $A(e)$) to denote the constant game returned by game A for valuation e. Such a constant game $e[A]$ is said to be an* **instance** *of A.*

Just as this is the case with propositions versus predicates, constant games in the sense of Definition 1 will be thought of as special, *constant* cases of games in the sense of Definition 4. In particular, each constant game A' is the game A such that, for every valuation e, $e[A] = A'$. From now on we will no longer distinguish between such A and A', so that, if A is a constant game, it is its own instance, with $A = e[A]$ for every e.

We say that a game A **depends** on a variable x iff there are two valuations e_1, e_2 that agree on all variables except x such that $e_1[A] \neq e_2[A]$. Constant games thus do not depend on any variables.

The notion of an elementary game that we defined for constant games naturally generalizes to all games by stipulating that a given game is **elementary** iff all of its instances are so. Hence, just as we identified classical propositions with constant elementary games, classical predicates from now on will be identified with elementary games. Say, $Even(x)$ is the elementary game such that $e[Even(x)]$ is the game $\top$ if $e(x)$ is even, and the game $\bot$ if $e(x)$ is odd.

Any other concepts originally defined only for constant games can be similarly extended to all games. In particular, just as the propositional operations of classical logic naturally generalize to operations on predicates, so do our game operations from Sect. 2. This is done by simply stipulating that $e[\ldots]$ commutes with all of those operations: $\neg A$ is the game such that, for every e, $e[\neg A] = \neg e[A]$; $A \sqcap B$ is the game such that, for every e, $e[A \sqcap B] = e[A] \sqcap e[B]$; etc. A little caution is necessary when generalizing the operation of prefixation this way. As we remember, for a constant game A, $\langle \Phi \rangle A$ is defined only when

Φ is a legal position of A. So, for $\langle\Phi\rangle A$ to be defined for a not-necessarily-constant game A, Φ should be a legal position of every instance of A. Once this condition is satisfied, $\langle\Phi\rangle A$ is defined as the game such that, for every valuation e, $e[\langle\Phi\rangle A] = \langle\Phi\rangle e[A]$.

To generalize the standard operation of substitution of variables to games, let us agree that by a **term** we mean either a variable or a constant; the domain of each valuation e is extended to all terms by stipulating that, for any constant c, $e(c) = c$.

Definition 5. *Let A be a game, $x_1, \ldots, x_n$ pairwise distinct variables, and $t_1, \ldots, t_n$ any (not necessarily distinct) terms. The result of **substituting** $x_1, \ldots, x_n$ by $t_1, \ldots, t_n$ in A, denoted $A(x_1/t_1, \ldots, x_n/t_n)$, is defined by stipulating that, for every valuation e, $e[A(x_1/t_1, \ldots, x_n/t_n)] = e'[A]$, where e' is the valuation for which we have:*

1. *$e'(x_1) = e(t_1)$, $\ldots$, $e'(x_n) = e(t_n)$;*
2. *for every variable $y \notin \{x_1, \ldots, x_n\}$, $e'(y) = e(y)$.*

Intuitively $A(x_1/t_1, \ldots, x_n/t_n)$ is A with $x_1, \ldots, x_n$ remapped to $t_1, \ldots, t_n$, respectively. Say, if A is the elementary game $x < y$, then $A(x/y, y/x)$ is $y < x$, $A(x/y)$ is $y < y$, $A(y/3)$ is $x < 3$, and $A(z/3)$—where z is different from x, y—remains $x < y$ because A does not depend on z.

Following the standard readability-improving practice established in the literature for predicates, we will often fix a tuple $(x_1, \ldots, x_n)$ of pairwise distinct variables for a game A and write A as $A(x_1, \ldots, x_n)$. It should be noted that when doing so, by no means do we imply that $x_1, \ldots, x_n$ are all of (or only) the variables on which A depends. Representing A in the form $A(x_1, \ldots, x_n)$ sets a context in which we can write $A(t_1, \ldots, t_n)$ to mean the same as the more clumsy expression $A(x_1/t_1, \ldots, x_n/t_n)$. So, if the game $x < y$ is represented as $A(x)$, then $A(3)$ will mean $3 < y$ and $A(y)$ mean $y < y$. And if the same game is represented as $A(y, z)$ (where $z \neq x, y$), then $A(z, 3)$ means $x < z$ while $A(y, 3)$ again means $x < y$.

The entities that in common language we call "games" are at least as often nonconstant as constant. Chess is a classical example of a constant game. On the other hand, many of the card games—including solitaire games where only one player is active—are more naturally represented as nonconstant games: each session/instance of such a game is set by a particular permutation of the card deck, and thus the game can be understood as a game that depends on a variable x ranging over the possible settings of the deck or certain portions of it. Even the game of checkers—another "classical example" of a constant game—has a natural nonconstant generalization $Checkers(x)$ (with x ranging over positive even integers), meaning a play on the board of size $x \times x$ where, in the initial position, the first $\frac{3}{2}x$ black cells are filled with white pieces and the last $\frac{3}{2}x$ black cells with black pieces. Then the ordinary checkers can be written as $Checkers(8)$. Furthermore, the numbers of pieces of either color also can be made variable, getting an even more general game $Checkers(x, y, z)$, with the ordinary checkers being the instance $Checkers(8, 12, 12)$ of it. By allowing rectangular (rather than just square-) shape boards, we would get a game that depends on four variables, etc. Computability theory texts also often appeal to nonconstant games to illustrate certain complexity-theory concepts such as alternating computation or PSPACE-completeness. The *Formula Game* or *Generalized Geography* ([14], Section 8.3) are typical examples. Both can be understood as games that depend on a variable x, with x ranging over quantified Boolean formulas in Formula Game and over directed graphs in Generalized Geography.

A game A is said to be **unistructural in** a variable x iff, for every two valuations e_1 and e_2 that agree on all variables except x, we have $\mathbf{Lr}^{e_1[A]} = \mathbf{Lr}^{e_2[A]}$. And A is (simply) **unistructural** iff $\mathbf{Lr}^{e_1[A]} = \mathbf{Lr}^{e_2[A]}$ for any two valuations e_1 and e_2. Intuitively, a unistructural game is a game whose every instance has the same structure (the $\mathbf{Lr}$ component). And A is unistructural in x iff the structure of an instance $e[A]$ of A does not depend on how e evaluates the variable x. Of course, every constant or elementary game is unistructural, and every unistructural game is unistructural in all variables. The class of unistructural games can be shown to be closed under all of our game operations (Theorem 1). While natural examples of nonunistructural games exist such as the games mentioned in the above paragraph, virtually all of the other examples of particular games discussed elsewhere in the present paper are unistructural. In fact, every nonunistructural game can be rather easily rewritten into an equivalent (in a certain reasonable sense) unistructural game. One of the standard ways to convert a nonunistructural game A into a corresponding unistructural game A' is to take the union (or anything bigger) U of the structures of all instances of A to be the common-for-all-instances structure of A', and then extend the $\mathbf{Wn}$ function of each instance $e[A]$ of A to U by stipulating that, if $\Gamma \notin \mathbf{Lr}^{e[A]}$, then the player who made the first illegal (in the sense of $e[A]$) move is the loser in $e[A']$. So, say, in the unistructural version of generalized checkers, an attempt by a player to move to or from a nonexisting cell would result in a loss for that player but otherwise considered a legal move. In view of these remarks, if the reader feels more comfortable this way, without much loss of generality (s)he can always understand "game" as "unistructural game".

Now we are ready to define quantifier-style operations on games. The blind group $\forall x, \exists x$ of quantifiers is only defined for games that are unistructural in x.

Definition 6. *Below $A(x)$ is an arbitrary game that in Clauses 5 and 6 is assumed to be unistructural in x. e ranges over all valuations. Just as in Definition 2, Φ ranges over nonempty positions, and Γ ranges over the legal runs of the game that is being defined. The notation $\Phi^{c\cdot}$ in clauses 3 and 4 means the result of removing from Φ all labeled moves except those of the form $\wp c.\alpha$ ($\wp \in \{\top, \bot\}$), and then deleting the prefix "c." in the remaining moves, i.e., replacing each such $\wp c.\alpha$ by $\wp\alpha$. Similarly for $\Gamma^{c\cdot}$.*

1. **Choice universal quantification** $\sqcap x A(x)$:

- $\Phi \in \mathbf{Lr}^{e[\sqcap x A(x)]}$ *iff* $\Phi = \langle \bot c, \Psi \rangle$, *where c is a constant and* $\Psi \in$ $\mathbf{Lr}^{e[A(c)]}$;
- $\mathbf{Wn}^{e[\sqcap x A(x)]}\langle \Gamma \rangle = \bot$ *iff* $\Gamma = \langle \bot c, \Upsilon \rangle$, *where c is a constant and* $\mathbf{Wn}^{e[A(c)]}\langle \Upsilon \rangle = \bot$.

2. **Choice existential quantification** $\sqcup x A(x)$:

- $\Phi \in \mathbf{Lr}^{e[\sqcup x A(x)]}$ *iff* $\Phi = \langle \top c, \Psi \rangle$, *where c is a constant and* $\Psi \in$ $\mathbf{Lr}^{e[A(c)]}$;
- $\mathbf{Wn}^{e[\sqcup x A(x)]}\langle \Gamma \rangle = \top$ *iff* $\Gamma = \langle \top c, \Upsilon \rangle$, *where c is a constant and* $\mathbf{Wn}^{e[A(c)]}\langle \Upsilon \rangle = \top$.

3. **Parallel universal quantification** $\wedge x A(x)$:

- $\Phi \in \mathbf{Lr}^{e[\wedge x A(x)]}$ *iff every move of* Φ *starts with "c." for some constant c and, for each such c,* $\Phi^{c.} \in \mathbf{Lr}^{e[A(c)]}$;
- $\mathbf{Wn}^{e[\wedge x A(x)]}\langle \Gamma \rangle = \top$ *iff, for each constant c,* $\mathbf{Wn}^{e[A(c)]}\langle \Gamma^{c.} \rangle = \top$.

4. **Parallel existential quantification** $\vee x A(x)$:

- $\Phi \in \mathbf{Lr}^{e[\vee x A(x)]}$ *iff every move of* Φ *starts with "c." for some constant c and, for each such c,* $\Phi^{c.} \in \mathbf{Lr}^{e[A(c)]}$;
- $\mathbf{Wn}^{e[\vee x A(x)]}\langle \Gamma \rangle = \bot$ *iff, for each constant c,* $\mathbf{Wn}^{e[A(c)]}\langle \Gamma^{c.} \rangle = \bot$.

5. **Blind universal quantification** $\forall x A(x)$:

- $\Phi \in \mathbf{Lr}^{e[\forall x A(x)]}$ *iff* $\Phi \in \mathbf{Lr}^{e[A(x)]}$;
- $\mathbf{Wn}^{e[\forall x A(x)]}\langle \Gamma \rangle = \top$ *iff, for each constant c,* $\mathbf{Wn}^{e[A(c)]}\langle \Gamma \rangle = \top$.

6. **Blind existential quantification** $\exists x A(x)$:

- $\Phi \in \mathbf{Lr}^{e[\exists x A(x)]}$ *iff* $\Phi \in \mathbf{Lr}^{e[A(x)]}$;
- $\mathbf{Wn}^{e[\exists x A(x)]}\langle \Gamma \rangle = \bot$ *iff, for each constant c,* $\mathbf{Wn}^{e[A(c)]}\langle \Gamma \rangle = \bot$.

Thus, $\sqcap x A(x)$ and $\wedge x A(x)$ are nothing but $A(1) \sqcap A(2) \sqcap \ldots$ and $A(1) \wedge A(2) \wedge \ldots$, respectively. Similarly, $\sqcup$ and $\vee$ are "big brothers" of $\sqcup$ and $\vee$. As for $\forall x A(x)$, as explained in Sect. 1, winning it for $\top$ (resp. $\bot$) means winning $A(x)$, at once, for all (resp. some) possible values of x without knowing the actual value of x. Playing or evaluating a game generally might be impossible or meaningless without knowing what moves are available/legal. Therefore our definition of $\forall x A(x)$ and $\exists x A(x)$ insists that the move legality question should not depend on the (unknown) value of x, i.e., that $A(x)$ should be unistructural in x.

As we did in Exercise 1, one can easily verify the following interdefinabilities:

$$\sqcup x A(x) = \neg \sqcap x \neg A(x); \qquad \sqcap x A(x) = \neg \sqcup x \neg A(x);$$
$$\vee x A(x) = \neg \wedge x \neg A(x); \qquad \wedge x A(x) = \neg \vee x \neg A(x);$$
$$\exists x A(x) = \neg \forall x \neg A(x); \qquad \forall x A(x) = \neg \exists x \neg A(x).$$

Exercise 4. Let $Odd(x)$ be the predicate "x is odd". Verify that:

1. $\langle \perp 3, \top 1 \rangle$ is a legal run of $\sqcap x (Odd(x) \sqcup \neg Odd(x))$ won by $\top$.
2. $\forall x (Odd(x) \sqcup \neg Odd(x))$ has exactly three legal runs: $\langle \rangle$, $\langle \top 1 \rangle$ and $\langle \top 2 \rangle$, all lost by $\top$. $\exists x (Odd(x) \sqcup \neg Odd(x))$ has the same legal runs, with $\langle \rangle$ won by $\perp$ and the other two by $\top$.
3. $\langle \top 9.1 \rangle$ is a legal run of $\bigvee x (Odd(x) \sqcup \neg Odd(x))$ won by $\top$.
4. $\langle \top 1.1, \top 2.2, \top 3.1, \top 4.2, \top 5.1, \top 6.2, \ldots \rangle$ is a legal run of $\bigwedge x (Odd(x) \sqcup \neg Odd(x))$ won by $\top$. On the other hand, every finite initial segment of this infinite run is lost by $\top$.

Exercise 5. Verify that, for every game $A(x)$, we have:

1. Where c is an arbitrary constant, $\langle \perp c \rangle \sqcap x A(x) = A(c)$ and $\langle \top c \rangle \sqcup x A(x) = A(c)$.
2. Where $A(x)$ is unistructural in x and Φ is a legal position of all instances of $A(x)$, $\langle \Phi \rangle \forall x A(x) = \forall x \langle \Phi \rangle A(x)$ and $\langle \Phi \rangle \exists x A(x) = \exists x \langle \Phi \rangle A(x)$.

The results of the above exercise will help us visualize legal runs of $\forall, \exists, \sqcap, \sqcup$-combinations of games in the style of the earlier Example 1:

Example 2. Let $E(x,y)$ be the predicate "$x + y$ is even", and G_0 be the game $\forall x ((E(x,4) \sqcup \neg E(x,4)) \rightarrow \sqcap y (E(x,y) \sqcup \neg E(x,y)))$, i.e., $\forall x ((\neg E(x,4) \sqcap E(x,4)) \vee \sqcap y (E(x,y) \sqcup \neg E(x,y)))$. Then $\langle \perp 2.7, \perp 1.2, \top 2.1 \rangle$ is a legal run of G_0, to which corresponds the following sequence of games:

$G_0 : \forall x ((\neg E(x,4) \sqcap E(x,4)) \vee \sqcap y (E(x,y) \sqcup \neg E(x,y)))$;
$G_1 : \forall x ((\neg E(x,4) \sqcap E(x,4)) \vee (E(x,7) \sqcup \neg E(x,7)))$,   i.e., $\langle \perp 2.7 \rangle G_0$;
$G_2 : \forall x (E(x,4) \vee (E(x,7) \sqcup \neg E(x,7)))$,   i.e., $\langle \perp 1.2 \rangle G_1$;
$G_3 : \forall x (E(x,4) \vee E(x,7))$,   i.e., $\langle \top 2.1 \rangle G_2$.

The run hits the true proposition $\forall x (E(x,4) \vee E(x,7))$ and hence is won by $\top$. Note that—just as this is the case with all non-choice operations—the $\forall, \exists$-structure of a game persists throughout a run.

When visualizing $\bigwedge, \bigvee$-games in a similar style, we are better off representing them as infinite conjunctions/disjunctions. Of course, putting infinitely many conjuncts/disjuncts on paper would be no fun. But, luckily, in every position of such (sub)games $\bigwedge x A(x)$ or $\bigvee x A(x)$ only a finite number of conjuncts/disjuncts would be "activated", i.e., have a non-$A(c)$ form, so that all of the other, uniform, conjuncts can be combined into blocks and represented, say, through an ellipsis, or through expressions such as $\bigwedge m \leq x \leq n A(x)$ or $\bigwedge x \geq m A(x)$. Once $\bigwedge, \bigvee$-formulas are represented as parallel conjunctions/disjunctions, we can apply the results of Exercise 3(3)—now generalized to infinite conjunctions/disjunctions—to visualize runs. For example, the legal run $\langle \top 9.1 \rangle$ of game $\bigvee x (Odd(x) \sqcup \neg Odd(x))$ from Exercise 4(3) will be represented as follows:

$\bigvee x \big(Odd(x) \sqcup \neg Odd(x) \big);$

$\bigvee x \leq 8 \big(Odd(x) \sqcup \neg Odd(x) \big) \vee Odd(9) \vee \bigvee x \geq 10 \big(Odd(x) \sqcup \neg Odd(x) \big).$

And the infinite legal run $\langle \top 1.1, \top 2.2, \top 3.1, \top 4.2, \top 5.1, \top 6.2, \ldots \rangle$ of game $\bigwedge x \big(Odd(x) \sqcup \neg Odd(x) \big)$ from Exercise 4(4) will be represented as follows:

$\bigwedge x \big(Odd(x) \sqcup \neg Odd(x) \big);$

$Odd(1) \wedge \bigwedge x \geq 2 \big(Odd(x) \sqcup \neg Odd(x) \big);$

$Odd(1) \wedge \neg Odd(2) \wedge \bigwedge x \geq 3 \big(Odd(x) \sqcup \neg Odd(x) \big);$

$Odd(1) \wedge \neg Odd(2) \wedge Odd(3) \wedge \bigwedge x \geq 4 \big(Odd(x) \sqcup \neg Odd(x) \big);$

...etc.

4 Interactive Computational Problems

Various sorts of games have been extensively studied in both logical and theoretical computer science literatures. The closest to our present approach to games appears to be Blass's [2] model, and less so the models proposed later within the "game semantics for linear logic" line by Abramsky, Jagadeesan, Hyland, Ong and others. See Sect. 27 of [6] for a discussion of how other game models compare with our own, and what the crucial advantages of our approach to games are that turn the corresponding logic into a logic of computability—something that is no longer "just a game". One of the main distinguishing features of our games is the absence of what in [1] is called *procedural rules*—rules strictly regulating who and when should move, the most standard procedural rule being the one according to which the players should take turns in alternating order. In our games, either player is free to make any (legal) move at any time. Such games can be called **free**, while games where in any given situation only one of the players is allowed to move called **strict**. Strict games can be thought of as special cases of our free games, where the structure (**Lr**) component is such that in any given position at most one of the players has legal moves. Our games are thus most general of all two-player, two-outcome games. This makes them the most powerful and flexible modeling tool for interactive tasks. It also makes our definitions of game operations as simple, compact and natural as they could be, and allows us to adequately capture certain intended intuitions associated with those operations. Consider the game *Chess∧Chess*. Assume an agent plays this two-board game over the Internet against two independent adversaries that, together, form the (one) environment for the agent. Playing white on both boards, in the initial position of this game only the agent has legal moves. But once such a move is made, say, on the left board, the picture changes. Now both the agent and the environment have legal moves: the agent may make another opening move on the right board, while the environment—in particular, adversary #1—may make a reply move on the left board. This is a situation where which player "can move" is no longer strictly determined, so the next player to move will be the one who can or wants to act sooner. A strict-game approach would impose some additional conditions uniquely determining the next player to move. Such conditions would most likely be artificial and not quite adequate, for the situation we are trying to model is a concurrent play on two boards against two independent adversaries, and we cannot or should not expect any coordination between their actions. Most of the compound tasks that we perform in everyday life are free rather than strict, and so are most computer communication/interaction protocols. A strict understanding of $\wedge$ would essentially mean some sort of an (in a sense interlaced but still) sequential rather than truly parallel/concurrent combination of tasks, where no steps in one component can be made until receiving a response in the other component, contrary to the very (utility-oriented) idea of parallel/distributed computation.

Our class of free games is obviously general enough to model anything that we would call a (two-agent, two-outcome) interactive problem. However, it is too general. There are games where the chances of a player to succeed essentially depend on the relative speed at which its adversary responds, and we do not want to consider that sort of games meaningful computational problems. A simple example would be a game where all moves are legal and that is won by the player who moves first. This is merely a contest of speed. Below we define a subclass of games called *static games*. Intuitively, they are games where speed is irrelevant: in order to succeed (play legal and win), only matters *what* to do (strategy) rather than *how fast* to do (speed). In particular, if a player can succeed when acting fast in such a game, it will remain equally successful acting the same way but slowly. This releases the player from any pressure for time and allows it to select its own pace for the game.

We say that a run Υ is a $\wp$-**delay** of a run Γ iff:

- for each player $\wp'$, the subsequence of $\wp'$-labeled moves of Υ is the same as that of Γ, and
- for any $n, k \geq 1$, if the nth $\wp$-labeled move is made later than (is to the right of) the kth non-$\wp$-labeled move in Γ, then so is it in Υ.

This means that in Υ each player has made the same sequence of moves as in Γ, only, in Υ, $\wp$ might have been acting with some delay. Then we say that a constant game A is **static** iff, whenever a run Υ is a $\wp$-delay of a run Γ, we have:

- if Γ is a $\wp$-legal run of A, then so is Υ,[3] and
- if Γ is a $\wp$-won run of A, then so is Υ.

This definition extends to all games by stipulating that a (not-necessarily-constant) game is **static** iff all of its instances are so.

Now we are ready to formally clarify what we mean by interactive computational problems: an **interactive computational problem (ICP)** is a static game, and from now on we will be using the terms "ICP" (or simply "problem") and "static game" interchangeably. This terminology is justified by one of the two main theses on which CL relies philosophically: *the concept*

---

[3] This first condition was a derivable one in the presentation chosen in [6]. See the footnote on page 190.

of static games is an adequate formal counterpart of our intuitive notion of "pure", speed-independent interactive computational problems. See Sect. 4 of [6] for a detailed discussion and examples in support of this thesis. According to the second thesis, *the concept of computability/winnability of static games, defined in the next section, is an adequate formal counterpart of our intuitive notion of effective solvability of speed-independent interactive problems.* This is thus an interactive version of the Church–Turing thesis.

Theorem 1.

1. Every elementary game is static and unistructural.

2. All of our game operations, ¬, ∧, ∨, →, ⊓, ⊔, ⨦, ⫯, ⅄, ⅄, ⊓, ⊔, ∀, ∃, ⋀, ⋁, *prefixation and substitution of variables, preserve both the static and the unistructural properties of games.*

The first clause of this theorem is straightforward; the second clause has been proven in [6] (Theorem 14.1) for all operations except ⅄, ⅄, ⋀ and ⋁ that were not officially introduced there but that can be handled in exactly the same way as ∧, ∨.

In view of Theorem 1, the closure of the set of all predicates under all of our game operations forms a natural class $\mathcal{C}$ of unistructural ICPs. For a reader who has difficulty in comprehending the concept of static games, it is perfectly safe to simply think of ICPs as elements of $\mathcal{C}$: even though the class $\mathcal{ICP}$ of all ICPs is essentially wider than $\mathcal{C}$, virtually all of our results—in particular, completeness results—remain valid with $\mathcal{ICP}$ restricted to $\mathcal{C}$. Class $\mathcal{C}$ has a number of nice features. Among them, together with unistructurality, is the effectiveness of the structure of any $A \in \mathcal{C}$, in the sense that the question whether a given move is legal in a given position is decidable—in fact, decidable rather efficiently.

5 Interactive Computability

Now that we know what ICPs are, it is time to clarify what their computability means. The definitions given in this section are semiformal. All of the omitted technical details are rather standard or irrelevant and can be easily restored by anyone familiar with Turing machines. If necessary, the corresponding detailed definitions can be found in Part II of [6].

As we remember, the central point of our philosophy is to require that agent ⊤ be implementable as a computer program, with effective and fully determined behavior. On the other hand, the behavior of agent ⊥ can be arbitrary. This intuition is captured by the model of interactive computation where ⊤ is formalized as what we call **HPM**.[4]

---

[4] HPM stands for "Hard-Play Machine". See [6] for a (little long) story about why "hard".

An HPM $\mathcal{M}$ is a Turing machine that, together with an ordinary read/write *work tape*, has two additional, read-only tapes: the *valuation tape* and the *run tape*. The presence of these two tapes is related to the fact that the outcome of a play over a given game depends on two parameters: (1) valuation and (2) the run that is generated in the play. $\mathcal{M}$ should have full access to information about these two parameters, and this information is provided by the valuation and run tapes: the former spells a (the "actual") valuation e by listing constants in the lexicographic order of the corresponding variables, and the latter spells, at any given time, the current position, i.e., the sequence of the (labeled) moves made by the two players so far, in the order in which those moves have been made. Thus, both of these two tapes can be considered input tapes. The reason for our choice to keep them separate is the difference in the nature of the input that they provide. Valuation is a *static* input, known at the very beginning of a computation/play and remaining unchanged throughout the subsequent process. On the other hand, the input provided by the run tape is *dynamic*: every time one of the players makes a move, the move (with the corresponding label) is appended to the content of this tape, with such content being unknown and hence blank at the beginning of interaction. Technically the run tape is read-only: the machine has unlimited read access to this (as well as to the valuation) tape, but it cannot write directly on it. Rather, $\mathcal{M}$ makes a move α by constructing it at the beginning of its work tape, delimiting its end with a blank symbol, and entering one of the specially designated states called *move states*. Once this happens, $\top\alpha$ is automatically appended to the current position spelled on the run tape. While the frequency at which the machine can make moves is naturally limited by its clock cycle time (the time each computation step takes), there are no limitations to how often the environment can make a move, so, during one computation step of the machine, any finite number of any moves by the environment can be appended to the content of the run tape. This corresponds to the intuition that not only the strategy, but also the relative speed of the environment can be arbitrary. For technical clarity, we can assume that the run tape remains stable during a clock cycle and is updated only on a transition from one cycle to another, on which event the moves (if any) by the two players appear on it at once in the order that they have been made. As we may guess, the computing power of the machine is rather rigid with respect to how this sort of technical details are arranged, and such details can be safely suppressed.

A *configuration* of $\mathcal{M}$ is defined in the standard way: this is a full description of the ("current") state of the machine, the locations of its three scanning heads and the contents of its tapes, with the exception that, in order to make finite descriptions of configurations possible, we do not formally include a description of the unchanging (and possibly essentially infinite) content of the valuation tape as a part of configuration, but rather account for it in our definition of computation branch as this will be seen below. The *initial configuration* is the configuration where $\mathcal{M}$ is in its start state and the work and run tapes are empty. A configuration C' is said to be an *e-successor* of configuration C if, when valuation e is spelled on the valuation tape, C' can legally follow C in the standard sense, based on the transition function (which we assume to be deterministic) of the machine and accounting for the possibility of the above-described nondeterministic updates of the content of the run tape. An *e-computation branch* of $\mathcal{M}$ is a sequence of configurations of $\mathcal{M}$ where the first configuration is the initial configuration and every other configuration is an *e*-successor of the previous one. Thus, the set of all *e*-computation branches captures all possible scenarios (on valuation e) corresponding to different behaviors by $\bot$. Each *e*-computation branch B of $\mathcal{M}$ incrementally spells—in the obvious sense—a run Γ on the run tape, which we call the *run spelled by B*.

Definition 7. *For ICPs A and B we say that:*

*1. An HPM $\mathcal{M}$ **computes** (**solves**, **wins**) A iff, for every valuation e, whenever Γ is the run spelled by some e-computation branch of $\mathcal{M}$, Γ is a $\top$-won legal run of $e[A]$ as long as it is $\bot$-legal.*

*2. A is **computable** iff there is an HPM that computes A. Such an HPM is said to be a **solution** to A.*

*3. A is **reducible** to B iff $B \to A$ is computable. An HPM that computes $B \to A$ is said to be a **reduction** of A to B.*

*4. A and B are **equivalent** iff A is reducible to B and B is reducible to A.*

One of the most appealing known models of interactive computation is *persistent Turing machines* (Goldin [4]). PTMs are defined as Turing machines where the content of the work tape persists between an output and the subsequent input events (while an ordinary Turing machine cleans up the tape and starts from scratch on every new input). The PTM model appears to be optimal for what is called *sequential interactive computations* [5], which into our terms translate as plays over games with strictly alternating legal moves by the two players, always by the environment to start. Our HPM model sacrifices some of the niceties of PTMs in its ambition to capture the wider class of free games and, correspondingly, not-necessarily-sequential interactive computations.

Just as the Turing machine model, our HPM model, as noted, is highly rigid with respect to reasonable technical variations. Say, a model where only environment's moves are visible to the machine yields the same class of computable ICPs. Similarly, there is no difference between whether we allow the scanning heads on the valuation and run tapes to move in either or only one (left to right) direction. Another variation is the one where an attempt by either player to make an illegal move has no effect: such moves are automatically rejected and/or filtered out by some interface hardware or software and thus illegal runs are never generated. Obviously in such a case a minimum requirement would be that the question of legality of moves be decidable. This again yields a model equivalent to HPM.

6 The Propositional Logic of Computability

Among the main technical goals of CL at its present stage of development is
to axiomatize the set of valid principles of computability or various natural
fragments of that set. This is a challenging but promising task. Some positive
results in this direction have already been obtained, yet more results are still
to come. We start our brief survey of known results at the simplest, propositional level. The system axiomatizing the most basic fragment of propositional
computability logic is called **CL1**. Its language extends that of classical propositional logic by incorporating into it two additional connectives: ⊓ and ⊔. As
always, there are infinitely many **atoms** in the language, for which we will be
using the letters $p, q, r, \ldots$ as metavariables. Atoms are meant to represent elementary games. The two atoms: ⊤ and ⊥ have a special status in that their
interpretation is fixed. Therefore we call them **logical** to distinguish them
from all other atoms that are called **nonlogical**. Formulas of this language,
referred to as **CL1-formulas**, are built from atoms in the standard way: the
class of **CL1**-formulas is defined as the smallest set of expressions such that
all atoms are in it and, if F and G are in it, then so are $\neg(F)$, $(F) \wedge (G)$,
$(F) \vee (G)$, $(F) \rightarrow (G)$, $(F) \sqcap (G)$, $(F) \sqcup (G)$. For better readability, we will
often omit some parentheses in formulas by standard conventions.

An **interpretation**, corresponding to what is more often called "model"
in classical logic, is a function $*$ that sends every nonlogical atom p to an
elementary game p^*. The mapping $*$ extends to all **CL1**-formulas by stipulating that it commutes with all connectives, i.e., respects their meaning
as game operations. That is, we have: $\top^* = \top$; $\bot^* = \bot$; $(\neg G)^* = \neg(G^*)$;
$(G \wedge H)^* = (G^*) \wedge (H^*)$; $(G \vee H)^* = (G^*) \vee (H^*)$; $(G \rightarrow H)^* = (G^*) \rightarrow (H^*)$;
$(G \sqcap H)^* = (G^*) \sqcap (H^*)$; $(G \sqcup H)^* = (G^*) \sqcup (H^*)$.

When $F^* = A$, we say that $*$ **interprets** F as A. We say that a
CL1-formula F is **valid** iff, for every interpretation $*$, the ICP F^* is computable. Thus, valid **CL1**-formulas are exactly the ones representing "always-
computable" problems, i.e., "valid principles of computability".

Note that, despite the fact that we refer to **CL1** as a "propositional logic",
interpretations of its formulas go beyond constant games, let alone propositions. This is so because our definition of interpretation does not insist that
atoms be interpreted as constant games. Rather, for the sake of generality, it
lets them represent any predicates.

To axiomatize the set of valid **CL1**-formulas, we need some preliminary
terminology. Understanding $F \rightarrow G$ as an abbreviation of $(\neg F) \vee G$, by a
positive (resp. **negative**) **occurrence** of a subexpression we mean an occurrence that is in the scope of an even (resp. odd) number of occurrences of
$\neg$. In the context of the language of **CL1**, by an **elementary formula** we
mean a formula not containing choice operators ⊓, ⊔, i.e., a formula of classical
propositional logic. A **surface occurrence** of a subexpression means an occurrence that is not in the scope of choice operators. The **elementarization**
of a **CL1**-formula F is the result of replacing in F every surface occurrence of

the form $G \sqcap H$ by $\top$ and every surface occurrence of the form $G \sqcup H$ by $\bot$. A **CL1**-formula is said to be **stable** iff its elementarization is a valid formula (tautology) of classical logic. Otherwise it is **instable**.

With $\mathcal{P} \mapsto C$ here and later meaning "from premise(s) $\mathcal{P}$ conclude C", deductively **CL1** is given by the following two rules of inference:

Rule (a): H $\mapsto F$, where F is stable and **H** is a set of formulas such that, whenever F has a positive (resp. negative) surface occurrence of a subformula $G_1 \sqcap G_2$ (resp. $G_1 \sqcup G_2$), for each $i \in \{1, 2\}$, **H** contains the result of replacing that occurrence in F by G_i.

Rule (b): $H \mapsto F$, where H is the result of replacing in F a negative (resp. positive) surface occurrence of a subformula $G_1 \sqcap G_2$ (resp. $G_1 \sqcup G_2$) by G_i for some $i \in \{1, 2\}$.

Axioms are not explicitly stated, but note that the set **H** of premises of Rule **(a)** can be empty, in which case the conclusion F of that rule acts as an axiom. A rather unusual logic, isn't it? Let us play with it a little to get a syntactic feel of it. Below, p, q, r are pairwise distinct nonlogical atoms.

Example 3. The following is a **CL1**-proof of $\big((p \to q) \sqcap (p \to r)\big) \to \big(p \to (q \sqcap r)\big)$:

1. $(p \to q) \to (p \to q)$ (from { } by Rule **(a)**)
2. $\big((p \to q) \sqcap (p \to r)\big) \to (p \to q)$ (from 1 by Rule **(b)**)
3. $(p \to r) \to (p \to r)$ (from { } by Rule **(a)**)
4. $\big((p \to q) \sqcap (p \to r)\big) \to (p \to r)$ (from 3 by Rule **(b)**)
5. $\big((p \to q) \sqcap (p \to r)\big) \to \big(p \to (q \sqcap r)\big)$ (from {2,4} by Rule **(a)**)

On the other hand, **CL1** does not prove $\big((p \to q) \sqcap (p \to r)\big) \to \big(p \to (q \wedge r)\big)$. Indeed, this formula is instable, so it could only be derived by Rule **(b)**. The premise of this rule should be either $(p \to q) \to \big(p \to (q \wedge r)\big)$ or $(p \to r) \to \big(p \to (q \wedge r)\big)$. In either case we deal with a formula that can be derived neither by Rule **(a)** (because it is instable) nor by Rule **(b)** (because it does not contain $\sqcap, \sqcup$).

Exercise 6. With *Logic* $\vdash F$ (resp. *Logic* $\nvdash F$) here and later meaning "F is provable (resp. not provable) in *Logic*", show that:
CL1 $\vdash \big((p \sqcap q) \wedge (p \sqcap q)\big) \to (p \sqcap q)$;
CL1 $\nvdash (p \sqcap q) \to \big((p \sqcap q) \wedge (p \sqcap q)\big)$.

As we probably just had a chance to notice, if F is an elementary formula, then the only way to prove F in **CL1** is to derive it by Rule **(a)** from the empty set of premises. In particular, this rule will be applicable when F is stable, which for an elementary F means nothing but that F is a classical tautology. And vice versa: every classically valid formula is an elementary formula derivable in **CL1** by Rule **(a)** from the empty set of premises. Thus we have:

Proposition 1. *The* $\sqcap, \sqcup$-*free fragment of* **CL1** *is exactly classical propositional logic.*

This is what we should have expected for, as noted earlier, when restricted to elementary problems—and $\sqcap, \sqcup$-free formulas are exactly the ones that represent such problems—the meanings of $\neg, \wedge, \vee, \rightarrow$ are exactly classical. Here comes the soundness/completeness result:

Theorem 2. (Japaridze [7]) **CL1** $\vdash F$ *iff* F *is valid* (*any* **CL1**-*formula* F).

Since the atoms of **CL1** represent predicates rather than ICPs in general, **CL1** only describes the valid principles of elementary ICPs. This limitation of expressive power is overcome in the extension of **CL1** called **CL2**. The language of the latter augments the language of the former in that, along with the old atoms of **CL1** which we now call **elementary atoms**, it has an additional sort of (nonlogical) atoms called **general atoms**. We continue using the lowercase letters $p, q, r, \ldots$ as metavariables for elementary atoms, and will be using the uppercase $P, Q, R, \ldots$ as metavariables for general atoms. We refer to formulas of this language as **CL2-formulas**. An **interpretation** now becomes a function that sends each nonlogical elementary atom (as before) to an elementary ICP and each general atom to any, not-necessarily-elementary, ICP. This mapping extends to all formulas in the same way as in the case of **CL1**. The concepts of validity, surface occurrence and positive/negative occurrence straightforwardly extend to this new language. The **elementarization** of a **CL2**-formula F means the result of replacing in F every surface occurrence of the form $G \sqcap H$ by $\top$, every surface occurrence of the form $G \sqcup H$ by $\bot$ *and*, in addition, replacing every positive surface occurrence of a general atom by $\bot$ and every negative surface occurrence of a general atom by $\top$.

The rules of inference of **CL2** are the two rules of **CL1**—that are now applied to any **CL2**-formulas rather than (just) **CL1**-formulas—plus the following additional rule:

Rule (c): $H \mapsto F$, where H is the result of replacing in F two—one positive and one negative—surface occurrences of some general atom by a nonlogical elementary atom that does not occur in F.

Example 4. The following is a **CL2**-proof of $P \wedge P \rightarrow P$:

1. $p \wedge P \rightarrow p$ (from { } by Rule **(a)**)
2. $P \wedge P \rightarrow P$ (from 1 by Rule **(c)**)

On the other hand, **CL2** does not prove $P \rightarrow P \wedge P$ (while, of course, it proves $p \rightarrow p \wedge p$). Indeed, this formula is instable and does not contain $\sqcap$ or $\sqcup$, so it cannot be derived by Rules **(a)** or **(b)**. If it is derived by Rule **(c)**, the premise should be $p \rightarrow P \wedge p$ or $p \rightarrow p \wedge P$ for some elementary atom p. In either case we deal with an instable formula that contains no choice operators and only has one occurrence of a general atom, so that it cannot be derived by any of the three rules of **CL2**.

Exercise 7. Verify that:

1. $\mathbf{CL2} \vdash P \vee \neg P$
2. $\mathbf{CL2} \not\vdash P \sqcup \neg P$
3. $\mathbf{CL2} \vdash P \rightarrow P \sqcap P$
4. $\mathbf{CL2} \vdash (P \wedge Q) \vee (R \wedge S) \rightarrow (P \vee R) \wedge (Q \vee S)$ (Blass's [2] principle)
5. $\mathbf{CL2} \vdash p \wedge (p \rightarrow Q) \wedge (p \rightarrow R) \rightarrow Q \wedge R$
6. $\mathbf{CL2} \not\vdash P \wedge (P \rightarrow Q) \wedge (P \rightarrow R) \rightarrow Q \wedge R$
7. $\mathbf{CL2} \vdash P \sqcap (Q \vee R) \rightarrow (P \sqcap Q) \vee (P \sqcap R)$
8. $\mathbf{CL2} \not\vdash (P \sqcap Q) \vee (P \sqcap R) \rightarrow P \sqcap (Q \vee R)$
9. $\mathbf{CL2} \vdash (p \sqcap Q) \vee (p \sqcap R) \rightarrow p \sqcap (Q \vee R)$

Theorem 3. (Japaridze [7]) $\mathbf{CL2} \vdash F$ *iff* F *is valid* (*any* $\mathbf{CL2}$-*formula* F).

Both **CL1** and **CL2** are obviously decidable, with a brute force decision algorithm running in polynomial space. Whether there are more efficient algorithms is unknown.

A next step in exploring propositional computability logic would be augmenting the language of **CL1** or **CL2** with recurrence operators. At present the author sees the decidability of the set of valid formulas in the δ, λ-augmented language of **CL1**, but has nothing yet to say about the δ, λ-augmented **CL2**.

7 The First-Order Logic of Computability

CL2 seamlessly extends to the first-order logic **CL4** with four quantifiers: $\forall, \exists, \sqcap, \sqcup$. The set of *variables* of the language of **CL4** is the same as the one that we fixed in Sect. 3. *Constants* $1, 2, 3, \ldots$ are also allowed in the language, and *terms* have the same meaning as before. The language has two—**elementary** and **general**—sorts of **ICP letters**, where each such letter comes with a fixed integer $n \geq 0$ called its **arity**. We assume that, for each n, there are infinitely many n-ary ICP letters of either (elementary and general) sort. Each **atom** looks like $L(t_1, \ldots, t_n)$, where L is an n-ary ICP letter and the t_i are any terms. The terms "elementary", "general", "n-ary" extend from ICP letters to atoms in the obvious way. If L is a 0-ary ICP letter, then the (only) corresponding atom we write as L rather than $L()$. $\top$ and $\bot$, as before, are two special (0-ary) elementary atoms called **logical**.

Formulas of this language, referred to as **CL4-formulas**, are built from atoms using $\neg, \wedge, \vee, \rightarrow, \sqcap, \sqcup$ in the same way as **CL1**- or **CL2**-formulas; in addition, we have the following formation rule: If F is a formula and x is a variable, then $\forall x(F), \exists x(F), \sqcap x(F)$ and $\sqcup x(F)$ are formulas.

An **interpretation** for the language of **CL4** is a function that sends each n-ary general (resp. elementary nonlogical) letter L to an ICP (resp. elementary ICP) $L^*(x_1, \ldots, x_n)$, where the x_i are pairwise distinct variables; in this case we say that $*$ **interprets** L as $L^*(x_1, \ldots, x_n)$. Note that, just as in the propositional case, we do not insist that interpretations respect the arity of ICP letters. Specifically, we do not require that the above $L^*(x_1, \ldots, x_n)$ depend on only (or all) the variables $x_1, \ldots, x_n$. Some caution is however necessary to avoid unpleasant collisions of variables, and also to guarantee that $\forall x$ and $\exists x$ are only applied to games for which they are defined, i.e., games that are unistructural in x. For this reason, we restrict interpretations to "admissible" ones. For a **CL4**-formula F and interpretation * we say that * is F-**admissible** iff, for every n-ary ICP letter L occurring in F, where * interprets L as $L^*(x_1, \ldots, x_n)$, the following two conditions are satisfied:

(i) $L^*(x_1, \ldots, x_n)$ does not depend on any variables that are not among $x_1, \ldots, x_n$ but occur in F.
(ii) Suppose, for some terms $t_1, \ldots, t_n$ and some i with $1 \leq i \leq n$, F has a subformula $\forall t_i G$ or $\exists t_i G$, where G contains an occurrence of $L(t_1, \ldots, t_n)$ that is not in the scope (within G) of $\sqcap t_i$ or $\sqcup t_i$. Then $L^*(x_1, \ldots, x_n)$ is unistructural in x_i.

The concept of admissible interpretation extends to any set S of **CL4**-formulas by stipulating that an interpretation * is S-admissible iff it is F-admissible for every $F \in S$. Notice that condition (ii) is automatically satisfied for elementary ICP letters, because an elementary problem (i.e., $L^*(x_1, \ldots, x_n)$) is always unistructural. In most typical cases we will be interested in interpretations that interpret every n-ary ICP letter L as a unistructural game $L^*(x_1, \ldots, x_n)$ that does not depend on any variables other than $x_1, \ldots, x_n$, so that both conditions (i) and (ii) will be automatically satisfied. With this remark in mind and in order to relax terminology, henceforth we will usually omit "F-admissible" and simply say "interpretation"; every time an expression F^* is used in a context, it should be understood that the range of * is restricted to F-admissible interpretations.

Every interpretation * extends from ICP letters to formulas (for which * is admissible) in the obvious way: where L is an n-ary ICP letter interpreted as $L^*(x_1, \ldots, x_n)$ and $t_1, \ldots, t_n$ are any terms, $\big(L(t_1, \ldots, t_n)\big)^* = L^*(t_1, \ldots, t_n)$; $\top^* = \top$, $(\neg G)^* = \neg(G^*)$; $(G \sqcap H)^* = (G^*) \sqcap (H^*)$; $(\forall x G)^* = \forall x(G^*)$, etc. When $F^* = A$, we say that * **interprets** F as A. We say that a **CL4**-formula F is **valid** iff, for every (F-admissible) interpretation *, the ICP F^* is computable.

The terms "negative occurrence" and "positive occurrence" have the same meaning as in the previous section. A **surface occurrence** of a subexpression in a **CL4**-formula is an occurrence that is not in the scope of choice operators $\sqcap, \sqcup, \sqcap, \sqcup$. When a **CL4**-formula contains neither choice operators nor general atoms, it is said to be **elementary**. The **elementarization** of a **CL4**-formula F is the result of replacing in F every surface occurrence of the form $G \sqcap H$ or $\sqcap x G$ by $\top$, every surface occurrence of the form $G \sqcup H$ or $\sqcup x G$ by $\bot$, every positive surface occurrence of a general atom by $\bot$ and every negative surface occurrence of a general atom by $\top$. A **CL4**-formula is **stable** iff its elementarization is a valid formula of classical first-order logic.

The definition of a *free occurrence* of a variable x in a formula is standard, meaning that the occurrence is not in the scope of $\forall x, \exists x, \sqcap x$ or $\sqcup x$. We will be using the expression $F(x/t)$ to denote the result of replacing all free occurrences of variable x by term t in **CL4**-formula F. A formula with no free occurrences of variables is said to be a **sentence**.

The rules of inference of **CL4** are obtained from those of **CL2** by replacing them by their "first-order versions", with Rule **(b)** splitting into two rules **(B1)** and **(B2)**, as follows:

Rule (A): $H \mapsto F$, where F is stable and H is a set of **CL4**-formulas satisfying the following conditions:
  (i) Whenever F has a positive (resp. negative) surface occurrence of a subformula $G_1 \sqcap G_2$ (resp. $G_1 \sqcup G_2$), for each $i \in \{1, 2\}$, H contains the result of replacing that occurrence in F by G_i;
  (ii) Whenever F has a positive (resp. negative) surface occurrence of a subformula $\sqcap xG$ (resp. $\sqcup xG$), H contains the result of replacing that occurrence in F by $G(x/y)$ for some variable y not occurring in F.

Rule (B1): $H \mapsto F$, where H is the result of replacing in F a negative (resp. positive) surface occurrence of a subformula $G_1 \sqcap G_2$ (resp. $G_1 \sqcup G_2$) by G_i for some $i \in \{1, 2\}$.

Rule (B2): $H \mapsto F$, where H is the result of replacing in F a negative (resp. positive) surface occurrence of a subformula $\sqcap xG$ (resp. $\sqcup xG$) by $G(x/t)$ for some term t such that (if t is a variable) neither the above occurrence of $\sqcap xG$ (resp. $\sqcup xG$) within F nor any of the free occurrences of x within G are in the scope of $\forall t, \exists t, \sqcap t$ or $\sqcup t$.

Rule (C): $H \mapsto F$, where H is the result of replacing in F two—one positive and one negative—surface occurrences of some n-ary general ICP letter by an n-ary nonlogical elementary ICP letter that does not occur in F.

In what follows, the lowercase p stands for a 1-ary (and hence nonlogical) elementary ICP letter, and the uppercase P, Q for 1-ary general ICP letters.

Example 5. The following is a **CL4**-proof of $\sqcap x \sqcup y (P(x) \rightarrow P(y))$:

1. $p(z) \rightarrow p(z)$ (from { } by Rule **(A)**)
2. $P(z) \rightarrow P(z)$ (from 1 by Rule **(C)**)
3. $\sqcup y (P(z) \rightarrow P(y))$ (from 2 by Rule **(B2)**)
4. $\sqcap x \sqcup y (P(x) \rightarrow P(y))$ (from {3} by Rule **(A)**)

On the other hand, a little analysis can convince us that **CL4** does not prove $\sqcup y \sqcap x (P(x) \rightarrow P(y))$, even though the "blind version" $\exists y \forall x (P(x) \rightarrow P(y))$ of this formula is derivable as follows:

1. $\exists y \forall x (p(x) \rightarrow p(y))$ (from { } by Rule **(A)**)
2. $\exists y \forall x (P(x) \rightarrow P(y))$ (from 1 by Rule **(C)**)

Exercise 8. Verify that:

1. $\mathbf{CL4} \vdash \forall x P(x) \rightarrow \sqcap x P(x)$
2. $\mathbf{CL4} \not\vdash \sqcap x P(x) \rightarrow \forall x P(x)$
3. $\mathbf{CL4} \vdash \sqcap x ((P(x) \wedge \sqcap x Q(x)) \sqcap (\sqcap x P(x) \wedge Q(x))) \rightarrow \sqcap x P(x) \wedge \sqcap x Q(x)$

A little excursus for the logicians. It was noted in Sect. 1 that the logical behavior of our parallel and choice operators is similar to yet not the same as that of the "corresponding" multiplicative and additive operators of linear logic (LL). Now we can be more specific. CL and LL agree on many simple and demonstrative formulas such as $P \rightarrow P \wedge P$ and $P \sqcup \neg P$ that both logics reject (Example 4, Exercise 7), or $P \vee \neg P$ and $P \rightarrow P \sqcap P$ that both logics accept (Exercise 7). CL also agrees with the version of LL called affine logic (LL with the weakening rule) on $P \wedge P \rightarrow P$ that both logics accept. On the other hand, the somewhat longer formulas of Exercises 8(3) and 7(4) are valid in our sense yet underivable in linear (or affine) logic. Neither the similarities nor the discrepancies are a surprise. The philosophies of CL and LL overlap in their striving to develop a logic of resources. But the ways this philosophy is materialized are rather different. CL starts with a mathematically strict and intuitively convincing semantics, and only after that, as a natural second step, asks what the corresponding logic and its axiomatizations (syntax) are. It would be accurate to say that LL, on the other hand, started directly from the second step. As a resource logic, LL was introduced syntactically rather than semantically,[5] essentially by taking classical sequent calculus and throwing out the rules that seemed unacceptable from some intuitive, naive resource point of view, so that, in the absence of a clear concept of truth or validity, the question about whether the resulting system was sound/complete could not even be meaningfully asked. In this process of syntactically rewriting classical logic some innocent, deeply hidden principles could have easily gotten victimized. Apparently the above-mentioned formulas separating CL from LL should be considered examples of such "victims". Of course, a number of attempts have been made to retroactively find a missing semantical justification for LL. Technically it is always possible to come up with some sort of a formal semantics that matches a given target syntactic construction, but the whole question is how natural and meaningful such a semantics is in its own right, and how adequately it captures the logic's underlying philosophy and ambitions. Unless, by good luck, the target system really *is* "the right logic", the chances of a decisive success when following the odd scheme "from syntax to semantics" can be rather slim. The natural scheme is "from semantics to syntax". It matches the way classical logic evolved and climaxed in Gödel's completeness theorem. And this is exactly the scheme that CL, too, follows.

Taking into account that classical validity and hence stability is recursively enumerable, obviously (the set of theorems of) **CL4** *is recursively enumerable.* [9] also proves that

Theorem 4. *The $\forall, \exists$-free fragment of* **CL4** *is decidable.*

This is a nice and perhaps not very obvious/expected fact, taking into account that the above fragment of **CL4** is still a first order logic as it contains

---

[5] A philosophically-minded reader would easily understand why the phase or coherent semantics do not count here.

the quantifiers $\sqcap, \sqcup$. This fragment is also natural as it gets rid of the only operators of the language that produce games with imperfect information.

Next, based on the straightforward observation that elementary formulas are derivable in **CL4** (in particular, from {} by Rule **(A)**) exactly when they are classically valid, we have:

Proposition 2. CL4 *is a conservative extension of classical first-order logic: an elementary* **CL4***-formula is classically valid if and only if it is provable in* **CL4***.*

The following theorem is the strongest technical result on CL known so far:

Theorem 5. (Japaridze [9]) **CL4** $\vdash F$ *iff* F *is valid* (*any* **CL4***-sentence* F). *Furthermore:*

Uniform-constructive soundness: *There is an effective procedure that takes a* **CL4***-proof of an arbitrary sentence* F *and constructs an HPM* $\mathcal{M}$ *such that, for every interpretation* *, $\mathcal{M}$ solves F^*.*

Strong completeness: *If* **CL4** $\not\vdash F$, *then* F^* *is not computable for some interpretation* * *that interprets each elementary atom as a finitary predicate and each general atom as a* $\sqcap, \sqcup$*-combination of finitary predicates.*

Here "**finitary predicate**" (or **finitary game** in general) is a predicate (game) A for which there is some finite set X of variables such that, for any two valuations e_1 and e_2 that agree on all variables from X, we have $e_1[A] = e_2[A]$. That is, only the values of those finitely many variables are relevant. A nonfinitary game generally depends on infinitely many variables, and appealing to this sort of games in a completeness proof could seriously weaken such a result: the reason for incomputability of a nonfinitary game could be just the fact that the machine can never finish reading all the relevant information from its valuation tape. Fortunately, in view of the strong completeness clause, it turns out that the question whether nonfinitary ICPs are allowed or not has no effect on the soundness and completeness of **CL4**; moreover, ICPs can be further restricted to the sort of games as simple as $\sqcap, \sqcup$-combinations of finitary predicates. Similarly, the uniform-constructive soundness clause dramatically strengthens the soundness result for **CL4** and, as this will be discussed in Section 8, opens application areas far beyond the pure theory of computing. Of course, both uniform-constructive soundness and strong completeness (automatically) hold for **CL1** and **CL2** as well, but the author has chosen to disclose this good news only in the present section.

Theorem 5, even though by an order of magnitude more informative than Gödel's completeness theorem for classical logic which it implies as a special case, is probably only a beginning of progress on the way of in-depth study of computability logic. Seeing what happens if we add parallel quantifiers and/or the recurrence group of operators to the language of **CL4**, or exploring some other—limited—$\wedge, \dot{\circ}, \lambda$-containing fragments of CL, remains a challenging but worthy task to pursue. Among the interesting fragments of CL is the one that only has general atoms and the operators $\sqcap, \sqcup, \sqcap, \sqcup, \circ\!-\,$, where $A \circ\!- B$ is defined as $(\flat A) \rightarrow B$. It was conjectured in [6] that the valid formulas of this language are exactly those provable in Heyting's intuitionistic calculus, with the above operators understood as the intuitionistic conjunction, disjunction, universal quantifier, existential quantifier and implication, respectively. The soundness part of this conjecture was successfully verified later in [10]. A verification of the remaining completeness part of the conjecture could signify a convincing "proof" of Kolmogorov's (1932) well-known but so far rather abstract thesis according to which intuitionistic logic is a logic of problems.

8 Applied Systems Based on CL

The original motivation underlying CL, presented in Sect. 1, was computability-theoretic: the approach provides a systematic answer to the question "what can be computed?", which is a fundamental question of computer science. Yet, a look at the uniform-constuctive soundness clause of Theorem 5 reveals that the CL paradigm is not only about *what* can be computed. It is equally about *how* problems can be computed/solved, suggesting that CL should have substantial utility, with its application areas not limited to theory of computing. In the present section we will briefly examine why and how CL is of interest in some other fields of study, such as knowledgebase systems, planning systems or constructive applied theories.

The reason for the failure of $p \sqcup \neg p$ as a computability-theoretic principle is that the problem represented by this formula may have no effective solution, that is, the predicate p^* may be undecidable. The reason why this principle fails in the context of knowledgebase systems, however, is much simpler. A knowledgebase system may fail to solve the problem *Female(Dana)* $\sqcup \neg Female(Dana)$ not because the latter has no effective solution (of course it has one), but because the system simply lacks sufficient knowledge to determine Dana's gender. On the other hand, any system would be able to "solve" the problem *Female(Dana)* $\vee \neg Female(Dana)$ as this is an automatically won elementary game so that there is nothing to solve at all. Similarly, while $\forall y \exists x Father(x, y)$ is an automatically solved elementary problem expressing the almost tautological knowledge that every person has a father, ability to solve the problem $\sqcap y \sqcup x Father(x, y)$ implies the nontrivial knowledge of everyone's actual father. Obviously the knowledge expressed by $A \sqcup B$ or $\sqcup x A(x)$ is generally stronger than the knowledge expressed by $A \vee B$ or $\exists x A(x)$, yet the language of classical logic fails to capture this difference, the difference whose relevance hardly requires any explanation. The traditional approaches to knowledgebase systems ([11, 13] etc.) try to mend this gap by augmenting the language of classical logic with special epistemic constructs, such as the modal "know that" operator **Know**, after which probably **Know**$A \vee$ **Know**B would be suggested as a translation for $A \sqcup B$

and $\forall y \exists x \mathbf{Know} A(x,y)$ for $\sqcap y \sqcup x A(x,y)$. Leaving it for the philosophers to argue whether, say, $\forall y \exists x \mathbf{Know} A(x,y)$ really expresses the constructive meaning of $\sqcap y \sqcup x A(x,y)$, and forgetting that epistemic constructs typically yield unnecessary and very unpleasant complications such as messiness and non-semidecidability of the resulting logics, some of the major issues still do not seem to be taken care of. Most of the actual knowledgebase and information systems are interactive, and what we really need is a logic of *interaction* rather than just a logic of knowledge. Furthermore, a knowledgebase logic needs to be *resource-conscious*. The informational resource expressed by $\sqcap x(Female(x) \sqcup \neg Female(x))$ is not as strong as the one expressed by $\sqcap x(Female(x) \sqcup \neg Female(x)) \wedge \sqcap x(Female(x) \sqcup \neg Female(x))$: the former implies the resource provider's commitment to tell only one (even though an arbitrary one) person's gender, while the latter is about telling any two people's genders.[6] Neither classical logic nor its standard epistemic extensions have the ability to account for such differences. CL promises to be adequate. It *is* a logic of interaction, it *is* resource-conscious, and it *does* capture the relevant differences between truth and actual ability to find/compute/know truth.

When CL is used as a logic of knowledgebases, its formulas represent interactive queries. A formula whose main operator is $\sqcup$ or $\bigsqcup$ can be understood as a question asked by the user, and a formula whose main operator is $\sqcap$ or $\bigsqcap$ a question asked by the system. Consider the problem $\sqcap x \sqcup y Has(x,y)$, where $Has(x,y)$ means "patient x has disease y" (with $Healthy$ counting as one of the possible "diseases"). This formula is the following question asked by the system: "Who do you want me to diagnose?" The user's response can be "Dana". This move brings the game down to $\sqcup y Has(Dana,y)$. This is now a question asked by the user: "What does Dana have?". The system's response can be "flu", taking us to the terminal position $Has(Dana, Flu)$. The system has been successful iff Dana really has flu.

Successfully solving the above problem $\sqcap x \sqcup y Has(x,y)$ requires having all relevant medical information for each possible patient, which in a real diagnostic system would hardly be the case. Most likely, such a system, after receiving a request to diagnose x, would make counterqueries regarding x's symptoms, blood pressure, test results, age, gender, etc., so that the query that the system will be solving would have a higher degree of interactivity than the two-step query $\sqcap x \sqcup y Has(x,y)$ does, with questions and counterquestions interspersed in some complex fashion. Here is when other computability-logic operations come into play. $\neg$ turns queries into counterqueries; parallel operations generate combined queries, with $\rightarrow$ acting as a query reduction operation; $\circ\!\!\downarrow, \lambda$ allow repeated queries, etc. Here we are expanding our example. Let $Sympt(x,s)$ mean "patient x has (set of) symptoms s", and $Pos(x,t)$ mean "patient x

---

[6] A reader having difficulty in understanding why this difference is relevant, may try to replace $Female(x)$ with $Acid(x)$, and then think of a (single) piece of litmus paper.

tests positive for test t". Imagine a diagnostic system that can diagnose any particular patient x, but needs some additional information. Specifically, it needs to know x's symptoms; plus, the system may require to have x taken a test t that it selects dynamically in the course of a dialogue with the user depending on what responses it received. The interactive task/query that such a system is performing/solving can then be expressed by the formula

$$\sqcap x\Big(\sqcup sSympt(x,s) \wedge \sqcap t\big(Pos(x,t) \sqcup \neg Pos(x,t)\big) \rightarrow \sqcup yHas(x,y)\Big). \quad (2)$$

A possible scenario of playing the above game is the following. At the beginning, the system waits until the user specifies a patient x to be diagnosed. We can think of this stage as systems's requesting the user to select a particular (value of) x, remembering that the presence of $\sqcap x$ automatically implies such a request. After a patient x, say $x = X$, is selected, the system requests to specify X's symptoms. Notice that our game rules make the system successful if the user fails to provide this information, i.e., specify a (the true) value for s in $\sqcup sSympt(X,s)$. Once a response, say, $s = S$, is received, the system selects a test $t = T$ and asks the user to perform it on X, i.e., to choose the true disjunct of $Pos(X,T) \sqcup \neg Pos(X,T)$. Finally, provided that the user gave correct answers to all counterqueries (and if not, the user has lost), the system makes a diagnostic decision, i.e., specifies a value Y for y in $\sqcup yHas(X,y)$ for which $Has(X,Y)$ is true.

The presence of a single "copy" of $\sqcap t\big(Pos(x,t) \sqcup \neg Pos(x,t)\big)$ in the antecedent of (2) means that the system may request testing a given patient only once. If n tests were potentially needed instead, this would be expressed by taking the $\wedge$-conjunction of n identical conjuncts $\sqcap t\big(Pos(x,t) \sqcup \neg Pos(x,t)\big)$. And if the system potentially needed an unbounded number of tests, then we would write $\wedge\sqcap t\big(Pos(x,t) \sqcup \neg Pos(x,t)\big)$, thus further weakening (2): a system that performs this weakened task is not as good as the one performing (2) as it requires stronger external (user-provided) informational resources. Replacing the main quantifier $\sqcap x$ by $\forall x$, on the other hand, would strengthen (2), signifying the system's ability to diagnose a patent purely on the basis of his/her symptoms and test result without knowing who the patient really is. However, if in its diagnostic decisions the system uses some additional information on patients such their medical histories stored in its knowledgebase and hence needs to know the patient's identity, $\sqcap x$ cannot be upgraded to $\forall x$. Replacing $\sqcap x$ by $\wedge x$ would be a yet another way to strengthen (2), signifying the system's ability to diagnose all patients rather than any particular one; obviously effects of at least the same strength would be achieved by just prefixing (2) with $\wedge$ or $\lozenge$.

As we just mentioned system's **knowledgebase**, let us make clear what it means. Formally, this is a finite $\wedge$-conjunction KB of formulas, which can also be thought of as the (multi)set of its conjuncts. We call the elements of this set the **internal informational resources** of the system. Intuitively, KB represents all of the nonlogical knowledge available to the system, so that (with a fixed built-in logic in mind) the strength of the former determines the query-solving power of the latter. Conceptually, however, we do not think of KB as a part of the system properly. The latter is just "pure", logic-based problem-solving software of universal utility that initially comes to the user without any nonlogical knowledge whatsoever. Indeed, built-in nonlogical knowledge would make it no longer universally applicable: Dana can be a female in the world of one potential user while a male in the world of another user, and $\forall x \forall y (x \times y = y \times x)$ can be false to a user who understands $\times$ as Cartesian rather than number-theoretic product. It is the user who selects and maintains KB for the system, putting into it all informational resources that (s)he believes are relevant, correct and maintainable. Think of the formalism of CL as a highly declarative programming language, and the process of creating KB as programming in it.

The knowledgebase KB of the system may include atomic elementary formulas expressing factual knowledge, such as $Female(Dana)$, or nonatomic elementary formulas expressing general knowledge, such as $\forall x (\exists y Father(x, y) \rightarrow Male(x))$ or $\forall x \forall y (x \times (y + 1) = (x \times y) + x)$; it can also include nonelementary formulas such as $\lfloor \sqcap x (Female(x) \sqcup Male(x))$, expressing potential knowledge of everyone's gender, or $\lfloor \sqcap x \sqcup y (x^2 = y)$, expressing ability to repeatedly compute the square function, or something more complex and more interactive such as formula (2). With each resource $R \in KB$ is associated (if not physically, at least conceptually) its **provider**—an agent that solves the query R for the system, i.e., plays the game R against the system. Physically the provider could be a computer program allocated to the system, or a network server having the system as a client, or another knowledgebase system to which the system has querying access, or even human personnel servicing the system. For example, the provider for $\lfloor \sqcap x \sqcup y Bloodpressure(x, y)$ would probably be a team of nurses repeatedly performing the task of measuring the blood pressure of a patient specified by the system and reporting the outcome back to the system. Again, we do not think of providers as a part of the system itself. The latter only sees *what* resources are available to it, without knowing or caring about *how* the corresponding providers do their job; furthermore, the system does not even care *whether* the providers really do their job right. The system's responsibility is only to correctly solve queries for the user *as long as* none of the providers fail to do their job. Indeed, if the system misdiagnoses a patient because a nurse-provider gave it wrong information about that patient's blood pressure, the hospital (ultimate user) is unlikely to fire the system and demand refund from its vendor; more likely, it would fire the nurse. Of course, when R is elementary, the provider has nothing to do, and its successfully playing R against the system simply means that R is true. Note that in the picture that we have just presented, the system plays each game $R \in KB$ in the role of $\perp$, so that, from the system's perspective, the game that it plays against the provider of R is $\neg R$ rather than R.

The most typical internal informational resources, such as factual knowledge or queries solved by computer programs, can be reused an arbitrary number of times and with unlimited branching capabilities, i.e., in the strong sense captured by the operator $\wedge$, and thus they would be prefixed with $\wedge$ as we did with $\sqcap x(Female(x) \sqcup Male(x))$ and $\sqcap x \sqcup y(x^2 = y)$. There was no point in $\wedge$-prefixing $Female(Dana)$, $\forall x(\exists y Father(x, y) \rightarrow Male(x))$ or $\forall x \forall y(x \times (y+1) = (x \times y) + x)$ because every elementary game A is equivalent to $\wedge A$ and hence remains "recyclable" even without recurrence operators. As noted in Sect. 1, there is no difference between $\wedge$ and λ as long as "simple" resources such as $\sqcap x \sqcup y(x^2 = y)$ are concerned. However, in some cases—say, when a resource with a high degree of interactivity is supported by an unlimited number of independent providers each of which however allows to run only one single "session"—the weaker operator λ will have to be used instead of $\wedge$. Yet, some of the internal informational resources could be essentially nonreusable. A provider possessing a single item of disposable pregnancy test device would apparently be able to support the resource $\sqcap x(Pregnant(x) \sqcup \neg Pregnant(x))$ but not $\wedge \sqcap x(Pregnant(x) \sqcup \neg Pregnant(x))$ and not even $\sqcap x(Pregnant(x) \sqcup \neg Pregnant(x)) \wedge \sqcap x(Pregnant(x) \sqcup \neg Pregnant(x))$. Most users, however, would try to refrain from including this sort of a resource into KB but rather make it a part (antecedent) of possible queries. Indeed, knowledgebases with non-recyclable resources would tend to weaken from query to query and require more careful maintainance/updates. The appeal of a knowledgebase entirely consisting of $\wedge,\lambda$-resources is its absolute persistence. Whether recyclable or not, all of the resources of KB can be used independently and in parallel. This is exactly what allows us to identify KB with the $\wedge$-conjunction of its elements.

Assume $KB = R_1 \wedge \ldots \wedge R_n$, and let us now try to visualize a system solving a query F for the user. The designer would probably select an interface where the user only sees the moves made by the system in F, and hence gets the illusion that the system is just playing F. But in fact the game that the system is really playing is $KB \rightarrow F$, i.e., $\neg R_1 \vee \ldots \vee \neg R_n \vee F$. Indeed, the system is not only interacting with the user in F, but, in parallel, also with its providers against whom, as we already know, it plays $\neg R_1, \ldots, \neg R_n$. As long as those providers do not fail to do their job, the system loses each of the games $\neg R_1, \ldots, \neg R_n$. Then our semantics for $\vee$ implies that the system wins its play over the "big game" $\neg R_1 \vee \ldots \vee \neg R_n \vee F$ if and only if it wins it in the F component, i.e., successfully solves the query F.

Thus, the system's ability to solve a query F reduces to its ability to generate a solution to $KB \rightarrow F$, i.e., a reduction of F to KB. What would give the system such an ability is built-in knowledge of CL, in particular, a **uniform-constructively sound axiomatization** of it, by which we mean a deductive system S (with effective proofs of its theorems) that satisfies the uniform-constructive soundness clause of Theorem 5 with "S" in the role of **CL4**. According to the uniform-constructive soundness property, it would be sufficient for the system to find a proof of $KB \rightarrow F$, which would allow it to (effectively) construct an HPM $\mathcal{M}$ and then run it on $KB \to F$ with a guaranteed success.

Notice that it is uniform-constructive soundness rather than simple soundness of the the built-in (axiomatization of the) logic that allows the knowledgebase system to function. Simple soundness just means that every provable formula is valid. This is not sufficient for two reasons. One reason is that validity of a formula E only implies that, for every interpretation *, a solution to the problem E^* exists. It may be the case, however, that different interpretations require different solutions, so that choosing the right solution requires knowledge of the actual interpretation, i.e., the *meaning*, of the atoms of E. Our assumption is that the system has no nonlogical knowledge which, in more precise terms, means nothing but that it has no knowledge of the interpretation *. Thus, a solution that the system generates for $KB^* \to F^*$ should be successful for any possible interpretation *. We call such an interpretation-independent solution, an HPM $\mathcal{M}$ that wins E^* for every interpretation *, a **uniform solution** to E, and correspondingly call a formula **uniformly valid** iff it has a uniform solution. The uniform-constructive soundness clause asserts that every provable formula is not only valid, but also uniformly valid. Going back to the example with which this section started, the reason why $p \sqcup \neg p$ fails in the context of computability theory is that it is not valid, while the reason for the failure of this principle in the context of knowledgebase systems is that it is not uniformly valid: its solution, even if it existed for each interpretation *, generally would depend on whether p^* is true or false, and the system would be unable to figure out the truth status of p^* unless this information was explicitly or implicitly contained in KB. Thus, for knowledgebase systems the primary semantical concept of interest is uniform validity rather than validity. But does having two different concepts of validity mean that we will have to deal with two different logics? Not really. According to Conjecture 26.2 of [6], *a formula of the language of CL is valid if and only if it is uniformly valid*. Our Theorem 5 with its uniform-constructive soundness clause signifies a successful verification of this conjecture for **CL4**-sentences: such a sentence is valid iff it is uniformly valid iff it is provable in **CL4**. There are good reasons to expect that this nice extensional equivalence between validity and uniform validity continues to hold for all reasonable extensions of the language of **CL4** and, in particular, its extension with $\flat, ?, \lambda, Y, \wedge, \vee$.

The other reason why simple soundness of the built-in logic would not be sufficient for a knowledgebase system to function—even if every provable formula was known to be uniformly valid—is the following. With simple soundness, after finding a proof of E, even though the system would know that a solution to E^* exists, it might have no way to actually find such a solution. On the other hand, uniform-constructive soundness guarantees that a (uniform) solution to every provable formula not only exists, but can be effectively extracted from a proof.

As for completeness of the built-in logic—unlike uniform-constructive soundness—it is a desirable but not necessary condition. So far a complete axiomatization has been found only for the fragment of CL limited to the language of **CL4**. We hope that the future will bring completeness results for more expressive fragments as well. But even if not, we can still certainly succeed in finding ever stronger axiomatizations that are uniform-constructively sound even if not necessarily complete. Extending **CL4** with some straightforward rules such as the ones that allow to replace $\flat F$ by $F \wedge \flat F$ and λF by $F \wedge \lambda F$, the rules $F \mapsto \flat F$, $F \mapsto \lambda F$, etc. would already immensely strengthen the logic. It should also be remembered that, when it comes to practical applications in the proper sense, the logic that will be used is likely to be far from complete anyway. Say, the popular classical-logic-based systems and programming languages are incomplete, and the reason is not that a complete axiomatization for classical logic is not known, but rather the unfortunate fact of life that often efficiency only comes at the expense of completeness.

But even **CL4**, as it is now, is already very powerful. Why don't we see a simple example to feel the flavor of it as a query-solving logic. Let $Acid(x)$ mean "solution x contains acid", and $Red(x)$ mean "litmus paper turns red in solution x". Assume that the knowledgebase KB of a **CL4**-based system contains $\forall x\big(Red(x) \rightarrow Acid(x)\big)$, $\forall x\big(Acid(x) \rightarrow Red(x)\big)$ and $\sqcap x\big(Red(x) \sqcup \neg Red(x)\big)$, accounting for knowledge of the fact that a solution contains acid iff the litmus paper turns red in it, and for availability of a provider who possesses a piece of litmus paper that it can dip into any solution and report the paper's color to the system. Then the system can solve the acidity query $\sqcap x\big(Acid(x) \sqcup \neg Acid(x)\big)$. This follows from the fact—left as an exercise for the reader to verify—that $\mathbf{CL4} \vdash KB \rightarrow \sqcap x\big(Acid(x) \sqcup \neg Acid(x)\big)$.

An implicit assumption underlying our discussions so far was that an interpretation is fixed in a context and does not change its values. Making just one more step and departing from this unchanging-interpretation assumption opens significantly wider application areas for CL, in particular, the more general area of planning and physical-informational (vs. just informational) resource management systems. We call such (CL-based) systems **resourcebase systems**. In this new context, interpretations in the old, unchanging sense can be renamed into **situations**, with the term "interpretation" reserved for the more general concept of possibly dynamic mapping from atoms to ICPs, mapping whose values may keep changing from situation to situation, with situations intuitively being nothing but "snapshots" of interpretations. Dynamic interpretations are indeed the common case in real world. Perhaps Dana is not pregnant in a given situation, so that $(Pregnant(Dana))^* = \bot$. But it may happen that the situation changes so that * reinterprets $Pregnant(Dana)$ into $\top$. Furthermore, probably Dana has full control over whether she gets pregnant or not. This means that she can successfully maintain the resource $Pregnant(Dana) \sqcap \neg Pregnant(Dana)$ which, unlike $Pregnant(Dana) \sqcup \neg Pregnant(Dana)$, generally no agent would be able to maintain if the situation was fixed and unmanageable. Thus, in the context of resourcebase systems, successful game-playing no longer means just correctly answering questions. It may involve performing physical tasks, i.e., controlling/managing situations. Think of the task performed by a ballistic missile. With t ranging over all reachable targets, this task can be expressed by $\sqcap tDestroyed(t)$. The user makes a move by specifying a target $t = T$. This amounts to commanding the missile to destroy T. Provided that the latter indeed successfully performs its task, the user's command will be satisfied: the situation, in which (the interpretation of) $Destroyed(T)$ was probably false, will change and $Destroyed(T)$ become true. The same example demonstrates the necessity for a planning logic to be resource-conscious. With only one missile available as a resource, an agent would be able to destroy any one target but not two. This is accounted for by the fact that $\sqcap tDestroyed(t) \rightarrow Destroyed(x)$ is valid while $\sqcap tDestroyed(t) \rightarrow Destroyed(x) \wedge Destroyed(y)$ is not.

The earlier-discussed CL-based knowledgebase systems solve problems in a uniform, interpretation-independent way. This means that whether the interpretation is unchanging or dynamic is technically irrelevant for them, so that exactly the same systems, without any modifications whatsoever, can be used for solving planning problems (instead of just solving queries) such as how to destroy target T or how to make Dana pregnant, with their knowledgebases (KB)—renamed into **resourcebases** (RB)—now containing physical, situation-managing resources such as $\sqcap tDestroyed(t)$ along with old-fashioned informational resources. See Sect. 26 of [6] for an illustrative example of a planning problem solved with CL. CL and especially extensions of its present version with certain new game operators, such as sequential versions of conjunction/disjunction, quantifiers and recurrence operators,[7] might have good potential as a new logical paradigm for AI planning systems.

The fact that CL is a conservative extension of classical logic also makes it a reasonable and appealing alternative to the latter in its most traditional and

---

[7] Here is an informal outline of one of the—perhaps what could be called *oblivious*—versions of sequential operators. The **sequential conjunction** $A\triangle B$ is a game that starts and proceeds as a play of A; it will also end as an ordinary play of A unless, at some point, $\bot$ makes a special "switch" move; to this move—it is OK if with a delay—$\top$ should respond with an "acknowledgment" move (if such a response is never made, $\top$ loses), after which A is abandoned, and the play continues/restarts as a play of B without the possibility to go back to A. The **sequential universal quantification** $\triangle xA(x)$ is then defined as $A(1)\triangle A(2)\triangle A(3)\triangle\ldots$, and the **sequential recurrence** λA as $A\triangle A\triangle A\triangle\ldots$ In both cases $\bot$ is considered the loser if it makes a switch move infinitely many times. As this can be understood, the dual operators: **sequential disjunction** $\triangledown$, **sequential existential quantifier** $\triangledown$ and **sequential corecurrence** $\curlyvee$ will be defined in a symmetric way with the roles of the two players interchanged. Note that, as a resource, λA is the weakest among $\lambda A, \curlywedge A, \delta A$: just like $\curlywedge A$ and δA, λA allows the user to restart A an arbitrary number of times; however, unlike the case with $\curlywedge A$ and δA, only one session of A can be run at a time, and restarting A signifies giving up the previous run(s) of it. See Sect. 2 of [10] for a more detailed discussion of how the three sorts of recurrence operations compare.

unchallenged application areas. In particular, it makes perfect sense to base applied theories, such as, say, Peano arithmetic (axiomatic number theory), on CL instead of classical logic. Due to conservativity, no old information would be lost or weakened this way. On the other hand, we would get by an order of magnitude more expressive, constructive and computationally meaningful theories than their classical-logic-based versions. Let us see a little more precisely what we mean by a CL-based applied theory. For simplicity, we restrict our considerations to the cases when the set AX of nonlogical **axioms** of the applied theory is finite. As we did with KB, we identify AX with the $\wedge$-conjunction of its elements. From (the problem represented by) AX—or, equivalently, each conjunct of it—we require to be computable in our sense, i.e., come with an HPM that solves it. So, notice, all of the axioms of the old, classical-logic-based version of the theory could be automatically included into the new set AX because they represent true and hence computable elementary problems. Many of those old axioms can be constructivized by, say, replacing blind or parallel operators with their choice equivalents. For example, we would want to rewrite the axiom $\forall x \exists y(y = x + 1)$ of arithmetic as the more informative $\sqcap x \sqcup y(y = x + 1)$. And, of course, to the old axioms or their constructivized versions could be added some essentially new axioms expressing basic computability principles specific to (the particular interpretation underlying) the theory. Provability (theoremhood) of a formula F in such a theory we understand as provability of the formula $AX \to F$ in the underlying axiomatization of CL which, as in the case of knowledgebase systems, is assumed to be uniform-constructively sound. The rule of modus ponens has been shown in [6] (Proposition 21.3) to preserve computability in the following uniform-constructive sense:

Theorem 6. *There is an effective function* $f: \{HPMs\} \times \{HPMs\} \to \{HPMs\}$ *such that, for any HPMs* $\mathcal{M}, \mathcal{N}$ *and ICPs A,B, if* $\mathcal{M}$ *solves A and* $\mathcal{N}$ *solves* $A \to B$, *then* $f(\mathcal{M}, \mathcal{N})$ *solves B.*

This theorem, together with our assumptions that AX is computable and that the underlying logic is uniform-constructively sound, immediately implies that the problem represented by any theorem F of the applied theory is computable and that, furthermore, a solution to such a problem can be effectively constructed from a proof of F. So, for example, once a formula $\sqcap x \sqcup y p(x, y)$ has been proven, we would know that, for every x, a y with $p(x, y)$ not only exists, but can be algorithmically found; furthermore, we would be able to actually construct such an algorithm. Similarly, a reduction—in the sense of Definition 7(3)—of the acceptance problem to the halting problem would automatically come with a proof of $\sqcap x \sqcap y(Halts(x, y) \sqcup \neg Halts(x, y)) \to \sqcap x \sqcap y(Accepts(x, y) \sqcup \neg Accepts(x, y))$ in such a theory. Does not this look like exactly what the constructivists have been calling for?..

* * *

As a conclusive remark, the author wants to point out that the story told in this paper was only about the tip of the iceberg called CL. Even though the phrase "*the* language of CL" was used in some semiformal contexts, such a language has no official boundaries and, depending on particular needs or taste, remains open to various sorts of interesting new operators. The general framework of CL is also ready to accommodate any reasonable weakening modifications of its absolute-strength computation model HPM,[8] thus keeping a way open for studying logics of sub-Turing computability and developing a systematic theory of interactive complexity.

References

1. J. van Benthem. *Logic in Games*. Lecture Notes, Institute for Logic, Language and Computation (ILLC), University of Amsterdam, 2001.
2. A. Blass. A game semantics for linear logic. *Ann Pure Appl Logic* 56:183-220, 1992.
3. J. Girard. Linear logic. *Theoret Comp Sci* 50:1-102, 1987.
4. D. Goldin. Persistent Turing machines as a model of interactive computation. *Lecture Notes in Comp Sci* 1762:116-135, 2000.
5. D. Goldin, S. Smolka, P. Attie, E. Sonderegger. Turing machines, transition systems and interaction. *Information and Computation* 194:101-128, 2004.
6. G. Japaridze. Introduction to computability logic. *Ann Pure Appl Logic* 123:1-99, 2003.
7. G. Japaridze. Propositional computability logic I-II. *ACM Transactions on Computational Logic* 7:202-262, 2006.
8. G. Japaridze. From truth to computability I. *Theoret Comp Sci* 357:100-135, 2006.

---

[8] Among the most natural modifications of this sort might be depriving the HPM of its infinite work tape, leaving in its place just a write-only buffer where the machine constructs its moves. In such a modification the exact type of read access to the run and valuation tapes becomes relevant, and a reasonable restriction would apparently be to allow—perhaps now multiple—read heads to move only in one direction. An approach favoring this sort of machines would try to model Turing (unlimited) or sub-Turing (limited) computational resources such as memory, time, etc. as games, and then understand computing a problem A with resources represented by R as computing $R \to A$, thus making explicit not only trans-Turing (incomputable) resources as we have been doing in this paper, but also all of the Turing/sub-Turing resources needed or allowed for computing A, the resources that the ordinary HPM, PTM or Turing machine models take for granted. So, with T representing the infinite read/write tape as a computational resource, computability of A in the old sense would mean nothing but computability of $T \to A$ in the new sense: having T in the antecedent would amount to having infinite memory, only this time provided externally (by the environment) via the run tape rather than internally via the work tape.

9. G. Japaridze. From truth to computability II.
   http://arxiv.org/abs/cs.LO/0501031, 2005.
10. G. Japaridze. Intuitionistic computability logic. *Acta Cybernetica* (to appear).
11. K. Konolige. On the relation between default and autoepistemic logic. In: *Proceedings of the International Joint Conference on Artificial Intelligence*. Detroit, MI, 1989.
12. R. Milner. Elements of interaction. *Communications of the ACM* 36:79-89, 1993.
13. R. Moore. A formal theory of knowledge and action. In: Hobbs J, Moore R (eds.) *Formal Theories of Commonsense Worlds*. Ablex, Norwood, N.J., 1985.
14. M. Sipser. *Introduction to the Theory of Computation*, 2nd Edition. Thomson Course Technology, Boston, MA, 2006.
15. A. Turing. On Computable numbers with an application to the entscheidungsproblem. *Proc London Math Soc* 2.42:230-265, 1936.
16. P. Wegner. Interactive foundations of computing. *Theoret Comp Sci* 192:315-351, 1998.

Part III

Applications

Human–Computer Interaction

Michel Beaudouin-Lafon

Université Paris-Sud, Orsay, France

1 Introduction

Human–computer interaction (HCI) is a multidisciplinary field "concerned with the design, evaluation and implementation of interactive computing systems for human use and with the study of major phenomena surrounding them" [24]. A *human–computer system*[1] is typically made up of two components: the *user interface* and the *functional core*. The user interface captures user input and turns it into calls to the functional core, which typically implements the algorithmic component of the system. The user interface also turns the results of its calls to the functional core into output to be presented to the user. A human–computer system therefore interacts with its user(s) through its user interface.

Human–computer systems are arguably the first truly interactive systems. In 1963, Ivan Sutherland's SketchPad [48] was the first system to use pen input on a CRT display, pioneering direct manipulation techniques that are still in use today. Forty years later, millions of people interact with graphical user interfaces on a daily basis, to the point where computers are often reduced to their input-output devices and applications to their user interface.

Yet human–computer systems are still created at great cost with algorithmic approaches. More than a decade ago, a study showed that on average 50% of the development cost of human–computer systems is spent on the user interface [37]. One of the main reasons was the lack of proper tools to develop such interfaces, their growing complexity and the inability to test them thoroughly. There is no reason to believe that the situation has changed substantially since then because the tools in use today are based on the same concepts as twenty years ago.

---

[1] Since the term "interactive system" that is normally used in HCI has a more general meaning in this book, this chapter uses the term "human–computer system" instead.

User interfaces are notoriously difficult to program, debug and maintain because they exacerbate many aspects of interactive systems. For example, traditional interactive systems, i.e., systems that interact with other computer systems, often rely on well-specified protocols so that it is fairly easy to anticipate future possible inputs. Human–computer systems, for they have a human in the loop, cannot rely on such strict protocols. In order to give the user a sense of control, they must be prepared to receive virtually any input at any moment, and react to it in a way that will be understandable to the user. Therefore the state space of a human–computer system is extremely large.

This chapter evaluates some unique aspects of human–computer systems with respect to the five characteristics of interactive systems outlined in the preface of this book:

- *Nonalgorithmic computational problem*: human–computer systems are often created by turning an algorithmic system into an interactive one in order to give the users more control over the process; at the same time, many human–computer systems are not meant to solve a particular algorithmic problem but instead to extend human capabilities in order to address more open-ended situations.
- *Dynamic interleaving of user input and system output streams*: human–computer systems feature intricate dependencies between input and output streams, with tight timing constraints and large abstraction mismatches between user, streams and computer.
- *Dependency on the environment*: the evolution towards novel forms of interaction, such as ubiquitous and pervasive computing, mixed and augmented reality, and tangible interfaces, extends the environment of human–computer systems to the physical world and blurs the distinction between physical and digital artifacts.
- *Parallel "computation" of user and computer*: the unique characteristics of human users as well as the distributed nature of many interfaces require multiple threads and various levels of parallelism and synchronization between user and computer.
- *Noncomputability of the environment*: humans are inherently noncomputable, but the learning and adaptation capabilities of users and computers can be leveraged to create more powerful human–computer systems.

The chapter covers a wide range of user interface styles and techniques, from traditional graphical user interfaces to advanced research, and considers the full life-cycle of human–computer systems from design to evaluation.

2 Computational Problem

> *Models of interaction capture the notion of performing a task or pro-*
> *viding a service, rather than algorithmically producing outputs from*
> *inputs.*[2]

This section shows that the type of problems addressed by human–computer systems has shifted from purely computational problems to open-ended problem solving. Nowadays, human–computer systems help users incrementally construct solutions to evolving problems rather than producing definitive answers to well-formed questions. Douglas Engelbart was probably the first to clearly articulate the vision that computers can "augment human intellect" and help solve problems that humans alone and computers alone could not solve [14]. For this vision to take shape, computer systems should be evaluated in terms of how well they support the creative and problem-solving process, not in terms of their pure algorithmic power.

Multiple approaches exist to support problem-solving with computer systems. The style of interaction may involve treating the computer as a tool that augments human capabilities, as a partner to which one delegates tasks, or as a medium to communicate with other users and solve problems collaboratively. The rest of this section describes these three *interaction paradigms*, presents a generic *conceptual model* that emphasizes the interactive nature of human–computer systems, and introduces *cognitive dimensions* to help understand the interactive nature of users' activities.

2.1 Interaction Paradigms

Early user interfaces were created to allow users to specify input values for algorithms, e.g., for ballistics calculations in the very early days of computer science. Even nowadays, some user interfaces are created solely for the purpose of specifying inputs and displaying the output of an algorithm, for example in biology for analyzing DNA. Users of these systems are nevertheless invariably frustrated by the limited amount of control they have over such user interfaces. They want to change parameters of the algorithm while it runs, or see its state or a partial output before it is finished. Adding such control over input and output is typical of turning an algorithmic software into an interactive one and drives the design of many human–computer systems.

The power of spreadsheet programs, for example, lies in their ability to embody a computation in a flexible environment where users can easily change input values as well as formulas and display correlations between input and output through plots and graphs. At some level, changing a cell in a spreadsheet just "re-runs the program", and is therefore algorithmic. At a higher level though, using a spreadsheet means changing cells to test several hypotheses, editing formulas to try variants of the computation, designing plots

---

[2] The quotes at the beginning of each section are from the preface of the book.

and graphs that give better insights into the problem under scrutiny. At this level, the spreadsheet program is used interactively, not algorithmically.

While spreadsheets are an example of tools that empower users by giving them direct control over a complex calculation, other styles of interaction exist where the roles of users and computers differ. The various interaction styles can be classified into three main *interaction paradigms*, as follows:

1. *First-person interfaces* are systems where the user directly engages with the *objects of interest* and uses tools and commands to manipulate these objects directly. In graphical user interfaces, the objects of interest refer both to the computational artifacts that exist inside the system and their representation on the screen. For example, in a desktop interfaces, the files and folders of a file system are represented by icons and windows on the screen. The user can interact with the computational artifacts through their representation using a pointing device, typically a mouse, and interaction objects such as menus and dialogue boxes. The system updates the graphical representation in response to its interpretation of the user actions, maintaining the consistency between the displayed state and the internal state of the system. Direct manipulation [44] and instrumental interaction [3, 5] are interaction models that give rules and guidelines for the design of such interfaces.

2. *Second-person interfaces* are based on the user delegating tasks to the system and the system reporting back on the progress of these tasks. The system is seen as a partner, and can only be effective if it has a good representation of the user and the user's tasks. This usually requires artificial intelligence techniques such as machine learning to adapt to the user and users' tasks dynamically (see also Sect. 6). Agent-based systems [34] fall into this category, as do most approaches based on natural language interaction, whether written or spoken, and avatars. Because of the sequential nature of interaction in these systems, they are often called *dialogue systems*.

3. *Third-person interfaces* are systems that mediate the communication among humans, i.e., users interact with the system in order to communicate with each other. E-mail, instant messaging and video-conferencing are examples of third-person interfaces. Shared whiteboards, and more generally shared editors, where users can interact simultaneously on the same objects, also fall into this category. The field of computer-supported cooperative work (CSCW) studies such systems [6].

All three paradigms emphasize the use of computers as a means to achieve a task, not an end. This is often misunderstood by computer scientists and software designers for whom the use of a computer is often an end rather than a means. The use of computers for human–human communication (third-person interfaces) clearly emphasizes this distinction: When exchanging email or instant messages or when collectively editing a shared document, the computer acts as a medium for communication, not a computational engine. First- and second-person interfaces are also widely used for open-ended tasks, in particular creative tasks such as text-editing, music composition, graphics and video editing (SketchPad [48] was arguably the first computer-aided design tool). With creative activities, the "problem" to be solved is not fully defined in the user's mind nor is the test to decide whether the problem is solved. Yet computers have been instrumental in the development of creative activities in many areas, from sound synthesis to special visual effects, from typography to music composition, from architecture to product design.

The rest of this chapter focuses mostly on first-person interfaces, primarily because they are the most widespread today. Nevertheless most of the arguments developed in the chapter apply to all three types of interfaces.

2.2 Conceptual Model

Figure 1 shows a generic conceptual model of a human–computer system. The user issues *commands* and receives *feedback* from the system to show that they are properly entered. The commands are then transformed into *operations* that modify the internal objects of the system and produces responses that are transmitted back to the user, typically by updating the screen display. For example, when the user drags the icon of a file towards the trash (command), the feedback is the ghost image of the icon being dragged and the highlighting of potential targets for the drag. Dragging an icon to the trash is interpreted as deleting the file represented by this icon. If the operation succeeds, the icon disappears from the screen and the trash looks fuller.

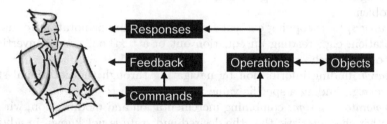

Fig. 1. Conceptual model of human–computer system

Feedback is an essential aspect of user interfaces. Without feedback of the keystrokes, one could not enter text reliably; without feedback of an icon being dragged, one could not use direct manipulation efficiently. As we will see in the next section, feedback requires a tight interleaving of user actions and system responses. Because of this tight coupling, a human–computer system is not purely algorithmic: user actions determine the feedback, and the feedback guides the next actions of the user. Since the system cannot know what the user has in mind, it cannot anticipate the user's next moves.

Moreover, many user interfaces, including graphical user interfaces, must maintain a permanent and up-to-date representation of the objects of interest. This representation is updated in response to user commands as well as when the state of the objects changes for other reasons. For example, an interface that displays the state of the file system must update its display when files are created and deleted, whether these operations are carried out by the user of the system or by a third party. Shared editors also exhibit this behavior: when another user edits the document, changes must be propagated to all other users. In practice, a standard way to program such interfaces is to use an *Observer* design pattern [18] that tracks changes to the objects and updates the display. This often requires modifying the software that implements the objects in order to provide proper notification of state changes, which is typical of turning an algorithmic software into an interactive one.

2.3 Cognitive Dimensions

Thomas Green [21, 22] has introduced a framework called *cognitive dimensions* that helps evaluate the design of information artifacts, including human–computer systems. This framework focuses on the representations used to depict the manipulated objects, called *notations*, and their *structure*. It introduces the following classification of users' activities [8]:

- *Incrementation:* adding further information to a notation without altering the structure in any way, e.g., adding a new formula to a spreadsheet;
- *Modification:* changing an existing notational structure, possibly without adding new content, e.g., changing a spreadsheet for use with a different problem;
- *Transcription:* copying content from one structure or notation to another notation, e.g., reading an equation out of a textbook, and converting it into a spreadsheet formula;
- *Search:* finding information by navigating through the notational structure, e.g., finding a specific value in a spreadsheet;
- *Exploratory design:* combining incrementation and modification, with the further characteristic that the desired end state is not known in advance, e.g., programming a spreadsheet on the fly or "hacking".

Different types of activities may involve using the same functions of the system, however each activity may raise specific requirements so that different commands are needed for each function. For example, when creating a presentation with, e.g., Microsoft Powerpoint, *incrementation* consists of creating new slides or adding content to existing slides, whereas *transcription* consists of copying content from an external source. The latter is facilitated by the ability to copy-paste text and diagrams across applications, while the former requires editing commands to create texts and diagrams within the application. Similarly, while *modification* and *exploratory design* both involve changing the design of the slides and their order, they may require different commands. Modification is typically used to create a presentation from an existing one and typically begins by saving the old file under a new name. Exploratory design, on the other hand, consists in exploring multiple alternatives and would be much facilitated if the user could bookmark and recall these alternatives rather than having to save them to different files. Finally, *search* can take many forms, from visual search of the thumbnails (performed by the user) to textual search through the outline of the presentation (performed by the system).

The spreadsheet and presentation software examples show that users are not primarily interested in having the system algorithmically produce definitive answers to well-formed questions, but rather that they use the system to incrementally construct solutions to evolving problems. In fact, it is precisely when problems are ill-defined that human–computer systems are needed: if the problem were well-defined, an algorithmic approach with no human in the loop would suffice.

Green's *cognitive dimensions* help better understand the problems users face when working with interactive software. While there are more than a dozen dimensions in the framework, we illustrate three of them here.

The cognitive dimension called *premature commitment* describes situations where the system imposes an order on the actions to be taken by users that forces them to make decisions ahead of time. Premature commitment is very frequent in computer systems and shows evidence of algorithmic behavior, i.e., situations where it is more convenient (for the system) to know all input at the beginning of the computation, while an interactive behavior would be preferable. For example, when saving a file for the first time, the system requires the user to enter the name of the file even though the user may not know the exact name he wants to use yet. Moreover, the user must commit his choice before knowing whether it creates a conflict with another file.

Another cognitive dimension is *viscosity* or resistance to change, i.e., how hard it is to make changes to previous work. For example, many text editors cannot change all bold text to italics in one command: the user has to go through the text by hand. The use of text and paragraph styles reduces this viscosity, however it still shows up when trying to edit a large document made of multiple files, where changes to a style have to be duplicated in each file. The combination of premature commitment and viscosity is particularly problematic: not only is the user asked to make a choice too early (premature commitment), but the cost of changing his mind is high (viscosity).

One last example of cognitive dimension is *progressive evaluation*, which describes whether it is possible to stop in the middle of a process and see the current result. This is again a case where the algorithmic approach causes problems since an algorithm is typically not interruptible and only gives its answer at the end of execution. Searching is a good example where progressive evaluation is useful: rather than having to wait until a whole database has been looked up, the system should present the matches as they are found. This gives the user a sense of progress, and if the right match shows up early, the user can interrupt the search. Another example is downloading a large file, where one would like to see what is being downloaded progressively in order to cancel the operation early if needed. Note that progress indicators (see Sect. 5.1) are a poor form of progressive evaluation.

The above three dimensions alone help better understand the mismatch between the capabilities of humans and computers, which is the major challenge for designers of human–computer systems. They also emphasize the users' need to keep options open, to make complex changes simply and to control the computational processes tightly.

In summary, human–computer systems are interactive by nature. Whether the system is used as a tool, as an agent or as a medium, its role is to complement, extend and augment the capabilities of the human users rather than give definite answers to well-defined problems.

3 Dynamic Streams

Interactions may consist of interleaved inputs and outputs modeled by dynamic streams; future input values can depend on past output values.

Human–computer systems are characterized by three types of dependencies: between input and output, between system state and interface, and between system and environment. After describing these dependencies, this section analyzes the mismatch between the low-level abstractions of input/output events and the high-level abstractions manipulated by both the user and computer. Finally it looks at current approaches to tackle these problems: event-based programming and formal models based on automata.

3.1 Three Types of Dependencies

Human–computer systems exhibit both dependencies between input and output streams: between later values of input streams and earlier values of output streams on the one hand, and between earlier values of input streams and later values of output streams on the other hand. The former corresponds to the fact that user actions depend on earlier system output. In graphical user interfaces, input commands such as clicking with the mouse are *always* interpreted relatively to the current display of the system as produced by earlier outputs. Such dependencies can be short-term as well as long-term: short-term dependencies correspond to the feedback provided by the system while the user specifies a command; long-term dependencies occur at the higher level of planning goals and subgoals and adjusting one's actions to the result of previous ones.

The other type of dependency, from earlier input to later output, is captured by the *side effects* that input actions have on the state of the interface, i.e., its internal objects. These are a special case of a more general form of dependency: the consistency between the internal system state of the system and the state displayed by the interface. These dependencies are the *raison d'être* of user interfaces, since users expect to see the effects of their actions and trust what they see. A good user interface will go out of its way to make these dependencies perceivable by the users, e.g., through animation. The fact that a dependency exists, i.e., that there is a causal path in the program, is not sufficient to make sure that it will be perceived and interpreted properly by the user. For example, minimizing a window may close it and display a window icon or button in a task bar. Without an animation, the user is unlikely to understand which icon or button now represents the window. This is worse when the state change is not initiated by the user. For example, if a window is opened on a remote file server and the server shuts down, a notification or animation must give the user a chance to understand what happened. Timing constraints are critical in that matter (see also Sect. 5.1): an animation will go unnoticed if it is too short and will get boring if it is too long; time delays between user action and system reaction must be bounded in order to perceive causality. In fact the perceived responsiveness of a user interface critically depends on properly accounting for these dependencies and the corresponding timing constraints.

In addition these side effects of user actions often need to be persistent. For example, a desktop interface must remember the positions of the icons on the display so that the next time the system is run, the icons will be at the same locations. This often creates problems with legacy applications where objects cannot be extended to include the necessary extra information to ensure full persistence. For example, the Unix file system cannot store icon locations as part of the i-nodes that represent the file system on disk, while the Macintosh file system can. As a result, desktop interfaces that run on top of Unix store icon locations in a separate database, which causes problems when files are manipulated by applications that are not aware of this database. This leads to the third type of dependency, between the system and its environment.

Human–computer systems often involve a variety of input and output streams which may have very diverse characteristics. For example, mice and keyboards provide low-bandwidth input, but sound and video input require much higher bandwidth. Video output to a display requires so much bandwidth that dedicated graphics hardware has become part of most computers in order to off-load the main CPU. With multimodal interaction [40] and ubiquitous computing [52, 53], the number and diversity of input and output streams keeps growing, and so do the dependencies among those streams.

3.2 Abstraction Mismatch

A common characteristic of the streams produced by a computer's input and output devices is their low level of abstraction: a mouse provides relative motion and button click events, a microphone provides raw sound samples, a video camera provides images made of pixels; for output, graphics cards implement primitives such as line segments, filled polygons and bitmap images. Even though the human and the computer both work at high levels of abstraction, the channels that connect them carry low-level information.

On the human side, Norman's action theory (see Sect. 6.1) refers to the *gulf of execution* and the *gulf of evaluation* to describe this abstraction mismatch [9]. The gulf of execution is the distance between the abstract desired goal of the task at hand and the actual physical actions required to (try to) reach this goal; the gulf of evaluation is the distance between the state of the system as perceived from its display and the user interpretation of whether the goal has been achieved.

A major goal of designing user interfaces is to reduce both gulfs. Well-designed metaphors, such as the well-known desktop metaphor, can be very effective in that matter: deleting files by dragging them to the trash requires less cognitive effort than remembering the name and syntax of a command-line interface. The dependencies between output streams and input streams are more explicit in graphical user interfaces than in many second-person interfaces because the commands directly refer, through pointing, to objects created by former system output. This reduces the gulf of execution by supporting more intuitive commands, such as moving objects by dragging them with the mouse. Conversely, perceiving the dependencies between the system's input and output streams, i.e., between user actions and system response, helps to reduce the gulf of evaluation. For example, seeing an icon disappear after it has been dragged to the trash makes it easy to understand what happened. With a Unix shell, the gulf of evaluation is larger: the response received for the file deletion command (`rm myfile`) is a simple prompt, which must be interpreted as "the command was executed successfully and therefore the file was deleted". Indeed, even advanced users often type an `ls` command (list files) after deleting a file to make sure it is really gone.

The abstraction mismatch exists on the computer side as well. Low-level input events must be interpreted into commands and operations, while feedback and responses must be translated into low-level display primitives. Dependencies among input streams must be extracted, e.g., clicking a mouse button while the Shift key is depressed, dependencies between input streams and output streams must be made perceivable by the user, e.g., highlighting folder icons while a file icon is being dragged over them, and dependencies between output streams must be enforced, e.g., images and sounds must be synchronized during an animation.

Extracting and creating these dependencies is especially difficult because the system must essentially behave as a real-time system: it must react to input events in bounded time. The time constants of the human perception systems range from a few milliseconds to a few hundred milliseconds. Although this may seem long when compared with the speed of today's computers, many applications do not match these constraints because of the abstraction mismatch. For example, browsing through a video or scrolling through a large collection of photos or a long document is rarely smooth unless explicit steps are taken to trade display quality for speed [49]. Indeed, there is no need to display an image at full resolution if the user is browsing but as soon as the user stops, the image must be refined to show all its details. Moreover, humans are very sensitive to jitter, i.e., to variations in response time over time, so that a "best effort" approach is not always the most appropriate.

3.3 Event-Based Programming

Even though the various types of dependencies between input and output streams in human–computer systems are well understood, the tools used to program user interfaces are still very primitive. The vast majority of user interfaces are organized around an *event loop* [39]: Input drivers append events to a global event queue every time the state of an input device changes. The application is supposed to retrieve and handle events as fast as it can. This is achieved by dispatching events to *event handlers* according to the event type, the event target (typically the object under the cursor) and the global state of the interface. The logic for this dispatching is often complex, hard to understand and hard to maintain: the code that handles a single interaction, such as a drag and drop, is scattered among several event handlers that have to communicate through global variables. As pointed out by Myers [35], the application becomes a "spaghetti of callbacks".

Many user interface toolkits such as GTk, Windows or the Macintosh toolbox are based on variants of the event-loop approach. They do provide an abstraction, called the *widget*, that encapsulates into a single object a presentation (how the widget looks on-screen), a behavior (how it reacts to input events) and an application interface (how it notifies the rest of the application of its state changes). Widgets work relatively well for simple interactions such as buttons, menus and scrollbars where interaction occurs within the same object. But widgets do not work for techniques such as drag-and-drop or direct-manipulation of application objects (icons, drawings, images, etc.) where interaction involves multiple objects.

The consequences on the quality of user interfaces are easy to see. For example, many applications use dialogue boxes that are *modal*, i.e., that force the user to terminate the interaction with the dialogue box before continuing or doing something else (an example of Green's premature commitment, see Sect. 2.3). In general, there is no good reason for the dialogue box to be modal. A file-saving dialogue box could stay open until the user decides under which name to save the file without preventing him or her from editing the file. The major reason why programmers use modal dialogue boxes is because it makes programming easier with the tools they have. If the file-saving dialogue were nonmodal, the programmer would have to manage its interaction with the rest of the system, e.g., handling the situation where the user issues the save-file command again (should it open a second dialogue box?) or reflecting changes in the file system that occur while the dialogue box is open. None of these problems are inherently difficult to solve but without proper tools, they do not justify, in the eyes of the programmer, the extra effort when compared with making the dialogue box modal.

Event-based programming is also at the root of the Model-View-Controler (MVC) pattern originally developed for the Smalltalk environment [27] and widely used in more recent frameworks such as Java Swing and .NET. The MVC pattern involves three objects: the *model* represents information that needs to be represented and interacted with, the *view* displays the information from the model, and the *controller* receives input events, transforms them into changes on the model which then notifies the view to update its display. An application contains a hierarchy of MVC triplets that may involve hundreds of objects. While more general than the widget model, the MVC model suffers similar problems: the events that make up a single interaction may be handled by multiple controllers that must coordinate their actions.

3.4 Formal Approaches

Several approaches have been attempted to use more formal models to describe the intricate relationships among input and output streams. Early work used augmented transition networks and recursive transition networks [20]. More recently, StateCharts [23] have been used as an alternative state machine model. Describing an interaction technique with a finite state automaton usually only requires a few states and transitions and is therefore manageable. Figure 2 shows a simple state machine for selecting objects with a click and moving them with drag-and-drop. Transitions are triggered by guarded events (in roman font in the figure). When a transition is fired, it may trigger an action (in italics in the figure). The major drawback of these approaches is that they do not deal with output. Output is always generated as a side effect, within the actions triggered by the transitions. This is not satisfying because it makes it impossible to prove anything about the dependencies between input and output.

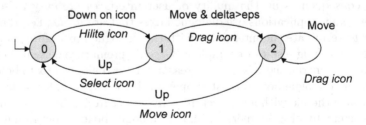

Fig. 2. State machine for selection and drag-and-drop

Another approach is based on cascading reactive devices [13]. ICON (Input CONfigurator) provides a visual interface where modules can be connected together to describe a configuration (see Fig. 3). This approach has the advantage that input and output are handled within the same framework. It has been used to describe a wide range of interaction techniques, from traditional widgets to advanced techniques such as toolglasses [7] or crossing-based interaction [1], as well as speech-based and multimodal interfaces.

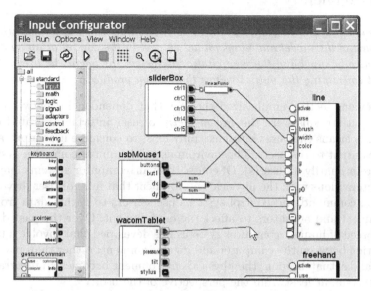

Fig. 3. ICON (image courtesy of Pierre Dragicevic)

Finally, Petri nets have also been used to describe various aspects of human–computer systems. The most advanced work in this area is ICO (Interactive Cooperative Objects) [41] and the associated PetShop tool [2]. ICOs use an object-oriented approach to describe the structure of the system and high-level Petri nets to describe its behavior. ICOs describe both input-to-output dependencies, i.e., how user actions affect the inner state of the application and which actions are enabled at any given time, and output-to-input dependencies, i.e., when and how the application displays information that is relevant to the user. The PetShop tool allows the interactive editing, verification and execution of the specification.

In summary, human–computer systems involve dynamic streams of various types with intricate dependencies between input and output streams and potentially tight time constraints. These streams carry low-level information, while both the user and computer operate at higher level of abstractions. This abstraction mismatch requires complex processing of input and output events that is not well supported by current programming tools. These tools promote simplified forms of interaction, e.g., based on widgets and modal dialogues, that do not encourage novel interaction techniques to be developed. Some approaches based on various kinds of transition networks, reactive devices and Petri nets have been studied in the literature and offer interesting perspective for better managing the dependencies among the interaction streams.

4 Environment

In models of interaction, the world or environment of the computation is part of the model and plays an active part in the computation by dynamically supplying the computational system, or agent, with inputs, and consuming the output values the system produces.

The previous section emphasized the fact that dependencies between input and output streams were the *raison d'être* of user interfaces. Stated differently, this means that user interfaces only exist to consume user input and to provide output to the users. The environment of a human–computer system is therefore primarily its user(s). Of course, human–computer systems may have other interactions with the physical environment that are not user driven. For example, command and control systems use sensors to gather data from the environment and actuators to affect the environment. Over the past decade, a new breed of human–computer systems has developed that involve a tighter integration between the computer and its environment: rather than just being sensed and actuated upon, the physical environment becomes an integral part of the system, at least from the perspective of the user.

Humans relate to the physical world in many ways. According to Gibson's ecological theory of perception [19], we directly perceive the *affordances* of objects for action, i.e., we instantly perceive whether an object can be picked up, sat upon, walked through, etc. Cultural affordances [38] extend Gibson's affordances with the fundamental, tacit knowledge that all individuals of a given culture have of their environment. Building on affordances is a powerful way to create interfaces that feel natural to use.

This section briefly introduces three related areas of research: ubiquitous and pervasive computing, mixed and augmented reality, and tangible interfaces. The *embodiment* [12] of digital artifacts into physical ones that characterizes all three approaches is the key to unlock the power of affordances. In terms of interactive computation, it means that the environment becomes symbiotic with the computer system.

4.1 Ubiquitous and Pervasive Computing

The vision for ubiquitous computing, or *Ubicomp*, put forward by Mark Weiser [52, 53], involves computers of all sizes and shapes seamlessly integrated into their environment so that they are used without even thinking about it. Weiser's group developed a first generation of such systems, based on tabs (pager-sized computers), pads (laptop-size computers) and boards (wall-size computers). A key aspect of the infrastructure underlying Ubicomp is transparent access to resources. The devices are networked and therefore it must be possible to start a task on some computer, e.g., a pad in one's office, and then move it to the board in the meeting room. The notion of an interactive application running on a system and used by a single user becomes obsolete. Instead, Ubicomp promotes a vision where services are available over the network to many users and are able to adapt to a variety of contexts of use. Ubicomp is clearly based on the interactive paradigm where the environment encompasses users, physical location and available physical resources for input and output.

Since Weiser's seminal work, the concept of Ubicomp has been explored and developed in a variety of directions. It has also taken on new names, such as *Pervasive Computing* and *Ambient Computing*. The main extension to the original concept is to make the environment more active: when sensors detect specific situations, such as someone entering a room or a meeting taking place, automated responses may take place, such as turning the lights on or setting up a shared whiteboard application on the laptops of the people in the meeting. The environment becomes a new component that interacts with the system. The downside of this approach is the sense of losing control over the physical environment: the users' interactions with the physical world are suddenly mediated by the computer system.

A milder approach consists of taking advantage of *peripheral awareness*, i.e., our ability to be aware of events occurring outside our focus of attention. Peripheral awareness is critical in our everyday life. It guides our actions, provides serendipity and allows us to react to the environment. A computer system can take advantage of the physical environment to deliver information through so-called *ambient displays* that are perceived through peripheral awareness. The concept was first elaborated by Weiser and Seely Brown under the name *calm technology* [54]. One of the first ambient display was LiveWire, a dangling string connected to an ethernet cable so that each network packet caused a tiny twitch of the motor to which the string was attached. High network traffic would make the string whirl madly, while slow traffic would make it spin onto itself slowly. Installed in a public space, the string could be seen and heard from several offices and provided a peripheral display of network activity. Since then, a number of ambient displays have been developed, most of which use large screens. While ambient displays are primarily output oriented, they can also take advantage of sensing technologies to adapt their content to the location and maybe even identity of nearby users. A good example is Rekimoto's augmented surfaces [42] where information can be seamlessly moved from a laptop to the desk and the wall display in the room, where other users can pick it up.

With ambient displays, and pervasive computing in general, the dependencies between output provided by the system and future user input are even more elusive than with traditional human–computer systems, yet such systems quickly become part of the fabric of our everyday life. They enrich the environment with information we use, sometimes even subconsciously, such as avoiding big downloads when the network is busy.

4.2 Augmented and Mixed Reality

Augmented reality and *mixed reality* [56, 30] share with Ubicomp the goal to better integrate the physical and computer worlds, but emphasize the use of everyday physical objects rather than relying on a pervasive computing infrastructure. The goal is to better take advantage of humans' skills to interact with familiar physical object.

The first augmented reality system was Wellner's Digital Desk [55], where a projector and camera installed above a traditional desk allowed mixing physical and digital information without the traditional PC devices such as keyboard, mouse and monitor. The camera could capture information from physical artifacts, such as the amounts on expense slips or a hand drawing, as well as simple interactions such as pointing and dragging; the projector could display digital information, such as a calculator or spreadsheet to compute and fill out an expense claim or a drawing program where the physical hand drawing captured by the camera could be duplicated, scaled and manipulated digitally.

With augmented and mixed reality, the seam between the physical and digital world becomes blurry; user interaction combines interaction with physical and digital artifacts; objects may exist both in the physical and electronic world, each representation complementing the other. For example, Mackay's work on augmented paper [31] enhances the capabilities of both paper documents and on-line documents by establishing links between them and allowing the user to interact with one form in order to affect the other. With the A-book [33], paper laboratory notebooks are augmented by capturing what is written on paper as well as digitally. A PDA can then be used as a *magic lens* to digitally interact with the content of the notebook, e.g., by creating links to on-line information, indexing the content or semi-automatically creating a table of contents (Figure 4). Even though the pen and paper are in the physical world and the user does not have the impression of interacting with a computer when taking notes, the system captures this input for later use when interacting through the PDA. Even when using the PDA, the display gives the impression that the underlying paper shows through the PDA when in fact it is a synthetic display, thereby merging the physical and digital worlds in the user's mental model.

The word "augmented reality" was originally coined as an opposite to "virtual reality" [56]. Whereas virtual reality immerses the user into a synthetic world and gets rid of the physical world, augmented reality takes the digital world and "explodes" it into the physical world. The systems described above augment physical objects, e.g., paper notebooks, or the environment, e.g., the physical desk. Another approach is to augment the users' *perception* of the physical world. This approach uses many of the technologies of virtual reality,

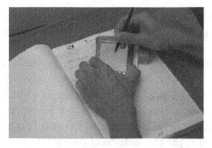

Fig. 4. A-book (image courtesy of Wendy Mackay)

such as head-mounted displays and position trackers, in order to superimpose synthetic images created by the computer onto the physical world. For example, maintenance operators wearing a special head-mounted device could have repairing instructions and diagrams directly overlaid (and registered with) the objects they operate on [15], or one could take a tour of a real city and see digital information overlaid on top of the monuments and landmarks. This approach is now called *augmented reality*, while the other two (augmenting the user or the environment) are now known as *mixed reality*. Either way, the goal is similar: to blur the distinction between physical and virtual in order to ease user interaction with the digital world.

4.3 Tangible Interfaces

Another, similar trend is called *tangible interfaces* [17, 50, 16]. Tangible interfaces attempt to create new physical objects that embody digital information or processes. One of the first examples of tangible interface is Durrell Bishop's *Marble answering machine*, where each new message on the answering machine generates a physical marble that the user can put on top of the machine to listen to it, take with her to remember the message, or put back into the machine to discard it.[3] Another example is Ullmer's *media blocks* [51], which are small pieces of wood that embody digital information, e.g., a video clip, a hand-drawn diagram or a text document. Printing a document simply consists of putting the media block holding that document on the printer itself. Creating a video can be done by spatially ordering the blocks that contain the respective clips.[4]

Tangible interaction is a slightly different approach from mixed reality since the latter attempts to use existing objects and extends them with computational capabilities. Here, new physical objects, such as the marble or the

---

[3] This design exercise inspired the opening scene of the movie *Minority Report*, where a machine carves a wood ball with the name of the author of a future crime.

[4] Incidentally, an augmented reality version of this video editing task, called Video Mosaic, was developed earlier with a variant of the Digital Desk and paper storyboards [30].

media block, embody digital information, such as a telephone message or a video clip, so that interaction with the physical object is interpreted as operations on the embodied information.

By building on human skills to manipulate physical objects, tangible interfaces blur the distinction between the system and the environment, between physical and digital. Carrying a marble in my pocket and putting it onto the answering machine are both physical actions, but only the latter is captured by the system and interpreted. In this case, the marble is passive and provides input when sensed by the system (this is typically achieved using RFID tags or similar technology). However, one could also imagine an active marble that beeps when it has been there too long without the message being played. Or a sensor in my apartment front door could warn me if I am passing the door with a marble in my pocket. It is then not clear, at least to the user, what is part of the "sytem" and what is part of the "environment". Augmented objects become part of an augmented world; they participate in events that may or may not be captured by the system. As long as they have a consistent behavior in both worlds, they exist as a single entity for the users.

In summary, new approaches to human–computer systems such as ubiquitous and pervasive computing, augmented and mixed reality and tangible interfaces redefine the traditional notions of the environment of a computer system. As we move away from explicit tasks and well-formed goals to implicit interaction, peripheral awareness and serendipitous activity, the physical and digital world merge and complement each other in complex and subtle ways.

5 Concurrency

In models of interaction, computation may be concurrent; a computing agent can compute in parallel with its environment and with other agents.

The human brain never stops. When interacting with computer systems, users always work in parallel with the system. They anticipate the system's response, e.g., by moving the cursor to the next interaction point even before the menu or dialogue box triggered by the previous action has appeared. They plan ahead future actions so that, often times, the next action is being planned while the current action is being carried out. The system, on the other hand, seems to be idle most of the time; if it conducts some computation in the background, this must not interfere with its ability to react to user input as quick as possible. This section examines two aspects of human–computer systems where concurrency is critical: providing timely reactions to user actions, and managing distributed interfaces.

5.1 Reaction Time, Progress Indicators and Animations

Users have expectations about the system reaction times and are quick to notice delays or criticize a system for being sluggish or nonresponsive. In fact, they expect a purely reactive system that produces a response in zero time once a command is submitted. The time scale for such instantaneous responses is that of human perception and varies according to the senses involved as well as the user's expectation. Typically, it is on the order of a few milliseconds to tens of milliseconds for visual or audio feedback of physical interactions such as clicking a button or dragging an icon. In such cases, any perceivable lag is problematic and it is better to degrade display quality in order to keep up with the pace than to introduce lag. When the reaction time is not related to a physical process, such as when popping up a dialogue box or displaying the results of a search, delays up to a second are acceptable. If the delay is longer, the system must display a progress indicator.

Progress indicators are inherently difficult to design and implement. They are a typical example of turning an algorithmic process that blindly computes a result into an interactive one that reports on its inner workings and is interruptible. When users trigger long processes, they want to know how long it is going to take. Ideally, the system should be able to display a countdown in real time. Users also want the ability to interrupt a long process, or even pause it and restart it later. A long computation should therefore always execute concurrently with the interaction thread in order to ensure that the system stays responsive.

Since it is often difficult to display a real-time countdown, an alternative is to display a percent-done indicator or progress bar. Even if the bar does not progress regularly and hence makes it difficult to predict the end time, it gives useful information to the user. If progress stops for a significant amount of time, an explanation should be given to the user, such as a network failure when trying to copy a large folder to a remote server. Instrumenting existing algorithms to provide such feedback can be difficult; in cases where even a percent-done indicator cannot be provided, a busy indicator should at least be displayed with the ability for the user to interrupt the process.

Ideally, long processes should compute their result incrementally so that it can be displayed as it is created, rather than have the user wait until the process is complete in order to see the final result. If the algorithm does not compute the result incrementally, it may be able to display its best result so far and update it as it progresses. Search processes are a good example: when a user enters a query to search for some data, it is best to display the partial results as they come in, even if this means updating the rankings or dropping results that turn out to be less relevant. This provides feedback to the user, who can also start working with an early and imperfect result right away and even stop the search if satisfied with it. This of course is only possible if the search proceeds in parallel with user interaction.

Even instantaneous interactions may give rise to parallel processing when using animation. Sudden display changes may be hard to perceive as they do not make the causality between a user action or external event and the corresponding system response explicit. Proper animations can greatly enhance the quality of an interface by helping users understand state changes caused by their actions. Minimizing a window, for example, should display the window shrinking into an icon so that the user can identify which icon now represents the window. Animation is also very useful when external events cause a change in the user interface. For example, a file server becoming unavailable could blink and then fade away so that the user has enough time to understand what happened. To be effective, animations should last on the order of one second and can use tricks from cartoons such as slow-in, slow-out in order to be perceived more easily [10]. Also, animations should degrade gracefully if the system is loaded [49]. Finally, the animation should proceed concurrently with the system's normal operation so that they do not slow the user down.

5.2 Distributed Interfaces

Distributed systems are becoming the norm rather than the exception for human–computer systems. The X Window System [43], for example, is based on a client–server model where the server provides services for sharing the input and output devices of a computer among various client applications. Clients send requests to the X server to create windows, draw into these windows, etc. The server sends events to the clients when user input occurs in one of their windows. The clients and the server all run concurrently, which can boost performance when they are on different machines.

With the advent of ubiquitous and pervasive computing, the amount of concurrency between the various components of a human–computer system is increasing. For example, a user may use a PDA to control a presentation running on a separate computer, as in Pebbles [36]. User interfaces that use gesture recognition, machine vision or speech recognition often offload some of the heavy digital signal processing onto dedicated servers in order to improve the performance and responsiveness of the system.

Finally collaborative systems are inherently distributed. Shared editors, for example, typically use a replicated or partially replicated architecture where similar replicas run at each site and exchange their respective users' input in order to update their state. Consistency management algorithms such as operation transformation [47, 26] ensure that the local states converge towards the same global state, detecting and sometimes solving conflicts. These algorithms usually rely on an optimistic approach, assuming that users will establish social protocols that minimize actual conflicts. These social protocols typically require that the activity of each user be visible to other users: a user is less likely to edit the same part of the document as another user if he is aware of the presence of the other user in this area. The concurrent activity of multiple users is made explicit in the interface so it can then be mediated by the social protocols. The tools that support social protocols may be separate from the collaborative application. For example, users can use instant messaging, telephone, or even their voice if they are collocated. In such cases, the causal chains can be extremely complex, involving both computer processes and the environment. In general, there is no hope that they can ever be computable algorithmically.

In summary, concurrency occurs at various levels in human–computer systems. Users operate concurrently with the system, the system is often distributed and each process generally has multiple threads, some for interaction, some for computation.

6 Noncomputability

The environment cannot be assumed to be static or even effectively computable; for example, it may include humans or other real-world elements.

Human–computer systems obviously have humans in the loop, whose actions are largely unpredictable. Most attempts at modeling human behavior to improve human–computer systems have failed, even in the simplest cases. For example, the wizards that try to help users in some applications are notoriously bad at anticipating the users' needs.

Machine learning and other artificial intelligence techniques are used increasingly to adapt human–computer systems to the observed user behavior. In many cases, their goal is to "replace the user", therefore trying to turn an interactive system into a noninteractive one. This is often framed in the context of first- vs. second-person interfaces where the latter attempt to delegate more and more tasks to the computer while the former attempt to empower the user with better tool [45]. A better approach probably is to try and combine the two approaches, as in *mixed initiative* systems [25].

However since humans are inherently noncomputable, there is always a limit to what the system can guess about the user's next steps. Instead of trying to get rid of interaction, one should use our knowledge of human behavior to serve interaction. This section therefore focuses on models and theories of human behavior and their consequences on the design of human–computer systems. It covers action theory, situated action, and co-adaptation and shows how to leverage the learning and adaptation capabilities of humans as well as computers.

6.1 Action Theory

Norman's *action theory* [9] gives an account of the psychological process a user goes through when interacting with a system (see Figure 5). The user

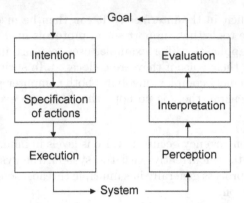

Fig. 5. Norman's action theory

has a goal, such as getting rid of a file. In order to reach the goal, the user forms an intention (delete the file), specifies the necessary actions (drag the icon of the file to the icon of the trash), and executes this action (using the mouse). According to the conceptual model introduced in Sect. 2.2, the system analyzes the input from the user and produces a response. The user then perceives the change (or lack of change) in the system state, interprets this change (the icon of the file has disappeared therefore the file is gone) and evaluates this outcome with respect to the original goal. If the goal is not reached, several strategies exist, e.g., the user can undo and try again or reach the original goal from the new current state. Finally, goals are often organized hierarchically, with goals subdivided into subgoals, e.g., cleaning up my computer desktop involves deleting some files, renaming others, etc.

This model is obviously a simplified, maybe simplistic, view of reality. Nevertheless it already shows that system input is driven by mental processes that are not accessible to the computer and are therefore unpredictable, and that future system input is determined, at least partially, by past system output in ways that are also unpredictable from the computer's perspective.

Many wizards, guided tours and interactive tutorials are based on this model: they walk users through a sequence of mostly predefined steps, assuming that they will reuse the same schema when confronted with the same situation. Some adaptive systems go further and try to infer the plan from the user's actions so as to take over from the user the next time they detect a similar pattern. A good example is Eager [11], a system that watches for repetitive actions such as making an index out of a list of messages and offers the user to continue when it has inferred a pattern. The main limitations of these systems are that they have a predefined library of plans, and they assume that users conform to these plans.

6.2 Situated Action

Suchman's theory of *situated action* shows that humans do not necessarily act according to plans [46]. Based on ethnographic observation of users, Lucy Suchman noted that the environment affects human behavior to cause users to modify their plans *in situ*, after they have formed them. For example, a user goes to the copier to make copies of a document, runs into a colleague and engages in a conversation with her, which makes her remember that she was supposed to meet with another person whose office is on the way to the copier. The person is not in her office and so she leaves a note asking him to come and see her. She finally gets to the copier but there is a line, so she gets back to her office and prints a new copy on her printer instead. When the colleague comes back into his office, he sees the note but the phone rings and keeps him busy for a while. He has to rush to a meeting and decides to send her an email instead.

Our activity is constantly shaped by the environment, our plans are constantly revised and adapted to the context: our actions are *situated*, they result from conflicting constraints and microdecisions in such a way that two identical situations may lead to different actions for reasons that are difficult to uncover, even less rationalize. There is a line at the copier; what makes me decide between waiting, coming back later, giving up on making the copy, delegating it to another person, etc.?

Human–computer systems should support humans, not force them to conform to the way computers work. They should support our nonpredictability by offering several ways of doing the same thing, by avoiding premature commitment, by allowing to go back in time and try something different, etc. They should be flexible enough to allow users to adapt the system to their needs, not the opposite. For example, users of paper forms often use the margins to write down extra information when the form does not cover a particular case. This flexibility if often lost with on-line forms, which have a fixed set of fields. It can be regained easily by adding free-form input fields for comments or notes. Of course, the system does not know what to do with that information, but it could make sure it is processed by a human user. This is, in fact, a simple form of co-adaptation.

6.3 Co-adaptation

Co-adaptation [32] is the process by which users adapt to a new technology, such as a new computer system, as well as adapt it to their own needs. It is based on the observation that users often reinterpret new technology in ways that were not anticipated by its designers. The appropriation of the system by its users includes understanding what the system can and cannot do and using features in unexpected ways. For example, email was created when system operators were exchanging files that needed processing and attached a message to the file to explain what to do with it. One day, someone realized that he could use the message for other purposes, unrelated to the file it was attached to. Only later on were messages decoupled from their attached files. Ironically, we now see the opposite process where files are attached to messages, and where email is used to exchange files.

Mackay [29] argues that users are innovators and that their adaptations of the technology can be turned into new features of future versions of the system. Observing the co-adaptation of a system is therefore a good source of information for system designers. The next step is to design systems that encourage co-adaptation, i.e., to design systems that are open and flexible enough that they can be redefined by their users. Spreadsheets are a very good example of such systems. They can be used for straight calculations, for hypothesis testing, for complex table layout, etc.

In general, introducing end-user programming capabilities into human–computer systems is a great way to open it for reinterpretation [28]. Macros and scripting languages are common forms of end-user programming that users can adopt fairly easily, especially when they use visual rather than textual descriptions. Defining the level of programmability of an interface is challenging. First, it requires exposing the inner workings of the system, potentially showing its weaknesses. Second, it must make sense for the end user, i.e., the exposed concepts must match the mental model that the user has formed of the system when using it.

Finally, opening a system for reinterpretation through macros and scripting develops its interactive aspect in new directions. Not only does the system input and output data during its execution, it is also able to change its own program at run-time. Self-modifying programs are certainly outside the scope of the traditional algorithmic approach, showing one more time the limits of this approach to model human–computer systems.

In summary, the environment of human–computer systems is made of humans and the physical world, neither of which is computable. Moreover, in order to support this environment, human–computer systems should be as flexible and open as possible, up to the point of allowing users to modify the system's code in order to adapt it to their needs.

7 Conclusion

This chapter has presented human–computer interaction from the perspective of the five characteristics of interactive systems: the nonalgorithmic computational problem they address, the dynamic interleaving of user input and system display streams, the dependency on the environment, the parallel "computation" of user and computer, and the noncomputability of the environment. It has been shown that human–computer systems feature all the characteristics of interactive systems and that many shortcomings of current systems are due to the use of algorithmic approaches to develop them.

The shift from algorithms to interaction should have happened long ago in human–computer systems, as the ingredients have been with us for so long in this area. Instead, commercial systems are more than ever developed in an algorithmic paradigm. For example, web applications are mostly based on form-filling and linear navigation of the results. At the same time, research turns to ever more interactive systems, such as mixed reality and ubiquitous computing where interaction is distributed among many devices and computers.

What is most needed for the shift to occur is tools. We need languages and libraries that truly implement reactive systems, tools for testing and verifying interactive systems, and sample applications that show the benefits that can be gained. This requires shifting the focus of the design process of human–computer systems from user interfaces to interaction phenomena [4]. With Moore's law making computers ever more powerful, computer systems should be easier, not harder to use. Interactive computation can unlock the true power of human–computer interaction by helping design systems that are simpler, more flexible, more open and better adapted to their users.

References

1. Johnny Accot and Shumin Zhai. More than dotting the i's — foundations for crossing-based interfaces. In *Proceedings ACM Conference on Human Factors in Computing Systems (CHI '02)*, pages 73–80. ACM Press, 2002.
2. Rémi Bastide, David Navarre, and Philippe Palanque. A tool-supported design framework for safety critical interactive systems. *Interacting with Computers*, 15(3):309–328, 2003.
3. Michel Beaudouin-Lafon. Instrumental interaction: an interaction model for designing post-WIMP user interfaces. In *Proceedings ACM Conference on Human Factors in Computing Systems (CHI '00)*, pages 446–453. ACM Press, 2000.
4. Michel Beaudouin-Lafon. Designing interfaction, not interfaces. In *Proceedings International Conference on Advanced Visual Interfaces (AVI '04)*, pages 15–22. ACM Press, May 2004.
5. Michel Beaudouin-Lafon and Wendy E. Mackay. Reification, polymorphism and reuse: Three principles for designing visual interfaces. In *Proceedings International Conference on Advanced Visual Interfaces (AVI '00)*, pages 102–109. ACM Press, 2000.
6. Michel Beaudouin-Lafon, editor. *Computer Supported Co-operative Work*, volume 7 of *Trends in Software*. John Wiley & Sons, 1999.
7. Eric A. Bier, Maureen C. Stone, Ken Pier, William Buxton, and Tony D. DeRose. Toolglass and magic lenses: the see-through interface. In *Proceedings ACM Conference on Computer Graphics and Interactive Techniques (SIGGRAPH '93)*, pages 73–80. ACM Press, 1993.
8. Alan F. Blackwell and Thomas R. G. Green. Notational systems – the cognitive dimensions of notations framework. In J.M. Carroll, editor, *HCI Models, Theories and Frameworks: Toward a Multidisciplinary Science*, pages 103–134. Morgan Kaufmann Publishers Inc., 2003.

9. Stuart K. Card, Allen Newell, and Thomas P. Moran. *The Psychology of Human-Computer Interaction.* Lawrence Erlbaum Associates, Inc., 1983.

10. Bay-Wei Chang and David Ungar. Animation: from cartoons to the user interface. In *Proceedings ACM Symposium on User Interface Software and Technology (UIST '93)*, pages 45–55. ACM Press, 1993.

11. Allen Cypher. Eager: Programming repetitive tasks by demonstration. In Allen Cypher, editor, *Watch What I Do: Programming by Demonstration.* MIT Press, 1993.

12. Paul Dourish. *Where the action is: the foundations of embodied interaction.* MIT Press, 2001.

13. Pierre Dragicevic and Jean-Daniel Fekete. The input configurator toolkit: towards high input adaptability in interactive applications. In *Proceedings International Conference on Advanced Visual Interfaces (AVI '04)*, pages 244–247. ACM Press, 2004.

14. Douglas C. Engelbart and William K. English. A research center for augmenting human intellect. In *AFIPS Conference Proceedings of the 1968 Fall Joint Computer Conference*, volume 33, pages 395–410, 1968.

15. Steven Feiner, Blair Macintyre, and Dorée Seligmann. Knowledge-based augmented reality. *Comm. ACM*, 36(7):53–62, 1993.

16. Kenneth P. Fishkin. A taxonomy for and analysis of tangible interfaces. *Personal Ubiquitous Comput.*, 8(5):347–358, 2004.

17. George W. Fitzmaurice, Hiroshi Ishii, and William A. S. Buxton. Bricks: laying the foundations for graspable user interfaces. In *Proceedings ACM Conference on Human Factors in Computing Systems (CHI '95)*, pages 442–449. ACM Press, 1995.

18. Erich Gamma, Richard Helm, Ralph Johnson, and John Vlissides. *Design patterns: elements of reusable object-oriented software.* Addison-Wesley Longman Publishing Co., Inc., 1995.

19. James J. Gibson. *The Ecological Approach to Visual Perception.* Boston: Houghton Mifflin, 1979.

20. Mark Green. A survey of three dialogue models. *ACM Trans. Graph.*, 5(3):244–275, 1986.

21. Thomas R. G. Green. Cognitive dimensions of notations. In *People and Computers V, Proceedings of the HCI '89*, pages 443–460. Cambridge University Press, 1989.

22. Thomas R. G. Green. Instructions and descriptions: some cognitive aspects of programming and similar activities. In *Proceedings International Conference on Advanced Visual Interfaces (AVI '00)*, pages 21–28. ACM Press, 2000.

23. David Harel. Statecharts: A visual formalism for complex systems. *Sci. Comput. Program.*, 8(3):231–274, 1987.

24. Thomas T. Hewett, chairman. ACM SIGCHI curricula for human-computer interaction. Technical report, ACM Press, 1992.

25. Eric Horvitz. Principles of mixed-initiative user interfaces. In *Proceedings ACM Conference on Human Factors in Computing Systems (CHI '99)*, pages 159–166. ACM Press, 1999.

26. Alain Karsenty and Michel Beaudouin-Lafon. An algorithm for distributed groupware applications. In *Proceedings International Conference on Distributed Systems (ICDCS '93)*, pages 195–202, 1993.

27. Glenn E. Krasner and Stephen T. Pope. A description of the model-view-controller user interface paradigm in the smalltalk-80 system. *Journal of Object Oriented Programming*, 1(3):26–49, 1988.

28. Catherine Letondal. Participatory programming: Developing programmable bioinformatics tools for end-users. In H. Lieberman, F. Paterno, and V. Wulf, editors, *End-User Development*. Springer/Kluwer Academic Publishers, 2005.

29. Wendy E. Mackay. Patterns of sharing customizable software. In *Proceedings ACM Conference on Computer Supported Cooperative Work (CSCW '90)*, pages 209–221. ACM Press, 1990.

30. Wendy E. Mackay. Augmented reality: linking real and virtual worlds: a new paradigm for interacting with computers. In *Proceedings International Conference on Advanced Visual Interfaces (AVI '98)*, pages 13–21, 1998.

31. Wendy E. Mackay. Is paper safer? the role of paper flight strips in air traffic control. *ACM Trans. Comput.-Hum. Interact.*, 6(4):311–340, 1999.

32. Wendy E. Mackay. Responding to cognitive overload: coadaptation between users and technology. *Intellectica*, 30(1):177–193, 2000.

33. Wendy E. Mackay, Guillaume Pothier, Catherine Letondal, Kaare Boegh, and Hans Erik Sorensen. The missing link: augmenting biology laboratory notebooks. In *Proceedings ACM Symposium on User Interface Software and Technology (UIST '02)*, pages 41–50. ACM Press, 2002.

34. Pattie Maes. Agents that reduce work and information overload. *Comm. ACM*, 37(7):30–40, 1994.

35. Brad A. Myers. Separating application code from toolkits: eliminating the spaghetti of call-backs. In *Proceedings ACM Symposium on User Interface Software and Technology (UIST '91)*, pages 211–220. ACM Press, 1991.

36. Brad A. Myers. Using handhelds and PCs together. *Comm. ACM*, 44(11):34–41, 2001.

37. Brad A. Myers and Mary Beth Rosson. Survey on user interface programming. In *Proceedings ACM Conference on Human Factors in Computing Systems (CHI '92)*, pages 195–202. ACM Press, 1992.

38. Donald A. Norman. Affordance, conventions, and design. *ACM interactions*, 6(3):38–43, 1999.

39. Dan R. Olsen. *Developing User Interfaces*. Morgan Kaufmann Publishers Inc., 1998.

40. Sharon Oviatt. Ten myths of multimodal interaction. *Comm. ACM*, 42(11):74–81, 1999.

41. Philippe Palanque and Rémi Bastide. Synergistic modelling of tasks, users and systems using formal specification techniques. *Interacting with Computers*, 9(2):129–153, 1997.

42. Jun Rekimoto and Masanori Saitoh. Augmented surfaces: a spatially continuous work space for hybrid computing environments. In *Proceedings ACM Conference on Human Factors in Computing Systems (CHI '99)*, pages 378–385. ACM Press, 1999.

43. Robert W. Scheifler and Jim Gettys. The X window system. *ACM Trans. Graph.*, 5(2):79–109, 1986.

44. Ben Shneiderman. Direct manipulation: A step beyond programming languages. In W. A S Buxton and R.M. Daecker, editors, *Human-computer interaction: a multidisciplinary approach*, pages 461–467. Morgan Kaufmann Publishers Inc., 1987.

45. Ben Shneiderman and Pattie Maes. Direct manipulation vs. interface agents. *ACM interactions*, 4(6):42–61, 1997.
46. Lucy A. Suchman. *Plans and situated actions: the problem of human-machine communication*. Cambridge University Press, 1987.
47. Chengzheng Sun and Clarence Ellis. Operational transformation in real-time group editors: issues, algorithms, and achievements. In *Proceedings ACM Conference on Computer Supported Cooperative Work (CSCW '98)*, pages 59–68. ACM Press, 1998.
48. Ivan E. Sutherland. Sketchpad a man-machine graphical communication system. In *Papers on Twenty-five years of electronic design automation*, pages 507–524. ACM Press, 1988.
49. Steven H. Tang and Mark A. Linton. Pacers: time-elastic objects. In *Proceedings ACM Symposium on User Interface Software and Technology (UIST '93)*, pages 35–43. ACM Press, 1993.
50. Brygg Ullmer and Hiroshi Ishii. Emerging frameworks for tangible user interfaces. In *Human-Computer Interaction in the New Millenium*, pages 579–601. Addison-Wesley Longman Publishing Co., Inc., 2001.
51. Brygg Ullmer, Hiroshi Ishii, and Dylan Glas. mediaBlocks: physical containers, transports, and controls for online media. In *Proceedings ACM Conference on Computer Graphics and Interactive Techniques (SIGGRAPH '98)*, pages 379–386. ACM Press, 1998.
52. Mark Weiser. The computer for the twenty-first century. *Scientific American*, pages 94–104, Sept. 1991.
53. Mark Weiser. Some computer science issues in ubiquitous computing. *Comm. ACM*, 36(7):75–84, 1993.
54. Mark Weiser and John Seely Brown. The coming age of calm technolgy. In P.J. Denning and R.M. Metcalfe, editors, *Beyond calculation: the next fifty years*, pages 75–85. Springer-Verlag, 1997.
55. Pierre Wellner. Interacting with paper on the DigitalDesk. *Comm. ACM*, 36(7):87–96, 1993.
56. Pierre Wellner, Rich Gold, and Wendy E. Mackay. Special issue on computer augmented environments: back to the real world. *Comm. ACM*, 36(7), 1993.

Modeling Web Interactions and Errors*

Shriram Krishnamurthi[1], Robert Bruce Findler[2], Paul Graunke[3,**], and
Matthias Felleisen[3]

[1] Brown University, Providence, RI, USA
[2] University of Chicago, Chicago, IL, USA
[3] Northeastern University, Boston, MA, USA

Summary. Programmers confront a minefield when they design interactive Web
programs. Web interactions take place via Web browsers. Browsers permit consumers
to whimsically navigate among the various stages of a dialog, leading to unexpected
outcomes. Furthermore, the growing diversity of browsers means the number of
interactive operations users can perform continues to grow.

To investigate this programming problem, we develop a foundational model of
Web interactions that reduces the panoply of browser-supported user interactions to
three fundamental ones. We use the model to formally describe two classes of errors
in Web programs. The descriptions suggest techniques for detecting both classes of
errors. For one class we present an incrementally-checked record type system, which
effectively eliminates these errors. For the other class, we introduce a dynamic safety
check that employs program annotations to detect errors.

1 Introduction

Over the past decade, the Web has evolved from a static medium into an
interactive one. A representative article claims that more than half of all
Web transactions are interactive [4], and this ratio only grows in favor of
interactivity. Indeed, entire corporations (including book retailers, auction
sites, travel reservation services, and so on) now interact primarily or solely
through the Web. These interfaces no longer present static content but rather
consume user input, perform computation based on these inputs, and generate
corresponding output. As a result, the Web has been transformed into an
important (and increasingly dominant) medium of interactive computation.

This rapid growth in the volume of interactively generated content might
suggest that Web page developers and programmers have mastered the mechanics of interactive Web content. In practice, however, as this chapter

---

* This research is partially supported by NSF grants CCR 0305949, ESI-0010064
  and CAI-0086264.
** Current affiliation: Galois Connections, Inc.

demonstrates, consumers still encounter many, and sometimes costly, program errors as they utilize these new services. Furthermore, many of these errors are caused precisely when users employ the *interactive* operations supported by Web browsers. A strong foundation for interactive computation must therefore study and address the world of Web programs.

A Web program's execution consists of a series of interactions between a Web browser and a Web server. When a Web browser submits a request whose path points to a Web program, the server invokes the program with the request via any of a number of protocols (CGI [19], Java servlets [7], or Microsoft's ASP.NET [18]). It then waits for the program to terminate and turns the program's output into a response that the browser can display. Put differently, each individual Web program simply consumes an HTTP request and produces a Web page in response. It is therefore appropriate to call such programs "scripts" considering that they only read some inputs and write some output. This very simplicity, however, is also what makes the design of multistage Web dialogs difficult.

First, multistage interactive Web programs consist of many scripts, each handling one request. These scripts communicate with each other via external media, because the participants in a dialog must remember earlier parts of a conversation. Not surprisingly, forcing the scripts to communicate this way causes many problems, considering that such communications rely on unstated, and therefore easily violated, invariants.

Second, the use of a Web browser for the consumer's side of the dialog introduces even more complications. The primary purpose of a Web browser is to empower consumers to navigate among a web of hyperlinked nodes at will. A consumer naturally wants this same power to explore dialogs on the Web. For example, a consumer may wish to backtrack to an earlier stage in a dialog, clone a page with choices and explore different possibilities in parallel, bookmark an interaction and come back to it later, and so on. Hence, a programmer must be extremely careful about the invariants that govern the communications among the scripts that make up an interactive Web program. What appears to be invariant in a purely sequential dialog context may not be so in a dialog medium that allows arbitrary navigation actions.

In this chapter, we make three contributions to the problem of designing reliable interactive Web programs. First, we develop a simple, formal model of Web interactions. Using this model, we can explain the above problems concisely. Second, we develop a type system that solves one of these problems in a provable manner (relative to the model). Third, because not all the checks can be performed statically, we suggest run-time checks to supplement the type system.

Section 2 describes a problem on an actual corporate Web site that succintly demonstrates the style of problems we study. Section 4 introduces a model of Web interactions suitable for understanding problems with sequential programs. Section 5 uses the model to demonstrate two major classes of mistakes. Section 6 introduces a standard type system for the Web that eliminates the first class of mistakes. Section 7 introduces a dynamic check into the programming language that warns consumers of potential problems. Sections 3 and 8 place our work in context.

2 A Sample Problem

We illustrate one of the Web programming problems with an example from the commercial world. Figure 1 contains snapshots from an actual interaction with Orbitz,[1] which sells travel services from many vendors. It naturally invites comparison shopping. In particular, a customer may enter the origin and destination airports to look for flights between cities, receive a list of flight choices, and then conduct the following actions:

1. Use the "open link in new window" option to study the details of a flight that leaves at 5:50 pm (step 1). The consumer now has two browser windows open.
2. Switching back to the choices window (step 2), the consumer can inspect a different option, e.g., a flight leaving at 9:30 am (step 3). Now the consumer can perform a side-by-side comparison of the options in two browser windows.
3. After comparing the flight details, the customer decides to take the first flight after all. The consumer switches back to the window with the 5:50 pm flight (step 4). Using this window (form), the consumer submits the request for the 5:50 pm flight (step 5).

At this point, the consumer expects the reservation system to respond with a page confirming the 5:50 pm flight. Alarmingly, even though the page indicates that clicking would reserve on the 5:50 pm flight, Orbitz instead selects the 9:30 am flight. A customer who doesn't pay close attention may purchase a ticket on the wrong flight.

The Orbitz problem dramatically illustrates our case. Sadly, this is not an isolated error. It exists in other services (such as hotel reservations) on the Orbitz site. Furthermore, as plain consumers, we have stumbled across this and related problems while using several vendor's sites, including Apple, Continental Airlines, Hertz car rentals, Microsoft, and Register.com. Clearly, an error that occurs repeatedly across organizations suggests not a one-time programming fault but rather a systemic problem. Hence, we must develop a foundational model to study Web interactions.

3 Prior Work

The Bigwig project [2] (a descendant of Bell Lab's Mawl project [1]) provides a radical solution to the problem. The main purpose of the project is to

---

[1] The screenshots were produced on June 28, 2002.

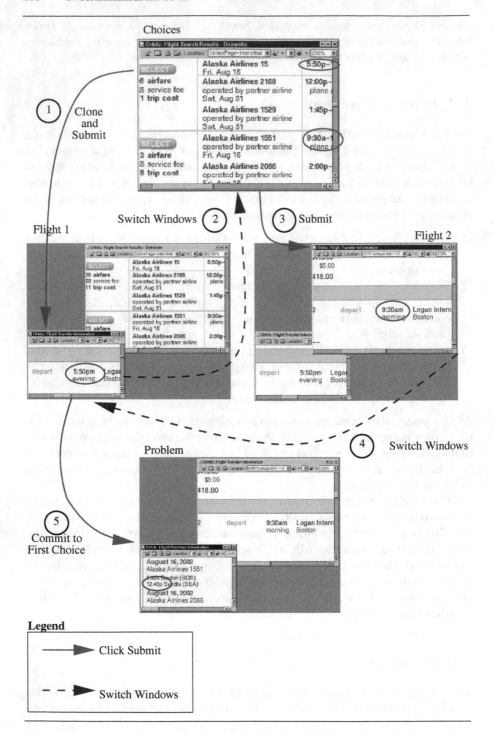

Fig. 1. Orbitz interactions

provide a domain-specific language for composing interactive Web sessions. The language's runtime system enforces the (informal) model of a session as a pair of communicating threads [3]. For example, clicking on the back button takes the consumer back to the very beginning of the dialog. While such a runtime system prevents damage, it is also overly draconian, especially when compared to other approaches to dealing with Web dialogs.

John Hughes [15], Christian Queinnec [22], and Paul Graham [13] independently had the deep insight that a browser's navigation actions correspond to the use of first-class continuations in a program. In particular, they show that an interaction with the consumer corresponds to the manipulation of a continuation. If the underlying language and server support these manipulations, a program doesn't have to terminate to interact with a consumer but instead captures a continuation and suspends the evaluation. Every time a consumer submits a response, the computation resumes the proper continuation. Put differently, the communication among scripts is now internalized within one program and can thus be subjected to the safety checks of the language.

Our prior work explored the implications of Queinnec's in two ways. First, we built a Web server that enables Web programs to interact directly with consumers [14]. Programming in this world eliminates many of the problems in a natural manner. Second, because this solution only applies if the server offers support for storing continuations, we explored the automatic generation of robust Web programs via functional compilation techniques [17]. While this idea works in principle, a full-fledged implementation requires a re-engineered library system and runtime environment for the targeted language.

Thiemann [26] started with Hughes's ideas and provides a monad-based library for constructing Web dialogs. In principle, his solution corresponds to our second approach; his monads take care of the "compilation" of Web scripts into a suitable continuation form. Working with Haskell, Thiemann can now use Haskell's type system to check the natural communication invariants between the various portions of a Web program. This work must accommodate effects (interactions with file systems, data bases, etc.), which it does in a somewhat unnatural manner. Specifically, for each interaction, the CGI scripts are re-executed from the beginning to the current point of interaction, which can be computationally expensive. This monad-based approach does, however, avoid the re-execution of effects, thereby preserving observed behavior relative to these effects.

4 Modeling the Web

As Web browsers proliferate, we expect that both the number and the nature of problems induced by interaction will grow. Browsers are likely to introduce interaction features that are especially convenient to a user but are equally unanticipated by the application developer. It becomes increasingly difficult to reason about the behavior of a program in the context of each particular browser; we would, therefore, benefit from a foundational model that encapsulates a wide variety of these interactions in a small set of primitives, akin to what Turing machines or lambda calculi do for standard computation. This section presents our first attempt at constructing such a model.

The model we present has four characteristics. First, it consists of a single server and a single client, because we wish to study the problems of *sequential* Web interactions. Second, it deals exclusively with dynamically generated Web pages, called forms, to mirror HTML's sublanguage of requests. Third, the model allows the consumer to switch among Web pages arbitrarily; as we show later, this suffices to represent the problem in Sect. 2 and similar phenomena. Finally, the model is abstract with respect to the programming language so that we can experiment with alternatives; here we use a lambda calculus for forms and basic data, though we could also have used a model such as Classic Java [10].

Our model lacks several properties that are orthogonal to our goals. First, the model ignores client-side storage, a.k.a. "cookies," which primarily addresses customization and storage optimizations. Server-side storage suffices for our goals. Second, Web programmers must address concurrency via locking, possibly relying on a server that serializes each session's requests or relying on a database. Distributing the server software across multiple machines complicates concurrency further. Third, monitoring and restarting servers improves fault tolerance. Fourth, the model does not allow the user to add fields to or drop fields from Web forms before submission. While the HTTP protocol permits this, browsers typically ensure that this does not happen. Accordingly, Web applications can protect themselves against dropped fields through a simple dynamic check that will not, in practice, ever fail. Finally, the model neither addresses nor introduces any security concerns, but existing solutions for ensuring authentication and privacy apply [8, 11].

4.1 Server and Client

Figure 2 describes the components of our model. Each Web configuration (W) consists of a single server (S) and a single client (C). The server consists of storage (Σ) and a dispatcher (see Fig. 4). The dispatcher contains a table P (for "programs") that associates URLs with programs and an evaluator that applies programs from the table to the submitted form. Programs are closed terms (M°) in a yet to be specified programming language.

The client consists of the current Web form and a set of all visited Web forms. Initially, the set is a singleton consisting of only the home page. It then grows as the consumer visits additional pages. The model assumes that the consumer can freely (nondeterministically) replace the current page with some previously visited page, or visit a new page. Since the current page is always an element of all previously visited pages, the consumer can also return to this page. We claim that this model of a consumer represents most

$$
\begin{aligned}
W &= S \times C & \{\text{ ``'', ``x'', ``why'', ``zee'' }\} && \subset \textit{String} \\
S &= \Sigma \times P & \{\, x, y, z \,\} && \subset \textit{Id} \\
P &= \textit{Url} \mapsto M^{\circ} & \{\, \textit{www.drscheme.org, www.plt-scheme.org }\} && \subset \textit{Url} \\
M^{\circ} &= \textit{programs} \\
C &= F \times \overrightarrow{F} \\
F &= (\textbf{form } \textit{Url } \overrightarrow{(\textit{Id } V_{\flat})}) \\
V_{\flat} &= \textit{Int } | \textit{ String}
\end{aligned}
$$

Fig. 2. Components of the Web model

interesting browser navigation actions, including some not yet conceived by browser implementors.[2]

The model distills a Web page to a minimal representation. Every page is simply a form (F). It contains the URL to which the form is submitted and a set of form fields. A field names a value that the consumer may edit at will. Figure 3 presents a concrete WebL form and its equivalent in HTML.

```
(form www.plt-scheme.org/my-program.ss
   (name "Paul") (time "1:30"))

<html>
 <body>
  <form action="www.plt-scheme.org/my-program.ss"
        method="post">
    <input type="text" name="name" value="Paul" />
    <input type="text" name="time" value="1:30" />
    <input type="submit" value="Submit">
  </form>
 </body>
</html>
```

Fig. 3. WebL form and equivalent HTML form

Figure 4 illustrates how the pieces of the model interact. The bold-faced letters correspond to the nonterminals in Fig. 2. The server and client may run on different machines, connected by a network. The client sends its current form to the server. The form names a program on the server; the server applies this program to the form and produces a response, possibly accessing the store

---

[2] Entering arbitrary URLs into the browser is a degenerate case of the user creating a brand new form, possibly with an incorrect number of fields (zero) or the wrong field names.

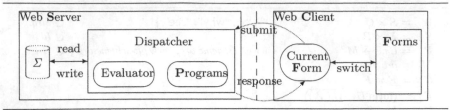

Fig. 4. The Web picture

in the process. Finally, the response replaces the current form on the client and appears in the client's set of visited forms.

To specify behavior, we use rewriting rules on Web configurations. Figure 5 contains rules that determine the behavior of the client and server as far as Web programs are concerned. Each rule is indexed by an operation and takes a server–client pair to a new server–client pair, reflecting the change caused by the operation.

$d_p : \Sigma \times F \longrightarrow \Sigma \times F$

fill-form $: W \longrightarrow W$
$\langle s, \langle (\mathbf{form}\ u\ \overrightarrow{(k\ v_0)}),\ \overrightarrow{f} \rangle \rangle \hookrightarrow \langle s, \langle (\mathbf{form}\ u\ \overrightarrow{(k\ v_1)}),\ \{(\mathbf{form}\ u\ \overrightarrow{(k\ v_1)})\} \cup \overrightarrow{f} \rangle \rangle$

switch $: W \longrightarrow W$
$\langle s, \langle f_0,\ \overrightarrow{f} \rangle \rangle \hookrightarrow \langle s, \langle f_1,\ \overrightarrow{f} \rangle \rangle\ \mathbf{where} f_1 \in \overrightarrow{f}$

submit $: W \longrightarrow W$
$\langle \langle \sigma_0,\ p \rangle,\ \langle f_0,\ \overrightarrow{f} \rangle \rangle \hookrightarrow \langle \langle \sigma_1,\ p \rangle,\ \langle f_1,\ \{f_1\} \cup \overrightarrow{f} \rangle \rangle$
$\mathbf{where}\ \langle \sigma_1,\ f_1 \rangle = d_p(\sigma_0, f_0)$

Fig. 5. Language transition relation

---

fill-form   allows the client to edit the values of fields in the current form. The form with the new data both becomes the current form and is added to the cache. This rule does not affect the server.

switch   brings to the foreground a (possibly) different Web form from the client's repository of visited forms. In practice, this happens in a number of ways: switching active browser windows, revisiting a cached page[3] using the back or forward buttons, or selecting a bookmark. This, too, does not affect the server.

---

[3] The actual behavior of revisiting a page depends on whether the page is cached or not. Returning to a non-cached page falls under the *submit* rule.

submit dispatches on the current form's URL to find a program in the table P. This program consumes the current server state and the submitted form to generate an updated server state and a response form. The server records this new state, while the new form is sent to the client and becomes the new current form. Figure 6 depicts this flow of control.

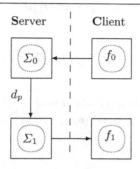

Fig. 6. Client–server control flow

The actual dispatching and evaluation (which is triggered by dispatching) are specific to the programming language, which we introduce next.

4.2 Functional Web Programming

Figure 7 specifies WebL, a core Web programming language. WebL extends the call-by-value λ-calculus [21] with integers, strings, and Web forms, which are records with a reference to a program. The language layer connects to the Web layer of the model (Fig. 2) by providing the two missing components: the syntax (M) and semantics of program evaluation, and the language-sensitive dispatch function d_p.

The **form** construct creates Web forms. The $M.Id$ construct extracts the value of a form field with the name Id. We specify the semantics of WebL with a reduction semantics [9]. There are two reductions: the β_v reduction substitutes an argument value for the formal parameter in the body of a function at an application, while the **select** reduction performs field lookup.

The bottom half of Fig. 7 specifies dispatching. It shows how d_p processes a submitted form $form_0$. First, it uses the URL in $form_0$ to extract a program from its table P. Second, it applies the program to the form and reduces this application to a value $form_1$. The store σ_0 remains the same, because thusfar WebL has no imperative constructs.

Syntax

$$M = V$$
$$| \ (M \ M)$$
$$| \ Id$$
$$| \ (\textbf{form} \ Url \ \overrightarrow{(Id \ M)})$$
$$| \ M.Id$$

$$V = V_b \ | \ (\lambda \ (Id) \ M) \ | \ F$$

Semantics

$$E = [] \ | \ (E \ M) \ | \ (V \ E)$$
$$| \ (\textbf{form} \ Url \ \overrightarrow{(Id \ V)} \ (Id \ E) \ \overrightarrow{(Id \ M)})$$
$$| \ E.Id$$

$(\beta_v) \quad E[((\lambda \ (x) \ body) \ v)] \longrightarrow_v E[body[x \backslash v]]$

$(\textbf{select}) \ E[(\textbf{form} \ url \ \overrightarrow{(n_i \ v_i)} \ (n_j \ v_j) \ \overrightarrow{(n_k \ v_k)}) . \ n_j] \longrightarrow_v E[v_i]$

Language to Web Connection

$d_p(\sigma_0, (\textbf{form} \ Url \ \overrightarrow{(Id \ v)})) = \langle \sigma_0, \ form_1 \rangle$

where $prog = P(Url)$ **and** $(prog \ (\textbf{form} \ Url \ \overrightarrow{(Id \ v)})) \longrightarrow_v^* form_1$

Fig. 7. Web programming language

4.3 Stateful Web Programming

Up to this point, scripts in our model can only communicate with each other through forms. In practice, however, Web scripts often communicate not only via forms but also through external storage (such as files and servlet session objects [7]). To model such stateful communications, we extend WebL with **read** and **write** primitives. Figure 8 presents these language extensions. The two primitives empower programs to read flat values from, and to write flat values to, store locations. The reduction relation $\longrightarrow_{v\sigma}$ is the natural extension of the relation $\longrightarrow_v$. The extended relation relates pairs of terms and stores rather than just terms. Consequently the dispatcher starts a reduction with the invoked program and the current store. At the end it uses the modified store to form the next Web configuration. Because only one program may modify the store at a time, the server model is sequential.

5 Problems with Web Applications

Our model of Web interactions can represent some common Web programming problems concisely. Here we present two of them. The first problem is that a Web script expects a different kind of form than is delivered. We dub this problem the "(script) communication problem." The second problem reveals

Syntax

$M = \cdots \mid (\textbf{read } Id) \mid (\textbf{write } Id\ M)$

Semantics

$\langle \sigma,\ e_0 \rangle \longrightarrow_{v\sigma} \langle \sigma,\ e_1 \rangle \quad \textbf{if} \quad e_0 \longrightarrow_v e_1$

$\langle \sigma,\ E[(\textbf{write } Id\ v_b)] \rangle \longrightarrow_{v\sigma} \langle \sigma[Id \backslash v_b],\ E[v_b] \rangle$

$\langle \sigma,\ E[(\textbf{read } Id)] \rangle \longrightarrow_{v\sigma} \langle \sigma,\ E[\sigma(Id)] \rangle$

$\textbf{where } Id \in dom(\sigma),\ v_b \in V_b$

Language to Web Connection

$\Sigma \sqsubseteq (Id \longrightarrow V_b)$

$d_p(\sigma_0, (\textbf{form } Url\ \overrightarrow{(Id\ s)})) = \langle \sigma_1,\ form_1 \rangle$

$\textbf{where } prog = p(Url)$

$\langle \sigma_0,\ (prog\ (\textbf{form } Url\ \overrightarrow{(Id\ s)}))) \rangle$

$\longrightarrow^*_{v\sigma} \langle \sigma_1,\ form_1 \rangle$

Fig. 8. Language extensions for storage

a weakness of the hypertext transfer protocol. Due to the lack of an update method, information on client Web pages becomes obsolete over time and, hence, may mislead the consumer. We dub this problem the "(HTTP) observer problem" indicating that the HTTP protocol does not permit a proper implementation of the Observer pattern [12] (which enables dependent observers to be notified of state changes).

5.1 The Communication Problem

Since standard Web programs must terminate to interact with a consumer, nontrivial interactive software consists of many small Web programs. If the software needs to interact N times with the client, it consists of $N+1$ scripts, and all scripts must communicate properly with their successors.[4] Worse, since the client can arbitrarily resubmit pages, the programmer cannot assume anything about the scripts' execution sequence.

Even without the difficulties of unusual execution sequences, splitting Web programs into pieces can introduce errors. Consider the example in Fig. 9. The server's table contains two programs with the filenames *start.ss* and *next.ss*.[5] The *start.ss* program prompts for the user's name and directs this information to *next.ss*. This second program attempts to verify some properties about the consumer. In doing so, it assumes that the input form contains both *name* and *phone* fields, and attempts to extract both. The attempt to extract the nonexistent *phone* field results in a runtime error. The diagram illustrates the problem graphically. When programmers mistakenly encode field names assumptions into the store—a mistake that is easily made with Java servlet and

---

[4] A good programmer may recognize opportunities for aggregating some of the programs. It is also possible to use a "multiplexer" technique that merges all these scripts into one single file and uses a dispatcher to find the proper subroutine. The problems remain the same, however, because the various pieces of the same program communicate via HTTP.

[5] Typically, ".ss" is the suffix for Scheme programs; we use it here to be suggestive since our Web programming language is based on Scheme.

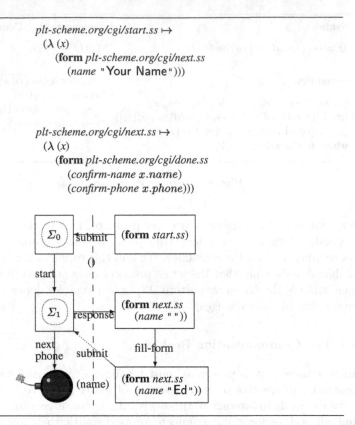

$$plt\text{-}scheme.org/cgi/start.ss \mapsto$$
$$(\lambda\,(x)$$
$$\quad(\textbf{form}\ plt\text{-}scheme.org/cgi/next.ss$$
$$\quad\quad(name\ \texttt{"Your Name"})))$$

$$plt\text{-}scheme.org/cgi/next.ss \mapsto$$
$$(\lambda\,(x)$$
$$\quad(\textbf{form}\ plt\text{-}scheme.org/cgi/done.ss$$
$$\quad\quad(confirm\text{-}name\ x.name)$$
$$\quad\quad(confirm\text{-}phone\ x.phone)))$$

Fig. 9. Collaborating programs

ASP.NET session objects—these safety errors concerning form field accesses become even more nefarious.

By now, programmers are well-aware of this problem and employ extensive dynamic testing to find these mistakes. In Sect. 6, we present a type system that discovers such problems statically and still allows programmers to develop complex interactive Web programs in an incremental manner.

5.2 The Observer Problem

In a model-view-controller (MVC) architecture, a change to the model triggers notification to all the views to update their display. Web programs do not enjoy this privilege, because HTTP does not provide for an update (or "push") method. Once a browser receives a page, it becomes outdated when the MVC model changes on the server, which may be due to additional form submissions from the consumer.

The Observer problem is often, but not always, due to a confusion of environments and stores, or form and server-side storage. A program that reserves flights needs to use both kinds of storage to represent different kinds of information [17]. Unfortunately, programmers who don't understand the difference may place information into the store when it really belongs in the Web form.

Figure 10 shows a reformulation of Orbitz's problem (see Sect. 2) in WebL. The first of these programs, *pick-flight*, asks the customer for a preferred flight time. The second program, *confirm-flight*, writes the selected flight time into external storage before asking the user to confirm the flight time. The third program, *receipt-flight*, reads the selected flight from storage and charges the customer for a ticket.

---

pick-flight ↦ (λ (*empty-form*) (**form** *confirm-flight* (*departure-time* "hh:mm")))

confirm-flight ↦ (λ (*first-form*)
        (**write** *your-flight first-form.departure-time*)
        (**form** *receipt-flight* (*confirm-time* (**read** *your-flight*))))

receipt-flight ↦ (λ (*confirmed-form*)
        (*buy-flight* (**read** *your-flight*))
        (**form** *next-action* (*itinerary* (**read** *your-flight*))))

Fig. 10. Stateful Web programs

It is easy to see that the WebL program models the problem in Sect. 2. Submitting two requests for the *confirm-flight* program results in two pages displaying different flight times on the client, yet only the flight time from the most recent request resides in the server's external storage. Submitting the outdated form that no longer matches the storage produces the mistake.

6 Type Checking Communication

Trying to extract a field from a form fails in WebL if the form does not contain the named field. To prevent such errors, languages often employ a type system (and/or safety checks). Our Web model shows, however, that straightforward type checking doesn't work, because programs consist of many separate scripts loosely connected via forms and storage. Checking all the scripts together is infeasible. Not only are these scripts developed and deployed in an incremental manner, they may also reside on different Web servers and/or be written in different programming languages. Furthermore, consumers can always edit a URL to generate a fresh request that the server has not seen before, akin to a user typing a fresh command at the read-eval-print loop of an interactive language implementation.

We therefore provide an *incremental* type system for Web applications. When the server receives a request for a URL not already in its table, it installs the relevant program to handle the request. Before installing the new program, the server type checks the program, which is a check for internal consistency. In addition, the server also derives constraints that this new program imposes on the other programs on the server with which it interacts. These constraints become external consistency checks. If either type checking or constraint resolution fails, the program is rejected, resulting in an error. In practice, a programmer may register several programs of one application and have them typed checked before they are deployed.

The type system for internal consistency checking heavily borrows from simply-typed λ-calculi with records [5, 20, 24]. Figure 11 defines the type system. In addition to the usual function type ($\longrightarrow$) and primitive types *Int* and *String*, the type language also includes types for Web forms. Similar to record types, **form** types contain the names and types of the form fields that, according to their intended usage, must have flat (marshallable) types. We overload the type environment to map both variables and store locations to types. An initial type environment Γ_0 maps locations in the external storage to flat types. Typed WebL differs from WebL only by requiring types for function arguments. That is, $(\lambda(x)M)$ becomes $(\lambda(x:\tau)M)$ in Typed WebL.

The type system also serves as the basis for external consistency checking. As the type checker traverses the program, it generates constraints on external programs. The type judgments, as shown in Fig. 11, have antecedents (above the bar) which, when conjoined, specify a condition. When this condition holds, the consequent (below the bar) also holds. Each judgment rules that a type environment (Γ) proves that a term has a particular type, and generates a (possibly empty) set of constraints. A constraint Url: (**form** $\overrightarrow{(Id\ \tau_b)}$) insists that the program associated with Url consume Web forms of type (**form** $\overrightarrow{(Id\ \tau_b)}$).

Most type rules in Fig. 11 handle constraints in a straightforward manner. Checking atomic expressions yields the empty set of constraints. Checking most expressions that contain subexpressions simply propagates the constraints from checking the subexpressions. The application rule says that if the function position generates constraint ξ_0 and the argument position generates constraint ξ_1, then the entire application expression will generate the union of these, i.e., the constraint $\xi_0 \cup \xi_1$. The only expressions that generate fresh atomic constraints are **form** expressions.

The expression (**form**: $Url\ \overrightarrow{(Id\ m)}$) constructs a **form** value, so its type is similar to a record type. This **form** expression also indirectly connects the program associated with Url to the form the consumer will submit later. If the type-checker looked up the program associated with Url immediately and compared the **form** type with the function's argument type, this would suffice.

Types

$Type \quad = Type \longrightarrow Type$
$\quad\quad\quad | \; (\mathbf{form} \; \overrightarrow{(Id \; Type_\flat)})$
$\quad\quad\quad | \; Type_\flat$
$Type_\flat = String \mid Int$

Type Judgments

$\Gamma \vdash M : Type, \; \varXi$
where
$\quad\quad \varXi = \{Url : (\mathbf{form} \; \overrightarrow{(Id \; \tau)})\}$

Type Derivation Rules

$$\Gamma \vdash string : String, \{\} \qquad \frac{\Gamma \vdash m : (\mathbf{form} \; \overrightarrow{(Id_a \; \tau_{\flat a})} \; (Id_x \; \tau_{\flat x}) \; \overrightarrow{(Id_b \; \tau_{\flat b})}), \xi}{\Gamma \vdash m.Id_x : \tau_{\flat x}, \xi}$$

$$\Gamma \vdash n : Int, \{\}$$

$$\frac{\Gamma(x) = \tau}{\Gamma \vdash x : \tau, \{\}} \qquad \frac{\overrightarrow{\Gamma \vdash m : \tau_\flat, \xi_m}}{\Gamma \vdash (\mathbf{form} \; Url \; \overrightarrow{(Id \; m)}) : (\mathbf{form} \; \overrightarrow{(Id \; \tau_\flat)}),}{\{Url : (\mathbf{form} \; \overrightarrow{(Id \; \tau_\flat)})\} \cup \overrightarrow{\xi_m}}$$

$$\frac{\Gamma, x : \tau_x \vdash m : \tau, \xi}{\Gamma \vdash (\lambda \, (x : \tau_x) \, m) : \tau_x \longrightarrow \tau, \xi}$$

$$\frac{\Gamma(l) = \tau_\flat}{\Gamma \vdash (\mathbf{read} \; l) : \tau_\flat, \{\}}$$

$$\frac{\Gamma \vdash m_0 : \tau_x \longrightarrow \tau, \xi_0 \quad \Gamma \vdash m_1 : \tau_x, \xi_1}{\Gamma \vdash (m_0 \; m_1) : \tau, \xi_0 \cup \xi_1} \qquad \frac{\Gamma(l) = \tau_\flat \quad \Gamma \vdash m : \tau_\flat, \xi}{\Gamma \vdash (\mathbf{write} \; l \; m) : \tau_\flat, \xi}$$

Fig. 11. Internal types for WebL

It would not, however, allow for independent development of connected Web programs. Instead, type checking the **form** expression generates the constraint Url: $(\mathbf{form} \; \overrightarrow{(Id \; \tau_\flat)})$, which must be checked later.

Figure 12 extends the definition of the server state S with a set of constraints $\varXi$. The function *Install-program* adds a new program m to the server's table p at a given Url if the program is internally and externally consistent. That is, the program must type check and the generated constraints must be consistent with the constraints already on the server. A set of constraints is consistent iff the set is a function from URLs to types. The *Constrain* function ensures that the program m is well typed, and it extends the existing set of constraints ξ_0 to include constraints generated during type checking ξ_1.

The incremental type checker catches communication errors, including the one demonstrated in Fig. 9. Adding type annotations results in the pair of programs in Fig. 13. Type checking produces types and constraints for both programs. The constraints, however, reveal a problem. Checking *start.ss* results in the following constraint:

$$\{ \; next.ss : (\mathbf{form} \, (name \; String)) \}$$

When the server installs *next.ss*, the *Constrain* function generates this constraint:

$$\{ \; next.ss : (\mathbf{form} \, (name \; String) \, (phone \; String)) \; \}$$

Server Extension and Additional Functions

$S = \Sigma \times P \times \Xi$

Install-program : $Url\ M\ W \longrightarrow W$

Install-program$(Url, m, \langle\langle\sigma, p, \xi\rangle, c\rangle) = \langle\langle\sigma, p[Url\backslash m], Constrain(\xi, Url, m)\rangle, c\rangle$
when *Consistent*(*Constrain*$(\xi, Url, m))$

Consistent : $\Xi \longrightarrow boolean$

Consistent$(\xi) \equiv$
  $(Url : (\textbf{form}\ \overrightarrow{(Id_0\ \tau_0)})) \in \xi\ \wedge$
  $(Url : (\textbf{form}\ \overrightarrow{(Id_1\ \tau_1)})) \in \xi \Longrightarrow$
  $\overrightarrow{(Id_0\ \tau_0)} = \overrightarrow{(Id_1\ \tau_1)}$

Constrain : $\Xi\ Url\ M \longrightarrow \Xi$

Constrain$(\xi_0, Url, m) =$
  $\xi_0 \cup \xi_1 \cup \{Url : (\textbf{form}\ \overrightarrow{(Id_{in}\ \tau_{in})})\}$
  where
  $\Gamma_0 \vdash m : (\textbf{form}\ \overrightarrow{(Id_{in}\ \tau_{in})})$
  $\longrightarrow (\textbf{form}\ \overrightarrow{(Id_{out}\ \tau_{out})}), \xi_1$

Fig. 12. Constraint checking

---

plt-scheme.org/cgi/start.ss $\longmapsto$
  $(\lambda\ ([x : (\textbf{form})])$
    $(\textbf{form}\ plt\text{-}scheme.org/cgi/next.ss$
      $(name\ "\textsf{Your Name}")))$

plt-scheme.org/cgi/next.ss $\longmapsto$
  $(\lambda\ ([x : (\textbf{form}\ (name\ String)\ (phone\ String))])$
    $(\textbf{form}\ plt\text{-}scheme.org/cgi/done.ss$
      $(confirm\text{-}name\ x.name)$
      $(confirm\text{-}phone\ x.phone)))$

Fig. 13. Typed collaborating programs

These two constraints are not *Consistent*, so the server rejects the *next.ss* program.

With type annotations, type checking, constraint generation, and constraint checking in place, the system provides three levels of guarantees. The first result shows that individual Web scripts respond to appropriately typed requests without getting stuck.

Proposition 1. *For all m in M, τ in Type, and set of Constraints ξ, if $\Gamma_0 \vdash m : \tau, \xi$ then for some v in V, $m \longrightarrow_v^* \nu$.*

The proof is essentially the same as the usual proof of strong normalization for the simply-typed lambda calculus.

The second proposition shows that the server does not apply Web programs to forms of the wrong type, as long as the server starts in a good state. Before we can state it, however, we need to explain what it means for a server state to be well-typed and for a submitted form to be well-typed. A server is well-typed when all the programs have function types that map forms to forms and when all the constraints are consistent:

server-typechecks$(\langle \sigma,\ p,\ \xi \rangle)$ iff *Consistent*(ξ) and for each *Url* in *dom*(p),

$\Gamma_0 \vdash p\ (Url) : (\textbf{form}\ \overrightarrow{(Id_1\tau_{b1})}) \longrightarrow (\textbf{form}\ \overrightarrow{(Id_2\tau_{b2})}), \xi_{Url}$ and

$\xi_{Url} \subset \xi$ and $Url{:}\ (\textbf{form}\ \overrightarrow{(Id\tau_{b1})}) \in \xi$

A form is well typed with respect to a server if it refers to a program on the server that accepts that type of form.

form-typechecks $(\langle \sigma,\ p,\ \xi \rangle, (\textbf{form}\ Url\ \overrightarrow{(Id\ v_b)}))$ iff

there are types $\overrightarrow{\tau_b}$ such that $\Gamma_0 \vdash v_b : \tau_b, \{\}$ and

$Url : (\textbf{form}\ \overrightarrow{(Id\ \tau_b)})$ is in ξ and

and $Url \in dom(p)$

Proposition 2. *If server-typechecks(s_0) and form-typechecks* (s_0, f_0) *then for some* $\langle s_1,\ \langle f_1,\ \overrightarrow{f} \rangle \rangle$,

$$\langle s_0,\ \langle f_0,\ \overrightarrow{f} \rangle \rangle \hookrightarrow_{submit} \langle s_1,\ \langle f_1,\ \overrightarrow{f} \rangle \rangle.$$

If the server's set of constraints is closed, the resulting configuration also guarantees the success of the next submission.

Proposition 3. *If* $\langle \langle \sigma,\ p,\ \xi \rangle,\ \langle f_0,\ \overrightarrow{f} \rangle \rangle \hookrightarrow_{submit} \langle s_1,\ \langle f_1,\ \overrightarrow{f} \rangle \rangle$,

server-typecheck($\langle \sigma,\ p,\ \xi \rangle$), form-typechecks($\langle \sigma,\ p,\ \xi \rangle,\ f_0$),

and for each constraint Url : $(\textbf{form}\ \overrightarrow{(Id\tau)})$ *in* ξ, *if Url is in dom(p) then*

server-typecheck(s_1) and form-typechecks(s_1, f_1).

In practice these checks only need to be performed upon demand. This strategy makes it possible to incrementally install programs that refer to other programs that have not yet been written and that are used only in rare cases, with the caveat that they are only checked when they are installed.

Alternative Web Programming Languages

It is not necessary to instantiate our model with a functional programming language. Instead, we could have used a language such as <bigwig>, which is the canonical imperative while-loop language over a basic data type of Web documents [25]. Furthermore, the <bigwig> language already provides an internal type system that derives and checks information about Web documents. Its type system is stronger than ours, allowing programmers to use complex mechanisms for composing Web documents.

The <bigwig> project and our analysis differ with respect to the ultimate goal. First, our primary goal is to accommodate the existing Web browser mechanisms. In contrast, <bigwig>'s runtime system disables the browser's navigation functionality. Second, we wish to accommodate an open world, where scripts in ASP.NET, Perl, or Python can collaborate. Our propositions show how type checks in the language and in the server can accommodate just this kind of openness. The `<bigwig>` project does not provide a model and therefore does not provide a foundation for investigating Web interactions in general.

Separating constraints on collaborating programs from the type checking of individual programs lends the system flexibility. For Typed WebL programs, the set of forms produced could be computed simply by examining the program's return type. For other languages the local type checking and the constraint generation may be less connected.

Extending our constraint checking to dynamically typed languages requires a type inference system capable of determining the types of all possible forms a program might produce. Though this is not necessary for Typed WebL, we choose to keep the constraint generation separate to emphasize the independence of the constraints from the languages used for individual scripts.

7 Addressing Outdated Observers

Section 5.2 describes the Observer problem, and points out that it is caused by the Web's lack of a "push" method. Some Web sites simulate pushing data by using a "meta" tag in HTML that forces the generated page to refresh its content periodically. A naïve implementation of this technique suffers from obvious scalability problems. More germane to our discussion, however, is that this does not actually implement the desired user interaction.

To understand this, consider the example in Sect. 2. The user opens a new window in step 1 to explore the flight departing at 5:50 pm. When the user examines a different flight in step 3, a push implementation would eventually *update* the information in the window for the 5:50 pm flight, to maintain its currency with the server's state. While this makes the flight reservation made after step 5 consistent with the information on the window, it means that the user's mental association of the first window with the flight at 5:50 pm has been silently invalidated by the update. This error is just as insidious as that in Sect. 2.

A better solution is to modify the server so that it detects when a submitted form does not reflect the server state. Roughly speaking, this corresponds to the execution of a safety check like the one for array indexing or list destructuring. If the "up-to-date" test fails, the server informs the consumer of the situation, which prevents the erroneous computation from causing further damage. Again, in analogy to safety checks, the server signals an exception and thus informs the consumer at the earliest opportunity that something went wrong. We believe that this approach is general because it is independent of the scripting language. Further, dynamic checking is an appropriate compromise because these kinds of situations depend on dynamic configurations rather than on static properties of the program.

To check on the datedness of a submitted form, the server must perform some additional bookkeeping. Specifically, determining if something is outdated requires a notion of time, and therefore the server must keep track of time [23]. For us, time is the number of processed submissions. The external storage Σ changes so that it maps locations not only to flat values but also to a timestamp for the last write, i.e., $\Sigma \sqsubseteq Id \longrightarrow Time \times V_\flat$ (compare to the signature in figure 8).

In addition, the server maintains a *carrier* set of all storage locations read or written during the execution of a script. When it sends each page to the consumer, the server adds the current time stamp and this set of locations as an extra hidden field on the page.

With this additional bookkeeping, the server can now check whether each request is up-to-date. When a request arrives, the server extracts both the carrier set and the page creation time. If any of the timestamps attached to the locations in the carrier set are out of date, then the submitted form may be inconsistent with the data in the current server store, and the server signals an exception identifying the out-of-date items:

> A *form* with carrier set *CS* and time stamp T submitted to a server with current state σ is **out of date** if and only if any of the locations in *CS* have a time stamp in σ that is larger than T.

The actual size of the carrier set will vary based not only on the script's function but also on its implementation (i.e., depending on how stateful it is).

Clearly, a naïve use of this test produces many false positives. For example, a script may use and modify the server state to compute a page counter, a set of advertisements, or other information irrelevant to the consumer. If a form is out of date only for "irrelevant" storage locations, the consumer should clearly not receive a warning. We therefore allow programs to specify whether reading or writing a location in the server state is a relevant or irrelevant action from the consumer's perspective. Assuming that language implementors make this change, the Web server can reduce the carrier set that it collects during a script execution and the number of warnings it issues.

8 Conclusion

This chapter introduces a formal model of sequential, interactive Web programs. We use the model to describe classes of errors that occur when consumers interact with programs using the natural capabilities of Web browsers. The analysis pinpoints two classes of problems with scripting languages and servers.

To remedy the situation, languages used for scripting should come with type checkers that compute the shape of expected forms on the input side and the shape of forms that the scripts may produce. These languages should also allow scripts to specify which actions on the server's state are relevant for the consumer. Furthermore, servers should be modified to integrate the type information from the scripts. In particular, servers should only submit forms to a script if the form is well-typed and its content is up-to-date.

Most combinations of Web servers and Web application programming languages fail to implement either kind of test. All of them, in particular, fail to check for the currency of data, even those whose authors are keenly aware of the problem described in Sect. 2. While we have implemented our model in a toy Web server, we have not (yet) ported the code to our PLT Web server [14]. Similarly, WASH/CGI [26] is based on a purely functional programming language in recognition of the problems involving state; the careful management of state appeares to address the problem of Section 2. This design is, however, deceiving. The true culprit is a lack of server-based checks that warn users about outdated information.

This formal model has already proven useful in other work. Web programs naturally give rise to temporal properties governing their execution over the course of a workflow, making model checking [6] an attractive verification technique. A naïve model construction based purely on the program source, however, fails to take into consideration the many interaction possibilities introduced by browsers, and thus fails to catch errors of the sort discussed in this paper. To model each browser primitive would, however, be onerous. Our work on model checking of Web programs [16] therefore uses the model of this paper to constrain the language of analysis, and can thus verify programs that operate in any browser so long as all their interaction primitives can be reduced to the ones presented in this paper.

In short, the formal model helps us to first reduce the complexity of Web interaction primitives to a small and manageable number. It then helps us describe common Web problems in terms of these primitives. We can then derive verification techniques to address these problems. We hope to exploit this knowledge to build better languages for programming applications that reside on servers and in Web browsers.

Acknowledgment

Thanks to Jacob Matthews for helping us experiment with WASH/CGI, and to Scott Smolka for his careful editorial work.

References

1. Atkins, D. L., T. Ball, G. Bruns and K. C. Cox. Mawl: A domain-specific language for form-based services. *Software Engineering*, 25(3):334–346, 1999.
2. Brabrand, C., A. Møller, A. Sandholm and M. Schwartzbach. A language for developing interactive Web services, 1999. Unpublished manuscript.
3. Brabrand, C., A. Møller, A. Sandholm and M. I. Schwartzbach. A runtime system for interactive Web services. In *Journal of Computer Networks*, pages 1391–1401, 1999.

4. BrightPlanet. DeepWeb.
   http://www.completeplanet.com/Tutorials/DeepWeb/.
5. Cardelli, L. Type systems. In *Handbook of Computer Science and Engineering*. CRC Press, 1996.
6. Clarke, E., O. Grumberg and D. Peled. *Model Checking*. MIT Press, 2000.
7. Coward, D. Java servlet specification version 2.3, October 2000.
   http://java.sun.com/products/servlet/.
8. Dierks, T. and C. Allen. The transport layer security protocol, January 1999.
   http://www.ietf.org/rfc/rfc2246.txt.
9. Felleisen, M. and R. Hieb. The revised report on the syntactic theories of sequential control and state. *Theoretical Computer Science*, 102:235–271, 1992. Original version in: Technical Report 89-100, Rice University, June 1989.
10. Flatt, M., S. Krishnamurthi and M. Felleisen. Classes and mixins. In *ACM SIGPLAN-SIGACT Symposium on Principles of Programming Languages*, pages 171–183, January 1998.
11. Freier, A. O., P. Karlton and P. C. Kocher. Secure socket layer 3.0, November 1996. IETF Draft   http://wp.netscape.com/eng/ssl3/ssl-toc.html.
12. Gamma, E., R. Helm, R. Johnson and J. Vlissides. *Design Patterns, Elements of Reusable Object-Oriented Software*. Addison-Wesley, 1994.
13. Graham, P. Beating the averages. http://www.paulgraham.com/avg.html.
14. Graunke, P. T., S. Krishnamurthi, S. van der Hoeven and M. Felleisen. Programming the Web with high-level programming languages. In *European Symposium on Programming*, pages 122–136, April 2001.
15. Hughes, J. Generalising monads to arrows. *Science of Computer Programming*, 37(1–3):67–111, May 2000.
16. Licata, D. R. and S. Krishnamurthi. Verifying interactive Web programs. In *IEEE International Symposium on Automated Software Engineering*, pages 164–173, September 2004.
17. Matthews, J., R. B. Findler, P. T. Graunke, S. Krishnamurthi and M. Felleisen. Automatically restructuring programs for the Web. *Automated Software Engineering*, 11(4):337–364, 2004.
18. Microsoft Corporation. http://www.microsoft.com/net/.
19. NCSA. The Common Gateway Interface. http://hoohoo.ncsa.uiuc.edu/cgi/.
20. Pierce, B. C. *Types and Programming Languages*. MIT Press, 2002.
21. Plotkin, G. D. Call-by-name, call-by-value, and the λ-calculus. *Theoretical Computer Science*, pages 125–159, 1975.
22. Queinnec, C. The influence of browsers on evaluators or, continuations to program Web servers. In *ACM SIGPLAN International Conference on Functional Programming*, pages 23–33, 2000.
23. Reed, D. P. Implementing atomic actions on decentralized data. In *ACM Transactions on Computer Systems*, pages 234–254, February 1983.
24. Rémy, D. Typechecking records and variants in a natural extension of ML. In *ACM Symposium on Principles of Programming Languages*, pages 77–88, 1989.
25. Sandholm, A. and M. I. Schwartzbach. A type system for dynamic Web documents. In *Symposium on Principles of Programming Languages*, pages 290–301, 2000.
26. Thiemann, P. WASH/CGI: Server-side Web scripting with sessions and typed, compositional forms. In *Practical Applications of Declarative Languages*, pages 192–208, 2002.

Composition of Interacting Computations

Farhad Arbab[1,2]

[1] Center for Mathematics and Computer Science (CWI), Amsterdam, The
   Netherlands
[2] Leiden University, Leiden, The Netherlands

Summary. The field of programming has been concerned with software composition since its very inception. Our models for software composition have brought us
up to a new plateau of software complexity and composition. To tackle the challenges
of composition at this level requires new models for software composition centered
on *interaction* as a first-class concept. Interaction has been studied as an insepara-
ble concern within concurrency theory. Curiously, however, interaction has not been
seriously considered as a first-class concept in *constructive models of computation*.

Composition of systems out of autonomous subsystems pivots on coordination
concerns that center on interaction. Coordination models and languages represent a
recent approach to design and development of concurrent systems. In this chapter,
we present a brief overview of coordination models and languages, followed by a
framework for their classification. We then focus on a specific coordination language,
called Reo, and demonstrate how it provides a powerful and expressive model for
flexible composition of behavior through interaction.

Reo serves as a good example of a constructive model of computation that treats
interaction as a (in fact, *the only*) first-class concept. It uniquely focuses on the
compositional construction of connectors that enable and coordinate the interactions
among the constituents in a concurrent system, without their knowledge. We show
how Reo allows complex behavior in a system to emerge as a composition of primitive
interactions.

1 Introduction

Naturalization of computing and information technologies into human enterprises propels the emergence of complex, dynamically evolving, distributed
information-intensive systems. The interest in understanding, design, specification, and validation of the architectures of these systems motivates the
study of models for a-posteriori composition of concurrent computations, their
interactions, and their coordination. The desire to compose running systems
by gluing together existing pieces of software and subsystems as reusable components, and to verify that they conform to such architectures, gives practical
relevance and urgency to this undertaking.

Software composition has been a concern since the inception of programming. Recognizing the need to go beyond the success of available tools is sometimes more difficult than accepting to abandon what does not work. Our models for software composition have served us well-enough to bring us up to a new plateau of software complexity and composition requirements beyond their own effectiveness. In this sense, they have become the victims of their own success. We now need to tackle dynamic composition of behavior by orchestrating the interactions among independent distributed subsystems or services whose actual code and algorithms must remain independent of one another. This requires new models for software composition centered on *interaction* as a first-class concept. Various aspects of interaction protocols have been studied in concurrency theory. Curiously, however, interaction has not been seriously considered as a first-class concept in *constructive models of computation*.

Different models of computation exist to serve different purposes. Turing machines, for instance, capture the essence of algorithmic computing as a sequence of mechanical operations that, if terminates, transforms its given input into an output. Turing machines were devised to explore the expressiveness of this notion of computing, and its limits. They are not (meant to be) useful for the actual construction of computing systems, hardware or software. Examples of *constructive models of computation* include the so-called von Neumann model, functional programming, logic programming, imperative programming, and object oriented programming.

Concurrent Turing machines do not add expressiveness over what a single universal Turing machine offers: whatever algorithmic computation a set of concurrent Turing machines can perform, can also be performed on a single Turing machine. In spite of this expressive equivalence, models of computation that have proven effective for construction of sequential programs are notoriously inadequate for construction of concurrent systems. Calculi such as CSP [1], CCS [2], the π-calculus [3, 4], process algebras [5, 6, 7], and the actor model [8] are among the various models of computation specifically aimed at the complexities that arise in the construction of concurrent systems.

Wegner's proposal of interaction machines [9, 10] and the claim that they model more than the algorithmic notion of computing captured by Turing machines have drawn considerable attention on interaction as a new paradigm in computing. However, interaction machines, as well as most subsequent work on interaction, e.g., by Goldin, et al. [11], and van Leeuwen and Wiedermann [12, 13], focus on expressiveness issues. As such, one may regard them as the "Turing machine level" work for the new paradigm of interaction. Wegner and Goldin have proposed interaction as a framework for modeling of complex systems [14].

Currently, what has emerged out of decades of experience with concurrency forms the mainstay of models and tools for construction and analysis of interactive computing systems. However, one should not misconstrue the lack of better tools and familiarity of existing ones as evidence for their adequacy.

The fact that we currently apply languages and tools based on various concurrent object oriented models, the actor model, and various process algebras, etc., simply means that they comprise the best in our available arsenal, but it does not mean that they necessarily embody the most appropriate models for tackling interaction in practice. If interaction identifies a distinctive shift within (or out of) concurrency, of a magnitude deserving recognition as a new paradigm, then this must surely have at least some nontrivial practical implications on suitable models and tools for construction of systems exploiting that distinction. What exactly are the properties that give rise to this distinction and how can they be utilized to offer more effective *constructive models of interaction*?

The most striking hallmark of *interaction* is that it is a phenomenon that involves two or more actors. This is in contrast to *action*, which is what a single actor manifests. A model of interaction must allow us to directly specify, represent, construct, compose, decompose, analyze, and reason about that which transpires among two or more engaged actors, without the necessity to be specific about their actions.

Contemporary models of concurrency predominantly treat interaction as a secondary or derived concept. Process calculi, for instance, are models for constructing processes. They offer operators for composing atomic processes or primitive actions into more complex processes. Interaction ensues only as a consequence of the unfolding of the behavior of the processes involved in a concurrent system. For example, as a process p unfolds and performs its actions, one of its primitive actions, such as a send, collides with a compatible primitive action, such as a receive, performed by another process q. It is this collision of actions that forms an interaction. Whether this collision occurs by dumb luck, divine intervention, or intelligent design, is irrelevant. A split-second earlier or later, perhaps in a different run, the same two actions could have collided with other actions of other processes, yielding entirely different interactions. Actions and their composition have explicit constructs used to define a system. Interaction is ephemeral and implicit, and plays no structural role in the construction of a system. Other contemporary models for software composition, such as the object oriented paradigm or the actor model, fair no better than process calculi in this regard.

A constructive model in the paradigm of interactive computing must treat interaction as a first-class concept. This means that it must offer (1) primitive interactions, and (2) rules of composition for combining (primitive) interactions into more complex interactions, without the need to specify (the actions of) the actors involved.

The coordination language Reo serves as a good example of a constructive model of interaction. In this chapter, we first present a brief overview of coordination models and languages, followed by a framework for their classification. We then describe Reo and demonstrate that it provides a powerful and expressive model for flexible composition of behavior through interaction. Reo uniquely focuses on the compositional construction of connectors that enable and coordinate the interactions among the constituents in a concurrent system, without their knowledge. Reo shows how complex behavior in a system can emerge as a composition of primitive interactions.

2 Coordination

When a group of people collaborate to achieve a common objective, it is quite usual for an individual to emerge or be designated as their leader. An important role of the leader is to coordinate the activities of the other collaborators to ensure that the group objective is achieved. A good deal of what a leader does to coordinate the activities of the others in the group is independent of the true nature of those activities and the group objective; furthermore, there is a great deal of overlap and congruence among the coordinating activities of the leaders of various groups working to achieve different objectives. Had this not been the case, management as a separate discipline would not have made any sense. The need for leadership and coordination among people increases as the number of collaborators and the complexity of their interactions increase. Analogously, our increasingly more complex computing applications involve intricate interactions among multitudes of constituents (e.g., agents, threads, processes, objects, components, etc.) and exhibit the need for explicit attention to their coordination and systematic mechanisms for its implementation. Whether this coordination is distributed or centralized is irrelevant here. What matters is recognizing that (1) the nature of coordination activity is different than and independent of specific applications, and (2) coordination activity in all applications involves a common set of primitive concepts.

Coordination languages, models, and systems constitute a recent field of study in programming and software systems, with the goal of finding solutions to the problem of managing the interaction among concurrent programs. Coordination can be defined as the study of the dynamic topologies of interactions among interaction machines, and the construction of protocols to realize such topologies that ensure well-behavedness. Analogous to the way in which topology abstracts away the metric details of geometry and focuses on the invariant properties of (seemingly very different) shapes, coordination abstracts away the details of computation in interaction machines, and focuses on the invariant properties of (seemingly very different) programs. As such, coordination focuses on patterns that specifically deal with interaction.

Coordination languages can be thought of as the linguistic counterpart of the ad hoc platforms that offer middle-ware support for software composition. The inability of traditional middle-ware software to deal with the cooperation model of a concurrent application in an explicit form contributes to the difficulty of developing working concurrent applications that contain large numbers of active entities with nontrivial cooperation protocols. In spite of the fact that the implementation of a complex protocol is often the most difficult and error prone part of an application development effort, the end

result is typically not recognized as a "commodity" in its own right, because
the protocol is only implicit in the behavior of the rest of the concurrent software. This makes maintenance and modification of the cooperation protocols
of concurrent applications much more difficult than necessary, and their reuse
next to impossible. In contrast to middle-ware software such as PVM [15],
MPI [16], COM+ [17], CORBA [18], etc., coordination models and languages
are meant to offer a systematic means to close the conceptual gap between
the cooperation model of an application and the lower-level communication
model used in its implementation.

Coordination languages are most relevant specifically in the context of
open systems, where the entities that participate in a system are not fixed
at the outset. Coordination is also relevant in design, development, debugging, maintenance, and reuse of all concurrent systems, where it addresses a
number of important software engineering issues. The current interest in constructing applications out of independent software components necessitates
specific attention to the so-called *glue-code*. The purpose of the glue-code is
to compose a set of components by filling the significant interface gaps that
naturally arise among them, simply because they are not (supposed to be)
tailor-made to work with one another. Using components, thus, means understanding how they individually interact with their environment, and specifying
how they should engage in mutual, cooperative interactions in order for their
composition to behave as a coordinated whole. Many of the core issues involved in component composition have already been identified and studied as
key concerns in work on coordination. Coordination models address such key
issues in component based software engineering as specification, interaction,
and dynamic composition of components. Specifically, *exogenous* coordination
models provide a very promising basis for the development of effective glue-
code languages because they enable third-party entities to wield coordination
control over the interaction behavior of mutually anonymous entities involved
in a collaboration activity from outside of those participating entities.

One of the best known coordination languages is Linda [19, 20], which is
based on the notion of a shared *tuple space*. Linda is not really a full programming language: its small set of primitives is meant to augment existing
programming languages. The tuple space of Linda is a centrally managed
resource and contains all pieces of information that processes wish to communicate with each other. Linda processes can be written in any language
augmented with Linda primitives. There are only four primitives provided by
Linda, which treat the tuple space as associative memory and operate on single tuples. The primitive **in** searches the tuple space for a matching tuple and
deletes it; **out** adds a tuple to the tuple space; **read** searches for a matching
tuple in the tuple space; and **eval** starts an active tuple (i.e., a process). Numerous other coordination models and language extensions, e.g., JavaSpace
of Jini [21, 22], are based on Linda-like models.

Besides the "generative tuple space" of Linda, a number of other interesting models have been proposed and used to support coordination languages and systems. Examples include various forms of "parallel multiset rewriting" or "chemical reactions" as in Gamma [23], models with explicit support for coordinators as in Manifold [24, 25], "software bus" as in ToolBus [26], and a calculus of generalized-channel composition as in Reo [27]. A significant number of these models are based on a few common notions, such as pattern-based, associative communication [28], that complement the name-oriented, data-based communication of traditional languages for parallel programming. See [29] for a comprehensive survey of coordination models.

Coordination languages have been applied to the parallelization of computation intensive sequential programs in the fields of simulation of fluid dynamics systems, matching of DNA strings, molecular synthesis, parallel and distributed simulation, monitoring of medical data, computer graphics, analysis of financial data integrated into decision support systems, and game playing (chess). See [30, 31, 32, 33] for some concrete examples.

3 Classification of Coordination Models

Some of the important properties of different coordination languages become clear when we classify them along the following three dimensions: focus of coordination, locus of coordination, and modus of coordination. Although a detailed description of most individual coordination models is beyond the scope of our interest in this chapter, an overview of the dimensions of this classification helps to clarify the issues they address, and thus the concerns of coordination as a field.

3.1 Focus

Focus of coordination refers to the aspect of the applications that a coordination model emphasizes as its primary concern. Significant aspects used by various models as their focus of coordination include data, control, and dataflow, respectively yielding *data-oriented*, *control-oriented*, and *dataflow-oriented* families of coordination models.

For instance, Linda uses a data-oriented coordination model, whereas Manifold is a control-oriented coordination language. The activity in a data-oriented application tends to center around a substantial shared body of data; the application is essentially concerned with what happens to the data. Examples include database and transaction systems such as banking and airline reservation applications. On the other hand, the activity in a control-oriented application tends to center around processing or flow of control and, often, the very notion of the data, as such, simply does not exist; such an application is essentially described as a collection of activities that genuinely consume their input data, and subsequently produce, remember, and transform "new data" that they generate by themselves. Examples include applications that involve work-flow in organizations, and multiphase applications where the content, format, and/or modality of information substantially changes from one phase to the next.

Dataflow-oriented models, such as Reo, use the flow of data as the only (or at least the primary) control mechanism. Unlike data-oriented models, dataflow models are oblivious to the actual content, type, or structure of data and are instead concerned with the flow of data from their sources to their destinations. Unlike control-oriented models, events that trigger state transitions are limited to only those that arise out of the flow of data.

3.2 Locus

Locus of coordination refers to where coordination activity takes place, classifying coordination models as *endogenous* or *exogenous*. Endogenous models, such as Linda, provide primitives that must be incorporated *within* a computation for its coordination. In contrast, exogenous models, such as Manifold and Reo, provide primitives that support coordination of entities from *without*. In applications that use exogenous models, primitives that affect the coordination of each module are outside the module itself.

Endogenous models are sometimes more natural for a given application. However, they generally lead to an intermixing of coordination primitives with computation code, which entangles the semantics of computation with coordination protocols. This intermixing tends to scatter communication/coordination primitives throughout the source code, making the cooperation model and the coordination protocol of an application nebulous and implicit: generally, there is no piece of source code identifiable as the cooperation model or the coordination protocol of an application, that can be designed, developed, debugged, maintained, and reused, in isolation from the rest of the application code. Figure 1 uses the dining philosophers problem to illustrate endogenous coordination in C-Linda. Observe that the decisions about the total number of philosophers (in this case, 4), the number of forks (also 4), and the actual scheme for prevention of deadlock (the "meal tickets" scheme, the number of available meal tickets, and the adherence to their use), which comprise the coordination protocol of this application, are all explicit concerns inside the code of philosophers.

On the other hand, exogenous models encourage development of coordination modules separately and independently of the computation modules they are supposed to coordinate. Consequently, the result of the substantial effort invested in the design and development of the coordination component of an application can manifest itself as tangible "pure coordinator modules" which are easier to understand, and can also be reused in other applications.

```
#define TRUE 1

philosopher(int i)
{
    while(TRUE) {
        think();
        in("meal ticket"); in("fork", i); in("fork", (i+1)%5);
        eat();
        out("fork", i); out("fork", (i+1)%5); out("meal ticket");
    } }

real_main()
{
    int i;
    for (i=0, i<5, i++){
        out("fork", i);
        eval(philosopher(i));
        if (i<4) out("meal ticket");
    }
}
```

Fig. 1. The dining philosophers in C-Linda

3.3 Modus

Modus of coordination refers to how coordination is carried out: how the coordination rules of an application are defined and enforced. The substance of the repertoire of coordination rules supported by different coordination models can be very different. Some, e.g., Linda, Manifold, and Reo, provide primitives for building coordination rules. Others propose rule-based languages where rules act as trigger conditions for action or as constraints on the behavior of active agents to coordinate them in a system. One way or the other, coordination rules provide a level of abstraction which hides much of the complexity of coordination activity from programmers. Explicit declarative rules can themselves be subjected to formal reasoning. Therefore, models that use more declarative coordination rules can support increased reasoning power.

A coordination model may allow only a single medium of coordination that enforces the rules; such is the case in Linda. Other Linda-like models allow multiple data-spaces, together with provisions for defining, selecting, or otherwise determining which coordinated entities are assigned to which data-space. Other coordination languages, such as Manifold and Reo, allow dynamic construction and reconfiguration of the coordination medium.

A related issue is the extent to which a model considers an "enforcer of the rules" or a "coordinator" to itself be amenable to other sets of (meta-) coordination rules. In many models, "the coordinator" is either implicit or is a single privileged entity that cannot be subjected to programmer defined rules. Other models allow more than one coordinator entities, which may or may not be subject to some form of meta-coordination rules. Few models, e.g., Manifold and Reo, treat coordinators as normal entities that can be subjected to the same coordination rules, thus eliminating the distinction between coordinators and meta-coordinators.

4 Reo

Reo is a channel-based exogenous coordination model wherein complex coordinators, called *connectors*, are compositionally built out of simpler ones. The simplest connectors in Reo are a set of *channels* with well-defined behavior supplied by users [27]. The emphasis in Reo is on connectors, their behavior, and their composition, not on the entities that connect, communicate, and cooperate through them. The behavior of every connector in Reo imposes a specific coordination pattern on the entities that perform normal I/O operations through that connector, without their knowledge. This makes Reo a powerful "glue language" for compositional construction of connectors to combine component instances into a software system and exogenously orchestrate their mutual interactions.

4.1 Components

Reo's notion of components and connectors is depicted in Fig. 2, where component instances are represented as boxes, channels as straight lines, and connectors are delineated by dashed lines. Each connector in Reo is, in turn, constructed compositionally out of simpler connectors, which are ultimately composed out of primitive channels.

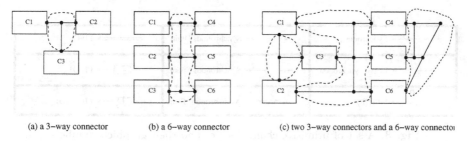

(a) a 3–way connector   (b) a 6–way connector   (c) two 3–way connectors and a 6–way connector

Fig. 2. Connectors and component composition

Every component instance consists of one or more active entities whose only means of communication with other entities outside of that component instance is through regular input/output of passive data. A component instance performs its I/O operations following its own timing and logic, independently of the others. None of these component instances is aware of the existence of the others, the specific connector used to glue it with the rest, or even of its own role in the composite system. Each connector represents a specific interaction protocol and ensures that this protocol is enforced among its connected component instances. The behavior of a connector is independent of the components that it connects.

4.2 Channels

Reo defines a number of operations for components to (dynamically) compose, connect to, and perform I/O through connectors. Atomic connectors are *channels*. The notion of channel in Reo is far more general than its common interpretation.

Reo defines a channel as a primitive communication medium with its own unique identity, that has exactly two ends together with a constraint that interrelates the timing and the content of the I/O operations through these ends. There are two types of channel ends: *source* end through which data enters and *sink* end through which data leaves a channel. A channel must support a certain set of primitive operations, such as I/O, on its ends; beyond that, Reo places no restriction on the behavior of a channel. Reo does not even insist that a channel must have one source and one sink; it also admits channels with two sources or two sinks. This allows an open-ended set of different channel types to be used simultaneously together in Reo, each with its own policy for synchronization, buffering, ordering, computation, data retention/loss, etc.

A Sampler of Channels

Figure 3 shows a sample set of primitive channel types and the graphical symbols we use to represent them.

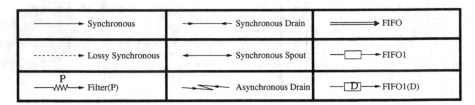

Fig. 3. A set of primitive channel types and their graphical symbols

A synchronous channel, Sync, graphically represented as a solid arrow, has a source- and a sink-end. This channel synchronizes the success of the two I/O operations on its two ends. In other words, it blocks a write operation on its source end or a take operation on its sink end, as necessary, to ensure that these two operations succeed atomically.

SyncDrain is a synchronous channel with two source ends; it has no sink end. This means no one can ever take any data out of this channel. Therefore, all data entered into this channel are lost. SyncDrain is a synchronous channel in exactly the same sense as a Sync channel: it synchronizes the two I/O operations on its ends. In this case they must both be write operations, and SyncDrain blocks either of the two, as necessary, to ensure that they succeed atomically.

FIFO is an asynchronous channel with a source end and a sink end with an unbounded buffer to contain data. Its buffer is initially empty. With an unbounded buffer, a write operation on its source end always succeeds, placing its data in the buffer. With a nonempty buffer, a take on the sink end of this channel succeeds and removes the oldest data item in the buffer. When the buffer is empty, a take operation on the sink end of this channel blocks, waiting for the status of the buffer to change.

LossySync is a synchronous channel with a behavior very similar to that of the Sync channel. Just as for a Sync channel, a take operation on the sink end of a LossySync blocks until a write is performed on its source end. Unlike the case of the Sync channel, all write operations on the source end of a LossySync immediately succeed: if there is a pending take on its sink end, then the written data item is transferred; otherwise, the write operation succeeds, but the written data item is lost.

A synchronous spout, SyncSpout, disposes data items out of its two ends only synchronously. The actual values it produces through its ends are non-deterministic.

FIFO1 is an asynchronous channel with a source end and a sink end and a bounded buffer with the capacity to contain at most 1 data item. Its buffer is initially empty. With an empty buffer, a write operation on its source end succeeds and fills the buffer. With a nonempty buffer, a take on the sink end of this channel succeeds and removes the data. Otherwise, I/O operations block waiting for the status of the buffer to change. FIFO1(D) is a variant of the FIFO1 channel whose buffer initially contains the data item D.

A Filter(P) channel is a synchronous channel with a source and a sink end that takes a pattern P parameter upon its creation. It behaves like a Sync channel, except that only those data items that match the pattern P can actually pass through it; others are always accepted by its source, but are immediately lost.

An asynchronous drain AsynchDrain is the dual of a SyncDrain: it allows the two write operations on its two ends to succeed only one at a time, i.e., never simultaneously together.

4.3 Connector

A connector is a set of channel ends organized in a graph of nodes and edges such that:

1. Zero or more channel ends coincide on every node.
2. Every channel end coincides on exactly one node.
3. There is an edge between two (not necessarily distinct) nodes if and only if there is a channel one end of which coincides on each of those nodes.

4.4 Nodes

A node is an important concept in Reo. Not to be confused with a location or a component, a node is a logical construct representing the fundamental topological property of coincidence of a set of channel ends, which has specific implications on the flow of data among and through those channel ends.

The set of channel ends coincident on a node A is disjointly partitioned into the sets $Src(A)$ and $Snk(A)$, denoting the sets of source and sink channel ends that coincide on A, respectively. A node A is called a *source node* if $Src(A) \neq \emptyset \land Snk(A) = \emptyset$. Analogously, A is called a *sink node* if $Src(A) = \emptyset \land Snk(A) \neq \emptyset$. A node A is called a mixed node if $Src(A) \neq \emptyset \land Snk(A) \neq \emptyset$. Figures 4.(a) and (b) show sink nodes with, respectively, two and three coincident channel ends. Figures 4.(c) and (d) show source nodes with, respectively, two and three coincident channel ends. Figure 4.(e) shows a mixed node where three sink and two source channel ends coincide.

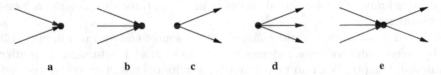

a   b   c   d   e

Fig. 4. Sink, source, and mixed nodes

The expressive power of Reo stems from the behavior of its nodes. Reo provides operations that enable components to connect to and perform I/O on source and sink nodes only; components cannot connect to, read from, or write to mixed nodes. At most one component can be connected to a (source or sink) node at a time. A component can write data items to a source node that it is connected to. The write operation succeeds only if all (source) channel ends coincident on the node accept the data item, in which case the data item is transparently written to every source end coincident on the node. A source node, thus, acts as a *replicator*. A component can obtain data items from a sink node that it is connected to through destructive (take) and nondestructive (read) input operations. A take operation succeeds only if at least one of the (sink) channel-ends coincident on the node offers a suitable data item; if more than one coincident channel end offers suitable data items, one is selected nondeterministically. A sink node, thus, acts as a nondeterministic *merger*. A mixed node is a self-contained "pumping station" that combines the behavior

of a sink node (merger) and a source node (replicator) in an atomic iteration
of an endless loop: in every iteration a mixed node nondeterministically selects
and takes a suitable data item offered by one of its coincident sink channel
ends and replicates it into all of its coincident source channel ends. A data
item is suitable for selection in an iteration, only if it can be accepted by all
source channel ends that coincide on the mixed node.

It follows that every channel represents a (simple) connector with two
nodes. More complex connectors are constructed in Reo out of simpler ones
using its *join* operation. Joining two nodes destroys both nodes and produces
a new node on which all of their coincident channel ends coincide.

This single operation allows construction of arbitrarily complex connectors
involving any combination of channels picked from an open-ended assortment
of user-defined channel types. The semantics of a connector is defined as a
composition of the semantics of its (1) constituent channels, and (2) nodes.
The semantics of a channel is defined by the user who provides it. Reo defines
the semantics of its three types of nodes, as mentioned above.

5 Coordination by Connectors

Figures 5.(a) and (b) show two Reo connectors. The enclosing thick boxes in
these figures represent hiding: the topologies of the nodes (and their edges)
inside the box are hidden and cannot be modified, yielding a connector with
a number of input/output ports, represented as nodes on the border of the
bounding box, which can be used by other entities outside the box to interact
with and through the connector.

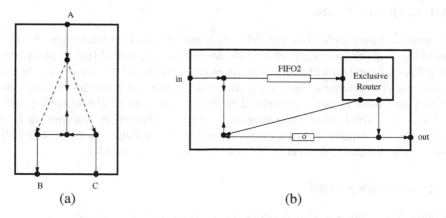

(a)   (b)

Fig. 5. An exclusive router and a shift-lossy `FIFO1`

The simplest channels used in these connectors are synchronous (`Sync`)
channels, represented as simple solid arrows. A `Sync` channel has a source and

a sink end, and no buffer. It accepts a data item through its source end if and only if it can simultaneously dispense it through its sink. A lossy synchronous (LossySync) channel is similar to a Sync channel, except that it always accepts all data items through its source end. If it is possible for it to simultaneously dispense the data item through its sink (e.g., there is a take operation pending on its sink) the channel transfers the data item; otherwise the data item is lost. LossySync channels are depicted as dashed arrows, e.g., in Fig. 5.(a). The edge connecting the bottom-most two nodes inside the enclosing box in Fig. 5.(b) represents an asynchronous channel with the bounded capacity of 1 (FIFO1), with the small box in the middle of the arrow representing its buffer. This channel can have an initially empty buffer, or as in Fig. 5.(b), contain an initial data value (in this case, the "o" in the box representing its buffer). Analogously, the edge connecting the top-most two nodes inside the enclosing box in Fig. 5.(b) represents an asynchronous FIFO channel with the bounded capacity of 2 (FIFO2), with its obvious semantics.

An example of the more exotic channels permitted in Reo is the synchronous drain channel (SyncDrain), whose visual symbol appears as the middle vertical edge in Fig. 5.(a) and the leftmost vertical edge in Fig. 5.(b). A SyncDrain channel has two source ends. Because it has no sink end, no data value can ever be obtained from this channel. It accepts a data item through one of its ends if and only if a data item is also available for it to simultaneously accept through its other end as well. All data accepted by this channel are lost. A close kin of SyncDrain is the asynchronous drain (AsyncDrain) channel (not shown in Fig. 5): it has two source ends through which it accepts and loses data items, but never simultaneously. SyncSpout and AsyncSpout are dual to the drain channel types as they have two sink ends [27].

5.1 Exclusive Router

Figure 5.(a) shows the Reo network for an exclusive router connector. A data item arriving at the input port A flows through to only one of the output ports B or C, depending on which one is ready to consume it. If both output ports are prepared to consume a data item, then one is selected nondeterministically. The input data is never replicated to more than one of the output ports. Figure 5.(a) shows that the exclusive router is obtained by composing two LossySync channels, a SyncDrain channel, and six Sync channels. See [34] for a more formal treatment of the semantics of this connector.

5.2 Shift-Lossy FIFO1

Figure 5.(b) shows a Reo network for a connector that behaves as a lossy FIFO1 channel with a shift loss-policy. This channel is called shift-lossy FIFO1 (ShiftLossyFIFO1). It behaves as a normal FIFO1 channel, except that if its buffer is full then the arrival of a new data item deletes the existing data item in its buffer, making room for the new arrival. As such, this channel implements a "shift loss-policy" losing the oldest contents in its buffer in favor of the latest arrivals. This is in contrast to the behavior of an overflow-lossy FIFO1 channel, whose "overflow loss-policy" loses the new arrivals when its buffer is full. The connector in Fig. 5.(b) is composed of an exclusive router (shown in Fig. 5.(a), an initially full FIFO1 channel, an initially empty FIFO2 channel, and four Sync channels. See [34] for a more formal treatment of the semantics of this connector.

The shift-lossy FIFO1 circuit in Fig. 5.(b) is indeed so frequently useful as a connector in construction of more complex circuits, that it makes sense to have a special graphical symbol to designate it as a short-hand. Figure 7 shows a circuit that uses two instances of our shift-lossy FIFO1. The graphical symbol we use to represent this circuit is intentionally similar to that of a regular FIFO1 channel, to hint at the similarity of the behavior of these two connectors. As seen in Fig. 7, our graphical symbol for a shift-lossy FIFO1 "channel" has a half-dashed box instead of the solid box of a regular FIFO1 channel: the sink-side half of the box representing the buffer of this channel is dashed, to suggest that it loses the older values to make room for new arrivals, i.e., it shifts to lose.

5.3 Write-Cue Regulator

Consider the connector in Fig. 6.(a), composed out of the three channels ab, cd, and ef. Channels ab and cd are of type Sync and ef is of type SyncDrain. This connector shows one of the most basic forms of exogenous coordination: the number of data items that flow from a to d is the same as the number of write operations that succeed on f. The analogy between the behavior of this connector and a transistor in the world of electronic circuits is conspicuous. A component instance connected to f can count and regulate the flow of data between the two nodes a and d by the timing and the number of write operations it performs on f. The entity that regulates and/or counts the number of data items through f need not know anything about the entities that write to a and/or consume data items from b, nor that its write actions actually regulate this flow. The two entities that communicate through a and d need not know anything about the fact that they are communicating with each other, nor that the volume of their communication is regulated and/or measured by a third entity at f.

5.4 Barrier Synchronizers

We can build on our write-cue regulator to construct a barrier synchronization connector, as in Fig. 6.(b). The four channels ab, cd, gh, and ij are all of type Sync. The SyncDrain channel ef ensures that a data item passes from a to d only simultaneously with the passing of a data item from g to j (and vice versa). This simple barrier synchronization connector can be trivially extended to any number of pairs, as shown in Fig. 6.(c).

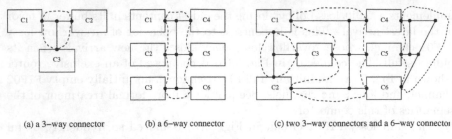

(a) a 3-way connector   (b) a 6-way connector   (c) two 3-way connectors and a 6-way connector

Fig. 6. Examples of connector circuits in Reo

5.5 Ordering

The connector in Fig. 6.(d) consists of three channels: ab, ac, and bc. The channels ab and ac are SyncDrain and Sync, respectively. The channel bc is of type FIFO1. The behavior of this connector can be seen as imposing an order on the flow of the data items written to a and b, through to c: the data items obtained by successive read operations on c consist of the first data item written to a, followed by the first data item written to b, followed by the second data item written to a, followed by the second data item written to b, etc. The coordination pattern imposed by our connector can be summarized as $c = (ab)^*$, meaning the sequence of values that appear through c consist of zero or more repetitions of the pairs of values written to a and b, in that order.

5.6 Sequencer

Consider the connector in Fig. 6.(e). The enclosing box represents the fact that the details of this connector are abstracted away and it provides only the four nodes of the channel ends a, b, c, and d for other entities (connectors and/or component instances) to (in this case) read from. Inside this connector, we have four Sync, an initialized FIFO1, and three FIFO1 channels connected together. The initialized FIFO1 channel is the leftmost one and is initialized to have a data item in its buffer, as indicated by the presence of the symbol "o" in the box representing its buffer. The actual value of this data item is irrelevant. The read operations on the nodes (with channel ends) a, b, c, and d can succeed only in the strict left to right order. This connector implements a generic sequencing protocol: we can parameterize this connector to have as many nodes as we want, simply by inserting more (or fewer) Sync and FIFO1 channel pairs, as required.

5.7 Variable

The Reo circuit in Fig. 7 implements the behavior of a dataflow variable. It uses two instances of the shift-lossy FIFO1 connector shown Fig. 5.b, to build a connector with a single input and a single output nodes. Initially, the buffers of its shift-lossy FIFO1 channels are empty, so an initial take on its output node suspends for data. Regardless of the status of its buffers, or whether or not data can be dispensed through its output node, every write to its input node always succeeds and resets both of its buffers to contain the new data item. Every time a value is dispensed through its output node, a copy of this value is "cycled back" into its left shift-lossy FIFO1 channel. This circuit "remembers" the last value it obtains through its input node, and dispenses copies of this value through its output node as frequently as necessary: i.e., it can be used as a dataflow variable.

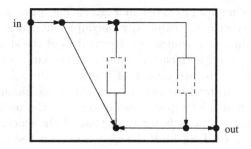

Fig. 7. Dataflow variable

The variable circuit in Fig. 7 is also very frequently useful as a connector in construction of more complex circuits. Therefore, it makes sense to have a short-hand graphical symbol to designate it with as well. Figure 8 shows three instances of our variable used in two connectors. Our symbol for a variable is similar to that for a regular FIFO1 channel, except that we use a rounded box to represent its buffer: the rounded box hints at the recycling behavior of the variable circuit, which implements its remembering of the last data item that it obtained or dispensed.

5.8 Time and Temperature Display

Figure 8.(a) shows a system composed of two components connected via a Reo connector. The two components are represented as thick-bordered boxes labeled Clock and Display in this figure. The clock component periodically— say every 30 seconds or so—produces a text string announcing the current time. The display component periodically reads and consumes a text string and displays it.

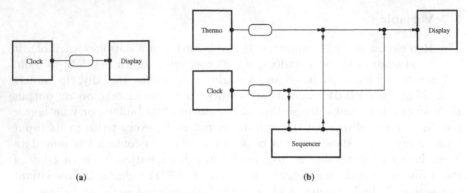

(a)   (b)

Fig. 8. A time/temperature display system

The connector used in Fig. 8.(a) between `Clock` and `Display` is the dataflow variable channel presented in Fig. 7. The purpose of the variable channel in this system is to temporally decouple the clock and the display, while facilitating their communication. Regardless of the state of the display, the clock can always write its current time into the channel, which may lose its old content, if any, to accommodate the new value. As frequently as it wishes, the display can read the current content of the channel, if any, which will be not older than the temporal resolution (i.e., the update cycle) of the clock. If the display's cycle is faster than that of the clock, the display will read the last value it read, again. If the clock's cycle is faster than that of the display, it may produce a new value before an older one is consumed by the display. The variable channel allows the new value to override the old. Thus, the system in Fig. 8.(a) periodically displays the current time.

Figure 8.(b) shows a system composed of three components connected by some Reo circuitry. Two of the components are the same clock and display of Fig. 8.(a). The third one, shown as the box labeled `Thermo` in this figure, is a thermometer that similar to the clock, periodically produces a text string announcing the current temperature. The two variable channels support communication and temporal decoupling of the clock and the thermometer components from the rest of the system. The input to the display component is regulated by a two-node version of the sequencer connector presented in Fig. 6.(e). Thus, the system in Fig. 8.(b) alternately displays current time and temperature.

The interesting point about this system is that none of the components involved is aware of the function of the system or of its own collaboration in realizing this "complex" coordinated behavior: the behaviors of the individual components are composed and coordinated exogenously (i.e., from outside of the components) by the Reo connectors to realize this collaborative behavior. Such "ignorant" components are highly generic and reusable, precisely because they are oblivious to whether they are used in a system like in Fig. 8.(a), or to build a system with a more complex coordination scheme as in Fig. 8.(b).

Reo has been used to model business processes, such as electronic auctions [35], coordination in biological systems [36], and composition of web services [37]. Reo circuits can be used to construct and compositionally reason about the properties of component connectors in soft-real-time applications, e.g., involving multimedia [38].

6 Expressiveness

Figure 6.(f) shows a simple example of the utility of our sequencer. The connector in this figure consists of a two-node sequencer, plus a pair of Sync channels and a SyncDrain channel connecting each of the nodes of the sequencer to the nodes a and c, and b and c, respectively. The connector in Fig. 6.(f) is another connector for the coordination pattern $c = (ab)^*$, although there is a subtle difference between the behavior of this connector and the one in Fig. 6.(d). See [27] for more detail.

It takes little effort to see that the connector in Fig. 6.(g) corresponds to the meta-regular expression $c = (aab)^*$. Figures 6.(f) and (g) show how easily we can construct connectors that exogenously impose coordination patterns corresponding to the Kleene-closure of any "meta-word" made up of atoms that stand for I/O operations, using a sequencer of the appropriate size.

Channel composition in Reo is a very powerful mechanism for construction of connectors. The expressive power of connector composition in Reo has been demonstrated through many examples in [27, 39]. For instance, exogenous coordination patterns that can be expressed as (meta-level) regular expressions over I/O operations performed by component instances can be composed in Reo out of a small set of only five primitive channel types[1]. A Turing machine consists of a finite state automaton for its control, and an unbounded tape. Since an unbounded tape can be simulated by two unbounded FIFO channels, adding FIFO to the above set of channel types makes channel composition in Reo Turing complete.

7 Dining Philosophers

We can vividly demonstrate the significance of exogenous coordination in system composition through the classical dining philosophers problem. In this section we use instances of two components, *Phil* and *Chop*, to (1) compose a dining philosophers application that exhibits the famous deadlock problem;

---

[1] In fact, Reo more naturally models infinite behavior through infinite streams (see Sect. 8). As such, composition of this set of primitive channels actually yields the equivalent of ω-regular expressions, rather than (finite) regular expressions. Therefore, for instance, the behavior of the connector in Fig. 6.(g), more accurately corresponds to the meta-regular expression $c = (aab)^\omega$, rather than $c = (aab)^*$.

and (2) compose another dining philosophers application that prevents the deadlock.

Figure 9 shows the C code of the two processes that we use as our *Phil* and *Chop* components in this example. The main program of our *Phil* component parses its command-line arguments to initialize its own id (which is actually not essential in this simplified example) and four output file descriptors: lt, lf, rt, and rf. All that a philosopher knows is that when its write operation on the file descriptor lt (for left-take) succeeds, it has obtained exclusive access to its left-hand chopstick; the success of its write operation on the file descriptor rt (for right-take) indicates that it has exclusive access to its right-hand chopstick; and the success of its write operations on the file descriptors lf (for left-free) and rf (for right-free) indicate its successful release of its left- and right-hand chopsticks, respectively. Thus, a philosopher instance enters an endless loop in which it thinks; then attempts to obtain its two chopsticks (first left then right); eats; and releases its chopsticks (for good form, in the reverse order of their acquisition).

```
#define TRUE 1                          #define TRUE 1

int                                     int
main(int argc, char *argv[])            main(int argc, char *argv[])
{                                       {
  /* Philosopher process */               /* Chopstick process */
  FILE *lt = NULL;                        FILE *t = NULL;
  FILE *lf = NULL;                        FILE *f = NULL;
  FILE *rt = NULL;                        int token = 0;
  FILE *rf = NULL;
  int id = 0;                             parse_chop_cmdline(argc, argv,
                                            &t, &f);
  parse_phil_cmdline(argc, argv,          while(TRUE) {
    &id, &lt, &lf, &rt, &rf);               scanf(t, "%d", &token);
  while(TRUE) {                            /* in use by token */
    think();                               scanf(f, "%d", &token);
    fprintf(lt, "%d\n", id);             }
    fprintf(rt, "%d\n", id);           }
    eat();
    fprintf(rf, "%d\n", id);
    fprintf(lf, "%d\n", id);
  }
}
```

Fig. 9. Philosopher and chopstick processes

The main program for our *Chop* component parses its command-line arguments to initialize two input file descriptors: t and f. All that a chopstick knows is that initially it is free and it can be alternately taken and freed.

Thus, a chopstick instance enters an endless loop in which it first reads a token (presumably, the id of its user philosopher) from its t (for take) file descriptor, and then reads a token from its f (for free) file descriptor. The success of its respective read operation indicates the acquisition or the release of a chopstick.

It is instructive to compare the code in Figs. 9 and 1. Contrary to the code in Fig. 1, there is no hint of any coordination or awareness of other instances anywhere in the philosopher (or the chopstick) process in Fig. 9. The only interaction of each process is through normal anonymous I/O of passive data with its environment. These processes are perfect candidate components for exogenous coordination. In Reo, any number of instances of these components can be composed in various ways and different configuration topologies.

In order to compose a system of dining philosophers in Reo, a separate program must instantiate an appropriate number of the processes in Fig. 9 and join their respective file descriptors with one another using appropriate channels and nodes. Figure 10.(a) shows the configuration of one such system representing four philosophers and four chopsticks around a virtual round table. In this figure, philosophers face the table, thus their sense of left and right is obvious. The file descriptors of philosophers and chopsticks constitute their respective ports, which Reo sees as nodes. Chopstick ports on the outer-edge of the table correspond to their t and the ones closer to the center of the table are their f file descriptors. The t port of each chopstick is connected to the rt and the lt ports of its adjacent philosophers (on its left and right, respectively), and its f port to their respective rf and lf ports. All channels are of type Sync.

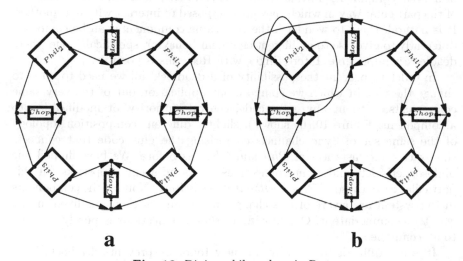

a   **b**

Fig. 10. Dining philosophers in Reo

Consider what happens in the node at the three-way junction connected to the t port of $Chop_1$. If $Chop_1$ is free and is ready to accept a token through its t port, as it initially is, whichever one of the two philosophers $Phil_1$ and $Phil_4$ happens to write its take request token first will succeed to take $Chop_1$. Of course, it is possible for $Phil_1$ and $Phil_4$ to attempt to take $Chop_1$ at the same time. In this case, the semantics of this mixed node guarantees that only one of them succeeds, nondeterministically; the write operation of the other remains pending until $Chop_1$ is free again. Because a philosopher frees a chopstick only after it has taken it, there is never any contention at the three-way junction connected to the f port of a chopstick.

The composition of channels in this Reo application enables philosophers to repeatedly go through their "eat" and "think" cycles at their leisure, resolving their contentions for taking the same chopsticks nondeterministically. The possibility of starvation is ruled out because the nondeterminism in Reo nodes is assumed to be fair. This simple glue code composed of nothing but common generic Sync channels directly renders a faithful implementation of the dining philosophers problem; all the way down to its possibility of deadlock. Because all philosophers are instances of the same component, they all attempt to fetch their chopsticks in the same order: left-first. If all chopsticks are free and all philosophers attempt to take their left chopsticks at the same time, of course, they will all succeed. However, this leaves no free chopstick for any philosopher to take before it can eat. No philosopher will relinquish its chopstick before it finishes its eating cycle. Therefore, this application deadlocks, as expected.

Observe that deadlock is not inherent in the behavior of any one of the individual components in this system—it is an *emergent behavior* arising out of the particular way in which they are composed to interact with one another. It is natural, then, to wonder if the very same components can be composed differently to give rise to a different emergent behavior, specifically, one where deadlock is impossible. Interestingly, with Reo, this is possible.

In order to prevent the possibility of a deadlock, all we need to do is to change the way in which we compose our application out of the very same components, without any extra code, central authority, or modification to a component. Figure 10.(b) shows a slightly different composition topology of the same set of Sync channels comprising the glue code that connects the exact same instances of *Phil* and *Chop* as before. We have flipped one philosopher's left and right connections to its adjacent chopsticks (in this particular case, those of $Phil_2$) *without its knowledge*. None of the components in the system are aware of this change, nor is any of them modified in any way to accommodate it. Our flipping of these connections is purely external to all components.

It is not difficult to see why this new topology prevents deadlock. If all philosophers attempt to take their left chopsticks now at the same time, one of them, namely $Phil_2$, will actually reach for the one on its right-hand-side. Of course, $Phil_2$ is unaware of the fact that as it reaches out through its left port to take its first chopstick, it is actually the one on its right-hand-side it competes to take. In this case it competes with $Phil_3$, which is also attempting to take its first chopstick. It makes no difference which one of the two wins this competition, one will be denied access to its first chopstick. This ensures that at least one chopstick will remain free (no philosopher attempts to take $Chop_2$ as its first chopstick) to enable at least one philosopher to obtain its second chopstick as well and complete its eating cycle.

Comparing the composition topologies in Figs. 10.(a) and (b), we see that in Reo (1) different glue code connecting the same components produces different emergent system behavior; and (2) coordination protocols are imposed by glue code on components that cooperate with one another through the glue code, without being aware of each other, their cooperation, or the glue code. The two systems in Figs. 10.(a) and (b) are made of the same number of constituent parts of the same types: the same number of component instances of the same kinds, and the same number of primitive connectors (Sync channels). The only difference between the two is in the *topology* of their interconnections. This topological difference is the only cause of the difference between the different emergent behavior in these two systems.

8 Abstract Behavior Types

An abstract data type (ADT) defines a data type as an algebra of operations with mathematically well-defined semantics, without specifying any detail about (1) the implementation of those operations or (2) the data structures they operate on. As such, ADT is a powerful abstraction and encapsulation mechanism that groups data together with their related operations into logically coherent and loosely-dependent entities, such as objects, yielding better structured programs. ADT has served as a foundation model for structured and object oriented programming for some thirty years.

The most basic inherent property of an ADT, i.e., that it provides a set of operations, subverts attempts to abstract away from their invocations in models where software composition reduces to a variant of ADT composition. Like procedure calls, operation invocations result in an asymmetric semantic dependency among ADTs that entangles interaction with composition of algorithms. For instance, when an ADT, T, invokes the *top* operation of a specific *stack* ADT, S, this "interaction" weaves the semantics of S (as defined by both the "state" of S as well as the entire set of operations defined in the *stack* ADT) into the semantics of T. The ADT T must "know" what it composes with in its interaction, i.e., the specific stack S as opposed to another, e.g., S', while clearly, S remains oblivious to its composition with T. However, at a more abstract level, it is useful to consider the fact that two entities interact, without considering that this interaction invokes an operation with certain semantics. For instance, which parties are involved in an interaction, what other interactions take place atomically with, or before/after this interaction, and the attributes of the communication (e.g., synchronous, asynchronous, buffered, rendezvous, etc.) involved in the interaction may constitute legitimate issues of concern at this level of abstraction. Expressing the semantics of "interaction composition" in a language like Reo requires a formal model of behavior that is more abstract than the ADT model.

The notion of abstract behavior type (ABT) as a higher-level analogue to ADT is introduced in [40] and proposed as a proper foundation model for both components and their composition. The ABT model supports a much looser coupling than is possible with the operational interfaces of ADTs, and is inherently amenable to exogenous coordination. Both of these are highly desirable, if not essential, properties for models of component behavior and composition of interactions.

An ABT defines an abstract behavior as a relation among the observable input/output that occur through a set of "contact points" (e.g., ports of a component instance) without specifying any detail about the operations that may be used to implement such behavior, or the data types those operations may manipulate for the realization of that behavior. This definition parallels that of an ADT, which abstracts away from the instructions and the data structures that may be used to implement the operational interface it defines for a data type. In contrast, an ABT defines a behavior in terms of a relation (i.e., constraint) on the observable input/output of an entity, without saying anything about how it can be realized.

There are several different ways to formalize the concept of ABT. For instance, process calculi, Petri nets, logic expressions, automata, or labeled transition systems can be used to describe transformations of input to output sequences of observables. Process calculi tend to emphasize processes rather than explicit expression of their input/output behavior. Petri nets are too low level to directly represent the rich set of behavioral relations involving nondeterminism, combination of synchrony and asynchrony, and compositionality that we are interested in. Automata can characterize the relation among the observable input/output sequences of an ABT. Indeed, the ABT model is properly formalized by *constraint automata* [34], precisely because they were devised to represent the operational semantics of Reo connector circuits for model checking.

Constraint automata can be considered generalizations of probabilistic automata, where data constraints, instead of probabilities, label state transitions and influence their firing. Timed-data-streams, which were introduced to define a coalgebraic semantics for Reo [39, 41], are also the referents in the language of constraint automata. Constraint automata seem to be more useful than labeled transition systems for modeling of systems composed of both synchronous and asynchronous components, and in practice, their composition tends to yield smaller models [42, 43].

For example, we show in [34] how the constraint automaton describing the behavior of the exclusive router circuit in Fig. 5.(a) is obtained by composing the eight constraint automata of its constituent channels and the constraint automaton for the merger inside its middle node. The resulting automaton has a single state and only two transitions. This is not so dramatic, because every one of the nine automata in this example has a single state and, therefore their product automaton also has a single state. If for simplicity we assume a single-ton data domain, then the constraint automaton representing the behavior of a FIFO1 channel has two states and two transitions. Composing the sink end of a FIFO1 with the source end of another must yield a FIFO2 channel (after *hiding* the joined node to make its dataflow events invisible). The product of the two constraint automata in this case has four states and six transitions. Hiding the joined node simplifies the composed automaton, yielding one with only three states and five transitions, which are precisely what we need to represent the observable behavior of a FIFO2 channel. Composing the constraint automaton representing the behavior of the ShiftLossyFIFO1 channel of Fig. 5.(b) in-volves forming the product of the automata of a merger, an exclusive router, and a SyncDrain channel, each of which has a single state, together with that of a FIFO1, which has two states, and a FIFO2, which has three states. Instead of six states, the resulting constraint automaton has only two states and three transitions (after hiding of its internal nodes), which are precisely what we need to represent the observable behavior of a ShiftLossyFIFO1 channel [34].

8.1 Relational View of ABT

The formalization presented in [40] defines an ABT as a (maximal) relation on a set of *timed data streams*, which emphasizes the relational aspect of the ABT model explicitly and abstracts away any hint of an underlying op-erational semantics of its implementation. This helps to focus on behavior specifications and their composition, rather than on operations that may be used to implement entities that exhibit such behavior and their interactions.

A *stream* (over A) is an infinite sequence of elements of some set A. The set of all streams over A is denoted as A^ω. Streams in $DS = D^\omega$ over a set of (uninterpreted) data items D are called *data streams* and are typically denoted as α, β, γ, etc. Zero-based indices are used to denote the individual elements of a stream, e.g., $\alpha(0), \alpha(1), \alpha(2), \dots$ denote the first, second, third, etc., elements of the stream α. We use the infix "dot" as the stream constructor: $x.\alpha$ denotes a stream whose first element is x and whose second, third, etc. elements are, respectively, the first and its successive elements of the stream α.

Following the conventions of stream calculus [44], the well-known opera-tions of head and tail on streams are called *initial value* and *derivative*: the initial value of a stream α (i.e., its head) is $\alpha(0)$, and its (first) derivative (i.e., its tail) is denoted as α'. Relational operators on streams apply pairwise to their respective elements, e.g., $\alpha \geq \beta$ means $\alpha(0) \geq \beta(0), \alpha(1) \geq \beta(1), \alpha(2) \geq \beta(2), \dots$.

Constrained streams in $TS = \mathbb{R}_+^\omega$ over positive real numbers representing moments in time are called *time streams* and are typically denoted as a, b,

c, etc. To qualify as a time stream, a stream of real numbers a must be (1) strictly increasing, i.e., the constraint $a < a'$ must hold; and (2) progressive, i.e., for every $N \geq 0$ there must exist an index $n \geq 0$ such that $a(n) > N$.

We use positive real numbers instead of natural numbers to represent time because, as observed in the world of temporal logic [45], real numbers induce the more abstract sense of *dense time* instead of the notion of *discrete time* imposed by natural numbers. Specifically, we sometimes need finitely many steps within any bounded time interval for certain ABT equivalence proofs (see, e.g., [39]). This is clearly not possible with a discrete model of time. Recall that the actual values of "time moments" are irrelevant in our ABT model; only their relative order is significant and must be preserved. Using dense time allows us to locally break strict numerical equality (i.e., simultaneity) arbitrarily while preserving the atomicity of events [40].

A *timed data stream* is a twin pair of streams $\langle \alpha, a \rangle$ in $TDS = DS \times TS$ consisting of a data stream $\alpha \in DS$ and a time stream $a \in TS$, with the interpretation that for all $i \geq 0$, the input/output of data item $\alpha(i)$ occurs at "time moment" $a(i)$. Two timed data streams $\langle \alpha, a \rangle$ and $\langle \beta, b \rangle$ are equal if their respective elements are equal, i.e., $\langle \alpha, a \rangle = \langle \beta, b \rangle \equiv \alpha = \beta \wedge a = b$.

Formalization of ABT in terms of timed data streams provides a simple yet powerful framework for the formal semantics of Reo. Timed data streams are used to model the flows of data through channel ends.[2] A channel itself is just a (binary) relation between the two timed data streams associated with its two ends. A more complex connector is simply an n-ary relation among n timed data streams, each representing the flow of data through one of the (non-hidden) n nodes of the connector.

The simplest channel, Sync, is formally defined as the relation:

$$\langle \alpha, a \rangle \ \text{Sync} \ \langle \beta, b \rangle \equiv \alpha = \beta \wedge a = b.$$

The equation states that every data item that goes into a Sync channel comes out in the exact same order. Furthermore, the arrival and the departure times of each data item are the same: there is no buffer in the channel for a data item to linger on for any length of time.

---

[2] The infinity of streams naturally models the infinite behavior of perpetual systems. Finite behavior can be modeled in at least three different ways. First, we can allow finite streams as well. Second, it can be modeled as a special case of infinite behavior, e.g., where after a certain time moment, only the special symbol $\perp$ appears as values in all time streams. Although viable, we ignore both of these schemes because they do not add conceptual novelty, yet dealing with the special cases that they involve requires a somewhat more complex formalism. The third way to model finite behavior is to ensure that after a certain point in time, the system has no observable behavior. This is possible with or without finite streams. See footnote 3 in Sect. 8.5.

A FIFO channel is defined as the relation:

$$\langle \alpha, a \rangle \text{ FIFO } \langle \beta, b \rangle \equiv \alpha = \beta \ \wedge \ a < b.$$

As in a synchronous channel, every data item that goes in, comes out of a FIFO channel in exactly the same order ($\alpha = \beta$). However, the departure time of each data item is necessarily after its arrival time ($a < b$): every data item must necessarily spend some non-zero length of time in the buffer of a FIFO channel.

A FIFO1 channel is similar to a FIFO:

$$\langle \alpha, a \rangle \text{ FIFO1 } \langle \beta, b \rangle \equiv \alpha = \beta \ \wedge \ a < b < a'.$$

Again, everything that goes in comes out in the same order ($\alpha = \beta$). But, not only the departure time $b(i)$ of every data item $\alpha(i) = \beta(i)$ is necessarily after its arrival time ($a(i) < b(i)$), but since the channel can contain no more than 1 element, the arrival time $a(i+1)$ of the next data item $\alpha(i+1)$ must be after the departure time $b(i)$ of its preceding element ($a < b < a' \equiv a(i) < b(i) < a(i+1)$).

A FIFO1(D) represents an asynchronous channel with the bounded capacity of 1 filled to contain the data item D as its initial value. The behavior of a FIFO1(D) channel is very similar to that of a FIFO1:

$$\langle \alpha, a \rangle \text{ FIFO1}(D) \ \langle \beta, b \rangle \equiv \beta = D.\alpha \ \wedge \ b < a < b'.$$

This channel produces an output data stream $\beta = D.\alpha$ consisting of the initial data item D followed by the input data stream α of the ABT, and for $i \geq 0$ performs its ith input operation some time between its ith and $(i+1)$st output operations ($b < a < b'$).

A SyncDrain channel merely relates the timing of the operations on its two ends:

$$\langle \alpha, a \rangle \text{ SyncDrain } \langle \beta, b \rangle \equiv a = b.$$

The replication that takes place at Reo nodes can be defined in terms of the ternary relation Rpl:

$$Rpl(\langle \alpha, a \rangle; \langle \beta, b \rangle, \langle \gamma, c \rangle) \equiv \beta = \alpha \ \wedge \ \gamma = \alpha \ \wedge \ b = a \ \wedge \ c = a.$$

The semicolon delimiter separates "input" and "output" arguments of the relation. The relation Rpl represents the replication of the single "input" timed data stream $\langle \alpha, a \rangle$ into two "output" timed data streams $\langle \beta, b \rangle$ and $\langle \gamma, c \rangle$.

The nondeterministic merge that happens at Reo nodes is defined in terms of the ternary relation Mrg:

$Mrg(\langle \alpha, a \rangle, \langle \beta, b \rangle; \langle \gamma, c \rangle) \equiv$

$$\begin{cases} \alpha(0) = \gamma(0) \land a(0) = c(0) \land Mrg(\langle \alpha', a' \rangle, \langle \beta, b \rangle; \langle \gamma', c' \rangle) & \text{if } a(0) < b(0) \\ \exists t : a(0) < t < min(a(1), b(1)) \land \exists r, s \in \{a(0), t\} \land & \text{if } a(0) = b(0) \\ \quad r \neq s \land Mrg(\langle \alpha, r.a' \rangle, \langle \beta, s.b' \rangle; \langle \gamma, c \rangle) \\ \beta(0) = \gamma(0) \land b(0) = c(0) \land Mrg(\langle \alpha, a \rangle, \langle \beta', b' \rangle; \langle \gamma', c' \rangle) & \text{if } a(0) > b(0). \end{cases}$$

8.2 ABT Composition

Because an ABT is a relation, two ABTs can be composed to yield another ABT through a relational composition similar to the join operation in relational databases. This yields a simple, yet powerful formalism for specification of complex behavior as a composition of simpler ones. Composition of simple interaction primitives into nontrivial behavior, such as the Reo circuits in the above examples, can be expressed as ABT composition [40].

Defining observable behavior in terms of input/output implants a dataflow essence within ABTs akin to such dataflow-like networks and calculi as [46, 47], and especially [48]. The coalgebraic model of ABT differs from all of the above-mentioned work in a number of respects. Most importantly, the ABT model is compositional. Its explicit modeling of ordering/timing of events in terms of separate time streams provides a simple foundation for defining complex synchronization and coordination protocols using a surprisingly expressive small set of primitives. Any behavior that can be expressed as ω-regular expressions over I/O operations can be composed in Reo out of a small set of only four primitive channel types (Sync, LossySync, FIFO1, and SyncDrain) [27]. Adding the unbounded FIFO to the above set of channel types makes channel composition in Reo Turing complete. This means that under ABT composition, the set of ABTs defining these primitive channels, plus the ABTs for merge and replication, is Turing complete.

The relational (as opposed to functional) nature of our formalism allows a composition of ABTs to mutually influence and constrain each other, yielding their collective behavior, analogous to how a set of constraints in a constraint satisfaction problem resolve into a solution. The use of coinduction as the main definition and proof principle to reason about both data and time streams allows simple compositional construction of ABTs representing many different generic coordination schemes involving combinations of various synchronous and asynchronous primitives that are not present (and not even expressible) in any of the aforementioned models.

8.3 Fibonacci Series

A simple example of how a composition of a set of components yields a system that delivers more than the sum of its parts is the computation of the classical Fibonacci series. To assemble a component based application to deliver this series we actually need only one (instance of one) adder component plus a number of channels.

Figure 11 shows a component (the outermost thick enclosing box) with only one output port (the only exposed node on the right border of the box). This is our application for computing the Fibonacci series. Peeking inside this component, we see how it is made out of an instance of an adder (labeled *AdderX*), a FIF01(1), a FIF01(0), a FIF01, and five Sync channels. *AdderX* represents a simple adder that repeatedly takes two input values, x and y, respectively through its input ports A and B, and produces a result, z, through its output port C, which is the sum of x and y.

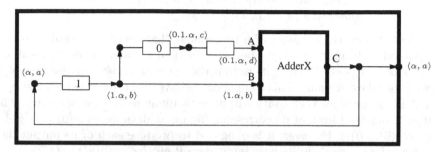

Fig. 11. Fibonacci series in Reo

Distinguishing semantics and behavior, as in [49], is useful here. In Sect. 8.4 we define a few ABTs that formalize (the semantics and) the observable behavior of some of the alternative adders mentioned in [49]. Semantically, we can use any one of the adders we define in Section 8.4 in the composition in Fig. 11. That is why the box representing the adder in this figure is labeled *AdderX*. However, the extra-semantic behavior of some of these adders makes them unsuitable for the specific circuit in Fig. 11. To understand how this circuit is expected to work, suppose *AdderX* has a behavior "compatible" with the circuit. We consider other alternatives in Sect. 8.5.

Intuitively, as long as the FIF01(0) channel is full, nothing can happen: there is no way for the value in FIF01(1) to move out. At some point in time, the value in FIF01(0) moves into the FIF01 channel. Thereafter, the FIF01(0) channel becomes empty and the two values in the FIF01(1) and the FIF01 channels become available for *AdderX* to consume. The intake of the value in FIF01(1) by *AdderX* inserts a copy of the same value into the FIF01(0) channel. When *AdderX* is ready to write its computed value out, it suspends waiting for some entity in the environment to accept this value. Transfer of this value to the entity in the environment also inserts a copy of the same value into the now empty FIF01(1) channel. At this point we are back to the initial state, but with different values in the buffers of the FIF01(1) and the FIF01(0) channels.

8.4 Adders

To illustrate the expressiveness of the ABT model and the utility of ABT composition, consider the adder component described in [49] and used in our Fibonacci example in Sect. 8.3. We define a few of the alternative versions of the behavior for this adder, below, each as a different ABT:

$$Adder1(\langle \alpha, a \rangle, \langle \beta, b \rangle; \langle \gamma, c \rangle) \equiv$$
$$\gamma(0) = \alpha(0) + \beta(0) \wedge$$
$$\exists t : max(a(0), b(0)) < t < min(a(1), b(1)) \wedge c(0) = t \wedge$$
$$Adder1(\langle \alpha', a' \rangle, \langle \beta', b' \rangle; \langle \gamma', c' \rangle).$$

*Adder*1 defines the behavior of a component that repeatedly reads a pair of input values from its two input ports, adds them up, and writes the result out on its output port. As such, its output data stream is the pairwise sum of its two input data streams. This component behaves asynchronously in the sense that it can produce each of its output data items with some arbitrary delay after it has read both of its corresponding input data items ($c(0) = t \wedge t > max(a(0), b(0))$). However, it is obligated to produce each of its output data items before it reads in its next input data item ($t < min(a(1), b(1))$).

$$Adder2(\langle \alpha, a \rangle, \langle \beta, b \rangle; \langle \gamma, c \rangle) \equiv$$
$$\gamma(0) = \alpha(0) + \beta(0) \wedge$$
$$c(0) = max(a(0), b(0)) \wedge$$
$$Adder2(\langle \alpha', a' \rangle, \langle \beta', b' \rangle; \langle \gamma', c' \rangle).$$

*Adder*2 behaves very much like *Adder*1, except that it produces the sum of every pair of input values atomically (i.e., synchronously) together with its consuming of its second input value ($c(0) = max(a(0), b(0))$).

$$Adder3(\langle \alpha, a \rangle, \langle \beta, b \rangle; \langle \gamma, c \rangle) \equiv$$
$$\gamma(0) = \alpha(0) + \beta(0) \wedge$$
$$a(0) < b(0) < c(0) < a(1) \wedge$$
$$Adder3(\langle \alpha', a' \rangle, \langle \beta', b' \rangle; \langle \gamma', c' \rangle).$$

*Adder*3 also behaves very much like *Adder*1, except that it always sequentially consumes an element from α first, then it consumes an element from β, then it produces their sum, before reading another element from α.

$$Adder4(\langle \alpha, a \rangle, \langle \beta, b \rangle; \langle \gamma, c \rangle) \equiv$$
$$\gamma(0) = \alpha(0) + \beta(0) \wedge$$
$$a = b = c \wedge$$
$$Adder4(\langle \alpha', a' \rangle, \langle \beta', b' \rangle; \langle \gamma', c' \rangle).$$

*Adder*4 behaves very much like *Adder*1, except that the consuming of every pair of input values and the production of their sum is one single atomic (synchronous) action.

$$Adder5(\langle \alpha, a \rangle, \langle \beta, b \rangle; \langle \gamma, c \rangle) \equiv$$
$$\gamma(0) = \alpha(0) + \beta(0) \wedge$$
$$c(0) = min(a(1), b(1)) \wedge$$
$$Adder5(\langle \alpha', a' \rangle, \langle \beta', b' \rangle; \langle \gamma', c' \rangle).$$

*Adder*5 behaves very much like *Adder*1, except that it produces the sum of every pair atomically together with its reading of the first of its next pair of input values.

These examples show how the diluted notion of local time and its explicit representation in timed data streams enable us to concisely define and distinguish subtle differences in the behavior of various components that arise out of the delicate temporal order of their observable actions. The ability to make such distinctions differentiates otherwise equivalent behavior of similar components whose "equivalent behavior" leads to the Brock–Ackerman anomalies [50] concerning the input-output relation of components in nondeterministic dataflow models.

8.5 Analysis of ABT Compositions

Suppose we use *Adder*4 of Sect. 8.4 to construct our Fibonacci circuit of Fig. 11. Formally, the ABT models of the component *Adder*4, channels, and Reo nodes that we presented earlier suffice for an analysis of the behavior of their composition in this example. We briefly sketch such a formal analysis here to demonstrate the utility of the ABT model and the significance of the distinction we made earlier between semantics and behavior.

Let $\langle \alpha, a \rangle$ be the output of our system, as indicated in Fig. 11. Form the ABT definition of the replicator (*Rpl*) inherent in the mixed node immediately on the left of this node, and the ABT definition of its three coincident Sync channels, we easily conclude that the output of *Adder*4 and the input of FIFO1(1) are also the same: $\langle \alpha, a \rangle$.

From the ABT definition of the FIFO1(1) channel, we conclude that the output of this channel is the timed data stream $\langle 1.\alpha, b \rangle$, where $b < a < b'$. From the ABT definition of the replicator (*Rpl*) inherent in the mixed node at the output on this channel and the ABT definition of its coincident Sync channels, we conclude that the input to the FIFO1(0) channel and the lower-input to *Adder*4 are also the same timed data stream.

From the ABT definition of the FIFO1(0) channel, we conclude that the output of this channel is the timed data stream $\langle 0.1.\alpha, c \rangle$, where $c < b < c'$. Given this as its input, the ABT definition of the FIFO1 channel yields $\langle 0.1.\alpha, d \rangle$ for its output, where $c < d < c'$.

The ABT definitions of the behavior of all of the above adders invariably yield $\alpha - 0.1.\alpha + 1.\alpha$, which is simply a short-hand for the series of equations:

$$\alpha(0) = 0 + 1 = 1$$
$$\alpha(1) = 1 + \alpha(0) = 1 + 1 = 2$$
$$\alpha(2) = \alpha(0) + \alpha(1) = 1 + 2 = 3$$
$$\alpha(3) = \alpha(1) + \alpha(2) = 2 + 3 = 5$$
$$\vdots$$

Thus, α indeed represents the Fibonacci series.

However, the ABT definition of the behavior of *Adder4* requires $a = b = d$, whereas the condition on the output of the FIFO1(1) channel, above, states that $b < a < b'$. This leads to the contradiction of having both $a = b$ and $b < a$. What this contradiction tells us is that our composed system using *Adder4* will produce no output at all! [3]

A closer examination reveals the reason: *Adder4* is a *synchronous* component; it must be able to consume both of its input values and produce its output, all in one single atomic step (i.e., transaction). The atomic reading of its lower input (b) together with the writing of its output (a) conflicts with the behavior of the FIFO1(1) channel. To comply with the behavior of *Adder4*, the FIFO1(1) channel must atomically both provide its output as the input to *Adder4*, and consume the output of *Adder4* as its own input. The ABT definition of the behavior of FIFO1(1) simply does not allow this to happen.

The only way to use such a synchronous adder as *Adder4* in this system, is to break this conflict, e.g., by replacing the Sync channel that connects the output of *Adder4* to the input of the FIFO1(1) channel, with a FIFO1 channel.

On the other hand, our circuit in Fig. 11 works perfectly if we use an adder with a different behavior, e.g., *Adder3*. The two adders produce the same data streams and the only difference between them is in their time streams. Using *Adder3*, we have $d < b < a < d'$. Because this equation implies $d < b$, which implies $d' < b'$, we can expand this equation as $d < b < a < d' < b'$, which complies with the $b < a < b'$ condition on the output of the FIFO1(1) channel, above. The timing conditions on the output of the FIFO1(0) channel ($c < b < c'$), and that of the FIFO1 channel ($c < d < c'$) conform with the temporal constraints of *Adder3* as well. The assumption of dense time allows an infinity of viable solutions to the resulting system of equations. In the context of *Adder3*, what matters is that the FIFO1 channel produces its output after it obtains the contents of the FIFO1(0) channel ($c < d$), but before the next input into the latter channel takes place ($c' < d'$ and $c' < b'$).

---

[3] This example shows that the composition of two ABTs may yield the empty relation, which simply means the result has "no externally observable behavior." Although "no externally observable behavior" can be interpreted as deadlock, there is nothing inherently wrong with or undesirable about it, because it can also be interpreted as normal termination. Thus, a composition that yields an empty ABT can be a perfectly legitimate way to model finite behavior in an otherwise perpetual systems. An example of such "desired deadlock" situations is presented in the inhibitor example in [27].

Whether this next input occurs before $Adder3$ writes it output $(c' < a)$, simultaneously $(c' = a)$, or after $(a < c')$, is irrelevant.

Similarly, we can show that the behavior of $Adder1$ or $Adder5$ is also compatible with the context of the circuit in Fig. 11 for producing the Fibonacci series. On the other hand, using $Adder2$ in this circuit may or may not work. The behavior specification of $Adder2$ allows it to always consume its B input (from the FIFO1(1) channel) first. In this case, the circuit indeed produces the Fibonacci series. But, $Adder2$ is also allowed to take its A input first. If $Adder2$ always takes its A input first, then the circuit hangs and produces nothing at all, due to the same timing conflict as with $Adder4$. If $Adder2$ internally decides afresh each time which input to take first, then the circuit will produce a finite sequence of the first $n \geq 0$ Fibonacci series, before it hangs and stops producing any further output.

Observe that all entities involved in this composed application are completely generic and, of course, neither knows anything about the Fibonacci series, nor the fact that it is "cooperating" with other entities to compute it. It is the specific glue code of this application, made by composing eight simple generic channels in a specific topology in Reo, that coordinates the communication of the components (in this case, only one) with one another (in this case, with itself) and the environment to compute this series. It is also worth noting that the possible or definite hanging behavior of this circuit with $Adder2$ or $Adder4$, for instance, is just another perfectly legitimate behavior. There is nothing inherent in such "deadlocks" that says they must necessarily be avoided. Any behavior of any circuit (including "deadlock") is objectively as valid and legitimate as any other. What constitutes (un)desirable behavior is a "subjective" matter for the context to decide. Additional circuitry may be necessary to ensure or prevent a particular behavior of a (sub-)circuit.

9 Petri Nets

Petri nets are frequently used to model interaction protocols and the behavior of complex systems. In some respects, Reo circuits resemble Petri nets. However, there are major differences between the two.

Petri nets are extensions of the finite state automata that incorporate a notion of concurrency. There are many different types of Petri nets, from basic nets defined by Carl A. Petri in 1962 to place/transition nets, colored Petri nets, stochastic Petri nets, etc., each of which extends the basic Petri net model with higher level concepts [51]. In this section, we consider only the elementary Petri nets, or the E/N systems. However, because we focus on the essential common features of all Petri nets, the distinctions we draw between Reo and the E/N systems also apply (with small alterations) to other Petri nets. Petri nets are formal systems and there exists an extensive body of work and theory behind them. Below, we give a brief informal description of the "dynamics" of Petri nets, which suffices for our purposes in this section.

Petri nets consist of *places* and *transitions* with interconnecting *arcs*. Places can either be empty or hold *tokens*. In lower-level Petri nets, e.g., E/N systems, tokens are not distinguishable from one another. In colored Petri nets, each token can have a color that distinguishes it from the others. Multiple places can hold tokens in a Petri net at the same time. In E/N systems, each place can hold at most one token, but in higher-level Perti nets, a place can hold multiple tokens as well. The well-formedness condition of Petri nets ensures that an arc emanating from a place ends with a transition, and an arc emanating from a transition ends with a place. Multiple arcs can emanate and/or end at the same place or transition. In graphical models of Petri nets, transitions are often represented as solid rectangles; arcs as arrows; and places as either (1) hollow circles, if they are empty, or otherwise (2) circles that contain smaller (colored) solid circles representing their (colored) tokens. See Figs. 12 and 14 for examples.

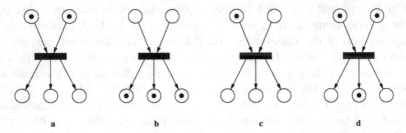

a   b   c   d

Fig. 12. Petri net transition firing in E/N systems

An *input place* of a transition t is one that is connected to t with an arc that ends at t. Similarly, an *output place* of a transition t is one that is connected to t with an arc that emanates from t. In Fig. 12, for instance, the places above each transition are its input places, and the ones below each transition are its output places. A transition can *fire* in an E/N system if and only if all of its input places contain tokens and all of its output places are empty. Firing of a transition consumes a token out of every one of its input places and deposits a token in every one of its output places. Fig. 12 illustrates firing in E/N systems. The transition in the Petri net in Fig. 12.(a) can fire, resulting in the Petri net in Fig. 12.(b). The transition in Fig. 12.(c) cannot fire because not all of its input places contain tokens. The transition in Fig. 12.(d) cannot fire because not all of its output places are empty.

The *places*, *transitions* and *arcs* in Petri nets can be seen as a fixed set of building blocks, each with a fixed behavior, for construction of Petri nets. In contrast, Reo defines a fixed set of composition rules and allows an arbitrary set of channels as primitives with arbitrary behavior, on which its composition rules can be applied to construct connector circuits. This readily allows incorporation of arbitrary computational entities into a composed Reo system. More importantly, it allows the harmonious combinations of synchrony and asynchrony in the same model which is not possible in Petri nets.

The similarity of the Petri net construction rules with Reo composition rules allows a direct translation of Petri nets into Reo circuits. Although direct translations of higher-level Petri nets into Reo circuits are also possible, here we consider only E/N systems.

Figure 13 shows the Reo equivalent constructs (the bottom row) for Petri net building blocks (the top row). An empty place corresponds to a `FIFO1` channel (see Fig. 3 in Sect. 4.2). A filled place containing a token • corresponds to a `FIFO1(•)` [4]. An arc corresponds to a `Sync` channel. A transition with a single incoming arc and $n > 0$ outgoing arcs corresponds to a node with one incoming and n outgoing `Sync` channels. A transition with $m > 1$ incoming and $n > 0$ outgoing arcs corresponds to a degenerate barrier synchronizer (Figs. 6.(b) and (c) in Sect. 5.4) Reo subcircuit with $m-1$ `SyncDrain` channels, m input nodes, and a single output node, as shown in the bottom-right of Fig. 13. All n `Sync` channels that correspond to the outgoing arcs of this transition are connected to the single output node of this subcircuit.

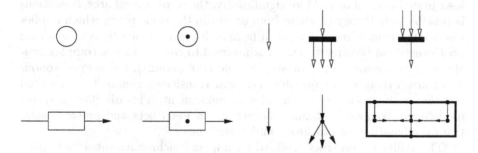

Fig. 13. Reo circuit equivalents for Petri net constructs

Using Fig. 13, it is straightforward to directly translate a Petri net into a Reo circuit. For example, applying this translation to the Petri net in Fig. 14.(a) yields the Reo circuit in Fig. 14.(b). (The gray box in Fig. 14.(b) represents a "degenerate barrier synchronizer" as shown in the lower-right corner of Fig. 13.) In this sense, every Petri net can be trivially considered to be a Reo circuit. The inverse translation, however, is far from trivial.

In Reo, synchrony and exclusion constraints propagate through (the synchronous subsections of) circuits. This is generally not the case in Petri nets, because their transitions are local. What sets Petri nets apart from classical automata is their transition nodes, which enable them to directly synchronize

---

[4] In higher-level Petri nets a place can hold multiple tokens. Instead of (initialized or empty) `FIFO1` channels, *bag channels* [27] must be used as their equivalents in Reo circuits (in the left two columns of the bottom row in Fig. 13).

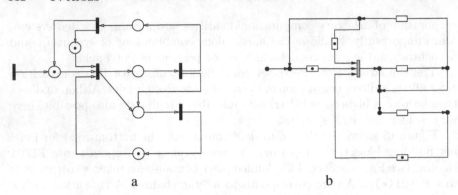

Fig. 14. Translation of Petri nets into Reo circuits

otherwise unrelated events (it is no accident that a nontrivial Petri net transition node translates into a barrier synchronizer in Reo). A Petri net transition node enforces synchronous *and* of several arcs/events. However, Petri nets have no primitive for the dual synchronous *or* of several arcs, and there can be no arc between two places, nor between two transitions. The latter disallows nested *and*s of arcs. More significantly, the *or* of several arcs/transitions is possible only if they emanate from or end in the same place, which implies the commitment of moving a token from or into that place. This means that arcs/events can be directly *and*-synchronized to compose more complex synchronous transitions (i.e., one-step atomic transactions), but a synchronous *or* of arcs/events is not possible, i.e., two transitions cannot be connected together without an intervening place/commitment. This disallows a direct modeling of composite atomic transactions in Petri nets and prevents arbitrary combinations of synchrony and asynchrony.

The ability to construct arbitrarily complex synchronous subcircuits (representing one-step atomic transactions) with asynchronous behavior in between, is unique in Reo and simplifies expressions of complex behavior. For example in the context of e-commerce, [35] and [52] show the construction of nontrivial Reo circuits that implement negotiation protocols for competition and collaboration in electronic auctions. The Petri net models of these same protocols would be substantially more complex and elaborate, because they would have to "simulate" all atomic transactions involved.

10 Synchronous Languages

Synchronous languages [53] like Esterel [54, 55], Lustre [56], and Signal [57], emerged in the 1980s for modeling and programming of reactive systems, signal processing, and critical control software. Because they involve synchronous dataflow networks, they address issues that are also of concern in Reo: specification of nontrivial synchronous behavior. However, there are significant differences between Reo and all synchronous dataflow networks, including synchronous languages.

Esterel [54, 55] is an imperative program generator language, essentially for defining the behavior of finite state automata. It is used to generate programs that constitute the reactive kernels of reactive systems, with actual interfaces and data handling specified in some other host language. Using Esterel, replication (of transitions, states, etc.) in the automata of complex systems are eliminated by the structural constructs of the language and computation. This makes it more convenient to describe the behavior of complex systems in Esterel, rather than directly as automata. Lustre [56] is a declarative dataflow kernel language very close to Esterel. They originally shared intermediate language and compilation tools. Signal [57] is another declarative synchronous language. Unlike Lustre, Signal is not a dataflow language, but deals with sequences of input and output signals and their relative order.

These languages have no specific explicit notion of time. Repetition of any event or signal abstractly indicates passage of time. In contrast, Reo has an explicit notion of dense time, represented separately from data, in its time streams. This allows direct expressions of temporal constraints (order, synchrony, and asynchrony) explicitly and independently of the data streams, which is not possible in synchronous languages. Synchronous languages have an implied notion of state, wherein actions and computation take place synchronously, taking "zero time" and transitions between states depend on their input/output data (but not time). Whereas synchronous and asynchronous behavior correspond to states and transitions in synchronous languages, both are specified in Reo uniformly as compositions of temporal and data constraints.

In synchronous languages, everything that happens in a "state" is synchronous and takes no time. However, in every state, the environment is always assumed to be ready to accept every output of that state (output enabledness). This prevents the propagation synchrony and exclusion. In Reo, the synchronous merge/replicate behavior inherent in its nodes allows two-way propagation of synchrony and exclusion constraints.

Synchronous languages originally produced executable code only for monoprocessor platforms, although recently some are being extended to produce code for distributed architectures as well. The execution model of the code generated by synchronous languages is generally different than the conceptual model of their program specification: they are not designed to allow dynamic changes to program specifications. In contrast, Reo connector circuits are inherently distributed, mobile, and dynamically reconfigurable.

11 Interaction as Building Block

The vast majority of classical models and paradigms for construction and study of complex systems use *actions* as their fundamental primitives. Examples include various object oriented programming models, the actor model [8],

CSP [1], CCS [2], the π-calculus [3, 4], and process algebras [5, 6, 7]. Because an action is something that a single actor performs, system construction in these models espouses a single-actor-at-a-time perspective. Complex global properties of a system involving more than one actor become difficult or impossible to verify and study, because they cannot be expressed explicitly in these models.

As a building block, an interaction can explicitly appear in the form of a relation that holds among a set of actors and constrains every one of them to coordinate their collective behavior. Such explicitly specified constraints can be composed together in various ways to yield more complex constraints (i.e., interaction protocols), without the need to specify the action sequences of any actors. A model that uses interaction as its primitive building blocks can offer a dual perspective wherein interaction among the actors/subsystems that comprise a complex system attains first class status with direct representation, making it easier to express and study its properties.

Reo is a good example of such a model. It offers (1) primitive interactions, in the form of channels, as building blocks, plus (2) composition rules for combining (primitive) interactions into more complex interactions (i.e., circuits), without the need to specify (the actions of) the actors involved. Indeed, every channel in Reo specifies a primitive interaction as a relational constraint that must hold between the I/O actions performed on its two ends, without saying anything about those actions or who performs them. These constraints specify the relative timing (i.e., synchrony/asynchrony) of (the success of) the I/O actions, and the desired data dependencies between them (e.g., buffering, ordering, selection, conversion, filtering, loss, and/or expiration of data). Reo's compositional operators indeed compose such relations to produce the more complex constraints that constitute the behavior of their resulting connectors. As an explicit, tangible piece of specification or program code, the same connector can be employed to engage entirely different sets of actors to yield entirely different systems. Perhaps more interestingly, the same set of actors can be composed together with different connectors, producing systems with very different emergent behavior [40].

In contrast to Reo which directly models interaction, process algebras (as well as process calculi, the actor model, object oriented models, etc.) directly model things that interact, rather than interaction itself. Interaction and communication protocols ensue only as ancillary consequences of the unfolding of the collective behavior of the processes involved in a concurrent system and have no explicit constructs to directly express them. The compositionality offered by process algebras convolutes composed interaction protocols: to learn how a process r that is a parallel composition of processes p and q interacts with its environment, one must unravel the actions of p and q and consider all of their possible combinations. Whereas process algebras explicitly compose and construct processes making the interaction relations amongst them implicit, Reo explicitly composes and constructs interaction relations and makes processes that engage in those relations implicit. Reo's liberal notion of channels and its fundamental notion of channel/connector composition allow, among other things, explicit construction of connectors that specify interaction protocols involving an expressive mix of synchrony and asynchrony.

The resounding similarity of Reo circuits with electronic circuits suggests new interaction-based approaches for the design of complex systems analogous to those used in computer aided design (CAD) of electronic circuits. Interaction protocols can be specified in a visual programming environment for Reo, the same way as CAD tools allow direct drawing of electronic circuits. Synthesis of electronic circuits from automata specifications is well-understood, and in some cases, modern CAD tools can synthesize a circuit from the Boolean logic expression that defines what it is expected to do. Using such high-level specifications instead of direct drawing of circuits relieves designers from the chore of actual detailed circuit design. Because, like electronic circuits, Reo circuits have a mathematically well-defined semantic basis, one hopes analogous synthesis of Reo circuits from higher-level (e.g., temporal logic or automata) specifications should be possible. On the other hand, interaction protocols (and Reo circuits) can express far more complex behavior than that of digital circuits, including combinations of synchrony and asynchrony, and relational, as well as simple (input/output) functional, interdependencies. In the light of this fact, it is far from obvious if synthesis of Reo circuits from suitable high-level automata specifications is possible at all, and if so, whether it can be done efficiently. As a first step in this direction, we have presented an algorithm for synthesis of Reo circuits from constraint automata specifications [58]. Synthesis of Reo circuits automatically yields decentralized implementation of interaction protocols for distributed systems from a high-level specification of their desired behavior.

12 Epilogue

The increased complexity of monolithic programs for more sophisticated applications quickly renders them prohibitively unmanageable. Viewing such systems as coordinated collaborations of interacting entities is a natural approach to tackle and break down this complexity. Furthermore, this view is congruent with contemporary issues that arise out of distribution, heterogeneity, mobility, and the intensifying requirement to reuse coarse-grain pieces of third-party software whose source code is unavailable, as building block components. Traditional models for software composition, such as procedure calls, module interconnection, object oriented method invocation, etc., break down this complexity using structural decomposition models that are based on simple, fixed interaction and coordination schemes. An application's interaction and coordination requirements that do not perfectly match with the patterns directly supported by such a model (e.g., synchronous method invocation) must then be explicitly programmed within the native interaction coordination scheme supported by the model. This motivates models for software

composition that provide richer and more flexible interaction and coordination primitives, and support mechanisms to compose them into more complex
interaction coordination protocols.

Specification and study of global properties of complex systems become
easier in a computational model that allows direct and explicit representation
of interaction. Coordination languages offer systematic middle-ware support
and models for software composition in concurrent settings. They focus on
interaction and the dominant role that it plays in compositional construction of parallel and distributed systems out of simpler computing devices. As
such, they illustrate the necessary shift of attention in the design of such systems, away from the algorithmic computation within individual computing
devices, onto their interactions with one another. However, as in other models
of concurrency, coordination languages generally do not treat interaction as a
first-class concept either.

Reo is a coordination language which serves as a good example of a constructive model of computation that treats interaction as a (in fact, the only)
first-class building block. Every channel in Reo directly specifies a primitive
interaction as a relational constraint, and Reo's calculus of channel composition allows construction of complex interaction protocols through arbitrary
combination of these primitive interactions. By its very nature, a channel
decouples the communicating parties at its two ends, making their communication indirect. Every channel independently coordinates the actions of the
parties at its two ends, yielding decentralized coordination.

Abstract behavior types offer a simple and flexible model for interaction
of components and their composition. An ABT is a mathematical construct
that defines and/or constrains the behavior of an entity (e.g., a component)
without any mention of operations or data types that may be used to realize that behavior. This puts the ABT model at a higher-level of abstraction
than abstract data types and makes it more suitable for components. The
endogenous nature of their composition means that it is not possible for a
third party, e.g., an entity in the environment, to compose two objects (or
two ADTs) "against their own will" so to speak. In contrast, the composition
of any two ABTs is always well-defined and yields another ABT.

The building blocks in the mathematical construction of the ABT model
are the (generally) infinite streams that represent the externally observable
sequences of I/O events that occur at an entity's interaction points (e.g.,
ports) through which it exchanges data with its environment. Such infinite
structures, and thus the ABT model, naturally lend themselves to coalgebraic
techniques and the coinduction reasoning principle. The ABT model supports
a much looser coupling than is possible with ADT and is inherently amenable
to exogenous coordination. Both of these are highly desirable, if not essential,
properties for component based and interactive systems.

The ABT model provides a simple formal foundation for definition and
composition of components and coordination of their interactions. However,
direct composition of component ABTs does not generally provide much of an

opportunity to systematically wield exogenous coordination. Reo is a channel-based exogenous coordination model that can be used as a glue language for dynamic compositional construction of connectors in (non-)distributed and/or mobile interactive system systems. Connector construction in Reo can be seen as an application of the ABT model. The behavior of a Reo node is defined as an ABT. A channel in Reo is just a special kind of an atomic connector. Because all Reo connectors are ABTs, the semantics of channel composition in Reo can be defined in terms of ABT composition.

Indirect communication and decentralized coordination have been identi-fied as essential ingredients for construction of large complex systems based on how successful complex biological systems involving simple agents, such as swarms, foraging ants, termite colonies, etc., have evolved in nature [59]. For instance, foraging ants indirectly and anonymously interact with each other to identify their path to a food source by depositing pheromones (evaporating scent chemicals) as they walk. Because ants tend to follow pheromone trails, successful paths to a food source emerge out of "random walks" by individual ants since they correspond to heavily traveled (and hence stronger and more attractive) pheromone trails. This is known as stigmergy, a feature of natu-ral systems in which the behavior of agents is shaped by interactions with anonymous other agents [59].

Indirect communication and decentralized coordination already exist in a coordination model like Linda, where the shared tuple space is used as a per-sistent medium for asynchronous anonymous communication among agents. A coordination language like Reo adds a new orthogonal dimension: it allows construction and reconfiguration of the very communication medium through which agents interact. Using Reo, part of the sophistication of the emergent behavior of a system can be programmed as inherent features of the tailor-made communication medium that it uses, analogous to how "programmed" features of a terrain such as obstacles, troughs, walls, and bridges can affect the behavior of foraging ants.

References

1. Hoare, C.: Communicating Sequential Processes. Prentice Hall International Series in Computer Science. Prentice-Hall, 1985.
2. Milner, R.: A Calculus of Communicating Systems. Volume 92 of Lecture Notes in Computer Science. Springer, 1980.
3. Milner, R.: Elements of interaction. Communications of the ACM **36**, 1993, pp. 78 89.
4. Sangiorgi, D., Walker, D.: The Pi-Calculus - A Theory of Mobile Processes. Cambridge University Press, 2001.
5. Bergstra, J.A., Klop, J.W.: Process algebra for synchronous communication. Information and Control **60**, 1984, pp. 109–137.

6. Bergstra, J.A., Klop, J.W.: Process algebra: specification and verification in bisimulation semantics. In Hazewinkel, M., Lenstra, J.K., Meertens, L.G.L.T., eds.: Mathematics and Computer Science II. CWI Monograph 4. North-Holland, Amsterdam, 1986, pp. 61–94.

7. Fokkink, W.: Introduction to Process Algebra. Texts in Theoretical Computer Science, An EATCS Series. Springer-Verlag, 1999.

8. Agha, G.: Actors: A Model of Concurrent Computation in Distributed Systems. MIT Press, 1986.

9. Wegner, P.: Interaction as a basis for empirical computer science. ACM Computing Surveys **27**, 1995, pp. 45–48.

10. Wegner, P.: Interactive foundations of computing. Theoretical Computer Science **192**, 1998, pp. 315–351.

11. Goldin, D., Smolka, S., Attie, P., Sonderegger, E.: Turing machines, transition systems, and interaction. Information and Computation Journal **194**, 2004, pp. 101–128.

12. van Leeuwen, J., Wiedermann, J.: On the power of interactive computing. In van Leeuwen, J., Watanabe, O., Hagiya, M., Mosses, P.D., Ito, T., eds.: Proceedings of the 1st International Conference on Theoretical Computer Science — Exploring New Frontiers of Theoretical Informatics, IFIP TCS'2000 (Sendai, Japan, August 17-19, 2000.. Volume 1872 of LNCS. Springer-Verlag, Berlin-Heidelberg-New York-Barcelona-Hong Kong-London-Milan-Paris-Singapore-Tokyo, 2000, pp. 619–623.

13. van Leeuwen, J., Wiedermann, J.: Beyond the turing limit: Evolving interactive systems. In Pacholski, L., Ruicka, P., eds.: SOFSEM 2001: Theory and Practice of Informatics: 28th Conference on Current Trends in Theory and Practice of Informatics. Volume 2234 of Lecture Notes in Computer Science. Springer-Verlag, 2001, pp. 90–109.

14. Wegner, P., Goldin, D.: Interaction as a framework for modeling. Lecture Notes in Computer Science **1565**, 1999, pp. 243–257.

15. (PVM) http://www.csm.ornl.gov/pvm.

16. (MPI) http://www-unix.mcs.anl.gov/mpi/.

17. (COM+) http://www.microsoft.com/com/tech/COMPlus.asp.

18. (CORBA) http://www.omg.org.

19. Carriero, N., Gelernter, D.: Linda in context. Communications of the ACM **32**, 1989, pp. 444–458.

20. Leler, W.: Linda meets Unix. IEEE Computer **23**, 1990, pp. 43–54.

21. (Jini) http://www.sun.com/jini.

22. Oaks, S., Wong, H.: Jini in a Nutshell. O'Reilly & Associates, 2000.

23. Banâtre, J.P., Le Métayer, D.: Programming by multiset transformations. Communications of the ACM **36**, 1993, pp. 98–111.

24. Arbab, F., Herman, I., Spilling, P.: An overview of Manifold and its implementation. Concurrency: Practice and Experience **5**, 1993, pp. 23–70.

25. Bonsangue, M., Arbab, F., de Bakker, J., Rutten, J., Scutellá, A., Zavattaro, G.: A transition system semantics for the control-driven coordination language Manifold. Theoretical Computer Science **240**, 2000, pp. 3–47.

26. Bergstra, J., Klint, P.: The ToolBus Coordination Architecture. In Ciancarini, P., Hankin, C., eds.: Proc. 1st Int. Conf. on Coordination Models and Languages. Volume 1061 of Lecture Notes in Computer Science., Cesena, Italy, Springer-Verlag, Berlin, 1996, pp. 75–88.

27. Arbab, F.: Reo: A channel-based coordination model for component composition. Mathematical Structures in Computer Science **14**, 2004, pp. 329–366.
28. Andreoli, J.M., Ciancarini, P., Pareschi, R.: Interaction Abstract Machines. In: Trends in Object-Based Concurrent Computing. MIT Press, 1993, pp. 257–280.
29. Papadopoulos, G., Arbab, F.: Coordination models and languages. In Zelkowitz, M., ed.: Advances in Computers – The Engineering of Large Systems. Volume 46. Academic Press, 1998, pp. 329–400.
30. Andreoli, J.M., Hankin, C., Le Métayer, D., eds.: Coordination Programming: Mechanisms, Models and Semantics. Imperial College Press, 1996.
31. Ciancarini, P., Hankin, C., eds.: 1st Int. Conf. on Coordination Languages and Models. Volume 1061 of Lecture Notes in Computer Science. Springer-Verlag, 1996.
32. Garlan, D., Le Métayer, D., eds.: 2nd Int. Conf. on Coordination Languages and Models. Volume 1282 of Lecture Notes in Computer Science. Springer-Verlag, 1997.
33. Omicini, A., Zambonelli, F., Klusch, M., Tolksdorf, R.: Coordination of Internet Agents: Models, Technologies, and Applications. Springer, ISBN 3-540-41613-7, 2001.
34. Baier, C., Sirjani, M., Arbab, F., Rutten, J.: Modeling component connectors in Reo by Constraint Automata. Science of Computer Programming 61, 2006, pp. 75–113 extended version.
35. Zlatev, Z., Diakov, N., Pokraev, S.: Construction of negotiation protocols for E-Commerce applications. ACM SIGecom Exchanges **5**, 2004, pp. 11–22.
36. Clarke, D., Arbab, F., Costa, D.: Modeling coordination in biological systems. In: Proc. of the International Symposium on Leveraging Applications of Formal Methods (ISoLA 2004), 2004.
37. Diakov, N., Arbab, F.: Compositional construction of web services using Reo. In: Proc. of International Workshop on Web Services: Modeling, Architecture and Infrastructure (WSMAI), INSTICC Press, 2004, pp. 49–58.
38. Arbab, F., Baier, C., de Boer, F., Rutten, J.: Models and temporal logics for timed component connectors. In: Proc. of the IEEE International Conference on Software Engineering and Formal Methods (SEFM), IEEE Computer Society, 2004, pp. 198–207.
39. Arbab, F., Rutten, J.: A coinductive calculus of component connectors. In M. Wirsing, D.P., Hennicker, R., eds.: Recent Trends in Algebraic Development Techniques, Proceedings of 16th International Workshop on Algebraic Development Techniques (WADT 2002). Volume 2755 of Lecture Notes in Computer Science., Springer-Verlag, 2003, pp. 35–56.
40. Arbab, F.: Abstract Behavior Types: A foundation model for components and their composition. Science of Computer Programming **55**, 2005, pp. 3–52 extended version.
41. Rutten, J.: Component connectors. In [60], 2004, pp. 73–87.
42. Mehta, N., Sirjani, M., Arbab, F.: Effective modeling of software architectural assemblies using Constraint Automata. Technical Report SEN-R0309, Centrum voor Wiskunde en Informatica, Kruislaan 413, 1098 SJ Amsterdam, The Netherlands, 2003.
43. Mehta, N.R., Medvidovic, N., Sirjani, M., Arbab, F.: Modeling behavior in compositions of software architectural primitives. In: Automated Software Engineering, IEEE Computer Society, 2004, pp. 371–374.

44. Rutten, J.: Elements of stream calculus (an extensive exercise in coinduction). In Brookes, S., Mislove, M., eds.: Proc. of 17th Conf. on Mathematical Foundations of Programming Semantics, Aarhus, Denmark, pp. 23–26, May 2001. Volume 45 of Electronic Notes in Theoretical Computer Science. Elsevier, Amsterdam, 2001.

45. Barringer, H., Kuiper, R., Pnueli, A.: A really abstract current model and its temporal logic. In: Proceedings of Thirteenth Annual ACM Symposium on principles of Programming Languages, ACM, 1986, pp. 173–183.

46. de Bakker, J., Kok, J.: Towards a Uniform Topological Treatment of Streams and Functions on Streams. In Brauer, W., ed.: Proceedings of the 12th International Colloquium on Automata, Languages and Programming. Volume 194 of Lecture Notes in Computer Science., Nafplion, Springer-Verlag, 1985, pp. 140–148.

47. Kok, J.: Semantic Models for Parallel Computation in Data Flow, Logic- and Object-Oriented Programming. PhD thesis, Vrije Universiteit, Amsterdam, 1989.

48. Broy, M., Stolen, K.: Specification and development of interactive systems. Volume 62 of Monographs in Computer Science. Springer, 2001.

49. Arbab, F.: Computing and Interaction. In [61], 2006.

50. Brock, J., Ackerman, W.: Scenarios: A model of non-determinate computation. In: Proceedings of the International Colloquium on Formalization of Programming Concepts, Springer-Verlag, 1981, pp. 252–259.

51. (Petri Nets World) http://www.informatik.uni-hamburg.de/TGI/PetriNets/.

52. Diakov, N., Zlatev, Z., Pokraev, S.: Composition of negotiation protocols for e-commerce applications. In Cheung, W., Hsu, J., eds.: The 2005 IEEE International Conference on e-Technology, e-Commerce and e-Service, 2005, pp. 418–423.

53. Halbwachs, N.: Synchronous programming of reactive systems. Kluwer Academic Publishers, 1993.

54. Berry, G.: The Esterel v5 language primer version 5.21 release 2.0. Technical report, INRIA, 1999. ftp://ftp-sop.inria.fr/meije/esterel/papers/primer.pdf.

55. Berry, G., Cosserat, L.: The synchronous programming languages Esterel and its mathematical semantics. In Brookes, Winskel, G., eds.: Seminar on Concurrency. Volume 197 of Lecture Notes in Computer Science. Springer Verlag, 1984, pp. 389–448.

56. Halbwachs, N., Caspi, P., Raymond, P., Pilaud, D.: The synchronous data flow programming language LUSTRE. Proceedings of the IEEE **79**, 1991, pp. 1305–1320.

57. le Guernic, P., Benveniste, A., Bournai, P., Gautier, T.: SIGNAL – a data flow-oriented language for signal processing. IEEE Transactions on Acoustics, Speech, and Signal Processing [see also IEEE Transactions on Signal Processing] **34**, 1986, pp. 362–3740.

58. Arbab, F., Baier, C., de Boer, F., Rutten, J., Sirjani, M.: Synthesis of Reo circuits for implementation of component-connector automata specifications. In Jacquet, J.M., Picco, G., eds.: Proc. of the 7th International Conference on Coordination Models and Languages (Coordination 2005). Volume 3454 of Lecture Notes in Computer Science., Springer-Verlag, 2005, pp. 236–251.

59. Keil, D., Goldin, D.: Modeling indirect interaction in open computational systems. In: Proc. 1st Int'l workshop on Theory and Practice of Open Computational Systems (TAPOCS), IEEE Computer Society Press, 2003.

60. Panangaden, P., van Breugel, F., eds.: Mathematical Techniques for Analyzing Concurrent and Probabilistic Systems. CRM Monograph Series. American Mathematical Society, 2004. ISSN: 1065-8599.
61. Goldin, D., Smolka, S., Wegner, P., eds.: Interactive Computation: The New Paradigm. Springer-Verlag, 2006 (this volume).

From Information-Centric to Experiential Environments

Rahul Singh[1] and Ramesh Jain[2]

[1] San Francisco State University, San Francisco, CA, USA
[2] University of California, Irvine, CA, USA

Summary. With progress in technology, information management systems are transitioning from storing well defined entities and relationships to the challenge of managing multifarious heterogeneous data. Underlying such data is often a rich diversity of information with emergent semantics. Recognizing this characteristic is essential to executing the transition from data to knowledge. In this context, this chapter presents the paradigm of experiential environments for facilitating user–data interactions in information management systems. Experiential environments emphasize obtaining information and insights rather than pure data lookup. To facilitate this aim, the paradigm utilizes the sentient nature of human beings, their sensory abilities, and interactive query–exploration–presentation interfaces to experience and assimilate information.

1 Introduction

In the good old days, just a decade or so ago, to exemplify the requirements and structure of a database, we typically considered a corporate database. Within it, entities, such as "employee", "address", or "salary" consisted of alphanumeric fields. Each such field represented some attribute that had been modeled. Users would pose queries, for example, to discover an employee attribute or to find all employees that satisfied certain attribute-related predicates.

Although in the new millennium users have vastly different expectations, most databases still retain the design philosophy of yesteryear: *Users ask queries to get answers in an information-centric environment.* This premise holds as long as all users have same or similar requirements. The database can then act as a resource that provides a well-defined environment for articulating queries on a fixed information structure. However, the emergence of Internet based systems, including the WWW, and progress in computing and storage technologies has fundamentally changed, the kind of data that is in common use today. This change is both quantitative and qualitative and has important consequences for paradigms used for interacting with data. Taken together, the situation contrasts sharply with the scenario that was common even just a decade ago and creates a mismatch between existing design paradigms and evolving requirements. A simple analysis of the nature of the data and expectations of users from current and next generation systems highlights the emerging issues:

- Volume of data is growing by orders of magnitude every year.
- Multimedia and sensor data is becoming more and more common.
- Different data sources provide facets of information which have to be combined to form a holistic picture.
- The goal of data assimilation increasingly requires that spatio-temporal characteristics of the data are taken into account.
- In many applications, real-time data processing is essential.
- Exploration, not querying, is the predominant mode of interaction, which makes context and state critical.
- The user is interested in experience and information, independent of the medium and the source.

In the chapter, we explore the paradigm of experiential computing for designing information management systems. The idea of experiential computing is built on the fact that humans are sentient observers. Therefore, this paradigm emphasizes interactivity and support for experiential user factors in the quest for information assimilation.

1.1 Issues Motivating the Need for Experiential Computing

Let's look at some of the basic issues that underlie this change. We motivate our perspective by noting three critical factors that influence the situation. These include: How the data is modeled and its implications (the data model), the presence of different data types and their implications (data heterogeneity), and finally, the expectation of users as they interact with the data (user requirements).

Data model: A data model can be thought of as an abstraction device through which a reasonable interpretation of the data can be obtained [53]. Keeping this in mind, we can identify two types of data sources, those that are *strongly modeled* and those that are *weakly modeled*. Conventional databases such as an inventory database or a corporate database are examples of strongly modeled sources of data. In them, data and relationships amongst data are stored with very specific goals in mind. Information from such databases can be retrieved (in the sense of normal queries) only in terms of the data and relations that are explicitly modeled or derivations based on them (e.g., joins on tables). Weakly modeled data sources on the other hand are less specific about the interpretations of the data that are made available through them. A general web-page is an example of a weakly modeled data source. While thematically coherent, a general web-page, unlike the above examples, does not seek to limit access to information present in it through a limited set of entities and relations.

Data heterogeneity: Data in traditional databases is synonymous with alphanumeric information. However, many contemporary applications are characterized by the fact that information is represented through different types of data like text (alphanumeric), images, audio, video, or other specialized data types. The proliferation of physically different data types (or data heterogeneity) is driven both by the increasing capabilities of computational systems as well as the increasing sophistication and ease of use of digital sensor technologies coupled with their decreasing cost. One of the important challenges in situations that involve heterogeneous data types lies in that the semantics associated with complex media (like video or images) is *emergent*, i.e., media is endowed with meaning by placing it in context of other similar media and through user interactions [44]. This has strong bearing on the systems that are designed to work with such data. For instance, the emergent semantics of complex media imply that such information is necessarily weakly modeled. To capture such issues, we distinguish two types of data: *alphanumeric* and *media-based*, where the latter may include alphanumeric data when occurring in conjunction with other data types.

User requirements: User requirements for the data fall into roughly two categories: *information* and *insight*. For example, in some cases, a user is just looking for some information, such as the location of a specific restaurant. In other cases the user may be interested in more complex insights such as how cosmopolitan is a particular city. These two types of requirements present completely different set of challenges for the design of information management systems.

1.2 Towards a New Paradigm

The matrix in Fig. 1 captures the relationships between the aforementioned issues. Each cell of this matrix lists the paradigms which can be used to address requirements at the intersection of these issues.

In this matrix, predictably, databases lie in the lower left quadrant at the intersection of information and strongly modeled sources; they are ideally suited for obtaining precise information in well specified domains. The bottom right quadrant is occupied by search engines. They are well tailored for generic searches across weakly modeled information sources. Such sources may either be alphanumeric or have heterogeneous data typically with textual annotations. The primary intention of search engines is to provide information through responses to specific (keyword-based) queries and not to directly facilitate exploration.

In this matrix, predictably, databases lie in the lower left quadrant at the intersection of information and strongly modeled sources; they are ideally suited for obtaining precise information in well specified domains. The

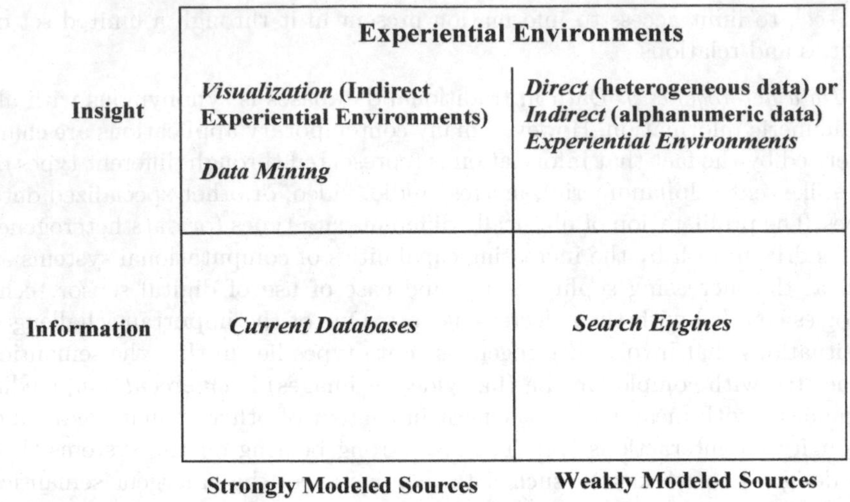

Experiential Environments		
Insight	*Visualization* (Indirect Experiential Environments) *Data Mining*	*Direct* (heterogeneous data) or *Indirect* (alphanumeric data) *Experiential Environments*
Information	*Current Databases*	*Search Engines*
	Strongly Modeled Sources	**Weakly Modeled Sources**

Fig. 1. Paradigms at the intersection of data modeling, data heterogeneity, and user requirements

bottom right quadrant is occupied by search engines. They are well tailored for generic searches across weakly modeled information sources. Such sources may either be alphanumeric or have heterogeneous data typically with textual annotations. The primary intention of search engines is to provide information through responses to specific (keyword-based) queries and not to directly facilitate exploration.

The top half of Fig. 1 consists of paradigms, many of which demonstrate characteristics that are partially or wholly experiential. This transition is reflected in the top left quadrant which consists of approaches that support gaining insights from precise sources. Techniques commonly employed for this goal include data mining and visualization. The latter is of special interest to us as it seeks to transform and present data in a manner that allow users to gain insights by "seeing" the patterns and relationships that may be present. This attribute, where the human senses are involved directly, as the reader will see from the ensuing sections, is a key characteristic of the experiential paradigm.

Finally, the top right quadrant addresses the intersection of insight and imprecise data sources. This intersection produces challenges which can be addressed through *experiential environments*, a new way of interacting with data that will become increasingly common in most data-intensive applications: In such cases, users encounter immense volumes of multifarious data from disparate, distributed, sometimes even unknown, data sources. To gain insights from such data, one must be immersed in it, just as one would be immersed in a real life situation to experience it first hand. Humans are sentient observers. They want to explore and experience information. Furthermore, they typically prefer to directly interact with the data without complicated intervening metaphors. This tendency probably stems from the fact that we humans are all immersed in the real world where the real world is really different attributes at different points surrounding us. We use our senses to measure or infer the various attributes. For example, our visual system is a powerful mechanism that allows us to infer different kinds of attributes about the environment surrounding us. Similarly, tactile senses allow us to measure other characteristics of the environment that are in close proximity to us. As these examples illustrate, we have complementary sensors to facilitate our explorations and experiences. Vision and sound are our sensors to infer about the world without the constraint of close proximity and we use these for experience as well as for communications. Other sensors, like touch, are used in situations where a certain amount of proximity and intimacy is required.

We develop the ideas initially proposed in [28] to point out two types of experiential environments that may be contemplated: The first of these is the *indirect experiential environments*. Within these environments, data is transformed to present it in manners where users can involve their senses to discern patterns and relationships. Techniques in information visualization as well as more evolved and integrated approaches such as the business activity monitoring application covered in Sect. 4.2 of this chapter fall in this category. The second type of experiential environment is called a *direct experiential environment*. The fundamental difference of such environments from those in the first category lies in their ability to deal with data types such as imagery or audio that can be directly presented to users. Therefore there is no interpretation or selection of transformations involved (Sect. 4 describes an example of such a system directed at the problem of personal multimedia information management). Finally, user-information interactions are also direct in that they do not use any intermediate metaphors or transformations.

1.3 From Data to Information and now to Insights: The Etudes of Experiential Computing

There is a very clear trend in the evolution of computing approaches from databases to search engines. Below [2] presents this trend by comparing the key characteristics of these systems. In Table 1, we extend Belew's observations to include experiential environments. Our extension highlights the trend from data to information and now to insights.

Traditional databases were designed to provide an environment where user could articulate their information needs using precisely specified logical relationships. The database would then respond by providing the information. On-Line-Analytical-Processing (OLAP) and visualization-based approaches are based on the same systems, but go farther by pulling out a volume of data and then using visualization tools to allow exploration of the retrieved dataset. Search engines directly adopted the basic concept of query from databases.

Table 1. Data to information (and now) to insights

	Database	Information retrieval	Experiential environment
Basic goal	Provide data	Provide information sources	Provide insight
Data type	Alphanumeric	Text	Multimedia
User query	Specific	General	Emergent
System provides	Data item	Pointer	Heterogeneous data
Retrieval method	Deterministic	Probabilistic	Hybrid
Success criterion	Efficiency	Utility	User satisfaction

Thus, in most of the current systems, a user articulates a query and gets an answer for it. If further information is needed, a new query must be articulated. Current information environments actually work against the human–machine synergy. Humans are very efficient in conceptual and perceptual analysis and relatively weak in mathematical and logical analysis; computers are exactly the opposite. In an experiential environment, users *directly use their senses to observe data and information of interest related to an event and they interact naturally with the data based on their particular set of interests in the context of that event.* Experiential environments have the following important characteristics:

- *They are direct:* These environments provide a holistic picture of the event without using any unfamiliar metaphors and commands. Within them, users employ intuitive actions based on commonly used operations and their anticipated results. In experiential environments, a user is presented data that is easily and rapidly interpreted by human senses and then the user interacts with the dataset to get a modified dataset.
- *They provide the same query and presentation spaces:* Most current information systems use different query and presentation spaces. Consider popular search engines. They provide a box to enter keywords and the system responds with a list of thousands of entries spanning over hundreds of pages. A user has no idea how the entries on the first page may be

related to the entries on the last, or how many times the same entry appears, or even how the entries on the same page are related to each other. Contrast this to a spreadsheet. The user articulates a query by changing certain data that is displayed in context of other data items. The user's action results in a new sheet showing new relationships. Here the query and presentation spaces are the same. These systems are called What-You-See-Is-What-You-Get or WYSIWYG.

- *They consider both the user state and context:* Information system should know the state and context of the user and present information that is relevant to this particular user in the given state and context. People operate best in known contexts and do not like instantaneous context switching. Early information systems, including databases, were designed to provide scalability and efficiency. These considerations led to designs that were stateless. The efficiency of relational databases is the result of this decision. This is also the reason why Internet search engines, which do not store user states, can be dissatisfying, as users seek to drill-down on information obtained from previous queries.
- *They promote perceptual analysis and exploration:* Experiential systems promote perceptual analysis and exploration. Because users involve their senses in analyzing, exploring, and interacting with the system, these systems are more compelling and understandable. Text based systems provide abstract information in visual form. Video games and many simulation systems are so engaging because they provide powerful visual environment, sound, and in some cases tactile inputs to users.

In this chapter, we begin by discussing the data engineering challenges that underlie the development of experiential environments in Sect. 2. This is followed by a description of event-based modeling in Sect. 3. In this section, we discuss how event-based organization and management of data facilitates development of contextual and personalized experiential environments. In Sect. 4, we present descriptions of two experiential systems in the areas of personal information management and business activity monitoring respectively. These examples illustrate how the ideas espoused in the previous sections can be realized in designing real-world systems. We conclude this chapter in Sect. 5 by reiterating the fundamental ideas behind the paradigm of experiential environments and outlining its broad applicability in the evolution of the next generation information and data management systems.

2 Data Engineering Challenges for Designing Experiential Environments

Experiential computing environments require supporting user interactions such as browsing, exploration, and queries on information represented through different media. The *direct* nature of experiential environments implies that the results of such interactions are expressed in the native format(s) of the underlying data. The data engineering challenges that are encountered in designing such systems span issues related to modeling and representation of heterogeneous data as well as design of user-data interfaces that support interactions that are direct and user context aware.

In experiential computing, the problem of *heterogeneity*, arises in many forms, including: *infrastructural heterogeneity* (due to different types of hardware and software platforms that may be involved), *logical heterogneity* (arising out of different data models or schemata used for providing a logical structure to the data), and *physical heterogeneity* (owing to the presence of fundamentally distinct types of data such as text, audio, images, or video). Amongst these, the problem of logical heterogeneity has typically been considered in traditional database research, while that of physical heterogeneity has been the focus in multimedia data modeling.

It can be postulated that physical heterogeneity leads to logical heterogeneity, since the need to capture specificities of each media would result in the development of different data models and schemata, which ultimately need to be integrated. This is reflected in the similarities that can be discerned between the approaches to addressing heterogeneity in database and multimedia research. For example, the idea of using local-as-view and global-as-view approaches [25] for specifying the correspondences between data at the source and in the global schema bears parallels to the principles of autonomy and uniformity suggested in [51] for media integration. However, till date, the issue of integration, when the heterogeneity is due to different media, has typically remained unaddressed both in multimedia and database research, as techniques have tended to concentrate on issues that arise in media-specific management. The result of this research focus manifests itself today in a large number of media specific solutions, such as those for images, audio, or video, but hardly any, that span different media.

Our emphasis in this chapter is on the problem of dealing with heterogeneity by starting from the physical level. Consequently, the following sections explicitly deal with issues that arise when information is represented using multiple and distinct media. As explained above, such a formulation subsumes the problem of dealing with logical heterogeneity. Furthermore, this approach allows us to address issues that occur due to the increasing availability of sensor-based data in applications varying from personal information management, to ubiquitous computing and sensor networks. We refer readers who are specifically interested in the issues of managing logical heterogeneity to introductory material well codified in textbooks such as [15, 38] along with the reviews [27, 31] and references therein. In this context, we also emphasize that the principles of experiential computing are not limited to the availability of multimedia information and are equally applicable to domains where the data is alphanumeric. In Sect. 4 this is illustrated through two examples, one of which deals with multimedia data in the domain of personal information management and the other, with alphanumeric data, in business intelligence.

2.1 Understanding (Physical) Heterogeneity

Fundamentally, multimedia data has a *gestalt* nature. This implies that it is comprised of more than one media that are semantically correlated and that the complete semantics conveyed in the data cannot be discerned by considering the data streams individually. The classical example of capturing an explosion using image-based data (video) and sound (audio) is often forwarded to underline this aspect. In the case of this example, either of the media (a flash of light or a loud sound) taken in isolation, is insufficient to determine that an explosion occurred. A unified data model is thus essential not only for preserving the semantic integrity of the information, but also for conveying the same by supporting query-retrieval and user interactions with the data. The principal characteristics of multimedia data that have influence on its modeling and subsequent usages include:

- *Semantic correlations across media:* As briefly described above, representing the semantic correlations across different media is fundamental to storage, processing, query-retrieval, and utilization of multimedia information. How do we represent heterogeneous multimedia data in a *general* and *unified* way that emphasizes the semantic correlations between the media? Different media, such as audio and images, have different form and characteristics. A unified data model needs to address these issues. This issue also expresses itself in terms of the problem of *multiple representations* where a single object, entity, or phenomenon may be captured and represented in different media formats. For example, the state of a patient's health may be recorded using biomedical imagery data including time-varying imaging, alphanumeric data detailing blood pressure, body-temperature, or patient-weight, and audio-transcripts. A data model should be capable of seamlessly resolving across the various representations.

- *Temporal characteristics of the data:* From surveillance videos, to personal photographs, to biomedical imagery (for example, tracking of synaptic activation in the brain), temporal and dynamic phenomena are commonly represented through multimedia data. The aforementioned applications and many others are characterized by data in which the time of occurrence or changes over time denote valuable information. A multimedia data model, therefore, should be able to represent, query, and reason about time and time-based relationships. Directly using traditional data models, such as the *entity-relationship* paradigm, to reason about dynamic data is complicated because such an approach is primarily designed to reflect a set of static relationships between entities. In dynamic environments not only the attributes associated with entities, but also the relationships between entities change with time. In modeling multimedia data, an additional challenge is faced in situations that require integrating semantically related dynamic and static media. This can happen for example, when information about a sporting event is available through a video-recording and a text report.

- *Spatial characteristics of the data:* Much of multimedia data has inherent characteristics that can be correlated with location. For example, automated traffic monitoring at intersections provides video footage distinct from those taken at highways. In bio-medical imaging the location (organ or tissue) is of critical importance for analysis and interpretation of the images. Personal videos of trips can be categorized by the geographical locations visited. These examples indicate that the semantics, the form, and the relationships expressed in multimedia data are often influenced by location and relationships such as adjacency, connectivity, proximity, or containment that can be defined over space.

- *User interactions with the data*: Current multimedia systems typically consider information in a manner that is independent of the user and context. Further, they make an implicit assumption that acquisition of knowledge by the user (based on the media) is a linear process and can be adequately represented by the rendering of the media alone. Therefore, they support limited interactions between the user and the data. This causes a significant loss in the totality of information being communicated between creation of the media and its consumption by users, as the media is presented in isolation from the context of its creation [49] as well as the context of the user. For instance, the rendering of a video is typically from a single perspective and users have little or no control in interactively exploring a scene using multiple perspectives. Additionally, in true *multi*-media settings, disparate data sources need to be united for presentation, query, and exploration in manners where the users are free to state their requests in natural form based on objects and event relationships of interest. The entire set of aforementioned issues is complicated by the fact that the semantics associated with complex media (like video or images) is emergent. Developing user–data interaction paradigms that address such issues requires support from underlying data models to impart the appropriate structure to the information.

2.2 Previous Research in Multimedia and Databases

In recent years, a number of data models have been developed to address the structure and semantics of media data like images and video [9, 10, 11, 12, 16, 20, 21, 33, 37, 46, 50] or sound [7, 55]. Such research has typically focused on the development of powerful features to describe the corresponding media and the use of similarity functions to answer queries based on these features [43]. This approach simplifies the general multimedia database problem, because a database is assumed to contain only a specific type of media data [13]. A related line of research has focused on developing models that support the structure of media data and the syntactic operations that are typically performed on them. For example [19] proposes as a basic abstraction the notion of "timed streams" of media elements like video, audio samples, and musical notes. This model considers issues like the temporal nature of media data (defined in terms of real time presentation constraints and media synchronization) along with operations like media derivation and media composition. Similarly [34] considers temporal access control issues like reverse, fast-forward, and midpoint suspension/resumption in their model. An object-relational model that builds upon [19] is proposed in [13] where a three-layered structure is defined. The lowermost layer consists of raw data (byte sequences). The middle layer consists of multimedia entities, called multimedia type, which can be images, image stacks, sound, video, or text. The top layer consists of logical entities that model the domain semantics and interact with entities representing multimedia types. Additionally, specialized entities, containing visual and spatial information can be defined at the top layer to be used for content-based querying. Layered architectures such as [56] or the one described above, break down the complexity of multimedia modeling by seeking clear distinction between raw data modeling, conceptual modeling, and presentation management.

The *Garlic* project at IBM [8, 24], uses an object-oriented data model as middleware to integrate multiple (potentially multimedia) databases. Translations of data types and schemas between individual repositories and Garlic are accomplished using repository wrappers. A repository of complex objects is provided for integration of multimedia data and legacy data. Query processing and data manipulation are supported through the Garlic system.

The papers reviewed above catalog a rich diversity of research approaches towards modeling information represented through multimedia data. However, to the best of our knowledge, *no research till date has attempted to address within a single framework, the problem of multimedia information management, in context of all the issues we enumerated early on in this section.* Towards this, in the following section we introduce the rudiments of event-based modeling that form the basis of our research in designing experiential systems.

3 Event-Based Unified Modeling of Multimedia Data

3.1 The Conceptual Model

The fundamental idea underlying the data model being considered by us is the notion of an *event* which may be defined as under [47]:

Definition 1. An event is an observed physical reality parameterized by space and time. The observations describing the event are defined by the nature or physics of the observable, the observation model, and the observer.

Certain key issues in this definition need to be highlighted. First, events are treated as a fundamental physical reality and the observations (or data) that describe them are defined to depend on the observation model and the observer. The observation model may include among others, the observation method (e.g., audio, video, images, or other data types such as alphanumeric data), sampling model (e.g., video-rate), and sampling period. The role of the observer is fulfilled by users involved in creation or consumption of the information. Events thus constitute the unifying notion that brings together heterogeneous data that is semantically correlated. This idea is illustrated in Fig. 2. Using events as the central semantic notion, a conceptual model can therefore be developed. As part of the conceptual model, the specification of an event covers three primary aspects:

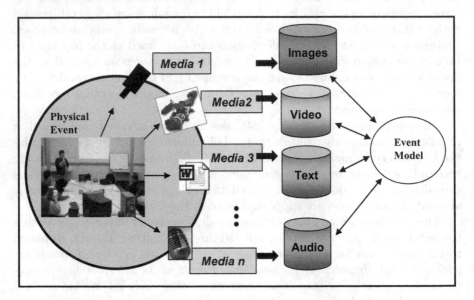

Fig. 2. Intuition behind the event-based unified multimedia data model

- *Event information:* The information component of the event may consist of specific attributes. Since events are spatio-temporal constructs, the event information component necessarily contains the time period of the activity and its spatial characteristics, e.g., its location. Additionally, information required to uniquely identify an event are also stored here. Further, entities like people or objects that participate in an event may be described here along with other types of domain specific information.
- *Event relations:* Events (and the activities underlying them) may be related to other events (activities) that occur in the system. Examples of such relations can be temporal and spatial co-occurrences, temporal sequencing, cause–effect relations, and aggregations of events. This information is modeled and described in the event relations component.
- *Media Support:* Each event is a unifying point for the various observations that describe it. These observations are available to us through different types of media data. Specific media data is said to support an event, if

it captures (describes) that event. We note that the exact form of the description depends on the characteristics of the media. For example, a basketball game may be described by video, photographs, and mixed text-image new article. Each of these descriptions exemplifies specific media that have different characteristics, while supporting the same event. Such media data may reside as multimedia files in a file system or in media specific databases. In the media support component, information such as media types, resource locators, or indexes corresponding to specific media that support the given event are stored. It should be noted that the conceptual model imposes no restrictions on the same media simultaneously supporting multiple events.

3.2 Multilevel Events

For broad usability, in the context of media-rich data, a data model and its physical implementations need to incorporate domain-level semantics so that users can interact with the information at the semantic level rather than at the level of nonintuitive media-specific features. This requires a model to span and seamlessly transition between low-level signal-centric modeling to high-level concept and semantic modeling. As an example of this, consider the problem of mapping an image with large number of "red" colored pixels to an entity with clear semantics associated with it, such as "tomato" or "sunset". This issue is synonymous with the problem of bridging the signal-to-symbol gap (the gap between the signal-level description of the content and the symbolic meaning associated with it).

One of the primary goals of event-based modeling is to relate media to semantically meaningful entities and concepts. This requires bridging the signal-to-symbol gap. To assist in building models that encompass such a transition, we distinguish between three types of events. We call the first of these *data events,* the second *elemental events,* and the last *semantic events.*

Data events model the physical characteristics of the information. For example, a photograph or video clip consists of pixels that contain illumination-intensity information of the scene. Similarly, an (digital) audio-clip consists of samplings of a sound wave. These are examples of data events. As these examples illustrate, the media support for each data event is a nonempty singleton set, consisting of a specific media instance. The reader will note that given the signal-level nature of data events, issues such as the nature or physics of the observable and the observation model have a strong bearing on their definition of data events.

An elemental event on the other hand is a conceptual entity and reflects an interpretation or analysis of information that is partially inspired by domain semantics while retaining the dependence on signal-level information (data events). For example, detecting a "person speaking" based on audio-visual data is an example of an elemental event. While being independent of data characteristics per se, the formulation of elemental events draws on detection of data features and may form the focal point for multimedia unification. In context of the earlier example, detecting that a person is speaking may be done by analyzing the sound-level (pure audio-based), analysis of lip movements (pure video-based), or through an analysis involving both audio and video. An elemental event therefore, may have either homogeneous or heterogeneous media support based on the constituent data events.

Finally, a semantic event captures the conceptual (or semantic) interpretation of the data and is based on the underlying elemental events. For instance, "giving a speech" is an example of a semantic event. This event may be based on the elemental event "person speaking" and be temporally related with other elemental events such as "coming to the podium". Thus, semantic events do not have direct media support, but function as a unifying point for all the underlying media.

The reader may note that denotation of data, elemental, and semantic levels in the multilevel event model does not imply that implementations are restricted to have only three levels in the transition from a signal-centric to a semantics-centric modeling of the information. Indeed, in an implementation, one or more of the levels defined above may consist of sublevels to assist in the transition. This will especially be true for the highest level where semantic events are represented. Conversely, an implementation may choose to collapse these three levels into a single layer. This could occur, for example, in situations where users directly annotate media to endow high-level semantics to it. In such a case the signal-to-symbol gap is bridged using cognitive input. The system described in Sect. 4 for personal multimedia information management takes this approach.

3.3 Modeling Time and Space

Time and Space are two of the fundamental attributes of the event model and how they are represented significantly impacts our ability to reason with the proposed model. It may be noted that modeling of time and space has received significant attention in both database and knowledge representation communities (see [54] and references therein) and our approach draws significantly from prior results in the area. In the context of temporal representation, a simple approach is to tag each attribute (or tuple) with a discrete timestamp. Its deficiency lies in that common algebraic operations like addition, multiplication, and division are not applicable to timestamps. Further, information that is not explicitly represented becomes difficult to query.

Research in temporal databases has also explored interval-based models of time. Such representations are ideally suited to describe events (such as a game or a meeting) that occur over a period of time. However, the modeling problem we are considering is significantly more complex and cannot be sufficiently addressed through interval-based models only. As an illustration, consider the example of parents taking a digital photograph of the "first smile" of their child. The photograph is in itself an event (a data event, in the three-layered hierarchy), that has an infinitesimal duration (manifested using a single timestamp). Further, based on that single photograph, an interval cannot be defined for the (semantic) event "first smile". In such cases either the fundamental nature of the event or lack of domain semantics precludes the use of interval representations. We therefore propose two temporal data types: infinitesimal time points and time intervals to temporally characterize events. In the following, we denote time points with a lowercase letter, potentially with subscripts (e.g., t_1, t_2) and time intervals with upper case letters $T = [t_1, t_2)$. Algebraic operators can be used to convert information among these types. For example, time intervals can be added or subtracted from time points to yield new time points. Further, time points can be subtracted to determine time intervals. Three classes of relationships can then be defined to reason about temporal data. These include:

- *Point–point relations*: Assuming a complete temporal ordering, two arbitrary time points t_1 and t_2 can be related as: $t_1 < t_2$ (**Before**); $t_1 = t_2$ (**Simultaneous**); $t_1 > t_2$ (**After**), and the negations $t_1 \geq t_2$ (**Not Before**); and $t_1 \leq t_2$ (**Not After**).
- *Point–interval relations:* The relations between an arbitrary time point t_1 and an arbitrary time interval $T = [t_a, t_b)$, are: $t_1 < T \Rightarrow t_1 < t_a$ (**Before**); $t_1 \in T \Rightarrow t_a < t_1 < t_b$ (**During**); $t_1 > T \Rightarrow t_1 > t_b$ (**After**), $t_1 \geq t_a$ (**Not Before**); and $t_1 \leq t_b$ (**Not After**).
- *Interval–interval relations:* Given two intervals $T = [t_a, t_b)$ and $U = [u_a, u_b)$, the possible relations between them are [1]: $t_b < u_a$ (**Before**); $t_a = u_a$ and $t_b = u_b$ (**Equal**); $t_b = u_a$ (**Meet**); $t_a < u_a$ and $t_b < u_b$ and $u_a < t_b$ (**Overlap**) $t_a > u_a$ and $t_b < u_b$ (**During**); $t_a = u_a$ and $t_b < u_b$ (**Start**); $t_a > u_a$ and $t_b = u_b$ (**Finish**); and the corresponding symmetric relationships (excluding the case for **Equal**).

These relations allow us to deal with relative position of intervals and are necessary to reason about effects that may influence the occurrence of each other (causality) or manifest themselves with delay. A graphical description of these relations is shown in Fig. 3.

The ability to reason about space, analogous to reasoning about time is a key component in a model that seeks to describe data collected in dynamic settings. Multimedia data, like photographs and videos have obvious spatial (geographic location) characterization associated with them. A wide range of examples from application areas can also be observed. For instance, in biomedical imaging, the location of a tumor in the body is a critical piece of information for diagnostics and treatment. Similarly, in weather forecasting, the localization of severe weather phenomena is critical.

Research in spatial databases suggests two alternative ways of representing space. The first involves describing space itself, i.e., describing every point in space. The second involves representing distinct entities. However, such a bifurcation introduces the problem of reconciling spatial granularity. This can potentially be resolved [23], by supporting concepts for modeling single

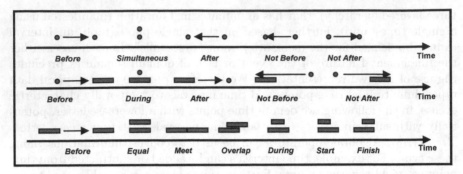

Fig. 3. Illustration of the three types of temporal relationships in the event-based model: The point–point relations are shown at the top, the point–interval relations are shown in the middle, and the interval–interval relations are shown at the bottom

objects (represented as points, lines, or regions) and spatially related collection of objects (represented as partitions or networks). One unified representation that can support this is the concept of *realm*, introduced in [22], where a realm is defined as a constrained finite set of points and line segments over a discrete grid, and conceptually represents the complete underlying geometry of one particular application space. The constraints ensure the necessity and sufficiency of the grid points for spatial representation. Abstractions such as points, lines, regions, partitions, and networks can either be described either as elements of a realm or represented on top of such elements. This approach appears to hold promise for modeling spatial attributes, by layering events in a hierarchy such that events in each layer share the same semantics of space. Other representations like TIN (triangulated irregular networks) [45] or constraint databases [30] can also be used to address such problems.

To facilitate reasoning with space, spatial algebras or spatial data types need to be defined, so that they capture the fundamental spatial abstractions, the relationships between them, and possible operations on them. In the spatial database community a variety of such approaches have been suggested (see [22, 23, 45] and references therein). Based on these we define the different types of spatial operations that are needed to reason about spatial characteristics of events to include: intersections of spatial types, topological relationships (*containment, intersection, adjacency, and enclosure*), operators defining numeric spatial attributes like *distance, area*, arithmetic operators on spatial types (*addition, subtraction*) that could be useful in aggregation relationships, operators returning atomic spatial data types (e.g., intersection of lines returning points, union of regions defining regions), operators defining directional relationships like *above, below, north_of*, and operators defining numeric relationships like *distance ¡ 5*. Researchers in spatial databases have identified various topological relations that may possibly exist. A simplification of these results was suggested in [23] which proposed the following five basic topological relationships derived from intersection of boundaries and interiors: *touch* (defined over line-line, point-line, point-region, line-region, and region-region), *in, cross, overlap,* and *disjoint.*

4 Putting it all Together: Experiential Environments for Real World Problems

In this section we consider two application domains where issues related to data heterogeneity, the importance of exploration, and the role of user–data interactions in information assimilation play a significant role. These application domains are: multimedia personal information management, and business activity monitoring. We also discuss the design of two systems based on the principles of experiential computing for these domains.

4.1 Application 1: Multimedia Personal Information Management

With advances in processing, storage, and sensor technologies over the last few decades, increasingly digital media of different types is being used to capture and store information. In the specific context of personal information, this trend has significantly accelerated in the recent past with the introduction of affordable digital cameras, portable audio recorders, and cellular phones capable of supporting, capturing, and storing text such as e-mails or instant messages, images, videos, and sound clips. These devices are setting a trend with people capturing increasing amounts of multimedia information to chronicle their day-to-day activities [4]. The emerging area of personal information management seeks to study challenges associated with management, presentation, and assimilation of such information.

4.2 Specificities of Personal Information Management in Media Rich Environments

The very nature of personal information management, especially in media rich environments, introduces specificities that need to be accounted for in a solution methodology. In this context, some key tendencies and requirements that can be gleaned from studies and prior research in the area include:

- *Support for context*: Personal information management systems have to serve the twin functions of *finding* and *reminding*. Rich contextual cues, such as time, space, thumbnails, or previews have been shown to help in search and presentation of personal information [3, 14, 52]. Additionally, user state and context can also be used as powerful aids, as discussed earlier in this chapter. Further, presentation of personal information is typically done not just in terms of isolated media, but by making it part of a specific personal context. Recent systems have attempted to provide support for this notion through the use of concepts such as landmarks (birthdays, deadlines, news events, holidays) [14] and storylines [16].

- *Co-location of related information*: The necessity of co-locating related information in a system, regardless of their format, can significantly reduce the cognitive load on users [14] and help them in assimilating the information by providing a holistic picture [28].
- *Query versus exploration*: Short (in terms of word length) and simple (in terms of Boolean operators involved) queries have typically been the norm in personal information management systems [14]. It has also been noted, that users of such systems tend to favor navigation and browsing over the use of powerful (but complex) search capabilities [6]. In [28], a review of media-rich applications including personal information, sports, and situation monitoring supports the importance of exploration over pure syntactic querying in forming insights based on the data.
- *Flexible information organization*: Specific media may simultaneously be part of different conceptual organizations defined by a user on the information space [17, 41, 40, 18]. Models, like directories or tables, that enforce rigid data categorization may constrain the way people like to structure and explore information. Such problems can be ameliorated by supporting flexible information organization.
- *Interactive interactions:* Given the multimodal nature of the available information and the observed user tendencies to eschew complex queries, highly interactive and iterative query strategies are essential for supporting fruitful user interactions with such systems. Recent efforts have moved in this direction. For example, in [14] and [48] interactive systems for managing personal information is proposed. In [52] the authors propose query-retrieval of digital images using spatial information and interactive queries. In all these cases, the systems emphasize interactive queries, direct presentation of results, and use of contextual cues such as time, participants [14, 48] and location [48, 52]. Evaluations of such systems indicate their efficacy both in terms of quantitative metrics as well as in terms of user satisfaction [14, 48].

4.3 An Experiential Approach to Managing Personal Information: The *eVITAe* Project

An analysis of the aforementioned problem specificities demonstrates a close relationship between the challenges that pervade personal multimedia information management and the emphasis areas of the experiential computing paradigm. For instance, issues such as context-support and co-location of related information are intimately tied to characteristics of experiential systems such as media independent information modeling and presentation and/or description of spatio-temporal relationships in the data. Similarly, the preference of users for interactive queries and flexible information organization observed in personal information management settings eminently fit the emphasis on interactivity that is central in experiential environments. The goal of the *eVITAe* (electronic-vitae) project [48] is to research the synergy amongst these issues and develop experiential systems for management of personal multimedia data. The prototype consists of three primary components namely *event entry, event storage, and event query and exploration environment* each of which are described below.

4.4 Event Entry

The role of event entry is to acquire all necessary information to create the event model. For example, such information may include time, location, participants, or any other domain specific event attribute. As has been pointed out [52], the primary ways of acquiring such information include (1) manual entry, (2) from data or data capture devices such as image headers and GPS enabled cameras [42], (3) from a digital calendar, (4) from surrounding information, and (5) by media analysis and association. Currently, *eVITAe* supports the first two approaches. To do so, batch processing scripts have been written to assimilate the media into the database. These scripts acquire the metadata about the media files and obtain the information such as authors (file owner), file name, creation time and a link to the actual media into the database. The reader may note that techniques such as clustering [36] and Bayesian networks [35] can also be applied to this problem.

4.5 Event Storage

The implementation of the event model in *eVITAe* can be described through the entity-relationship diagram shown in Fig. 4. The key element in this diagram is the entity *Event* which, as its name suggests, corresponds to the key notion of the event-based conceptual model. It should be noted that the notion of an event here compresses the three-layered event model into a single layer. The *Event name* is a surrogate for a unique identifier that is generated for each event when it is created. An event is further described by a set of entities that are shown on the left side of Fig. 4. In the following, we briefly describe each of these entities in terms of the role they play in the event model:

Spatial characterization: The entity *Space* is used to describe the spatial characteristics associated with events and is stored as latitude and longitude. The location information can be used in visualization and querying using map-based interfaces (see following section for details). Since, directly working with latitude–longitude information is cumbersome to most users, a look-up mechanism is created to map the latitude-longitude data to names of established places, such as cities along with their associated information like zip code, state and country. This helps users to interact with location-based information naturally and obviates the complexity associated with direct usage of latitude/longitude information

Representation of media: The entity *Media* is used to denote the media data which supports a given event. The media data may be referred to by a

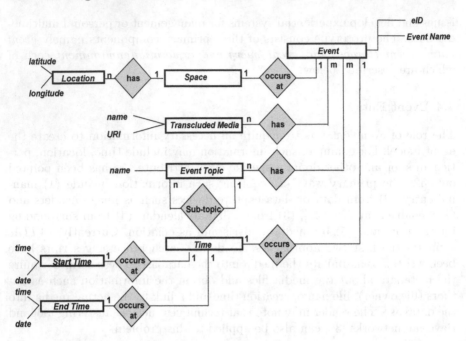

Fig. 4. ER-diagram describing the event-model used for personal multimedia modeling

URL, a foreign key, or an index into a media-specific database (e.g., an image database). Further, additional information such as the media type may also be part of the description of this entity. It may be noted, that the model allows multiple media to support a given event as well as allowing a specific media to support different events.

Representation of participants: In the context of personal media, social information, such as presence of an individual, can play an important role in information organization. This is emphasized by studies such as [32], where it was found that users associate their personal photographs with information on events, location, subject (defined as a combination of *who*, what, when, and where), and time. The entity *Participants* is used to depict such information. It allows, for instance, retrieval of all events (and associated media) where a specific person was present.

Temporal characterization: The entity *Time* is used to model the temporal context of an event. Each event, in the ER-diagram is associated with a start-time and an end-time. In the case of point events, the start-time equals the end-time. It should be noted, that the physical implementation as described by the ER-model implicitly stores the *valid time* associated with events. This is because of the fact that in the contemporary setting many devices used for capturing personal information such as digital cameras (both for still photography and video capture), time-aware audio recorders, and electronic communications such as e-mails and instant messages allow direct and immediate information capture as an event occurs. However, if the domain semantics require keeping track of the *transaction time*, for instance, to have data available only for a specific time period after it has been published, the model can be extended in a manner similar to that used for valid time.

4.6 Event Presentation and Interaction Environment

In *eVITAe*, an integrated multimodal interaction environment is used as a unified presentation–browsing–querying interface. Two views of this environment are presented in Fig. 5 and depict its main components. The system employs direct manipulation techniques [26] to facilitate a natural user–system interaction. In this paradigm, users can directly perform different kinds of operations on items (events) of interest. Furthermore, combining the query and presentation space alleviates the cognitive load from the user's part unlike traditional query environments. Time and space are the primary attributes of the event definition, and hence are depicted as the primary exploration dimensions. Auxiliary panels are used to show the details of the events, and their attributes. Options for zooming, filtering, extraction, viewing relations, and details-on-demand are provided to help users interact with the information space. In the following, we discuss in greater details, the key aspects of the presentation and exploration environment:

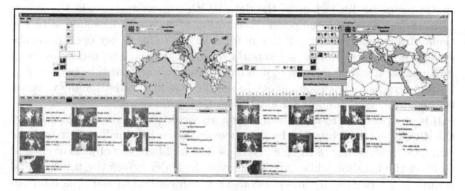

Fig. 5. Two views of the event presentation and exploration environment in *eVITAe*: The screenshot on the left shows the overview of the information. The one on the right shows details of the event on spatial and temporal zoom-in. In both the views the top left pane is the *eventCanvas* where a chronologically ordered view of events is presented. The top right pane is used for visualization and interactions with the spatial aspects of the data. The bottom left pane is called the *mediaDetail-Canvas*. Here, details of the specific media instances supporting an event are shown. Finally, the lower right pane, called the *attributeCanvas*, shows the nonmedia data, such as participant names or event descriptions, associated with a selected event

Event representation: In the *eventCanvas* pane, events are represented through a recursive graphical representation called an *event-plane*. It consists of a rectangle which spans the duration of the event. The media, supporting an event, are represented by icons on the event-plane. Within an event-plane, the icons representing the media are chronologically ordered in terms of their capture times. The recursive nature of the event-plane is used to capture aggregate relationships where an event may comprise of other events. Such relationships, when they exist, are depicted using nested event planes. The primary purpose of such a representation is to provide users with a high-level view of the information that is independent of media specificities. When an event is selected, details about information associated with it such as the supporting media or alphanumeric attributes are automatically brought up in the *mediaDetailCanvas* and the *attributeCanvas* respectively. When a user needs to explore a specific event in detail, the media supporting an event is displayed in the *mediaDetailCanvas* by clicking on the event-plane icon of the corresponding event. When an event is thus selected, any available non-media attributes or alphanumeric meta-data related to it are simultaneously displayed in the *attributeCanvas*. Users have the option to see the actual media by clicking on a media icon in the *eventCanvas*. Selection of a specific media instance via clicking spawns a window which triggers the appropriate application for that particular kind of media.

Interactions with the temporal aspects of information: Events are defined over space and time. The *eVITAe* system not only captures this notion through event modeling, but also provides intuitive ways to visualize the spatio-temporal dimensions of the data. With respect to time, in the *eventCanvas* (see Fig. 5), a temporal distribution of events is presented with the events being ordered chronologically from left to right. A key operation supported in the *eventCanvas* is temporal zooming. Through it, users can zoom into a particular time interval to find more details about that time period (Fig. 5, right screenshot) or zooming out to see the overall distribution of events on the temporal axis. Support for local zooming (zooming within a specific interval) is also provided to allow focusing on a specific period for details, without the display getting cluttered by details over the entire timeline. Further, the semantic fisheye-view technique [29] is used to highlight the objects of current focus in the timeline while the user moves the slider across the timeline and zooms into a particular time interval. User can also select multiple intervals in the timeline, thereby creating multiple foci of the fish eye view.

Interactions with spatial information: Spatial information is displayed in the top-right panel of the *eVITAe* interface (see Fig. 5) and shows the overall distribution of events over space. The spatial display supports option to zoom down to a particular location by dragging a rectangle which contains that location (Fig. 5, right screenshot), and options to zoom out by clicking on the zoom out icon to get an overall picture of the information space. Furthermore, panning of the entire space is also supported. The spatial canvas in *eVITAe* has been implemented using an open source JavaBeans package called OpenMap [5]. A Mercator projection [39], in which meridians and parallels of latitude appear as lines crossing at right angles and areas farther from the equator appear larger, is used to display the various maps.

Interactions with alphanumeric information: The presentation of alphanumeric information such as names of participants in an event or event descriptions is done using the *attributeCanvas*. Queries on events with respect to alphanumeric information can also be issued here. For example, to find all events having a specific participant a user would select the attribute "participants" in the *attributeCanvas* and type the name of the desired participant. The database is then queried for this information and the query results are displayed by highlighting the pertinent events in the *eventCanvas*.

Dynamic and reflective user interface: In a system having multiple simultaneous views of the data, such as *eVITAe* it is important to be able to establish relationships between different views of the dataset, such that any activity in one view is reflected in all the others. Such a capacity is essential for maintaining context as users interact with the information in different manners within each view. In *eVITAe* all the views of the data are tightly coupled through the database. For example, selecting an event in the timeline view leads to that event getting highlighted in the spatial view. Simultaneously, the details of that event are displayed in the *mediaDetailCanvas* and different attributes of the events are brought-up in the *attributeCanvas*. This in conjunction with support for rapid, incremental, and multimodal interactions enables users to explore and "experience" the information from different perspectives.

4.7 Application 2: Business Activity Monitoring Application

Applications such as business activity monitoring (BAM) and homeland security must draw from a large network of disparate data sources, including databases, sensors, and systems in which data is entered manually. The goal of BAM is to allow a unified interface so that a manager can use it to monitor the status of activities at different locations and to analyze the causes of past events. In all such applications, real time data analysis must be combined with real time data assimilation from all sources to present a unified model of the situation in an intuitive form. Techniques and tools developed for traditional database applications, such as payroll databases, are not adequate for this problem because a typical user is interested in exploratory formulations, such as understanding what could be the problem situations and why did they occur. In this context we note that data mining techniques are suitable when a hypothesis has been formed, but tools must first help in generating that hypothesis.

A cornerstone of our approach to this problem has been to create an environment that provides a holistic picture of all available information. By looking at the holistic picture, hypothesis can be formulated and then studied. Towards this we have developed an approach for implementing BAM systems that uses event-based domain model and the metadata to construct a new index that is independent of the data types and data sources. Specific event models have been developed for sales, inventory, and marketing domains. These models draw information from different databases, often from across the world, and unify this data around the domain events for each specific case. The reader may note that data in this problem does not display significant physical heterogeneity. However, the information assimilation challenges remain acute owing to the complexity and logical heterogeneity of the information.

All the events are stored in a database that is called *eventbase*. Similar to the problem of personal information management, the links to all original data or data sources are very important. These links are used to present appropriate media in the context of corresponding events. A strong interactive environment has been developed for users to interact with this system and gain insights through observations and analysis. The advantages of the approach include: (a) pre-processing important information related to events and objects based on domain knowledge, (b) presenting information using domain based visualization, and (c) providing a unified access to all information related to an event in terms of valid time. As an interactive environment for the system, an interface called the *EventViewer* has been developed which offers multidimensional navigational and exploration capabilities. An application screen of the *EventViewer* for the BAM application is shown in Fig. 6.

For an event three basic characteristics are its name and class, the location, and the time. As shown in the top left part of the screen in Fig. 6, a user can navigate through the class ontology hierarchy. Navigation through the location and time dimensions is either through zooming or by moving along different directions using simple natural controls. These traversals are very similar to those in video games. One can select parts of a map ranging from part of a room to the map of the world. Similarly, on the time line, one could be in the range of microseconds to centuries, or even larger scales when required. Once a user selects specific event classes, a region on the map, and a time interval, the system responds by presenting all events (and their selected attributes), satisfying these constraints. This information is presented by using the following three representations: (1) as a list in the space provided for event lists, (2) as symbols displayed on the location map, and (3) as symbols displayed at appropriate time points on the time line. These three representations are tightly linked. For instance, if an item in the list is selected, it gets simultaneously highlighted in the location and time displays. Such an approach to information search is a quintessential example of the WYSIWYG search philosophy.

A major goal of the BAM environment, as mentioned earlier, is to provide an intuitive feel of what events may have occurred and how they are related to other events and information. By presenting events on a map as well as on a time line, the context of the events is maintained and displayed to a

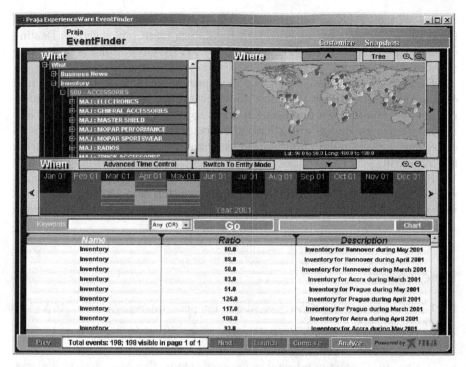

Fig. 6. Screenshot of an *EventViewer* for demand activity monitoring

user. A user can then refine the search criteria and as the criteria are refined, the results change appropriately. This instantaneous feedback allows users to experiment with the data set and develop insights and form hypotheses. When a user is interested in knowing more about a specific event, he or she can explore that event by double clicking on its representation in any of the three display areas. The system then provides all the data sources (like audio, video, or text) related to the selected event.

5 Conclusions

Traditional interface to database systems have been designed under the assumption that their role is to provide precise information as a response to precise queries. This model implicitly assumes that exact queries can be issued to obtain all relevant information. Therefore, such interfaces are not required to be interactive. Homogeneity in data, relatively small data volumes, and strongly structured application domains ensure the success of such information centric approaches. However, the volume and nature of the data being stored in databases today is significantly different than what was common a decade or more ago. Moreover, databases are being used for different roles now; the evolution in technology has put databases in the heart of systems where people seek not just data but information and insights. Dealing efficaciously with this new scenario requires query environments to become more exploratory and interactive.

Towards this, in this chapter, we have presented the idea of experiential environments for facilitating user–data interactions. In this paradigm, information is presented in a manner that seeks to take advantage of the sentient nature of human beings along with their cognitive and sensory abilities to experience and assimilate information. As examples, two experiential systems for supporting user interactions in different application contexts are presented. With the ever increasing availability of heterogeneous, media-rich data and requirements for supporting information assimilation across them, we believe, that the ideas of experiential environments will find active use in both research and development.

References

1. J. Allen. Maintaining Knowledge About Temporal Intervals. *Comm. ACM*, Vol. 26, No. 11, 1983.
2. R. Belew. Finding Out About: A Cognitive Perspective on Search Technology and the WWW. Cambridge University Press, Cambridge, U.K., 2000.
3. D. Barreau. Context as a Factor in Personal Information Management Systems. J. Am. Soc. For Information Science, Vol. 46, No. 5:327-339, 1995.
4. "Log your Life Via Your Phone", March 10, 2004, http://news.bbc.co.uk/2/hi/technology/
5. BBN Technologies. OpenMap - Open Systems Mapping Technology, 1999
6. D. Barreau and B. Nardi. Finding and Reminding: File Organization from the Desktop, *SIGCHI Bulletin* 27, No. 3:39-43, 1995.
7. T. Blum, D. Keislar, J. Wheaton, and E. Wold. Audio Databases with Content-based Retrieval. Proc. IJCAI Workshop on Intelligent Multimedia Information Retrieval, 1995.
8. M. Carey et al. Towards Heterogeneous Multimedia Information Systems: The Garlic Approach. Fifth Int'l Workshop on Research Issues in Data Engineering – Distributed Object Management, 1995.
9. C. Carson, M. Thomas, S. Belongie, J. Hallerstein, and J. Malik. Blobworld: A System for Region-Based Image Indexing and Retrieval, Proc. Int. Conf. on Visual Information, 1999.
10. K. Chakrabarti, K. Porkaew, and S. Mehrotra. Efficient Query Refinement in Multimedia Databases. ICDE, 2000.
11. L. Chen, M. Tamer Özsu, and V. Oria. Modeling Video Data for Content Based Queries: Extending the DISIMA Image Data Model. MMM-2003: 169-189, 2003.
12. N. Dimitrova et al. Applications of Video-Content Analysis and Retrieval. IEEE MultiMedia 9(3): 42-55, 2002.
13. J. D. N. Dionisio and A. Cardenas. A Unified Data Model for Representing Multimedia, Timeline, and Simulation Data", *IEEE Trans. Knowledge and Data Engineering,* Vol. 10, No. 5, 1998.

14. S. Dumais, E. Cutrell, J. Cadiz, G. Jancke, R. Sarin, and D. Robbins. Stuff I've Seen: A System for Personal Information Retrieval and Re-Use, ACM Conf. on Research and Development in Information Retrieval, 2003.
15. R. Elmasri and S. Navathe. *Fundamentals of Database Systems*, Addison-Wesley, 2004.
16. M. Flickner, H. Sawhney, W. Niblack, J. Ashley, Q. Huang, B. Dom, M. Gorkani, J. Hafner, D. Lee, D. Petkovic, D. Steele, and P. Yanker. Query by Image and Video Content: The QBIC System, *IEEE Computer*, 1995.
17. E. Freeman and S. Fertig. Lifestreams: Organizing your electronic life. In AAAI Fall Symposium: AI Applications in Knowledge Navigation and Retrieval, Cambridge, MA, 1995.
18. J. Gemmel, G. Bell, R. Lueder, S. Drucker, and C. Wong. MyLifeBits: fulfilling the Memex vision. *ACM Multimedia*, pp. 235-238, 2002.
19. S. Gibbs, C. Breiteneder, and D. Tsichritzis. Data Modeling of Time-Based Media, *Proc. SIGMOD*, pp. 91-102, 1994.
20. W. I. Grosky, P. Stanchev. An Image Data Model. VISUAL 2000: pp. 14-25, 2000.
21. A. Gupta, T. Weymouth, and R. Jain. Semantic Queries with Pictures: The VIMSYS Model, *Proc. 17th Int'l Conf. on Very Large Databases*, 1991.
22. R. H. Guting and M. Schneider. Realms: A Foundation for Spatial Data Types in Database Systems, *Proc. 3rd Int'l Symp. on Large Spatial Databases*, pp. 14-35, 1993.
23. R. H. Guting. An Introduction to Spatial Database Systems, *VLDB Journal*, Vol.3, No. 4, 1994.
24. L. M. Haas, R. J. Miller, B. Niswonger, M. T. Roth, P. M. Schwarz, E. L. Wimmers. Transforming Heterogeneous Data with Database Middleware: Beyond Integration, *IEEE Data Engineering Bulletin*, 1997.
25. A. Y. Halevy. Answering Queries Using Views: A Survey, *VLDB Journal*, Vol. 10, No. 4, pp. 270-294, 2001.
26. E. L. Hutchins, J. D. Hollan, D. A. Norman. *Direct Manipulation Interfaces, User Centered System Design*. Lawrence Erlbaum Associates, 1986.
27. R. Hull. Managing Semantic Hetrogeneity in Databases: A Theoretical Perspective, ACM Conf. on Principles of Database Systems, pp 51- 61, 1997.
28. R. Jain. Experiential Computing, *Comm ACM*, Vol. 46, No. 7, 2003.
29. P. Janecek and P. Pu. A Framework for Designing Fisheye Views to Support Multiple Semantic Contexts. International Conference on Advanced Visual Interfaces (AVI '02), ACM Press, 2002.
30. P. C. Kanellakis and D. Q. Goldin. Constraint Programming and Database Query Languages, Proc. 2nd Conf. on Theoretical Aspects of Computer Science, 1994.
31. M. Lenzerini. Data Integration: A Theoretical Perspective, Proc. SIGMOD, pp. 233-246, 2002.
32. II. Libermann and H. Liu. Adaptive Linking Between Text and Photos Using Common Sense Reasoning, In Adaptive Hypermedia and Adaptive Web-Based Systems, deBra P, Brusilovsky P, and Conejo R (eds.), Springer-verlag, Berlin, pp. 2-11, 2002.

33. J. Li and M. Ozsu. STARS: A Spatial Attributes Retrieval System for Images and Video, Int'l. Conf. on Multimedia Modeling, pp. 69-84, 1997.
34. T. Little and A. Ghafoor. Interval-Based Conceptual Models for Time-Dependent Multimedia Data. *IEEE Trans. Knowledge and Data Engineering*, Vol. 5, No. 4, pp. 551-563, 1993.
35. J. Luo, E. Savakis, S. Etz, and A. Singhal. On the Application of Bayes Network to Semantic Understanding of Consumer Photographs, ICIP, 2000
36. A. Loui and A. Savakis. utomated Event Clustering and Quality Screening of Consumer Pictures for Digital Albuming. *IEEE Trans. Multimedia*, Vol. 5, No. 3, 2000
37. B. S. Manjunath and W. Y. Ma. Texture Features for Browsing and Retrieval of Image Data. *IEEE Trans. Pattern Analysis and Machine Intelligence*, Vol 18, No 8, pp 837-842, 1996
38. H. Garcia-Molina, J. D. Ullman, J. Widom *Database Systems. The Complete Book*, Prentice Hall, 2002
39. http://science.nasa.gov/Realtime/rocket_sci/orbmech/mercator.html
40. T. Nelson. Xanalogical Structure, Needed Now More Than Ever: Parallel Documents, Deep Links to Context, Deep Versioning, and Deep Re-Use", *ACM Computing Surveys*, Vol. 31, 1999
41. J. Rekimoto. Time-machine computing: a time-centric approach for the information environment", Proceedings of the 12th annual ACM symposium on User interface software and technology, pp. 45 – 54, 1999.
42. http://www.dcviews.com/press/Ricoh_RDC-i700G.htm
43. S. Santini and A. Gupta. Principles of Schema Design for Multimedia Databases. IEEE Trans. On Multimedia, Vol. 4, No. 2, 2002.
44. S. Santini, A. Gupta, and R. Jain. Emergent Semantics Through Interaction In Image Databases, *IEEE Trans. Knowledge and Data Engineering*, Vol. 13, No. 3, pp. 337-351, 2001.
45. S. Shekhar and S. Chawla. *Spatial Databases: A Tour*, Prentice Hall, 2003.
46. H-Y. Shum, M. Liao, S-F. Chang. Advances in Multimedia Information Processing - PCM 2001, *Proc. nd IEEE Pacific Rim Conf. on Multimedia*, 2001.
47. R. Singh, Z. Li, P. Kim, D. Pack, and R. Jain. Event-Based Modeling and Processing of Digital Media, Proc. 1st ACM SIGMOD Workshop on Computer Vision Meets Databases (CVDB), 2004.
48. R. Singh, R. L. Knickmeyer, P. Gupta, and R. Jain. Designing Experiential Environments for Management of Personal Multimedia, *ACM Multimedia*, 2004.
49. H. Sridharan, H. Sundaram, and T. Rikakis. Computational Models for Experiences in the Arts and Multimedia, ETP, 2003.
50. D. Stan, I. K. Sethi. eID: a system for exploration of image databases. Inf. Process. Manage. 39(3): 335-361, 2003.
51. V. S. Subrahmanian. Principles of Multimedia Database Systems, Morgan Kauffman, 1998.
52. K. Toyama, R. Logan, A. Roseway, and P. Anandan. Geographic Location Tags on Digital Images, *ACM Multimedia*, pp. 156-166, 2003.
53. D. C. Tsichritzis and F. H. Lochovsky. Data Models, Prentics-Hall, New Jersey, 1982.

54. G. Widerhold, S. Jajodia, and W. Litwin. Dealing with Granularity of Time in Temporal Databases CAiSE91, pp. 124-140, 1991.
55. E. Wold, T. Blum, D. Keislar, and J. Wheaton. Content-based Classification, Search and Retrieval of Audio IEEE Multimedia, Vol 3, No. 3, pp 27-36, 1996.
56. M. J. Wynblatt. Control Layer Primitives for the Layered Multimedia Data Model, *ACM Multimedia*, 1995.

Modeling and Simulation of Large Biological, Information and Socio-Technical Systems: An Interaction Based Approach

Chris Barrett, Stephen Eubank, and Madhav Marathe

Virginia Polytechnic Institute and State University, Blacksburg, VA, USA.

Summary. We describe an interaction based approach for computer modeling and simulation of large integrated biological, information, social and technical (BIST) systems. Examples of such systems are urban regional transportation systems, the national electrical power markets and grids, gene regulatory networks, the World-Wide Internet, infectious diseases, vaccine design and deployment, theater war, etc. These systems are composed of large numbers of interacting human, physical, informational and technological components. These components adapt and learn, exhibit perception, interpretation, reasoning, deception, cooperation and non-cooperation, and have economic motives as well as the usual physical properties of interaction.

The theoretical foundation of our approach consists of two parts: (i) mathematics of complex interdependent dynamic networks, and (ii) mathematical and computational theory of a class of finite discrete dynamical systems called *Sequential Dynamical Systems* (SDSs). We then consider engineering principles based on such a theory. As with the theoretical foundation, they consist of two basic parts: (i) Efficient data manipulation, including synthesis, integration, storage and regeneration and (ii) high performance computing oriented system design, development and implementation. The engineering methods allow us to specify, design, and analyze simulations of extremely large systems and implement them on massively parallel architectures. As an illustration of our approach, an interaction based computer modeling and simulation framework to study very large interdependent societal infrastructures is described.

1 Introduction

This chapter considers an interaction based approach for modeling and simulation of large scale integrated biological, information, social and technical (henceforth referred to as BIST) systems. BIST systems consist of a large number of interacting physical, biological, technological, informational and human/societal components whose *global system* properties are a result of interactions among representations of *local* system *elements*. Examples of such systems are urban regional transportation systems, national electrical power markets and grids, the Internet, peer to peer networks, ad hoc communication and computing systems, gene regulatory networks, public health, etc. The complicated interdependencies and interactions are inherent within and among constituent BIST systems. This is exemplified by the recent cascading failure of the electric grid in the northeastern United States. Failure of the grid led to cascading effects that slowed down Internet traffic, closed down financial institutions and disrupted the transportation and telecommunication systems.

In the past, mathematical models based on differential equations have often been used to model complex physical and social systems. Although such models are valuable in terms of providing simple first order explanations, they are not particularly useful in providing a generative computer model or a causal explanation of the associated dynamic phenomena. For instance, epidemiologists have traditionally used coupled differential rate equation based models on completely mixed populations to understand the spread of diseases. These simple models provide a good prediction for a number of important epidemiological parameters such as number of sick, infected and recovered individuals in a population. Nevertheless, such epidemiological models have a number of well known shortcomings. They include: an ad hoc value of the reproduction number, the inability to predict anything about the early phase of disease spread, and an inability to account for spatial and demographic diversity in urban populations. Even more important, the models do not provide any causal explanation nor do they lead to a generative computational model. As a result, questions such as identifying potential individuals that can be vaccinated to contain the epidemic are very hard to analyze; see [22, 33, 46] for additional discussion.

Here, we describe an interaction based approach for modeling and simulation of BIST systems. The approach uses an endogenous representation of individual agents together with explicit interaction between these agents to generate and represent the causal ecologies in such systems. The approach was developed over the last 12 years by our group and provides a common framework for three seemingly diverse areas: (i) representation and analysis of large scale distributed BIST systems, (ii) next generation computing architectures, and (iii) associated distributed information and data integration architectures.

The interaction-based approach is based on a mathematical and computational discrete dynamical systems theory called Sequential Dynamical System (SDS). SDSs provide a formal basis for describing complex simulations by composing simpler ones. They are a new class of discrete, finite dynamical systems and emphasize questions of what is being computed by systems of interacting elements, as opposed to the traditional approach of how *hard* it is to compute a given procedure or class. Nevertheless, a traditional Turing machine based approach is used for characterizing the computational complexity of the interacting elements.

We complement the theoretical discussion by describing **Simfrastructure**: a practical microscopic interaction-based modeling framework to study very large interdependent societal infrastructures formed by the interaction between the built urban infrastructure and spatial movement patterns of individuals carrying out their day-to-day activities. Simfrastructure has been used to model extremely large infrastructures consisting of millions of interacting agents consisting of more than 10 million individual elements. For example, the transportation module within Simfrastructure can represent every individual in the Chicago region at a temporal resolution of 1 second, and a spatial resolution of approximately 7 meters. This region spans approximately 250 square miles and has more than 400 counties. There are more than 9 million individuals taking roughly 25 million trips each day. The time varying social contact network consists of more than 25 million edges and vertices. The size, scope and multiple time scales of system representation naturally motivates a high performance computing implementation and requires new engineering design principles. Individual modules of this system routinely run on clusters comprised of 128 nodes; several of the individual simulations are also being executed on 1000+ node systems.

1.1 Relationship to Interactive Computing

There are at least two reasons why the topic of computer modeling and simulation of large BIST systems is pertinent to interactive computation. First, as discussed above, interaction based computer models are natural and the only way to represent and comprehend the complex dynamics of many BIST systems. In the past, computer simulation of physical phenomenon has been a key driver in the development of current high performance computing systems. Our view is that interaction based modeling and simulation of BIST systems will serve as a key driver for the development of next generation interactive computing platforms. Second, and perhaps more pertinent to this book, we believe that an interaction based modeling of BIST systems will yield new mathematical and computational techniques that advance the state of the art of interactive computation. Recently, computer scientists have proposed automata theoretic models, programming languages, and calculi that attempt to treat interaction, as an atomic element of computation. Several chapters in the book address these topics in detail. BIST systems naturally display many attributes of interactive computing such as providing a service rather than solving a specific algorithmic task, inclusion of environment within the computational representation, etc. Thus a deeper understanding of these inherent properties of BIST systems will provide new ideas for developing a interactive computing

To further appreciate this, consider for example interdependent societal infrastructure systems spanning large urban areas. They are the center of economic, commercial and social activities. The design of these urban areas, their rapid population growth, and sharing of the limited resources by their inhabitants has led to increased social interactions [47, 8]. Large scale information delivery, and access systems developed by today's computing companies such as Google, Yahoo, Akamai, etc. are examples of emerging socio-technical information infrastructure systems. Such regional and global scale infrastructure systems are spatially distributed, managed by different federal, state, and commercial entities and operate at multiple time scales. Despite this heterogeneity, based on certain basic economic and legal principles, these interdependent systems usually work seamlessly to provide uninterrupted services to the millions of individuals residing in the urban region. Under any reasonable definition, these are complex systems whose global behavior is a result of complicated interactions between constituent elements. For example, the spatial distribution of individuals in an urban region, their movement patterns, and their phone-calling patterns, all have a direct bearing on the structure and the design of wire-line and wireless telecommunication networks. A systematic understanding of such systems must therefore be able to represent the complex interdependencies between individual constituent elements and their dynamics. The focus is on understanding consequences of certain decisions or representing the interactions between individuals and the infrastructures rather than solving specific algorithmic question. The constituent BIST systems (e.g., transportation and urban populations) are tightly coupled and co-evolve: they are naturally viewed as large population ecologies. Computational models developed to represent these systems will necessarily have to clarify the role of interaction between constituent elements and the environment. This includes questions of what is being computed, the meaning and role of environment and acceptance of nondeterminism as an elementary phenomenon.

1.2 Organization

The remainder of the chapter is organized as follows. Section 2 contains basic definitions and preliminary results. In Sect. 3, we discuss the theoretical foundations of interaction based simulation and modeling of BIST systems. Section 4 contains a discussion of the engineering principles necessary for design and implementation of large BIST system simulations. In Sect. 5 a practical operational system based on the theoretical and engineering foundations described in Sect. 3.1 – 4 is discussed. Finally, Sect. 6 contains concluding remarks and directions for future work.

2 Terminology and Preliminary Results

Informally, computer simulation is the art and science of using computers to calculate interactions and transactions among many separate algorithmic representations, each of which might be associated with identifiable "things" in the real world (at least in a world outside the simulation program). Because of the widespread use of computer simulations, it is difficult to give a precise definition of a computer simulation that is applicable to all the various settings where it is used. Nevertheless, it is clear that simulation has two essential aspects: dynamics generation and mimicry of the dynamics of another system by the dynamics of the simulation program. Thus we view simulations as comprised of the following: (i) a collection of entities with state values and local rules for state transitions, (ii) an interaction graph capturing the local dependency of an entity on its neighboring entities, and (iii) an update sequence or schedule such that the causality in the system is represented by the composition of local mappings.

A **Sequential Dynamical System** (SDS) $\mathcal{S}$ over a given domain $\mathbb{D}$ of state values is a triple $(G, \mathcal{F}, \pi)$, whose components are as follows:

1. $G(V, E)$ is a finite undirected graph without multiedges or self loops. G is referred to as the **underlying graph** of $\mathcal{S}$. We use n to denote $|V|$ and m to denote $|E|$. The nodes of G are numbered using the integers 1, 2, ..., n.
2. For each node i of G, $\mathcal{F}$ specifies a *local transition function*, denoted by f_i. This function maps $\mathbb{D}^{\delta_i+1}$ into $\mathbb{D}$, where δ_i is the degree of node i. Letting $N(i)$ denote the set consisting of node i itself and its neighbors, each input of f_i corresponds to a member of $N(i)$.
3. Finally, π is a permutation of $\{1, 2, \ldots, n\}$ specifying the order in which nodes update their states using their local transition functions. Alternatively, π can be envisioned as a total order on the set of nodes.

A *configuration* $\mathcal{C}$ of $\mathcal{S}$ can be interchangeably regarded as an n-vector $(c_1, c_2, \ldots, c_n)$, where each $c_i \in \mathbb{D}$, $1 \leq i \leq n$, or as a function $\mathcal{C} : V \rightarrow \mathbb{D}$.

Computationally, each step of an SDS (i.e., the transition from one configuration to another), involves n substeps, where the nodes are processed in the *sequential* order specified by permutation π. The "processing" of a node consists of computing the value of the node's local transition function and changing its state to the computed value. The following pseudocode shows the computations involved in one transition.

---

for $i = 1$ **to** n **do**
  (i) Node $\pi(i)$ evaluates $f_{\pi(i)}$. This computation uses the *current* values of the state of node $\pi(i)$ and those of the neighbors of node $\pi(i)$. Let x denote the value computed.
  (ii) Node $\pi(i)$ sets its state $s_{\pi(i)}$ to x.
end-for

We use $F_{\mathcal{S}}$ to denote the *global transition function* associated with $\mathcal{S}$. This function can be viewed either as a function that maps $\mathbb{D}^n$ into $\mathbb{D}^n$ or as a function that maps $\mathbb{D}^V$ into $\mathbb{D}^V$. $F_{\mathcal{S}}$ represents the transitions between configurations, and can therefore be considered as defining the dynamic behavior of SDS $\mathcal{S}$. A **fixed point** of an SDS $\mathcal{S}$ is a configuration $\mathcal{C}$ such that $F_\mathcal{S}(\mathcal{C}) = \mathcal{C}$.

The **phase space** $\mathcal{P}_\mathcal{S}$ of an SDS $\mathcal{S}$ is a directed graph defined as follows: There is a node in $\mathcal{P}_\mathcal{S}$ for each configuration of $\mathcal{S}$. There is a directed edge from a node representing configuration $\mathcal{C}$ to that representing configuration $\mathcal{C}'$ if $F_\mathcal{S}(\mathcal{C}) = \mathcal{C}'$.

It is possible to obtain restricted versions of SDSs by appropriately restricting the domain $\mathbb{D}$ and/or the local transition functions. We use the notation "(x, y)-SDS" to denote an SDS where "x" specifies the restriction on the domain and "y" specifies the restriction on the local transition functions. Thus for example, (BOOL, SYM)-SDS are SDS in which domain of state values is Boolean and each local transition function is symmetric. (BOOL, THRESH)-SDS are SDSs in which the domain of state values is Boolean and each local transition function is a simple-threshold function. And finally, (BOOL, NOR)-SDS are SDSs in which domain of state values is Boolean and each local transition function is the NOR function. A **Synchronous Dynamical System** (SyDS), is a special kind of SDS, *without* node permutations. In a SyDS, during each time step, all the nodes *synchronously* compute and update their state values. Thus, SyDSs are similar to classical CA with the difference that the connectivity between cells is specified by an arbitrary graph. The restrictions on domain and local transition functions for SDSs are applicable to SyDSs as well.

Example 1. Consider a (BOOL, NOR)-SDS shown in Fig. 1 (left). Let $\pi = (a, b, c)$. Each node a, b and c execute the local function $NOR(x, y, z)$. Phase space associated with the dynamical system when vertices are updated in the order a,b and c is shown in Fig. 1 (right). Each tuple in the ellipse denotes the states of the nodes a, b and c in that order. Notice that the phase space does not have a fixed point. It turns out that SDS with NOR local functions can never have fixed points.

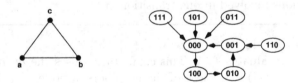

Fig. 1. Figure illustrating SDS and its phase space described in Example 1

SDSs naturally capture the three essential elements of a computer simulation. The use of simple functions to represent each agent/entity is just an equivalent alternate representation of each individual as automata. The fact that each function depends locally on the state values of neighboring agents is intended to capture the intuition that individual objects comprising a real system usually have only local knowledge about the system. Finally, a permutation is an abstraction of the need to *explicitly* encode causal dependency.

The basic SDS model can easily be generalized in a number of ways including: (i) partial orders or schedules specified using formal languages, (ii) allowing stochastic local functions or interaction graphs, (iii) time varying SDS in which the topology or the local functions vary/evolve in time. These generalizations are important while modeling realistic BIST systems; see [7, 37, 54, 45, 52, 53] for additional details and examples.

Computational SDS (cSDS) arise naturally when each local function is viewed procedurally. cSDS are useful for formal specification, and analysis of infrastructure simulation systems and extend the algebraic theory of dynamical systems in two important ways. First, we pass from extremely general structural and analytical properties of composed local maps to issues of provable implementation of SDS in computing architectures and specification of interacting local symbolic procedures. This is related to successive reductions of cSDS to procedural primitives, which leads to a notion of cSDS-based distributed simulation compilers with provable simulated dynamics (e.g., for massively parallel or grid computation). Second, the aggregate behavior of iterated compositions of local maps that comprise an SDS can be understood as a (specific) simulated algorithm together with its associated and inherent computational complexity. We have called this the *algorithmic semantics* of an SDS (equivalently, the algorithmic semantics of a dynamical system or a simulation). It is particularly important to view a composed dynamical system as computing a specifiable algorithm with provable time and space performance.

2.1 SDSs as Elementary Models of Interactive Computation

The basic definition of SDS together with the above generalizations form an elementary model of interactive computation. The introductory chapter in this book identifies four distinguishing features of interactive computing, namely

- Computational Problem: A computational problem entails performing a task or providing a service, rather than algorithmically producing an answer to a question
- Observable Behavior: A computing component is now modeled not as a functional transformation from input to output, but rather in terms of an observable behavior consisting of interaction steps
- Environments: The world or environment of the computation is part of the model, playing an active part in the computation by dynamically supplying the computational system, or agent, with the inputs, and consuming the output values from the system. The environment cannot be assumed to be static, or even effectively computable; for example, it may include humans or other elements of the real world
- Concurrency: Computation is concurrent; the computing agent computes in parallel with its environment and with other agents that may be in it

SDS and its extensions adequately captures these four essential and distinguishing features and can be used to model practical BIST systems. The following example illustrates this point.

Example 2. **TRANSIMS** is a large-scale Federal Highway Administration (FHWA) funded transportation simulation project [9] that we co-developed over the last 10 years. In this project, an SDS-based approach was used to microsimulate every vehicle in an urban transportation network (see [82] for an SDS specification). Each roadway is divided into discrete cells. Each cell is 7.5 meters long and one lane wide. Each cell contains either a vehicle (or a part of a vehicle) or is empty. The microsimulation is carried out in discrete time steps with each step simulating one second of real traffic. In each time step, a vehicle on the network makes decisions such as accelerate, brake or change lanes, in response to the occupancy of the neighboring cells. We can represent the above model using the SDS framework. For ease of exposition, we assume a single lane circular road that can be modeled as a one dimensional array of cells. In this representation, each cell represents a 7.5 meter segment of the road. The variable *gap* is used to measure the number of empty cells between a car and the car ahead of it. In the following, let v denote the speed of the vehicles in number of cells per unit time, $v_{\max}$ denote the maximum speed and *rand* as a random number between 0 and 1. Finally, p_{noise} denotes the probability with which a vehicle is slowed by 1 unit. Each iteration consists of the following three sequential rules that are applied in parallel to all the cars:

1. Acceleration of free vehicles: **If** $v < v_{\max}$, **Then** $v = v + 1$.
2. Braking due to cars in front: **If** $v > gap$, **Then** $v = gap$.
3. Stochastic Jitter: **If** $(v > 0)$ **AND** $(rand < p_{\text{noise}})$, **Then** $v = v - 1$.

To illustrate how an SDS based model can be constructed, let us consider a simple circular one lane road. One vehicle occupies one cell and has a given velocity. Let us assume that a vehicle can travel at one of three velocities: 0, 1 and 2. There are m vehicles and their initial positions are chosen at random. They are labeled 1 through m by the order in which they initially appear on the road. There is a schedule π that determines the update ordering. A vehicle at cell i with speed v is updated as shown in Table 1. This defines the local function at a node in the time evolving graph. Thus a vehicle at cell i with speed 1 that has two free cells ahead moves one cell ahead and gets the new speed of 2. At each time step t we can derive the associated dependency graph $G(t)$. The graph $G(t)$ has vertices $1, 2, \ldots, m$ corresponding to the vehicles. Two vehicles k and l are connected by an edge if the distance between them at time t is less than or equal to $v_{\max} = 2$. If the distance is larger they are independent by construction. (A vehicle only depends on what is ahead on the road.) Thus, for the configuration in Fig. 2, we derive the dependency graph shown in Fig. 2.

Table 1. The update rule for a single vehicle

(Cell,Speed)	$i+1$ taken	$i+1$ free, $i+2$ taken	$i+1$, $i+2$ free
$(i,0)$	$(i,0)$	$(i,1)$	$(i,2)$
$(i,1)$	$(i,0)$	$(i+1,1)$	$(i+1,2)$
$(i,2)$	$(i,0)$	$(i+1,1)$	$(i+2,2)$

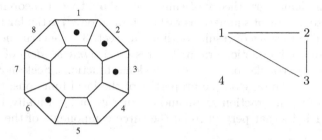

Fig. 2. A circular one-lane road divided into cells. A dot indicates that the given cell is occupied by a vehicle. The dependency graph $G(t=0)$ associated to configuration to the left is shown to the right

Discussion

- The computational problem at hand is to represent traffic dynamics in a city. There is no explicit algorithmic description of this problem. Traffic is an *emergent* or *simulated* property. As discussed in [70, 76], traffic can be viewed as a chaotic system and thus even its simple properties are unlikely to be *predictable*.
- The description of the driver is not merely contained in the local rules, but is obtained via composing the time varying explicit interactions with other drivers. This notion of disaggregated normative agent is discussed further in Sect. 4.1. Moreover, this interaction is dynamic and the neighborhood changes all the time. In other words, the environment is not static. The driver interacts continually with the environment and co-evolves with it.
- The computation is inherently concurrent. The update order chosen is important. For instance, in the case of the single-lane system, updating the states from front to back acts like a perfect predictor and thus never yields clusters of vehicles. On the other hand, updating from back to front yields more realistic traffic dynamics [68, 70, 76].

The complete **TRANSIMS** system is described in Sect. 5 and models a number of other interesting features, including activity based traffic modeling, game theoretic behavior of individual travelers, co-evolution and effects of large scale transformational changes such as building new highways. The above example describes a simplified version of one of the **TRANSIMS** modules and is intended to convey the richness inherent in such systems. Nevertheless, the example drives the main point: SDSs and its extensions can serve as elementary models of interactive computation.

3 Theoretical Foundations

We describe an elementary theory of interaction based simulations abstracted as SDS. An elementary theory of simulation should yield theorems that are applicable to a class of simulations rather than to only particular members of this class. The first set of results outlined in Sect. 3.1 concern the structural properties of the interaction graph. The results are *independent* of the update order and the particular properties of the local functions. Section 3.2 outlines results that depend only on the properties of the local functions; they are independent of the interaction graph and the update order. Finally, in Sect. 3.3, we discuss results that pertain to all the three components of the definition.

3.1 Effect of BIST Network

Recently there has been a resurgence of research in complex networks, driven by a number of empirical and theoretical studies showing that network structure plays a crucial role in understanding the overall behavior of complex systems. See [23, 5, 2, 28, 33, 35, 34, 39, 71, 83] and the references therein for recent results in this active area. Another recent direction of research has been to determine random graph models that can generate such networks. Unfortunately, many of these random graph models, such as the preferential attachment model, are not suited for social network analysis.

Construction of BIST Networks Construction of BIST networks is challenging: in some cases data is easily available to construct the networks, while in the majority of other cases, although such data exists, it is not freely available. In yet other cases, the network has to be constructed by integrating a number of different databases. Finally, in case of social and ad hoc networks, it is impossible at the current time to gather enough data to construct such networks. Thus simulation based tools are required for generating such networks. We describe two networks here: the social contact network and the mobile ad hoc network. One is a social network, the other is formed by social interactions and the links are really a matter of convention, but nevertheless is best classified as a infrastructure network. Important examples of other BIST networks that have to be constructed by integrating various information sources and simulations include the route level IP network, the gene annotation networks and protein–protein interaction networks.

Example 3. Consider a social network that captures the interaction between individuals moving through an urban region [33, 7]. This information can be abstractly represented by a (vertex and edge) labeled bipartite graph G_{PL}, where P is the set of people and L is the set of locations. If a person $p \in P$ visits a location $l \in L$, there is an edge $(p, \ell, label) \in E(G_{PL})$ between them, where $label$ is a record of the type of activity of the visit and its start and end points. Each vertex (person or location) can also have labels. A person's various labels correspond to his/her demographic attributes such as age, income, etc. The labels attached to locations specify the location's attributes such as its x and y coordinates, the type of activity performed, maximum capacity, etc. Note that there can be multiple edges between a person and a location recording different visits. Figure 3 shows an example of a bipartite graph. Part (a) of Fig. 3 shows an example of a bipartite people-location graph G_{PL} with two types of vertex representing four people (P) denoted by filled circles and four locations (L), denoted by squares. Figure 3 parts (b) and (c), show two distinct projections of the basic network that can be defined and constructed from this information. The graphs G_P and G_L induced by G_{PL}. G_P is the temporal people–people–spatial-proximity graph. It connects two individuals by edges if they were in spatial proximity during some time of the day. G_L is the building–building temporal graph. Two buildings are joined by an edge in a time period if an individual left one of the buildings in that period and arrived at the other building in the same time-period. Figure 3 part (d) shows the static projections of G_P^S and G_L^S resulting from ignoring time labels.

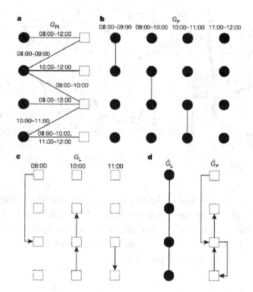

Fig. 3. Figure depicting a social contact network described in Example 3. (a) shows the bipartite graph G_{PL}. (b) and (c) show two distinct temporal projections of G_{PL}, namely G_P and G_L and (d) shows the static projections G_P^S and G_L^S resulting from ignoring time labels

We point out that simulations appear to be the only way to construct such networks. Contrast this with the electrical grid: although it might be hard to obtain the data, the data certainly exists with government agencies and private companies.

Example 4. A synthetic vehicular ad hoc telecommunication network is obtained by assigning one or more wireless devices to drivers, vehicles and other individuals in an urban region. Each vertex in the ad hoc telecommunication network corresponds to a transceiver and two nodes are joined by an edge if and only if they are within each other's radio range. Note that to construct such a network, one needs the following: a detailed time varying location of transceivers, information on the characteristics of the transceiver and time varying activity related to the transceiver (on and off patterns). Again, as in the case of social contact networks, it is hard to get data for such networks and simulation based data integration and creation methods appear to be necessary. We used the section of downtown Portland, Oregon, shown in Fig. 4 for illustration. More details on the structural properties of realistic vehicular ad hoc networks can be found in [13, 14, 25].

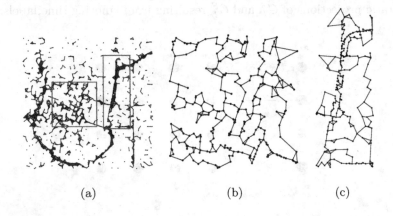

(a)   (b)   (c)

Fig. 4. Versions of an ad hoc telecommunication network formed by assigning transceivers to individuals in cars on a section of Portland road network discussed in Example 4. (a) Network topology when all the transceivers were assigned the same power. (b) and (c) show parts of the network when power control algorithms in [58] were applied to reduce the overall interference

Important Notes:

- Notice how various components of network constructions played a role in the above examples. In Example 3, the underlying population and the infrastructure remained invariant. We simply varied the interaction criteria.

In Example 4, the synthetic individuals had to be endowed with additional attributes such as a mobile wireless device. The interaction criteria is different and is defined with respect to the wireless device and is in this case the radio range of the individual transceivers (transmitter and a receiver).

- The two networks have differing levels of fidelity in terms of temporal evolution. In Example 3, if the intended application is disease propagation, then time scales could be relatively large, on the order of minutes to hours. In contrast, the telecommunication ad hoc network formed needs to be represented and computed at extremely small time scales (milliseconds), since loss in radio range implies loss in data packets. Notice that as society becomes ever more digital, social networks can more appropriately be defined not only over individuals but also over digital devices capable of handling specific tasks.

- While we have not elaborated it here, individual transceivers can choose to send messages to other specific transceivers (e.g., text messages on a phone): this yields yet another social network with communication devices as nodes and an edge between two devices when they send a message to each other. Such a network rides on the top of the rapidly evolving communication network that is described here.

Measurement and Analysis of BIST networks Once a complex network is constructed, we study the following interrelated questions: (i) discovering new measures that provide information about the network's structure and dynamics, and (ii) fast and provable algorithms for computing network measures over very large social and infrastructure networks. Some important observations based on results in [14, 33, 34, 35] include: (i) Social and infrastructure networks are not necessarily scale free or small world networks [33, 34, 35], (ii) structural measures for real infrastructure and social networks are often different from similar measures for classical random networks, and (iii) social networks have high local clustering. In contrast, many physical networks such as power and transport networks have very low clustering coefficient.

We illustrate the range of static analysis by describing important structural results pertaining to social contact networks such as the ones described in Example 3. See [33, 34, 35] for a more comprehensive discussion on this subject. In the bipartite graph G_{PL} for the city of Portland, there are 1615 860 (1.6 million) individuals, 181 230 (181K) locations, and 6060 679 (6.1 million) edges. Figure 5(a) and (b) shows the degree distributions of the locations and people in the bipartite graph, G_{PL} for the Portland data. Note that a large part of the degree sequence of locations follows a power-law distribution, i.e., $n_k \propto k^{-\beta}$, where n_k denotes the number of locations of degree k; for the Portland data, $\beta \approx 2.8$. The degree distribution of people is roughly Poisson. The degree sequence of people in the people-people graph G_P is shown in Fig. 5(c) and looks quite different than the degree sequence of G_{PL}. The graph G_P for Portland is not fully connected, but has a giant component with

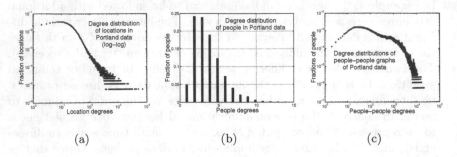

(a)   (b)   (c)

Fig. 5. (a) and (b) Degree distributions of locations and people in the bipartite graph G_{PL} for Portland data. The location degrees range from 1 to 7091, people degrees range from 1 to 15. (c) Degree distribution of people–people graph projection obtained from the original bipartite graph

1 615 813 people. The clustering coefficient p of G_P: it is about 0.57 which is substantially higher than clustering coefficients for infrastructure networks.

Next, we describe two structural measures that provide further evidence into how *well connected* today's urban social networks are. First, consider graph expansion. We consider the two standard notions of expansion in the graph G_P. The edge expansion of a subset $S \subseteq P$ is defined as the ratio

$$\frac{|\{e = (u,v) : (u,v) \text{ is an edge and } u \in S, v \notin S\}|}{|S|}.$$

The vertex expansion of a subset $S \subseteq P$ is defined as the ratio $|\{u \notin S : (u,v) \text{ is an edge and } v \in S\}|/|S|$. The edge (vertex, respectively) expansion of G_P is the minimum, taken over all $S \subset P, |S| \leq |P|/2$, of the edge (vertex, respectively) expansion of S. The vertex and edge expansions are important graph-theoretic properties that capture fault-tolerance, speed of data dissemination in the network, etc. Roughly, the higher the expansion, the quicker the spread of any phenomena (disease, gossip, data, etc.) along the links of the network. Random sampling based estimates of vertex and edge expansion are shown in Fig. 6. The Y-axis plots the smallest expansion value found among the 500 000 independent samples; the X-axis plots the set size S as a percentage of the total number of vertices in the graph (the sampling probability). The plots labeled "Vertex expansion-2" and "Edge expansion-2" in Fig. 6 show the expansion in the graph G_P, while the plots marked "Vertex expansion-1" and "Edge expansion-1" show the same quantity on a sparser people-people graph—the graph is made sparser by only retaining edges between individuals who came in contact for at least one hour. The graphs make two points: (i) as expected expansion becomes smaller as the contact graph gets sparser, and (ii) even for sparse contact networks the expansion values are quite high.

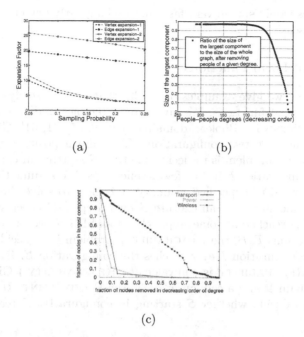

(a)   (b)

(c)

Fig. 6. (a) Expansion of the people–people graph: the plots marked "Vertex expansion-2" and "Edge expansion-2" show the vertex and edge expansion for the graph G_P, while "Vertex expansion-1" and "Edge expansion-1" show the corresponding quantities in the graph obtained by retaining only those edges that involve an interaction of at least 1 hour. This leads to a much sparser graph and correspondingly lower values of vertex and edge expansions. (b) Plots showing the relative ease with which we can break infrastructure networks by removing nodes of high connectivity. (c) In contrast to (b), figure (c) shows that urban social networks are very hard to shatter

Another important structural measure (informally called *shattering*) is to determine the ability to disconnect a social or an infrastructure network by removing high connectivity nodes. Figure 6(b) and (c) show these plots for three infrastructure networks and urban social networks respectively. Notice the remarkable difference between the plots: they show that while infrastructure networks are prone to targeted failures, social networks are very robust. Targeted failures correspond to removal of high degree nodes. For social networks, this corresponds to removing individuals by quarantining or vaccinating them in case of epidemics, with large number of social contacts. This connectivity property of the social network turns out to be the *Achilles heel*: while strong connectivity is important for the day-to-day functioning of the social system, it is a weakness in controlling the spread of infectious diseases. In other words, The high expansion and inability to shatter social networks implies that contagious diseases would spread very fast, and making early detection imperative to control disease.

3.2 Effect of Local Functions

In this section, we give examples of results that depend solely on the properties of the local functions. We give three examples and restrict ourselves to local functions with Boolean domains; see [19, 15, 21, 51]. Given an SDS S over a domain $\mathbb{D}$, two configurations $\mathcal{I}$, $\mathcal{B}$, and a positive integer t, the t-REACHABILITY problem is to decide whether S starting in configuration $\mathcal{I}$ will reach configuration $\mathcal{B}$ in t or fewer time steps. We assume that t is specified in binary. (If t is specified in unary, it is easy to solve this problem in polynomial time since we can execute S for t steps and check whether configuration $\mathcal{B}$ is reached at some step.) Given an SDS S over a domain $\mathbb{D}$ and two configurations $\mathcal{I}$, $\mathcal{B}$, the REACHABILITY problem is to decide whether S starting in configuration $\mathcal{I}$ ever reaches the configuration $\mathcal{B}$. (Note that, for $t \geq |\mathbb{D}|^n$, t-REACHABILITY is equivalent to REACHABILITY.) Given an SDS S over a domain $\mathbb{D}$ and a configuration $\mathcal{I}$, the FIXED POINT REACHABILITY problem is to decide whether S starting in configuration $\mathcal{I}$ reaches a fixed point.

1. The REACHABILITY and t-REACHABILITY problems are solvable in polynomial time for (BOOL, NOR)-SDSs for which the number of independent sets in the underlying graph is polynomial. For any (BOOL, NOR)-SDS, every transient in the phase space is of length 1 and the phase space does not have fixed points.

2. Given an n-node (FINRING, LINEAR)-SDS S over a finite domain $\mathbb{D}$, the FIXED POINT REACHABILITY problem for S can be solved using a number of algebraic operations that is polynomial in n and $|\mathbb{D}|$. When the domain $\mathbb{D}$ is Boolean and the operators of the unitary semi-ring are OR (+) and AND (*), each linear local transition function is either XOR (exclusive or) or XNOR (the complement of exclusive or). Thus, the FIXED POINT REACHABILITY problem for such SDSs can be solved efficiently.

3. Let $S = (G, \mathcal{F}, \pi)$ be a (BOOL, THRESH)-SDS whose underlying graph G has n nodes and m edges. From any initial configuration $\mathcal{I}$, S reaches a fixed point after at most $\lfloor (m + n + 1)/2 \rfloor$ steps. Thus, t-REACHABILITY, REACHABILITY and FIXED POINT REACHABILITY problems for (BOOL, THRESH)-SDSs can be solved in polynomial time.

3.3 Composite Analysis of SDS

Finally, we consider examples of composite analysis of SDS. Following [17], we say that a system is predictable if basic phase space properties such as reachability and fixed point reachability can be determined in time which is polynomial in the size of the system specification. It can be shown that very simple SDSs are computationally universal for the appropriate space/time complexity class (see [15, 21]). For example there exist constants d_2, p_2 and n_2 such that the t-REACHABILITY, REACHABILITY and FIXED POINT REACHABILITY problems for (BOOL, SYM)-SDSs are **PSPACE**-hard, even when all of the following restrictions hold: (a) The maximum node degree in the underlying graph is bounded by d_2. (b) The pathwidth (and hence the treewidth) of the underlying graph is bounded by p_2. (c) The number of distinct local transition functions used is bounded by n_2.

Due to the particular proof technique used, these results naturally extend to yield general computational universality. For instance, we show that the reachability problem for *very simple* SDS (e.g., SDS in which the domain of state values is Boolean and each node computes the same symmetric Boolean function) is **PSPACE**-hard: this implies that the systems are not easily predictable. In fact, the results imply that no prediction method is likely to be more efficient than running the simulation itself. By allowing an exponential memory at each node or allowing exponentially many nodes, one can obtain **EXPSPACE**-hardness results. An important implication of this (stated informally) is the following: *the optimal computational strategies for determining the structural properties of such complex dynamical systems are interaction based simulations.* Moreover the systems for which the hardness results hold are so simple (essentially, local transition functions can be simple threshold or inverted thresholds) that any realistic socio-technical system is likely to have such systems embedded in them. See [17, 66, 40, 85] for additional discussion on this topic.

As another illustration of the general complexity theoretic results that can be obtained as regards to SDSs, we consider the predecessor existence problem. Given an SDS S and a configuration C, the PREDECESSOR EXISTENCE (or PRE) problem (a.k.a pre-image existence problem) is to determine whether there is a configuration C' such that S has a transition from C' to C. Apart from the decision version, we also consider the problems of counting the number of predecessors (the counting version, denoted by #-PREDECESSOR EXISTENCE), deciding if there is a unique predecessor (the unique version, denoted by UNIQUE-PREDECESSOR EXISTENCE) and if there are two predecessors of the given configuration (the ambiguous version, denoted by AMBIGUOUS-PREDECESSOR EXISTENCE). Using the concept of *simultaneous local reductions*, it is possible to obtain results that simultaneously characterize the complexity of the PREDECESSOR EXISTENCE, #-PREDECESSOR EXISTENCE, UNIQUE-PREDECESSOR EXISTENCE and AMBIGUOUS-PREDECESSOR EXISTENCE problems for SDS and SyDS. The results are summarized in Fig. 7 and are proved in [20]. These are local transformations that simultaneously yield the hardness for decision, counting, unique and ambiguous versions of the problem. Such a reduction allows us to tightly relate the computational complexity of these problems; see [30, 49, 50] for more discussion on simultaneous local reductions. The easiness results are obtained using generic algorithms that exploit the underlying structure of the interaction graph and the seman-

The PRE problem is **NP**-complete for the following restricted classes of SDSs. In most cases, the #-PREDECESSOR EXISTENCE problem is #**P**-complete, the AMBIGUOUS-PREDECESSOR EXISTENCE problem is **NP**-complete and UNIQUE-PREDECESSOR EXISTENCE problem is **D^P**-complete (using randomized reductions).

1. **Identical and/or restricted class of functions:**
   a) (BOOL, THRESH)-SDSs where each node computes the same k-simple-threshold function for any $k \geq 2$,
   b) (BOOL, TALLY)-SDSs in which each node computes the same k-tally function for any $k \geq 1$,
2. **Restricted graphs:**
   a) SDSs over the Boolean domain where at most one local transition function is not symmetric and the underlying graph is a *star*,
   b) SDSs over the Boolean domain and the underlying graph is a *grid*,
   c) (BOOL, SYM)-SDSs whose underlying graphs are *planar*.

The PRE problem is in **P** for the following classes of SDSs.

1. for (FIELD, LINEAR)-SDSs, (BOOL, AND)-SDSs and (BOOL, OR)-SDSs with no restrictions on the underlying graph,
2. for (BOOL, SYM)-SDSs when underlying graphs have bounded treewidth,
3. for SDSs when underlying graph is simultaneously bounded degree and and bounded treewidth with no restriction on the local transition functions (other than that the functions are over finite domain).

Fig. 7. Example of complexity theoretic results that can be proven for special classes of SDS. Note the interplay between the graph structure and function complexity. Although the results are shown only for PRE problem and its variants, it is possible to obtain similar results for other problems such as Garden of Eden states, etc. These results also imply analogous results for Discrete Hopfield networks, concurrent transition systems and other related models

tics of the local transition functions. The algorithms are generic in the sense that the same basic algorithm can be used to compute solution to the decision, counting, ambiguous and unique versions of the problem by merely supplying the appropriate semantics for the semi-ring operations that are carried out; see [80].

3.4 Formal Specifications and Local Simulation Compliers

Discrete dynamical systems are a natural mathematical language for formally specifying large scale interacting systems. Recently SDS and abstract state machines (ASM)[1] have been used for formally specifying the several modules of the telecommunication system [24, 59]. Ideally, we would like to express the BIST systems using *higher level SDSs*, i.e., SDSs with more expressive

---

[1] See http://www.eecs.umich.edu/gasm/.

local functions and interaction networks. In contrast, *simpler* SDSs, i.e., SDSs with less expressive local functions and regular interaction networks are likely to be more suitable for finding efficient mappings of the SDSs on HPC architectures. This is because the language (model) that is most convenient to describe the underlying system might not necessarily be the best model for actual simulation of the system on a HPC architecture. Thus it is conceivable that such simpler systems obtained via translation could be mapped on HPC architectures and the resulting maps could be analyzed for performance bottlenecks. Simpler systems can potentially also be used to verify the correctness of the ensuing protocols. To achieve this, such translations should be efficient and preserve the basic properties across the original and the translated system. The constructions given as part of the simulation results in [19, 21] can be viewed as *local simulation compilers* that transform one type of SDS to a simpler kind of SDS in such a way that (i) the translation is local and efficient and (ii) relevant features of the phase space of the original SDS are captured appropriately in the phase space of the simpler SDS. In recent years (see [40, 85, 42, 63] and the references therein), several authors have suggested building *cellular automata based computers* for simulating physics. We believe that *SDS based computers* are better suited for simulating BIST systems. In [62], Margolus proposes a DRAM based architecture for large scale spatial lattice computations, also see DeHon [32]. Simulation compilers as discussed above will form the basis for implementing Simfrastructure like simulations on massively parallel architectures such as FPGAs. See [82] for a recent study.

3.5 Implications for Other Computational Models

The complexity theoretic results for SDS can be used to yield lower (and upper) bounds on the complexity of reachability problems for other computational models of discrete dynamical systems. These include:

1. Classical cellular automata (CA), (see for example, [85]) systolic arrays proposed by Kung et al. [56] and *graph automata* [72], which are a widely studied class of dynamical systems in physics and complex systems and have been used in massively parallel computing architectures.
2. Concurrent transition systems (CTS) have been widely studied as formal models of concurrent processes. They have been used to specify communication protocols and concurrent programs in the context of distributed computing.
3. Discrete *recurrent Hopfield networks* [36, 73, 73] which are used in machine learning and image processing.

The results can be used to characterizations of the complexity of state executability problems for CTSs, discrete Hopfield networks and cellular automata in terms of (i) the power of individual automata, (ii) the size of the alphabet for encoding messages, (iii) the interconnection topology and (iv) the method of communication (e.g., channels, action symbols).

4 Engineering BIST Systems

An important factor in building simulations of BIST systems is the size and scope of the systems that need to be represented. For example, infrastructure simulations should be able to represent over 10^6 entities and cover large geographical areas, the size of medium sized metropolis. A telecommunication simulation system representing a medium sized city should be able to represent 10^9 transceivers and 10^{12} packets per hour. As a result, building such systems requires new engineering principles for a high resolution HPC oriented representation. Classical methods for representing agents and their interactions will not scale beyond a certain point. Another interesting problem involves methods related to spatio-temporal data collection, integration and validation. Building such simulations involves, on the one hand, integrating large numbers of databases, streaming datasets and results from earlier simulation runs in a consistent manner and on the other hand, developing efficient methods for storing and analyzing data that is produced by such simulations. We discuss two interrelated topics below.

4.1 Concept of Agency: A Disaggregated Interactive, Normative Representation

Another issue to consider while implementing large simulations is that of agent encapsulation. In the past, most work on agent-based simulations has been implemented using object oriented computing languages and as a result people have a found natural one-to-one mapping of agents onto objects. This simplifies the task of debugging and implementing the agent based simulation architecture. Unfortunately, this approach does not scale while implementing large BIST systems. The notion of agency is much more abstract than usually studied in the literature and is based on the notion of composition and interaction. By composition, we mean that the functionality associated with an agent is obtained by composing (both structurally and functionally) its various incarnations or avatars. By interaction, we mean that a specific functionality of an agent depends on the behavior of other agents interacting with it. For instance, in the traffic simulation (**TRANSIMS**), an agent is sometimes a driver and sometimes a parent and sometimes an office worker. When assuming the role of a driver, the agent's speed is not only dependent on his own rules but the speed of other drivers around him. The SDS based view again provides a natural mathematical framework to represent this notion of agency.

PARameterized Approximate Local and Efficient aLgorithms (**PARALEL**) provide a way to address the scaling issue. As discussed above, in simulating large systems with tens of thousands (or more) of interacting elements, it is computationally infeasible to explicitly represent each entity in detail using, perhaps, naive one agent-one encapsulated software object representational ideas. A common method of simulating such systems is to use parameterized representations of entities. The goal is to capture different behaviors of the system using different sets of parameters. The concept corresponds to having a normative representation of each abstract agent. A parameterized representation allows efficient use of computational resources. Indeed, even in systems with only tens of thousands of entities, the set of potential interactions among the entities is so large that parameterized representations are desirable, if not absolutely necessary to simulate the interactions in an efficient manner. The basic ideas behind agent abstraction are found in the concept of **PARALEL** algorithms:

- **PAR**ameterized, in that a single basic algorithm with a correct set of input parameters is capable of representing a class of algorithms,
- **A**pproximate, in that their behavior closely approximates an exact algorithm achieving a given task,
- **L**ocal, in that the information required by such algorithms is local as opposed to global, and
- **E**fficient, in that they are very fast and can be executed efficiently on both sequential and distributed shared memory multiprocessor architectures a-**L**-gorithms.

The concept of local algorithms is akin to the recently independently introduced concept of decentralized algorithms [55] and also to the classical concept of distributed algorithms. The approximate behavior is also pertinent at two levels. At the basic level an approximate algorithm closely models the behavior of each physical entity. At a global level, an approximate solution implies that the composed local algorithms representing each agent along with the update mechanism approximate the global system dynamics. The global level of approximation is more important, although the local level cannot be completely ignored.

Example 5. **Normative drivers in traffic simulations.** Consider the rules for a driver update given in Example 2. In spite of their simplicity, these rules produce fairly realistic traffic flow characteristics and can in the limit, approach the fluid dynamics models studied in traffic flow theory [68, 70, 76]. The traffic pattern evolution as a function of the density $\rho = m/n$ (m is the number of cars in a given a period of time on a road segment of length n measured in number of cells) exhibits a threshold value for congestion. Figure 8 shows illustration of traffic flow characteristics produced by the above set of rules for a one-lane road with periodic boundary conditions. See [69] for additional discussion.

4.2 Efficient Storage and Regeneration

The simulations of BIST systems described here produce extremely large quantities of data. For example, simulating an ad hoc packet switched network with a million moving transceivers for even 15 minutes produces time

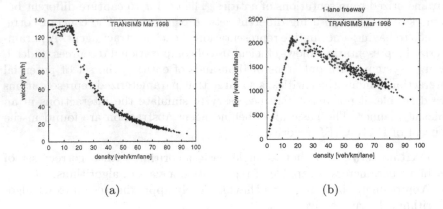

(a)   (b)

Fig. 8. Figures representing various traffic flow characteristics

varying network requiring gigabytes of memory and packet level data requiring terabytes of memory. It is therefore impossible to exhaustively store the data generated while running these simulations. This motivates the need for computationally efficient data storage and methods with the following requirements: (i) efficiency in terms of space and time complexity and in many cases capability to run in an online setting, and (ii) the stored data should have enough information to allow recreation of certain dynamic features observed while running the simulations. We can equivalently view this as a semantic compression step.

The next step is efficient (re)-generation of data (including networks). Generation of random graphs and random data sets allow us to test scalability as well as the semantic properties of simulations. Re-generated data is necessary to recreate data that could not be stored while running the larger simulations. Re-generation methods can be viewed as reduced simulations; they allow one to generate certain dynamics of interest without resorting to expensive runs of the large simulation. For example, in [12] a system is described to store and regenerate statistically equivalent packet streams arriving at their destination succinctly using signal theoretic and statistical methods. The size of the stored model is much smaller than the original data. The regeneration step uses the Markov Chain Monte Carlo method. The regenerated packet sequences are statistically indistinguishable from the original packet sequence when compared using basic quality of service measures such as throughput, jitter, skips, repeats, etc. The methods appear to yield compression ratios of over 100 000 while being able to recover many of the measures within 1% error. Similar methods can be devised to store and regenerate large BIST networks. The compression methods store structural properties of the network. The regeneration methods then use stochastic methods to re-generate the graphs. The random graphs so generated are "similar" to the original networks and can be constructed in a fraction of the time required to construct original networks.

5 A Practical Interaction Based System: Modeling Interdependent Urban Infrastructures

As an example of the theoretical framework described in the preceding sections, we will describe **Simfrastructure**: a high-performance service oriented agent based modeling and simulation system for representing and analyzing interdependent infrastructures. See [4, 26, 27, 29, 44, 57, 61, 31, 75, 86] and additional references in the following sections for other examples of similar efforts. Simfrastructure can represent and analyze interdependent urban infrastructures including transportation, telecommunication, public health, energy, financial (commodity markets)[2]. In conjunction with a representation of the urban population dynamics and the details of the built infrastructure, such modeling systems can be viewed as *functioning virtual cities*. A unique feature of tools such as Simfrastructure is their ability to represent entire urban populations at the level of individuals, including their activities, movements and locations. The ability to generate an urban population, move each person on a second-by-second basis, and monitor the individual's interaction with others and the physical infrastructures enables the understanding of infrastructure operations and interdependencies at an extreme but practical level of detail.

A connected collection of such urban infrastructure simulations allow analysis of urban infrastructure interdependencies through integrated functional data flow architectures. In brief, this functionality derives from population-mobility data generated by the simulation and modeling framework for the transportation sector. The simulation produces a synthetic population with demographics assigned to every individual. We track the second-by-second activities and locations of each individual by tying population information to detailed maps of urban infrastructures. This information drives each of the infrastructure simulations and is shared among the various infrastructure sector modules through a common interface. This also allows us to provide feedback between modules regarding infrastructure changes that arise in one sector during the course of a simulation and are likely to affect the behavior of other infrastructures. With the ability to simulate multiple infrastructures and their interdependencies in large urban regions, these systems provide planners and decision makers with an unprecedented modeling and analysis capability. Figure 9 shows a schematic view of the interdependent infrastructure simulation architecture.

---

[2] See http://ndssl.vbi.vt.edu/ for more details.

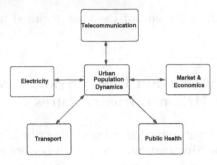

Fig. 9. A schematic diagram of Simfrastructure: an interdependent urban infrastructure simulation and modeling framework

5.1 A Service Oriented Architecture of Simfrastructure

We have recently completed a design and initial prototype implementation of Simfrastructure using web services based globally scalable architecture. The new design of the system specifically aims to scale Simfrastructure to represent entire countries and over time entire global populations. The only way to achieve such unprecedented scalability is to use web services architecture combined with Grid Computing infrastructure. We have recently demonstrated the design by constructing extremely detailed proto-populations of individuals residing in states along the US Eastern seaboard consisting of approximately 100 million individuals. This architecture takes care of ensuring that the simulations have the data that they need to operate, allow direct discovery of available services, and facilitate the integration of new services. The system design allows simulation modules to be run on any available computation resource in a way that is transparent to the user. The use of existing web services standards, allows any architecture or programming language to be supported.

The newly developed architecture makes it easy for organizations to add their own simulations and analysis tools into the system. One novel aspect of the architecture is the ability for different organizations to host the same simulation applied to different geographic areas. These instances will be able to communicate through web services to collaborate on a larger problem. For instance, a transportation system simulation could be run at each Metropolitan Planning Organization (MPO) covering the local urban region. The simulations running at each MPO could then exchange the traffic exiting each local area and entering an adjacent area. This exchange could be expanded to include bus, rail, and air traffic to aid in epidemiological modeling at the national level. Note that the system formed in this way is not predetermined, but is self-organized based on the currently available services.

The architecture also allows the implementation of a particular service to be easily updated or replaced without affecting current users of the service. Multiple providers of a service can coexist, each with a different trade-off (e.g., resolution vs. execution time). The request for a service will be decoupled from the execution of the service so that a user simply makes a request that a service be performed. Attached to the request are conditions that must be met such as monetary cost, completion time, security requirement, etc. These requests need not be computational, but may be for services provide by other individuals or organizations. Software brokers examine these requests and match them to available resources.

Currently, Simfrastructure has working models for the following infrastructures: (i) Synthetic populations and urban environments, (ii) transportation, (iii) commodity markets, (iv) integrated telecommunication, (v) public health, and (vi) electrical power. Below we describe each of these modules briefly. We will end the section with illustrative use cases.

5.2 Synthetic Protopopulations and Urban Environment Representation

A detailed population mobility and the associated built urban infrastructure is the central piece of such simulations. It provides a common interface for the flow of information between all the infrastructure sector simulations. All information describing the synthetic population and elements of the built urban environment resides in this module. In addition, changes in the urban infrastructure that arise during the course of a simulation and constrain activities and locations of the population pass between the modules through this module, where sector-specific information is transformed into a common format. The module makes information available to the other infrastructure simulations in the form of a consistent data structure, called proto-populations: they are synthetic populations whose resolution, fidelity and quality can be varied depending on the nature of the application.

A protopopulation is a collection of synthetic people, each associated with demographic variables drawn from any of the demographics available and extracted from the census [16, 77, 78]. Protopopulations can represent a person, a vehicle, or an infrastructure element such as a hospital or a switch. Here, for illustration, we will concentrate on creation of synthetic urban populations. Figure 10 shows a schematic diagram. Joint demographic distributions can be reconstructed from marginal distributions available in typical census data using an iterative proportional fitting (IPF) technique. Each synthetic individual is placed in a household with other synthetic people and each household is placed geographically in such a way that a census of the synthetic population is statistically indistinguishable from the original census, if aggregated to the block group level. Synthetic populations are thus statistically indistinguishable from the census data. Since they are synthetic, the privacy of individuals within the population is protected. The *synthetic individuals* carry with them a complete range of demographic attributes collected from the census data, including variables such as income level and age. Next, a set of activity templates for households is created, based on several thousand responses to an activity

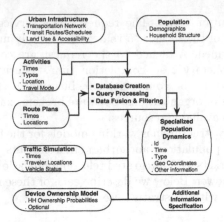

Fig. 10. Schematic diagram showing how various databases are integrated to create a synthetic population

or time-use survey. These activity templates include the types of activities each household member performs and the time of day they are performed.

Each synthetic household is then matched with one of the survey households, using a decision tree based on demographics such as the number of workers in the household, number of children of various ages, etc. Next, the synthetic household is assigned the activity template of its matching survey household. For each household and each activity performed by this household, a preliminary assignment of a location is made based on observed land-use patterns, tax data, etc. This assignment must be calibrated against observed travel-time distributions. However, the travel-times corresponding to any particular assignment of activities to locations cannot be determined analytically. Indeed, the urban transportation system is a canonical example of complex system wherein global behavior arises from simple local interactions. Using techniques from combinatorial optimization, machine learning and agent based modeling we then refine the population, their activity locations and their itineraries [9].

The time varying, spatially placed, synthetic population constructed in the above manner can be enhanced for other uses. For instance, we used data fusion techniques to assign these individuals: telecommunication devices (cell phones, pagers, etc.), time varying demand for electricity, water and other such commodities. Note that such data is impossible to collect and can only be created using methods described here.

This produces synthetic individuals that just like real individuals can now call other individuals, consume various resources during the day and carry out other activities like eating, socializing, shopping, etc. An important point to note here is that such data is impossible to collect by mere measurements or surveys: it is the output of the agent based models such as the ones developed in [9].

5.3 Transportation Sector

Large scale microscopic simulation of transportation systems has become possible over the last few years. See [31, 75, 9] for examples of efforts in this regard. A prototypical question that can be studied with such simulations is the economic and social impact of building a new freeway in a large metropolitan area. Systems such as **TRANSIMS** conceptually decompose the transportation planning task into three time scales.

First, a large time scale associated with land use and demographic distribution as a characterization of travelers. In this phase, demographic information is used to create *activities* for travelers. Activity information typically consists of requests that travelers be at a certain location at a specified time. They include information on travel modes available to the traveler. A synthetic population is endowed with demographics matching the joint distributions given in census data. Observations are made on the daily activity patterns of several thousand households (from survey data). These patterns are used as templates and associated with synthetic households with similar demographics. The locations at which activities are carried out are estimated while taking into account observed land use patterns, travel times, and dollar costs of transportation. Second, an intermediate time scale consists of planning routes and trip-chains to satisfy the activity requests. This module finds minimum cost paths through the transportation infrastructure consistent with constraints on mode choice. An example constraint might be: "walk to a transit stop, take transit to work using no more than two transfers and no more than one bus" [9]. Finally, a very short time scale is associated with the actual execution of trip plans in the network. This is done by a simulation that moves cellular automata corresponding to the travelers through a very detailed representation of the urban transportation network [68] . Examples 2 and 5 have already discussed some of these aspects. The simulation resolves traffic down to 7.5 meters and times down to 1 second. It provides an updated estimate of link costs, including the effects of congestion, to the router and location estimation algorithms, which produce new plans. This feedback process continues iteratively until convergence to a steady state in which no one can find a better path in the context of everyone else's decisions. The resulting traffic patterns are matched to observed traffic.

A substantial effort has been spent on calibration and validation of the output produced by **TRANSIMS**; see [9, 68] for details. First, the design of the system is based on SDS. Second, various microscopic and macroscopic quantities produced by **TRANSIMS** have been validated in the city of Portland; including (i) traffic invariants such as flow density patterns and jam wave propagation, (ii) macroscopic quantities, such as activities and population densities in the entire city, number of people occupying various locations in a time varying fashion, time varying traffic density split by trip purpose and various modal choices over highways and other major roads, turn counts, number of trips going between zones in a city, etc.

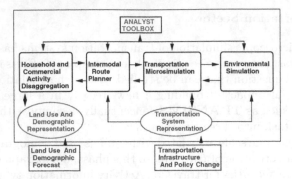

Fig. 11. Data flow in the **TRANSIMS** simulation system, proceeding from left to right. Input data comes from the US census and metropolitan planning organizations. We generate a synthetic population whose demographics match the census; give each household an appropriate set of activities; plan routes through the network; and estimate the resulting travel times. The dotted lines represent feedback pathways, along which data flows from right to left, in the system

An Interaction Based Viewpoint. The **TRANSIMS** system has been designed using an interaction-based approach to capture the causes of observed traffic patterns. For each individual, his endogenous attributes are derived the census data and his endogenous goals are derived from the activity patterns. His endogenous procedures or behavior consist of methods for finding specific locations to perform his desired activities, specific algorithms for finding routes to go from one location to another and specific rules used for driving. When such an endogenous individual interacts with the infrastructure and other individuals, we get traffic. The particular locations that an individual chooses, or the routes he takes are not determined solely by his endogenous attributes; they are a result of his goals, methods and his interaction with other individuals and the infrastructure. Similarly, the causal explanation of traffic or the question of who is at a given location at a given time, is given not only by the description of the individuals and the infrastructure, but also by the interaction amongst them. Thus consequences of large transformational changes such as a cascading power failure or infectious diseases can be understood in terms of the net effect of the interactions.

This is very different than traditional statistical models that fit parameters to given observations. Such systems that rely on observation and direct measurement of traffic cannot extrapolate into hypothetical scenarios precisely because they have no representation of the multitude of forces and interactions that lie behind each observation. As a simple example, the **TRANSIMS** methodology tells us how many people would be likely to use a new freeway if it were constructed. In doing so it captures what by now is well known as induced/latent demand. An observationally based system cannot extrapolate well beyond the circumstances in which it has been observed. Similarly, this approach will allow us to simulate the effects of changes in behavior or use of infrastructure on the overall social dynamics.

5.4 Telecommunication Sector

The telecommunication modeling environment is an extension of the **AdHop-Net** [13, 24], designed to model extremely large, complex telecommunication networks made up of cellular networks, public switched telephone networks (PSTNs), Internet (IP) networks, and ad hoc mesh networks. It is an end-to-end simulation system, meaning that all aspects of the communication system are represented. Although simulations have been used for over four decades for representing and analyzing telecommunication systems, the use of high performance computing oriented simulations of very large telecommunication systems is a relatively new subject area; see [4, 29] for examples.

The system has been specifically designed to be interoperable with other infrastructure simulations and is useful for representing the complete system comprising the information and communication networks. It is also designed for technological scaling—as we move towards ubiquitous computing, telecommunication and computing networks with billions of heterogeneous transceivers. Such an integrated system can be used to evaluate federal policies on the use and operation of telecommunication infrastructures, especially in regards to potential effects of the policies on national security. It can also be used to discover and respond to new vulnerabilities that could occur while deploying ad hoc and integrated networks, i.e., networks of mobile radio devices that present a constantly evolving telecommunication network.

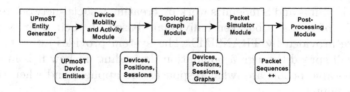

Fig. 12. Overall design of the telecommunication modeling module

The modeling environment decomposes the telecommunication system into four basic time scales. The first module places devices and individuals throughout the urban region. It then generates the positions of transceivers at various times of the coarse simulation clock. This module also allows transceivers to become idle for some period of time and to rejoin the network at a later time. The module also provides for new transceivers to join the network and existing transceivers to leave the network permanently. Wireline devices are placed permanently at various locations based on the publicly available information.

In the second step, each device (e.g., phone, computers, etc) is assigned data sessions: the sessions are consistent with the kind of devices, their locations and their users. The sessions generated are statistically identical to the sessions generated in an urban region of interest. The next step consists of constructing a (time-varying) telecommunication network. Due to the various technologies used, these networks are dynamic and their topology varies significantly depending on the kind of technology used. This corresponds to intermediate time scale. Finally, at the finest time scale, voice or data is moved over the dynamic network; this aspect uses packet/voice data simulation methods based on flow techniques or discrete dynamical systems. The data is then stored succinctly using signal theoretic methods; Markov chain methods are then used to regenerate statistically equivalent packet streams. An auxiliary module is concerned with construction, analysis and regeneration of integrated telecommunication networks. The module synthesizes publicly available data sets in conjunction with population mobility information to construct the complete set of networks used in a telecommunication system: wireline, wireless, ad hoc and the packet switched IP networks.

5.5 Public Health

The public health module (called **EpiSims**) of the integrated system simulates the spread of disease in urban areas. It details the demographic and geographic distributions of disease and provides decision makers with information about (1) the consequences of a biological attack or natural outbreak, (2) the resulting demand for health services, and (3) the feasibility and effectiveness of response options. See [22, 33, 34] for further details. **Simdemics**, an extension of EpiSims, is designed to model general reaction diffusion process such as vector borne diseases and simulation of social norms and fads.

Both EpiSims and Simdemics work by creating a social-network representing details of contacts between individuals based on their activity patterns which are provided by TRANSIMS. The system provides estimates of how disease will spread through a population depending on how it is introduced, how vulnerable people are, what responses are applied, and when responses are implemented.

The module simulates the movement of each individual from location to location in a large urban area as he or she goes about daily activities. The individuals are synthetic; they do not represent specific people, but a census taken on the entire synthetic population would be statistically indistinguishable from the actual census. On the other hand, the locations visited by individuals are real street addresses and reflect actual land-use patterns in the city.

The modeling environment associates a state of health with each individual being simulated. An individual's demographics determine his/her response to exposure and infection. For example, anyone over the age of 32 is assumed to have been vaccinated for smallpox. Exposure occurs in either of two ways: through contact with an infectious person or by visiting a contaminated location. The simulation user can introduce contamination at a location as an exogenous event in the simulation. Whether a person is infectious depends on when that person was exposed and their individual response to infection. By varying a few parameters, users can model many different diseases.

A simulated person's state of health may affect his or her actions. They may seek treatment at a nearby hospital or clinic, or they may stay home instead of pursuing certain activities. In addition, the user may specify actions that affect simulated people, such as mass or targeted vaccination/treatment/prophylaxis and isolation. Targeted responses are automated within the simulations: people are chosen at a user-specified rate from a list of symptomatic people; their contacts are found by following their schedule; and the contacts are then treated and/or isolated.

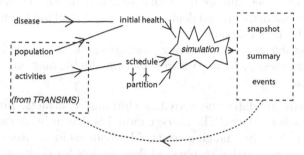

Fig. 13. Data flow in the epidemiology simulation system. Input data comes from two sources: the user's disease model and information about the social network. Stand-alone tools operate on the disease model and the population's demographics to produce the initial state of health for everyone in the simulation. Another tool converts a list of activities and locations organized by person into a schedule of events (primarily arrivals and departures) organized by location. The final preparation step estimates an optimal partition of resources among computational nodes. The simulation itself executes events in strict time order and propagates disease in accordance with the user's disease model

5.6 Commodity Markets

Sigma is an agent-based, microscopic, computational modeling framework to study commodity markets. Systems such as Sigma offer several advantages to an economist interested in studying commodity markets, including (i) exact knowledge of what is exogenous and what is endogenous in the experiment, (ii) complete control on the amount of information accessible to the players, (iii) clear delineation of what information is public and private as well as what assumptions are reasonable to include. The economist can not only study the system in equilibrium, but can also study the transient dynamics that lead to equilibrium conditions.

Sigma uses an interaction based computing approach to study the micro-level behavior of the market and its players. The computational framework provides user, the ability to control individuals' preferences, behavior, market elements, trading mechanisms, etc. This facilitates the study of different economic structures, strategies, policies and institutions in isolation. It can currently simulate a restructured electricity market. Three kinds of markets are modeled; centralized, decentralized, and a real-time (spot) market. The models employ economic theory-based methods and capture the dynamics of supply and demand in a market driven economy. New approaches that facilitate a wide range of experiments with a high degree of realism, include:

1. flexible methods of aggregating individual consumers and producers into hierarchies in order to represent buyers and suppliers in residential, commercial, and wholesale markets;
2. heterogeneous demand profiles with elastic and inelastic components using time, location,activity, and demographic data for all individual consumers in a synthetic population;
3. user-selectable economic clearing mechanisms to accommodate an array of market types, including Vickrey auction, double auction, and marginal price clearing.

The system simulates the activities (bidding, contracts, prices, etc.) of individual market players. The market model is driven by dynamic demand profiles that reflect the changing needs of individuals in an urban population. The model can be coupled to physical flow models for commodities that require physical clearing (such as electricity). The tool uses population dynamics and activity location data from a population dynamics simulation such as TRANSIMS. This information ties the market simulations to the urban infrastructure. Markets, among other things, are sensitive indicators of infrastructure disruptions and can be used to gauge public mood and awareness in crisis situations. The overall design of Sigma is depicted schematically in Fig. 14. The framework, due to scaling requirements, has a parametric representation for buyers as well as sellers. This allows one to represent a number of realistic, individualistic, behavioral features that are typically assumed away in classical economic literature due to mathematical intractability. These include dropping classical Cournot oligopolists' assumptions, perfect rationality, information symmetry between consumers and generators, etc.

Sigma is a detailed simulation based analysis tool for simulating large commodity markets such as electricity markets. Markets are among other things, sensitive indicators of infrastructure disruptions and can be used to gauge public mood and awareness in crisis situations. It can be used to analyze effects of different regulatory changes, the impact of changes in consumer behavior on the clearing price, impact of price caps on demand and supply, market efficiency, generators' bidding strategies, etc. Another important use for such tools is their ability to analyze the effect of different market clearing rules on clearing prices.

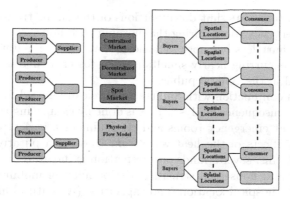

Fig. 14. Schematic diagram of the commodity market simulation system

The system simulates the activities (bidding, contracts, prices, etc.) of individual market players. The market model is driven by dynamic demand profiles that reflect the changing needs of individuals in an urban population. The model can be coupled to physical flow models for commodities that require physical clearing. The tool uses population dynamics and activity location data from a population dynamics simulation such as TRANSIMS. This information ties the market simulations to the urban infrastructure. The overall design of such a tool is depicted schematically in Fig. 14. It consists of three main components that form a coupled system:

1. the electrical power grid, with associated elements including generators, substations, transmission grids and their related electrical characteristics;
2. a market consisting of market entities, including buyers, sellers, the power exchange (where electricity trades are carried out at various time/size scales), the independent system operator (ISO) and the market clearing rules and strategies;
3. an activity based individual power demand creator that yields spatio-temporal distribution of the power consumed.

Such simulations, due to scaling requirements, have a parametric representation for buyers as well as sellers. They allow for a number of realistic behavioral features that are typically assumed away in classical economic literature due to mathematical intractability. These include dropping classical Cournot oligopolist's assumptions, perfect rationality, symmetric information between consumers and generators, etc.

5.7 An Illustrative Use Case

The following use case built around EpiSims and Simfrastructure demonstrates how such modelling tools can be used for situational awareness and consequence analysis in the event of epidemics. In this scenario, during a heat wave in a city, terrorists shut down portions of the public transit system and a hospital emergency room during the morning rush hour. At the same time, they spread a harmless but noticeable aerosol at two commuter rail stations. These events, occurring nearly simultaneously, foster a chaotic, if not panic-stricken, mood in the general public.

EpiSims in conjunction with Simfrastructure can be used for situation assessment and consequence analysis. This is done by estimating the demand by demographics at emergency rooms and clinics under a variety of hypotheses to distinguish effects of the heat wave from those of a putative bio-attack. To accomplish this, several kinds of information is integrated: (i) population demographics and household structure, (ii) population mobility and transit timetables, (iii) hospital locations and capacities, (iv) natural history of various infectious diseases, (v) historical heat wave casualties, and (vi) (potential) surveillance data. We then estimate the demographics (age, gender, and home location) of people likely to have been in the two stations when they were "attacked". These are the people who would show up first for treatment if indeed a bio-attack had occurred. They also would serve as the subpopulation to seed with disease in a simulation. Biases in their demographics compared to a random sample of the population will induce persistent biases in the set of people infected at any time that cannot be captured by models assuming homogeneous mixing. We estimate demand at hospitals, assuming that people would arrive at a hospital near their home location. We further estimate whether each hospital had sufficient capacity to meet the demand. Historically, the most likely casualties of a heat wave are elderly people living alone with few activities outside the home. This information, combined with demographic and household structure data, allows us to estimate demand for health services created by the heat wave by demographic and location. For situation assessment, we note the obvious differences between these two demand patterns. In an actual event, comparison with admissions surveillance data would allow quick disambiguation between the two.

We estimate the likely spread of disease for several different pathogens by demographic and location. Furthermore, we can implement several suggested mitigating responses, such as closing schools and/or workplaces, or quarantining households with symptomatic people. Knowledge of the household structure permits an exceptionally realistic representation of the consequences of these actions. For example, if schools are closed, a care-giver will also need to stay home in many households. Or if households are quarantined when a member becomes symptomatic, we can estimate the immediate economic impact using the household incomes for exactly those households affected. Similarly, the economic impact of casualties with known demographics leads to a cost–benefit analysis for proposed interventions. In a similar study that we recently undertook, we found enormous differences in cost for interventions with similar numbers of casualties. Information on casualties can be fed back into the representation of the urban environment to evaluate effects on interdependent infrastructure.

The use case demonstrates the need for an interaction based modeling and simulation approach: such an approach captures physical interdependencies between infrastructures as well as implicit human-mediated interdependencies existing between infrastructures. For example, the demand for cooling on a hot summer day can strain the energy distribution system, forcing it to operate in a less robust regime. Furthermore, the consequences of decisions made to mitigate accidents depend on the demand being serviced at the moment. Thus a decision to brown-out New York's financial district while maintaining service to residential areas has completely different effects at midnight on a Saturday than at 2 pm on a Wednesday. Practical decision support environments based on modeling environments such as Simfrastructure can evaluate such situation-dependent consequences.

6 Concluding Remarks

We described an interaction based approach to modeling and simulations of large scale socio-technical, biological and information systems. The theoretical foundations of this approach were based on sequential dynamical systems (SDS) and theory of large scale complex networks. Engineering principles are derived from such a theory. These engineering principles allow us to design simulations for extremely large systems and implement them on massively parallel architectures. As an illustration, we described Simfrastructure: a practical interaction based modeling tool to study large interdependent urban infrastructures. Large scale high performance computing oriented simulations for these systems are already operational; the simulations and the underlying systems would greatly benefit from further advances in interactive computing.

We are also currently exploring two broad research areas to further develop the interaction based design and analysis of extremely large heterogeneous systems: (i) discrete microscopic modeling and simulation of biological systems [52, 45, 54] and (ii) robust nanoscale design and computation.

Acknowledgements: We sincerely thank our colleagues, collaborators and the team members of the projects discussed here. Simfrastructure is being jointly developed with Karla Atkins, Keith Bisset, Richard Beckman, V. Anil Kumar, Achla Marathe, Henning Mortveit and Paula Stretz at Virginia Tech. The mathematical and computational theory of SDS was developed jointly with Harry B. Hunt III, S. Ravi, Daniel Rosenkrantz and Richard Stearns at University at Albany, Henning Mortveit at Virginia Tech and Christian Reidys at Los Alamos. The network theory is being jointly developed with Anil Vullikanti, Aravind Srinivasan, Srinivasan Parthasarathy and Nan Wang at University of Maryland and Ravi Sundaram (Northeastern) and Mayur Thakur (University of Missouri, Rolla).

References

1. R. Axtell, J. Epstein. *Growing Artificial Societies: Social Science From the Bottom Up.* MIT Press / Brookings Institution, 1996.
2. R. Albert, A. Barabási. Statistical mechanics of complex networks, *Rev. Mod. Phys.* 74, 2002, pp. 47-97.
3. K. Atkins, C. Barrett, C. Homan, A. Marathe, M. Marathe, S. Thite. Marketecture: A Simulation-Based Framework for Studying Experimental Deregulated Power Markets, *Proc. 6th IAEE European Conf. Modeling in Energy Economics and Policy*, Zurich, 2004.
4. L. Bajaj, M. Takai, R. Ahuja, R. Bagrodia. Simulation of Large Scale Communication Systems. *Proc. MILCOM'99*, 1999.
5. A. Barabási, R. Albert. Emergence of scaling in random networks. *Science*, 286, 1999.
6. C. Barrett, S. Eubank, M. Marathe, H. Mortveit, C. Reidys. Science and Engineering of Large Scale Socio-Technical Simulations, *Proc. 1st Int'l Conf. on Grand Challenges in Simulations*, held as a part of Western Simulation Conference, San Antonio Texas, 2002.
7. C. Barrett, S. Eubank, V. Anil Kumar, M. Marathe. Understanding Large Scale Social and Infrastructure Networks: A Simulation Based Approach, *SIAM News* 37(4), 2004. Appears as part of Math Awareness Month on The Mathematics of Networks.
8. M. Batty. Hierarchy in Cities and City Systems, CASA Working paper series 85-11-4, 2005. To appear in *Hierarchy in natural and Social Sciences*, D. Pumain, Ed., Kluwer Academic Publishers.
9. C. Barrett, R. Beckman, K. Berkbigler, K. Bisset, B. Bush, K. Campbell, S. Eubank, K. Henson, J. Hurford, D. Kubicek, M. Marathe, P. Romero, J. Smith, L. Smith, P. Speckman, P. Stretz, G. Thayer, E. Eeckhout, W. Williams. TRANSIMS: Transportation Analysis Simulation System. *Tech. Report LA-UR-00-1725*, Los Alamos National Laboratory Unclassified Report, 2001.
10. C. Barrett, C. Reidys. Elements of a Theory of simulation I: Sequential CA over random graphs *Appl. Math. and Comput.* 98:241–259, 1999.
11. C. Barrett, H. Mortveit, C. Reidys. Elements of a Theory of simulation II: Sequential dynamical systems. *Appl. Math. and Comput.* 107(2-3), pp. 121–136, 2000.
12. G. Istrate, A. Hansson, S. Thulasidasan, M. Marathe, C. Barrett. RESTORED: A Methodology for Semantic Compression of TCP Traces. *Tech. Report*, Los Alamos National Laboratory, submitted.
13. C. Barrett, M. Marathe, H. Mortveit, S. Ravi, C. Reidys, J. Smith. AdHopNet: Advances in Simulation-based Design and Analysis of Ad-Hoc Networks *Tech. Report LA-UR 00-1567*, Los Alamos National Laboratory, 2000.
14. C. Barrett, M. Marathe, J. Smith, S. Ravi. A mobility and traffic generation framework for modeling and simulating ad hoc communication networks. *ACM Symp. on Applied Computing* (SAC), 2002, pp. 122-126.
15. C. Barrett, H. Hunt III, M. Marathe, S. Ravi, D. Rosenkrantz, R. Stearns. Analysis Problems for Sequential Dynamical Systems and Communicating State Machines. *Proc. Int'l Symp. on Math. Foundations of Computer Science* (MFCS'01), Czech Republic, pp. 159–172, 2001.
16. R. Beckman, K. Baggerly, M. McKay. Creating synthetic base-line populations, *Transportation Research Part A – Policy and Practice* 30, pp. 415–429, 1996.

17. S. Buss, C. Papadimitriou, J. Tsitsiklis. On the Predictability of Coupled Automata: An Allegory About Chaos. *Complex Systems* 1(5), pp. 525–539, 1991.

18. D. Brand, P. Zafiropulo. On Communicating Finite State Machines. *J. ACM* 30(2), pp. 323–342, 1983.

19. C. Barrett, H. Hunt III, M. Marathe, S. Ravi, D. Rosenkrantz, R. Stearns, P. Tosic. Gardens of Eden and fixed points in sequential dynamical systems. *Proc. Int'l Conf. on Discrete Models - Combinatorics, Computation and Geometry* (DM-CCG), Paris, pp. 95–110, 2001.

20. C. Barrett, H. Hunt III, M. Marathe, S. Ravi, D. Rosenkrantz, R. Stearns, M. Thakur. Complexity of Predecessor Existence Problems for Finite Discrete Dynamical Systems. *Tech. Report*, Virginia Tech, 2004. Preliminary Version appeared in Discrete Models of Complex Systems (DMCS) 2002.

21. C. Barrett, H. Hunt III, M. Marathe, S. Ravi, D. Rosenkrantz, R. Stearns. Reachability Problems for Sequential Dynamical Systems with Threshold Functions. *Theoretical Computer Science*, 1-3, pp. 41-64, 2003.

22. C. Barrett, J. Smith, S. Eubank, Modern Epidemiology Modeling, in *Scientific American*, 2005.

23. A. Broder, R. Kumar, F. Maghoul, P. Raghavan, S. Rajagopalan, R. Stata, A. Tomkins, J. Wiener. Graph structure in the web. *Computer Networks*, 33, 2000.

24. C. Barrett, M. Marathe, H. Mortveit, C. Reidys. SDS Based Specification of Large IP Networks *Tech. Report*, Los Alamos National Laboratory, 2001.

25. C. Barrett, M. Drozda, D. Engelhart, V. Anil Kumar, M. Marathe, M. Morin, S. Ravi, J. Smith. Structural Analysis of Ad Hoc Networks: Implications for Protocol Performance, *Proc. IEEE Int'l Conf. on Wireless and Mobile Computing, Communications and Networking*, 2005.

26. K. Carley, D. Fridsma, E. Casman, N. Altman, J. Chang, J. Kaminski, D. Nave, A. Yahja. BioWar: Scalable Multi-Agent Social and Epidemiological Simulation of Bioterrorism Events. *Prof. NAACSOS Conf.*, Pittsburgh, PA, 2003.

27. R. Breiger, K. Carley, Eds., *NRC workshop on Social Network Modeling and Analysis*, pp. 133-145, National Research Council, 2003.

28. F. Chung, L. Lu. Connected components in a random graph with given degree sequences. *Annals of Combinatorics*, 6:125–145, 2002.

29. J. Cowie, D. Nicol, A. Ogielski. Modeling 100 000 Nodes and Beyond: Self-Validating Design. *DARPA/NIST Workshop on Validation of Large Scale Network Simulation Models*, 1999.

30. N. Creignou, S. Khanna, M. Sudan. *Complexity Classifications of Boolean Constraint Satisfaction Problems*. SIAM Monographs on Discrete Mathematics and Applications, 2001.

31. DYNAMIT. Massachusetts Institute of Technology, Cambridge, Massachusetts. http://mit.edu/its/dynamit.html, 1999.

32. A. DeHon. Very Large Scale Spatial Computing *Proc. Third Int'l Conf. on Unconventional Models of Computation* (UMC'02), 15-19, pp. 27–37, 2002.

33. S. Eubank, H. Guclu, V. Anil Kumar, M. Marathe, A. Srinivasan, Z. Toroczkai, N. Wang. Modeling Disease Outbreaks in Realistic Urban Social Networks, *Nature*, 429, pp. 180-184, 2004.

34. S. Eubank, V. Anil Kumar, M. Marathe, A. Srinivasan, N. Wang. Structural and Algorithmic Aspects of Large Social Networks, *Proc. 15th ACM-SIAM Symp. on Discrete Algorithms* (SODA), pp. 711-720, 2004.

35. S. Eubank, V. Anil Kumar, M. Marathe, A. Srinivasan, N. Wang. Structure of Social Contact Networks and their Impact on Epidemics. to appear in *AMS-DIMACS Special Volume on Epidemiology*, 2005.
36. P. Floreen, P. Orponen. Complexity Issues in Discrete Hopfield Networks *Comp. and Learning Complexity of Neural Networks: Advanced Topics*, Edited by I. Parberry, 1994.
37. J. Epstein. *Generative Social Science: Studies in Agent-Based Computational Modeling*, Princeton University Press, Forthcoming, 2005.
38. I. Foster and G. Kesselman, Eds. *The Grid: Blueprint for a New Computing Infrastructure*, 2000.
39. C. Faloutsos, P. Faloutsos, M. Faloutsos. On Power-Law Relationships of the Internet Topology, *Proc. ACM SIGCOMM*, 1999.
40. M. Garzon. *Models of Massive Parallelism: Models of Cellular Automata and Neural Networks*, EATCS Monographs on Theoretical Computer Science, Springer Verlag, 1995.
41. D. Goldin, S. Smolka, P. Attie, E. Sonderegger. Turing Machines, Transition Systems, and Interaction *Information and Computation*, 194(2), pp. 101-128, 2004.
42. H. Gutowitz, Ed. Cellular Automata: Theory and Experiment North Holland, 1989.
43. D. Harel, O. Kupferman, M. Vardi. On the complexity of verifying concurrent transition systems. *Proc. 8th Int. Conf. Concurrency Theory* (CONCUR'97), Warsaw, Poland, July 1997, Vol. 1243 LNCS, pp. 258–272, 1997.
44. Y. Haimes, B. Horowitz. Modeling Interdependent Infrastructures for Sustainable Counterterrorism. Journal of Infrastructure Systems, pp. 33-41, 2004.
45. L. Hartwell, J. Hopfield, S. Leibler, A. Murray. From Molecular to Modular Cell Biology, *Nature*, Vol. 402, pp. C47-C51, 1999.
46. H. Hethcote. The Mathematics of Infectious Diseases *SIAM Review*, 42(4):599–653, 2000.
47. B. Hillel. Cities as Movement Economies. *Urban Design Int'l* 1, pp. 49-60, 1996.
48. J. Hopfield. Neural Networks and Physical Systems with Emergent Collective Computational Abilities. *Proc. of National Academy of Sciences of the USA*, No. 81, pp. 3088-3092, 1982.
49. H. Hunt III, R. Stearns, M. Marathe. Relational Representability, Local Reductions and the Complexity of Generalized Satisfiability Problem. *Tech. Report No. LA-UR-00-6108*, Los Alamos National Laboratory, 2000.
50. H. Hunt III, R. Stearns, M. Marathe. Strongly Local Reductions and the Complexity/Efficient Approximability of Algebra and Optimization on Abstract Algebraic Structures, *Proc. Int'l Conf. on Symbolic and Algebraic Computations* (ISAAC), pp. 183-191, 2001.
51. H. Hunt III, D. Rosenkrantz, C. Barrett, M. Marathe, S. Ravi. Complexity of Analysis and Verification Problems for Communicating Automata and Discrete Dynamical Systems. *Tech. Report No. LA-UR-01-1687*, Los Alamos National Laboratory, 2001.
52. T. Ideker, T. Galitski, L. Hood. A New Approach to Decoding Life, *Ann. Review of Genomics and Human Genetics*, Vol. 2, pp. 343-372, 2001.
53. G. Istrate, M. Marathe, S. Ravi. Adversarial models in evolutionary game dynamics. *Proc. 12th ACM-SIAM Symp. on Discrete Algorithms* (SODA'2001), Washington, DC, pp. 719–720, 2001.

54. H. Kitano. Computational Systems Biology, *Nature* 420, pp. 206-210, 2002.
55. J. Kleinberg. Navigation in a Small World. *Nature* 406, 2000.
56. H. Kung. Why Systolic Architectures. *IEEE Computers*, 15(1), pp. 37-42, 1982.
57. R. Little. Controlling Cascading Failure: Understanding the Vulnerabilities of Interconnected Infrastructures. *J. Urban Technology*, 9(1), 109-123, 2002.
58. R. Liu, E. Lloyd, M. Marathe, R. Ramanathan, S. Ravi. Algorithmic Aspects of Topology Control Problems For Ad-hoc Networks, *ACM/Baltzer J. Mobile Networks and Applications* (MONET), 10, pp. 19-34, 2005.
59. M. Liu, M. Subramaniam. An Approach for Formal Specification and Verification of Large Scale Simulation Systems Using Abstract State Machines, *Los Alamos National Laboratory Tech. Report*, 2005.
60. R. Laubenbacher, B. Pareigis. Decomposition and simulation of sequential dynamical systems, *Advances in Applied Math*, 30, pp. 655-678, 2003.
61. E. Lee, A. Wallace, J. Mitchell, D. Mendon, J. Chow. Managing disruptions to critical interdependent infrastructures in the context of the 2001 WorldTrade Center attack, in *Beyond September 11: An account of post-disaster research* M. F. Myers, Ed. Boulder, CO: Natural Hazards Research and Applications Information Center, University of Colorado, Program on Environment and Behavior, Special Publication 39, pp. 165-198, 2003.
62. N. Margolus. An Embedded DRAM Architecture for Large-Scale Spatial-Lattice Computations *Proc. 27th Annual Int'l Symp. on Computer Architecture* (ISCA), pp. 149-158, 2000.
63. N. Margolus, T. Toffoli. *Cellulae Automata Machines: A New Environment for Modeling*, Cambridge: MIT press, 1987.
64. R. Milner. *Communicating and Mobile systems: the π-calculus* Cambridge University Press, 1999.
65. R. Milner. Elements of Interaction, *Comm. ACM* 36:1, pp. 78-89, 1993.
66. C. Moore. Unpredictability and Undecidability in Dynamical Systems. *Physical Review Letters* 64(20), pp 2354-2357, 1990.
67. H. Mortveit, C. Reidys. Discrete, Sequential Dynamical Systems. *Discrete Mathematics* 226:281–295, 2001.
68. K. Nagel, M. Schrekenberg. A Cellular Automata Model for Freeway Traffic. *J. de Physique I*, France, 2:2221, 1995.
69. K. Nagel, P. Stretz, M. Pieck, S. Leckey, R. Donnelly, and C. Barrett. TRANSIMS Traffic Flow Characteristics. *Transportation Research Board Annual Meeting*, 1998.
70. K. Nagel, M. Paczuski. Emergent traffic jams. *Physical Review E*, 51:2909-2918, 1995.
71. M. Newman, The structure and function of complex networks. *SIAM Review* 45, 167–256, 2003.
72. C. Nicthiu, E. Remila. Simulations of graph automaton. *Proc. Mathematical Foundations of Computer Science (MFCS'98) Satellite workshop on graph automata*, Th Worsch and R. Wolmar Eds, Universität Karlsruhe, pp. 69-78, 1998.
73. P. Orponen. Computational Complexity of Neural Networks: A Survey, *Nordic J. of Computing* 1(1), pp. 94-110, 1994.
74. A. Rabinovich. Complexity of Equivalence Problems for Concurrent Systems of Finite Agents. *Information and Computation* 127(2), pp. 164–185, 1997.

75. B. Raney, N. Cetin, A. Völlmy, A. Vrtic, K. Axhausen, K. Nagel, An Agent-Based Microsimulation Model of Swiss Travel: First Results, *Networks and Spatial Economics* 3, pp. 23–41, 2003.

76. M. Schreckenberg, A. Schadschneider, K. Nagel, N. Ito. Discrete stochastic models for traffic flow. *Physical Review E* 51:29-39, 1995.

77. P. Speckman, K. Vaughn, E. Pas. Generating Household Activity-Travel Patterns (HATPs) for Synthetic Populations. *Transportation Research Board Annual Meeting*, 1997.

78. P. Speckman, K. Vaughn, E. Pas. A Continuous Spatial Interaction Model: Application to Home-Work Travel in Portland, Oregon. *Transportation Research Board Annual Meeting*, 1997.

79. Y. Sheffi. *Urban Transportation Networks: Equilibrium Analysis with Mathematical Programming methods.* Prentice Hall, 1985.

80. R. Stearns, H. Hunt III. An algebraic model for combinatorial problems. *SIAM J. Computing* 25, No. 2, 448-476, 1996.

81. S. Shukla, H. Hunt III, D. Rosenkrantz, and R. Stearns. On the Complexity of Relational Problems for Finite State Processes. *Proc. Int'l Colloquium on Automata Programming and Languages* (ICALP), pp. 466-477, 1996.

82. J. Tripp, A. Hansson, M. Gokhale, H. Mortveit. Partitioning Hardware and Software for Reconfigurable Supercomputing Applications: A Case Study, *Proc. Supercomputing* (SC'05), 2005.

83. D. Watts, S. Strogatz. Collective dynamics of 'small-world' networks, *Nature*, vol. 393, pp. 440-442, 1998.

84. P. Wegner. Interactive Foundations of Computing, *Theoretical Computer Science* 192, pp. 315-351, 1998.

85. S. Wolfram, Ed. *Theory and applications of cellular automata*, World Scientific, 1987.

86. http://dimacs.rutgers.edu/Workshops/Opening/abstracts.html
http://www.mel.nist.gov/div826/msid/sima/simconf/march04/phsi.pdf
http://www.iupui.edu/ ilight/symposium04/ILIGHTPPT/measrespon.pdf
http://www.mgmt.purdue.edu/centers/seas/Research/Research.htm.

Part IV

New Directions

The Multidisciplinary Patterns of Interaction from Sciences to Computer Science

Andrea Omicini, Alessandro Ricci, and Mirko Viroli

ALMA MATER STUDIORUM—Università di Bologna a Cesena, Italy

> *We have to study the interactions as well as the parts.*
> John H. Holland, "Emergence: From Chaos to Order" [23, page 14]

Summary. Interaction is a fundamental dimension for modelling and engineering complex computational systems. More generally, interaction is a critical issue in the understanding of complex systems of any sort: as such, it has emerged in several well-established scientific areas other than computer science, like biology, physics, social and organizational sciences.

In this chapter, we take a multidisciplinary view of interaction by drawing parallels between researches outside and within computer science. We point out some of the basic patterns of interaction as they emerge from a number of heterogeneous research fields, and show how they can be brought to computer science and provide new insights on the issue of interaction in complex computational systems.

1 The Many Facets of Interaction

Interaction is a fundamental dimension for modelling and engineering complex computational systems. In particular, in a world where software systems are made of an ever-increasing amount of objects, components, processes, or agents, and where the Internet, with billions of interacting clients and servers, represents the most widespread application environment, it is quite apparent that interaction is today the most relevant source of complexity for software systems of any sort.

Obviously, complexity is not a peculiar feature of software systems: instead, the notion of complex system crosses the strict boundaries between different scientific disciplines, ranging from physics to biology, from economics to sociology and organization sciences. Rather than making complexity a hazy and fuzzy concept, such a multidisciplinary interest has produced a flow of innovative and stimulating research that has started debating and penetrating the intricacies of complexity as a whole, trans-disciplinary concept. Starting from the pioneering work of Simon [44] on complex artificial systems (whose acceptation of complexity and complex system is the one implicitly adopted here), this has led to the recognition that there exist some "laws of complexity" that characterize any complex system, independently of its specific nature [26]. No matter if we are modelling the behaviour of a human organization, the life of an intricate ecosystem, or the dynamics of a huge market-place, we can expect to find some repeated patterns, some shared schema, some common laws that makes all these systems look similar when observed at the right level of abstraction.

Analogously, when we focus on artificial, computer-based systems, exploiting a multidisciplinary approach in order to understand complex software systems comes to be almost mandatory, rather than useful or merely inspiring. This holds, also and in particular, when trying to fully understand the role of interaction within complex software systems. In this perspective, we argue that one should first look at the many scientific research fields dealing with complex systems of any sort, and devise out the multifaceted aspects of interaction they exhibit. Along this line, in this chapter we liberally draw from the findings of some relevant fields dealing with complex systems, and try to outline the many diverse patterns of interaction as they independently emerge from such a wide range of different research fields. Then, we discuss how results coming from such heterogeneous sources can be used to draw some fundamental conclusions about the nature and role of interaction within complex software systems. Whenever the sake of clarity demands it, we focus on multiagent systems (MAS), as they encompass the widest range of sources of complexity (intelligence, autonomy, mobility, decentralised control, etc.) among the modern software paradigms.

First of all, Sect. 2 introduces a suggestive view on interaction as it comes from the world of physics. There, the issue of interaction has slowly emerged as a relevant one—from Newton's reflections on mediators of forces, to the N-body problem—to become a key one in the last century, when physicists focused on the one hand on devising out the mediator particles for fundamental forces, on the other hand on defining the general theory encompassing all known fundamental laws that govern interaction between basic particles. Then, according to the view currently promoted by the most advanced research, all physical processes could possibly be explained in terms of the *interactions* among vibrating filaments of energy, called *strings* [19]. So, even at the most fundamental level of human science—the world of fundamental physics—it is interaction that works as both the source of complexity and the potential source of solutions. Even though the above point may be argued (and with some reasons) to be more speculative than scientifically well-founded, it seems at least indicative of the fact that dealing with complex systems first of all means understanding and modelling the patterns of interaction among the basic system components.

The distinction between the "replicator" and "interactor" units of selection that has characterized a good deal of the last decades' discussions in the field of evolutionary biology is also quite revelatory [25], as discussed in Sect. 3. Roughly speaking, the scientific debate has led to a recognition that causality of natural selection (and thus, evolution of biological systems) resides in the entities that interact with their environment and make replication differential (interactors), rather than in the individual entities that pass on their structure in replication (replicators) [17]. Then, it is not merely that complex systems demand that investigations focus on interaction. By taking biological systems as meaningful examples of complex systems, we see that their evolution over time cannot be understood except in terms of the interactions of their individual components with the environment. This agrees with the Brooks' revolution in robotics [5], where interaction with the environment is proposed as the main source for intelligent behaviour of artificial systems, as well as with recent trends of computational research such as agent-oriented software engineering [3], which promote the *environment* as a first-class entity in the engineering of situated computational systems [34]. More generally, this says that the interaction between components of whichever sort and their environment is a fundamental dimension for modelling and engineering complex software systems.

Biological systems tell us something else about the nature of the interaction with the environment. By taking into account the well-studied behaviour of ant colonies [18], it is quite easy to see how some key features of complex systems—such as emergent behaviours, some forms of global intelligence, and system self-adaptation to changing environment conditions—can stem from stigmergic coordination, that is, the result of interactions occurring among individuals (ants) *through* the environment (through pheromones, in the case of ants) [21, 24]. Such sorts of complex systems, in short, exhibit independent and autonomous individual components, that interact with each other mainly by modifying the surrounding environment, through *mediators* (e.g., the pheromones) that physically embody an information content, and whose characteristics (e.g., the rate of decay) affect the nature of interaction among components, as well as the global behaviour of the system and its evolution over time.

Mediated interaction, the nature of the mediators, and their intrinsic influence over the global system behaviour, emerge as key issues for understanding complex systems—and, quite possibly, for modelling and engineering computational systems. Given the social nature of biological systems like ant colonies or hives, it does not come as a surprise that mediated interaction and the related issues are addressed in even more detail in the context of psychological and organizational sciences. Accordingly, in Sect. 4 we show how activity theory (AT) [29, 49] provides a promising framework for understanding the nature of interaction in complex systems seen as organizations. Central to AT is the notion of *artifact*, which serves as a *mediator* for any sort of interaction in human activities. Artifacts can be either physical, such as pens, walls and traffic lights, or cognitive, such as operating procedures, heuristics, scripts, individual and collective experiences, and languages. As mediating tools, artifacts have both an *enabling* and a *constraining* function, in that they expand the ability of the individuals to interact and affect the environment, but at the same time, as the vehicles for interaction, they limit this ability according to their own nature and structure.[1] The findings of AT can be recast in terms of computer science, by implicitly interpreting complex software systems as complex organizations. In order to make the system work and dynamically adapt to the changes of the world where it functions, mediating artifacts should exhibit properties such as malleability, controllability, predictability and inspectability. These features would allow and in principle promote dynamic adaptability of systems, intelligent self-organization, and support individual intelligence [36].

In Sect. 5 we draw from recent anthropological studies on the history of human societies to suggest how mediating artifacts should be reified within complex software systems. There, it has been shown that when the size of a human society grows over a certain number, direct interaction and sharing of power among peers is not functional any longer, threatening the survival of the society [11]. In response to such a growth in scale, that makes social systems unmanageable and unsuccessful in the long term, social *institutions* are always created (political and religious hierarchies, armies, administrative structures) which typically take the form of social *infrastructures*, that embody social laws and norms, and regulate the life of the societies. In term of computer-based systems, this corresponds to the recent trend toward *governing* infrastructures [35] which make it possible to govern the complexity of software systems by harnessing their interactions. This is illustrated by the notions of coordination service [48] and of e-institution [33] among others.

2 Interaction as a Fundamental Dimension of Systems

2.1 Interaction in Physics

Research in physics explores the nature and dynamics of the most complex system we can experience and observe: our physical world. By adopting a birds-eye view over the history of physics (that most physicists would probably execrate, but that may fit our needs as computational scientists, here), it is quite interesting to see how the issue of interaction developed here.

From Democritus to Mendeleev's periodic table, the first two thousand years of research on physics (in its most general form, thus including physical chemistry and the related disciplines) has been dominated by the interest in the nature and properties of fundamental "atomic" particles, the microscopic bricks of matter from which the macroscopic structure and dynamics of the whole Universe could be inferred. However, Newton's mechanics revolution

---

[1] As a simple example, a spear-thrower extends the reach of a hunter's arm, but also prevents him having both hands free.

positioned the problem of interaction as a core concern, perhaps for the first time. Each individual physical entity of a system does not simply behave according to some intrinsic properties, but continuously interacts with other individual entities in the system, so that the cumulative effects of all the interactions determine the global system behaviour.

Despite the simplicity of Newton's laws, the three-body problem (and its N-body generalisation[2]) already suggested how much complexity can emerge from interaction. However, it was Newton's philosophical reasoning that led to the first speculations about the nature of interaction between physical bodies, and about the existence of *mediators* enacting forces working between distant bodies as a form of implicit "communication". This inspired vision resulted in the attempt to encompass the whole spectrum of the fundamental forces of Nature within a single general framework, along the two directions of quanto-mechanics (at the microlevel) and Einstein's general relativity theory (at the macrolevel). Along this line, physicists strongly focused on the interaction issue: on the one hand, they tried to devise out and observe specific mediator particles for every known fundamental force, on the other hand they aimed at defining a unifying Theory of the Whole that could account for all the known fundamental laws of interaction.

The conflict between quantum-mechanics and relativity views may be resolved by the theory of strings, which not by chance introduces a suggestive view of interaction as a first-class issue in the world of fundamental physics [20]. According to string theorists, the whole universe is made of elementary particles, called strings, which are filaments of energy that have a spatial extension (they are not zero-sized particles) and vibrate. Their shape, and the various ways in which they can vibrate determine their observable properties, and produce (and explain) the huge variety of particles that fundamental physics has discovered or conjectured in the last centuries—in particular, mediators like gluons and gravitons. Also, the fact that strings are dimensional particles makes their mutual interaction an event that is nonatomic in space and time. The modalities of interaction among vibrating strings seem so complex that the conceptual and practical tools available to physicists today often fail to satisfactorily model the resulting physical processes.

What concerns us here, is one of the fundamental assumptions of string theory: that is, that all physical processes can be explained in terms of interactions among vibrating strings [19]. As a result, it is no longer possible to explain phenomena in the physical world in terms of the individual behaviour and properties of individual entities (e.g., their position and speed), which are then put together according to quite simple interaction patterns/laws—as in the case of classical Newtonian mechanics. Instead, the world of strings look rather like a place where complexity is largely a result of articulated interac-

---

[2] The well-known N body problem can be formulated as follows: given N bodies, their initial positions, masses, and velocities, finding their subsequent motions as determined by classical, Newtonian mechanics.

tion patterns between the individual components. So, even at the most fundamental level of human science—the world of fundamental physics—interaction (among strings, at the current state of knowledge) works as both a source of complexity and a potential source of solutions.

2.2 Interaction in Computational Systems

The trend toward interaction in physics research has been parallelled in computational sciences, in particular by the intuitions of Robin Milner [31] and by the remarkable work by Peter Wegner [50, 51]. One of the starting points of Wegner's work was the incoherent situation of computer science as it emerged at the end the 1980s: a world where algorithms and Turing machines dominated the theoretical scene, while computers everywhere were operating under a completely different computational paradigm, yet to be even recognized. In short, Wegner argued that Turing machines actually expressed only the scale of complexity of algorithms as executed by sequential machines with no interaction whatsoever, apart from initial input and final output. At the same time, practical experience with any computer featuring an even trivial operating system provided evidence of an interactive way to compute that was not accounted for in any way by Turing's model.

The resulting claim, with formal support recently added to the already quite convincing evidence [16], was that computation should be conceived as spreading over two orthogonal dimensions—*algorithmic* and *interactive* computation—that give rise to different levels in the expressiveness of computational systems. While Turing machines were perfect models for algorithmic computation, they could say nothing (or, at least, not so much) about interactive computation, and new, more general models were required, such as the persistent turing machine (PTM) [16]. After Milner first emphasized the role of interaction in computational systems [31], Wegner made interaction emerge as a first-class issue, which is at the core of both computer research and technology.

The above parallel between the history of ideas in physics and computer science might then be argued (and maybe with some reasons) to be more speculative than scientifically well-founded. However, it seems to indicate that the understanding of complex systems cannot come from the mere study of the nature and inner dynamics of the basic system constituents, but requires instead that the nontrivial patterns of their mutual interaction be devised out and suitably modelled.

3 Interaction and Environment

3.1 Interactors in Evolutionary Biology

Evolutionary biology is a particularly interesting field for us here, given the fact that it deals with the long-term behaviour of complex living systems.

Evolutionary biology aims at understanding and explaining the way in which first-class components of biological systems (such as cells, organisms, species) change over time—where the notion of time spans from the small scale of individual living organisms up to the geological scale. After nearly one century and a half, one of the reference works in the field is still the monumental *Origin of Species* by Charles Darwin [8], a milestone of human knowledge indeed. According to the basic Darwinian theory, the process of natural selection is grounded on three basic facts (overproduction of offspring, variation, and heritability) plus one core mechanism, that is, differential reproductive success within evolving local environments. Besides the obvious general relevance of such a matter, what is really of interest here is the subject of the intense and passionate discussion that has kept going on during the last decades among evolutionary biologists. The matter of discussion, labelled as the *replicator approach vs. interactor approach* issue, focused on how "differential selection" actually occurs, and what is the unit of (differential) selection.

In general, a replicator can be described as an "entity that passes on its structure directly in replication", and an interactor as an "entity that directly interacts as a cohesive whole with its environment in such a way that replication is differential" [25, page 318]. The so-called "replicator approach" sees all evolution as proceeding through genes as units of reproduction, with the interacting entities (the organisms) merely built up as a result. Along this line, the founders of modern gene selectionism, such as Dawkins [9] and Williams [53], advocated the prominence of replicators in the selection process: the real unit of selection is represented by the genes, struggling for their eternal life, indefinitely reproducing themselves through higher-level organisms working as mere passive recipients, vehicles for gene existence. By contrast, the "interactor approach" obviously acknowledges the role of replication in selection (already assumed by Darwin long before the gene replication mechanism was known), but advocates the prominence of interactors as units of reproduction. Along this line, selection is obviously defined in terms of *both* notions (replicator *and* interactor) as the result of the differential proliferation/extinction of interactors in terms of the differential perpetuation of replicators.

However, according to Stephen Gould, causality in selection resides in interaction with the environment, and not in replication [17, page 615].[3] In particular, the key point in Gould's theory is that genes (the replicators) do not interact *directly* with the environment—so, they are not exposed directly to change. Rather, genes indirectly operate via the organisms (the interactors) that live, behave, interact and die—and typically reproduce, thus perpetuating replicators as a secondary effect. In doing so, interactors build up the process of differential selection that determines the evolution of biological systems over time: interaction with the environment can then be viewed as the main force that drives biological evolution.

---

[3] See also [17, page 623]: "units of selection must, above all, be interactors".

3.2 The Role of the Environment in Computational Systems

At a first glance, what happened in the evolutionary biology field resembles some of the research developments that occurred in computational sciences in the last decades, and in particular in the MAS field. At the very beginning (after Darwin, but before Mendel's gene theory was commonly understood and accepted) the very notion of replicator was an empty box: heritability of features was accepted, but no scientific explanation of how this could happen was available. As a result, when the gene replication mechanism was finally understood and modelled, and used as a basis for the whole Darwinian theory, excitement put all the emphasis upon such a mechanism—so, for instance, explaining everything in terms of genes and their duplication was quite natural. Only subsequently, after Hull and Gould, organisms—rather than genes—were finally recognized as the units of selection, and interaction with the environment was understood as a primal issue in natural selection.

More or less in the same way, the power of the notion of agency made research on MASs focus for a long time on the individual agent issues—and in particular on principles of the agent inner architecture and functioning. Even the revolutionary work of Brooks on robotic agents [5], with its notion of *situated intelligence* pointing out the inextricable relation between intelligent behaviour and the environment, was not immediately appreciated. Only in the last few years, interaction with the environment has finally been recognized as an essential issue for understanding agent and MAS evolution over time. It is not by chance that only in 2004 was the first workshop on "Environments for MultiAgent Systems" held, at the 3rd world-wide MAS conference [52]. The recognition of the role of the environment in the MAS field recently came from subfields such as agent-oriented software engineering (AOSE) [3]. There, AOSE methodologies promoted the environment as a first-class entity in the engineering of situated computational systems, putting the interaction of agents with their environment at the core of the engineering process [34]. Under this perspective, agents are the interactors of MASs, and it is their observable behaviour while interacting with the environment—their *situated interaction*, along Brooks' line—rather than their inner structure, that determines the evolution of the system as a whole.

3.3 Interaction through the Environment

When trying to understand how interaction with the environment affects the properties and behaviour of complex systems, social biological systems can be used as a powerful source of inspiration. In the context of animal societies, like ant or termite colonies, *stigmergy* is a well-known form of indirect interaction occurring through the environment—and exploiting the physical properties of the environment. There, individuals (such as ants or termites) interact by exploiting shared environmental structures and mechanisms to store and sense some sorts of signs (such as pheromones in the case of ant-based systems), as well as processes transforming them (such as evaporation/aggregation of pheromones) which also depend on the nature of the environment [18].

Complex social systems of this kind, in short, exhibit independent and autonomous individual components, which interact with each other in several nontrivial ways, but mainly by locally modifying the surrounding environment. The modification is through *mediators* (e.g., the pheromones) that physically embody an information content, and whose characteristics (e.g., the rate of decay) affect the nature of interaction among components, and, in the end, the global behaviour of the system and its evolution over time. The many desirable features of such systems—like emergent behaviours, some forms of global intelligence, and system self-adaptation to changing environment conditions—that can stem from stigmergic coordination, has inspired a number of stigmergy-based approaches to the coordination of computational systems [21, 24]. Other models, like the ones based on computational fields [30], or generalizing stigmergy [41], add some more to the notion of situated interaction, which is going to be clearly developed in the next section through the specific notion of mediated interaction.

4 Mediated Interaction

4.1 Mediated Interaction in Human Organizations

Activity theory [29, 49, 13] and distributed cognition [27] are two approaches to the study of human social activities that have deeply focused on the role of interaction within complex human organizations. The first result clearly emerging from these social/psychological theories is that *every individual as well as social activity in complex societies is mediated* [46, 2].

This is particularly clear in the context of activity theory (AT), where *mediation* is among the basic principles that constitute the core of the AT framework: human activity is always mediated by a number of tools or *artifacts*, both external and internal. The mechanism underlying artifact mediation is the formation of *functional organs*, i.e., the combination of natural human abilities with the capacities of external components—artifacts—to perform a new function of to perform an existing one more efficiently.

Then, any activity can be characterized by a *subject*, an *object* and by one or more *mediating artifacts*: (i) a subject is an agent or group engaged in an activity; (ii) an object is held by the subject and motivates the activity, giving it a specific direction (the objective of the activity); (iii) the mediation artifacts are the tools that enable and mediate subject actions toward the object of the activity. The mediating artifacts can be either physical or abstract/cognitive; from cognitive examples such as symbols, rules, operating procedures, heuristics, individual/collective experiences, languages, to physical entities, such as maps, blackboards, synchronizers, semaphores, and so on. The definition is clearly oriented to bring to the foreground not only individuals (subjects) and their cognitive aspects, but also the context where they play, and the continuous dynamic processes that link subjects and the context.

According to AT, mediating tools have both an *enabling* and a *constraining* function. On the one hand, they expand the possibilities of individuals to manipulate and transform different objects. On the other hand, the object is perceived and manipulated not "as such" but within the limitations set by the tool. Mediating artifacts shape the way human beings interact with reality. According to the principle of internalisation/externalisation, shaping external activities ultimately results in shaping internal ones. Artifacts embody a set of social practices, and their design reflects a history of particular use: they usually reflect the experiences of other people who have tried to solve similar problems at an earlier time and invented/modified the tool to make it more efficient.

Mediating artifacts are created and transformed during the development of the activity itself and then they carry with them a particular culture, the historical remnants of that development. So, the use of tools is a means for the *accumulation* and *transmission* of *social knowledge*. They influence not only the external behaviour, but also the mental functioning of individuals using them.

Latest research in AT—applied in particular in the context of CSCW (Computer Supported Cooperative Work)—focuses on the characterization of activities and artifacts in the context of collective human work [2]. AT describes cooperation as a collaborative activity with one objective but distributed between several actors, each performing one or more actions according to the shared goal of the work. The relationships between the individual work activities and the work activities of his/her fellow workers is subject to a division of work, and is regulated by different rules and norms, more or less explicit. According to this research, a collaborative activity can be structured in three *hierarchical levels*: *co-ordinated*, *co-operative*, and *co-constructive* [2, 12]. Mediating artifacts are *used* to encapsulate and automatise the routine flow of interaction between the participants to the collaborative activities at the co-ordination level. By contrast, they are *designed* and *forged* at the co-operation level, where participants focus on a common objective of the activity, and then on the means (the artifacts) for realizing it.

The notion of *dynamic transformation* between the three hierarchical levels of collaborative activities is also central to AT [2]. Transformations are strictly related to the stability of the means of work and of the object of work. Upward transformations correspond to the activity of evaluating and re-thinking either the means of work, or the object of the work itself. Instead, downward transformations correspond to the resolution of conflicts and problems, which is reified in the lower levels, possibly embodied in a newly-forged mediating artifact. Correspondingly, *reflection* on the means of work—going from co-ordination to co-operation—and *routinization*—going from co-operation to co-ordination—are the most important transformations. The former happens when the coordinated flow of work, relying on stable means of work such as scripts, rules, mediating artifacts in general, needs to be co-operatively re-established according to the object of work; the reasons can be either co-ordination breakdown, or a deliberate re-conceptualization of the way the work is currently achieved. The latter works in the opposite directions, by re-establishing co-ordinated work where the means of collaboration are stabilized, and new/adapted mediating artifacts are provided to be exploited by participants in the co-ordination stage.

4.2 Mediated Interaction in Computational Systems

Activity theory has recently found its applications within computational sciences, in particular in CSCW [32] and agent-oriented software engineering [40]. More generally, the conceptual framework of AT can find its use beyond the scope of human collaborative activities, wherever systems can be conceived as made of independent entities, which autonomously act within a structured context to achieve their own goals as well as collective objectives. This is for instance the sort of context that is typical of distributed and concurrent systems, in particular those modelled or built according to the agent paradigm.

AT is a source of a number of interesting ideas for computational systems. As far as interaction is concerned, we can synthesize at least three major points:

Beyond direct interaction — First of all, interaction is always mediated. Direct interaction is only an interpretation, which only works when the medium of the interaction can be abstracted away without any loss in the understanding of the state and dynamics of the interaction. *Environment* plays a key role here, since it generally works as the natural *locus* of the mediation: the central issue becomes how to control and instrument the environment where computational systems live and work, in order to enable and coordinate the interaction among the computational entities that are there immersed.

Mediating artifacts — Mediated interaction is encapsulated within first-class entities, the mediating artifacts. Mediating artifacts play a twofold role: constructive/enabling, and constraining/governing. On the one hand, they are the means that enable interaction, and allow software engineers to define and shape the space of component interaction. On the other hand, by determining admissible interactions, they constrain the components' observable behaviour, and make it possible to govern the space of interaction.

- Mediating artifacts are then essential tools in the modelling and engineering of complex computational systems, and are subject of theories and practices that are typically different from the ones adopted for interacting components. The central role of abstractions working as mediating artifacts is already evident in several approaches coming from computer science, software engineering and artificial intelligence. The notion of coordination medium within the area of coordination models and languages [6, 15]—like Linda tuple spaces [14] or TuCSoN tuple centres [38]—blackboards in distributed artificial intelligence [7], channels in the core calculi for interaction [31] or component composition [1], connectors in software architectures [43].

Analysis and synthesis of the interaction space — The notions of mediated interaction and mediated artifact deeply impact on methodologies for the construction of computational systems, at every stage of the engineering process. The three levels for collaborative activities in AT—co-construction, co-operation, co-ordination—can be seen as representing distinct stages of an interaction-oriented engineering process, covering the specification, design, validation, run-time verification and modification of mediating artifacts.

- Dynamic transformation between the three levels is the crucial point for both the analysis and the synthesis in the interaction-oriented engineering process: on the one hand, mediating artifacts are the subject of dynamic observation—observing their state and history makes it possible to analyse and understand the dynamic behaviour of complex systems; on the other hand, mediating artifacts are the basic bricks for computational systems—they are designed and forged to shape and govern the space of component interaction.

- Dynamics also means that systems can be changed at run-time, by suitably observing, understanding and modifying mediating artifacts, so as to intervene on the dynamics of system interaction. By featuring properties such as predictability, inspectability, controllability, malleability and linkability [40], mediating artifacts promote engineering practices aimed at promoting social intelligence, system adaptation and self-organization of computational systems [37].

5 Institutions and Infrastructures

5.1 Institutions and Infrastructures in Human Societies

The most recent accounts of the research by cultural anthropologists tend to recognize some repeated patterns in the formation and evolution of human societies in the last ten thousands years—not only in the European and North-American history, but around the globe. In particular, the many different forms taken by human societies are often divided in half a dozen of categories, that differs under many aspects: number of members, settlement pattern, basis of relationships between members, and (in general) form of government [11].

However, it can be easily seen that most of the above issues are so to say "dependent" variables, where the main "independent variable" is the number of people constituting a society. How people are settled, how they relate each other, how they resolve conflicts, etc., are mostly dependent on the number of members of the society.

Under certain favourable conditions (such as the abundance of food), successful societies (that is, those forms of human organization that guarantee more chances of survival to its members, and thus, to themselves) tend to grow in size. When they grow over certain limits, the institutions that govern them are forced to change—and societies change with them. For instance, in a band (the tiniest form of society, with dozens of members at most) or a tribe (hundreds of members), power is shared among peers, and conflict resolutions between members is handled informally on a case by case basis: no formal rules nor recognized institutions (apart from shared habit and oral tradition) help in composing conflicts. By contrast, larger societal forms like chiefdoms (with thousands of members) typically evolve by requiring some forms of central government (with chiefs exerting their powers over other members) and institutions (with bureaucrats ruling some aspects of social life, like exacting tributes, or resolving conflicts between members). The largest known forms of human organizations (states) typically develop military forces, police, written rules (laws), and all the well-known (to us) social institutions that shape and govern modern forms of human societies.

In the end, this is clearly a problem of *scale*: direct interaction and sharing of power among (human) peers does not work at the large scale. By freely reinterpreting the results from [11], this is due to several reasons:

Mutual recognition — Any form of cooperation (or even conflict avoidance) between members of a society depends on their capability to recognize each other as members of the *same* society, even if they do not know each other directly. When mutual recognition can no longer be based on direct knowledge, as in the case of large number of members, only formally defined social institutions (common, county, nation, state, . . .) can ensure mutual recognition by providing a social, shared notion of identity, not based on kinship or friendship of any kind.

Monopoly of force — When the number of the society members is too high, the number of possible conflicts grows so much that the use of force by conflicting members to resolve conflicts becomes potentially disruptive for the society as a whole. The development of centralised institutions monopolising force and preventing/solving potentially violent disputes through both administrative and military infrastructures (judiciary, prisons, police, army) become inescapable when a society grows in size.

Delegation of Power — In small societies, decision making can be a globally shared process where everybody is involved in the discussion and in the final deliberation. In the case of large societies, this may obviously lead to an unbearably inefficient process, and has typically produced many forms of delegation of power to a small number of selected members (leaders, majors, kings, presidents) or institutions (oligarchs, senates, parliaments), that can ensure timely convergence of the decision process.

Redistribution of goods — While trading in small societies can be handled on a peer-to-peer basis, the exchange of goods needs a more complex organization in larger societies. Political and economical conventions, regulations, norms and laws are required, and call for suitable institutions to enact them, and rule economic interaction among a vast number of society members.

Distribution of space and resources — Resources available to a small society, like living space, can be distributed on an ad hoc basis, and accessed almost freely. When population increases, and its density grows, distribution of space (and access to shared resources like water and food) requires a more structured societal organization, and the introduction of new notions like private property, right to access, right to use and so on.

5.2 Institutions and Infrastructures in Computational Systems

So, what are we going to learn for software systems, from the long history of successful complex systems like human societies? A number of interesting results have the potential to be applied to computational systems in general. For the sake of simplicity, however, in the following we will refer in particular to MASs, as they present the deepest similarities with human societies among the many classes of computational systems known today.

First of all, we recognize that large systems composed of many individual members cannot be based on peer-to-peer relations: interactions between members have to be governed and ruled by suitable *institutions*. How much is "large" for a software system we cannot derive from here: a human in a human society is not the same as an agent in a MAS. What is not likely to change, however, is that *at some scale*—whichever it is, thousands, millions or billions of agents—the same sorts of problems are likely to arise in increasingly complex MASs that already rose in human society growing in size over time, and eventually make the development of social institutions almost mandatory.[4] On the other hand, this also corresponds in MAS research to the recent trend toward institutions meant to govern the complexity of software systems by harnessing interaction among components—as illustrated by the nowadays emerging notions of *e-institution* [33], and *logic-based electronic institution* [47] among the many others.

Institutions for large agent societies have to provide solutions to problems such as the ones for large human societies pointed out above: mutual

---

[4] The argument that agents have not the same limitations as humans is exact but, at the same time, misleading: limitations (for instance, in memory) might be different (for instance, in size), but they exist indeed. So, there will always exist an appropriate scale of complexity where agents (and agent societies) encouter the same sort of problems as humans (and human societies).

recognition between members of a MAS, support for specialized agent roles, resolution of conflicts between agents, concerning for instance access to shared resources, enaction of global laws governing the behaviour of agents and promoting cooperative attitude—or at least, efficient decision making in large MASs.

As an aside it has also to be noted that institutions in human societies (the army, the police, the parliament, the judiciary) are not individual human beings—as obvious as it may seem. Institutions are made of humans, but none of them is an individual human. Even more, this simple consideration is not limited to collective institutions: even kingship, for instance, is an institution that cannot be identified or confused with the individual, temporary king. Correspondingly, institutions in MASs are (in principle) not agents: agents may participate in them and make them work, but no agent is an institution.[5] Instead, agent institutions are naturally embodied in agent infrastructures, governing agent interactions within a MAS—as pointed out by the notion of *governing infrastructure* in [35].[6]

In the same way as infrastructures in human societies provide services to individuals and organizations (the communication, the health care, the security, the physical mobility infrastructures, among the many others), agent infrastructures are meant to provide services to agents and agent societies. Correspondingly, in the same way as traffic lights or street signs govern car traffic (allowing the more or less peaceful coexistence of car drivers), runtime abstractions provided by an agent infrastructure can be used by MASs to rule agent access to shared resources, and to allow several potentially conflicting agents to achieve their respective, unrelated goals in a coordinated way.[7] By further developing the conclusions of previous section, this is most properly achieved through the use of mediating artifacts, provided by agent infrastructures as runtime abstractions, as in the case of workflow engines for MASs [39], or of the general notion of *coordination services* [48].

The final point here is then clear: institutions, and the infrastructures that enforce them, are required to rule and govern the interactions among members of large, complex societies—without them, these societies are doomed to instability, chaos and final failure. Accordingly, the modelling and engineer-

---

[5] The fact that institutions can be interpreted (as in [4]) or even implemented (as in [45]) as agents can be of some use, sometimes, but does not affect the general principle that institutions are not agents.

[6] In the same way as they are not agents, institutions are not even infrastructures: rather, agent institutions are naturally *implemented upon* agent infrastructures.

[7] While *agentification* of resources—that is, the view of resources as agents—is usable and useful in particular cases, it is not the most suitable and effective approach in general. In fact, as argued for instance in [42], agents *use* resources (through virtual physical actions), while they *speak* to other agents (through communicative actions): resources have interfaces, agents have not. In the end, agentification is nothing but the obvious result of the bias toward communication (against physical action) of current agent research.

ing of complex computational systems like MASs require the definition and enaction of *computational institutions*, embodied in hardware/software infrastructures which provide suitable runtime abstractions to mediate and govern the interaction between the individual components of a system.

6 Final Remarks and Conclusions

Many other possible sources of inspiration are not accounted for by this chapter: the implications of the Heisenberg *uncertainty principle* [22], basically stating that the interaction involved in the observation of phenomena intrinsically affects their behaviour; the part of modern biology concerning modelling and simulation of biological processes, and known as systems biology, which aims at system-level understanding of biological systems [28]; the notion of emergence [23], some theories of economics, and surely many others, even from the computer science field. But the goal here is not to be exhaustive.

Instead, our aim in this chapter is first of all to point out how the study of interaction as a first class subject of research is at the core of a number of diverse scientific areas dealing with complex systems; then, to show that the patterns emerging from such a heterogeneous range of scientific disciplines can be exploited as transdisciplinary bridges fruitfully connecting different areas, and bring their results to computer science.

Along this line, we try to devise an as-simple-as-possible conceptual path:

1. Interaction as a first-class subject of study — Complex systems cannot be described, understood or built by merely dealing with the nature and behaviour of their individual components—in the same way as fundamental physics cannot be understood by merely focusing upon the nature of individual particles. Instead, the study of interaction *per se* is a central issue, which calls for special, interaction-oriented paradigms, models, technologies and methodologies aimed at modelling and engineering complex systems.
2. Environment, or the situatedness of interaction — The individual components of a system cannot be studied or understood separately from the environment where they live and interact—in the same way as evolution of human societies cannot be understood separately from the environment where they live. Studying the environment of a system, its nature and dynamics, and its interaction with the system components, is a fundamental precondition to the understanding of the essence and evolution over time of complex systems of any sort.
3. Mediated interaction, and the artifacts — Interaction is always mediated, and the nature of mediators affects interaction—in the same way as the nature of pheromones determines the behaviour of ants and ant colonies. The notions of mediator and mediating artifact are essential tools in the analysis and synthesis of the space of interaction within complex systems.

4. Institutions and infrastructures — Institutions are required to rule and govern the interactions among participants of large, complex systems—in the same way as they are required by contemporary human societies. In order to enact institutions, infrastructures are needed which mediate and govern the interaction between the individual participants of a complex system, by encoding and enforcing institutional rules, norms and laws.

As the reader may easily note, the above interaction-related patterns do not require for their general description any reference to the nature of the complex system involved: be it either a physical, a biological, a social, or a computational system, all the above considerations straightforwardly apply. Drawing from the wide range of disciplines dealing with the study of complex systems, computational sciences can finally find new paths for overcoming complexity, and possibly constructing the artificial systems of tomorrow.

References

1. F. Arbab. Reo: A channel-based coordination model for component composition. *Mathematical Structures in Computer Science*, 14:329–366, 2004.
2. J. Bardram. Designing for the dynamics of cooperative work activities. In *1998 ACM Conference on Computer Supported Cooperative Work (CSCW'98)*, pages 89–98. ACM Press, 14–18Nov. 1998.
3. F. Bergenti, M.-P. Gleizes, and F. Zambonelli, editors. *Methodologies and Software Engineering for Agent Systems: The Agent-Oriented Software Engineering Handbook*. Kluwer Academic publishers, June 2004.
4. G. Boella and L. W. van der Torre. Attributing mental attitudes to normative systems. In J. S. Rosenschein, M. J. Wooldridge, T. Sandholm, and M. Yokoo, editors, *2nd International Joint Conference on Autonomous Agents and Multiagent Systems (AAMAS 2003)*, pages 942–943. ACM Press, 14-18July 2003. Poster.
5. R. A. Brooks. Intelligence without representation. *Artificial Intelligence*, 47(1-3):139–159, 1991.
6. P. Ciancarini. Coordination models and languages as software integrators. *ACM Computing Surveys*, 28(2):300–302, June 1996.
7. D. D. Corkill. Blackboard systems. *Journal of AI Expert*, 9(6):40–47, 1991.
8. C. Darwin. *The Origin of Species*. Murray, London, 6th edition, 1872.
9. R. Dawkins. *The Selfish Gene*. Oxford University Press, Oxford, UK, 1976.
10. G. Di Marzo Serugendo, A. Karageorgos, O. F. Rana, and F. Zambonelli, editors. *Engineering Self-Organising Systems: Nature-Inspired Approaches to Software Engineering*, volume 2977 of *LNAI*. Springer, May 2004.
11. J. Diamond. *Guns, Germs, and Steel: The Fates of Human Societies*. W.W. Norton & Company, March 1997.
12. Y. Engeström, K. Brown, L. C. Christopher, and J. Gregory. Coordination, cooperation, and communication in the courts: Expansive transitions in legal work. In M. Cole, Y. Engeström, and O. Vasquez, editors, *Mind, Culture, and Activity*, chapter 28. Cambridge University Press, Oct. 1997.

13. Y. Engeström, R. Miettinen, and R.-L. Punamaki, editors. *Perspectives on Activity Theory.* Cambridge University Press, 1999.

14. D. Gelernter. Generative communication in Linda. *ACM Transactions on Programming Languages and Systems,* 7(1):80–112, Jan. 1985.

15. D. Gelernter and N. Carriero. Coordination languages and their significance. *Communications of the ACM,* 35(2):97–107, Feb. 1992.

16. D. Q. Goldin, S. A. Smolka, P. C. Attie, and E. L. Sonderegger. Turing machines, transition systems and interaction. *Information and Computation,* 194(2):101–128, Nov. 2004.

17. S. J. Gould. *The Structure of Evolutionary Theory.* The Belknap Press of Harvard University Press, Mar. 2002.

18. P.-P. Grassé. La reconstruction du nid et les coordinations inter-individuelles chez bellicositermes natalensis et cubitermes sp. la theorie de la stigmergie: essai d'interpretation des termites constructeurs. *Insectes Sociaux,* 6:41–83, 1959.

19. B. R. Greene. *The Elegant Universe. Superstrings, Hidden Dimensions, and the Quest for the Ultimate Theory.* Knopf Publishing Group, March 2000.

20. B. R. Greene. *The Fabric of The Cosmos: Space, Time, and the Texture of Reality.* Alfred A. Knopf, New York, NY, USA, Feb. 2004.

21. Hadeli, P. Valckenaers, C. Zamfirescu, H. Van Brussel, B. Saint Germain, T. Hoelvoet, and E. Steegmans. Self-organising in multi-agent coordination and control using stigmergy. In Di Marzo Serugendo et al. [10], pages 105–123.

22. W. Heisenberg. *Collected Works: Scientific Review Papers, Talks, and Books.* Springer, 1984.

23. J. H. Holland. *Emergence: From Chaos to Order.* Basic Books, New York, NY, USA, 1999.

24. O. Holland and C. Melhuis. Stigmergy, self-organization, and sorting in collective robotics. *Artificial Life,* 5(2):173–202, 1999.

25. D. L. Hull. Individuality and selection. *Annual Review of Ecology and Systematics,* 11:311–332, 1980.

26. S. A. Kauffman. *Investigations.* Oxford University Press, March 2001.

27. D. Kirsh. Distributed cognition, coordination and environment design. In *European Cognitive Science Society,* pages 1–11, 1999.

28. H. Kitano. *Foundations of Systems Biology.* MIT Press, 2002.

29. A. N. Leontjev. *Activity, Consciousness, and Personality.* Prentice Hall, 1978.

30. M. Mamei and F. Zambonelli. Self-organization in multi-agents systems: A middelware approach. In Di Marzo Serugendo et al. [10], pages 233–248.

31. R. Milner. Elements of interaction: Turing Award lecture. *Communications of the ACM,* 36(1):78–89, Jan. 1993.

32. B. Nardi, editor. *Context and Consciousness: Activity Theory and Human-Computer Interaction.* MIT Press, 1996.

33. P. Noriega and C. Sierra. Electronic institutions: Future trends and challenges. In M. Klusch, S. Ossowski, and O. Shehory, editors, *Cooperative Information Agents VI,* volume 2446 of *LNAI.* Springer, 2002.

34. A. Omicini. SODA: Societies and infrastructures in the analysis and design of agent-based systems. In P. Ciancarini and M. J. Wooldridge, editors, *Agent-Oriented Software Engineering,* volume 1957 of *LNCS,* pages 185–193. Springer, 2001.

35. A. Omicini and S. Ossowski. Objective versus subjective coordination in the engineering of agent systems. In M. Klusch, S. Bergamaschi, P. Edwards, and P. Petta, editors, *Intelligent Information Agents: An AgentLink Perspective*, volume 2586 of *LNAI: State-of-the-Art Survey*, pages 179–202. Springer, 2003.

36. A. Omicini and A. Ricci. Reasoning about organisation: Shaping the infrastructure. *AI*IA Notizie*, XVI(2):7–16, June 2003.

37. A. Omicini, A. Ricci, M. Viroli, C. Castelfranchi, and L. Tummolini. Coordination artifacts: Environment-based coordination for intelligent agents. In N. R. Jennings, C. Sierra, L. Sonenberg, and M. Tambe, editors, *3rd international Joint Conference on Autonomous Agents and Multiagent Systems (AAMAS 2004)*, volume 1, pages 286–293, New York, NY, USA, 19–23July 2004. ACM.

38. A. Omicini and F. Zambonelli. Coordination for Internet application development. *Autonomous Agents and Multi-Agent Systems*, 2(3):251–269, Sept. 1999.

39. A. Ricci, A. Omicini, and E. Denti. Virtual enterprises and workflow management as agent coordination issues. *International Journal of Cooperative Information Systems*, 11(3/4):355–379, Sept./Dec. 2002.

40. A. Ricci, A. Omicini, and E. Denti. Activity Theory as a framework for MAS coordination. In P. Petta, R. Tolksdorf, and F. Zambonelli, editors, *Engineering Societies in the Agents World III*, volume 2577 of *LNCS*, pages 96–110. Springer-Verlag, Apr. 2003.

41. A. Ricci, A. Omicini, M. Viroli, L. Gardelli, and E. Oliva. Cognitive stigmergy: A framework based on agents and artifacts. In M.-P. Gleizes, G. A. Kaminka, A. Nowé, S. Ossowski, K. Tuyls, and K. Verbeeck, editors, *3rd European Workshop on Multi-Agent Systems (EUMAS 2005)*, pages 332–343, Brussels, Belgium, 7–8 Dec. 2005. Koninklijke Vlaamse Academie van Belie voor Wetenschappen en Kunsten.

42. A. Ricci, M. Viroli, and A. Omicini. Environment-based coordination through coordination artifacts. In Weyns et al. [52], pages 190–214. 1st International Workshop (E4MAS 2004), New York, NY, USA, July 2004, Revised Selected Papers.

43. M. Shaw, R. DeLine, D. V. Klein, T. L. Ross, D. M. Young, and G. Zelesnik. Abstractions for software architecture and tools to support them. *IEEE Transaction on Software Engineering*, 21(4):314–335, 1995.

44. H. A. Simon. *The Sciences of the Artificial*. The MIT Press, 3rd edition, Oct. 1996.

45. L. Stein. Interaction, computation, and education. In this volume.

46. T. Susi and T. Ziemke. Social cognition, artefacts, and stigmergy: A comparative analysis of theoretical frameworks for the understanding of artefact-mediated collaborative activity. *Cognitive Systems Research*, 2(4):273–290, Dec. 2001.

47. W. W. Vasconcelos. Logic-based electronic institutions. In J. A. Leite, A. Omicini, L. Sterling, and P. Torroni, editors, *Declarative Agent Languages and Technologies*, volume 2990 of *LNAI*, pages 223–242. Springer, May 2004. 1st International Workshop (DALT 2003), Melbourne, Australia, 15July2003. Revised Selected and Invited Papers.

48. M. Viroli and A. Omicini. Coordination as a service: Ontological and formal foundation. *Electronic Notes in Theoretical Computer Science*, 68(3):457–482, Mar. 2003. 1st International Workshop "Foundations of Coordination Languages and Software Architecture" (FOCLASA 2002), Brno, Czech Republic, 24Aug.2002. Proceedings.

49. L. S. Vygotskij. *Mind and Society*. Harvard University Press, 1978.

50. P. Wegner. Why interaction is more powerful than algorithms. *Communications of the ACM*, 40(5):80–91, May 1997.

51. P. Wegner. Interactive foundations of computing. *Theoretical Computer Science*, 192(2):315–351, Feb. 1998.

52. D. Weyns, H. V. D. Parunak, and F. Michel, editors. *Environments for Multi-Agent Systems*, volume 3374 of *LNAI*. Springer, Feb. 2005. 1st International Workshop (E4MAS 2004), New York, NY, USA, July 2004, Revised Selected Papers.

53. G. C. Williams. *Adaptation and Natural Selection*. Oxford University Press, Oxford, UK, 1966.

Coordination

Peter J. Denning[1] and Thomas W. Malone[2]

[1] Naval Postgraduate School, Monterey, CA, USA
[2] MIT, Cambridge, MA, USA

1 Introduction

Interactive computation seems like one of the oldest and most familiar aspects of computing. It was introduced in the first time-sharing systems in the late 1950s. In what way is interactive computation, as suggested by this book's title, a new paradigm?

Since those early days, the theory of computation has dwelt on machines and algorithms for mathematical functions. We might call these "function machines". The theory provided us with a deep and rich understanding of algorithmic complexity and the limitations of various classes of function machines. It gave us the Church–Turing thesis, which postulates that any effective procedure can be realized as a function machine. Its treatment of interaction has been limited to concurrent systems of interacting function machines. Real systems, however, are far more than networks of function machines; they are symbiotic communities of machines and humans. Humans contribute many things that function machines cannot do, such as recognizing context, making new distinctions, and creating new abstractions. Human–machine systems routinely carry out sophisticated computational tasks that the old theory says are not computable. As computational theorists grapple with this anomaly, they are extending the theory in refreshing directions and are introducing entirely new ways to think about computation and its limits. This is the revolution the editors are celebrating in this book.

Our purpose in this chapter is to present two complementary views of coordination in real human–machine systems. Coordination is the heart of interaction. Coordination is one of the six fundamental areas of computing principles. It is concerned with managing the interactions among multiple activities so that they achieve a single, collective result. Those who design, build, and evaluate interactive systems have employed coordination principles for many years. Coordination plays a similarly fundamental role in management science. Coordination principles will undoubtedly play a central role in the new theoretical paradigms.

2 The Great Principles Framework

Let us begin by situating coordination within a conceptual framework for the computing field, Fig. 1 (Denning 2003). The ultimate purpose of computing is to support information operations in a wide variety of application domains. Over the past 60 years, the computing field has developed about 30 core technologies that constitute the platforms on which applications are built. The core technologies rely on fundamental principles of two kinds: mechanics and

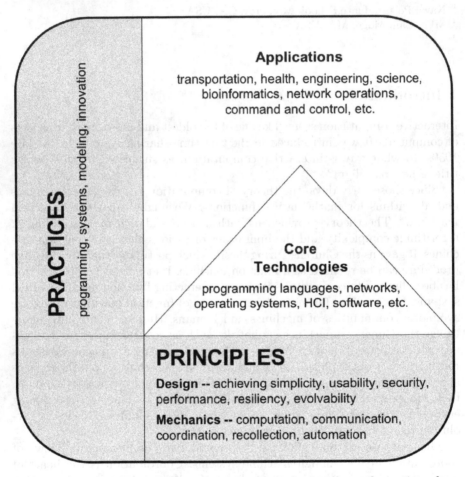

Fig. 1. The Great Principles framework consists of principles and practices along separate dimensions, supporting core technologies of computing, which in turn support applications. The principles are of two kinds: mechanics—how computations and computers work—and design—how to build them to work well. These principles pervade core technologies that in turn support many application areas. Practices, the embodied skills of computing professionals, apply at all levels

design. The mechanical principles are fundamental laws and recurrences, the cause-and-effect relationships of computers and algorithms; the design principles are time-tested guides for solving computational problems and organizing computing systems. The core practices are the areas of competence that computing professionals must have in order to build core technologies and applications on a solid base of principles. The space of applications is defined by principles and practices on separate dimensions. The principles express the what of computing, the practices the how.

This picture reveals computing to be a much broader field than programming. Although programming is a critical core practice, it is not the defining practice of the field. You cannot understand the field without understanding programming and programmers, but you cannot see the whole of the field if you think that applications are constructed simply by acts of programming.

The fundamental mechanical principles of computing can be viewed from five perspectives:

- Computation: What can be computed and how; limits of computing.
- Communication: Sending messages from one point to another.
- Coordination: Multiple entities cooperating toward a common result.
- Recollection: Storing and retrieving information.
- Automation: Performing cognitive tasks by computer.

These categories are not disjoint. For example, a network protocol can be studied under Communication in its role as a method of transmitting data, and under Coordination as a method of synchronizing sender and receiver. We often refer to the categories as the five windows because they are like five portals into the same room. Each window sees the contents of the room in a distinctive way. Some elements of the room are visible through multiple windows. The windows do not partition the room into five disjoint subsets.

These five windows completely cover the field. Imagine the block diagram of a typical computer. It consists of a CPU (central processing unit), a memory subsystem, and an I/O subsystem. The CPU corresponds to the Computation function; the memory to the Recollection function; and the I/O to the Communication function. Now observe that computers never stand alone; they are always interconnected in some way to other computers or to humans. This network of computers and humans corresponds to the Coordination function. Finally, the purpose of a network of computers is to work on tasks we delegate to it; the business of deciding what can be delegated, and how, corresponds to the Automation function. Thus the principal functions of computing systems coincide with the five windows.

3 Coordination

Coordination is concerned with multiple agents acting together (interacting) to accomplish a common goal. The agents can be computational processes or humans. Coordination implies some sort of feedback so that the agents can tell whether their actions are effective and can correct when necessary.

In this chapter, we describe two complementary approaches to understanding the fundamental principles of coordination. The first focuses on three basic kinds of dependencies among activities—flow, sharing, and fit—and the different coordination processes that can manage these dependencies. The other approach focuses on a single basic coordination molecule—the action loop—from which all coordination patterns can be built. Like the windows of computing mechanics, these two windows of coordination have distinctive views. The dependency view focuses on the flow of resources; the action loop view focuses on the flow of commitments. The two views work together synergistically.

4 Dependency Patterns and Coordination Processes

Coordination can be defined as the management of dependencies among activities (Malone and Crowston, 1994). An activity is a set of tasks performed by a human or computational process. A dependency relation between activities A and B exists when the completion of one activity (say B) depends in some way on the other activity (A). For example: (1) Activities A and B are events and A must precede B. (2) B needs information from A before acting. (3) A and B both need to use the same processor. (4) A and B produce parts that are combined into a single assembly. (5) B is software that customizes itself to the profile of activity A. (6) A's input to B must be in formats recognized by B.

It is useful to view such dependencies as arising from resources that are related to both activities. For example, activity A might produce a resource that activity B needs; both activities compete for the same resource; or both activities update the same resource.

More precisely, Fig. 2 shows the three topological possibilities for directed graphs involving two activities and one resource. We label these three basic dependency patterns: *flow, sharing,* and *fit* (see Crowston, 1991; Zlotkin, 1995; Malone, et al., 1999):

- *Flow dependencies* arise whenever one activity produces a resource that is used by another activity. This common dependency is the focus of most existing process mapping techniques, such as flow charts.
- *Sharing dependencies* occur whenever multiple activities all use the same (usually limited) resource. This kind of dependency arises when two activities need to be done by the same person, when they need to use the same computer processor, or when they both use money from the same account. It also arises when activities draw from a common resource even when access is not limited, for example, travel agents working from a common flight schedule. Although this kind of dependency is often not depicted in

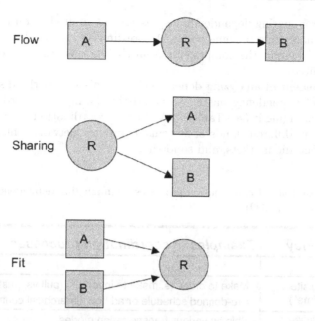

Fig. 2. The three fundamental dependency patterns can be depicted as directed graphs. In a *flow* dependency, one activity (A) produces a resource (R) used by another activity (B). In a *sharing* dependency, multiple activities all use the same resource. In a *fit* dependency, multiple activities jointly produce a single resource. All three dependencies are focal points for coordination

process maps, allocating shared, limited resources is clearly a critical aspect of many management activities and of the design of many computer systems.

- *Fit dependencies* arise when multiple activities collectively produce, contribute to, or update a single resource. This kind of dependency arises when several engineers are designing different modules of a software system, when an assembly line is fitting parts into a car, or when different travel agents are booking seats on the same flight. Although not always depicted on process maps, this kind of dependency is a critical aspect of many assembly and shared update operations.

The dependency patterns shown in Fig. 2 are certainly not the only ones possible, but as far as we can tell all other dependencies can be analyzed as specializations or combinations of these three. The flow dependency appears to be the most elementary of all because flows are involved in managing all the other types of dependencies.

Dependencies are managed with coordination processes or protocols that supplement the activities. A coordination protocol manages the resource involved in the dependency. For example, a coordination protocol for a flow dependency may move a resource from one activity to another. A coordination protocol for a sharing dependency may assign the limited resource among the contenders according to some policy. A coordination protocol for a fit dependency may assemble the components from the various activities contributing to the resource.

A key benefit of analyzing dependencies in this way is the discovery that each kind of dependency has a characteristic "family" of coordination processes for managing it (see Table 1). And these coordination processes are the same in many different kinds of systems: computer networks, human organizations, economic markets, and so forth.

Table 1. Examples of coordination processes for managing dependencies (adapted from Malone et al, 1999)

Dependency	Examples of coordination processes
Flow	
Prerequisite ("right time")	Make to order vs. make to inventory (pull vs. push) Pre-defined schedule or ad hoc hierarchical control
Accessibility ("right place")	Ship by various transportation modes Assemble at point of use
Usability ("right thing")	Conform to standards Negotiate individual requirements Participatory design
Sharing	FIFO queueing Preemptive priority queueing Budget allocation Managerial decision Market-like bidding
Fit	Predefined standards ("plan") Case by case negotiation ("emerge") Slotted synchronization Mutual exclusion locks Resolve conflicts by common manager or peer negotiation

The flow dependency, which accounts for the majority of coordination mechanisms, has three subdependencies: (1) The *prerequisite* dependency concerns the timing of the flow—how it is initiated (e.g., push or pull) or how often it is initiated (e.g., on a schedule or on demand). (2) The *accessibility* dependency concerns how the resource is made available to the activity that uses it (e.g., A ships it to B, or A makes it at B's location). (3) The *usability* dependency concerns making sure the resource is usable by B (e.g., the resource might meet some widely shared standard or A and B might negotiate the specifications individually each time). These three subdependencies correspond to the three elements of the common business phrase, *"right thing in the right place at the right time"*; in fact, they offer a rigorous working definition of this intuitive but often-imprecise business term.

Sharing dependencies are managed by a variety of coordination mechanisms that offer different ways to allocate a limited resource among contenders. These include FIFO queueing, priority queueing, budgets, managerial decision, multiple-reading, and market-like bidding. In a job shop, for instance, three workers could use a simple "first come first serve" mechanism to share a machine. Or, they could budget the machine time among themselves with assigned time slots. Or, they could use a priority scheme in which jobs of higher priority preempt other jobs at the machine. Or, the machine's owner could sell time to the highest bidder. A computer operating system has a very similar family of alternatives for scheduling the use of a computer processor, memory, and other resources. (See Coffman and Denning, 1973; Dellarocas, 1996, 1997.)

Fit dependencies are managed by a variety of coordination mechanisms that offer different ways to combining the contributions from the source activities. These include slotted access (each contributor has a specific location for its contribution), mutually-excluded (locked) access, or update access. An automobile assembly line illustrates slotted access: each station installs a part at a unique position, allowing many parts to be installed concurrently without conflict. An airline database illustrates mutually excluded update access: records must be locked by one updater at a time. The database illustrates a further coordination issue: some activities update it (a fit dependency) and others read it (a sharing dependency on the database lock); the reads and writes must be coordinated to avoid conflicts or errors in reading inconsistent data.

The use of the term "dependency" here differs somewhat from other computer science uses of the term. For example, in operating systems, databases, and networks we are concerned about the ordering of certain events, mutually exclusive use of shared data, buffer overflow, and deadlocks. Solutions to these problems often involve more than one of the flow-sharing-fit dependencies. For example, a mutual exclusion lock is both a sharing dependency (value of the lock) and flow dependency (obtaining the lock if it is free). Updating a record in a database or an item in a buffer is both a fit dependency (contributing to a common resource) and a flow dependency (obtaining the lock). A deadlock can be viewed as a failed combination of fit, sharing, and flow dependencies. The protocols for managing these dependencies are often dominated by their flow dependency components, which involve exchanges of signals or messages.

Computing systems also manage dependencies besides those built on exchange of signals or messages. For example, a procedure that checks its inputs for proper type and range is checking a usability subdependency of flow. A type-checking compiler manages flow dependencies (inheritance from higher types) and fit dependencies (a collection of types contributing to the whole program). Similarly, a linking loader implements flow and fit dependencies among modules. A CPU scheduler manages the sharing dependency of a processor among tasks. A seat-assignment program in an airline flights database manages fit dependencies among travel agents. A web page that customizes its display for a particular browser implements a flow dependency from the browser to the page.

These examples show that the coordination mechanisms we see in computing systems and networks are the managers of dependencies; but they are not the actual dependencies. The language of dependencies is like a higher level language and the mechanisms are like a lower level language. A designer expresses the dependencies and then implements coordination mechanisms to manage them.

Thus, a single dependency can be an abstraction for a very complex coordination process to manage it, and there may be many possible coordination processes for the same dependency. For example, the relation between a web server at one node of the Internet sending a page to a web browser at another node might be represented as a single flow dependency from the server to the browser. But this high-level flow dependency is an abstraction of many possible coordination processes that might involve dozens of low-level packets flowing in both directions.

The dependency-based approach can be used to analyze, design, and invent coordination processes for computer systems as well as for organizations. For example, it has been used to classify over 5000 business processes and activities; see the MIT website <ccs.mit.edu/ph> and Malone, Crowston, and Herman (2003). It helped invent a new way to hire people in a large financial services organization (Klein, et al., 2003). It has helped to integrate the software components in computer systems (Dellarocas, 1996, 1997).

5 Action Loops

The action loop directly describes a universal pattern of interaction between two entities as they coordinate to accomplish a task. It was first described by Winograd and Flores as "conversation for action" (1986) and matured into the Action Workflow technology (see <www.actiontech.com>). The action loop is linguistic: it is a conversational pattern followed by two parties. The loop consists of four segments, each representing a time interval closed by a speech act. (See Fig. 3.) Request–promise interactions that occur numerous times in daily life are the most common examples.

The action loop started as an expression of a universal pattern of human coordination—a model of interactions between individuals, personally and within organizations. The commitments of individual members to fulfill their roles in action loops create a coordination network, built from interconnected action loops, to support a common mission. (See Winograd and Flores, 1986; Denning, 1992; Denning and Medina-Mora, 1995.)

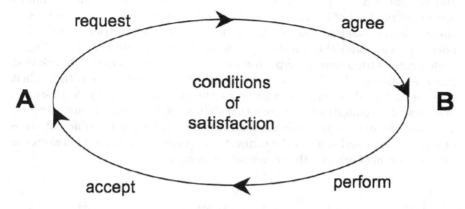

Fig. 3. The action loop is a fundamental pattern of coordination. It connects two parties: B fulfills a request from A. The two agree on the conditions of satisfaction, a clear statement of intention of what is to be accomplished and by when. The four loop segments are terminated by speech acts—"I request," "I agree," "I deliver," and "I am satisfied." The loop can represent a high-level coordination as when A is a customer and B a merchant; it can represent a low-level coordination as when A asks an office mate for a report; and it can represent a pair of machines carrying out a protocol. The fourth segment represents the opportunity for A to give feedback about B's performance; it can be direct, as in an acknowledgement, or indirect, as when B consults data about how many customers (A's) accepted its offer

When he first described action loops, Fernando Flores noted that some of the components might be collapsed and not explicit. For example: A says "Pass the salt." B passes the salt. A nods. There is only one explicit speech act; agreement and performance are collapsed into one action; and satisfaction is expressed with a nod. The important aspect is the closure of the loop. If any component is missing, the loop will not close, and various breakdowns will appear, such as a missed coordination, wasted effort, A distrusting B, or B branding A as ungrateful.

The action loop is also a model of human–computer interactions and of protocols between machines and software components, all of which rely on closed interaction loops. The failure of a loop to close produces breakdowns such as user thinking the computer has hung up, or a protocol between two computers stalls and freezes the system. In this sense, the action loop is the fundamental building block of coordinated action at all levels from interacting machines to interacting people in organizations.

The term workflow has come to mean the management of coordination among people in an organization. The action loop has added a new dimension to the study of workflow systems. These systems need to be viewed at two levels: the level of commitments and the level of information and resource flow. At the level of commitments we see individuals entering into agreements and coordinating with one another by action loops to fulfill their commitments. At the level of information and resource flow we see computing agents, clients, servers, and communication systems that store, retrieve, and transport data and materiel handled by people in the commitment network. Figure 4 illustrates with a university payroll process as an information network that processes forms. This diagram shows mainly flow dependencies with implicit sharing and fit dependencies relative to the databases. Figure 5 illustrates one view of a commitment network that drives the information-flow network. This view focuses on the action loops that are involved in the different steps of the processes and some of the connections (interaction points) between the information network and the coordination network.

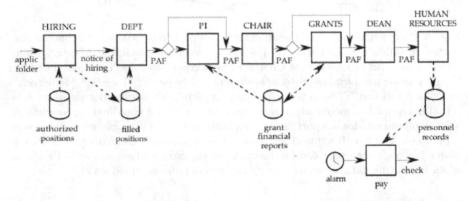

Fig. 4. The information network supporting a university pay process consists of a series of functions (boxes) that convey data (forms) and consult with databases (cylinders) and clocks. Intentions to pay someone are created during the hiring process and recorded in databases. They are enacted at set intervals when paychecks are produced. (PAF = personnel action form, PI = principal investigator)

How general is the action loop? The examples above work for coordination in business organizations. But what about nonbusiness examples such as baseball teams or orchestras, spontaneous teams, and even "flash mobs"? Although these groups have different purposes, their coordination structures can always be viewed as having action loops. A baseball team, for example, consists of nine players promising the manager to play positions, giving nine action loops with fairly general conditions of satisfaction (e.g., "play third base"); additional action loops arise spontaneously during plays such as catching the ball and throwing players out.

There is often a direct correspondence between action loops in the commitment network and flow dependencies in the information-resource network. The resource that flows from A to B is described by the conditions of satisfaction. The prerequisite aspect of the flow dependency is determined by whether the loop is an offer (initiated by B, a "push") or by a request (initiated by A, a

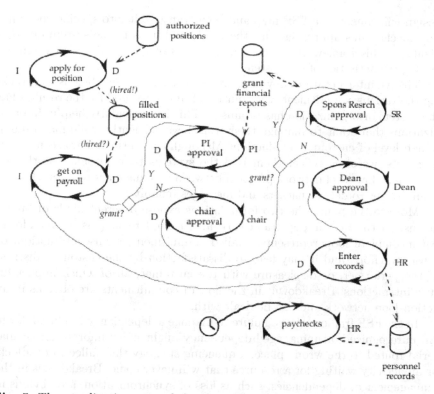

Fig. 5. The coordination network for the university pay process consists of action loops that are connected when a person playing a performer role in one loop makes requests in another. The cylinders represent databases of the information structure that answer questions needed to complete some action loops. This coordination process drives the information network shown in Fig. 4. (I = individual, D = department hiring agent, SR = sponsored research agent, HR = human resources agent)

"pull"). The accessibility aspect is managed by B's delivery act. The usability aspect is managed by the initial agreement on conditions of satisfaction and the final accept.

6 Synergy of the Two Frameworks

Flow-sharing-fit (FSF) dependency networks and action loop (AL) networks are interpretations of coordination and interaction. Each is a notation for presenting, describing, designing, and analyzing coordination. But the two approaches emphasize different things and are useful in different ways.

The FSF interpretation provides a general framework for coordination that avoids the detail of many coordination mechanisms. A dependency is an abstraction of a family of coordination mechanisms. A system or organizational design will construct a FSF map and then translate it into specific coordination mechanisms appropriate for the local conditions in the system or organization. This framework focuses on the flows of information and resources among the activities of the system.

The AL interpretation provides a framework for making obvious and tracking the various commitments that must be fulfilled to produce the results that the system or organization has promised. This is particularly helpful in organizations that want to manage their workflows efficiently while maintaining a high level of customer satisfaction. Although commitments are seen as human acts, we often reflect them into the systems that automate work. For example, a low-level network protocol between two machines reflects a human commitment to deliver packets and messages reliably.

More to the point, the two formulations expose different kinds of breakdowns. In the action-loop framework an incomplete loop is a breakdown. An incomplete loop represents a failed commitment, a miscoordination, or a wasted effort; and it may lead to dissatisfaction by the customer, distrust of the performer, or displeasure with the customer, all of which impact future interactions. Breakdowns in the flow of commitments are obvious in an action-loop network and can be dealt with.

In the FSF framework the failure to manage a dependency is a breakdown. An unrecognized or unmanaged dependency might mean information or material routed to the wrong place, a queueing strategy that failed, a deadlock, or an activity waiting for a resource that will never come. Breakdowns in the management of dependencies, such as loss of synchronization, are obvious in this framework and can be dealt with.

Another point of differentiation is that the two systems represent different approaches to hierarchical decomposition. For example, an action-loop network can be replaced by a single, more abstract loop if the network has a single customer and can be treated as a single, abstract performer. An FSF approach can analyze coordination recursively at many different levels. For instance, the entire sales and logistics departments of a company can be viewed as part of the coordination process used to manage the flow dependency of the company's products to its customers. But within the sales and logistics departments there are many detailed activities and resources which can, themselves, be analyzed in terms of FSF dependencies and the coordination processes needed to manage them.

Given these differences, an analysis of a system using both perspectives is likely to detect more breakdowns and surface more possibilities for innovation than either approach alone. As suggested in Fig. 6, we often achieve a more complete view of a system by looking at two levels: the network of commitments, and the network of dependencies. The two networks interact; events in one trigger (or correspond to) events in the other.

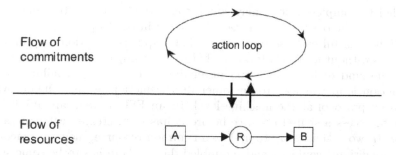

Fig. 6. Action loops are especially useful for visualizing, designing, and managing commitments toward their completions. Flow-sharing-fit dependencies are especially useful for managing coordination between activities and resources. Each framework makes certain kinds of breakdowns obvious; for example, broken loops and unmanaged dependencies

7 Can There Be Coordination Without Feedback?

Effective coordination implies some sort of feedback that enables actors to change if behaviors are ineffective. This statement deserves more scrutiny because it is easy to think of examples where there is coordination without apparent feedback:

- Scout ants leave enzyme trails that lead worker ants to food.
- Bees' dances tell other bees where pollen can be found.
- The weather service broadcasts a hurricane warning, asking thousands of people to take shelter or evacuate.
- Railroads and airlines publish timetables of trains and flights.
- Companies market their products.
- Search for Extra Terrestrial Intelligence, SETI, sends an inscribed plaque on a deep-space probe, hoping that another intelligence will read and decipher it.

In each of these cases, we find there is some form of indirect feedback that supports the coordination. Ants and bees have evolved their coordination practices over many generations; only the successful practices survive. People are educated or trained in advance of hurricanes to know what actions they should take in case of a warning; the warning triggers those actions. Railroads, airlines, and companies watch sales and discontinue unprofitable services and products. SETI hopes that one day, in a distant future, a response will come from another race.

The definition of the action loop allows for these indirect forms to complete the loop in the fourth segment. Action loops always occur in some context that gives the conditions of satisfaction meaning and purpose. That context is the result of previous actions, conversations, and declarations. The feedback needed to complete a loop may come from other actors in the context, not necessarily the ones who are directly engaged in the loop.

It is a useful exercise to analyze what happens in action loop and FSF systems without feedback. It seems that eliminating feedback inevitably leads to some kind of breakdown and unreliability. For example, failure to close an action loop will lead to customer dissatisfaction at the human level or a frozen protocol at the machine level. In an FSF system, an activity that tries to access a shared resource before it has been created will generate an error. If two activities try to update a common resource, they may encounter race conditions, conflicts, and scrambled data. There has to be some sort of feedback to insure that flow, sharing, and fit work correctly.

8 Delegations to Computational Coordination Structures

The two-level structure shown in Figs. 4 and 5 illustrates one of several possible ways for humans to delegate responsibilities to a computational structure. In that example, the making and fulfilling of promises was retained by humans (Fig. 5) and the movement of information on forms and files was delegated to an information structure (Fig. 4). In general, four levels of delegation are possible:

- **HH: human–human:** People coordinate directly in their social and linguistic networks without delegating anything to a computer, except possibly for the transport of signals and data through communication systems.
- **HHA: human–human with computer assistance:** A coordination network is represented as a computational structure, and individual interaction events (such as speech acts, clock triggers, and external signals) trigger state changes in the structure. The structure moves and processes data, and tracks progress, helping the participants continue to move toward completion of their commitments.
- **HC: human–computer:** The performer role of a loop is assigned to a computational process. The language for interacting with the process organizes the HC interface, HCI.
- **CC: computer–computer:** Both the requester and performer roles are delegated to (different) processes. The interactions between them follow prescribed multiparty algorithms called protocols. All the issues of concurrency and distributed computation fall under this heading.

The HHA level emerged in the 1980s under the title Computer Supported Cooperative Work, CSCW. For example, in the 1980s Action Technologies marketed an email system, The Coordinator, which tracked action loops; and Lotus Notes offered sophisticated dynamic conversation databases. There are now numerous other CSCW products, including graphical tools for mapping and managing coordination networks (like Fig. 5); project time-line schedulers; email filters, chat for unstructured, free form, real-time conversations;

group brainstorming systems; blackboard systems for collaboration and classroom management, and decision support systems for managers. Each of these systems is built around a model of the type of work supported; each helps the participants track the progress of the work toward completion or some form of resolution.

Since the first time-sharing systems of the late 1950s, the HC interaction, HCI, has been recognized as an important area of computing. A partial list of the HCI areas includes: command languages that evoke actions from the computer; design of functions such as mouse, window, or direct graphical manipulation, that make an interface language user-friendly and error resistant; "ergonomic" designs that minimize movements and steps; systems that help users navigate (or browse) through large complex spaces of objects; search engines for the World Wide Web; hypertext, the backbone of the World Wide Web; virtual reality; and schemas (such as the "desktop") that organize the workspace. The desktop metaphor, which has dominated user interfaces for a generation, has recently come under attack by designers who find it unsuited to many common HC interactions, for example, finding all one's documents on a particular topic. Two prominent examples of alternatives are the Lifestream model (Carriero-Gelernter, 2001) and the Apple Computer's Spotlight, which integrates keyword searches into the computer desktop.

The CC interaction has an even longer historical record. Computer systems almost always consisted of multiple interacting computers connected by a network. In the 1950s, operating systems designers worked out structures for organizing computing systems as sets of interacting, autonomous computational processes. They created coordination tools such as interrupts, time-slicing, context switching, semaphore signaling, message transfer, and scheduling methods such as priority and round-robin. In the 1960s the basic science of interprocess coordination was articulated under the heading of concurrency control: race conditions, determinacy, termination, queueing, congestion, synchronization, serialization, mutual exclusion, deadlock control, language constructs (such as monitors and cooperating sequential processes, CSP), correctness proofs for distributed computation, generic coordination patterns, and remote procedure call. Coordination became one of the fundamental responsibilities of an operating system. Since the 1960s, the theory of concurrency has developed extensively and has reached well beyond the sphere of operating systems. (See Coffman and Denning, 1973.)

9 Pushing the Limits of Delegation

Much of the progress described above depends on the successful delegation of human tasks to computers. How far can we push this? What limits our ability to delegate?

Everyone agrees that any mechanical, repetitive, mindless human process can be delegated to a computational process. The computational process can carry out exactly the same steps, with less error and at higher speed, and produce exactly the same results. Sometimes we can create a computational process that gives the same results as a human process but with a different method; for example, recent Bayesian spam filters have been successful even though no one knows whether humans use Bayesian learning to decide which emails are important. But there are many things we do not know how to delegate to a computer such as finding someone in a crowd, designing a new product, formulating a scientific hypothesis, performing a virtuoso concerto, composing music, or adjudicating a dispute. Writers Hubert Dreyfus (1992) and Don Norman (1994) have made long lists of things that humans do easily, but they doubt computers will ever be able to do them. Thus it appears there are limits to what can be delegated.

Even if we restrict the question of what can be delegated to pure coordination, there are limits. Can we delegate the fulfillment of a promise to a computer? This is a central issue in the study of software agents. Let us distinguish between low commitment and high commitment promises. A low commitment promise is a statement of intention. For example, if you say to your spouse, "I'll quit work early on Christmas Eve and be home for the family," your spouse may know from experience that a last-minute, high-paying client might demand your services on Christmas Eve. Your spouse knows you have good intentions but knows better than to trust your promise completely. In contrast, a high commitment promise is one that you're willing to go out of your way to deliver, going outside established processes and norms if need be. In a famous example, a Fedex plane made an emergency landing in Texas. The pilot was so concerned about delivering the packages on time, he hired a helicopter to ferry them to the nearest airport. To that point, no one had ever contemplated using a helicopter to transport Fedex packages. It appears that low commitment promises are easily delegated to computers; indeed, many people treat many automatic processes in this way. It appears that high commitment promises cannot be successfully delegated: the computer can't read the larger context, evaluate alternatives hidden there, or evaluate the risk of departing from established norms. In between these two extremes are many gradations. The more context can be made explicit, the better the job a computer can do in departing from established norms in finding alternative ways to fulfill promises.

10 The Role of Math in Understanding Coordination

The history of coordination shows that mathematical understanding has been very important to the advancement of the principles. Discrete and combinatorial math were among the earliest math to be deployed—graphs, trees, counting arguments, generating functions, models for asynchronous computation, and algorithm analysis. These were augmented by methods from predicate logic, used to state precise propositions describing the correct function of a distributed system, and by temporal logic that added predicates about time ordering of events. These maths are commonly used in theoretical computer science.

Coordination, however, frequently takes place in an environment of uncertainty about the exact timing of events. We don't know exactly at what moment a user will make a request of a machine, or exactly when the machine will respond. We don't know exactly how many users will overload a system, or packets will overload a network. To deal with these uncertainties, we routinely turn to probability theory, queueing theory, and scheduling theory to help. In the early 1970s, for example, we learned how to use "Markovian queueing networks" to predict throughput and response time of real computing systems quite accurately, and we developed extremely fast algorithms ("mean value analysis") to calculate these predictions from a model with many servers and workloads. We used this math to evaluate response times of web systems that cache web documents in local servers and to determine the capacity of web stores. We subsequently used the same math to understanding the performance of network protocols such as TCP/IP. We used scheduling theory to tell us how to organize tasks in real-time systems so that they could be completed within their deadlines after their triggering events. These maths do not play a prominent role in theoretical computer science.

This may account for why some theoretical computer scientists look at the area of coordination and see "practice" rather than "foundations". The math is there but it's not the math they are accustomed to looking for.

11 Personal Perspectives on Coordination History

Denning: My first memories of computers date back to 1951 when as a young boy I was captivated by the newspaper stories of "electronic brains being deployed in the Census Bureau". Even then, computers were portrayed as machines to interact with. Later in the 1950s I built simple computers for science fairs and discovered that some modes of interaction (clicking, buzzing, sparking, oscilloscopes, graphical output) were more attention-getting than others (silent vacuum tubes, voltmeters). When I arrived at MIT in 1964 to begin my formal education as a computer scientist, I joined Project MAC, which was dedicated to interactive computation. In those days I was primarily concerned with issues of concurrency control (the CC subdomain); but I was also interested in how interactive computing increased programmer productivity, reduced programming bugs, gave birth to text editing, and enabled direct graphical manipulation—the beginnings of HCI. I was fascinated with the invention of hypertext, mouse, and windows by Ted Nelson and Doug Engelbart in the later 1960s. Interactive computing, and the underlying technical issues of coordination, has been an integral part of the computing world I lived in for my entire career.

By 1970, Ed Coffman and I became convinced that the principles of operating systems, especially those bearing on coordination, had advanced sufficiently that operating systems should be considered as a fundamental core field on its own and not an application of other knowledge. We recorded our understanding in the book *Operating Systems Theory* (1973), which became a classic and remained in print until 1995. We showed fundamental theorems in concurrency, notably those relating to determinacy, synchronization, and deadlocks. We drew heavily on the pioneering work of Dick Karp, Ray Miller, Anatol Holt, and Edsger Dijkstra from the 1960s, which was continued by Jack Dennis in his computation structures group at Project MAC in the 1960s and 1970s. Three major concurrent computation models emerged from that research: cooperating sequential processes, dataflow, and actors. All continue to be important today. The computation structures group sponsored conferences on coordination and concurrency as early as 1970. Solutions to synchronization and deadlock problems were extended from operating systems into database systems (atomic transactions) and communication systems (protocols). All these technologies became the subject of formal verification, which stimulated the development of verification logics including temporal logics. Some of this knowledge appears to have been lost. For example, Coffman and I stated a fundamental theorem about determinacy, well-known in those days; the theorem is today being rediscovered by security researchers seeking to prove that various constraints lead to noninterference between concurrent processes.[1]

The 1980s, which I witnessed from a ringside seat at NASA-Ames, were a time of tremendous advancement for coordination, HCI, and concurrency. In the area of coordination, the field of CSCW was born with studies of email systems that supported action loops, of systems for facilitating brainstorming and speculation, of the collaboratory for supporting research, and of human work and interaction that might be supported by computers (Doug Englebart). The business world discovered and embraced workflow technologies; Action Technologies started the workflow industry and (in the early 1990s) IBM bought Lotus Notes to incorporate workflow into its enterprise systems. HCI became its own field of study with advances in graphics interface, hypertext, speech recognition, some aspects of natural language translation, and design issues such as usability and ergonomics. Concurrency advanced in two fronts with the development of computational science and high performance

---

[1] Given a set of processes each implementing a fixed but unknown function; a set of memory cells, each readable by some processes and writeable by others; and a precedence relation partially ordering the executions of the processes. The output cells of every process are disjoint from input and output cells of every other process than can run concurrently with it. Then for every possible execution sequence of these processes, the final values in the memory cells are uniquely determined by the initial values. In fact, the sequence of values written in each memory cell is unique. As a corollary, any system of processes that exchange values through FIFO queues (rather then memory cells) will be determinate.

computing applied to the "grand challenges of science." One front was continued advancement in graphics, especially visualization of complex data and graphics accelerators for personal computers—all intended to improve the interaction with humans. Virtual reality, the search for completely immersive sensory environments, emerged during this time. The other front was in massively parallel supercomputers, notably the Connection Machine and Hypercube. The standalone massively parallel computers disappeared because the only customer willing to pay $400M a shot was the US government. However, other systems for massive computation emerged including Beowulf and grid computing. New languages (such as Occam, which embedded Hoare's CSP) were invented to support them.

The 1990s continued the breathtaking advancements. New forms of coordination were developed for the Internet and Web (the ultimate triumph of hypertext). These included e-commerce (the on-line store, shopping cart), the auction (eBay), journalism (the web log), publishing (the digital library), public key infrastructure, and the search engine (to locate items in the vast Internet). Security researchers invented protocols to increase trust, and belief logics to verify them. Large-systems researchers examined how massive groups of autonomous processes might generate unsuspected "emergent" behavior. Performance analysts extended their methods to enable prediction of throughput and response time for task requests in these new systems. Computers as multimedia centers provided new paradigms for distribution of music (peer-to-peer) music file sharing, production of CDs and DVDs, editing of images and movies, and even new approaches for first courses in computer science.

When I devised the great principles framework for computing (2003), I included coordination (interaction) as one of the six principal categories. My own career had provided ample evidence that many fundamental principles are in this area.

Malone: Like Peter, my imagination was stimulated by early newspaper accounts of "electronic brains", I did science fair projects about computers, and I was deeply inspired by the pioneering visions of Ted Nelson and Doug Engelbart for interactive computing. I sent my first email message when I arrived as a graduate student at Stanford in 1975. I had the privilege of joining Xerox PARC in 1979 when it was a science-fiction wonderland of networked personal computers, display-oriented editors, and laser printers—technologies that we now take for granted and hardly notice. At PARC, I worked on a system for sharing tasks among idle, networked personal computers using a market-like bidding mechanism for task assignment (Malone, Fikes, Grant, and Howard, 1988). I also participated in one of the first conferences on Computer–Human Interaction (CHI).

After coming to MIT in 1983, I was among the earliest researchers involved in developing the field of Computer-Supported Cooperative Work (CSCW). I led the team at MIT that developed an early system for using "intelligent agents" to filter and route email messages using "if-then" rules (Malone, Grant, Turbak, Brobst, and Cohen, 1987).]

Based on all these experiences, I developed a growing conviction that there were deep—and not widely appreciated—commonalities in how the activities of different actors could be coordinated in many different kinds of systems, including computer networks, human organizations, and economic markets. This conviction led me to begin articulating in the late 1980s the possibilities for a field of "coordination theory" or "coordination science" that would understand, catalog, and analyze the fundamental principles of coordination.

Now, almost two decades later, I believe significant progress has been made toward this goal: Numerous papers and books have been published on the topic of coordination. I have co-authored an article and co-edited a book that attempt to provide an overview for the field (Malone and Crowston, 1994; Olson, Malone, and Smith, 2001). With my colleagues I created a Center for Coordination Science at MIT, developed an on-line repository of knowledge about business processes and coordination (Malone, Crowston, and Herman, 2003), and used this approach to develop tools that help (semi-)automatically create software systems (Dellarocas, 1996, 1997). In spite of all this progress, however, I believe much work remains to be done to fulfill the promise of this approach.

12 The Future

In the foregoing we have emphasized the pervasive, fundamental nature of the principles of coordination, particularly their influence in HCI, CSCW, workflow, and concurrent computing. In truth, coordination principles affect every core technology of computing: it is hard to imagine a computer or process that does not interact either with humans or with other processes.

Interaction provides for a synergy between computation and human capabilities that enhances both and overcomes some limitations. Computers extend human capabilities by carrying out large computations, without error, that humans could not hope to complete in their lifetimes. (But not all: many important problems are computationally intractable.) Humans extend computing capabilities by providing answers to noncomputable questions at interaction points in a program. (But not all: many questions are too complex for a human to answer.) An old computability theorem says the power of a computer can be extended by an oracle that can answer a noncomputable question: the oracle-plus-computer is more powerful than computer alone. (But not without limit: there is always another question that cannot be answered by oracle-plus-computer.) Our experience with interaction confirms this: in the synergy of the interaction, the human looks like an oracle to the computer.

What can we expect in the future? Here are some places where we expect to see continued advancements in the theory and practice of coordination.

- **Computer Supported Cooperative Work, CSCW.** Language-action research will continue to interact with computing to yield new understandings of recurrent patterns of human conversation and work. These will lead to new systems for manually and automatically mapping networks of commitments in organizations, tracking cooperative work toward completion of commitments, and understanding the nature of knowledge work. On-line repositories of business processes will represent common patterns in how different activities are related. With help from the XML description languages of the Web, these systems will make explicit more "layers" of context, thus increasing the computer's ability to help people do some tasks and to completely automate other tasks where users have high levels of trust in the computer's ability to deal with unforeseen circumstances.

- **Trust.** Trust has become an important issue in commerce, security, and safety critical systems. Systems are called "trustworthy" when users see solid evidence that the computer will perform as expected in all or most circumstances. Trust itself is a commitment by a user to accept the risk and rely on the system to perform its duties. Can linguistic studies of trust as a commitment shed light on how to design systems that people are willing to trust? How much does trustworthiness depend on the user believing that the computer can sense context and take appropriate action in situations not foreseen by the designers? How can tools like on-line reputation systems help people know when to trust other humans with whom they have only interacted electronically? (See Resnick, Zeckhauser, Friedman, and Kuwabara, 2000.)

- **Delegations and agents.** Coordination exists as a fundamental principle of computing because people delegate tasks to computational processes. The processes must interact with each other and with users. The modern field of "agents" is concerned with how computational processes can interact to carry out a delegated task. What are limits on delegation? Many questions about limits rely on philosophy to answer since we need to understand what humans understand and how they come to understand before we can design a computational process that replaces a human capability. Dreyfus, for example, argues that software agents cannot be experts according to the same criteria as humans judge experts (Dreyfus, 2003).

- **Reverse Turing tests.** Much has been made of the Turing test to establish whether a computer is intelligent by measuring how long it might take a human to determine that the entity on the other side of an interaction is a computational process rather than another human. Recently, researchers have turned this upside down. To make sure that the entities logging in to one's accounts are humans and not attacking automated systems, researchers at the Carnegie-Mellon Captcha Project have found simple visual and aural tasks that humans can do easily but no known algorithm can do. This line of research may eventually help deal with difficult problems such as spam, worms, and viruses, which are initiated by humans but carried out on massive scales by automated processes.

- **Dealing with uncertainty:** Many events in interactive environments occur at unpredictable times. Two systems of analysis have been developed for performance prediction of systems of interacting components subject to random delays: queueing and scheduling theory; and emergent behavior theory. As other interaction research reveals more about formal structures of patterns of interaction, we may be able to apply queueing theory to make performance predictions for these systems. For example, using queueing methods such as G-networks (Gelenbe 2000) and Petri nets, it may be possible to analyze a network of action loops configured to implement a customer request (as in Fig. 5) to predict response time and throughput and locate bottlenecks. Emergent phenomena are system-wide behaviors that are not explicitly programmed in to any system component or rules of interaction. Examples are "Internet packet storms" and the spread of innovations (Huberman and Lukose, 1997). Statistical methods enable the detection, explanation, and analysis of such phenomena. With either type of analysis, networks of human interactions may become more analyzable and predictable.

- **Protocols:** Protocols are algorithms that specify how two or more computational processes can coordinate their actions. Early protocols included IP and TCP in the Internet. Interaction researchers are examining protocols to control massive autonomous parallelism in the Internet (also known as grid supercomputing); deep-space Internet communications; money flows in e-commerce transactions; certificate flows in public key infrastructure; belief logics for verifying trust; and security of systems. The range of protocol research will expand as more patterns of human and machine interaction are formalized.

- **Cross-organizational systems:** Increasingly, one of the biggest challenges for computer science will be dynamically weaving together complex cross-organizational systems from components on many different machines, owned by many different people and organizations, as the needs arise. All of the research areas listed so far will be needed to do this well, along with others such as service oriented architectures and the semantic web. Solving this problem is also likely to benefit from the creation of extensive on-line libraries of common processes—including coordination processes—that can be used to help assemble complex applications rapidly and, in some cases, automatically.

- **Real-time systems:** Many critical functions such as electric power distribution, water distribution, network routing tables, air traffic control, international money transfer depend on complex, distributed systems of agents that must respond quickly (and within set time limits) to specified events. Many of these systems are known to be vulnerable to cascading failures. Interaction research can team with systems and control engineering to yield solutions to these problems.

- **Human–computer interaction, HCI:** HCI research has been taking up fascinating new questions in recent years. Usability of systems is a prominent example. We are learning to make assessments of usability and connect them to reliability and safety of systems during heavy human–computer interaction. We are learning to design systems for customer satisfaction (e.g., on-line shopping) and customer support. We are learning how to build virtual reality simulators that train people to be effective actors in selected domains. We are learning to measure the effectiveness of training by examining the human–computer interaction that occurs in a VR simulation. This research area is a marriage between computer science and the entertainment industry.

- **Interface metaphor.** There are many complaints about the "death of the desktop metaphor". This is the convention of using windows, icons, menus, mouse, pointer, folders, and trash. Many people are finding it inadequate for the way they are using computers today: storing every email, every document, every photo, every sound track in a computer. They do not think of these things as parts of a desktop. There has been a great debate going on for several years on what should replace the desktop metaphor. Research and experiments with such alternatives will be a continuing part of interaction research.

- **Systems with delayed feedback.** Systems in which the parties receive direct feedback in the context of an action loop are the ones most familiar to us. However, we note that there are many modes of indirect feedback, for example, adjustments in train schedules based on the history of customer purchases of seats. We can grade systems by the time delay from the stimulating events, such as posting of a train schedule, to the feedback, such as the determination that a train should be discontinued. What are the limits of these systems as a function of the feedback delay? In what ways do they become unstable when feedback is slowed? What categories of interaction cannot be handled when feedback is slow?

- **Inventing new organizations.** The history of computing so far has focused on innovations at various layers of the "technology stack," such as hardware, operating systems, applications, and user interfaces. But some of the most important innovations ahead of us may be at the next layer up: the human organizations that use these technologies. With dramatically cheaper communication, for instance, it is now possible for huge numbers of people, even in very large organizations, to have enough information to make sensible decisions for themselves, instead of just following orders from someone above them in a hierarchy (Malone, 2004). We are only just now beginning to explore the vast design space of these decentralized organizations that computer technology is making possible.

These questions are pervaded by a qualitative difference from early research in interaction systems. This is the inclusion of human behaviors in the systems studied. We are no longer studying only interactions between machines, which are predictable and formalizable, we are studying interactions between humans mediated by machines, between humans and machines, and between machines in networks to which humans have delegated tasks. The addition of a human dimension has opened many new possibilities for design and uses of systems. We are turning increasingly to statistical and queueing methods in analyzing these systems; the purely formal methods rooted in discrete mathematics are insufficient for the questions we now ask, especially those dealing with uncertainty. We are extending the range of networked systems to which many of our familiar analytic methods can be applied.

We welcome these developments. They are good for computer science. They immerse us with the human dimension to computing and the attendant difficulties of design; they will make us better designers. Many of the new research areas are partnerships between other areas that have not interacted much in the past; for example between linguistic philosophers and designers of workflow systems, or between video entertainers and builders of virtual reality training systems, or between computing engineers and control engineers. Interaction research is encouraging interaction among researchers! This can only enrich our field.

References

1. Action Technologies. "Overview of Business Process Management" <http://www.actiontech.com/bpm/>.
2. G. Agha. *Actors: A Model of Concurrent Computation in Distributed Systems.* MIT Press, 1987.
3. F. Arbab. "What Do You Mean, Coordination?" *Bulletin of Dutch Association for Theoretical Computer Science* (NVTI), March 1998. <http://www.cwi.nl/ farhad/NVTIpaper.ps>
4. F. Arbab. "Coordination of interacting concurrent computations." *Interactive Computation: The New Paradigm* (D. Goldin and P. Wegner, eds). Springer-Verlag, 2006.
5. N. Carriero, and D. Gelernter. "A computational model of everything." *Comm. ACM 44*, 11, Nov 2001, pp. 77-81.
6. Captcha Project. Tests that humans can pass but not current computer programs. <http://www.captcha.net>.
7. E. Coffman and P. Denning. *Operating Systems Theory.* Prentice-Hall, 1973.
8. F. Commoner, H. Anatol, E. Shimon, and A. Pnueli. "Marked directed graphs." *J. Computers and Systems Science 5*, October 1971.
9. C. Dellarocas. *A coordination Perspective on Software Architecture: Towards a Design Handbook for Integrating Software Components.* Ph.D. thesis, Dept. of Electrical Engineering and Computer Science, Massachusetts Institute of Technology, February 1996 (Excerpts of Chapter 4 reprinted in Malone, Crowston, & Herman, 2003).
10. C. Dellarocas. "Towards a design handbook for integrating software components." *Proc. 5th Int'l Symp. on Assessment of Software Tools* (SAST '97), Pittsburgh, PA, June 2-5, 1997, pp. 3-13.
11. P. Denning. Work is a closed loop process. *American Scientist 80*, July-August 1992, pp. 314-317.

12. P. Denning. Great Principles of Computing. *Comm. ACM 46*, 10, Nov 2003,pp. 15-20.

13. P. Denning and R. Medina-Mora. Completing the loops. ORSA/TIMS *Interfaces 25*, May-June 1995, pp. 42-57.

14. E. Dijkstra. *Selected Writings on Computing: A Personal Perspective.* Springer-Verlag, 1982.

15. H. Dreyfus. *What Computers Still Can't Do.* MIT Press, 1992.

16. H. Dreyfus. *On the Internet.* Routledge, 2001.

17. F. Flores. The Leaders of the Future. In *Beyond Calculation* (P. Denning and R. Metcalfe, eds). Copernicus, 1997, pp. 175-192.

18. E. Gelenbe. "The first decade of G-networks." *European J. Operational Research 126*, October 2000, pp. 231–232.

19. B. Huberman and R. Lukose. Social Dilemmas and Internet Congestion. *Science 277*, July 1997,pp. 535-537.

20. R. Karp and R. Miller. "Properties of a model for parallel computations: determinacy, termination, and queueing." *SIAM J. of Appl. Math 14*, November 1966, pp. 1390-1411.

21. R. Karp and R. Miller. "Parallel program schemata." *J. Computers and Systems Science 3*, May 1969, pp. 147-195.

22. M. Klein, G. A. Herman, J. Lee, E. O'Donnell, and T. W. Malone. "Inventing new business processes using a process repository." In Malone, T. W., Crowston, K. G., & Herman, G. (Eds.) *Organizing Business Knowledge: The MIT Process Handbook.* Cambridge, MA: MIT Press, 2003.

23. T. W. Malone. *The Future of Work: How the New Order of Business Will Shape Your Organization, Your Management Style, and Your Life.* Boston, MA: Harvard Business School Press, 2004.

24. T. W. Malone and K. Crowston. The interdisciplinary study of coordination. *ACM Computing Surveys, 26* (1), March 1994, pp. 87-119.

25. T. W. Malone, K. G. Crowston, J. Lee, B. Pentland, C. Dellarocas, G. Wyner, J. Quimby, C. S. Osborn, A. Bernstein, G. Herman, M. Klein, and E. O'Donnell. Tools for inventing organizations: Toward a handbook of organizational processes. *Management Science, 45*, March 1999, pp. 425-443.

26. T. W. Malone, K. G. Crowston, and G. Herman (Eds.) *Organizing Business Knowledge: The MIT Process Handbook.* Cambridge, MA: MIT Press, 2003.

27. T. W. Malone, R. E. Fikes, K. R. Grant, and M. T. Howard. Enterprise: A market-like task scheduler for distributed computing environments. In B. A. Huberman (Ed.), *The Ecology of Computation*, Amsterdam: North Holland, 1988.

28. T. W. Malone, K. R. Grant, F. A. Turbak, S. A. Brobst, and M. D. Cohen. Intelligent information sharing systems, *Comm. ACM, 30*, 1987, pp. 390-402.

29. D. Norman, *Things That Make Us Smart.* Perseus Books, 1994.

30. What is Lotus Notes? See <http://www-10.lotus.com/ldd/whatisnotes>

31. G. M. Olson, T. W. Malone, and J. B. Smith, (Eds.) *Coordination Theory and Collaboration Technology.* Mahwah, NJ: Erlbaum, 2001.

32. P. Resnick, R. Zeckhauser, E . Friedman, and K. Kuwabara, "Reputation Systems," *Comm. ACM 43*, no. 12, Dec. 2000, pp. 45-48.

33. T. Winograd and F. Flores. *Understanding computers and cognition· A new foundation for design.* Norwood, NJ: Ablex, 1986.

Social Interaction, Knowledge, and Social Software

Eric Pacuit[1] and Rohit Parikh[2]

[1] ILLC, Amsterdam, The Netherlands
[2] Brooklyn College and CUNY Graduate Center, New York, NY, USA

1 Introduction

In [31] a theory of *human computation*, analogous to Turing's theory of *machine computation*, is discussed. The issue there is whether there might be an analogue to Church's thesis in this human domain. Examples of human algorithms discussed include the making of scrambled eggs. By comparison, Lynn Stein in this volume discusses the making of a peanut butter and jelly sandwich. Neither she nor us in this volume have any concern with Church's thesis as such, although that might prove to be a fascinating topic for a future paper. Rather the issue here is *interaction*, which occurs most naturally in multiagent algorithms, unlike the making of scrambled eggs or peanut butter sandwiches where one agent normally suffices.[1] Such multiagent algorithms, examples of which are building a house, or playing bridge, are examples of what we shall call *social software* after [32]. In that paper, one of us asked "Is it possible to create a theory of how social procedures work with a view to creating better ones and ensuring the correctness of the ones we do have?" The present chapter will survey some of the logical and mathematical tools that have been developed over the years that may help address this question.

Social procedures occur at two levels. One is the purely personal level where an individual is able to perform some complex action *because* social structures have been set up to enable such an action. Taking a train (which requires a system) or even a bath (where the city must supply not only the water but also a system of pipes to carry it) are examples of such situations where an individual is doing something simple or complex which is enabled by existing social structures. Procedures which are *truly* social are those which require more than one individual even in their execution. A piano duet is a simple example, but holding an election or passing a bill through the Senate are more complex ones. Computer programs, whether sequential or distributed, have logical and algorithmic properties which can be analyzed by means of

---

[1] However, as the adage goes, it does take many cooks to *spoil* the broth!.

appropriate logics of programs. Similarly, these social procedures also have logical properties which can be analyzed by means of the appropriate logical tools, augmented by tools from game theory, perhaps even from psychology.

There are several ways to compare social software with distributed computing. In both cases the issue of knowledge arises. When several processes, whether human or computer, are taking part in a common procedure, then they need to know *enough* of what others are doing so as to be able to do their part when the time comes. Indeed, Halpern and Moses' fundamental paper on common knowledge was written in the context of distributed computing, although *other* authors like Aumann (game theory, see [2, 3]) and Lewis (social agreement, see [17]) had a different setting. Thus knowledge matters and we shall give a quick survey of current formal theories of knowledge.

However, unless the agents have the same goal, or at least compatible goals, there may be some element of strategizing where each agent tries to maximize its own benefit (sometimes represented as *utility*) while keeping in mind what other agents are apt to do. This makes game theory relevant.

In the context of social programming where an overarching social agent (say, a government) is trying to make agents act in a socially beneficial way, the social agent will still need to take into account the fact that while its own goal is *social welfare*, the goal of the individual agent is his own *personal welfare*. Thus agents have to be guided to act in beneficial ways. A simple example of this is the system of library fines to ensure that borrowers do not keep books too long and prevent other borrowers from having access to them.

Finally, agents may sometimes act in concert with other agents, i.e., form coalitions. There is an extensive theory of co-operative games but our primary purpose here will be to give a brief account of the logical theory of coalitions due to Marc Pauly.

Thus what we hope to do in this chapter is to survey some of these logical and analytical tools and indicate a few applications.

These tools are:

1. Logic of knowledge
2. Logic of games
3. Game theory and economic design

In the following sections we shall give brief descriptions of these three tools and then indicate some applications. We assume that the reader has some mild acquaintance with game theory (although we shall not actually use very much), and [16] is a good reference for that field. Moore [18] gives a survey of economic design. The sections are reasonably independent and the applications depend mainly on reasoning about knowledge.

2 Models of Knowledge and Belief

Formal models of knowledge and beliefs have been discussed by a diverse list of communities, including computer scientists ([7, 42, 27]), economists ([5, 2, 4]) and philosophers ([21, 11]). In this section we provide a brief overview of some of the models found in the computer science and game theory literature.

2.1 Epistemic Logic

Starting with Hintikka's *Knowledge and Belief* [21] there has been a lot of research on the use of logic to formalize the uncertainty faced by a group of agents. A detailed discussion of epistemic and modal logic and its applications in computer science can be found in the textbooks [7, 27].

The main idea of epistemic logic is to extend the language of propositional logic with symbols (K_i) that are used to formalize the statement "agent i knows ϕ" where ϕ is any formula. For example, the formula $K_i\phi \to \phi$ represents the widely accepted principle that agents can only know true propositions, i.e., if i knows ϕ, then ϕ must be true.

Formally, if At is a set of atomic propositions, then the language of multi-agent epistemic logic $\mathcal{L}_n^K(\text{At})$ (or $\mathcal{LK}$ if At, n are understood from the context) has the following syntactic form:

$$\phi := A \mid \neg\phi \mid \phi \wedge \psi \mid K_i\phi$$

where $A \in \text{At}$. We assume that the boolean connectives $\vee, \to, \leftrightarrow$ are defined as usual. The formula $L_i\phi$, defined as $\neg K_i\neg\phi$, is the dual of $K_i\phi$. Given that the intended meaning of the formula $K_i\phi$ is "agent i knows ϕ", $L_i\phi$ can be read as "ϕ is epistemically possible for agent i". There are a number of principles about knowledge—listed below—expressible in the language of epistemic logic that have been widely discussed by many different communities. Since our focus is on social software and not on epistemic or modal logic, we shall simply assume those schemes which correspond to the most widely prevalent understanding of the formal properties of knowledge. When more restricted properties of knowledge are entertained, *negative introspection* is the first axiom to be dropped. Let $\phi, \psi \in \mathcal{LK}$ be arbitrary formulas.

K $K_i(\phi \to \psi) \to (K_i\phi \to K_i\psi)$ *Kripke's axiom*
T $K_i\phi \to \phi$ *Truth*
4 $K_i\phi \to K_iK_i\phi$ *Positive introspection*
5 $\neg K_i\phi \to K_i\neg K_i\phi$ *Negative introspection*
D $\neg K_i\bot$ *Consistency*

Note that D is a consequence of T.

We now turn to the semantics of epistemic logic. The main idea is that a formula $K_i\phi$ is true provided that ϕ is true in all situations that i considers possible. This definition was first put forward by Leibniz and is discussed in detail by Hintikka [21]. This intuition can be formalized using a Kripke structure.

Definition 1. *A* **Kripke model** *is a triple* $\langle W, \{R_i\}_{i \in \mathcal{A}}, V \rangle$ *where* W *is a nonempty set, for each* $i \in \mathcal{A}$, $R_i \subseteq W \times W$, *and* $V : \text{At} \to 2^W$ *is a valuation function.*

In order to make sure that the axiom schemes $K, T, 4, 5, D$ hold, the relations R_i must all be equivalence relations. Elements $w \in W$ are called states, or worlds. We write wR_iv if $(w, v) \in R_i$. The relation R_i represents the uncertainty that agent i has about the "actual situation". In other words, if wR_iv and the actual situation is w, then for all agent i knows, the situation may be v. Notice that R_i represents the uncertainty each agent has about the actual situation and the agents' uncertainty about how the other agents view the situation, but it does not settle which basic facts are true at which states. For this, we need the valuation function V, where $w \in V(A)$ is interpreted as A *is true at state* w. We write $\mathcal{M}, w \models \phi$ to mean that ϕ is true at state w in $\mathcal{M}$. Truth is defined recursively as follows. Let $\mathcal{M} = \langle W, \{R_i\}_{i \in \mathcal{A}}, V \rangle$ be a model and $w \in W$ any state.

1. $\mathcal{M}, w \models A$ if $A \in V(s)$
2. $\mathcal{M}, w \models \phi \wedge \psi$ if $\mathcal{M}, w \models \phi$ and $\mathcal{M}, w \models \psi$
3. $\mathcal{M}, w \models \neg\phi$ if $\mathcal{M}, w \not\models \phi$
4. $\mathcal{M}, w \models K_i\phi$ if for each $v \in W$, if wR_iv, then $\mathcal{M}, w \models \phi$.

If the model $\mathcal{M}$ is understood we may write $w \models \phi$. If $\mathcal{M}, w \models \phi$ for all states $w \in W$, then we say that ϕ is **valid in** $\mathcal{M}$ and write $\mathcal{M} \models \phi$. Note that principle **4** is justified by the fact that i can only know ϕ if ϕ is true in every state where, for all i knows, he might be.

Common knowledge can be defined via the "everyone knows" operator. Let $E\phi = K_1\phi \wedge K_2\phi ... \wedge K_n\phi$, where $\mathcal{A} = \{1, ..., n\}$ is the set of agents. Thus $E\phi$ says that all n agents know ϕ. Then ϕ is "common knowledge" is expressed by the infinite conjunction $\phi \wedge E\phi \wedge E^2\phi \wedge ...$ For a more detailed discussion about reasoning about common knowledge see [15, 7]. See [17, 6] for a philosophical discussion of common knowledge.

2.2 Aumann Structures

One of the first attempts to formalize knowledge in economic situations is by Aumann [2]. As in the previous section, let W be a set of worlds, or states. In this section we reason semantically. Let S be the set of all states of nature. A state of nature is a complete description of the exogenous parameters (i.e., facts about the physical world) that do not depend on the agents' uncertainties.

In the previous section we defined an object language that could express statements of the form "agent i knows ϕ", and interpreted these formulas in a Kripke model. In this section we have no such object language. Reasoning about agents is done purely semantically. Thus we are making essential use of the fact that we can identify a proposition with the set of worlds in which it is true. Intuitively, we say that a set $E \subseteq W$, called an **event**, is true at state w if $w \in E$.

In [2], Aumann represents the uncertainty of each agent about the actual state of affairs by a partition over the set of states. Formally, for each agent $i \in \mathcal{A}$, there is a partition $\mathcal{P}_i$ over the set W. (A partition of W is a pairwise disjoint collection of subsets of W whose union is all of W.) Elements of $\mathcal{P}_i$ are called **cells**, and for $w \in W$, let $\mathcal{P}_i(w)$ denote the cell of $\mathcal{P}_i$ containing w. Putting everything together,

Definition 2. *An* **Aumann model based on S** *is a triple* $\langle W, \{P_i\}_{i \in \mathcal{A}}, \sigma \rangle$, *where W is a nonempty set, each $\mathcal{P}_i$ is a partition over W and $\sigma : W \to S$.*

So, σ is analogous to a valuation function, it assigns to each world a state of nature in which every ground fact (any fact *not about the uncertainty of the agents*) is either true or false. If $\sigma(w) = \sigma(w')$ then the two worlds w, w' will agree on all the facts, but the agents may have different knowledge in them. Elements of W are *richer* in information than the elements of S.

The event that agent i knows event E, denoted $\mathsf{K}_i E$, is defined to be

$$\mathsf{K}_i E = \{w \mid \mathcal{P}_i(w) \subseteq E\}$$

In other words, for each agent $i \in \mathcal{A}$, we define a set valued function $\mathsf{K}_i : 2^W \to 2^W$ using the above definition. It is not hard to show, given this definition and the fact that the $\mathcal{P}_i$s are patitions, that for each $i \in \mathcal{A}$ and each $E \subseteq W$,

$E \subseteq F \Rightarrow \mathsf{K}_i(E) \subseteq \mathsf{K}_i(F)$	*Monotonicity*
$\mathsf{K}_i(E \cap F) = \mathsf{K}_i(E) \cap \mathsf{K}_i(F)$	*Closure under intersection*
$\mathsf{K}_i E \subseteq E$	*Truth*
$\mathsf{K}_i(E) \subseteq \mathsf{K}_i(\mathsf{K}_i(E))$	*Positive introspection*
$\overline{\mathsf{K}_i(E)} \subseteq \mathsf{K}_i(\overline{\mathsf{K}_i(E)})$	*Negative introspection*
$\mathsf{K}_i(\emptyset) = \emptyset$	*Consistency.*

These are the analogues of the $K, T, 4, 5$ and D axiom schemes from the previous section. In fact, there is an obvious translation between Aumann structures and Kripke structures. In [14], Halpern formally compares the two frameworks pointing out similarities and important differences.

There is a more fine-grained model of uncertainty discussed in the game theory literature, usually called a Bayesian model. In a Bayesian model, the uncertainty of each agent is represented by probability functions over the set of worlds, and so we can express exactly *how* uncertain each agent is about the given situation. A detailed discussion and pointers to the relevant literature can be found in [5, 3].

Finally, a set E is a *common knowledge* set if $\mathsf{K}_i(E) = E$ for all i.[2] Event F is common knowledge at state w if there is a set E such that E is a

---

[2] Note that this definition makes heavy use of the richer state space W. Within E, agent i is not only aware of certain objective facts, she is also aware of some of the *knowledge* of other agents.

common knowledge set, and $w \in E \subseteq F$. Note that this definition of common knowledge is very transparent compared to the more syntactic one from the previous section.

2.3 History-Based Models

History based structures, also called *interpreted systems*, have been extensively discussed in the distributed computing literature (see [7] Chap. 4, 5 and 8 for a thorough discussion). This section will present the framework of Parikh and Ramanjam found in [35, 36]. In [36], Parikh and Ramanajam argue that this framework very naturally formalizes many social situations by providing a semantics of messages in which sophisticated notions such as Gricean implicature can be represented.

We begin by assuming the existence of a global discrete clock (whether the agents have access to this clock is another issue that will be discussed shortly). At each moment, some event takes place. Let E be a fixed set of events. As discussed in the previous section, it is natural to allow that different agents are aware of different events. To that end, assume for each agent $i \in \mathcal{A}$, a set $E_i \subseteq E$ of events "seen" by agent i. Before defining a history we need some notation: Given any set X (of events), X^* is the set of finite strings over X and X^ω the set of infinite strings over X. A **global history** is any sequence, or string, of events, i.e., an element of $E^* \cup E^\omega$. Let $h, h', \ldots$ range over E^* and $H, H', \ldots$ range over $E^* \cup E^\omega$. A **local history** for agent i is any element $h \in E_i^*$. Notice that local histories are always assumed to be finite.

Given two histories H and H', write $H \preceq H'$ to mean H is a *finite prefix* of H'. Let hH denote the concatenation of finite history h with possibly infinite history H. Let H_k denote the finite prefix of H of length k (given that H is infinite or of length $\geq k$). Given a set $\mathcal{H}$ of histories, define $\mathsf{FinPre}(\mathcal{H}) = \{h \mid h \in E^*, h \preceq H, \text{ and } H \in \mathcal{H}\}$. So $\mathsf{FinPre}(\mathcal{H})$ is the set of finite prefixes of elements of $\mathcal{H}$. A set $\mathcal{H} \subseteq E^* \cup E^\omega$ is called a **protocol**. Intuitively, the protocol is simply the set of possible histories that could arise in a particular situation. Following [36], little structure is placed on the set $\mathcal{H}$. I.e., the protocol can be *any* nonempty set of histories, provided only that if a history H is in the protocol $\mathcal{H}$, then so is any prefix of H. Notice that this notion of a protocol differs from standard usage of the term protocol which is taken to mean a procedure executed by a group of agents. Certainly any procedure will generate a set of histories, but not every set of histories can be generated by some procedure. Therefore, this definition of protocol is more general than the standard definition. It *is* useful as [36] use it to interpret even notions like Gricean implicature.

Given a particular finite global history H and an agent i, i will only "see" the events in H that are from E_i. This leads to a natural definition of agent uncertainty.

Definition 3. *For each $i \in \mathcal{A}$ define $\lambda_i : \mathsf{FinPre}(E^\omega) \to E_i^*$ to be the **local view function** of agent i.*

In systems in which agents cannot access a global clock. $\lambda_i(H)$ is obtained by mapping each event in E_i to itself and all *other* events to the empty string. Thus if $\lambda_i(H) = h$ for some finite history H, and event $e \in E_i$, which is visible to i, takes place next, then $\lambda_i(He) = he$, otherwise $\lambda_i(He) = h$. Let H and H' be two global histories in some protocol $\mathcal{H}$. We write $H \sim_{i,t} H'$ if according to agent i, H is "equivalent" to H' at time t, i.e., $\lambda_i(H_t) = \lambda_i(H'_t)$. It is easy to see that for each time $t \in \mathbb{N}$, $\sim_{i,t}$ is an equivalence relation.

Definition 4. *Given a history based multiagent frame for a set of agents $\mathcal{A}$ and events E, $\mathcal{F}_H = \langle \mathcal{H}, E_1, \ldots, E_n \rangle$, a **history based model** is a tuple $\langle \mathcal{H}, \lambda_1, \ldots, \lambda_n, V \rangle$, where each λ_i is a local view function and $V : \mathsf{FinPre}(\mathcal{H}) \rightarrow 2^{\Phi_0}$ is a valuation function.*

Finally, a few comments about whether agents have access to the global clock. We say that a history based frame $\mathcal{F}_H$ is **synchronous** if all agents have access to the global clock. Formally this is achieved by assuming a special event $c \in E$ with $c \in E_i$ for each $i \in \mathcal{A}$. This event represents a clock tick. In synchronous history based models, the local view function maps each event seen by agent i in some finite history H to itself, and all other events to the clock tick c. Notice that in such a case, for any finite global history H and local view function λ_i, the length of $\lambda_i(H)$ and the length of H are always equal.

Given these tree-like structures, it is natural to define a language in which we can express both knowledge-theoretic and temporal facts. Formally, we add a unary modal operator $\bigcirc$ and a binary modal operator U to the language $\mathcal{LK}$. Denote this language by $\mathcal{L}_n^{KT}$. $\bigcirc\phi$ is intended to mean that ϕ *is true after the next event* and $\phi U \psi$ is intended to mean that ϕ *is true until ψ becomes true*. Other well known temporal operators can be defined. Details can be found in [36] and [13, 7].

Truth is defined at finite histories. Thus, for $H \in \mathcal{H}$, $H, t \models \phi$ is intended to mean that in history H at time t, ϕ is true. Boolean connectives and atomic propositions are obvious.

1. $H, t \models \bigcirc\phi$ iff $H, t+1 \models \phi$
2. $H, t \models \phi U \psi$ iff there exists $m \geq t$ such that $H, m \models \psi$ and for all l such that $t < l < m$, $H, l \models \phi$
3. $H, t \models K_i\phi$ iff for all $H' \in \mathcal{H}$ such that $H \sim_{i,t} H'$, $H', t \models \phi$.

In the above definition of truth of K_i formulas (item 3 above), it is assumed that the agents all share a global clock. This assumption is made in order to simplify the presentation. A sound and complete axiomatization for knowledge and time under various assumptions can be found in [13], using a slightly different framework.

3 Logic of Games

The logic of games [33] is an offshoot of propositional dynamic logic or PDL. PDL was invented by Fischer and Ladner [8] following Pratt's work on first order dynamic logic.

In dynamic logic a program is thought of as running in a state space, and a program α is thought of as starting in some state s and arriving at some state t if and when it finishes. The program need not be deterministic so that starting with the same s it might instead arrive at some t'. This allows us to see α as a binary relation $R_\alpha = \{(s,t)|\alpha$ can go from s to $t\}$. This converts α into a modality and allows us to define the constructs $[\alpha]$ and $\langle\alpha\rangle$, which are the program theoretic versions of the modal operators box and diamond. The formula $\langle\alpha\rangle A$ holds at state s if there is *some* run of the program α starting at s which results in a state t which satisfies A. $[\alpha]A$ holds if *every* terminating run does so.

However, our interest here is in *games* which can no longer be represented as binary relations, instead the semantics is more like the Scott–Montague semantics for modal logic in which Kripke's axiom **K** is no longer valid. The reason roughly is this. If α is a *program* and $\langle\alpha\rangle(A \vee B)$ holds then $\langle\alpha\rangle A$ or $\langle\alpha\rangle B$ must hold. For if there is an α-computation which results in $A \vee B$ then there must be one which results in A or one which results in B. ($\langle\alpha\rangle(A\vee B) \to \langle\alpha\rangle(A) \vee \langle\alpha\rangle(B)$ is an axiom equivalent to Kripke's **K**). But this need not hold with a game. It may well be that one player, say I, has a winning strategy to achieve $A \vee B$ in the game α without having a winning strategy to achieve either A reliably or B reliably. For instance a game of chess may reach a point where Black can ensure a checkmate in three moves, but it is White's moves which decide whether that checkmate is by queen or by rook—Black cannot ensure a checkmate by queen nor a checkmate by rook. Thus game logic is a non-normal (non-**K**) logic corresponding to PDL.

3.1 Syntax and Semantics

We have a finite supply $g_1,\ldots,g_n$ of atomic games and a finite supply $P_1,\ldots,P_m$ of atomic formulae. Then we define games α and formulae A by induction.

1. Each P_i is a formula.
2. If A and B are formulae, then so are $A \vee B$, $\neg A$.
3. If A is a formula and α is a game, then $(\alpha)A$ is a formula.
4. Each g_i is a game.
5. If α and β are games, then so are $\alpha;\beta$ (or simply $\alpha\beta$), $\alpha \vee \beta$, $\langle\alpha^*\rangle$, and α^d. Here α^d is the dual of α.
6. If A is a formula then $\langle A\rangle$ is a game.

We shall write $\alpha \wedge \beta$, $[\alpha^*]$ and $[A]$ respectively for the duals of $\alpha \vee \beta$, $\langle\alpha^*\rangle$ and $\langle A\rangle$. If confusion will not result then we shall write αA for $(\alpha)A$. For example, $\langle g_i^*\rangle A$ instead of $(\langle g_i^*\rangle)A$.

Intuitively, the games can be explained as follows. $\alpha; \beta$ is the game: play α and then β. The game $\alpha \vee \beta$ is: player I has the first move, she decides whether α or β is to be played, and then the chosen game is played. The game $\alpha \wedge \beta$ is similar except that player II makes the decision. In $\langle \alpha^* \rangle$, the game α is played repeatedly (perhaps zero times) until player I decides to stop. She need not declare in advance how many times is α to be played, but she is *required* to eventually stop, and player II may use this fact as part of his strategy. Player I may not stop in the *middle* of some play of α. Similarly with $[\alpha^*]$ and player II. In α^d, the two players interchange roles. Finally, with $\langle A \rangle$, the formula A is evaluated. If A is false, then I loses, otherwise we go on. (Thus $\langle A \rangle B$ is equivalent to $A \wedge B$.) Similarly with $[A]$ and II. The formula $(\alpha)A$ means that player I has a winning strategy to play game α in such a way that formula A is true if and when the game ends (or if the game does not end, the fault for that lies with II).

Formally, a model of game logic consists of a set W of worlds; for each atomic P a subset $\pi(P)$ of W; and for each primitive game g a subset $\rho(g)$ of $W \times P(W)$, where $P(W)$ is the power set of W. $\rho(g)$ must satisfy the monotonicity condition: if $(s, X) \in \rho(g)$ and $X \subseteq Y$, then $(s, Y) \in \rho(g)$. For clearly if an agent can play the game so as to be sure to be in X at the end, then the agent can also ensure Y by simply ensuring X. We shall find it convenient to think of $\rho(g)$ as an operator from $P(W)$ to itself, given by the formula

$$\rho(g)(X) = \{s | (s, X) \in \rho(g)\}$$

It is then monotonic in X. We define $\pi(A)$ and $\rho(\alpha)$ for more complex formulae and games as follows:

1. $\pi(A \vee B) = \pi(A) \cup \pi(B)$
2. $\pi(\neg A) = W - \pi(A)$
3. $\pi((\alpha)A) = \{s | (s, \pi(A)) \in \rho(\alpha)\} = \rho(\alpha)(\pi(A))$
4. $\rho(\alpha; \beta)(X) = \rho(\alpha)(\rho(\beta)(X))$
5. $\rho(\alpha \vee \beta)(X) = \rho(\alpha)(X) \cup \rho(\beta)(X)$
6. $\rho(\langle \alpha^* \rangle)(X) = \mu Y(X \subseteq Y \wedge \rho(\alpha)(Y) \subseteq Y)$
7. $\rho(\alpha^d)(X) = W - \rho(\alpha)(W - X)$
8. $\rho(\langle A \rangle)(X) = \pi(A) \cap X$.

It is easily checked that $\rho(\alpha \wedge \beta)(X) = \rho(\alpha)(X) \cap \rho(\beta)(X)$, $\rho([A])(X) = (W - \pi(A)) \cup X$, and $\rho([\alpha^*])(X) = \nu Y((Y \subseteq X) \wedge (Y \subseteq \rho(\alpha)(Y))$ where νY means "the largest Y such that". This is easily seen by noticing that $\rho([\alpha^*])(X) = W - \rho(\langle \alpha^* \rangle)(W - X) = W - $ the smallest Z such that $(W - X) \subseteq Z$ and $\rho(\alpha)(Z) \subseteq Z$.

We shall have occasion to use both ways of thinking of ρ, as a map from $P(W)$ to itself, also as a subset of $W \times P(W)$. In particular we shall need the (easily checked) fact that $(s, X) \in \rho(\beta; \gamma)$ iff there is a Y such that $(s, Y) \in$

$\rho(\beta)$ and for all $t \in Y$, $(t, X) \in \rho(\gamma)$. Similarly, $(s, X) \in \rho(\beta \vee \gamma)$ iff $(s, X) \in \rho(\beta)$ or $(s, X) \in \rho(\gamma)$.

So far we have made no connection with PDL. However, given a language of PDL we can associate with it a game logic where to each program a_i of PDL we associate two games $\langle a_i \rangle$ and $[a_i]$. We take $\rho(\langle a \rangle)(X) = \{s : \exists t(s, t) \in R_a$ and $t \in X\}$ and $\rho([a])(X) = \{s : \forall t(s, t) \in R_a$ implies $t \in X\}$ and the formulae of PDL can be translated easily into those of game logic. Note that if the program a is to be run and player I wants to have A true after, then if she runs a, only $\langle a \rangle A$ needs to be true. However, if player II is going to run the program a then $[a]A$ needs to be true for I to win in any case. Note that if there are no a-computations beginning at the state s, then player II is unable to move, $[a]A$ is true and player I wins. In other words, unlike the situation in chess, a situation where a player is unable to move is regarded as a loss for that player in both PDL and game logic.

However, game logic is more expressive than PDL. The formula $\langle [b^*] \rangle \texttt{false}$ of game logic says that *there is no infinite computation of the program* b, a notion that cannot be expressed in PDL.

Finally, let us show how well-foundedness can be defined in game logic. Given a linear ordering R over a set W, consider the model of game logic where g denotes $[a]$ and R_a is the inverse relation of R. Then R is well-founded over W iff the formula $\langle g^* \rangle \texttt{false}$ is true. Player I cannot terminate the game without losing, but she is required to terminate the game sometime. The only way she can win is to keep saying to player II, *keep playing!*, and hope that player II will sooner or later be deadlocked. (The subgame $[a]$ of $\langle [a]^* \rangle$ is a game where player II moves, and in the main game $\langle [a]^* \rangle$, player I is responsible for deciding how many times is $[a]$ played.) Thus I wins iff there are no infinite descending sequences of R on W.

However, despite its power, game logic can be translated into μ-calculus of [19] and by the decision procedure of [20], is decidable. An elementary decision procedure for dual-free game logic exists as does a completeness result, whose axiomatization is given below.

3.2 Completeness

The following axioms and rules are complete for the "dual-free" part of game logic.

The axioms of game logic

1. All tautologies
2. $(\alpha; \beta)A \Leftrightarrow (\alpha)(\beta)A$
3. $(\alpha \vee \beta)A \Leftrightarrow (\alpha)A \vee (\beta)A$
4. $(\langle \alpha^* \rangle)A \Leftrightarrow A \vee (\alpha)(\langle \alpha^* \rangle)A$
5. $(\langle A \rangle)B \Leftrightarrow A \wedge B$

Rules of inference

1. Modus ponens
$$\frac{A \quad A \Rightarrow B}{B}$$

2. Monotonicity
$$\frac{A \Rightarrow B}{(\alpha)A \Rightarrow (\alpha)B}$$

3. Bar induction
$$\frac{(\alpha)A \Rightarrow A}{(\langle \alpha^* \rangle)A \Rightarrow A}$$

The soundness of these axioms and rules is quite straightforward. The completeness proof given in [33].

The completeness problem for game logic *with* dual has now been open for about 20 years.

4 Coalitional Logic

In his dissertation [40], Marc Pauly extended game logic to a logic for reasoning about coalitional powers in games. This section will describe his basic framework. The interested reader is referred to [40, 39] for a more detailed discussion.

In game logic, the formula $[\alpha]\phi$ is intended to mean that player II has winning strategy in the determined, zero-sum game α. The intuition driving the semantics for game logic is that when $w\rho_\alpha X$ holds, player I (alone) can force the outcome of the game α to end in one of the states in X. Pauly drops the assumption of determinacy of the games, weakening the power of the individual players. In Pauly's semantics, typically a *coalition* of agents is needed for the outcome to end in some state in a set X.

The first step is the introduce a language that can express facts about coalitions of players. Given a finite set of agents $\mathcal{A}$, the language of coalitional logic has the following syntactic form

$$\phi := A \mid \neg\phi \mid \phi \vee \psi \mid [C]\phi$$

where $A \in \mathsf{At}$ is an atomic proposition and $C \subseteq \mathcal{A}$. The other boolean connectives are defined as usual. The intended interpretation of $[C]\phi$ is that the group of agents in C have a joint strategy to ensure that ϕ is true.

The semantics is essentially a Scott–Montague neighborhood model with a neighborhood function for each subset of agents. Let W be a set of states. An **effectivity function** is a map

$$E : (2^{\mathcal{A}} \times W) \to 2^{2^W}$$

We write $wE_C X$ if $X \in E(C, w)$. The intended interpretation of $wE_C X$ is that in state w, the agents in C have a joint strategy to bring about one of the states in X. An effectivity function is **playable** iff for all $w \in W$,

1. For all $C \subseteq \mathcal{A}$, $\emptyset \notin E(C, w)$
2. For all $C \subseteq \mathcal{A}$ $W \in E(C, w)$
3. E is $\mathcal{A}$-**maximal**, i.e., for all $X \subseteq W$, if $X \in E(\mathcal{A}, w)$ then $\overline{X} \notin E(\emptyset, w)$
4. E is **outcome-monotonic**, i.e., for all $X \subseteq X' \subseteq W$, $w \in W$, and $C \subseteq \mathcal{A}$, if $X \in E(C, w)$ then $X' \in E(C, w)$
5. E is **superadditive**, i.e., for all subsets X_1, X_2 of W and sets of agents C_1, C_2 such that $C_1 \cap C_2 = \emptyset$ and $X_1 \in E(C_1, w)$ and $X_2 \in E(C_2, w)$, we have $X_1 \cap X_2 \in E(C_1 \cup C_2)$.

Pauly [40] shows that these conditions are exactly the conditions needed to formalize the intuitive interpretation of the effectivity functions. Given any strategic game G, we can define an effectivity function generated by G. Essentially, we say that a set X is in $E_G(C)$ for some set $C \subseteq \mathcal{A}$ iff there is a strategy that the agents in C can play such that for any strategy that the other players follow, the outcome will be some element of X. Pauly showed that the above conditions charactize all effectivity functions generated by some game.

Theorem 1 (Pauly [40]). *An effectivity function E is playable iff it is the effectivity function E_G of some strategic game G.*

We can now formally define a coalitional model.

Definition 5. *A **coalitional model** is a tuple $\langle W, E, V \rangle$ where W is a nonempty set of states, E is a playable effectivity function, and $V : \mathsf{At} \to \mathcal{P}(S)$ is a valuation function.*

Given such a model, truth is defined as follows

$$\mathcal{M}, w \models A \quad \text{iff } A \in \mathsf{At} \text{ and } w \in V(A)$$
$$\mathcal{M}, w \models \neg\phi \quad \text{iff } \mathcal{M}, s \not\models \phi$$
$$\mathcal{M}, w \models \phi \vee \psi \text{ iff } \mathcal{M}, s \models \phi \text{ or } \mathcal{M}, w \models \psi$$
$$\mathcal{M}, w \models [C]\phi \quad \text{iff } w E_C \phi^{\mathcal{M}}$$

where $\phi^{\mathcal{M}} = \{w \in W \mid \mathcal{M}, w \models \phi\}$. Pauly shows [40] that the following axiom system is sound and complete for the class of coalitional models.

$$(\bot) \ \neg[C]\bot$$
$$(\top) \ [C]\top$$
$$(N) \ \neg[\emptyset]\neg\phi \to [N]\phi$$
$$(M) \ [C](\phi \wedge \psi) \to [C]\psi$$
$$(S) \ ([C_1]\phi_1 \wedge [C_2]\phi_2) \to [C_1 \cup C_2](\phi_1 \wedge \phi_2)$$

provided $C_1 \cap C_2 = \emptyset$. We also assume modus ponens and that from $\phi \leftrightarrow \psi$, we can infer $[C]\phi \leftrightarrow [C]\psi$.

5 Some Applications

Our primary purpose in this survey has been to give a survey of tools used in studying social software. However, we now proceed to give some examples of applications. The first two examples are *light*.

5.1 A Knowledge Interaction

Suppose that Bob is giving a seminar and would like Ann to attend his talk; however, he only wants Ann to attend if she is interested in the subject of his talk, not because she is just being polite.

Why can't Bob just *tell* Ann about his talk?

We suggest that Bob would like to satisfy three conditions.

1. $K_a(S)$ (Ann knows S, where S stands for the proposition that Bob is giving the seminar.)
2. $K_b K_a(S)$ (Bob knows that Ann knows S.)
3. $\neg K_a K_b K_a(S)$ (Ann does *not* know that Bob knows that she knows S.)

Let us examine the three conditions. Clearly the first is necessary, for if Ann does not know about the seminar she cannot go, even if she wants to. The second, while not crucial, gives Bob peace of mind.

It is the last one which is interesting. Ann could have two reasons for going. She could go because she is interested in the talk. Or she could go to please Bob or out of fear that he will be offended if she does not go. If she knows that Bob knows that she knows, she will have to allow for an expectation on his part that she should go.

If Bob just *tells* her about the seminar, then common knowledge of S will be created, including the dreaded formula $K_a K_b K_a(S)$. So Bob cannot just *tell* her.

But he *can* ask a friend discreetly to tell her. Then he will be more confident that she will not feel pressured to come. This solves his problem of achieving the three conditions 1–3.

A similar example arises with a joke about a butler in a hotel who enters a room to clean it, and surprises a woman guest coming out of the bath. "Excuse me, sir, and he withdraws."

Why "*sir*"? Because she can reason that if he is mistaken about the gender, then he could not have seen her clearly, and there is no reason for her to be embarrassed—or to complain to the hotel. The butler very intelligently saves her from embarrassment by deliberately creating a false belief in her. (In other words $\neg K_g K_b(F)$ and even $B_g \neg K_b(F)$ where F stands for the fact that the guest is female, and B is the belief operator.)

Such issues will arise again in the section on knowledge based obligation.

It is generally accepted that what people do depends on what they believe, what they prefer, and what their options are. Their beliefs tell them what the options are and how they should be weighed. Thus if Bob has the option of meeting Jane for dinner or not, but does not know if she is pretty or ugly, then in a sense he knows what his options are, to meet her or not. But there is also a sense in which he does not know how to weigh the options. Now if he knows that Jane is ugly, he can safely have dinner with her without worrying that his own wife will be suspicious.

In the same way, in our earlier example, Ann does have the option of going to the seminar or not—once she knows about it. But how she weighs that option will depend on whether she knows that Bob knows that she knows.

5.2 The Two Horsemen and Letters of Recommendation

Suppose we want to find out which of two horses is faster. This is easy, we race them against each other. The horse which reaches the goal first is the faster horse. And surely this method should also tell us which horse is *slower*, it is the other one. However, there is a complication which will be instructive.

Two horsemen are on a forest path chatting about something. A passerby Mary, the mischief maker, comes along and having plenty of time and a desire for amusement, suggests that they race against each other to a tree a short distance away and she will give a prize of $100. However, there is an interesting twist. She will give the $100 to the owner of the *slower* horse. Let us call the two horsemen Bill and Joe. Joe's horse can go at 35 miles per hour, whereas Bill's horse can only go 30 miles per hour. Since Bill has the slower horse, he should get the $100.

The two horsemen start, but soon realize that there is a problem. Each one is trying to go slower than the other and it is obvious that the race is not going to finish. There is a broad smile on Mary's face as she sees that she is having some amusement at no cost. Each horseman can make his horse go at any speed upto its maximum. But he has no reason to use the maximum. They try to go as slow as they can and so they end up in a stalemate with both horses going at 0 miles per hour. Let x, y be the speeds respetively at which Bill's horse and Joe's horse are going. Then [0,0] is a Nash equilibrium here.

However, along comes another passerby, let us call her Pam, the problem solver, and the situation is explained to her. She turns out to have a clever solution. She advises the two men to switch horses. Now each man has an incentive to go fast, because by making his competitor's horse go faster, he is helping his own horse to win! Joe's horse, ridden by Bill, comes first and Bill gets the $100 as he should. The Nash equilibrium has shifted to [35,30].

For a practical analogue of the two horses example, consider the issue of grades and letters of recommendation. Suppose that Prof. Meyer is writing a letter of recommendation for his student Maria and Prof. Shankar is writing one for his student Peter. Both believe that their respective students are good, but only good. Not very good, not excellent, just good. Both also know that only one student can get the job or scholarship. Under this circumstance, it is clear that both of the advisers are best off writing letters saying that their respective student is excellent. This is strategic behaviour in a domain familiar to all of us. Some employers will try to counter this by appealing to third parties for an evaluation, but the close knowledge that the two advisers have of their advisees cannot be discovered very easily. And unfortunately, we know no obvious analogue to the strategem of exchanging horses. Certainly, if someone were to find such an analogue, it would revolutionize the whole process of writing letters of recommendation.

5.3 Banach–Knaster Cake Cutting Procedure

The following problem has often been mentioned in the literature. Some n people have to share a cake and do not have access to any measuring device. Moreover, they do not trust each other. Can they *still* divide the cake in a way which seems fair to all? The Banach–Knaster last diminisher procedure goes as follows.

Player 1 cuts out a piece p which she claims is a fair share for her. After that p is inspected by the other $n - 1$ people. Anyone who thinks the piece too big may put something back into the main cake. After all $n - 1$ have looked at it, one of two things must have happened. Either no one diminished p, in which case player 1 takes p and leaves to eat it. Or else one or more people *did* diminish p in which case the *last diminisher* takes the reduced p and leaves. In any case, the game is now down to $n - 1$ people and can be repeated.

It is proved in [33] that this procedure is correct in the sense that each of the n players has a winning strategy to make sure that he gets his fair share. The technique used uses an n person (rather than two-person) version of game logic of Sect. 3.

5.4 Consensus

In 1979 Robert Aumann proved a spectacular result [1]. Suppose that two people A, B with the same prior probability distibution receive *different* information about some event E. It is then likely that their probabilities for E will diverge and that $p = p_A(E)$ could be different from $q = p_B(E)$. What Aumann showed was that if the values p and q are *common knowledge* then they must be equal. This result (somewhat extended) has the following curious consequence: suppose that A is planning to sell B a stock at a selling price s and B is plannning to buy. Assuming that they are both motivated by money and not, say by love or hate for the stock, the future price which A expects the stock to have is *less* than s and the future price which B expects the stock to have is *more* than s. But this fact is common knowledge as it is of course common knowledge that the sale is taking place. But this violates the theorem, the future prices *cannot* be different and the sale cannot take place! This is indeed a paradoxical result.

Aumann's result was extended by Bacharach, Cave, and Geanakoplos and Polmarchakis [10]. The last two showed that in Aumann's framework, if p, q

were not common knowledge they *could* be different, but that if the values $p_A(E)$ and $p_B(E)$ were repeatedly exchanged by A, B, and repeatedly revised, then the process of revision would eventually make them equal. A result by Parikh and Krasucki [34] extends the same phenomenon to n agents who communicate pairwise in a strongly connected graph. It is shown that personal values of probabilities and other strongly convex functions eventually become equal when people communicate in pairs, provided that no one is left out of the chain.

5.5 Logic of Communication Graphs

In [29], Pacuit and Parikh introduce a multimodal epistemic logic for reasoning about knowledge and communication. The language is a multiagent modal language with a communication modality. The formula $K_i\phi$ is interpreted as "according to i's current information, i knows ϕ", and $\Diamond\phi$ will be interpreted as "after some communications among the agents, ϕ becomes true". Thus for example, the formula

$$K_j\phi \rightarrow \Diamond K_i\phi$$

expresses that if agent j (currently) knows ϕ, then after some communication agent i can come to know ϕ. The following example illustrates the type of situations that the logic of communicationg graphs is intended to capture.

Consider the current situation with Bush and Porter Goss, the director of the CIA. If Bush wants some information from a particular CIA operative, say Bob, he must get this information through Goss. Suppose that ϕ is a formula representing the exact whereabouts of Bin Laden and that Bob, the CIA operative in charge of maintaining this information knows ϕ. In particular, $K_{\text{Bob}}\phi$, but suppose that at the moment, Bush does not know the exact whereabouts of Bin Laden ($\neg K_{\text{Bush}}\phi$). Presumably Bush *can* find out the exact whereabouts of Bin Laden ($\Diamond K_{\text{Bush}}\phi$) by going through Goss, but of course, *we* cannot find out such information ($\neg\Diamond K_e\phi \wedge \neg\Diamond K_r\phi$) since we do not have the appropriate security clearance. Clearly, then, as a *prerequisite* for Bush learning ϕ, Goss will also have come to know ϕ. We can represent this situation by the following formula:

$$\neg K_{\text{Bush}}\phi \wedge \Box(K_{\text{Bush}}\phi \rightarrow K_{\text{Goss}}\phi)$$

where $\Box$ is the dual of diamond. And this is because there is no direct link between Bush and Bob, only a chain going through Goss.

It is assumed that a set At of propositional variables are understood by (in the language of) all the agents, but only specific agents know their actual values at the start. Thus initially, each agent has some private information which can be shared through communication with the other agents. Now, if agents are restricted in whom they can communicate with, then this fact will restrict the knowledge they can acquire.

Let $\mathcal{A}$ be a set of agents. A **communication graph** is a directed graph $\mathcal{G}_\mathcal{A} = (\mathcal{A}, E)$ where $E \subseteq \mathcal{A} \times \mathcal{A}$. Intuitively $(i, j) \in E$ means that i can directly receive information from agent j, but *without* j knowing this fact. Thus an edge between i and j in the communication graph represents a one-sided relationship between i and j. Agent i has access to any piece of information that agent j knows. We have introduced this "one sidedness" restriction in order to simplify our semantics, but also because such situations of one sided learning occur naturally. A common situation that is helpful to keep in mind is accessing a website. We can think of agent j as creating a website in which everything he *currently* knows is available, and then if there is an edge between i and j then agent i can access this website without j being aware that the site is being accessed. Another important application of course is spying, where one person accesses another's information without the latter being aware that information is being leaked. Naturally j may have been able to access some other agent k's website and had updated some of her own information. Therefore, it is important to stress that when i accesses j's website, he is accessing j's current information which may include what another agent k knew initially.

The semantics combines ideas both from the subset models of [28] and the history based models of Parikh and Ramanajum (see [35, 36] and Sect. 2.3). The reader is refered to [29] for the details of the semantics. The satisfiability problem for the logic of communication graphs is shown to be decidable. Furthermore, as one may suspect, there is a connection between the structure of the communication graph and the set of valid formulas in a model (based on the communication graph). The following formula

$$\bigwedge_l K_j\phi \wedge \neg K_l\phi \rightarrow \Diamond(K_i\phi \wedge \neg K_l\phi)$$

where i, j are distinct agents, l ranges over agents distinct from these two and ϕ is a ground formula, states that it is possible for i to learn ϕ from j without any other l learning ϕ. Intuitively, this should be true if i has access to j's website without interference from anyone. It is shown in [29] that if there is an edge from i to j in a graph $\mathcal{G}$ then the above formula scheme is valid in the model based on $\mathcal{G}$.

5.6 Knowledge-Based Obligation

We start with the intuition that agents cannot be expected to perform actions, the need for which they are not aware of. In [30], Parikh, Pacuit and Cogan present a multiagent logic of knowledge, action and obligation. The semantics extends the history based models described in Sect. 2.3. In [30], various deontic dilemmas are described that illustrate the dependency of an agent's obligation on knowledge. For instance a doctor cannot be expected to treat a patient unless she is *aware* of the fact that he is sick, and this creates a secondary obligation on the patient or someone else to *inform* the doctor of his situation. In other words, many obligations are situation dependent, and are only relevant in the presence of the relevant information. This creates the notion of *knowledge-based obligation*.

Both the case of an absolute obligation (although dependent on information) as well as the notion of an obligation which may be over-ridden by more relevant information are considered. For instance a physician who is about to inject a patient with drug d may find out that the patient is allergic to d and that she should use d' instead. Dealing with the second kind of case requires a resort to nonmonotonic reasoning and the notion of *weak knowledge* which is stronger than plain belief, but weaker than absolute knowledge in that it can be over-ridden. Consider the following examples:

(a) Uma is a physician whose neighbor is ill. Uma does not know and has not been informed. Uma has no obligation (as yet) to treat the neighbor.

(b) Uma is a physician whose neighbor Sam is ill. The neighbor's daughter Ann comes to Uma's house and tells her. Now Uma does have an obligation to treat Sam, or perhaps call in an ambulance or a specialist.

(c) Mary is a patient in St. Gibson's hospital. Mary is having a heart attack. The caveat which applied in case (a) does not apply here. The hospital has an obligation to be aware of Mary's condition at all times and to provide emergency treatment as appropriate. When there is a knowledge based obligation, but also the obligation to *have* the knowledge, then we have an obligation *simpliciter*.

(d) Uma has a patient with a certain condition C who is in the St. Gibson hospital mentioned above. There are two drugs d and d' which can be used for C, but d has a better track record. Uma is about to inject the patient with d, but unknown to Uma, the patient is allergic to d and for this patient d' should be used. Nurse Rebecca is aware of the patient's allergy and also that Uma is about to administer d. It is then Rebecca's obligation to inform Uma and to suggest that drug d' be used in this case.

In all the cases we mentioned above, the issue of an obligation arises. This obligation is circumstantial in the sense that in other circumstances, the obligation might not apply. Moreover, the circumstances may not be fully known. In such a situation, there may still be enough information about the circumstances to decide on the proper course of action. If Sam is ill, Uma needs to know that he is ill, and the nature of his symptoms, but not where Sam went to school.

Suppose that you want to formalize Uma's reasoning in the above examples, and *formally prove* that she is obliged to treat Sam in example (b). This has in fact been one of the goals of standard *deontic logic*. See [23, 22] and references therein for an uptodate discussion of deontic logic. Getting back to formalizing Uma's reasoning, one of the main points discussed above is that Uma's obligation arises only after she learns of her neighbor's illness. In other words, her obligation depends on her having the appropriate knowledge. In much of the deontic logic literature, an agent's knowledge is only informally represented or the discussion is focused on representing epistemic obligations, i.e., what an agent "ought to know", see [26] for a recent discussion. The logic in [30] is intended to capture the *dependency* of individual obligation on knowledge. The semantics extends the history based models described in Sect. 2.3 with PDL-style action modalities and a deontic operator. Refer to [30] for a detailed discussion of the semantics.

6 Conclusion

We end this paper with an amusing story about Mark Twain.

> 'There was a mystery,' said I. 'We were twins, and one day when we were two weeks old—that is, he was one week old and I was one week old—we got mixed up in the bathtub, and one of us drowned. We never could tell which. One of us had a strawberry birthmark on the back of his hand. There it is on my hand. This is the one that was drowned. There's no doubt about it.'
> 'Where's the mystery?' he said.
> 'Why, don't you see how stupid it was to bury the wrong twin?' I answered.
> (Mark Twain in a 1906 interview reported by the *New York Times*)

The *New York Times* reporter was not fast enough on his feet to hoist Twain on his own petard and ask what difference it made which twin was buried if people could not tell them apart (even after the drowning). But Twain's joke, like other deep jokes (by Groucho Marx or by the Sufi Mullah Nasruddin) leads into important issues like why we need names for people, why the government needs social security numbers, why identity theft is possible. *Who am I?* is normally a question which typically a Zen Buddhist asks. But *Who are you?* is a question which others ask quite often. And this is because societal algorithms depend very much on *identity*. The bank does not want to allow others to withdraw funds from our accounts, or to allow us to withdraw funds from the accounts of others. Questions can be raised here at two levels. One level is why algorithms work only when identity is established. But a deeper level is what game theoretic reasons lie behind such algorithms in the first place. For instance in the play *Romeo and Juliet* when a Montressor has killed a Capulet, it is fine to kill another Montressor to revenge oneself. So the identity which matters here is not personal, but based on clan. There is a game between the two clans, where a threat to kill one member of a clan may be a deterrent on another. This is perhaps a foolish "algorithm", where one Montressor is killed instead of another, but favours are also often dealt out for similar reasons. These issues of the importance of (personal or tribal) identity to the correctness and relevance of games are deep and belong to another (future) paper. But we hasten to point out that they *are* urgent. When Sunni Arabs explode a bomb at a Shia mosque in Iraq, they may have nothing against the individual Shias praying at the mosque. They are *sending a message* to the *group*. If we want to solve such problems, we will surely need to go into the question of interactions where what matters is group identity and not personal identity.

References

1. R. Aumann. Agreeing to Disagree, *Annals of Statistics*, 4:1236 – 1239.
2. R. Aumann. Interactive Epistemology I: Knowledge, *International Journal of Game Theory*, 28:263–300, 1999.
3. R. Aumann. Interactive Epistemology II: Probability, *International Journal of Game Theory*, 28:301–314, 1999.
4. A. Brandenburger, Knowledge and Equilibrium in Games, *Journal of Economic Perspectives*, Vol. **6**, 1992, pp. 83–101.
5. G. Bonanno, and P. Battigalli. Recent results on belief, knowledge and the epistemic foundations of game theory, *Research in Economics 53*, 2 (June 1999), 149–225.
6. M. Chwe, *Rational Ritual : Culture, Coordination, and Common Knowledge*, Princeton University Press, 2001.
7. R. Fagin, J. Halpern, Y. Moses, and M. Vardi. *Reasoning about Knowledge*, The MIT Press, 1995.
8. M. J. Fischer and R. E. Ladner. Propositional dynamic logic of regular programs *J. Comput. Syst. Sci.*, 18(2), pp. 194–211.
9. R. W. Floyd. Assigning meanings to programs, *Proc. Symp. Appl. Math.*, Volume **19**, pp. 19–31.
10. J. Geanakoplos and H. Polemarchakis. We Can't Disagree Forever, *Journal of Economic Theory*, **28(1)**, 1982.
11. P. Gochet and P. Gribomont. Epistemic logic, In *The Handbook of History and Philosophy of Logic*, D. Gabbay and J. Woods, Eds., vol. 4. Elsevier, forthcoming.
12. D. Harel, D. Kozen and J. Tiuryn. *Dynamic Logic*, MIT Press, 2000.
13. J. Halpern, R. van der Meyden and M. Vardi. Complete Axiomatizations for Reasoning about Knowledge and Time, *SIAM Journal on Computing*, Vol **33**, No. 3, 2004, pp. 674–703.
14. J. Halpern. Set-theoretic completeness for epistemic and conditional logic, *Annals of Mathematics and Artificial Intelligence 26* 1999, pp. 1–27.
15. J. Halpern and Y. Moses, Knowledge and common knowledge in a distributed environment, *Journal of the ACM*, **37:3**, 1990, pp. 549-587.
16. M. Osborne and A. Rubinstein. *A Course in Game Theory*, MIT Press, 1994.
17. D. Lewis, *Convention: A Philosophical Study*, Harvard University Press, 1969.
18. J. Moore. Implementation in Environments with Complete Information, In J.J. Laffont, *Advances in Economic Theory: Proceedings of the Congress of the Economiteric Society*, Cambridge University Press, 1992.
19. D. Kozen. *Results on the propositional μ-calculus*, Proc 9th ICALP, Springer LNCS #140, 1982, pp. 348–359.
20. D. Kozen and R. Parikh, *A decision procedure for the propositional μ-calculus*, Proc. CMU Conf. on the Logic of Programs, Springer LNCS #164, pp. 313–325.

21. J. Hintikka. *Knowledge and Belief: An Introduction to the Logic of the Two Notions*, Cornell University Press, 1962.
22. R. Hilpinen. Deontic Logic, in *Blackwell Guide to Philosophical Logic*, Ed. Lou Goble, Blackwell, 2001, pp. 159–182.
23. J. Horty. *Agency and Deontic Logic*, Oxford 2001.
24. C. A. R. Hoare. An axiomatic basis for computer programming, *Comm. ACM* 12, pp. 576–580, 583.
25. B. Kooi. *Knowledge, chance and change* Ph.D. thesis, 2003.
26. A. Lomuscio and M. Sergot. Deontic interpreted systems, *Studia Logica*, **75**, 2003, pp. 63–92.
27. J.J. Meyer and W. van der Hoek. *Epistemic Logic for Computer Science and Artificial Intelligence* Cambridge Tracts in Theoretical Computer Science 41, Cambridge University Press, 1995.
28. L. Moss and R. Parikh. Topological Reasoning and the Logic of Knowledge, *TARK IV*, Ed. Y. Moses, Morgan Kaufmann, 1992.
29. E. Pacuit and R. Parikh. The Logic of Communication Graphs, *Proc. DALT 2004*, Joao Alexandre Leite, Andrea Omicini, Paolo Torroni, Pinar Yolum (Eds.), Revised Selected Papers, Springer LNCS #3476, 2005, pp. 256–269.
30. E. Pacuit, R. Parikh, and E. Cogan. The Logic of Knowledge Based Obligations, Presented at DALT 2004, forthcoming in *Knowledge, Rationality and Action* 2005.
31. R. Parikh Effectiveness, *the Philosophical Forum* XII, 1980, pp. 68–81.
32. R. Parikh. Social software, *Synthese*, pp. 187–211, September 2002.
33. R. Parikh. The Logic of Games and its Applications, *Annals of Discrete Math.*, 24, 1985, pp. 111–140.
34. R. Parikh and P. Krasucki. Communication, Consensus and Knowledge, *J. Economic Theory*, **52**, 1990, pp. 178–189.
35. R. Parikh and R. Ramanujam. Distributed Processing and the Logic of Knowledge, in *Logic of Programs*, Springer LNCS #193, June 1985, pp. 256–268.
36. R. Parikh and R. Ramanujam. A Knowledge based Semantics of Messages, *J. Logic, Language and Information*, **12**, 2003, pp. 453–467.
37. R. Parikh. Levels of Knowledge, Games, and Group Action, *Research in Economics*, vol 57, 2003, pp. 267–281.
38. R. Parikh. Logical omniscience, in *Logic and Computational Complexity* Ed. Leivant, Springer LNCS #960, 1995, pp. 22–29.
39. M. Pauly. A Logical Framework for Coalitional Effectivity in Dynamic Procedures, in *Bulletin of Economic Research*, **53(4)**, pp. 305–324.
40. M. Pauly. Logic for Social Software, Ph.D. Thesis, University of Amsterdam. ILLC Dissertation Series 2001-10, ISBN: 90-6196-510-1.
41. V. Pratt. Semantical considerations on Floyd-Hoare logic, In *Proc. 17th Symp. Found. Comput. Sci.* pp. 109–121. IEEE.
42. A. M. Zanaboni. *Reasoning about knowledge: Notes of Rohit Parikh's lectures.* Published in Italy: Cassa di Risparmio di Padova e Rovigo, June 1991. Based on lectures given at the 3rd International School for Computer Science Researchers, Acireale, June 1991.

Interaction, Computation, and Education

Lynn Andrea Stein

Franklin W. Olin College of Engineering, Needham, MA, USA

It seems to me that education has a two-fold function to perform in the life of man and in society: the one is utility and the other is culture.

Martin Luther King, Jr.

The purpose of education has always been to every one, in essence, the same— to give the young the things they need in order to develop in an orderly, sequential way into members of society.

John Dewey

1 Introduction

This chapter is not quite like any of the other chapters in this volume.

Education is, at its essence, about the transmission of culture. This volume as a whole documents a fundamental shift in the culture of computation: from a focus on algorithmic problem solving to a perspective in which interaction plays a central role. Many of the papers in this volume provide formal foundations for the interactive approach to computation or explore the systems that are a part of this conceptualization of the field. They speak in the language of computer science and use that language to describe a variant vision, one more responsive to the artifacts and theories at the center of much computational progress today. They are intended for current practitioners and they expand existing models to embrace this new paradigm.

In contrast, this chapter focuses on fundamental stories. The story is the ultimate cultural transmission, proto-education that speaks in a visceral language to directly address our understanding of phenomena. Most computer science work is done in programming languages or in mathematical formulae or architectural diagrams, building theories or systems that demonstrate the author's point. But before any of this work—informing the common understanding—is a shared story that carries the culture of computation, our touchstone, our common premises. This is a story first told by the likes of Babbage and Turing and von Neumann, a story that allowed the separation of the computational from worlds of mathematics and science and engineering, a story that enabled many of the technological revolutions of the last half-century. It is also a story that has remained essentially unchanged even in the face of the cultural shift documented by the remainder of this volume. The purpose of this chapter is to examine that story explicitly—to bring it to light and analyze how and why it has served us so far—and to introduce an alternative narrative that better fits the world this volume describes.[1]

Education is cultural transmission. In the computer science classroom, we don't often tell stories explicitly. Nonetheless, we all carry a basic shared understanding of computation on which all the rest of our work is built. By casting this common understanding in the language of a story, we are able to reify it, to make it directly manipulable, and to examine its contributions and its limitations. By introducing an alternate narrative better suited to the world of interactive computation, we can replace the core of the cultural transmission on which computer science education relies.

This begins by describing the traditional computational story in the form of a parable often used in introductory computer science classes. These are the venues in which we indoctrinate new members of the computational society. The stories we tell there are the stories on which our field is built, and we expect these stories to serve our students well as they mature into computational professionals. The next section of this chapter describes the central computational story as it is told to newcomers, but it also relates that story to the practice of computing over the last half century.

Section 3 raises the specter of several computational artifacts that do not fit well into the conventional computational story. While the oldest of these dates back almost as far as the computational narrative itself, problematic systems have been playing roles of increasing prominence in the past decade. These systems have provoked the sea change documented by this volume, and Sect. 4 of this chapter provides an alternative narrative in terms of which these systems and developments can be more easily understood.

If we have a better narrative for computation—the interactive narrative, rather than the traditional one—then it stands to reason that this should be taught in our introductory courses. The second half of this chapter explores just this theme, describing two pedagogic examples from a new curriculum based on this story of interaction and exploring their implications. The curricular examples here are extracted from [Stein, CS101], a dynamic body of work rethinking the introductory computer science curriculum. After all, the role of stories in the conduct of science is to guide and inform our practices.

---

[1] In fact, many of the changes documented by these papers have deep roots, because interaction is as old as computation (or older); it has simply been forgotten, ignored, or overlooked because of the enormous power of computation's central narrative.

If we are training new generations of scientists, we have an obligation to train them in science informed by stories that are authentic—true to the phenomena we study and build—and useful.

It may seem strange to include a paper about stories in a volume about computer science. Or, perhaps, computer scientists—whose stories are more commonly writ in languages the computer can execute—should know better than others the importance of getting those stories right.

2 A Parable of Programming

Consider the following problem: presented with a jar of peanut butter, a jar of jelly, two slices of bread, and some knives, construct a peanut-butter and jelly sandwich.[2] This is like the functional specification of a traditional sequential program.

In the early days of computation, this kind of problem would have been solved very explicitly in terms of steps: First, open the jar. Pick up a knife. Now load some peanut butter onto the knife, then store the peanut butter on the bread. Go back and load some more peanut butter; store it. And so on. A slight augmentation was the idea of an explicit looping construct, which allowed the loading and storing to be repeated until some boundary condition was met, e.g., until the bread was covered.[3] This program—suitably extended to achieve the desired result—in many ways reflects the first activities recognizable as computer programming.

In the 1960s and 1970s, computing moved from the explicit sequencing of steps to what is now called "high level programming". This approach allows the programmer to collect a sequence of steps and to encapsulate it so that it can be regarded as a single step. (This is often called "procedural abstraction".) For example, we might want to repeat the peanut-butter spreading procedure on the other piece of bread. In fact, we'd really like to repeat it with the jelly in place of the peanut butter; this is easily accomplished with a parameterized procedure, i.e., one that allows the spreadable substance to be supplied at the time that the procedure is to be executed.

The idea of encapsulating sequences of steps into larger—higher level, more abstract—steps allowed for very significant advances in computation. It meant that software designers could increasingly think in terms of these very high-level steps, and that implementors could build systems by recursively decom-

---

[2] The trick, missed by several Europeans in random trials, is that the peanut butter goes on one slice of bread and the jelly on the other. Otherwise, the poor-quality white bread required for an authentic PBJ disintegrates as the second substance is applied. But this is beside the point.

[3] This idea had been present in certain prior procedural formats, including Euclid's algorithm for finding the greatest common denominator, El Kowarizmi's algorithm for the addition of numbers with many digits, or more prosaic forms such as recipes ("beat until stiff") or mechanical processes ("sand until smooth").

Fig. 1. Sequential computation is like making a peanut butter and jelly sandwich

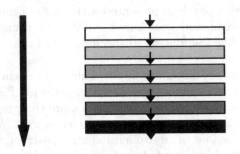

Fig. 2. Sequential computation: Beginning with some input, execute a sequence of steps that terminates, producing a result

posing these steps into sequences of simpler steps, over and over, until finally the simplest steps were machine-performable. Much of the history of computing in the 1970s consists of building better tools to support the automating of machine performance of increasingly higher-level steps and the concomitant raising of the level at which software designers could operate.

A further transition in programming practice surrounds the adoption of object oriented programming. This technique centers around the idea that that there is benefit to encapsulating data and performable behavior within a single reusable program constituent. For example, the jelly (and its spreadability) might be useful not only for my sandwich today but also on my muffin tomorrow morning. With the original descriptions of object-oriented programming came a vision of self-activating (autonomous) objects. These are objects containing (or controlling) their own threads of control: An alarm clock, a garbage collector, etc.

Alan Kay has always insisted that the idea of active objects was a part of his vision of object oriented programming from the beginning, but by the late 1980s, it was clear that "concurrent" was a subspecies of object-oriented programming, at best (for example, [Kay, 1997] vs. [Yonezawa and Tokoro, 1987]). Other attempts to activate objects, [Agha and Hewitt, 1987], for example, were similarly sidelined, and this notion was largely lost in the translation of object-oriented philosophies into practice. Object-oriented programming languages and techniques may lead to a more flexible program organization, but object-oriented programming per se still largely fits the sequentialist, result-oriented, calculate-the-answer paradigm.

In each of these versions, the success of our program is measured by the peanut butter and jelly sandwich that is produced. We can ask questions about it: Is it an optimal peanut butter and jelly sandwich? We can also measure the process that led to its creation: How many knives were dirtied in the process? This model of computation, based on Turing's machine and the mathematical calculations of the original human computers of the early twentieth century, has informed our thinking for more than half a century. It is what might be called the calculation model of computation—sequencing steps to produce a result—and its hallmarks are algorithm and functional specification.

No matter how we build our programs, there have been some very significant advances enabled by this sequentialist, result-oriented story of computation (both within and outside of computer science). It is quite clear that some of these advances would have been unlikely without certain of the clarifying abstractions embodied by this paradigm. (For example, control of hardware was greatly facilitated by the digital abstraction and von Neumann architecture.) However, these abstractions hide as much as they reveal. In today's changing computational climate, this calculate-the-answer kind of computation has moved from empowering to limiting our vision.

3 Computations and Interactions

The structures contributed by the calculation model of computation were tremendously empowering in the first half of this century. Turing's and von Neumann's abstractions enabled computer science to focus on the organization of sequences of steps into larger functional units without worrying about transient voltage levels or multiple simultaneous transitions within the hardware. This way of thinking about computation also let us ignore the occasional power fault, the mechanical misfire, delays in operator feedback, or other human activities.

The power of the step-by-step construction metaphor made much of modern computation possible. Although some early computers were used in actual physically coupled control systems—realtime guidance of mechanical operations—more frequently they were used to assist humans in decision-making—calculating the answers to mathematical questions, such as the trajectories of ballistic missiles—in a manner well modeled by the peanut butter and jelly story of sequential computation.[4] Perhaps if more emphasis had

---

[4] For an elaboration of this argument, see [Stein, 1999a, *Metaphor*]. For a discussion of early computing and control systems, see [Mindell, 2002] and for an early history of computing, see [Campbell-Kelly and Aspray, 1997]

been placed earlier on embedded computation and control systems—systems for which interaction was a more significant factor—the sequential calculation model would not have become computation's dominant metaphor for decades. But it is equally possible, given some of the difficulties encountered by those using digital computers for control or attempting to build embedded cybernetic systems, that without the sequential calculation model of computing we would not have had much computing at all.

At the same time, the peanut butter and jelly story encourages us to ignore the fact that computers are actually built out of analog components. It obscures the fact that each component is fallible. It hides the ways in which the computer is physically coupled into the world, and largely ignores any systems—human or mechanical or otherwise—within which the computation is embedded. In short, it hides the reality that computational systems are interactive communities—communities of interacting entities—themselves embedded in still larger communities of interaction.

With the advent of timesharing systems, of increasingly networked computers, of computational boxes containing more than one central processing unit, it became less and less true that these other things "don't matter". The activity of another user on the same timesharing system does impact my computation, though the virtual machine model goes to great lengths to minimize this interaction. Similarly, computations that necessarily take place across multiple computers—the web is only the most visible example—are poorly explained in terms of the traditional computational story.

One example of a computation that is ill-explained in traditional terms is the operating system.[5] Its basic structure is an interactive control loop that continually processes whatever command you type at it (or whatever requests are made by various software and hardware systems). If you look inside the operating system, you will find what are in essence multiple interactive control loops—ongoing interacting subsystems—constituting a community that is the operating system. For example, an operating system has a virtual memory subsystem that keeps track of what is in memory and also allows the use of some disk space as though it were additional memory. Another piece of the operating system processes keystrokes as they are typed and passes that information on to the appropriate constituent or application. Perhaps the computer in question is networked; in this case, the operating system may well supply services for communicating over that network. There are of course

---

[5] Goldin asserts that the operating system is the first system in which the limitations of the Turing machine model were noted: "They do not ever stop computing—and thus diverge and are useless according to TM theory." She calls this the "OS conundrum" (personal communication). Others apparently came to this realization through different pathways: I imagine that those who work in the areas of networks and controls have always had their suspicions regarding the inadequacy of the conventional computational story, and I learned early on in my own work with robots that I wasn't particularly interested in the answer the robot produced when it finally stopped.

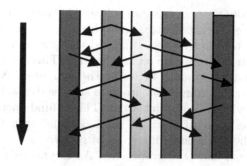

Fig. 3. Computation as interaction: Many persistent entities communicate and coordinate over time

many other pieces of the operating system. In some operating systems, these pieces are all executed within a single thread of control, and this decomposition into simultaneous autonomous systems is more metaphoric. In other systems, these pieces are more literally co-occurrent (or at least interwoven). In almost all systems, there is an asynchronous interrupt system; also, peripheral devices with their own processors managing the services that they supply are increasingly common.

This suggests that there must be an alternate story of computation, one that takes ongoing interaction as primary. Such a story of computation-as-interaction must also support thinking about levels of abstraction and recursive decomposition. For example, if we look inside one of the pieces of an operating system, we see that the virtual memory subsystem is composed of a community of interacting entities (including, for example, different levels of cache). From the outside—from the perspective of network services or keyboard I/O—the virtual memory system is a single entity resolving page references. In fact, significant negotiation among constituent entities occurs whenever a page is referenced. From inside the virtual memory system, we can more clearly see this recursive decomposition into subcommunities. Similarly, though the operating system is itself built out of many interacting entities, it looks like a single monolithic system from the perspective of those outside the operating system (like the user or an application program). The operating system provides the illusion of a single interactive entity.[6]

But an operating system is an unusual program, and perhaps we do not need to reconsider computation's central narrative for its sake alone. Consider, then, a more traditional application: word processing. When I first learned to

---

[6] If this final image—the illusion of a single interactive entity—seems reminiscent of Minsky's *Society of Mind* [1986], this is not coincidental. The interactive story is equally applicable to what we know of cognitive architectures and neuroscience; indeed, it may be a more currently useful bridge to these disciplines than the more orthodox computationally based cognitive science revolution of the 1970s. For a further discussion of these ideas, see [Stein, 1999a, *Metaphor*].

word-process, I wrote my text using an editor. This produced a file with some text in it. Next, I gave that file to a spell-checker. This produced a file with (hopefully) better text in it. Then, I handed that file off to a text formatter (such as nroff or latex), producing yet another file. (This one is much harder for a human to read, but presumably better for the computer.) Nowadays, this file needs to be handed to a conversion program such as dvips. I can then see my paper (using a previewer) and print it out. This is fundamentally a sequence-of-steps calculation story. It starts at the beginning with the information I produce, and at the end results in a stack of paper.

This is no longer how I word-process. As I type this paper, the word processor I'm using dynamically reformats my page so that it looks at all times the way that it would if I were previewing or printing it. At the same time, if I type "hte", the word processor reverses the "h" and the "t", producing "the". It also underlines misspelled words and what it views as questionable grammar. One could imagine that it simultaneously went off and searched the web, suggesting references I might want to add to my paper. All of these things are happening concurrently and asynchronously with the work that I am doing. It is reasonable to imagine that this word processor is built out of components that are themselves concurrent interacting entities; if we went inside each one, we might find it to be a community of communities. Stepping back, the word processor is itself a member of a community consisting of me, my computer's operating system and perhaps those papers out on the web. None of these things is particularly well-explained by the sequenced steps of the calculation metaphor of computation.

In the peanut butter and jelly model of computation, all inputs are present at the beginning. Output is what you produce at the end. A computation is described this functional—one shot input/output relationship—specification. The interesting questions concern time-to-completion and resource utilization. Classic computational systems are built by sequential, functional composition.

In contrast, in interactive systems input is continually arriving; output is continually being produced. Behavioral specifications include the services provided—what kind of responses can you expect on an ongoing basis?—and the invariants maintained—what is guaranteed to stay the same over time? Questions include latency and throughput. Interactive systems are built by spatial or conceptual coupling, i.e., by concurrent co-operation.

In a conventional computation, the end is the moment of success. When an interactive system—an operating system, a network, a robot—stops, it is usually because something has gone wrong. What, after all, is the end result that the World-Wide Web is trying to produce? The old story simply doesn't fit our artifacts.

What is needed, then, is a new story of computation that can explain these systems. This new story should be as simple as the peanut butter and jelly parable, because it is about the key ideas in computing. But it should be powerful enough to explain how systems work even when those systems are based fundamentally on interactions, as our networks and operating systems and robots and even desktop applications clearly are. We explore one such narrative in the next section.

4 Expanding the Parable

We—all of us, every day—live in a concurrent world. Things happen when our backs are turned, and many of us do more than one thing at a time. The calculation model of computation is really quite different from many of our everyday experience. In the calculation metaphor, the outside world doesn't really have a role to play in the sequence of steps that constitutes our computation. The buzz and hum of everyday life is irrelevant to the unrelenting progress of computation-as-calculation.

This kind of computation is not like following a recipe; it is like organizing the operation of a café or restaurant. The problem confronting the system designer is to figure out how to serve customers food on an ongoing basis. Similarly, the web, the modern word processor, and the operating system provide services on an ongoing basis. In the restaurant (and in these other systems), these services must be provided simultaneously. It wouldn't do to wait for the first customer to finish before taking the second's order. Input doesn't arrive all at the beginning; instead, customers are continually walking in the door. Output isn't what you do just before you close; it's a steady production. (Input is what you monitor; output is what you do.)

Programming is constituting a community of interacting entities. Populating the restaurant requires asking: Who are the members of the community? How do they interact? What is each one made of? These are the central questions of the new computational metaphor.

To populate our restaurant, we need to identify the members of our community. One possible organization involves a division of labor into the wait staff, the kitchen staff, and the business staff. These correspond roughly to such canonical pieces as a user interface, a computational engine, and a manager of an external resource such as a database or network services.

The second question is: How do they interact? The key notions here are ideas such as interface and protocol. An interface is the interactive equivalent of a functional description, specifying what an entity requires and what it produces, what behavioral contracts the entity can be expected to subscribe to. A protocol describes the precise choreography of an interaction, including what each party does in what temporal sequence and how information moves back and forth. For example, we might design a data-structure based protocol (depicted in Fig. 4) for the waiter to communicate orders to the kitchen by writing the customer's order on a piece of paper, then hanging the paper in the kitchen staff's window. The state of that paper (often including its physical location) serves as a cue to the kitchen staff as to what food preparation remains on the order. When the food is delivered to the waiter, the scrap of paper is thrown away (garbage collected).

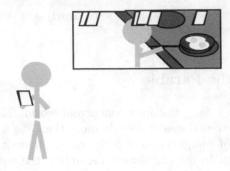

Fig. 4. The orders written by the waiter are the foundation for a data-structure-based protocol between the kitchen and the wait staff. As each order is processed and picked up, the corresponding piece of paper is discarded

Fig. 5. Bin sorting: Sort the balls from the input bucket into a fixed set of output baskets

Of course, computational protocols come in many different varieties; the important point is that the protocol determines how these two entities interact. Similarly, we might design protocols for other interactions within the system—the waiter and the business manager, for example—so that the restaurant maintains a sufficient supply of peanut butter.

Once we design the community and its interactions, we need to apply the traditional technique of recursive decomposition. Of each entity, we ask how it is made. For example, the wait staff might really consist of the maître d'hôtel, one or more waiters, someone to clear the table, etc.[7] Among them, each has a distinct set of responsibilities and certain protocols for interaction. From the kitchen's perspective, the wait staff may be approximated as a single entity that periodically delivers order request and retrieves platters of food; from among the wait staff, the reality of a community is visible. Similarly, from the customer's perspective, the entire restaurant might be seen as a single entity. It might be a one-man shop, with a single person literally playing each of these roles. Or it might be a large, well-staffed restaurant, but one whose complex interactions are largely invisible to the customers.

---

[7] Such an extensive wait staff would be quite unusual in a café or luncheonette, but might be appropriate in a more elaborate restaurant.

Stepping outside of the restaurant, we see that it is itself embedded in a community. That community involves the customers who come to eat. It also involves the restaurant's suppliers, the tax collector, the landlord, and many others. The same model and questions—Who are the members? How do they interact? What's inside each?—apply.

The restaurant model of computation involves sequences of steps; you can't run a restaurant without cooking some recipes. But the recipes are not the heart of the restaurant. Instead, the pieces of this model are ongoing persistent autonomously active entities: the staff. They are coupled together using various interaction protocols. The entire system is evaluated based on ongoing behavior, rather than any end result. (A restaurant ends when it closes down; at that point, it is no longer functioning properly.) Computation today is like running a restaurant.

5 Educational Implications

Introductory computer science education is the place where we as a community articulate the principles that underlie our field. It is in this course that we lay out the foundations of computation and teach students to think in computational terms. The peanut butter and jelly model has—literally and figuratively—been a central part of this course. If computation today is more appropriately construed as a restaurant, we must rethink the story that we tell our community's newest members.

5.1 A Traditionally Sequential Example

In this section, I will describe an example that begins as a traditionally sequential story. By recasting this example in interactive terms—reconstituting it as an interactive community rather than a sequence of steps—I will demonstrate how the shift in metaphor leads to a transformation of traditional curricular materials. Transferring the problem from the traditional calculation-based metaphor into this new interactive framework turns it into a very different kind of problem. What begins as a very simple sequential program winds up as an equally accessible description of a problem usually viewed as too complex for first-semester college students. The moral of this story is that concurrency is not inherently more difficult than sequential programming; it is, however, a radically different way of approaching problems.

Bin Sorting

The traditional sequential problem on which this example is based is bin sort: Given a collection of items associated with a fixed finite set of keys, sort them according to these keys. In simpler terms, imagine a bucket of balls of different colors; the programmer's task is to sort these balls into baskets, one corresponding to each color represented. A traditional approach would use a program with the following structure:[8]

SEQUENTIAL BINSORT

1. Pick up a ball from the input bucket.
2. Consider the first basket.
3. If the color of the ball matches the color of the current basket, put the ball into the basket and go to step 1.
4. Otherwise (the color does not match, so) consider the next basket.
5. Go to step 3.

This program can be executed by a single thread of computation. It will eventually wind up placing each ball in the appropriately colored basket. That is, its functional specification matches the requirements of the problem. All input is available at the beginning of the problem; the computation's result is its final state. In short, this is a conventional algorithmic computation lifted directly from the standard—peanut butter and jelly paradigm—literature.

The analysis performed in a traditional sophomore-level algorithms class further assures us that this task will be completed on average in $nk/2$ iterations (where n is the number of balls and k the number of baskets) and at worst will require nk iterations. These are the kinds of questions that we would expect the traditional computational metaphor to evoke.

A community of sorters

Contrast the bin sort algorithm with a more communal decomposition of the same problem. Instead of breaking the problem into steps, we break it into entities—one for each basket (or color). Next, we arrange these entities in a line, with buffers between them, as in Fig. 6. Each entity follows the interactive rule:

COMMUNITY BINSORT

1. Pick up a ball from your input buffer.
2. If the color of the ball matches the color of *your* basket, put the ball into *your* basket.
3. Otherwise (it is not your color), *put it into your output buffer*.

---

[8] This program outline leaves out the termination condition. In fact, termination represents an asymmetry between the traditional (calculation) model of computation and the interactive one. As will be seen below, if the read is blocking, no explicit termination condition is needed in the interactive program; therefore, I have omitted it here as well.

Fig. 6. A community-of-interacting-entities solution to the bin sorting problem

This is very close to being a subset of the SEQUENTIAL BINSORT rule; new text has been highlighted in this pseudocode. In addition, the control flow in this rule is a simple *go back to line 1* implicit at the end of this code. That control flow is not made explicit because the default behavior for an interactive entity is to keep processing—often to keep looping over its inputs—forever. A conventional algorithmic computation runs through its steps until completion and only hands off control to any other piece of code when it completes its task. In contrast, an interactive entity continually processes input and continually produces output. It can be coupled with other entities not through temporal sequencing but through spatial interaction (in this case, shared buffers).

By making the original bucket of balls the input buffer for one of the entities and stringing the others along, we have a parallel program that is in many respects strikingly similar to the traditional sequential decomposition described above. It differs by containing multiple active entities—multiple threads of control—and simultaneous activity. It requires essentially the same number of total steps as the original bin sort, though the activity is distributed across the community of active entities, or agents.

Importantly, this new framing of the problem lends itself to a somewhat different set of questions: comparisons of the relative workloads of the first vs. last of these agents, or even the question of workload itself; discussion of how long it takes each ball to stop moving down the line of entities; etc. Of course, these questions are precisely the kinds of questions that one begins to ask about parallel and concurrent programs.

Significantly, this new program decomposition is not too complex for beginning computational students, bringing these questions into reach of our disciplines newest members. However, this is only the beginning of what the new computational metaphor can do.

Expanding the community

In the interactive decomposition of the bin sorting problem, one of the entities has privileged access to the original bucket of balls. There is no particular reason why this should be so. Instead, we can change the program so that each entity uses the original bucket as its input buffer and as its output buffer. The rule for this is a minor variation on the COMMUNITY BINSORT rule:

COMMUNITY BINSORT 2

1. Pick up a ball from your input buffer.
2. If it is your color, put it into your basket.
3. Otherwise (it is not your color), put it *back into your input buffer*.

In addition to the change highlighted in the BINSORT rule, this modification requires a change in the topology of the community, i.e., its interconnections. The new topology is shown in Fig. 7(a) and involves only one shared bucket. In this configuration, each entity picks up a ball from the (single) shared central bucket, keeps it if it matches, and otherwise returns it to that bucket.

Fig. 7. Variants on the interactive bin-sorting community. (a) A randomized version. (b) A hierarchical version. (c) An on-line hierarchical version: network routing!

This is a parallel randomized bin sort. The algorithm is not one usually presented to undergraduates (at any level). The reason why randomized algorithms are usually deferred until graduate[9] courses is that concurrency itself is not considered an undergraduate topic. However, decomposed in this fashion, it is completely accessible. For example, most school children would have no trouble understanding that the blue-basket entity might continually pick up and put down a green ball, preventing it from ever reaching the green basket. That is, randomized sort is not guaranteed to complete.

---

[9] What in the US is called a graduate course is in many other parts of the world referred to as a postgraduate course.

Nor does this example end here. We can take the output baskets of each of these entities and use them as input buffers for other sets of entities. (Again, the entities each use the COMMUNITY BINSORT 2 rule; the network topology is shown in Fig. 7(b).) This results in a hierarchical sort: The first level of entities sorts by major color family, the second by shading within that color family, etc. Given its homogeneously parallel decomposition, this problem scales easily, meshing coarse-grained with increasingly fine-grained sorts. At this point, we are moving beyond what the traditional sequential decomposition can easily accommodate.

One final twist shifts this problem firmly from the purely sequential world to the on-line, interactive model. In previous versions of the problem, we have used a fixed bucket of balls as input. In the interactive model of computation, where input is a continual process, there is no reason for this.

Imagine instead that the balls in this problem were supplied over a conveyer belt. Again, the computational entities are arranged in the topology of Fig. 7(b) and run the code for COMMUNITY BINSORT 2. Now, however, there is no end to the supply and therefore no final state by which to judge the performance of our computational community. Instead, we ask questions about more engineering terms: latency and throughput, correctness and completeness. How long does each ball spend travelling through the system? Is it guaranteed to eventually find its home? Are ordering constraints preserved?

If these questions sound vaguely familiar, this is no coincidence. From a traditionally sequential bin-sorting problem, we have moved to the world of network routing. The final version of this program is a simplified form of the programs that run our worldwide communication networks.

5.2 Morals

This problem started out as a very traditional von Neumann sequence-of-steps kind of problem. By shifting the metaphor—by thinking of the problem as the interaction of a community of agents—we teach our students the basics of network routing. They can explore many of the issues that arise in real-life computational networks. Shifting the metaphor makes things that were very inaccessible to beginning students much more accessible. In courses that I and others have taught using this approach [Stein, CS101], first semester students with no prior programming experience learn in a single term to build client-server chat programs and networked video games. These are not things that first-semester students typically do. The reason that they are able to accomplish this is that the basic language to think about these things is not very difficult once you realize that a computation is built out of a community of interacting entities.

Another major point of this example is that concurrency is not a topic to be afraid of. We all live in a concurrent world. In teaching computer science, we tell our students to ignore their instinctual understanding of concurrency.

"Forget how the world works; this is computer science," we say. Ignore turn-taking and sign-up sheets, ganging up or cooperating to solve problems. In essence, we put blinders on our students. Then, sometime around their third year of university training, we start to remove those blinders as we introduce them to topics like operating systems or user interfaces or embedded systems. At that point, our students have generally absorbed our lessons and become good sequentialist computer scientists. For many of them, there is only a single thread of control, one thing happening at a time, in a vacuum.

Instead, we ought to teach our students—from the beginning—to marshal their intuitions about interacting communities. They come to computation with instincts about managing the world's complexities, about surviving in a world full of simultaneous interactions, about organizing cooperation so that interactions solve problems. We can teach our students how to translate that tremendous body of intuition into computational practice.

5.3 Echo to Internet Chat: Syllabus in a Nutshell

The bin sorting/network routing example illustrates the way in which a traditionally sequential problem can be completely transformed by recasting it in an interactive framework. In courses that I have taught, students typically see only the interactive (routing) version. In this section, I describe a different example, one that is woven through the course and explains students' progression from a simple infinite echo loop to networked video games.

The simplest program

This example begins with the simplest interactive program:

                        while (true) echo

This program replaces the quintessential first program of the historical paradigm,

                        print "Hello, world!"

The echoer is an "atomic unit" of computation that continually reads its input and reproduces that signal on its output. It goes on forever; beginning and ending are relatively unimportant special cases. It interacts; it can be coupled to other entities, such as the user (by way of keyboard and screen). Embedded in such a context, it takes on the appearance of a traditional "standalone" program.

Looking inside this program, we may choose to divide it into two separate entities, one responsible for user input (the "source") and the other for output (the "sink"). For example, if echo is decomposed into read and write, the "source" entity is the reader and the "sink" entity is the writer. In the same kind of pseudocode used in the last section, this might look like:

ECHOER

1. read *something* from the user's input
2. write that *something* to the user's screen

which can be decomposed into SOURCE and SINK as follows:

SOURCE
1. read *something* from the user's input and hand it to SINK

SINK

1. on receipt of *something* from SOURCE, write it to the user's screen

These entities form a simple community, communicating with one another, but also with the user. Like other entities, humans are members of the community who interact with program components. Unlike other entities, human users represent a special class of community members with decidedly different bandwidth, latency, and other computational properties. Accounting for these differences and accommodating them is the foundation of the underappreciated field of user interface design.

This illustrates the ways in which a single apparent entity (ECHOER) may in fact be constructed out of several entities cooperating. Each of these entities interacts with the other according to some predetermined protocol ("hand it to SINK"/"on receipt...\"). There are actually many ways to implement this handoff, and exploration of the tradeoffs between a supplier-driven and recipient-driven versions are well within the understanding of introductory students. For example, the supplier-driven version is like the Fruit-of-the-Month Club, with automated deliveries and occasional piles of rotted fruit when the recipient is on vacation. The recipient-driven version avoids oversupply at the doorstep, but can lead to long waits in line at the fruit supplier. These are exactly the kinds of questions that designers of such protocols address, and they are easily accessible to the beginning undergraduate.

Variations on a theme

Once our protocol is chosen, we can design alternate entities that conform to either side of it, making it possible, e.g., to read from a stored file or to write to a printer.

FILE SOURCE

1. read *something* from the **file** and hand it to **a** SINK

PRINTER SINK

1. on receipt of *something* from **a** SOURCE, write it to the **printer**

These constituent entities may be mixed and matched as long as their interface protocol is adhered to.

Indeed, we can extend this idea further. If we create an entity that subscribes to both the source (producer) and sink (consumer) side of the protocol, we can insert a transformer entity into the community:

TRANSFORMER

1. on receipt of *something* from a SOURCE
2. *transform it*
3. hand *the transformed* something to a SINK

For example, the transformation entity might modify any strings it receives by converting them to upper case or translating them into pig latin.[10]

UPPER-CASER TRANSFORMER

1. on receipt of *something* from a SOURCE
2. *focus on the first letter*
3. *turn the current letter into its upper case equivalent*
4. *if this is not the last letter, focus on the next letter and go back to step 3*
5. hand the transformed *something* to a SINK

PIG-LATIN TRANSFORMER [11]

1. on receipt of *something* from a SOURCE
2. *remove the first letter*
3. *append a hyphen to the end of the word*
4. *append the removed first letter to the end of the word, after the hyphen*
5. *add "ay" at the end*
6. hand the transformed *something* to a SINK

---

[10] Pig latin is an English language children's game in which words are transformed by moving the initial consonant to the end and adding "ay". For example, "igpay atinlay" is pig latin for "pig latin". Most languages and cultures have similar word-transformation games.

[11] The astute reader will observe that this transformer doesn't really give good rules for pig latin. For example, it doesn't properly handle words beginning with a vowel or a multiletter consonant formation: "order" translates as "rder-oay", which is certainly wrong, as is "ruitcake-fay" for "fruitcake". In addition, both the pig latin transformer and the upper caser transformer make undocumented assumptions about the form of their input, etc. Remedying these issues in the pseudocode would add nothing to the presentation of ideas here and so is left as an exercise for the reader. Complete code is included in [Stein, CS101].

If the transformation component is suitably designed, multiple transformations can be coupled together in sequence—capitalization and pig-latin translation together, for example—or in some kind of alternation.

Further broadening the program, we can create an augmented transformation entity that includes transmission of the string over the network.

NETWORK TRANSFORMER (FIRST HALF)[12]

1. on receipt of *something* from a SOURCE
2. *send the* something *over the network (to the other half of this TRANSFORMER)*

NETWORK TRANSFORMER (SECOND HALF)

1. *when the* something *is received over the network (from the other half of this transformer)*
2. hand the transformed *something* to a SINK

Note that, from the outside, the FIRST HALF looks like any other SINK while the SECOND HALF looks like a conventional SOURCE. By connecting this to a user-interface SOURCE on one computer and a user-interace SINK on another, we can construct a program that reads input from one user and writes the same (or, if we want to add transformers, a transformed) signal as output to another user. This is still basically the same program, except that the input and output computers are now separated. Conceptually, it is still a single interactive entity. And yet, this is also Internet chat.

Telling the larger story

Progressing from echo to chat, as we do during the course of the semester, introduces many topics that are not traditionally part of introductory computer science. The structure of these programs opens the opportunity for an exploration of issues of information transfer (including push and pull), explicit dispatch vs. event-driven programming, concurrency, user interfaces, networking, component architectures, and a whole host of other issues not usually considered accessible to the introductory student.

This approach also explains the role of users in computational systems. In the traditional world, where computation is concerned with "what do I do next?" it is hard to explain how people fit in. But if computation is a community of interacting entities, people are easily explained as members of the community in which the computation is embedded. The boundary between

---

[12] The intricacies of network communication are omitted here, but once we are writing code in a sufficiently high level language, there's actually not that much hidden under that particular rug. Working versions of these transformers are included in [Stein, CS101]

what happens inside the computer and the world into which it is coupled is blurred; we can shift that line in either direction, allocating more or less of the problem to the mechanical computer. In other words, this approach makes the issue of user interfaces a study of the special case in which one of the computational entities is human.

Part of the reason for this transformation of the curriculum is that the community-based approach to program design slices the traditional curriculum along entirely different lines from the traditional, calculation-oriented curriculum. Shifting the metaphor shifts the fundamentals of the field. It changes the ways in which we approach questions and even which questions we consider important. If computation is a community, we care less about how to get from here to there and more about how to interact with other entities. We design fewer algorithms and more protocols. We worry less about functions and more about constraints or invariants, i.e., what stays the same through time. We ask about throughput and latency rather than time-to-completion. And yet, we maintain the fundamental ideas of computational design in terms of abstraction and recursive decomposition.

6 Summary

Computation is not a sequence of steps to produce a result at the end. Computation is embodied in ongoing interactive entities. It is composed of a community of such entities; their interactions are what make computation happen. Input is what you observe; output is what you do. Computations are evaluated based on ongoing behavior, commitments kept, services provided, invariants maintained.

A significant fraction of this paper discusses rethinking introductory computer programming. This is because the introductory course is where we make our metaphors explicit, where we lay out what computation is all about. By recasting the course in terms of a new metaphor for computation, I was able to teach beginning students about ideas traditionally considered too complex and inaccessible for that level. Curricularly, this changes every subsequent course, without actually changing the course sequence. Everything that we teach our students takes on new meaning. This approach makes it easier to contextualize traditionally hard-to-fit-in topics such as user interfaces. It facilitates the teaching of operating systems and networking, because they are not simultaneously learning about concurrency and about the mechanisms to implement concurrency on a sequential processor. Rethinking the computational metaphor turns the discipline on its side, giving us new ways to understand a wide range of phenomena.

But this chapter is not about how to teach the introductory course, even though this metaphoric shift has profound implications there. This chapter is about changing the ways in which computer scientists think about computation. Many subdisciplines have their own language for describing this way of thinking about computation. In artificial intelligence, the recent attention to embodiment, to agents, to behaviors, is indicative of this shift. The computer systems community uses terms like server, transaction, thread. Other research communities that rely on similar notions—by still other names—are those that study networking, distributed systems, information management, human–computer interaction and computer-supported collaboration, web computing, and embedded. Each of these research communities has its own terminology for describing the interactive community metaphor, impeding the opportunities for cross-field discourse and collaborative problem solving.

By recasting all of computational science in terms of the interactive community, we have shifted the center of the field. Efforts to make multiple CPUs look like a single processor—as in automatic program parallelization—now seem peripheral. Research on user interfaces, or on component architectures such as CORBA or COM, take on new centrality given their focus on coupling subsystems together. The heart of current computational thinking is in agents, servers, services, and distributed systems.

This way of approaching computation also has profound implications for the kinds of thinking we do. For our students, it means that we harness their native intuition about how to survive in an inherently concurrent and asynchronous world. We never put on the blinders of calculational sequentialism. We never assume that our programs operate in a world unto themselves; instead, our programs are constructed to function in a dynamic, concurrent world with which they continually interact.

In other disciplines, we find that the new metaphors we are using are more appropriate for bidirectional cross-disciplinary communication. Just as computation is a reference model for understanding cognitive and biological science, so what we learn about the robustness of biological systems inspires us in the construction of "survivable" computational systems. Both natural and artificial computations produce behavior by virtue of the interactions of a community.

Many disciplines study systems of interaction. The cognitive sciences look at how natural intelligence works. Organizational science analyze the ways in which corporations and other large administrative entities function. Several of the social sciences study the ways in which human communities work. Each of these fields has the potential to contribute to, and to benefit from, a computational science of interaction.

References

1. Gul Agha and Carl Hewitt. "Actors: A Conceptual Foundation for Concurrent Object-Oriented Programming." In *Research Directions in Object-Oriented Programming*, Bruce Shriver and Peter Wegner, eds., MIT Press, Cambridge, MA, 1987, pp. 49 - 74

2. Martin Campbell-Kelly and William Aspray. *Computer: A History of the Information Machine*, HarperCollins, 1997.
3. John Dewey. "Individual Psychology and Education." *The Philosopher* **12**, 1934.
4. Alan Kay. "The Computer Revolution Hasn't Happened Yet." Keynote address at the *ACM SIGPLAN Conference on Object Oriented Systems, Languages, and Applications*. Atlanta, Georgia. 1997.
5. Martin Luther King, Jr. "The Purpose of Education." *Maroon Tiger*, January-February 1941.
6. L. F. Menabrea. *Sketch of the Analytical Engine Invented by Charles Babbage*, Bibliothèque Universelle de Genève, October, 1842, No. 82. Translated with notes by Ada Augusta, Countess of Lovelace.
7. David A. Mindell. *Between Human and Machine: Feedback, Control, and Computing before Cybernetics*, Baltimore: Johns Hopkins University Press, 2002.
8. Marvin Minsky. *The Society of Mind*, New York: Simon & Schuster, 1985.
9. Lynn Andrea Stein. "Challenging the Computational Metaphor: Implications for How We Think," *Cybernetics and Systems* **30** *(6)*:473-507, 1999 (a).
10. Lynn Andrea Stein. "What We Swept Under the Rug: Radically Rethinking CS1," *Computer Science Education* **8** *(2)*:118-129, 1999 (b).
11. Lynn Andrea Stein. *Rethinking CS101*. Web site at http://www.cs101.org includes textbook, syllabi, problem sets, teaching materials, as well as publications.
12. Lynn Andrea Stein. *Introduction to Interactive Programming*, to appear. Currently at http://www.cs101.org/ipij.
13. Alan Turing. "On Computable Numbers, with an application to the Entscheidungsproblem", *Proc. Lond. Math. Soc.* (2) 42 pp 230-265, 1936; correction ibid. 43, pp 544-546, 1937.
14. John von Neumann. *First Draft of a Report on the EDVAC*, Contract No.W-670-ORD-4926 between the United States Army Ordnance Department and the University of Pennsylvania. Moore School of Electrical Engineering, University of Pennsylvania, June 30, 1945.
15. Akinori Yonezawa and Mario Tokoro. *Object-oriented concurrent programming*, MIT Press, Cambridge, MA, 1987.

List of Contributors

Susanne Albers
Department of Computer Science
University of Freiburg
Georges-Köhler-Allee 79
79110 Freiburg, Germany
salbers@informatik.uni-freiburg.de

Farhad Arbab
CWI
Kruislaan 413
1098 SJ Amsterdam
The Netherlands
farhad@cwi.nl
&
LIACS
Leiden University
Niels Bohrweg 1
2333 CA Leiden
The Netherlands
farhad@liacs.nl

Chris Barrett
Virginia Bio-Informatics Institute &
Computer Science Dept.
Virginia Polytechnic Institute and
State University
1880 Pratt Drive, Building XV
Blacksburg, VA 24061-0497, USA
cbarrett@vbi.vt.edu

Michel Beaudouin-Lafon
Université Paris-Sud
LRI - Bât 490
91405 Orsay, France
mbl@lri.fr

Manfred Broy
Institut für Informatik
Technische Universität München
D-80290 München, Germany
broy@in.tum.de

Peter Denning
Computer Science, Code CS
Naval Postgraduate School
Monterey, CA 93943, USA
pjd@nps.edu

Stephen Eubank
Virginia Bio-Informatics Institute &
Physics Dept.
Virginia Polytechnic Institute and
State University
1880 Pratt Drive, Building XV
Blacksburg, VA 24061-0497, USA
seubank@vbi.vt.edu

Matthias Felleisen
College of Computer Science
308B, West Village H
Northeastern University
Boston, MA 02115, USA
matthias@ccs.neu.edu

Robert Bruce Findler
Department of Computer Science
University of Chicago
1100 E. 58th Street
Chicago, IL 60637, USA
robby@cs.uchicago.edu

Dina Goldin
Computer Science Department
Box 1910
Brown University
Providence, RI 02912, USA
dqg@cs.brown.edu

Paul Graunke
College of Computer Science
Northeastern University
Boston, MA 02115, USA
ptg@ccs.neu.edu

Yuri Gurevich
Microsoft Research
One Microsoft Way
Redmond, WA 98052, USA
gurevich@microsoft.com

Ramesh Jain
Donald Bren School of Information
and Computer Sciences
University of California, Irvine
Irvine, CA 92697, USA
jain@ics.uci.edu

Giorgi Japaridze
Computing Sciences Dept.
Villanova University
800 Lancaster Ave.
Villanova, PA 19085, USA
giorgi.japaridze@villanova.edu

Shriram Krishnamurthi
Computer Science Department
Box 1910
Brown University
Providence, RI 02912-1910, USA
sk@cs.brown.edu

Orna Kupferman
School of Computer Science & Engr.
Hebrew University
Jerusalem 91904, Israel
orna@cs.huji.ac.il

Thomas Malone
Sloan School of Management
30 Wadsworth Street
MIT
Cambridge, MA 02142, USA
malone@mit.edu

Madhav V. Marathe
Virginia Bio-Informatics Institute &
Computer Science Dept.
Virginia Polytechnic Institute and
State University,
1880 Pratt Drive, Building XV
Blacksburg, VA 24061-0497, USA
mmarathe@vbi.vt.edu

Robin Milner
The Computer Laboratory
University of Cambridge
J J Thomson Avenue
Cambridge CB3 0FD, UK
Robin.Milner@cl.cam.ac.uk

Andrea Omicini
DEIS
Alma Mater Studiorum
Università di Bologna
via Venezia 52
47023 Cesena, Italy
andrea.omicini@unibo.it

Eric Pacuit
ILLC
University of Amsterdam
Plantage Muidergracht 14
Amsterdam, The Netherlands
epacuit@science.uva.nl

Rohit Parikh
Brooklyn College and CUNY
Graduate Center
365 Fifth Avenue
New York, NY 10016-4309, USA
rparikh@gc.cuny.edu

Alessandro Ricci
DEIS
Alma Mater Studiorum
Università di Bologna
via Venezia 52
47023 Cesena, Italy
a.ricci@unibo.it

Rahul Singh
Department of Computer Science
San Francisco State University
San Francisco, CA 94132, USA
rsingh@cs.sfsu.edu

Scott Smolka
Dept. of Computer Science
SUNY at Stony Brook
Stony Brook, NY 11794-4400, USA
sas@cs.sunysb.edu

Lynn Andrea Stein
Franklin W. Olin College of Engr.
1000 Olin Way
Needham, MA 02492, USA
las@olin.edu

Jan van Leeuwen
Department of Information and
Computing Sciences
Utrecht University
Padualaan 14
3584 CH Utrecht, The Netherlands
j.vanleeuwen@cs.uu.nl

Moshe Y. Vardi
Department of Computer Science
Rice University
Houston, TX 77251-1892, USA
vardi@cs.rice.edu

Mirko Viroli
DEIS
Alma Mater Studiorum
Università di Bologna
via Venezia 52
47023 Cesena, Italy
mirko.viroli@unibo.it

Peter Wegner
Computer Science Department
Box 1910
Brown University
Providence, RI 02912, USA
pw@cs.brown.edu

Jiří Wiedermann
Institute of Computer Science
Academy of Sciences of the Czech
Republic
Pod Vodárenskou věží 2
182 07 Prague 8, Czech Republic
Jiri.Wiedermann@cs.cas.cz